T0305552

Cooperation Networks and Economic Development

For most Western audiences, Cuba is a touristic paradise stuck in time and virtually detached from world technology networks by the US embargo – anything but a hub of industrial innovation and high value-added biotechnology.

However, a closer look reveals more subtle but equally powerful stories that challenge the homogenizing assumptions of conventional economics and open up scope for more sophisticated reflections on Cuban economy and industry. From this kind of enquiry emerges the case of the internationally respected Cuban biotech industry as the most successful case of science and technology policy in the country's economic history.

The book takes an interdisciplinary approach, exploring issues such as interdependency, purpose and history as natural constituencies of the innovation process. It also examines the dynamic and crucial role played by the state in the formation of innovative business enterprises. This book will be of interest to academic researchers in the fields of innovation and economic development.

Andrés Cárdenas O'Farrill received his first economics degree at the University of Havana. He started his career as an economist by working at the Cuban Ministry for Economy, where he became interested in the world of renewable energy. He gained his second economics degree at the University of Leipzig and his PhD at the University of Bremen. He is currently a Research Associate of the Academic-Industry Research Network – **theAIRnet**.

Routledge Studies in Development Economics

For more information about this series, please visit www.routledge.com/series/SE0266

Cooperation Networks and Economic Development
Cuba's High-Tech Potential

Andrés Cárdenas O'Farrill

Routledge
Taylor & Francis Group

LONDON AND NEW YORK

First published 2021
by Routledge
2 Park Square, Milton Park, Abingdon, Oxon OX14 4RN

and by Routledge
605 Third Avenue, New York, NY 10017

First issued in paperback 2022

Routledge is an imprint of the Taylor & Francis Group, an informa business

© 2021 Andrés Cárdenas O'Farrill

Publisher's Note
The publisher has gone to great lengths to ensure the quality of this reprint but
points out that some imperfections in the original copies may be apparent.

British Library Cataloguing-in-Publication Data
A catalogue record for this book is available from the British Library

Library of Congress Cataloging-in-Publication Data
A catalog record has been requested for this book

ISBN 13: 978-1-03-239983-6 (pbk)
ISBN 13: 978-1-138-55898-4 (hbk)
ISBN 13: 978-0-203-71334-1 (ebk)

DOI: 10.4324/9780203713341

Typeset in Bembo
by Newgen Publishing UK

Access the Support Material: www.routledge.com/9781138558984

To great-aunt Margarita Vélez Vega
To my little daughter Luana (the light)
To my beloved father (we miss you terribly)

Contents

Conclusions   356

Annexes   366

Figures

Tables

Abbreviations

ANAP	National Association of Small Farmers
API	active pharmaceutical ingredients
BioCEN	National Centre for Bioproduction
CECMED	National Regulatory Agency (Cuba)
CENCEC	National Clinical Trials Coordinating Centre (Cuba)
CENPALAB	National Centre for Production of Laboratory Animals
CENSA	National Centre for Animal and Plant Health
CIDEM	Centre for Medical Research and Development
CIE	Centre for Immunoassay
CIGB	Genetic Engineering and Biotechnology
CITMA	Ministry for Science and Technology (Cuba)
CMEA	Council for Mutual Economic Assistance
CNC	Centre for Neurosciences
CNIC	National Centre for Scientific Research
CQF	Pharmaceutical Chemistry Centre
CRO	Clinical Research Organisation
DARPA	Defense Advanced Research Projects Agency (US)
DCA	dynamically coherent agents
DIA	dynamic incoherent agents
EMA	European Medicine Agency
ERSO	Electronics Research and Service Organisation (Taiwan)
FDA	Food and Drug Administration (US)
FIPCO	full integrated pharmaceutical companies
ICID	Institute for Digital Research
IFN	Interferon
INRA	National Land Reform Institute
ITRI	Industrial Technology Research Institute (Taiwan)
JUCEPLAN	Central Planning Board
KAIST	Korea Advanced Institute of Science and Technology.
KIST	Korea Institute of Science and Technology
LAGS	Laboratory of Synthetic Antigens
MINSAP	Ministry for Public Health (Cuba)
MITI	Ministry of International Trade and Industry (Japan)

NFO	non-firm organization
NIH	National Health Institutes (US)
NSSI	National and Sectoral System of Innovations
OI	organizational integration
OSDE	Enterprise Management Central Organisations (Spanish)
SDPE	System of Economic Direction and Planning
SOE	state owned enterprises
UBPCs	basic units of cooperative production
WHO	World Health Organisation
WIPO	World Intellectual Property Organisation

Preface and acknowledgements

The first notions about the existence of a biotechnology industry in Cuba came to me in the form of intermittent media reports in my early teens at the end 1980s and beginning of the 1990s. Back then, the sugar (and later tourism) industries were seen as the most conspicuous resources that the country should properly exploit in order to become more prosperous. In fact, tourism became the country's survival flag during the worst years of the economic crisis that impacted Cuba after the collapse of the Soviet Union. I still remember how many young and qualified professionals emigrated from respectable sectors to the tourism industry in order to improve their standard of living. At that time it was pretty common to see a medical doctor or an engineer driving a taxi, or becoming owner of a small (more or less improvised) restaurant, or just leaving the country. Everybody seemed to be convinced of the fact that things like sugar and tourism were destined to be the means to make our way in the world.

However, the sugar industry was almost dismantled in 2002. (At the time of finishing this monograph, 2019, new efforts are being made to accomplish a partial reactivation after a rise in sugar price took place in 2008, but never like before.) This product had been the country's export insignia since its days as a Spanish colony. It continued to be so after the end of the colony and during the republican life until 1959. The revolutionary government that came to power in 1959 sought to achieve the elimination of the monoculture based on sugar in the medium term and to lead the country to industrialization, but the way proved to be tougher than was thought. The dependence on sugar was re-established during the 1960s and further institutionalized from the 1970s onwards. The persistence of low sugar prices from the 1990s on did the rest of the job until 2002.

On the other side, in the tourism industry income per tourist was negative in most of the period 1995–2011, despite the increasing number of visitors. Sticky inefficiencies have kept the productivity and the aggregate value at relatively low levels compared to the amount of investment in the sector. That scenario has not changed much during the last decade. While its proximity to the United States had made Cuba a popular attraction for tourists during the second, third and fifth decades of the twentieth century, political conflicts after 1959 saw a deterioration of the industry during the next three decades until the 1990s, when the number of visitors reached pre-revolutionary levels again. The re-establishment of diplomatic relations with the United States in 2015 boosted the industry, but President Trump's new hostile attitudes toward the island changed the game again. The current situation might change with a new President but the industry would still need to deal with its own demons.

Even while the balance of the industry should not be necessarily deemed as negative, tourism itself does not seem to be leading the country to an industrial future. In actual fact, clear signals of stagnation are there. In addition, nickel prices, the other important Cuban commodity, seem unable to recover the high trends registered in the past. At the end, serious questions about the sustainability of this commodity-based model have begun to be asked. The country experienced growth after 2005, but so far it is still hard to see how a model based fundamentally (although not exclusively, as we will see) on the exploitation of natural resources and non-tradable services should become a sustainable source of growth and development.

In the middle of this situation, however, other areas of the economy have been improving. Take, for example, health indicators: in 2007 the Cuban population was protected against 13 diseases, far beyond the goals established by the World Health Organisation (WHO); and illnesses like diphtheria, polio, hepatitis B and others had been completely eradicated or drastically reduced. The current country infant mortality scores among the lowest in the developing world; and for that matter, around the world.

The explanation of these positive outcomes is the existence of an efficient government-controlled health system, which, notwithstanding its shortcomings, has become a reference for many developing countries and an interesting case study for academics around the world. Indeed, the Cuban health system follows a concept of integral and preventative medicine that helps specialists detect many conditions early on and save money and lives. It is worth mentioning the huge investment in a qualified workforce, which is by now one of the largest around the world (measured in terms of doctors per capita).

However positive these policies are though, other things are needed. As the Director of the Cuba-based Center of Molecular Immunology (CIM) stated in 2009, "a full-coverage vaccination program with state-of-the-art vaccines would still be very difficult without a vaccine production capability." There is not much publicly available information regarding the numbers for the Cuban biopharmaceutical industry, but it is known that during the last 30 years, more than $1 billion (including $338 million in 2005 and $567 million in 2010) were invested to create an industry complex that, at the time of BioCubaFarma creation in 2012, hosted 24 research organizations, 58 manufacturing facilities and employed 12,000 workers, among them 7000 scientists.

What was once called the "billion dollar gamble," in reference to the seemingly unrealistic goal of creating such an industry in a country like Cuba, has become a sophisticated sector that between 1995 and 2010 increased Cuba's exports of biopharmaceutical products fivefold and has developed innovative products such as a vaccine against type-B bacterial meningococcal disease and a synthetic antigen vaccine against Haemophilus influenzae type b (the first in the world). Currently, this industry covers more than 60 percent of the domestic needs and has been at times (2007 to the best of our knowledge) Cuba's second largest exporter after the nickel industry. In actual fact, the country has succeeded by creating a high-tech industry with pretty decent levels of performance, when considering the acute scarceness of its resources. The efficient answer given by the Cuban medical and biopharmaceutical sectors to the worldwide sanitary crisis created by the ongoing events arising from the virus Covid-19 (these events are worth mentioning but will not be discussed in the book as the latter was written well before) are a testament to the qualities of the industry

However, none of these outcomes can be explained by employing a conventional economic theory. The Cuban case seems to contradict every single assumption of a theoretical framework that has paradoxically become a mantra in the course of the last four decades. Understandably, most policymakers and academics around the world that have been trained in this mantra might feel the need to pose an obvious question: e.g. how can we explain those outcomes in a country with extreme underdeveloped markets, until very recently an almost absurdly state-controlled economy, with strongly restricted private property rights systems, lacking a developed and open financial market, with no venture capital industry and virtually disconnected from the world technology flows by virtue of the US embargo, in place for more than half a century?

Indeed, according to the conventional wisdom, it is hard to imagine that such a cash-demanding, high-tech industry as biotechnology can be successfully developed under such conditions. Of course, some economists would invoke notions of totalitarianism, culturalism, political corruption and red-tape. But notwithstanding the inadequacy of these explanations, the truth is that the question deserves to be further explored.

To be sure, the Cuban biotechnology industry is the exception of the Cuban industrial landscape. The rest of the sectors have a long way to go. But precisely for that reason, the analysis of this case becomes more interesting. What did policymakers do in this case that they missed in other sectors? Would it be possible to apply this organizational experience to other Cuban and other countries' industries? What kind of specific experiences would be useful for other (developing and developed) countries? How could the Cuba biopharma industry develop such innovative products in such a cost-effective manner? What kind of theoretical framework could we use to explain this case? These are the sort of questions that have served as motivation for this enquiry.

This material has been the result of several years of research that started back in 2008, during my PhD research. It's been both a beautiful and hard journey and its completion has been the result of emotional or material support received by good and helpful people. In this sense I would like to say thanks to my family, particularly my father, who, even in the distance, has been a source of intellectual exchange and encouragement. I would also like to say thanks to the Friedrich Ebert Stiftung (Foundation Friedrich Ebert) for the financial support and for the permanent network. Very special thanks to Professors William Lazonick and Ha Joon Chang for the chance of sharing my ideas and for the inspiration.

It is also important to thank Prof. Konrad Soyez, Dr. Tirso Saenz, Dr. Maria Amparo Pascual, Dr. Pedro Saura (posth.), Dr. Patricia Hernández, Prof. Wolfram Elsner, Prof. Pedro Valdés Sosa, Laudelina Rodriguez Lastre, Gustavo Santos, Oda Siqveland, Elda Molina, WTO Secretariat, Jeanette Brooks, Camila Pineiro, Cristina Puerta, Diana Sharafieva, Lucía Iglesias, Chamu Dissanayaka, Silvia Pedraza, Jorge Pérez-López, Andrew Popp, Dr. Rafael Pérez Cristá (posth.), Alfredo Rodriguez Diaz, Prof. Agustin Lage, Prof. Hudson Freeze, Prof. Peter Agre, Prof. Harald zur Hausen, Dr. James Larrick, Ian Taylor, Nathan Steele, Rosana Maynegra Diaz, Becky Albrecht, all those involved in the edition process: Emily Kindleysides, Elanor Best, Natalie Tomlinson, Lisa Lavelle, Katie Hemmings, Martin Nobe, Kiruthiga Sowndararajan, Mathivanan, Kawiya Bakthavatchalam and too many others that helped in one way or another. I do not want to let anyone out and that's impossible.

The inevitable errors in such a large and ambitious work are, in form and content, all mine.

1 General introduction and methodological considerations

1.1 Introduction

To study specific cases may have many advantages, as well as disadvantages. A potential disadvantage has to do with the extent to which such a study can be useful to gain understanding about a given field; in a word, relevance. The field of economics in particular has been too focused on traditional econometric models and similar statistical tools in order to gain precision across a large number of standardized data. But is precision relevance? As Erik Reinert states, "[in] today's standard economics the focus is on mathematics and precision more than on the object of analysis itself, the economy."[1] However, real world economic problems are complex phenomena. We find "extremely difficult trade-offs, across time and even generations, under conditions of uncertainty."[2] Any policy recommendation depends on contextual and specific issues.

In order to gain some theoretical understanding of these issues, we need to rely on factual knowledge. To obtain factual knowledge the scholar must move between different levels of analysis, which implies the use of heterogeneous (and difficult to standardize) pieces of evidence. This makes the analysis more complex and less precise. However, if we assume all dissimilarities away, then we will not be able to differentiate between a shoemaker in Guatemala and Microsoft, as both would be averaged out as the typical representative firm of the orthodox discourse. Or we will end up believing that a poor African farmer, all other things being equal, will be able to achieve the same success as a European engineer just by working hard.

If we are to gain some relevant understanding about complex economic problems, then we must assume the complexity in them by considering the qualitative differences between elements, agents and phenomena. As Reinert states, "[a] system where all agents and all inputs are qualitatively identical, applied in a world devoid of context, will necessarily produce sameness of results." It would be like classifying human beings exclusively according to weight and height, because they are quantifiable, while leaving out the rest of the elements (personality, ideology, power and capabilities, their context, natural environment, religion etc.). We need qualities, classification systems, taxonomies, historical narratives etc., in order to advance rational explanations on economic problems necessarily rooted in historic specific contexts. To be sure, we are not excluding quantitative analysis (in this study we advance a form of quantification), as it is the complement of qualitative analysis, but we are "asking for room to bring qualitative analysis back to academics economics."[3] An economic argument does not need to be quantitative in order to be economic.

With the above-mentioned elements in mind, we will try to do something unusual, at least in economics, in this study, if by no means new: we will explicitly rely on historical pieces of evidence to build this case. Not only the evidence related to it but also evidence from many other cases, in order to gain cross-case validation with respect to the causal chain of events that has led to specific outcomes in the case under study. And this is precisely the major advantage of case studies: causal explanation. While traditional econometric models establish relationships, they do not provide causality in the sense that they do not allow the researcher to explore the causal path described by a theory. To be sure, the causal explanations provided by cases are very imperfect, but they can provide valuable knowledge on specific aspects of a given phenomenon. This is what this study expects to achieve by exploring the interesting story of the Cuban biotech.

Notice that the analysis of the Cuban biotech basically focuses on the development of the industry prior to the creation of the Biotechnological and Pharmaceutical Industries Enterprise Group (BioCubaFarma), a state holding created in 2012 as a result of the most recent government's economic reforms. This year will be taken as a sort of demarcation line for the analysis, among other things because we are more interested in the process of formation of the industry, and its theoretical implications, rather than with the updated description of its current structure. In this sense, the accurateness of the description applies until the creation of the new holding. Also notice that the phenomena under study are constantly evolving, which makes catching up with the latest developments particularly challenging due to the natural vagaries of the publishing process and the inevitable time lags which result therefrom. That is the reason why, in our opinion, it is healthier to focus the energy in extracting patterns and lessons than trying to obsess ourselves with actuality. Having said that, however, the book will provide relevant general information about what has happened after 2012 in order to keep up to date with the latest events within the industry. The new entity BioCubaFarma derives from the merger of all institutions of the Scientific Pole in western Havana, the biotechnological side of the industry, and all companies within the Quimefa Group, which represented the traditional Cuban pharmaceutical industry. We will only briefly discuss the theoretical implications of what has happened after that merger because this new holding is still in process of accommodation.

Chapters 2, 3 and 4 will be devoted to the proposition of a possible theoretical framework that might help to understand the case under study. In Chapter 2 we will explore the idea of the economy as a complex system. We start to build our theoretical body on the notion of complex economic systems seen as purposeful, interdependent and path dependent. It is argued that the concept of self-organization (as traditionally employed in much of the literature) tends to overshadow the important role played by governments in the innovation process. There is evidence of the government not simply creating the conditions for innovation, but also actively funding early ground-breaking research, as well as building the necessary networks between state non-firm organizations and the business, private and public, sector to allow the commercial development to occur. For that reason, this research consciously includes the *government agency* in the theoretical discourse on complexity. It is argued that government should not be conceived as an exogenous agent but as a central network agent within a complex economy.

At this point we introduce network theory as a way of dealing with the representation and analysis of complex economic systems. Relying on this theory, it is hypothesized that economic systems (such as many other complex social and non-social systems) can be conceived as hub dominated networks, where the most central nodes play the role of integrators of the whole system. In this context we introduce the network-related concept of *centrality* as a way of measuring the positional advantages of each node within the network of agents.

In Chapter 3 we introduce the notion of the *government* as a central agent within a complex economic system. While Chapter 2 is intended to explore the theoretical implications of seeing the economy as a complex system, Chapter 3 is intended to conceptualize the role of the state in a complex economic system. This is carried out by linking insights and categories of the complex systems literature with insights and evidence provided by fields such as development and innovation economics, institutional economics and business history, which have been hitherto relatively ignored by the field of complexity economics. As part of this conceptualization we propose a typology which is intended to help to capture the *status* of the *government agency* within a complex economic network.

The chapter provides also historical evidence and important elaborations provided by an ever-growing number of scholars in the fields of development and innovation economics, but also in a well established literature in fields such as political sciences and sociology that clashes with the idea of a non-developmental state behind most of the successful developmental efforts in modern Western (and non Western) history. Even in today's advanced economies, which, as a logical consequence of the increasing specialization and technological advancement show a great deal of decentralization in the process of decision making, the government continues to play a critical role in the development of frontier technologies.

In Chapter 4 we establish a link of the notion of a hub dominated network introduced in Chapter 2 with a theoretical framework in economics that can justify the usage of the analogy. We found that the Neo-Schumpeterian notion of *national (sectoral) systems of innovation* as a network of heterogeneous agents, embedded in a certain institutional environment, reflects this analogy very well. Likewise, we further conceptualize on the idea of government based non-firm organizations as the hubs of the national (sectoral) systems of innovation.

In this chapter we introduce the theory of the innovative enterprise as a theory opposed to the notion of the optimizing firm (Lazonick 2002). Traditional theories of the firm conceive firms as economic agents that take technologies and markets as given phenomena, and support the strategy of companies adapting themselves to given conditions (optimizing firm). In contrast, the theory of the innovative firm is based on the idea that innovation is a truly uncertain processes, where relevant information is not just hidden or asymmetric but unknown to the participants in the process. Therefore innovative firms must develop the ability to overcome technological and market uncertainties during the process of developing new capabilities. Without establishing how organizational resources are invested in path-breaking technologies it is not possible to explain why some economies prosper and others do not.

This theory conceives the firm not as an isolated agent, but as embedded in an ecology of agents and relations. This symbiosis opens promising prospects for the creation of new relational concepts that can comprise categories extracted from different levels of aggregation into the same level of analysis. We propose that one of these concepts could be the *organizational integration* as defined in the context of the theory of innovative business enterprise. The general idea behind this concept is that when an economy shows good performance it is because governments, businesses and other organizations are working together. Then we could talk about organizational success. In this context, we propose that the concept of *organizational integration* can be related to the notion of *centrality* as defined in network theory (Chapter 2).

Furthermore, in order to proceed with the case, we intend to explore the historical context in which the Cuban biopharmaceutical industry has emerged. In doing so, we analyse in detail the industrial strategies of the post-1959 period, by emphasizing elements such as the organizational structures underlying the strategies and the degree of coordination in targeted industries, and also in how these factors might be related to the development of the biotechnology industry. We divide our quest in two parts: Chapter 5 covers the first 30 years of the Cuban revolution, which match the period until the collapse of the Soviet Union. This event marks a new era in Cuban economic life, of which the detailed organizational challenges, innovations and shortcomings are discussed in Chapter 6.

In Chapter 5 we will see that the main problem for the period 1959–89 is the lack of functional integration between economic actors. Even when the levels of centralization achieved during the period reached schizophrenic pitches, paradoxically, the lack of coordination between the state and productive agents was pervasive during the period, making it impossible to activate targeted flows of information between them, and preventing policy targets from being accomplished. As already mentioned, the objective of the first stage of this period (1959–63) was to free the country from dependence on sugar and to industrialize it. Some of the introduced policies had an undeniable developmental dimension, but the strategy failed for the indicated reasons, as well as due to the role played by the American embargo.

Nevertheless, some manufacturing industries were introduced during the period 1959–89. Things like the first Cuban microcomputer were built in the period. However, most of the manufacturers were not able to mature technologically or commercially. There was no organized and well integrated system of innovation in place; one that was capable of consciously developing better, cheaper and more commercial products. Some initiatives, such as the "Movement of Inventors and Innovators" existed, and they certainly were (and are) responsible for many innovations in the production system, but this movement was usually disconnected from the science system, even from firms in the same industry (e.g. suppliers). Centralized governments plans were only interested in quantity; leaving quality and innovation outside.

At the same time, the first research institutes were created. These institutes were to later become the core of the biotechnology industry. Likewise, an impressive health system was developed, which also contributed to the later development of the industry under study. However, even with all these advances, the country remained highly dependent on the sugar industry in it most traditional form. The industrial structure was unable to compete in international markets, as the collapse of the Soviet Union, its main trading partner, in 1990 clearly showed. At that time, Cuba lost 85 percent of its trading links and succumbed to the worst economic crisis experienced by the country in peacetime. The new challenges were to save some of the undeniable social achievements of the process, while finding new sales opportunities and new foreign investors and creating new institutions.

These new challenges are addressed in Chapter 6. In this chapter we address the question of whether the new changes introduced since 1990 have contributed to creating a sustainable growth model for the country. In our view, the balance is mixed. While industry and firm decision makers were given a good deal of strategic control over the allocation of the resources, holding companies were transformed into the main technology and expertise absorbers of the economy, and a much better organizational integration was to be observed in the system, financial commitment remained (with exception of the biopharmaceutical complex) almost exclusively concentrated on natural resources-based industries such as tourism and mining. The economy began to experience positive growth rates beginning in 1994, but the stagnation of the tourism industry and the permanent reduction of nickel international prices have imposed the need to rethink the current development strategy.

In fact, the country has experienced a worrisome deindustrialization. In 1989, 90 percent of the country's exports were manufactured products, while in 2005 only 30 percent belonged to this category. While most of the industries developed in the previous period were not competitive the solution, in our view, should have been to upgrade them instead of stopping their development. Currently, like 20 years before, the Cuban economy continues looking for a sustainable way to progress. That being said, over the course of that same period, one industry did not follow the decreasing path of the rest of the economy: the biotechnology industry. In Chapter 7 we will get into details about the mechanisms working here. An optional network analysis of the Cuban bio-tech will be presented in Annex 4, but it is not essential for the comprehension of the central idea of the book. This network analysis is more a quantitative exploration of the new conceptual frameworks introduced in the study, and it is aimed at those interested in expanding on the subject. For those who go there, notice that it is about a framework under construction, necessarily populated with imperfection. For those who don't feel like going there, Chapter 7 will be more than enough.

Chapter 7 will be devoted to presenting the case and to the qualitative (within-case) analysis of the causal chain of events, which led to the cre-ation of the most important components of the case. The analysis will pro-ceed by describing the network according to its node subgroups. The historic–institutional context will be analysed in some detail in which the most important organizations under study were developed; and the possible causal mechanisms behind the evolution and outcomes of the industry. These mechanisms will be subtly contrasted with the great deal of historical evidence provided by a great variety of country and sector-specific cases.

In this chapter we will see that even when the pervasive lack of regular data makes it difficult to establish an accurate picture about the outcomes of Cuba's biotechnology industry, the available evidence allows to assume that this industry is being able to deliver cost–effective products to the national health system when compared to other countries of similar and even higher income groups. A number of key health indicators and a number of prize-winning innovative products provide the challenge of explaining these outcomes in a rational manner.

We will see that this industry, in contrast to most (biopharma) industries worldwide, but also in contrast to most of the Cuban industrial landscape, has been characterized by a high level of integration between its agents. The para-mount rule of the Cuban industry is cooperation rather competition, where government non-firm organizations (particularly regulatory agencies) have played an important role. Similar to other technology development experiences, this type of organization has played crucial incubating and brokering roles within the Cuban biotech network, by allowing open flows of knowledge and resources across the boundaries of heterogeneous organizations.

As we will discuss later, these results show that in order to carry out their regulatory functions, these agencies need to embody a high set of complex coord-inating abilities. For example they need the ability to rapidly transmit informa-tion and knowledge to others directly tied to them, either simultaneously or not. This connecting role demands the continuous creation of standard interfaces and protocols such as regulatory frameworks and other shared platforms, in order to encourage less costly, long-term teamwork. Shared standards and protocols, but also shared manufacturing or commercialization capabilities, are common place in Cuban health biotechnology and play a paramount role in this performance. This has allowed the creation of important economies of scale and scope, along with network effects, supplier based innovations, etc.

Standardization is nothing new, and, as mentioned in other chapters, has always been the basis of economies of scale and broad technologic development. However the emergence of complex technologies imposes particular challenges to this process. These technologies display high levels of input and demand heterogeneity (the biotech industry a paramount example) which opens the possibilities of knowledge recombination (and thus innovation) by exploiting the potentials offered by modular (as opposed to integrated) forms of organization. At the same time, the high levels of tacitness involved in these industries exercise important pressures for integration in order for created knowledge to be able to be absorbed and cumulated.

In contrast, for example, alliances in the worldwide biopharma industry tend to be short and less innovative. This dilemma has been shown by several authors to be one of the major obstacles in the development of the biopharmaceutical sector worldwide (e.g. Pisano 2006; Wessner et al. 2001). They argue that modularity has led to the commoditization of knowledge, which has made profitable for many products-less firms to rely on proprietary patenting, even at the cost of blocking innovation within the industry. This scenario imposes the need of e.g. reviewing patent laws, government support in creating partnership programs, and providing interdisciplinary training in order to build long-term bridges between agents. Seen from this perspective, we argue that it makes sense to take into account the sectoral features of the industry in order to better understand the organizational arrangements; and institutional environments that allow using the advantages of both vertical integration and modularity.

In our view, the Cuban case is giving a clue in two important dimensions. First, this case is showing that, far from depending on expensive intellectual property commoditization and blocking mechanisms, organizational integration carried out by government agencies may help firms to deal with the high levels of uncertainty surrounding product development in the industry. Second, the fact that the government has not only been a key participant in the development of Cuba's biotechnology industry, but also in other high-tech industries worldwide, is telling us that the Cuban case could actually be considered the confirmation of a huge, but hitherto ignored body of historic case evidence, rather than a rare case of authoritarian success in a small Caribbean island.

Summarizing, the present study seeks to explore the possibilities of catch up development and innovation through national and sectoral networking. A special emphasis will be given to the role and position of the state as institution within these phenomena. This will be concretely done by analysing *the set of institutions*[4] *and causal mechanisms, which have determined the existence and positive performance of the biotechnology industry in Cuba.* Likewise, this study will propose a theoretical framework that could explain the outcomes of this case; which might also apply to the analysis of other cases. In other words, this research is intended primarily to describe the variety of actors surrounding a given phenomena (what question) and to explain how these actors contribute to a given outcome (how or why question).

To address these descriptive and explanatory questions, this research has been conceived as a case study intended to gain in-depth knowledge of the phenomena under analysis, while making direct observation of it. Below we will discuss some important aspects of this methodology and the way it relates to the Cuban biotech case. However, the reader does not need to go through it in order to make sense of the book. The methodological discussion could just be of some interest for those who want to explore the issue in more detail, and it is aimed at them. However, you can skip it if you feel you know enough of the subject, or if you just find methodological information dry and boring. It won't affect the main point of the general text.

The same applies to the general text, if you find the mix of theoretical issues and historical examples too overloaded, just go to Chapters 5, 6 and 7, which deal with Cuba specifically. If, on the other hand, you are interested in theoretical issues and comparative history, then go to Chapters 2, 3 and 4.

1.2 Research design and data collection

To conceptually clarify the just mentioned methodological position, this study will be referred to as an *explanatory* case study[5] in the terminology of George and Bennett (2005); or *confirmatory*, in the terminology of Gerring (2007). This method allows the researcher to have access to the sort of detailed information that enables the construction of a causal pathway which can explain outcomes previously predicted by a given theoretical framework. That is, the purpose of this study is essentially to test a theory or set of hypotheses by intensive studying a single event (the case), which means explaining the causal mechanisms for that event to be able to happen. In other words, it will be attempted to demonstrate that the case under study fits, with an acceptable degree of plausibility, both the predictions made and the evidence provided by a given theoretical framework.

Specifically, this study rests on the following operational causal hypothesis: *government-based non-firm organizations play a crucial role in the process of organizational integration within the Cuban biotech industry.* This hypothesis formulation follows the terminology employed by Gerring (2007), where a hypothesis is intended to identify the "causal pathway, or connecting thread, between $X1$[6] and Y" (p. 73). $X1$ is the independent variable and Y the dependent one. It is important to note that this $X1/Y$ relation may be qualitative or quantitative[7] (for a full discussion, see ibid., pp. 71–4).

If a researcher is attempting to explain a "puzzling outcome, but has no preconceptions about its causes, then the research will be described as *Y-centered*" (ibid., p. 71). When trying to explain the effects of a particular cause, the research will be described as "*X-centered*" (ibid.). If a researcher is looking to examine a particular causal relationship, the research will be described as "*X1/Y-centered*, for it connects a particular cause with a particular outcome" (ibid.). "X- or Y-centered research is exploratory; [because] its purpose is to generate new hypotheses. X1/Y-centered research, by contrast, is confirmatory/

disconfirmatory [like the case under study]; [because] its purpose is to test an existing hypothesis" (ibid.).

Our causal hypothesis arises from the data collected in the direct observation and in-depth analysis of the case, but it also rests on general insights provided by the discipline of complexity economics, and on concrete empirical evidence and concepts provided by theories in the fields of evolutionary-institutional innovation (e.g. the concept of organizational integration), and development economics. In general, the study has an interdisciplinary nature, which not only implies the use of different theories and fields, but also the existence of multiple sources and types of information. However, we could say that the previously mentioned sources match the two most distinctive types of data/information employed to construct (external and internal) validity in case studies (Yin 2003a,b).

To synthesize, the first type of data corresponds to the within-case (qualitative and quantitative) evidence and has been gathered from a systematic review of specialized publications, in-depth interviews and consultation with key representatives of the industry, government agencies, industry public information databases, contemporary and historical literature on the subject, archival historical documents, company reports, economic journals, international databases (WHO, World Bank, consultancy firms etc.) and other trade publications. This information provided a reasonable background to trace causal chains within the case, in order to achieve *internal validity* (Gerring 2007). As we will see, most of this data is of relational nature (see below, Network method).

The second source of data has been gathered by reviewing cross-case evidence obtained basically from specialized sectoral and economics literature such as research papers and monographs, archival information from public databases, direct exchange with other researchers, historical documents and governments reports. Cross-case evidence offers the possibility of clarifying how the intensively studied case represents some broader population of cases. Usually, even exploratory case studies culminate in cross-case confirmatory analysis (ibid.). This helps to provide *external validity* to the single case.

The above-mentioned research program is also consistent with the foundational institutionalist methodology proposed by Wilber and Harrison (1978). It basically consists of exercising concrete observations of a particular event and finding its recurrent themes and practices in order to gain understanding about that event. In turn, understanding or explaining an event involves a process of contextual validation, which means that the researcher inductively formulates initial hypotheses or interpretations on the basis of the analysis of other case studies, survey data, etc. These tentative hypotheses are then to be continually cross-checked against new data and evidence. This approach is perfectly consistent with other institutional programs being taken as reference by the present study (e.g. historical-transformation methodology; see below, section Historical specificity).

In addition, employing diverse theories and types of information offers the chance of establishing cross-verification techniques (more than one method, or theory, or more than a tool within a method etc.) to strengthen validity. This double (sometimes triple) checking of results minimizes (if not completely avoids) some limitations inherent to case study methodology (selection bias, lack of generalization, verification bias, equifinality, indeterminacy etc.). Some authors call it triangulation or cross examination (Denzin 2006).

1.3 On prediction and testing

At the same time, although in a more modest scale, this study will explore the possibilities of sketching some new insights and typologies, which might complement the proposed theoretical framework. This concept-generating capacity is a consubstantial feature of the case studies method because "[t]he relationships discovered among different elements of a single [always unique] case have a prima facie causal connection[8] [...]" (Gerring 2007, p. 41, see also Yin 2003a, 2003b and George and Bennett 2005). The suggested insights will be explicitly oriented, however, to help to accomplish our primary research goal, namely, to confirm the predictions made by an existing body of theory.

It is important to point out that the term "prediction" is being employed here in the sense given to it by Herbert Simon while discussing the relation of premises and conclusions in economic theory (see Archibald, Simon and Samuelson 1963). According to him the scientific theories are not meant to advance predictions (in the sense of knowing the future or testing homogenized variables) but explanations. In this view the real predictions are actually a test of the validity of the explanation. In this sense, testing consists not only of exclusively finding some relationship between a set of assumptions and the conclusions arrived at (as it is usually econometric models) but also to check the whole causal chain of the explanation.

The term of "testing" should not necessarily (although it could) be associated to the search of correlations in statistical sense. Correlation does not explain causality. In this study, testing is about making close observations of the elements and variables supposed to lead to a given outcome; in order to confirm, as much as possible, that our explanation is, at least, plausible. As Simon noted, "[t]hat X and Y are taken as premises [assumptions] and Z as a conclusion is not just a matter of taste in formulation of the theory," but should actually reflect the fact that "[t]he formulation fits our common, if implicit, notions of explanation" (Archibald, Simon and Samuelson 1963, p. 229). The point in testing is to make these "notions of explanation" as explicit as possible to be sure that they are real and not imaginary.

To be sure, assumptions are always simplifications, but they should try to be as good as possible.[9] Like good maps, theories rest on simplifications of the less relevant elements for the explanation to be able to be advanced. However, one cannot design a map by deliberately changing the location of rivers and mountains just to make it easier, no matter what level of abstraction one employs. However, as Simon further admits, for most of the economists, the "proposition Z is the [only one to be] empirically tested [...], while X and Y [can remain] not directly observable" (ibid., p. 230). This misconception still persists today and represents, with all its consequences, the rule (rather than the exception) in the economic profession.

This is not to say that statistical relationships are unimportant. Statistical quantification is important in its own right and perfectly compatible with case studies. However, when testing or proposing theories, we need to be sure that our assumptions reflect as much as possible the real world. As Simon proposes, "[l]et us make the observations necessary to discover and test true propositions" (ibid.). However, the reality is that in many case studies this straightforward suggestion may become complicated by the fact that; many of the necessary assumptions to be found in the real world are difficult, or in many cases impossible to standardize. In contrast, correlations are generally linked to causal relationships (not causal mechanisms!) between random homogeneous variables, which are statistically independent from each other.

However, in practice we find too many diverse and interrelated pieces of evidence at the same time, all (although not necessary equally) relevant to a case. But even when one can find a homogenized sample of data (and thus statistically relevant) as part of within-case evidence, the sort of empirical regularities arrived at and described by statistics cannot identify the active mechanisms or contribute "to any profounder information about the interactions of forces behind an observed pattern" (Danermarkt et al. 2002, p. 153). Thus, in many cases the *what/how* questions go unanswered.

A different kind of pattern modeling is proposed by the institutional methodologist approach proposed by Wilber and Harrison (1978). This approach calls for the construction of pattern models that arise from connecting all the validated hypotheses. This model should identify the heterogeneous range of explanatory factors at work and the patterns of interaction between these factors. In this context, it is the case study research, the type of method that "may allow one to peer into the box of causality to locate the intermediate factors lying between some structural cause and its purported effect" (Gerring 2007, p. 45).

However, as Simon again reminds us, to trace the causal pathway of a proposition "may involve more empirical work at the level of the individual [cases] than most conventionally-trained economists find comfortable" (Archibald, Simon and Samuelson 1963, p. 230). This could (although not necessarily) be interpreted as we will need to apply certain qualitative tools in order to certify the validity of the observations made. This involves studying and becoming aware of history, politics, technology, culture, institutions etc. It also involves the creation of qualitative categories (typologies, taxonomies), which help us to better deal with contingent theories. This may sound far-fetched for an orthodox economist, but it is in fact what has characterized the profession for more than 500 years (Reinert 2007). Of course, as noted above, it is not possible to study all the components of a phenomenon. We have to necessarily confine to those components (or causal variables) that seem to provide greater explanatory power. The point is that we are looking for causal explanations rather than for empirical regularities in form of statistic co-variation.

1.4 Research tools

The argument of this research relies basically on two analytic tools: *cross-level reasoning* and *process tracing*. The first tool has to do with the use of evidence other than the one obtained in the within-case analysis. As already suggested, in order for case studies to be integrated in a broader field of study, at least a preliminary notion must exist about how single case results are likely to fit into a broader set of cases (Wilber and Harrison 1978). That's the reason why this study also relies strongly on the tool denominated *cross-level reasoning* (Gerring 2007, pp. 84–5), which is the use of cross-case evidence (comparative study cases, large sample studies, historic comparative cases, other single cases etc.). After all "case study is, by definition, a study of some phenomenon broader than the unit under investigation" (ibid., 85).

Given that cross-case research is always more representative of the population of interest than case study research (provided a sensible process of case selection has been carried out), the combination of within- and cross-case evidence builds better prospects to achieve some degree of *external validity*. This helps to deal, at least partially, with warranted and traditional criticisms made to single case studies on the quality of the inferences made (e.g. generalization and verification bias). For example, in the process of testing hypotheses of theories, overcoming the lack of generalization[10] is crucial. In the present study, we attempt to deal with this problem by presenting sectoral and cross-sectoral information that is to be compared with the Cuban biotech sector.[11]

The fact is that regardless the field or tool, case studies and cross-case studies are to be conceived as two sides of the same coin, because they complement each other in the iterative task of causal investigation. Realist cross-case arguments rely necessarily on within-case assumptions, and vice versa. "Neither [of them] works very well when isolated from the other" (Gerring 2007, p. 84). Among the scholars on case study methodology, there is a growing consensus that the strongest means of drawing inferences from case studies is the use of a combination of within-case analysis and cross-case comparisons within a single study or research program (George and Bennett 2005; Flyvbjerg 2011). It is difficult to conceive "cross-case research that does not draw upon case study work, or case study work that disregards adjacent cases"; given that both "are distinct, but synergistic tools in the analysis of social life" (Gerring 2007, p. 85).

The second tool endeavours to trace causal mechanisms by providing historical traces of the cases. Historical explanation is not simply a description of a sequence of events, but the attempt to find regular patterns between the set of events (Robert 1996, cited in George and Bennett 2005). However a distinction must be established between universalistic and probabilistic laws.

While the universalistic laws model[12] is deductive in form, no explanation using probabilistic laws (like in the social sciences) can be strictly deductive. Instead, for the process of hypothesis formation and validation to take place, deductive/inductive logic needs to be complemented by such form of inference as abduction.[13] In order to establish a possible explanatory sequence of the causal mechanisms behind complex historical events, social scientists tend to *trace* "the sequence of events that brought them about" (ibid., p. 226). This analytical tool will be employed in our research and is what case study scholars call *process tracing*[14] (George and Bennett 2005; Gerring 2007).

Process tracing is about finding the causal path of a social phenomenon, i.e. "to infer and construct a causal chain account of how various conditions and variables interacted over time to produce the historical outcome" (George and Bennett 2005). According to Gerring (2007) the most important aspect of this tool is that "multiple types of evidence are employed for the verification of a single inference – bits and pieces of evidence that embody different units of analysis (they are each drawn from unique populations)" (p. 173).

Given that the causal path behind a certain phenomenon may be (and usually is) composed of individual observations that are non-comparable, they cannot be analysed as a unified sample. Process tracing necessarily involves looking for causal chains, sometimes long chains.

> Rather than multiple instances of X1 → Y [as is the case in statistical research], one examines a single instance of X1 → X2 → X3 → X4 → Y. (Of course, this causal path may be much longer and more circuitous, with multiple switches and feedback loops).
>
> (ibid., p. 173)

The construction of a highly plausible causal chain, which is consistent with the evidence, and survives comparison with alternative explanations, will help achieve *internal validity* and to reduce (if not eliminate) the difficulties faced by the uses of counterfactuals in complex socioeconomic phenomena.[15]

1.5 Case selection

Case study selection is a very important step in case studies, because it can simply enable or prevent the researcher from achieving its research objectives. The present research pursues to confirm a theory or theoretical framework and it attempted to classify the case under study according to this objective. Cases studies can be classified according to several methods of case selection, e.g. typical case, pathway case, deviant case, crucial/critical case, diverse case etc. (a detailed discussion can be found in Gerring 2007 and George and Bennett 2005, see also Flyvbejerg 2011).

The Cuban case can be included in several groups according to the analysis level and the research stage. However, most significant here is the classification of the case according to the research objectives. In this sense, and as already mentioned, the case was thought to be a *deviant case* at early stages. A deviant case is expected to provide

> information on unusual cases, which can be especially problematic or especially good in a more closely defined sense. To understand the limits of

existing theories and to develop new concepts, variables, and theories that are able to account for deviant cases.

(Flyvbjerg 2011, p. 307)

Indeed, seen under the light of the findings and generalizations of orthodox economic theory, the case of the Cuban biotechnology seems like a freaky event that does not fit any theory. As mentioned above, seen from an orthodox perspective, Cuba's underdeveloped financial markets, lack of private venture capital and strongly restricted private intellectual property rights cannot be thought of as incentives to develop such a cash-demanding high-tech industry. This is the last thing a neo-liberal economist would recommend as a model.

A closer look, though, reveals that these handicaps may not necessarily be obstacles for technology development. In fact, it has become common place among most industry officials to name certain organizational structures as the key to the success. In Cuba these structures are seen as an innovation, and they certainly are, not only when seen from the perspective of mainstream economic theories, but also from the perspective of the rest of Cuba's typical organizational structure.

However, when one takes a deeper and broader look at the functioning of the industry worldwide, then one begins to understand why the Cuban case is performing so well. In addition, if we examine more heterodox economic approaches (e.g. Lazonick 2002; Chang 2003), and contrast the evidence provided by them with the Cuban case, then our study begins to look less and less deviant. To be sure, as expected from a deviant case (in the sense of not fitting any theory), this case has allowed us to develop new concepts and to understand the limits of certain theories. However, it ceases to be entirely unusual (if still inevitably singular and idiosyncratic) to become more what the case literature calls a *critical (or crucial) case*.

Flyvbjerg (2011) defines crucial cases as the kind of cases that enable one to "achieve information that permits logical deductions of the type, 'If this is (not) valid for this case, then it applies to all [most of] (no) cases'" (p. 307). The concept was introduced by Harry Eckstein as a case "that *must closely fit* a theory if one is to have confidence in the theory's validity, or, conversely, *must not fit* equally well any rule contrary to that proposed" (Eckstein 1975, p. 118). Gerring (2007) states that "[s]ince the publication of Eckstein's influential essay, the crucial-case approach has been claimed in a multitude of studies across several social science disciplines and has come to be recognised as a staple of the case study method" (p. 115).

Several authors also agree in considering crucial the type of cases where particularly single cases can serve well the purpose of theory testing (George and Bennett 2005). Referring to the need to overcome the generalization bias, Flyvbjerg (2011) argues that "a *critical case* can be defined as having strategic importance in relation to the general problem" (p. 307). The chances of better applying the method depend on the degree of precision of the theories and their predictive consequences. In this sense, Gerring (2007) warns not to misconceive the critiques from an inductive point of view.

On the other hand, it could be that during the process of discriminating variables, some valid ones are left out, which can weaken the strength of the analysis. In this case, George and Bennett (2005) suggest applying a process-tracing procedure to a wide range of alternative hypotheses that theorists, and even participants in the events, have proposed, not only to the main hypotheses of greatest interest to the researcher. While this process can never be completely satisfactory and encompassing (risk of indeterminacy, equifinality[16] etc.), it should be pursued to the best of the possibilities of the researcher. With this caveat in mind, we will proceed to continue explaining the method.

Crucial cases in practice are classified in *most-likely* and *least-likely* cases because, as most authors recognize, truly crucial cases rarely occur in nature or the social world (George and Bennett 2005; Eckstein 1975). According to George and Bennett (2005) "in a most likely case, the independent variables[17] posited by a theory are at values that strongly posit an outcome or posit an extreme outcome" (p. 121). These cases are designed to "cast strong doubt on theories if the theories do not fit" (ibid., p. 121). They are supposed to fulfil all conditions for a predicted outcome to be achieved, and yet do not achieve it because they actually lack the crucial dimension, the condition of theoretical interest. "'If it is not valid for this case, then it is not valid for any (or only few) cases'" (Flyvbjerg 2011, p. 307). For example, if a statement affirms that sugar is the only product which is powdered and white, then it would be useful to bring some salt, which is very likely to fulfil the statement, in order to demonstrate that not all white, powdered products are sugar.

Conversely, in the least-likely cases "the independent variables in a theory are at values that only weakly predict an outcome or predict a low-magnitude outcome" (George and Bennett 2005, p. 121). In an easier words, Flyvbjerg (2011) observes that "'If it is valid for this case, it is valid for all (or many) cases'" (p. 307). These cases are designed to "strengthen support for theories that fit even cases where they should be weak"; *and in our view, the Cuban case fulfils the condition*. Let us explain.

The cases exemplified by the framework we chose to be confirmed are cases that widely differ from the Cuban one in almost anything (i.e. form, content and function that things are expected to exert). For example, firms shown as examples by the theory are mostly private firms, with a lot of power over their corporate funds and over their intellectual property. They are well connected to leaders in international high-tech flows, with the financial capacity and the freedom to attract the best qualified workforce around the world. Additionally, some of them have the power of setting domestic prices, are embedded in highly developed infrastructures and are located almost exclusively in industrialized and quite decentralized capitalistic societies (although the dichotomy soc vs. cap needs to be revised). These same societies are endowed with well developed and open financial markets and are prone to free trade. Nothing can be more different than the Cuban firms in biotechnology. Still, they have succeeded reasonably well.

The point is that, if Cuban firms were able to succeed in high-tech development (at this time, only biotech), and we are still able to explain this by using the theory, then the theory must be at least plausible. This could be telling us that the causal mechanisms described by the theory show some degree of cross-case validity and therefore are acceptable as (provisional) explanation. "Theories that survive such [...] test may prove to be generally applicable to many types of cases [middle-range contingent generalisations], as they have already proven their robustness in the presence of countervailing mechanisms" (George and Bennett 2005, p. 122).

This sort of validation may be useful when studying economic institutions in the context of economic science, because it gives us elements to recognize the importance of acknowledging historical specific traces of national economies. We do not live in a world of nations succeeding by copying and applying identically a set of known institutional environments. And yet, similar mechanisms are demonstrable across the differences. However, to better understand the mechanisms, it may be necessary to engage in more historical-comparative methodologies that describe how different and historical specific institutional settings have developed across the time, and been able to reproduce similar causal mechanisms.

1.6 Historical specificity in case studies in economics

Contrary to what many believe today, the assessment of the methodological implications of taking into account the *historical specificity* in economics had its beginnings a long time ago.[18] In this list we need to mention the German Historical School, which includes names like Werner Sombart, Gustav von Schmoller, Max Weber and Friedrich List, with his influential classic of 1841 *National System of Political Economy*,[19] in which the central premise stemmed from Alexander Hamilton's argument (1791)[20] for industry protection in the United States. Another important exponent of the argument of historical specificity is Karl Marx, whose brilliant analysis of capitalism was made by relying on direct observations of the British industrialization. He shares this approach with the German School, although from a very different ideological position (a detailed comparative analysis is found in Hodgson 2001).

Beyond its limitations,[21] the German school raised and addressed some of the key conceptual and methodological problems of social sciences (particularly economics). It enjoyed prominence for a long period of time (until the Second World War) and served as a starting point for the English and Irish Historical Schools, and also for the American Institutionalism (Veblen, Commons). After the Second World War, the influence of this school began to wane in favor of neoclassical economics. However, the historical approach still found strong followers in development economics of different tendencies (Lewis, Rostow, Kutznets, Prebish, Furtado, Gerschenkron, Hirschman and more recently

Chang, Burlamaqui, Lall, Lazonick, Reinert etc.). Even Alfred Marshall, one of the founding fathers of neoclassical economics, acknowledged the influence of this school.

Few schools of economic thought have had such longevity and prominence, and, by comparison, such subsequent neglect. Yet today modern economic theory is dominated globally and completely – even in Germany – by a highly formalized technical concern. Even in fields such as development economics and economic history, where historical approach is crucial, "contemporary discussion on economic development policy-making has been peculiarly a-historical" (Chang 2003, p. 7).

Conventional economics has focused fundamentally on a methodology based on the neoclassical *constrained optimization* (Lazonick 2002; Foster 2005) models to understand the behavior of the firm. These models examine how business enterprises as individual economic agents make resource allocation decisions at a particular point of time under extreme tight and unrealistic market conditions. By focusing on constrained optimization, conventional economists exclude historic and institutional evolution of the economic analysis and this invalidates the economic development as a primary object of *intellectual endeavor.*

The advent of today's traditional constrained optimization methodology contributed to the separation between what was called political economy after Stanley Jevon's *The Theory of Political Economy* (1871) and Marshall's *Principle of Economics* (1890); and the political economy as practiced by the Classical School. Even when the fundaments of the marginal revolution are to be found in the Classical School, it can be said that there was no insurmountable tension between (wrongly called) normative and positive issues because it was (somewhat tacitly assumed) that both belong to the realm of science. Adam Smith himself, as a moral philosopher, made a number of normative statements in his works.

However, the *law of diminishing returns* as elaborated by eighteenth-century French economist Jacques Turgot,[22] and by nineteenth-century British economists David Ricardo and Thomas Malthus on the one side; and the *law of diminishing marginal utility* as defined by nineteenth-century German economist Hermann Heinrich Gossen[23] relying on Bentham's Utilitarianism, paved the way for the marginal revolution (led by Stanley Jevons[24] in England, Carl Menger[25] in Austria, Leon Walras[26] in France and Vilfredo Pareto[27] in Italy) of the late nineteenth century. The combination of these two elements gave sense to the idea of a natural balancing mechanism of supply and demand, namely the market price (as previously suggested by Adam Smith).

This notion of equilibrium builds the core of the methodology of orthodox economics, which was given further theoretical and mathematical rigor by the models of Hicks,[28] Samuelson[29] and Arrow and Debreu[30] (neoclassical synthesis[31]). As already commented, *economics* (in contraposition to political economy) ended up being a science of automatic, market-based regulated *exchange* between atomistic and identical agents, which left out the important, inherent tendency toward disequilibrium existent in the economic systems. In this context, historic specific elements such as technology, government policies, political culture etc. became part of the things politicians and other "non-economic" actors were supposed to deal with.

However, life has shown that such a vision is unable to explain even the most ubiquitous economic questions. The division between economics and political economy has proved to be spurious and prejudicial, in terms of both theory and policy. In fact, economic systems are part of complex and interrelated sets of heterogeneous societal elements, which remains in constant disequilibrium. This has been gradually reflected by a broad spectrum of insights provided by Veblenian, Schumpeterian and neo-Schumpeterian economists, business historians, evolutionary-based institutionalists, innovation economists, development economists and complexity economists. For example, the institutional methodology proposed by Wilber and Harrison (1978) advocates for holistic explanations that take into account the complexity of economic reality; and recognizes the need to contextualize economics models building by acknowledging the social and historical specificity of particular situations.

In many of these insights (if not with the same intensity) the argument in favor of including the *historical element* in the economic analysis has been clearly advanced, in order to better deal with the complex nature of economic systems. This has had a strong impact in defining the methodological foundations of the work of some important contemporary scholars (although still a minority).

For instance, in recent times, the utilization of case studies and qualitative historical-comparatives studies in the fields of economics has experienced an authentic renaissance, mostly as a reaction to the a-historical methodology employed by the neoclassical economics in the last three decades. Particularly during the last decade or so, many scholars have confirmed, beyond any doubt, the validity and usefulness of the historical scrutiny of the economic performance.

Among many other papers and essays that can be included, we can mention such relevant works as Chang's *Kicking Away the Ladder* of 2003; Reinert's *How Rich Countries Got Rich... And Why Poor Countries Stay Poor* of 2007; Cimoli, Dosi and Stiglitz as editors and co-writers of 2009's *Industrial Policy and Economic Development: The Political Economy of Capabilities Accumulation;* Lazonick's *Sustainable Prosperity in the New Economy? Business Organisation and High-Tech Employment in the United States* of 2008; or the 1999 study funded by the US National Academy of Sciences titled *Funding a Revolution: Government Support for Computing Research.* These works, and many others, have successfully addressed the problem of historical specificity, while at the same time identifying relevant cross-case causal mechanisms behind the innovative behaviors of firms and industries, which in the end lead to economic development.

Chang (2003) defends the validity of the historical approach by observing that knowledge of historical facts about developmental experiences carried out by industrialized countries elsewhere allows (developing, but also developed) countries to "make informed choices about policies and institutions that may be appropriate for them" (p. 140). Understanding the role of policies and institutions in economic development implies "throwing out historical myths and overly abstract theories that are blinding many theoretician and policymakers" (ibid.).

In fact, the theory of the innovative firm (Lazonick 2002), one of the central elements of the theoretical approach being employed in the present case study, explicitly proposes to use the *historical-transformation methodology* in which relevant theories are the result of an "iterative intellectual approach in which theoretical postulates are derived from the study of the historical record and the resultant theory is used to analyze history as an ongoing and unfolding process" (p. 4). A similar point has been made by the Other Canon School (Reinert 2007), which aims at employing "observable facts, experience and lesson-drawing as the starting point for theorizing about economics" (p. 30).

Allowing historical specificity to re-enter the discourse on economics does not mean learning from the past only by passively collecting or cataloging historical facts, but by fundamentally providing *working hypotheses* or *persistent historical patterns* (for future research) by analyzing specific study cases. Comparative historical analysis is essential in order to understand the *socio-institutional* conditions under which the innovative enterprise came into being and became a catalyser of progress.

Notes

1 Reinert E, *How Rich Countries Got Rich…and Why Poor Countries Stay Poor*, Constable, London, 2007, p. 35.
2 Ibid.
3 Ibid., p. 46.
4 The definition of institutions refers not only to formal and informal rules, but also includes organizations (seen as a set of formal and informal institutions) such as firms, universities, government agencies etc. (see G Hodgson, What are institutions, *Journal of Economic Issues*, Vol XL, No. 1, 2006, pp. 8–13).
5 To find a definition of case study has been (and still is) one of the biggest challenges of the social science methodological debate. We follow here the general definition given by George/Bennett which defines case study by as "the detailed examination of an aspect of a historical episode to develop or test historical explanations that may be generalizable to other events" (see AL George and A Bennett, Case *Studies* and *Theory Development* in the *Social Sciences*, MIT Press, Cambridge, MA, 2005, p. 5). This definition is also compatible with the one given by Robert Yin as an empirical inquiry that investigates a contemporary phenomenon within its real-life context, in which multiple sources of evidence are used. A very detailed discussion on the subject can be found in George and Bennet (see also B Flyvbjerg, Case Study, In: Denzin and Lincoln eds., The Sage Handbook of the Qualitative Research, 4th edition (Thousand Oaks, CA: Sage, 2011, Chapter 17, pp. 301–16 or J Gerring, Case Study Research Principles and Practices, Cambridge University Press, 2007.
6 All hypotheses involve at least one independent variable (X) and one dependent variable (Y). For convenience, this author labels "the causal factor of special

theoretical interest X1, and the control (background) variable, or vector of controls (if there are any), X2" (Gerring, p. 71).

7   "Note that to pursue an X1/Y-centered analysis does *not* imply that the writer is attempting to prove or disprove a monocausal or deterministic argument. The presumed causal relationship between X1 and Y may be of any sort. X1 may explain only a small amount of variation in Y. The X1/Y relationship may be probabilistic. X1 may refer either to a single variable or to a vector of causal factors. This vector may be an interrelationship (e.g., an interaction term). The only distinguishing feature of X1/Y-centered analysis is that a specific causal factor(s), a specific outcome, and some pattern of association between the two are stipulated. Thus, X1/Y-centered analysis presumes a particular hypothesis – a proposition. Y- or X-centered analysis, by contrast, is much more open-ended".

(ibid., pp. 71–2)

8   According to Gerring "[…] the world of social science may be usefully divided according to the predominant goal undertaken in a given study, either hypothesis *generating* or hypothesis *testing*" (p. 39). He argues, however that "[c]ase studies enjoy a natural advantage in research of an exploratory nature" (p. 40) because the introduction of new interpretations and insights easier, in fact almost obligatory, when carrying out in-depth analysis of unique events. In his words

"It is the very fuzziness of case studies that grants them an advantage in research at the exploratory stage, for the single-case study allows one to test a multitude of hypotheses in a rough-and-ready way. Nor is this an entirely conjectural process. The relationships discovered among different elements of a single case have a prima facie causal connection: they are all at the scene of the crime. This is revelatory when one is at an early stage of analysis, for at that point there is no identifiable suspect and the crime itself may be difficult to discern".

(ibid., p. 41)

9   Herbert Simon proposed a methodological principle that he called "principle of continuity of approximation." It asserts: "If the conditions of the real world approximate sufficiently well the assumptions of an ideal type, the derivations from these assumptions will be approximately correct […]Unreality of premises is not a virtue in scientific theory; it is a necessary evil-a concession to the finite computing capacity of the scientist that is made tolerable by the principle of continuity of approximation" (see GC Archibald; HA Simon; PA Samuelson, Discussion, *The American Economic Review*, Vol. 53, No. 2, Papers and Proceedings of the Seventy-Fifth Annual Meeting of the American Economic Association, May 1963, p. 231)

10 We refer here to contingent generalization instead of abstract generalizations (see George and Bennett, see also Hodgson, How *Economics Forgot History*: The *Problem of Historical Specificity* in *Social Science*, Routledge, London/New York, 2001, pp. 3–21).

11 This is important because at earlier stages of the research, the Cuban case was thought to be a theoretical anomaly or deviant case (according to the standard theory) and we ended up defining it as a crucial (least-likely) case (see above Case selection). We suggest that the phenomena at play in the latter are somewhat expressed in the former.

12 This refers to the definition "covering law" given by Carl Hempel. For a discussion, see B. Danermark et al., *Explaining Society: Critical Realism in Social Sciences*, Routledge, London and New York, 2002, pp. 106–9). See also George and Bennett, p. 226).

13 The concept was introduced into modern logic by the founder of American Pragmatism; Charles Sanders Peirce. It differs from induction in that we start from a rule describing a pattern; and it differs from deduction in that the conclusion is not logically given in the premise. Essentially abduction is about recontextualizing, i.e. to observe, describe, interpret and explain within a frame of a new context (B Danermark et al., *Explaining...* pp. 89–95).

14 According to George and Bennett a number of earlier writers have made the same point, referring to process-tracing variously as "a genetic explanation" (Ernest Nagel), "a sequential explanation" (Louis Mink), "the model of the continuous series" (William Dray), "a chain of causal explanations" (Michael Scriven), "narrative explanations" (R. F. Atkinson), and "the structure of a narrative explanation" (Arthur Danto). Roberts chooses to call this explanatory process "colligation," drawing on earlier usages of this term and clarifying its meaning (p. 226).

15 One of the central assumptions for the use of counterfactuals is that the causal variable identified operated independently of other causal variables. This assumption is often difficult to substantiate, a fact that makes the use of a counterfactual problematic (ibid., pp. 231–3). In the field of development economics, Chang reflects on this subject while analyzing the success of industrial policy in East Asia. According to this author it is logically possible (to hypothesize the role of market forces in the East Asian miracle), but if that were to be the case, these countries must have had some country-specific "countervailing forces" that were so powerful that they cancelled out all the harmful effects of market-distorting industrial policy and still generated the highest growth rates in human history (6-7% annual growth rate in per capita income over four decades, before China's miracle). He finds this highly implausible. Are these skeptics really seriously suggesting, continues Chang, that, without industrial policy, these powerful countervailing forces would have made the East Asian countries grow at – what? – 9%, 10%, or even 12%, when no country in history has ever grown at faster than 7% for an extended period, industrial policy or not? Anyhow, concludes Chang, no convincing story built around these countervailing forces has been offered [...] Of course [...], it is impossible to definitely prove that East Asia could have done better or worse without industrial policy [...] However, not all counterfactuals are equally plausible, and the counterfactual supposed by the critics of industrial policy is highly implausible. This nudges us towards the conclusion that industrial policy worked in East Asia. Moreover, once we go beyond the late-20th century East Asian experiences, there is quite a lot of evidence that further strengthens (although once again cannot "prove") the case for industrial policy (see the whole quotation in HJ Chang, 'Industrial policy: Can we go beyond an unproductive confrontation?', A Plenary Paper for ABCDE (Annual World Bank Conference on Development Economics), Seoul, South Korea, 2009, June 22–4, pp. 5–13).

16 A principle of open system, which consists of the possibility that different initial conditions can lead to the same end state. The term was coined by the Austrian-born system theorist Ludwig von Bertalanffy (1904–1968).

17 Note that this refers to qualitative variables, which may contain several attributes, some of them not even quantifiable.

18 Geoffrey Hodgson provides an accomplished and very detailed analysis in *How Economics…*

19 Friedrich List's contemporaries did not regard him as a member of the historical school, largely because he was not a university academic and he lived much of his life outside Germany. However, his inclusion in the school is appropriate because he focused with acute vision on the contrasts between different types of national economic system. He brought attention to the historical and specific features of national economic development (ibid., p. 73).

20 In the 1791 *Report on the Manufacturers of the United States,* the first US Secretary of the Treasury, Alexander Hamilton, recreates the toolbox employed by Henry VII during the XVI century England.

21 The major limitation of this school is said to have failed to articulate a relationship between the particular and the general. "Here universal theories are rejected in favour of particular theories based on 'simple description' of specific phenomena. This type of blunt appeal to historical facts as a basis for a historically confined economic theory was typical of much subsequent writing by the older historicists" (Hodgson, *How Economics…*, p. 59). In particular, the successes of their "Austrian" opponents, in the controversies of the *Methodenstreit* of the 1880s and thereafter, were partly due to these weaknesses. This also explains the neoclassical reaction against this school, personified in the Robinns essay. The first methodological counter-attack by the historically inclined economists was flawed, and an adequate methodological response did not emerge. A principal weakness in the earlier historical school tradition (not necessarily later traditions of that School) was an excessive faith in empiricism and inductive methods. However, the fact is that the neoclassical approach succeeded by both ignoring and burying the problem of historical specificity, but has failed to come up with new ways of addressing the problem. The most recent financial crisis and the massive and scandalous failure of the one-size-fits-all policies inspired by the neoclassical-based Washington Consensus around the world prove that assertion.

22 An important work is Reflections on the Formation and Distribution of Wealth (English version) written in 1786 and published in 1769–76.

23 His most important book was *Die Entwickelung der Gesetze des menschlichen Verkehrs, und der daraus fließenden Regeln für menschliches Handeln* (*The Development of the Laws of Human Intercourse and the* Consequent Rules of Human Action) published in 1854.

24 In his *General Mathematical Theory of Political Economy* (published in 1862) he outlined the marginal utility theory.

25 He was the founder of the Austrian School and a formidable opponent of the German historical School. *His methodological debate with Gustav Schmoller was the most important element of the so-called Methodenstreit (see Die Irrtümer des Historicismus in der Deutschen Nationalökonomie (The flaws of the historicism) published in 1884.*

26 His masterwork was *Elements of a Pure Economics*, written in 1872. Walras derived his notions of static equilibrium from the *Elements of Statics,* published in 1803 by the French mathematician Louis Poinsot.

27 In his work *Manual of Political Economy* (1906) he introduced the notion of *Pareto-optimality,* which is the condition under which markets reach equilibrium so that no further trades can be made without making someone worse off. The Pareto optimal is not necessarily the point at which value is maximized for the entire group, as there might be some trades that would harm some people for the benefit

of others, but would nonetheless raise the sum total utility of the group (see E Beinhocker, *The Origin of Wealth: Evolution, Complexity, and the Radical Remaking of Economics*, Harvard Business School Press, MA, 2006, p. 36). Together with Walras, Pareto belonged to the Lausanne School of economics, sometimes referred to as the *Mathematical School,* and both represent the second generation of the Neoclassic Revolution

28 His main work is *Value and Capital,* which was essentially a synthesis of the works of Walras, Marshall, and Pareto into a coherent theory.

29 In his *Foundations of Economic* he took Hicks's theory, added his insights on revealed preferences; and turned it into a dazzling mathematical theory that become the standard model for the workings of markets.

30 Arrow and Debreu connected Walras's notion of a general equilibrium with Pareto's concept of optimality in a very general way, thus creating the Neoclassical theory of general equilibrium. According to Beinhocker "[a]t the height of the Cold War, it was eventually interpreted in the political realm (albeit incorrectly) as final mathematical proof of the superiority of market capitalism over socialism" (p. 38).

31 This synthesis was essentially microeconomic at the beginning, but during the 1960s and 1970s, economists such as Milton Friedman and Robert Lucas (Chicago School) began to apply the techniques of neoclassical microeconomics to macroeconomics, and concepts such as rational utility-maximizing consumers and optimal equilibriums became a core part of orthodox macroeconomic theory as well.

References

Alexander Hamilton's Final Version of the Report on the Subject of Manufactures (5 December 1791), *Founders Online*, National Archives, available at: https://founders. archives.gov/documents/Hamilton/01-10-02-0001-0007. [Original source: Syrett H (1966), *The Papers of Alexander Hamilton*, vol. 10, *December 1791–January 1792*, New York: Columbia University Press, 1966, pp. 230–340.]

Archibald GC, Simon H and Samuelson P (1963), Problem of methodology: Discussion, *The American Economic Review*, Papers and Proceedings of the Seventy-Fifth Annual Meeting of the American Economic Association 53 (2): 227–36.

Beinhocker E (2006), *The Origin of Wealth: Evolution, Complexity, and the Radical Remaking of Economics.* Boston, MA: Harvard Business School Press.

Bhaskar R (1978), A Realist Theory of Science. Hassocks: Harvester Press.

Borgatti S et al. (2009), Network analysis in social sciences, *Science* 13 (February): 892–95.

Chang HJ (2003), *Kicking Away the Ladder.* London: Anthem Press.

Cimoli M et al. (eds.) (2009), *Industrial Policy and Economic Development: The Political Economy of Capabilities Accumulation.* Oxford: Oxford University Press.

Danermark B et al. (2002), *Explaining Society: Critical Realism in Social Sciences.* London and New York: Routledge.

Denzin N (2006), *Sociological Methods: A Sourcebook,* 5th edition. New Brunswick, N.J.: Aldine Transaction.

Eckstein H (1975), Case studies and theory in political science. In: FI Greenstein and NW Polsby (eds.), *Handbook of Political Science*, vol. 7. Political Science: Scope and Theory. Reading, MA: Addison-Wesley, pp. 94–137.

Flyvbjerg B (2011), Case study. In: N Denzin and Y Lincoln (eds.), *The Sage Handbook of the Qualitative Research*, 4th edition. Thousand Oaks, CA: Sage, pp. 301–16.

Foster J (2005), From simplistic to complex systems in economics, *Cambridge Jornal of Economics* 29 (6): 873–92.

George AL and Bennett A (2005), *Case Studies and Theory Development in the Social Sciences.* Cambridge, MA: MIT Press.

Gerring J (2007), *Case Study Research Principles and Practices.* Cambridge: Cambridge University Press.

Hodgson G (2001), *How Economics Forgot History: The Problem of Historical Specificity in Social Science.* London/New York: Routledge.

Hodgson G (2006), What are institutions?, *Journal of Economic Issues* XL (1): 1–25

Hughes et al. (1999), *Funding a Revolution: Government Support for Computing Research.* Washington, D.C.: National Academy Press.

Jevons W (2013) [1871], *The Theory of Political Economy*, Fourth Edition, Palgrave Macmillan.

Lazonick W (2002), Innovative enterprise and historical transformation, *Enterprise & Society*, 3 (1): 3–47.

Lazonick W (2008), *Sustainable Prosperity in the New Economy? Business Organisation and High-Tech Employment in the United States.* Kalamazoo, Michigan: W.E. Upjohn Institute for Employment Research.

Pisano G (2006), *Science Business: The Premise, the Reality, and the Future of Biotech.* Boston, MA: Harvard Business School Press.

Reinert E (2007), *How Rich Countries got Rich… and Why Poor Countries Stay Poor.* London: Constable.

Roberts C (1996), *The Logic of Historical Explanation.* The Pennsylvania State University Press.

Wasserman S and Faust K (1994), *Social Network Analysis: Methods and Applications.* Cambridge: Cambridge University Press.

Wessner C et al. (eds.) (2001), *Capitalizing on New Needs and New Opportunities: Government-Industry Partnerships in Biotechnology and Information Technologies.* Washington, D.C.: National Academy Press.

Wilber C and Harrison R (1978), The methodological basis of institutional economics: Pattern models, storytelling and holism. *Journal of Economic Issues* XII (1): 61–89.

Yin R (2003a), *Applications of Case Study Research*, 2nd edition. Thousand Oaks, CA: Sage.

Yin R (2003b), *Case Study Research: Design and Methods*, 3rd edition. Thousand Oaks, CA: Sage.

Part I

Theory and conceptualization

2 Economies as networks

2.1 The economy as a complex system

Even while advancing an all-encompassing definition of complex systems is far from being a trivial task, there seems to be some, if neither universal nor definitive, consensus about their common features. Herbert Simon, one of the founding fathers of the field, defined a complex system as

> one made up of a large number of parts that interact in a non-simple way. In such systems, the whole is more than the sum of the parts, not in an ultimate, metaphysical sense, but in the important pragmatic sense that, given the properties of the parts and the laws of their interaction, it is not a trivial matter to infer the properties of the whole.
>
> (Simon 1962, p. 468)

In addition to Herbert Simon, the application of the complex system perspective in economics specifically can be also found in the earlier contributions of economists such as Gunnar Myrdal (cumulative circular causation),[1] Nicholas Georgescu-Roegen (entropy)[2] and Friedrich Hayek (dispersed knowledge).

The idea of the world as a historically contingent, organic and evolutionary entity has, though, a longer tradition in economics. Notions of fundamental uncertainty and continuous structural change are also to be found in Adam Smith, Joseph Schumpeter, Karl Marx, Thorstein Veblen, Adolph Wagner, Frank Knight, Nicholas Kaldor and John M. Keynes, among others. Suffice it to recall that most of them understood that society and technology shape one another, i.e., co-evolve, in non-linear ways, which leads to the emergence of different patterns of behaviors and organization. Veblen (1898) refers to "a cumulative process of adaptation of means to ends that cumulatively change as the process goes on, both the agent and his environment being at any point the outcome of the past process" (p. 391).

The material life of a community is both the cause and effect of changes in that community's habit of thought. This constitutive relationship crystallizes as a progression of conflicts between different vested interests, constantly engaged in political negotiations about the attributes of society and technology, which involves social power relationships, ethical and moral views, political agendas or commercial interests. These insights have been relatively recently, 25 years ago, re-absorbed into the complexity economics program advanced by the Santa Fe Institute in California, and expanded elsewhere, which has taken advantage from recent improvements in computational power to develop new techniques and experiments that help to explore and model economic evolution in a more realist manner.

The term of "complexity economics" was, in a sort of serendipitous way, coined by Arthur (1999) and it has since then become an interesting area of investigation within economic sciences. Looking at the economy from this perspective means to examine in detail "how individual behaviors might react to the patterns they together create" (Arthur 2015, p. 3). Similarly, complexity is defined in more general terms not as a theory but as "a movement in the sciences that studies how the interacting elements in a system create overall patterns, and how these overall patterns in turn cause the interacting elements to change or adapt" (ibid.). This way of thinking has certainly expanded to other areas such as political economy, behavioral economics or innovation and development economics, sometimes arriving at conflicting, if not necessarily insurmountable, conclusions about the role of certain agents within the economic system.

Even when the framework called "complexity economics" etymologically relates to the concept it intends to capture, it is neither the only nor the first framework making "complex systems" assumptions about the economic system. For example, in this study we explore the idea of government and market as consubstantial entities, which is an assumption made by the complexity framework (Colander and Kuper 2014). However this assumption has also been explicitly advanced in the past by Adam Smith, Friedrich List or Karl Polanyi and by Evans (1995), Hodgson (2001), Chang (2002), among others, in recent times. In addition, the extent to which current advocates of the complexity view apply the framework greatly depends on the particular views they have about the topic under discussion. In this study the framework will be conceived as a project in construction, always open for corrections and additions, just as some of its most enlightened practitioners advocate (Arthur 2015; Colander and Kuper 2014).

As above suggested, at the core of the concept of complex systems is the ability of multi-agent structures to generate non-equilibrium-based self-regulative scenarios, whose emergent features qualitatively differ from the features of the single agents of which these structures are made. Reflecting on this, Foley (2003, p. 2) points out that complex systems share the capacity of configuring their components parts in a "large number of ways, constant change in response to environmental stimulus and their own development." He further states that these multi-agent structures show "a strong tendency to achieve recognizable patterns in their configurations."

Other similar definitions include Rocha (2000), which defines a complex system as any system composed of a large number of interacting components (agents, processes, etc.) whose aggregate activity is nonlinear (not derivable from the summations of the activity of individual components). According to Amaral and Ottino (2004) a complex system is a system with a large number of elements, building block or agents, capable of interacting with each other and with the environment. Foster (2005) identifies complex systems as "dissipative structures that import free energy and export entropy" capable to self-organize themselves and to maintain their boundaries.

Many processes are highly cross-linked in nature and in society as well. In many systems, however, we can distinguish a set of fundamental building blocks, which interact nonlinearly to form compound structures or functions with an identity that requires more explanatory devices from those used to explain the building blocks. Examples of these systems are gene networks that direct developmental processes, immune networks that preserve the identity of organisms, social insect colonies, neural networks in the brain that produce intelligence and consciousness, ecological networks, social networks comprised of transportation, utilities, and telecommunication systems, as well as economies.

When defining the economy from a complex system perspective, however, an important issue of contention arises regarding self-organization. As already pointed out, one of the most relevant characteristics attributed to complex systems consists of the ability of self-organization. Amaral and Ottino (2004) points out that "the common characteristic of all complex systems is that they display organization without any *external* organizing principle being applied" (p. 148). Rocha (2000) argues that "self-organization is seen as the process by which systems of many components tend to reach a particular state, a set of cycling states, or a small volume of their state space, with no external interference."[3] In most of the explanations the element of non-external interference is emphasized. However, although this definition applies to a wide range of disciplines, the concrete form that it takes will be actually dependent on the kind of system under study.

In the field of economics, the idea of self-organization is inextricably linked to the notion of spontaneous order advanced by Friedrich von Hayek (and somewhat different to the original notion of the term intended by Michael Polanyi), the foremost representative of the Austrian School. In this notion, the degree of complexity that social systems display is such that they cannot be conceived as the creation of any single agency, since no individual is able to possess the complete knowledge that is embodied in the system (Hayek 1973, pp. 11–16). This undoubtedly profound and sophisticated notion rejects, of course, any state role in the good functioning of a complex economy. Therefore, the best way to efficiently allocate resources in a complex economy consists of allowing individuals to pursue their objectives through free market competition (what Hayek termed as catallactics[4]) while preventing them from being imposed a hierarchy of ends by any single authority (taxis[5]). The behavioral rules governing both the free exchange and the creation of skills and knowledge result from a spontaneous selection process rooted in the individuals' interactions.

To be sure, in Austrian and neo-Austrian views, the state role should consist of encouraging and improving by law (previously existent) general rules that allow the spontaneous order to work properly. That is, government size is not as important as its function. But in definitional terms, the government agency is regarded as a political entity outside the economic system, which should not interfere with its self-organization process. In the Austrian perspective there can be neither short- nor long-term goals that the state can meaningfully pursue at systemic level.

However, as also proposed by the present study (see Chapters 3 and 4), the notion of a self-organizing national innovation system, in terms of Hayek's definition, counters all historical accounts on economic development. The historical evidence shows how the government agency, in different places and times, has been involved in the creation (or annihilation) and development (or retardation) of new technologies and promising industries. Its function has not been merely that of an external, impartial agent but that of an essential component of the system, thus reflecting, and at the same time helping, to constitute the changing balance of social forces within society.

While the institutional forms that these efforts have taken differ (e.g. welfare state, neo-liberal state, democratic state, dictatorial state, corporative state, developmental state, socialist state, capitalist state etc.) the point is that the state and the political system are embedded in an ensemble of social relations. Therefore, it is difficult to talk about a self-organizing economic system on the one hand and about a government agency external to the system on the other. Actually, the state as institution has a polymorphic nature, which means that its projects and strategies are unavoidably related to a wide balance of forces within and beyond the state. That is, the links between government strategy and economic system need to be seen in relational terms (opposed to the traditional hierarchical terms).

As part of his strategic-relational approach, Jessop (2010) defines[6] the state as an "ensemble of power centres and capacities that offer unequal chances to different forces within and outside the state and that cannot, *qua* institutional ensemble, exercise power" (p. 45). In other words, it is not the state, as such, that exercises power. Instead, "its powers (plural) are activated by changing sets of state officials located in specific parts of the state in specific conjunctures" (ibid.). That is, state powers are always "conditional or relational" and their realization depends on the complex interdependencies between the state, the political system, and the rest of the society.

This does not mean that the state lacks autonomy as a system. In autopoietic[7] terms, the constellation of subsystems that make a society are autonomous in the sense that they define and defend their own boundaries vis-à-vis their self-defined external environments. However, this notion of autopoiesis (third order) emphasizes the point that "these systems are not hermetically sealed off from their environments but experience changes therein as perturbations that affect their own operation" (Jessop 1990, p. 358). That means that "the development of a given autonomous structure is conditioned by its relation to other structures" and, at the same time, this given structure "follows its own logic" (which also co-evolves along with the structure it sustains). Thus the history of the relation of this structure "with its environment is imprinted in its present organization and modus operandi [...]" (p. 359).

Seen from this perspective, it could be plausible to interpret the available historical evidence in such a way that, even when the state is not to be conceived above society, it achieves its autonomy as an agent in that it is able to articulate the different social subsystems or structures treated as autonomous structures.[8] The government agency is characterized by a "structurally inscribed strategic selectivity" (Jessop 2010, p. 45), which makes it the only agent with the potential (if not the actuality) to stand for the whole society.

However the state is not there to find optimal combinations of existing system resources since there is no optimal solution in terms of socioeconomic development. In complex processes such as economic development and innovation, the final outcome is uncertain. Optimal solutions are only plausible in the short term, when there is a known set of future outcomes and known probabilities associated with each occurrence. However, complex processes such as innovation and economic development usually mean breaking new ground, entering unknown territory, and will require abilities and resources that are hidden, scattered, badly utilized or simply non-existent. It is the need to recognize and exploit new opportunities in the middle of uncertainties "[w]hat makes the public sector entrepreneurial[...]" (Hayter et. al 2018, p. 677). That is, the state does not promote development in that it only adapts to a given set of choices, but is meant to become an entrepreneurial agent by "reformulating the choice set itself" (Chang 1999, p. 194).

In other words, all forms of state are meant to provide a hegemonic vision or general line "that seek to reconcile the particular and the universal by linking the state's purposes to a broader – but always selective – political, intellectual and moral vision of the public interest" (Jessop 2010, p. 48). Given that the process is inevitably selective, conflict management is expected to play an important role. For that reason, consensus should not be understood as a harmonious condition, because consensus usually arises from a conflict-ridden process that frequently leaves out potentially significant players. Consequently, all state forms (and their interaction with their environment) can be said to be contingent (if not necessarily in the short term) and ever-evolving, since they are just one element of a complex social order and have limited capacities to intervene in other parts of the whole, even when, simultaneously, they are expected to maintain institutional integration and social cohesion. Jessop (1990) calls this peculiar circumstance "an inevitable feature of the state paradoxical position as both part and whole of the society" (p. 361).

If some sort of self-organization is present in the economic systems (seen from a complex perspective) then it should include the state in some way. The state action should be seen as a constitutive element of the operational codes that help to define the boundaries of the economic system. But, if the self-organization process includes the state, does it make any sense to continue to talk about state intervention in the economy? The answer is yes. Even when the state is part of the economic system, it has relative autonomy with respect to the economy because of its paradoxical position as an agent, which consists (at least nominally) of achieving strategic coordination among the different societal subsystems in order to enforce collectively binding decisions. In fact, it could be said that the government agency, as institution, helped build the (self-regulative and evolving) discourse of all societal subsystems (although selectively), and at the same time, is independent enough to intervene in them. This seemingly paradoxical state of affairs only makes sense if society is seen relationally.

The present study defends a notion of economy as a complex, self-regulatory system, which includes the government agency as an indissoluble element of the system.[9] However, in order to avoid confusion, the present study will only refer to "self-organization" in the sense of Hayek. This should allow a better differentiation between this traditional concept and the notions advanced by the study. Chapter 3 is intended to further develop some of these notions.

2.2 Innovation as a relational process

As discussed in the section above, economic systems are far from being isolated societal systems formed by independent and identical agents. Economic development and innovation are processes that presuppose the existence of a widespread division of labor and comprise an ever increasing variety of participants. These essentially collective processes are very much embedded within social, cultural and political systems; which results in cumulative and complex interdependencies, which, contrary to much that is presumed by conventional wisdom, do not allow taking for granted the existence of unambiguous and totally predictable outcomes.

Actually, innovation involves path dependent search and experimentation in the middle of strong uncertainty. This process is not simply driven by firms, but also their interaction with a number of *non-firm organizations* (states, public organizations, civil society organizations, unions, research organizations etc., henceforth NFO) with very different functions and points of interest (Evans 1995; Malerba 2002; Freeman 2008; Cimoli et al. 2009).

This interdependency reflects the relational property of innovation and economic development. Both need to be understood as very "complex bargaining process[es]," where the markets[10] are not likely to be the "primary matchmakers" (Lazonick 2011, p. 40). The success of these processes becomes very dependent of what Lazonick (2002, 2008, 2011) calls "*organizational integration*" (see Chapter 4). The idea is also found in Simon (1991), who contends that it is organizations (rather than markets), that played a major role in economic development and innovation.

Thus seen, it makes sense to represent economic systems as a network of interdependent elements, whose outcomes depend on their positions in the network. In contrast to what many orthodox economists believe, heterodox approaches (evolutionary, institutional, neo-Schumpeterian, development economics, complexity economics, economic history) are telling us that economic systems are actually complex systems in continuous evolution; composed of interdependent and heterogeneous entities, whose real value lies in the connection they can establish among themselves, rather than in their separate individual capabilities (Kirman 2011; Elsner 2010; Coe et al. 2008; Freeman 2008; Beinhocker 2006; Fster 2005; Dopfer et al. 2004; Lazonick 2002, 2008; Chang (2002, 2010).

The fundamental difference between a network-based explanation and a non-network explanation of a process is the inclusion of concepts and information on *relationships* among units in a study (Wasserman and Faust 1994, p. 6). This means that the relevant theoretical concepts and data are to be conceived relationally. The term *relational* means that relations established by linkages among units are a fundamental component of the theory. During the last decades several relationally defined theoretical concepts have made their entrance into the academic discourse of economics. For instance, concepts such as organizational learning, tacit knowledge, national (sectoral) system of innovation, or knowledge transfer are relational definitions.

However, today, a good part of the mainstream academic discourse in economics tends to ignore relational information. Most of the methodological individualistic orthodox economics (although this has been gradually reduced in the last decades) tends to focus on punctual attributes of autonomous individual units, the associations between these attributes, or the usefulness of one or more attributes for predicting the level of another attribute (Wasserman and Faust 1994; Hodgson 2000; Reinert 2007). This has built the base for the application of the most standards statistical methods in the social sciences (including economics). Without disregarding the utility of such methods, it must be said, however, that the historical evidence revealing the existence of synergies and direct interdependencies between economic agents has been frequently left outside of the explanation (Reinert 2007). However, the reality is one of firms, industries and economies that exchange and produce resources in very complex and interconnected ways, the firm being only a very proximate unit of analysis (Coe 2008).

Of course, it does not mean that firms do not matter. Firms are themselves networks like any other economic entities. Undoubtedly, to develop in-house R&D competencies within the enterprises remains essential for technology acquisition and technical innovation (Dosi et al. 1994; Freeman 2008). However, it is not only about R&D, but also about a wide range of scientific and technical services (STS) which reinforce and interact with R&D and in the early stages can often substitute for it.

Although a firm may manufacture a product, the process usually involves other partners or subcontracting firms; and a range of consultants and specialists in the service sector may be also involved. They include quality control, market research, design, testing, production engineering, technical information services, and a number of training activities. Not to mention the role of the government agency in both delivering most of these services and connecting previously unrelated actors within the economy, and also assuming the financial and technological risks of in the development of innovative breakthroughs (Mazzucato 2013; Lazonick 2011; Chang 2002, 2003, 2010).

As Foster (2005) points out, "modern production systems are bewildering networks of connections," which means that the functional boundaries of the firm are not as clear as can be thought (p. 889). Therefore, even if firms are usually clearly defined legal entities with specific legally established boundaries; it makes sense to think of them as networks embedded within networks, with varying degrees of imbrications and interconnections (Coe et al. 2008). The boundaries between internalization and externalization of functions are in a "continuous state of flux, involving a complex reconfiguring of organisational boundaries," which is critical for the development of new products and processes (ibid., p. 277).

New and more sophisticated products are only possible because new combinations of a huge variety of inputs are carried out; very often also within new organizational settings. Knowledge developed in one sector spill over "apparently unconnected sectors providing the point that new knowledge is created by linking previously unconnected facts or events" (Reinert 2007, p. 94). A proof of the existence of these mechanisms could be found in the so-called "complex product industries," which encompasses industries such as the electronic, computer, ICT, automotive, aerospace, software or biotechnology (Marengo et al. 2009, also called complex product system in Dosi et al. 2003). Complex products are those made of many different components whose production typically involves different underlying bodies of technological knowledge (ibid., p. 2). Their "multi-components and multi-technology nature" usually involves the participation of many different companies (ibid., p. 2).

Networks express the need to coordinate and integrate all these extraordinarily intricate, uncertain operations, as rapidly and efficiently as possible. At the core of this need is the fact that time- and quality-based competition depends on eliminating waste in the form of time, effort, defective units, and inventory in manufacturing-distribution systems (Coe et al. 2008). Economics of scale, scope; and network effects all depend on "synergies created in such system of networks" (Reinert 2007, p. 104). These advantages in terms of economies of scale and scope derives, as already pointed out, from the larger chances that networks offer for technology recombination among complementary components. They provide the kind of increasing returns that makes industrial advancement and economic growth possible. The more fluid the networking process, the better the chances for innovation.

When the networking process functions properly, we are in the presence of what Lazonick (2011) calls "organisational success." One of the concepts intended to describe a successful networking process is called *organizational integration*. The concept arises from the field of innovation economics and gives an idea of the extent to which governments, businesses, and other NFOs are all working together to develop and utilize a society's productive resources (the concept will be treated in more detail in Chapter 4).

The present research is particularly (although by no means exclusively) interested in the contribution of government-based NFOs in the process just mentioned above. But which specific properties are suitable to complex economic systems that make possible the idea of the government agency as an indissoluble part of that system? In the first section of the chapter we saw that while most of the complex systems (e.g. physical, chemical, biological, social and economic systems) that display organized complexity, all share common properties, they differ in important aspects. Reflecting on this, Foster (2005), relying on Foley (2003), identifies some general properties for an economic system to be defined as a complex adaptive system, which will be detailed hereafter. For the sake of the argument being made in the present study, we have chosen three properties to illustrate our point.

2.3 The economy as a purposeful system

The first property is that of a dissipative structure,[11] one that converts "information into knowledge for the *purpose*[12] of creating, maintaining and expanding the organised complexity of the system" (Foster 2005, p. 875). This notion could be interpreted as the existence of intentionality in the making of an economic system, which arises from the fact that knowledge and enquiry are the results of both "conscious prefiguration and self-reflexive reasoning, with regard to future events or outcomes" (Hodgson 2006, p. 5). Of course, this does not mean that these future outcomes (or the way to achieve them) are a certain thing; nor does this exclude the emergence of unintended events. Still, it could be spoken of conscious prefiguration in that there is a deliberate or purposive disposition toward some state of affairs. Specifically referring to the government role in the creation of new economic spaces of opportunity during U.S. history, Cohen and DeLong (2016) put it bluntly in the introduction of their impassionate defense of industrial policy when they talk about "intelligent designs" as a result of "collective choices" and a common vision instead of "the emergent outcomes of innumerable individual choices" or "the unguided result of mindless evolution" (p 1).

Likewise, seminal contributions on evolutionary technology policy concur with the view that "although the emergence of novelty is unpredictable, the processes which translate novelty into coherent patterns of change are not, and it is on this distinction that the role of technology policy hinges" (Metcalfe 1995, p. 28). This kind of intentionality is at the core of evolutionary institutional economics, because institutions facilitate ordered thought, expectations, and action by giving form and consistency to human activities (Hodgson 2006). No wonder why terms such as *institution* and *organization*[13] are key elements when it comes to understand both growth and innovation.

Again, this is not to say that the outcomes of all human affairs are necessarily deliberate and intended. As Beinhocker (2006) asserts, the combination of sensitivity to initial conditions, path dependence, and immense dynamic complexity makes the economy hard to forecast in any way but the very short term.[14] Michael Polanyi persuasively argued that knowledge has a manifestly tacit dimension, even with the most deliberative of acts.[15] The explanatory relevance of tacit and socially complex resources in understanding firm/industry organization and behavior can be found in a huge amount of literature on organizational capabilities (Penrose 1959; Teece et al. 1997; Nonaka and Krogh 2009).

However, the point is that we should not take a complex socioeconomic system as a purely self-organized entity without any external enforcement, but rather as a mix of both mechanisms. As Hodgson (2006) points out, the literature on self-organization and spontaneous orders provides the essential insight that institutions and other social phenomena can arise in an non-designed way through structured interactions between agents. This characteristic is rooted in the emergent properties of complex systems (Hodgson 2000; Elsner 2010). Some rules can be self-enforcing through endogenous sanction mechanisms agreed through *habituation* (Elsner 2010). However, as already mentioned, much of the literature on self-organization and spontaneous order tend to make "an excessive emphasis on the (albeit essential) idea of self-organization, to the detriment of other vital mechanisms of institutional emergence and sustenance" (Hodgson 2006, p. 14).

The notion of self-organization within the social system can be traced back to David Hume and Adam Smith, through the Austrian school of economics from Carl Menger to Hayek (Hodgson 2006, 2009); and it is a key topic in the modern analysis of complex socioeconomic systems. However the concepts of self-organization or spontaneous order alone are insufficient for an understanding of all institutions, simply because many institutions are the result of deliberate actions (Chang 2002; Vasconcelos 2010).

True, the understanding of economic systems as complex systems suppose the acceptance of unintended emergent properties. For example, innovation and technological change can be rightly labeled as open-ended processes (Elsner 2010). However, innovation is not based on luck alone. As one of the great and pioneering system theorists Russell Ackoff suggested in his 1972's pioneering work *On Purposeful Systems,* in a purposeful system, participants intentionally and collectively formulate objectives that are part of the common purpose into a larger system, the end result being the common purpose different from what the individual component parts would have achieved.

In this context Ackoff calls attention upon the fact that "purposeful members of a system [behave] at a sub-purposeful level" (Ackoff and Emery 2006, p. 220). He makes his case by explaining the relationship between "division of labor, responsibility and authority" while stating that

> without the first, no part of a system could hope to effectively carry out any of the particular functions of a purposeful system, and without observance of the second and third no part would be likely to survive as part of a purposeful system.
>
> (ibid.)

For instance, a report about the impact of US federal investment in research let clear that policymakers have an array of tools that they can use to try to influence the behavior of complex innovation processes (National Research Council 2011). In actual fact, all institutions depend on other institutions, which mean that even self-organizing systems depend on external institutions that are required to enforce the internal rules.[16]

As Nightingale (2004) points out, "innovation requires the construction of predictability, and it is this feature, and not the derivative features of tacitness or bounded rationality, that structures innovative activity" (p. 18). While accepting the unpredictable nature of innovation, he also states that "because predictability isn't natural, both firms and nations need to invest in this infrastructure to exploit research, innovate, import technology or access the international science system"(ibid., p. 20).

In the same mood, Rocha (2000) speaks of "*selected self-organisation,*" because "the self-organising system must be structurally coupled to some external system which acts on the structure of the first inducing some form of explicit or implicit selection of its dynamic classifications" (p. 4). He states that selected self-organization requires both self-organization and a selective process to be specified. In evolutionary economics, a discussion still persists on the nature of the selection process (see e.g. Hodgson 2002). In this sense, Metcalfe (1995) makes an early appeal to handle carefully the notion of selective environment. While in the simplest cases it can be equated with the traditional market mechanism à la Hayek, this is only one level of mode selection. A more accurate representation could state that "[a]ny framework in which agents interact in order to choose between competing patterns of behaviour has selective properties" (Metcalfe 1995, p. 29).

It would be interesting to add that classic institutionalist John Commons preferred the term "artificial selection" to the term "natural selection" when describing the institutional making of economics (Commons 1924, 1934). According to Commons, the concept of natural selection omits the role of human intentionality in the economic system. In this context, Commons places special emphasis in the commanding role of the government as authoritative entity within the economic system.

Even when some criticism to Commons's theory points out that the distinction between state and society, or state and nation, seems to disappear – and that it tends to downplay the importance of inter-organizational relations and therefore the existence of organic institutions (in Menger terms) – the same criticism could be made of the Austrian, Veblens and New institutional traditions "that overly focus on organic institutions" (Chavance 2012, p. 43; Hodgson 2002). At the end, the point to be made is that Commons's view on the role of political institutions in the functioning of the complex economic system needs to be taken into account, when we consider the historical evidence.

Hodgson (2009) reaffirms that a newly formed spontaneous order alone cannot enforce rule fulfilment. This is because mechanisms to ensure cooperation depend on the ability to reward its members; however, this new created order does not yet have the capacities to grant such advantages. Consequently, they need to be built on pre-existing institutions to secure initial compliance. For example, one of the "design principles" mentioned by Ostrom (2010) in her analysis of the field evidence of polycentric governance in complex common-pool resource environments is that the rights of local users to make their own rules are recognized by the government (p. 13).

Even when it is still an open question whether there is any other institution, with the exception of the state, capable of fulfilling this role, historical evidence shows nevertheless, that the state has been an integral part of the formation of complex socioeconomic systems (see Polanyi 1944; Chang 2002, 2003; Evans et al. 1985, 1995; Reinert 2007; Cimoli et al. 2009; Ruttan 2006). In the presence of incomplete and imperfect information, persistent uncertainty, high transaction costs, asymmetrically powerful relations, and agents with limited insight, powerful institutions are necessary to (at the very minimum) enforce rights and to propose trajectories. Of course, technology policy can fail. The process is necessarily politically and administratively constrained and there cannot be a presumption that policymakers have a better understanding of technological information. Rather, what they have is the (potential) ability to coordinate across a wide range of institutions.

2.4 The economy: A system as a whole

Complementing the aforementioned, we have the second property formulated by Foster (2005), which is that such complex an economic system

> is a whole in itself, as well as being a component part of some systems and oppositional to others—it is the connections that are forged between systems that permit the emergence of organised complexity at higher levels of aggregation.
>
> (p. 875)

Indeed, as already suggested, firms are embedded in networks, industries and sectors, which make technological and organizational innovations dense and highly interdependent and complementary phenomena.

For instance, "case studies of the role of research in innovation reveal an extremely complex process in which research is an important element of the process but not the only important element. Everything is connected to everything else" (National Research Council 2011, p. 12). Innovation is referred to as an "ecosystem," in which "all things flow in different ways at different times depending on who is looking when and where in the process" (ibid.). They continue by saying that "in a complex system such as the innovation ecosystem, there is no reason to believe that optimizing the performance of any one part of the system will optimize or even necessarily improve the performance of the system as a whole" (ibid.), implying that research cannot be treated as an independent variable.

But the notion of system interconnection goes beyond the technology-industry level and penetrates the realm of politics. As West et al. (in Chesbrough et al. 2006) point out in their analysis of the Open innovation paradigm, innovation is practiced within a context of certain "political and economic institutions." Chang (2002) convincingly makes the case of a program for an *Institutional Political Economy (IPE)* that conceives market and other institutions as a result of conscious political deliberation. This program draws attention to the institutional complexity of markets by arguing that the form that they take is conditional of the set of rights and obligations (explicitly or implicitly) accepted by the members of a given society. This is, sociocultural and contextual processes and interactions do play a central role in the form markets and economic systems take.

For the just mentioned reasons, Chang (2002) argues that this very institutional complexity makes it impossible to define a definitive boundary between markets and the state. In fact, there is a large institutional variety besides markets and state intervention through which economic activities can be organized. In some countries or industries what looks like market failure for some, can look like organizational success for others (Lazonick 2002).

2.5 The historical dimension of economic evolution

The third property of complex economic systems has to do with the need to place them in an explicit historical time dimension (Foster 2005). Theoretical questions concerning the emergence of institutions, innovation diffusion, selection and system maintenance do not happen in a-historical contexts. We already discussed the importance of historic specificity from a methodological perspective in Chapter 1. Rather, in this section we will examine the implications of assuming historic specificity as a property of complex economic systems. But before going into this, we will add few complementary comments on the methodological side as a point of departure for the subsequent analysis.

Several authors have argued against the a-historical nature of modern mainstream economic theories. For instance, Hodgson (2001) illustrates in a magisterial fashion how the problem of "historical specificity" was ignored by the mainstream economics that emerged after World War II. He argues that "all socio-economic systems are necessarily combinations of dissimilar elements. These combinations will in turn depend on historical and local circumstances" (ibid., p. 44). To acknowledge the importance of historic specific phenomena leads to the need of creating theoretical devices that match the given context.

The contributions to solve this problem date from the fifteenth century with the works of, for example, Antonio Serra and Giovanni Botero. Another significant contribution to the theoretical exploration of the historical specificity came in the nineteenth century from Marx on the one side; and from the German historical school (List, Sombart, Weber) on the other. According to Hodgson (2001), Marx and the German historical schools emphasized that the premises of the study of economic systems "must be based on a real object, rather than being arbitrary assumptions" (ibid., p. 60). These explorations exerted a big influence in the further development of the American institutional school (Veblen, Common, Ayers).

To avoid any misunderstanding, it should be observed that to call attention to historical specificity does not mean to reject the importance of general statements when studying the functioning of economic systems. The present study is not advocating any post-modernistic[17] or extreme relativistic view on the social sciences at all. On the contrary, *our point of departure is that explanatory unifications and general frameworks that explain real causal mechanisms are unavoidably central purposes of science.* As Hodgson (2001) also points out, "science cannot proceed without some general or universal statements and principles" (p. 54). He also makes clear that to be able to deal "with complex (socio-economic) systems, we require a combination of general concepts, statements and theories, with particular concepts, statements and theories, relating to particular types of system or subsystem" (p. 55).

In fact, the paramount objective of the present study is to prove that the mechanisms behind the functioning of a specific institutional framework (Cuban biotechnology industry) fit very well the set of mechanisms described by more general (and historically informed) theoretical frameworks (e.g. national and sectoral system of innovation perspectives, theory of the innovative firm). Even if these specific mechanisms differ from the ones employed by other countries, a much closer evaluation might be telling us that what actually matters in the understanding of economic systems is the developmental function played by the institution and not only the historic specific form of that developmental institution.

For example, a general framework could be that there exists strong historical evidence about the systematic use of industrial policies to advance economic development, but to understand the development of a given economic system; we cannot merely say that. Actually we would need to know the historic specific institutions and type of organizations that shape that system, if we are to be able to make sound explanations and reasonable policy recommendations. To make use of some cross-country evidence in historical perspective is aimed precisely at looking for more encompassing general mechanisms, which might be expressed in very different and specific institutional frameworks. In this sense Chang (2003) talks about "persistent historical patterns" (p. 6) and Reinert (in Cimoli et al. 2009) refers to "mandatory passage point[s] in human history" (p. 100).

2.5.1 Meso-economics: Institutions as analytical unit

The most important implication of considering economic systems as historically conditioned systems is the existence of institutions. Hodgson (2006) defines institutions as "systems of established and prevalent social rules that structure social interactions. Language, money, law, systems of weights and measures, table manners, and firms (and other organizations) are thus all institutions" (p. 2).

These rules are preceded and constituted by shared habits, which in the old institutional tradition (Veblen) are seen as the propensity to engage in a "previously adopted or acquired behaviour," provided the proper stimulus is triggered (p. 6).

To become rule-following behaviors, these shared habits need to be *institutionalizable*, i.e. to be codifiable in order to be able to acquire normative character. In a world populated with bounded rationality, uncertainty and division of labor (i.e. fragmented value-added chains) on the one side, and overwhelming complementarity on the other, most socioeconomic processes necessarily presupposes the interaction between highly heterogeneous agents. The process of continuous repetition of a these interactions, provided the proper stimulus is activated, leads to the emergence of certain rules that create mutually consistent prospects among the agents about certain behaviors and decisions. This habituation process may at some point take the form of explicit cooperation,[18] which builds the basis for these rules or shared knowledge to become institutions. Cooperation makes it possible for institutions to be durable, and it provides room for joint learning and mutually adapting expectations (Elsner 2010; Hodgson 2006).

The institutions reinforce in turn the original habits by creating certain incentives and constraints for individual agents. The rationalization of these repeated behaviors builds the foundation for intentionality (see Section 2.3). That is, deliberate actions or purpose are not to be seen outside the complex interdependence between them and more (custom, convention-charged) non-deliberate forms of behavior. In other words, culture and history matter in that they provide the material and cognitive environment in which individual agents think and act.

History also matters because the problem-solving potential of institutions increases as the interactions become recurrent and sequential (i.e. in historical time). Therefore, the process is unavoidably path-dependent, which leads to lock-ins, which is an important property of non-linear dynamic systems (fixed points and attractors).[19] Of course, at the same time, the individual agency also acts upon institutions given the fact that organizational cultures are not homogeneous entities but are formed by different coexisting (and sometimes conflicting) traditions, and thus open to interpretation. That introduces a possible disruptive element within the complex economic system and builds the foundation for selective institutional change. This reflects the uncertain and evolving nature of the process, which in turn, reinforces new habits and creates new expectations and behaviors.

The fact that habits are reinforced by institutions means that the latter do not only constrain the behavior of pre-formed, unchanging individual agents, but also can, in fact, mold individual agent motivations through a historical collective and cumulative learning process.[20] This is what Hodgson (2006) calls "reconstitutive downward causation" and what Chang (2002) calls "the constitutive role of institutions." Evolutionary institutional economics conceives institutionalization as a process that depends on a system of historically determined (and politically legitimated) sets of social rights and obligations, and as the most conspicuous outcome of the complex interdependencies in the economy. Therefore, it makes sense to talk of institutions as the most appropriate level of analysis when studying complex social systems and indeed, as the central analytic unit of complex phenomena such as innovation and economic development (Hodgson 2000; Elsner 2010). This, in turn, has important implications.

Taking institutions as a point of departure means that the analysis of economic systems involves the interaction of a wide diversity of entities, which cannot be explained by relying on the conventional micro-macro dichotomy. As Elsner (2010) argues, to fruitfully comprehend complex evolutionary theorizing, modeling, simulations, lab experimentation, real world clusters and networks may require a specific theoretical space.

The search of a new level of analysis is inextricably related to the concept of *emergence*. The central point of the notion of emergence is that the properties of new phenomena cannot be reduced to the properties of their isolated constituents. When complex systems interact new characteristics of the new whole emerge that cannot be predicted from the knowledge of its components. More important, as discussed above, is the existence of a two-way causation between systems. Newly emerged systems influence and are influenced by their constituents.

As Hodgson (2000) states, if we accept that socioeconomic systems have emergent properties, which cannot be explained by the features of their constituent parts, then macro-behavior cannot be expressed in terms of individual actions, as the orthodox discourse does (methodological individualism). Neither can it be explained as the simple additive outcome of individual actions (aggregation fallacy). By rejecting these assumptions, we can advance an alternative and more realistic set of assumptions in order to overcome the limitations of orthodox interpretations of economic behavior, e.g.; the existence of a wide diversity of economic agents, which do not follow any one-size-fits-all rationality. The proposed framework to deal with emergence in socioeconomic systems has been coined by many evolutionary-institutional economists as the *meso* level of analysis (e.g. Hodgson 2000; Dopfer et al. 2004; Elsner 2010).

The fundamental feature of the meso analysis is that it takes institutions as its unit of analysis. That fills an important conceptual gap because it is institutions that "simultaneously constitute and are constituted by human action" (Hodgson 2000, p. 118). "Institutions are sustained by subjective ideas in the head of agents" and at the same time represent "objective structures" faced by the agents too (ibid.). In addition, institutions usually show a degree of invariance over long periods of time, and may last longer than individuals, which offers an additional reason to pick institution as a "bedrock unit" (ibid., p. 119). The elements just mentioned contrast with the orthodox logic of taking individuals (or individual entities, e.g. firms) as irreducible units of analysis. Notice that this does not mean that the role of the part is being given up to the dominance of the whole because institutions are actually emergent structures, which result from the complex interactions between *part* and *whole*. This aspect could help to overcome "the philosophical dilemma between realism and subjectivism in social science. Actor and institutional structure, although distinct, are thus connected in a circle of mutual interaction and interdependence" (Hodgson 2006, p. 8)

Last but not least, the meso level gives the possibility of explaining socio-economic phenomena without having to constrain the explanation to only one type of behavior or entity. If we consider institutions as the result of the interaction of different socioeconomic levels; and as systems of rules that exists in all socioeconomic levels, then it is plausible; and even necessary to combine insights from different levels of analysis. Indeed, an institutional analysis of the socioeconomic system requires a more interdisciplinary treatment of its properties. In fact, in this research we will consciously combine apparently unrelated theoretical approaches including important insights of business strategy, economic history, political science, sociology, development and innovation economics, etc.

2.5.2 Implication for the analysis of economic growth

The omission of the problem of historical specificity has had strong implications in the understanding of the phenomena studied by both development and innovation economic. For instance, recent research in the field of development economics unveils a number of misunderstanding and omissions in relation to the understanding of the role of the state in leading their countries ahead in the industrial path (Chang 2002, 2010); Reinert 1999, 2007; Cimoli et al. 2009; Woo-Cumings 1999; Jäntti and Vartiainen 2009, Hauknes and Smith 2003). Reinert (1999) confirms that the industrial powers of Europe and North America seem to be unified in a common misconception about their own past and "about the role of the State in bringing them out of poverty" (p. 272).

Many point out that the one-size-fits all approach of the Washington Consensus has actually inflicted much damage in the structures of the developing countries (e.g. Chang 2002; Reinert 2007). Indeed, to ignore that different economic systems demand different policies and approaches according to their development stage has actually resulted in deindustrialization, low growth rates, poverty and increasing inequality (ibid.). As Reinert (1999) sustains, "the record of the past economic policies of the presently industrialized countries has to a large extent been 'unlearned'" (p. 272). In actual fact, mainstream universal assumptions of minimal government intervention, perfect information, institutions-free markets superiority or private property rights have proven to be inadequate to understand phenomena such as economic development in developing countries. To counteract these realities Chang (2002) suggests that to study "the historical facts about the developmental experiences of the developed countries" would contribute to reject "historical myths and overly abstract theories that are blinding many theoreticians and policymakers" (p. 140).

Similarly, the lack of historical perspective has been an obstacle to improve the understanding of the processes of technological learning and innovation. As several authors argue, novel technologies arise from the combination of existing technologies; however, not all technologies are actively used or combined at the same time (Arthur 2009; Levinthal 1998). The process implies the creation of new organizational structures and societal arrangement, whose design is "historically contingent" (Arthur 2009, p. 186). "There is [...] nothing predetermined about the arrangements that fall into place and define the structure of the economy" (ibid., p. 198). To ignore these elements means to ignore that, in actual fact, the acquisition of more productive knowledge happens to be intrinsically related to the country's ability to build socially accepted institutions which help to absorb, use and develop technological and organizational knowledge in order to build the foundation for economic development.

At the same time, present choices affect the direction of the future evolution of technological and organizational innovations. This evolution includes the way in which technical skills are accumulated, economies of scale reaped and so on, which in turn will differ from each other depending of the technology or sector involved (Cimoli et al. in Cimoli et al. 2009, p. 30).

This sort of systemic irreversibility is also a characteristic of complex economic systems and helps to explain the different patterns of specialization among the nations. From a complexity perspective, Foster (2005) argues that such systems "exhibit some degree of structural irreversibility owing to the inherent hierarchical and 'bonding' nature of the connections between components that are formed as structural development proceeds" (p. 875). This is, at the same time, the cause "that precipitates a structural discontinuity" (ibid., p. 875) when novel technologies enter into an economy's "active collection of technologies" (Arthur 2009, p. 177). This process, which arises as human and technical needs create what Arthur (2009) calls "opportunity niches" (pp. 174–6); is nothing but the confirmation of the transitory nature of these systems and the essence of the Schumpeterian concept of creative destruction.

Given that the learning process is fundamentally an idiosyncratic process, it is not a surprise that historically, the national dimension has played such a crucial role in the accumulation of technological and managerial capabilities. As Chang (2010) argues, the process of technological change is far from being a market-induced process. Given that in the innovation practice, relevant information is not hidden or asymmetric but unknown to the participants in the process, it would not always be possible for a country to follow "market" signals closely in order to enter or remain in an industry. In actual fact, firms and sectors with uncertain prospects will need to be created, subsidized, and nurtured, possibly for decades, if industrial upgrading and innovation are to be achieved. This applies specially (but by no means exclusively) to developing countries involved in the catch-up process.

Indeed, as Reinert (2007) points out, the economics of the twentieth century has lost "two important dimensions: time (history) and space (geography)" (p. 36). The world of "automatic and timeless harmony" advanced by the modern standard economics led to the omission of crucial elements such as the increasing returns; i.e. the fact that some economic activities display better innovation opportunities; and hence better growth opportunities than others; and the process of cumulative causations that create structural change (synergies) (ibid.).

2.6 The conception of networks at work

We have just mentioned that new technologies emerge from the combination of already existing ones. The complementarities that arise from this process demand a wider division of labor and at the same time a closer integration between large numbers of heterogeneous agents. These interactions can be represented by network dynamics that are bound in space and time and can change with the environment and co-evolve with the agents (Foster 2005; Coe et al. 2008). Networks are formed and evolve on the basis of the addition or deletion of either agents or the links between them.

As networks successfully (or unsuccessfully) evolve (and more and better products can be delivered), an economy's value creation increases. The proliferation of various forms of inter-firm collaboration along the value chain; including alliances, joint ventures, acquisitions and cooperative agreements among firms of high innovative industries is well documented (see e.g. for the biotechnology).

Although they have unquestionably become far more complex organizationally, production networks are in fact anything but new. Rather, they reflect the *fundamental structural and relational nature of the process of value creation within an economy*. Reinert (2007) provides a very well documented account of the synergies and diversity of activities observed by sixteenth-century economist Giovanni Botero[21] in Venice and by seventeenth-century economists Antonio Serra and Ludwig von Seckendorf[22] in Venice and in the Dutch Republic respectively. Consequently, the notion of *network* does not reveal any new hybrid category existing in the "void between markets and hierarchies, as some continue to argue," but it actually represents "the fundamental structural and relational nature of how production, distribution and consumption of goods and services are—indeed always have been—organized" (Coe et al. 2008, p. 272).

Synergic mechanisms within an economic system can be found in all registered development efforts, encompassing a broad body of experiences, ranging from the Venetian Arsenal as part of the Venetian system of innovation, the Dutch system of innovation (Reinert 2007), through the American system of manufacturing and the Japanese manufacturing system to the modern semiconductor, IT and biotechnology industries. Early development economists during the second half of the twentieth century, such as Albert Hirschman and François Perroux, understood the role played by interdependence in the industrialization process. All these instances emphasize the fact *that added value arises from the connections between elements, rather than just from the elements themselves* (Foster 2005), or, in other words, "[t]he fact that the linkage effects of two industries viewed in combination are larger than the sum of the linkage effect of each industry in isolation [...]" (Hirschman 1958, p. 104). Such an approach also emphasizes the growing complex nature of the interdependencies that exist behind innovation and economic development.

As Coe et al. (2008) points out, "adopting an explicitly networked approach allows us to identify a wide range of *non-firm actors* as constituent parts of the overall production system" (p. 275). It also takes us beyond the linear progression of the innovation process, by helping us to unveil the "complex circulations of capital, knowledge and people that underlie the production of all goods and services." Moreover, a multidimensional network perspective brings into view the connections and synergies between processes of value creation in different production networks.

2.6.1 The network approach

Newmann (2006) defines a network as "a set of items, which we will call vertices or sometimes nodes, with connections between them, called edges" (p. 2). According to the literature, the term *node* alternate with terms such as *vertex, agents, actors,* etc; and the term *edge* can alternate with terms such as *link, linkages, connection, etc.* A node with a high (small) number of links to other nodes is said to have a high (small) degree.

Similarly, Hanneman and Riddle (2005) defines a social network as a set of actors (or points, or nodes, or agents) that may have relationships (or edges, or ties) with one another. Networks can have few or many actors (individuals, organizations, nations, groups etc.) and one or more kinds of relations between pairs of actors (resources, beliefs, friendship ties etc.) (see also Boratti et al. 2009; Borgatti and Halgin 2011; Borgatti and Foster 2003; Wasserman and Faust 1994; Freeman 1979). Similar definitions can be found in other author across the literature on network analysis (e.g. Barabásí and Albert 1999; Newman 2010; Vega-Redondo 2006).

Network theory can be considered to be part of graph theory, and it has to do with the study of graphs (and their properties) as a representation of symmetric and asymmetric binary relations[23] between discrete[24] objects (nodes). Directed graphs (or networks) are among the most ubiquitous ways to models natural and social structures. Much of the theoretical wealth of network analysis rests on its ability to (1) analyze both network dynamics (e.g., small-worldness, scale free) and (2) node positions (e.g., centrality); and relating these to group and node outcomes (Borgatti and Hagin 2011).

The just mentioned features tend to be relatively isolated from each other in terms their role in the research agendas of different fields. Currently, network research agenda divide, according to the emphasis in one or another feature, in two groups: physical network and social network research. The network research in the physical sciences tend to focus on describing the universal properties of complex network structures in the real world, i.e. biological, genetic, physical or social systems (Borgatti et al. 2009; Newman 2010; Vega-Redondo

2006). For example, properties such as small world and scale-free networks are believed to be present in many real complex networks. The main objective of this agenda is to create models of networks that can help us to understand the meaning of these properties – how they came to be as they are, and how they interact with one another. Examples of relevant exponent of this school could be found in Erdös and Renyi (1959); Newman (2010); Watts and Strogatz (1998); Barabási and Albert (1999); Vega-Redondo (2006); and Schweitzer et al. (2009).

On the other hand, the social network research is usually carried out by social scientists and tends to focus mostly on the outcomes of individual nodes[25] (not to be confused with statistically independent attributes) than with the network as a whole (Borgatti et al. 2009; Newman 2006). A typical social network analyst question could be: which nodes are best connected to others or have most influence? (Newman 2006 p. 2). At the level of the individual node, a node's outcomes and future characteristics depend in part on its position in the network structure.

The purpose of this research agenda is to develop a family of node-level measures to better understand the structural importance or prominence of a node in the network. Among the relevant exponents of the social network school we can mention Granovetter (1973); Freeman (1979, 1977, 1979); Wasserman and Faust (1994); Krackhardt (1999); Borgatti (2005); Bonacich (2007). In social sciences, network analysis is intended to find explanations for the same kinds of outcomes that have been the traditional focus of the social sciences (Borgatti et al. 2009).

This *node-level approach is the one being advanced in the present study (see* Annexes*)*. As is the case for most social scientists, our main interest is to understand the role of the individual node, regardless of whether the node itself represents an individual or a collective (such as a firm). This research is intended to analyze the kind of *institution* that better contributes to knowledge diffusion within (and therefore to the development of) the Cuban biotechnology industry.

2.6.2 Hub dominated networks vs. ideal "random" networks

While this study follows a node-level approach, it also acknowledges the utility of the properties developed by the physical network approach in understanding the dynamic of socioeconomic systems. The objective of this section is to briefly refer to these properties and to make a preliminary comment on their relation with the issues analyzed by the present study. Note, however, that we do not intend to make any further development of these properties in this work, but merely to reflect on the possible impact that further research could have on the subject under study.

As already suggested, the central claim of this school is that most of the systems studied by contemporary science form complex networks and also tend to display some analogous topological properties. The central goal of this perspective is to suggest appropriate ways to measure these properties, and to create models of networks that can help us to understand the meaning of these properties (Newman 2006).

There exists a variety of these models, but they could be synthesized into two groups: random and non-random (very detailed and highly technical discussions on the subject can be found in Newman 2006 and Vega-Redondo 2006). To the first group belongs the models of Erdös and Renyi (1959, 1960) and Watts and Strogatz (1998). A common feature of these models is that the probability that two vertices are connected is random and uniform. The models' starting points are a fixed number of nodes that are randomly connected. A second aspect is that these models assume that the probability of finding highly connected nodes is practically absent.[26]

However, real world networks, including economic networks, are far from being random, static and homogeneous. This problem was assessed by the second group, whose central exponent is the scale-free[27] models of Barabási and Albert (1999) and Ravasz and Barabási (2003). In these models networks are represented as open and ever-growing systems (in contrast with the fixed number of random models). Indeed, in economic networks the number of actors constantly varies, representing this feature the very source of structural change within the system (Foster 2005).

In addition, and more relevant for the sake of the argument being made here, non-random models introduce the property of *preferential attachment* within the network. This means that "the probability with which a new vertex connects to the existing vertices is not uniform"; and that "there is a higher probability that it will be linked to a vertex that already has a large number of connections" (Barabási and Albert 1999, p. 511, see also Hébert-Dufrene et al 2015). As a result, we have complex systems (including the economy) as sets of incomplete and ever growing networks, where some nodes tend to become *hubs* (highly connected nodes) through which most connections are routed. Certainly a much more compatible notion of the real world, Ravasz and Barabási (2003) assert that hubs "play a key role in keeping complex networks together" (p. 6).

Complementing the notion of hubs as important actors within the networks is the *hierarchical network* model advanced by Ravasz and Barabási (2003). The essential idea behind this model is that the *clustering coefficient* of a node tends to decrease as the degree (number of connections to other nodes) increase,[28] the clustering coefficient being the measure of connectivity between the immediate neighbors of a given node.[29] Ravasz and Barabási (2003) show that the clustering coefficient of the hubs decreases linearly with the degree. This means that while the small nodes are part of highly cohesive, densely interlinked clusters, the hubs are not, as their neighbors have a little chance of linking to each other. Therefore, the hubs play the important role of bridging the many small communities of clusters into a single, integrated network (ibid., p. 6). The presence of such a hierarchical architecture reinterprets the role of the hubs in complex networks because is telling us that the crucial function of hubs is not only to be linked to everybody, but fundamentally to link those who cannot connect with everybody.

The notion of *hub dominated network* helps to achieve a representational understanding of the high degrees of heterogeneity and complementarities that exist within both economies and innovation systems. As Foster (2005) points out, there are clear parallels between the neo-Schumpeterian theory and the notion of hub-dominated networks. Indeed, the literature on national (sectoral) systems of innovation and the recent research in development economics have presented enough historic evidence on "the role of corporate strategy and government policy in developing networking relationships with [and between] external sources of information, knowledge and advice" (Freeman 2008, p. 78). Especially the role (although not exclusively) of government-based NFOs as selection and diffusion agents within an economy (Malerba 2002; Cimoli et al. 2009; Chang 2003; Coe 2008; Mazzucato 2011; Lazonick 2011; Ruttan 2006).

From a firm perspective, the literature on evolutionary systems integration contends that complex product industries require the existence of system integrating organizations or system integrators; with the ability to coordinate the activity of these industries (Dosi et al. 2003; Prencipe et al. 2005). According to this perspective, these integrators are said to be the most crucial nodes within these complex production networks. However, this literature makes little reference to the role of NFOs within complex industries.

A more detailed discussion on the nature and role of NFOs will be found in Chapters 3 and 4. For now, only some brief comments will be made. From a sectoral system of innovation perspective, Malerba (2002) defines sectoral structures as a "web of relationships among heterogeneous agents with different beliefs, competencies and behavior, and that relationship affect agents actions" (p. 256). Within this context, Malerba (2002) emphasizes the role of "non-firm organisations such as universities, financial institutions, government agencies, local authorities and so on" (p. 255) as the source of "innovation and change in several sectors (such as pharmaceuticals and biotechnology, information technology and telecommunications)" (p. 256).

The issue had already been pointed out by Nelson (1993) (National System of Innovation, see Chapter 4) and has been further emphasized by other scholars. For instance, Cimoli et al. (2009) state that, even when the historical experience shows a great variety of country-and sector-specific policies and institutional combinations, one subtle historical regularity "is the centrality of public agencies, such as universities, and public policies in the generation and establishment on new technological paradigms" from "nineteenth-century Europe and the US all the way to contemporary times" (p. 28). In the field of development economics, Chang (2003, 2009) have also made a compelling case in this regard.

2.6.3 Social network research

During the previous sections we explored the idea of the economic systems as intentional, hub dominated complex networks, where these hubs exert determinant influence in the successful organizational integration of the system, and therefore in its innovative outputs. In order to take this assumption further, it is important to determine what kind of institutions (and organizations) play the role of hubs. In other words, to find out how *central* is each organization within the network. To do this, we need to rely on a social network analysis, which is the one that, in contrast to the physical network research, provides a number of graph-theoretic properties expressed in a number of construct indices to analyze individual node's outcomes. As already mentioned, *this research focuses essentially on the role of individual nodes (particularly NFOs), because this study is intended to analyze the role of specific institutions in a given phenomenon.* The core assumption is that non-firm organization play a very important (and not marginal, as usually assumed by the mainstream) role as hubs of the innovation system.

However, this is not to say that this study employs network theories and measurements as explanatory factors or variables in understanding individual behavior. This study is not establishing any quantitative correlation between independent variables (in traditional sense, e.g. regression analysis). As Wasserman and Faust (1994) point out, such analysis "still uses individual actors as the basic modelling unit"; and "does not focus on the network structure" (p. 9). This sort of analysis is still the most widely used in traditional social sciences research, however, even if useful in many circumstances, it is ill-suited to analyze relational phenomena. One of the most important limitations in this regard is the assumption of sampling independence of observations on individual units, which allows the considerable machinery of statistical analysis to be applied to a range of research questions by employing the traditional case by variables (ibid.).

In contrast, research embracing theories that incorporate network ideas argue that social units are not acting independently from one another, but rather influence each other. As already mentioned, whether the approach employed seeks to study individual action in the context of structured relationships, or studies structures directly, social network concepts are operationalized in relational terms (Wasserman and Faust 1994, p. 6). In the present study, the network analysis is employed in one of the senses illustrated by Wasserman and Faust (1994), namely to "express relationally defined theoretical concepts by providing formal definitions, measures and descriptions, to evaluate models and theories in which key concepts and propositions are expressed as relational processes or structural outcomes..." (p. 5). *This is, to test relational (and history-based) economic theories and concepts expressed in a particular case.*

2.6.4 The notion of centrality

As suggested above, historically, social network analysis made by social scientists has been more frequently concerned in the study of node properties (Borgatti et al. 2009). This focus on node-level outcomes is probably driven by the explanatory role of this tool in social sciences, in contrast to the research goal of the physic approach. At the same time, Borgatti et al. (2009) also acknowledges that both perspectives can learn from each other. After all, these differences reflect the very nature of the scientific enterprise, namely such old tensions as universalism vs. particularism, or simplicity vs. complexity. Another reason could be that in most of the social sciences, research is very likely to be based on the role of strategic players (government, firms, industries, non-firm organizations, formal and informal institutions) in certain collective outcomes.

Similarly, the present study is interested in measuring the structural import-ance of a node in a network (for example, how important a person is within a social network, how important a room is within a building, or how important a road is within an urban network). "Perhaps the most fundamental axiom in social network research is that a node's position in a network determines in part the opportunities and constraints that it encounters, and in this way plays an important role in a node's outcomes" (ibid., p. 12). In this regard, the most important measure is *centrality*. This is one of the most widely employed definitions in social network research and much of the language used to describe this notion is a sign of its sociological origin.[30]

Basically, the notion of centrality addresses the question: which are the most important or central vertices in a network (Freeman 1979, Wasserman and Faust 1994; Hanneman and Riddle 2005; Borgatti et al. 2009; Opsahl et al. 2010; Newman 2010)? Even when the notion had already been reportedly employed in social research, there seems to be a consensus about the point that Freeman (1979) is the author who most successfully has synthesized and formally represented this notion. The concept has been improved and modi-fied by several authors; and several other complementary measures have been introduced since then (see Borgatti 2005 for a review), but the essential features remain more or less close to Freeman's definition. For instance, Borgatti (2005) has pointed out that Freeman's centrality syntheses provided the "canonical definitions" for the field (p. 2).

Freeman (1979) intuitively links the concept of centrality to "the point at the centre of a star or the hub of a wheel" (p. 218). Someone located at the center of the star is "universally assumed" to have a privileged central struc-tural position with respect to the others. Given the multidimensionality of the term "importance," however, it is not surprising to find various definitions (and therefore) measures of centrality. All of them aim at quantifying the prominence of an individual actor embedded in a network, but they differ on the criteria used to achieve that.[31]

These definitions show high potential to capture important features of the innovation system, and the role played by different organizations in this system; for instance the ability to broker information and resources. Burt (2005) notes that the notion of brokerage assumes that information takes time and there-fore it is expected to circulate first within groups rather that between groups (within divisions rather between divisions, within firms rather than between firms, within industries rather than between industries etc.). This means that, even if innovation is of high quality, not all economics agents are simultaneously aware of opportunities provided by other agents (bounded rationality, asym-metric information, uncertainty).

In this context, agents that invest time and energy in obtaining information from each side and linking them are much more prone to bring together non-redundant sources of information. They provide more value than highly connected (i.e. highly clustered) agents, whose information flows tend to be overlapping rather than additive. Therefore, the more disconnected (and diverse) the contacts of a given socioeconomic agent, the greater the chances of adding value by brokering connections among others. Burt (2005) calls this kind of brokering agent the "entrepreneur in the literal sense" (p. 207).

Indeed, bringing together different and unrelated pieces of knowledge is the essence of entrepreneurship. As Hobday and Perini (in Cimoli et al. 2009) argue based on the Asian experience, the primary role of entrepreneurship is to make it possible processes such as technology transfer, catch-up and learning to happen. Mazzucato (2011) uses the term entrepreneurial state to describe the important brokering role played by government non-firm organizations in fostering radical innovation and economic development.[32] Block (2008) employs the notion of Developmental Network State to describe similar phenomena. This is one of the reasons why it can be said, as already argued above, that value creation within the economy has a fundamental relational nature.

Other definitions of centrality may help address the question of "how long it will take for information to spread from a given node to the other nodes in the network." The underlying rationale for the desirability of information spreading is that nodes obtain some value (gain) from the information (Kim 2010).

If new technologies (and institutions) are built upon already existent technologies (and institutions), then to diffuse the relevant information (and knowledge) as soon as possible across the system will contribute decisively to increase the prospects for organizational learning (and thus for organizational integration) within an innovation system. A confirmation of this statement can be found in the solid amount of evidence provided by innovation literature scholars with regard to the role of government (non-firm) organizations in the diffusion of new practices and technologies (for both developed and developing countries) (Mazzoleni and Nelson in Cimoli et al. 2009; Bell and Pavitt 1993; Perez and Soete 1988).

Mazzoleni and Nelson (in Cimoli et al. 2009) state that government have been usually successful in identifying economic sectors and technologies where the role of non-firm organizations (NFO) has been crucial. Block (2008) points out further arguments defending the idea of government NFOs when diffusing innovation and knowledge across sectors and the economy.

Notes

1 See G Myrdal, *American Dilemma: The Negro Problem and Modern Democracy.* New York/London: Harper & Row, 1944, pp. 1065–70.
2 N Georgescu-Roegen, *The Entropy Law and the Economic Process*, Harvard University Press: Cambridge, Massachusetts, 1971.

3 The citations of this work, in this and other chapters of the present study, correspond to an online copy of the original version uploaded by the author. Available at http://informatics.indiana.edu/rocha/ps/sa2.pdf

4 Hayek employed the term catalactics or *catallaxy* "to describe the order brought about by the mutual adjustment of many individual economies in a market" (F Hayek, Law, Legislation and Liberty, University of Chicago Press, 1973, p. 108). He defined it as "the special kind of spontaneous order produced by the market through people acting within the rules of the law of property, tort and contract" (p. 109).

5 Hayek established a distinction between an order that result from a deliberate arrange, e.g., an organization (taxis) and a spontaneous order (cosmos), ibid., pp. 35–52.

6 Jessop's approach strongly relies on the relational state theory of Nicos Poulantzas, which in turn relied on Gramsci's notion of cultural hegemony. According to Poulantzas, the state is a social relation that reproduces society's internal divisions and contradictions among and within each and every branch of the state system (see N Poulantzas, Political Power and Social Classes. NLB, London and New York, 1978 and B Jessop, State *Theory: Putting Capitalist States in Their Place*, Cambridge, Polity Press, 1990).

7 The concept stems originally from the biological sciences and was re-interpreted and introduced (not without resistance of its original creators) in social science by the well-known German sociologist and system theorist Niklas Luhmann (1927–1998). We rely, however, on the type of autopoiesis – third order autopoiesis – defined by Jessop. A discussion about the distinction between the three types can be found in G Teubner and A Febbrajo (eds), State, Law, and Economy as Autopoietic Systems, Giuffrè, Milan, 1992.

According to Jessop's notion,

> "an autopoietic system is self-constituting in so far as it defines and defends its own boundary vis-à-vis its self-defined external environment. It is also self-organizing because it has its own distinctive operational codes and programs. Hence, while an autopoietic system may respond to changes in its environment and even change its organization in so doing, it does so in terms of its own codes and programmes".

(State theory..., p. 4)

8 Jessop defines this property of the state as "structural coupling" and it refers to "the co-evolution of autonomous structures which share at least part of the same social space" (ibid., p. 358).

9 In addition to Jessop, the analysis of the dialectic between politics (embodied in the state policies) and economy is found in the work of a number of scholars (e.g. Marx, Weber, Polanyi, French Regulation School, Deane, Evans, Chang, Lazonick etc.).

10 We refer to the market in orthodox sense, which means an institution free from political influence and capable of setting partial equilibrium prices. As we will see, the notion of free market is highly implausible because no market can be said to be independent of other societal entities.

11 The term of dissipative structure refers to an open system operating in non-equilibrium which can reach to some extent a reproducible steady state. This state results either from evolution, from artifice, or by a combination of both. The term was coined by the Russian-born Belgian physical chemist Nobel laureate Ilya Prigogine, whose pioneering research led to important research in complexity and self-organizing systems.

12 This notion of purpose include, but goes definitely beyond the notion of "purposive action" accepted from Hayek, Law... in his discussion on self-spontaneous order (p. 39). Hayek accepted the notion of purpose as "acquired regularities of conduct conducive to the maintenance of the order" (ibid.). This is acceptable "so long as we do not imply an awareness of purpose of the part of the elements" (ibid.). He was so reluctant to the use of the term (and of its possible implications) that he preferred to use the term "function" instead of "purpose" (ibid.).

13 In this study we tend to use the terms *institution* and *organization* as different entities, however this is made only with the purpose of better studying the role of organizations in the economic systems. However, conceptually, organizations are also to be defined as institutions as they match the definition of "a socially embedded system of rules" (Hodgson, What *Are* ... p. 8). At the same time, it is to be noted that Hodgson, while discussing North's definition of institution, also speaks of organizations as "special kind of institutions" in that they "involve (a) criteria to establish their boundaries and to distinguish their members from non-members, (b) principles of sovereignty concerning who is in charge, and (c) chains of command delineating responsibilities within the organization" (ibid.). For further discussion see Hodgsonm, What *Are*... pp. 8–13).

14 The impossibility of long-range forecasting in the economy, however, is not a barrier to the field's growth as a science because science is about explaining, not forecasting, and understanding the dynamic nature of the economy will significantly help in developing testable explanations of economic phenomena (see Beinhocker).

15 See M Polany, The Tacit Dimension. First published Doubleday & Co. Reprinted Peter Smith, Gloucester, Mass, 1966, 1983.

16 Similar to what we mentioned earlier, Hodgson, What *Are*... mentions that even proponents of the self-spontaneous school argued in favor of external enforcement. He states that "Menger ([1871] 1981) himself recognized a distinction between 'organic' (self-organizing) and 'pragmatic' (designed) institutions. But many subsequent authors ignore the latter to concentrate on the former" (p. 13).

17 A further discussion on the damage caused by this perspective in the social science, in particular in the heterodox economics and in sociology see Hodgson, How *Economics*... pp. 34–9.

18 Some authors understand cooperation as a coordination that sacrifices the potential short-run one-shot extra gain. See W Elsner, The process and a simple logic of ´meso´. Emergence and the co-evolution of institutions and group size, *Journal of Evolutionary Economics* 20(3): 445–77, 2010.

19 The economy is a dynamical system because the state of the system at the current moment is a function of the state of the system at the previous moment. Moreover, it is non-linear because small changes in the variables that regulate the system (initial conditions) may be magnified over time by positive or negative feedback loops. Positive feedback reinforces, accelerates, or amplifies changes, whether it is a virtuous cycle or downward spiral. Negative feedback dampens change, controls things, and brings things back in line. Attractors are equilibrium states the result of the combination of different feedback loops, to which a dynamic system is pulled or attracted cyclically. They are seen as stable equilibrium or as unstable equilibrium, depending on whether a small change in the initial condition tends to disrupt the equilibrium or not. Fixed points are final steady states toward which dynamic systems evolve.

20 In neoclassical and new institutionalist theories individual motivations are thought of as ultimate data. Here institutions are able to shape individual behavior by punishing or rewarding particular types of behavior, but they are not able to change the motivations itself. In the program of the IPE advanced by HJ Chang, motivations are not seen as given but as being fundamentally shaped by the institutions surrounding individuals. That is, individuals inevitably internalize some of the values, worldviews and moral codes embodied in the institutions and thereby have themselves changed. See HJ Chang, Breaking the mould: an institutionalist political economy alternative to the neo-liberal theory of the market, *Cambridge Journal of Economics* 26(5): 539–59, 2002.

21 His most famous work, according to Reinert, p. 92, is On the Greatness of Cities, originally published in 1588.

22 He visited the Delft cluster, which was in the seventeenth century a leader in the production of glass lenses (ibid., 93).

23 Binary relation is the mathematical definition for pairs of objects. The term is employed in graph theory to denote adjacency.

24 Graph theory is considered to be an important part of discrete mathematics. Discrete objects (such as graphs) are mathematical structures that can assume only distinct, separated values. The term "discrete mathematics" is therefore used in contrast with "continuous mathematics," and therefore excludes subjects such as calculus and analysis.

25 Social network analysis also discuss network structures at the network level in order to assess features such as connectivity (e.g., density), but have not paid much attention to the probability of near-universal descriptions. This study focuses on node-level properties as it is intended to find out the kind of institution that better contribute to organizational integration within the Cuban biotech industry. Specifically, following the framework of national (sectoral) system of innovation, this study intends to explore the role of non-firm organizations in this phenomenon.

26 It is assumed that the probability of a node n with degree k decreases exponentially with k.

27 Scale free refers to the networks that follow the power law, which means that the probability that a randomly selected node with k links (i.e., degree k) follows $P(k) \sim k^n$, where n is the degree exponent (see E Ravasz and AL Barabási, Hierarchical organization in complex networks, *Phys. Rev. E* 67: 026112, 2003.

28 According to Ravasz and Barabási, a network has a hierarchical topology when the clustering coefficient $C(k)$ of a node with k links follows the scaling law. This law is represented as $C(K) \sim 1/k$.

29 The index was introduced by Watts and Strogatz and represented a step forward in term of the realism of the random models in comparison with other models. For a discussion see D Watts and S Strogatz, Collective dynamics of "small-world" networks, *Nature*, June, **393** (6684), 440–2, 1998.

30 A historical examination of social network research can be found in Borgatti et al. Other examinations including empirical, theoretical, and mathematical developments can be found in Wasserman and Faust (pp. 10–17). See S Borgatti et al., Network analysis in social sciences, *Science* 13, February: 892–95, 2009. A more comprehensive account can be found in M Newman, Networks: An Introduction. Oxford: Oxford University Press, 2010 (Chapter 3).

31 Something similar happens with the concept organizational integration, which is the one being linked to centrality in this research. The formal-mathematical definition

of the latter is outside the scope of this work. This does not necessarily add up to the understanding of the central issue and could therefore result very abstract for many readers. Further exploration of the subject, however, can be found in the Annexes. There we provide more technical definitions, if not necessarily exhaustive, of the network theory concepts, particularly the core centrality concepts, dealt with in this work, along with the practical application to the case of the Cuban biotechnology industry. Note, however, that it is not the central aim of this study to develop any formal (mathematical) notions of network theory, but instead to rely on its definitions in order to explore their economic meaning and interpretation in terms of the present research.

32 Even if this concept is firstly intended to developed nations, there is actually a significant overlapping between this concept and the one referring to the developmental state (see Chapter 4).

References

Ackoff R (1971), Toward a system of systems concepts, *Management Science* 17(11): 661–71.

Ackoff R and Emery F [1972](2006), *On Purposeful Systems.* Fourth Paperback printing. New Brunswick: Aldine-Transaction.

Amaral L and Ottino J (2004), Complex networks: Augmenting the framework for the study of complex systems, *European Physical Journal* B **38**: 147–62.

Arthur B (1999), Complexity and the economy, *Science* 284: 107–9.

Arthur B (2009), *The Nature of Technology: What It Is and How It Evolves.* New York: Free Press.

Arthur B (ed.) (2015), *Complexity and the Economy.* New York: Oxford University Press.

Barabási A and Albert R (1999), Emergence of scaling in random networks, *Science* 286 (15) (October): 509–12.

Beinhocker E (2006), *The Origin of Wealth: Evolution, Complexity, and the Radical Remaking of Economics.* Cambridge, MA: Harvard Business School Press.

Bell M and Pavitt K (1993), Technological accumulation and industrial growth: Contrasts between developed and developing countries, *Industrial and Corporate Change* 2(1): 157–210.

Block F (2008), Swimming against the current: The rise of a hidden developmental state in the United States, *Politics & Society* 36(2) (June): 169–206.

Bonacich P (1987), Power and centrality: A family of measures, *Amererican Journal of Sociology* 92(5): 1170–82.

Borgatti S (2005), Centrality and network flow, *Social Networks* 27: 55–71.

Borgatti S and Foster P (2003), The network paradigm in organizational research: A review and typology, *Journal of Management* 29(6): 991–1013.

Borgatti S and Halgin D (2011), On network theory, *Organization Science,* Articles in Advance, 1–14.

Borgatti S et al. (2009), Network analysis in social sciences, *Science* 13 (February): 892–5.

Burt R (2005), The social capital of structural holes. In: M Guillén et al. (eds.), *The New Economic Sociology.* New York: Russell Sage Foundation, pp. 148–93.

Chang HJ (1999), The economic theory of the developmental state. In: M Woo-Cumings (ed.), *The Developmental State.* Ithaca and London: Cornell University Press, pp. 182–99.

Chang HJ (2002), Breaking the mould: An institutionalist political economy alternative to the neo-liberal theory of the market, *Cambridge Journal of Economics* 26(5): 539–59.

Chang HJ (2003), *Kicking Away the Ladder.* London: Anthem Press.

Chang HJ (2009), Industrial Policy: Can We Go Beyond an Unproductive Confrontation?, A Plenary Paper for ABCDE (Annual World Bank Conference on Development Economics), Seoul, South Korea, June 22–24.

Chang HJ (2010), *23 Things They Don't Tell You about Capitalism.* London: Penguin Group.

B (2012), John Commons's organizational theory of institutions: A discussion, *Journal of Institutional Economics* 8(1): 27–47.

Chesbrough H et al. (eds.) (2006), *Open Innovation: Researching a New Paradigm.* Oxford: Oxford University Press.

Cimoli M et al. (eds.) (2009), *The Political Economy of Capabilities Accumulation: The Past and Future of Policies for Industrial Development.* New York: Oxford University Press.

Coe N et al. (2008), Global production networks: Realizing the potential, *Journal of Economic Geography* 8(3): 271–95.

Cohen S and DeLong JB (2016), Concrete Economics: The Hamilton Approach to Economic Growth and Policy. Cambridge, MA and London: Harvard Business Review Press.

Colander D and Kupers R (2014), *Complexity and the Art of Public Policy: Solving Society's Problems from the Bottom Up.* Princeton and Oxford: Princeton University Press.

Commons J (1924), *Legal Foundations of Capitalism.* New York: Macmillan.

Commons J (1934), *Institutional Economics.* New York: Macmillan.

Dopfer et al. (2004), Micro–meso–macro, *Journal of Evolutionary Economics* 14: 263–79.

Dosi G et al. (1994), The process of economic development: Introducing some stylized facts and theories on technologies, firms and institutions, *Industrial and Corporate Change* 3(1): 1–45

Dosi G et al. (2003), The economics of systems integration: Towards an evolutionary interpretation. In: A Prencipe et al. (eds.), *The Business of Systems Integration.* Oxford: Oxford University Press, pp. 95–114.

Elsner W (2010), The process and a simple logic of "meso". Emergence and the co-evolution of institutions and group size, *Journal of Evolutionary Economics* 20(3): 445–77.

Erdös P and Renyi A (1959), On random graphs, *Publicationes Mathematicae* 6: 290–7.

Erdös P and Renyi A (1960), On the evolution of random graphs, *Publications of the Mathematical Institute of the Hungarian Academy of Sciences* 5: 17–61.

Evans P (1995), *Embedded Autonomy: States and Industrial Transformation.* Princeton, NJ: Princeton University Press.

Evans P et al. (eds) [1985] (1999), *Bringing the State Back In.* Cambridge: Cambridge University Press.

Evans P (1995), *Embedded Autonomy: States and Industrial Transformation.* Princeton University Press.

Foley D (2003), *Unholy Trinity: Labour, Land and Capital.* London: Routledge.

Foster J (2005), From simplistic to complex systems in economics, *Cambridge Journal of Economics* 29(6): 873–92.

Freeman Ch (1995), National system of innovation in a historical perpective, *Cambridge Journal of Economics* 19: 5–24.

Freeman Ch (2008), *System of Innovation.* UK, USA: Edward Elgar.

Freeman L (1977, 1979), A set of measures of centrality based on betweenness, *Sociometry* 40: 3541.

Freeman L (1979), Centrality in social networks: Conceptual clarification, *Social Networks*, 1 (1978, 1979): 215–39.

Georgescu-Roegen N (1971), *The Entropy Law and the Economic Process (1971)*. Cambridge, MA: Harvard University Press.

Granovetter M (1973), The strength of the weak tie, *American Journal of Sociology* 78(6): 1360–80.

Hanneman R and Riddle M (2005), *Introduction to Social Network Methods*. Riverside, CA: University of California, Riverside (published in digital form at http://faculty.ucr.edu/~hanneman/

Hauknes J and Smith K (2003), Corporate Governance and Innovation in Mobile Telecommunications: How Did the Nordic Area Become a World Leader?, STEP Report, Oslo, R-12.

Hayek F (1973), *Law, Legislation and Liberty*. Chicago: University of Chicago Press.

Hayter CS et al. (2018), Public-sector entrepeneurship, Oxford Review of Economic Policy 34(4): 676–94.

Hébert-Dufresne L et al (2015), Complex networks as an emerging property of hierarchical preferential attachment, Physical Review E 92, 062809.

Hirschman A (1958), *The Strategy of Economic Development*. New Haven: Yale University Press.

Hodgson G (2000), Form micro to macro: the concept of emergence and the role of institutions. In: L Burlamaqui et al. (eds.), *Institutions and the Role of the State*. UK, USA: Edward Elgar, pp. 103–28.

Hodgson G (2001), *How Economics Forgot History: The Problem of Historical Specificity in Social Science*. London: Routledge.

Hodgson G (2002), Darwinism in economics: From analogy to antology, *Journal of Evolutionary Economics*, 12: 259–281

Hodgson G (2006), What are institutions, *Journal of Economic Issues* Vol XL(1): 1–25

Hodgson G (2009), On the institutional foundation of law: The insufficiency of custom and private ordering, *Journal of Economic Issues* XLIII(1): 143–66.

Jäntti M and Vartiainen J (2009), The Finnish Developmental State and its Growth Regime, UNU-WIDER, United Nations University, Helsinki, Research Paper No. 2009/35

Jessop B (1990), *State Theory: Putting Capitalist States in Their Place*. Cambridge: Polity Press.

Jessop B (2010), Redesigning the state, reorienting state power, and rethinking state theory. In: C Jenkins and K Leicht (eds.), *Handbook of Politics: State and Society in Global Perspective*. New York: Springer, pp. 41–61.

Kim JY (2010), Information diffusion and closeness centrality, *Sociological Theory and Methods* 25(1): 95–106.

Kirman A (2011), *Complex Economics: Individual and Collective Rationality*. London: Routledge.

Krackhardt D (1999), The ties that torture: Simmelian tie analysis in organizations, *Research in the Sociology of Organizations* 16: 183–210.

Lazonick W (2002), Innovative enterprise and historical transformation, *Enterprise & Society* 3(1): 3–47.

Lazonick W (2008), Sustainable *Prosperity in the New Economy? Business Organization and High-Tech Employment in the United States*. Kalamazoo, Michigan: W.E. Upjohn Institute for Employment Research.

Lazonick W (2011), The Innovative Enterprise and the Developmental State: Toward an Economics of "Organizational Success." Paper prepared for: Institute for New Economic Thinking Annual 2011 conference Crisis and Renewal: International Political Economy at the Crossroads Mount Washington Hotel Bretton Woods, NH, April 8–11, 2011.

Levinthal D (1998), The slow pace of rapid technological change: gradualism and punctuation in technological change, *Industrial and Corporate Change* 7: 217–47.

Malerba F (2002), Sectoral systems of innovation and production, *Research Policy* 31: 247–64.

Marengo L et al. (2009), Appropriability, Patents, and Rates of Innovation in Complex Products Industries, LEM, Working paper series.

Mazzucato M (2013), *The Entrepreneurial State*. London: Demos.

Metcalfe JS (1995), Technology systems and technology policy in an evolutionary framework, *Cambridge Journal of Economics* 19: 25–46.

Myrdal G (1944), *American Dilemma: The Negro Problem and Modern Democracy*. New York/London: Harper & Row.

National Research Council (2011), *Measuring the Impacts of Federal Investments in Research: A Workshop Summary*. Washington, DC: The National Academies Press.

Nelson R (1993), *National Innovation Systems: A Comparative Study*. Oxford: Oxford University Press.

Nelson R and Rosenberg N (1993), Technical innovation and national systems. In: Nelson R (ed.), *National Innovation Systems*. Oxford: Oxford University Press.

Newman M (2006), A measure of betweenness centrality based on random walks, *Social Networks* 27: 39–54.

Newman M (2010), *Networks: An Introduction*. Oxford: Oxford University Press.

Nightingale P (2004), Technological Capabilities, Invisible Infrastructure & the Unsocial Construction of Predictability: The Overlooked Fixed Costs of Useful Research. Paper to be presented at the DRUID Summer Conference 2004 on Industrial dynamics, innovation and, Elsinore, Denmark, June 14–16.

Nonaka I and Krogh G (2009), Tacit knowledge and knowledge conversion: Controversy and advancement in organizational knowledge creation theory, *Organization Science* 20(3) (May–June): 635–52.

Opsahl T et al. (2010), Node centrality in weighted networks: Generalizing degree and shortest paths, *Social Networks* 32(3) (July): 245–51.

Ostrom E (2010), Beyond markets and states: Polycentric governance of complex economic systems, *American Economic Review* 100 (June): 1–33.

Penrose E (1959), *The Theory of the Growth of the Firm*. New York: Oxford University Press.

Perez C and Soete L (1988), Catching up in technology: Entry barriers and windows of opportunity. In: G Dosi et al. (eds.), *Technological Change and Economic Theory*. London: Pinter Publishers, pp. 458–79.

Polanyi K [1944] (2001), *The Great Transformation: The Political and Economic Origin of Our Time*. Boston: Beacon Press.

Polanyi M [1966] (1983), *The Tacit Dimension*. New York: Doubleday & Co. Reprinted Gloucester, Mass: Peter Smith.

Poulantzas N (1978), *Political Power and Social Classes*. London and New York: NLB.

Prencipe A et al. (eds.) (2005), *The Business of Systems Integration*. Oxford: Oxford University Press.

Ravasz E and Barabási A-L (2003), Hierarchical organization in complex networks, *Physical Review E* 67: 026112.

Reinert E (1999), The role of the state in economic growth, *Journal of Economic Studies* 26(4/5): 268–326.

Reinert E (2007), *How Rich Countries Got Rich… and Why Poor Countries Stay Poor.* London: Constable.

Rocha L (2000), Syntactic autonomy, cellular automata, and RNA editing: Or why self-organization needs symbols to evolve and how it might evolve them. In: JLR Chandler and G Van de Vijver (eds.), *Closure: Emergent Organizations and Their Dynamics.* New York: Annals of the New York Academy of Sciences, Vol. 901, pp. 207–23.

Ruttan V (2006), Is war necessary for economic growth?, *Historically Speaking-Issues* (merged papers), Clemons Lecture, University of Minnesota, October 9.

Simon H (1991), Organizations and markets, *Journal of Economic Perspectives* 5: 25–44.

Schweitzer F et al. (2009), Economic networks: The new challenges, *Science* 325 (July 24): 422–5.

Teece DJ et al. (1997), Dynamic capabilities and strategic management, *Strategic Management Journal* 18(7): 509–33.

Teubner G and Febbrajo A (eds.) (1992), *State, Law, and Economy as Autopoietic Systems.* Milan: Giuffrè.

Vasconcelos G (2010), From Hayek's spontaneous orders to Luhmann's autopoietic systems, *Studies in Emergent Order* 3: 50–81.

Veblen T (1898), Why is economics not an evolutionary science, *Quarterly Journal of Economics*, July, 373–97.

Vega-Redondo F (2006), *Complex Social Networks.* New York: Cambridge University Press.

Wasserman S and Faust K (1994), *Social Network Analysis: Methods and Applications.* Cambridge: Cambridge University Press.

Watts D and Strogatz S (1998), Collective dynamics of "small-world" networks, *Nature* 393(6684) (June): 440–2.

Woo-Cumings M (1999), *The Developmental State.* Ithaca, N.Y.: Cornell University Press.

Further reading

Amatori F, Millward R and Toninelli A (2005), Reappraising State-Owned Enterprise: A Comparison of the UK and Italy. New York: Routledge.

Bonacich, P (2007), Some unique properties of eigenvector centrality, *Social Networks* 29(4): 555–64.

Burt R (2005), The social capital of structural holes. In: M Guilln et al. (eds.), *The New Economic Sociology.* New York: Russell Sage Foundation, pp. 148–93.

Dopfer K (2005), *Economics, Evolution and the State: The Governance of Complexity.* UK, USA: Edward Elgar.

Freeman Ch (1995), National system of innovation in a historical perpective, *Cambridge Journal of Economics* 19: 5–24.

Lee J and Kim S. (2011), Exploring the role of social networks in affective organizational commitment: Network centrality, strength of ties, and structural holes, The American Review of Public Administration 41(2): 205–23.

Pisano G (2006), *Science Business: The Premise, the Reality, and the Future of Biotech.* Boston, MA: Harvard Business School Press.

Rapoport A (1957), Contribution to the theory of random and biased nets, *Bulletin of Mathematical Biophysics* 19: 257–77.

Simon H (1955), On a class of skew distribution functions, *Biometrika* 42: 425–40.

Teichova A and Matis H (eds.) (2003), *Nation, State and the Economy in History.* New York: Cambridge University Press.

von Hippel E (2005), *Democratizing Innovation.* Cambridge: MIT Press.

3 The state as networker

3.1 The need of a conceptualization of government agency

As already pointed out, besides complexity economics, other areas of the economic science have embraced the complexity way of thinking, sometimes arriving at conflicting, if not insurmountable, conclusions. One example is the conception on the role of the state. This chapter is attempting to establish a more explicit theoretical bridge between *government agency* and complexity economics. One of the challenges of the current research agenda on economics includes a more accurate theoretical account on the role of the state within a complex economic system.

In contrast to mainstream economics, evolutionary-institutional based complexity economics acknowledges the need to conceive the economy as a dynamic, non-equilibrium and open network of relations. However, the role of the state has not been sufficiently conceptualized, at least with the aims of reflecting the available historical evidence. One of the aims of this research is to legitimize the *conceptual link* between notions such as e.g. *networks, dominant hub, adaptability, complex systems* on the one side; and *embedded autonomy, SOE, developmental state, entrepreneurial state, industrial policy, national systems of innovation, innovative firm* on the other side.

It is quite disconcerting to see how, despite the huge amount of evidence regarding the role of industrial policy since the industrialization period (and even before) to the *new economy* or *knowledge economy*, almost no word has been given to it. Not to mention the absence of conceptualization on the *government agency* within the complex socioeconomic networks. Even when the stance taken by the current literature on complexity economics on the subject has been (if seldom) much more realistic and less prejudiced (Kirman 2011; Pelikan and Wegner 2003; Dopfer 2005; Dopfer and Potts 2008; Beinhocker 2006), it has remained close to the neo-liberal spirit of the state as *shaper of the environment*[1] (Hayek 1960). At the same time, however, this should not be a surprise since "it is the neo-Austrian economists who have been the heterodox group most open to the complex system perspective" (Foster 2005 p 879).

For example, Kirman (2011) rightly argues that "we should be building models in which interaction and interdependence are the central motor of the economy" (p. 8). However, he does not mention the terms "government" or "state" anywhere (not even in a minimal form) while acknowledging that

> Hayek's vision as information as dispersed throughout, with each individual having her or his own limited amount [...] but with the system organizing itself as individuals interact is in the spirit of the sort of model I have in mind.
>
> (Kirman 2011, p. 7)

He considers the interaction between individuals (not institutions and individuals) as the central element when understanding "many macroeconomic phenomena" (ibid.).

Beinhocker (2006, pp. 415–51) asserts that, in complexity economics, "the question is not states versus markets—it is how to combine states *and* markets to create an effective evolutionary system" (p. 427), but at the same time he very much embraces the Hayekian state and market notion. He also acknowledges that the notion of complexity is beyond the "traditional market failures and would have us be sceptical of market solutions that depend on traditional theory's usual array of unrealistic assumptions" (p. 424). But, even when he implicitly admits the institutional variety behind different development experiences, he does not make any explicit attempt to define the markets in a way other than the traditional a-historical tradition does (see below).

Slembeck (in Pelikan and Wegner 2003) correctly argues that the complex interdependencies arising from division of labor and specialization "tend to induce conflicts that need social coordination and can be solved only by collective action" (p. 141). He also argues that for this collective action to be able to happen, a commonly accepted basis needs to be created out of the diverging interests, beliefs and ideologies that are present in the policymaking process. However, he sees generally politicians and economists as two very different (even opposed) entities, living in "different worlds," with the economists' side typically (and somewhat naturally) ignoring the distributional effects of policymaking and politicians that always follow their own interests (ibid., p. 147). But the latter clashes somehow with the evolutionary spirit of Slembeck's argument, because, even if this might be the case, there is a lot of historical evidence suggesting that politicians do not necessarily look after their personal interests. It also omits the fact that actually these two spheres, although with their own logics, tend to interact most of the time, shaping one another (Hodgson 2000, 2009; Chang 2002; Gindis 2009).

A more recent contribution made by Colander and Kupers (2014) reasserts the above-mentioned points. The authors go, to the extent of our knowledge, beyond most of the complexity literature in terms of application of the framework in the design of public policy. It is a well-thought analysis that openly accepts the endogenous nature of the government entity within the economic system but, in our view, it is still too much concerned with avoiding rent-seeking behavior and harmful government intervention. The latter are undoubtedly, and for very good reasons, necessary goals, but the emphasis of the whole argument clearly tilts towards the "predatory state" narrative advanced by the neoclassical political economy and rational choice analysis of the 1970s and the 1980s (Buchanan et al. 1980; Krueger 1974; Colander 1984; Colclough and Manor 1991; for a critique see Chang 1999).

Even when Colander and Kupers (2014) envision the state as a "natural partner" within a complex economy, they reaffirm their affinities by calling their approach "activist laissez faire" policy (p. 31). They claim that those who believe in free markets are generally "much closer to a complexity frame than those who primarily put their faith in governmental planning and control" (ibid.). Therefore, "complexity may often well be equated with laissez-faire" (ibid.). That means, in order for the state to fit within this framework it needs to be removed from most of its hierarchical nature as much as possible. In this view, situating the state in horizontal relationship with other institutions would help to create an "ecostructure" (supported by the state), which would make it easier for the state to "delegate many of its coordination roles to other collective choice institutions" (p. 27).

However, while flat hierarchies work well in some contexts (e.g. Ostrom's polycentric governance of common pool-resources) they do not necessarily work well everywhere. Later in this chapter we will consider a different complexity-based way of looking at hierarchy. For now, let's notice that it may be problematic to deal with the government role as just another "means through which individuals solve collective problems" (ibid., p. 7) without qualifying the kind of collective problem a community could face. It is not the same providing for some coordination mechanism in order to protect a common forest area, for instance, as providing for a minimum education level for the children of a country or community. Specifically in terms of economic development, the 200-year-old US history of state and local economic development tells a different story about the undoubtedly complex interplay between hierarchies and coordination (Coan 2017).

This is not to say that the state does all the work alone from a superior position, but to say that in a world full of assets with limited mobility those who control such assets will have strong incentives to oppose structural change, which will lead to inevitable conflicts. Evidence shows that in many successful economies, structural transformation arising from these conflicts has been carried out in a highly and deliberate politicized way. How do recent experiences of East Asian industrial policies, and beyond, fit within this framework? Stops this kind of industrial policy being relevant just because absolute central control is an illusion? Should we refrain from studying the theoretical implications that, existing and past, governance mechanisms with markedly top-down features have for the complexity discourse? Or should we just accept that our conceptual projections in social sciences are, no matter how blurred ideologies can become, necessarily rooted in certain ideological preferences, whose normative implications express, quite often if not always, different valid aspects of a complex subject.

The idea of providing societal governance frameworks that ensure personal freedom and autonomy, and which prevent sedimented bureaucracies from stifling human creativity, is one worth of advocating for. But the idea of "private organizations [operating] more as state organizations" and "state organizations that would operate more as private organizations" (ibid.) simply resembles too much the neoliberal-based new public management models with its claims of political independent bodies, contracting-out management, public–private partnerships and customer (instead of citizen) services. To be sure, none of these things are necessarily undesirable and have proven to work very well in some contexts, but this is not the grand story of the new public management models.

Very concisely, new public management had its heyday during the 1980s and 1990s in the industrialized Anglo-Saxon area, later extending to other places. Its major intellectual influences are to be found in the public choice theory and agency theory (Ferlie 2017). This model of management is concerned with the notion government should create market-based arenas of choice in which individuals, as customers, can make decisions based on their own self-interest. But as we begin to think about citizens as being analogous to customers, and government as analogous to a market, the need to talk about or act upon the "public interest" largely disappears (Denhardt and Denhardt 2007).

There is a clear difference between public interest as shared values and the notion of collective problem solving advanced by Colander and Kupers (2014). The context in which the later is employed reveals a close relation to the public school idea of collective action as an aggregation of private decision-makers; closer to Proudhon's spirit than Rousseau's. This framework denies *de facto* any notion of public interest or renders it, in the best case, as a by-product of individual choices in a market-based arena.

However, despite how elusive the notion of public interest can be, we immediately know of its existence when we experience the general discontent that arises if supposedly common principles are believed to be violated, just as historical events such as the Enclosures, or recent events such as the financial crisis of 2008, and its long aftermath, have persuasively shown. The philosophy of new public management overshadows the idea of shared values by obliterating basic differences between public and non-public agents, which has hurt citizen's ability of holding organizations and public bodies accountable, therefore generating serious democratic and organizational deficits everywhere (for an in-depth discussion see Ferlie 2017; Ritchie 2014; Andrew et al. 2011; Drechsler and Randma-Liiv 2014; Evans and Rauch 1999). This model emerged at the same time as the complexity economics agenda, and it is plausible to speculate about the influence the former has had in the practitioners of the latter.

Again, the main point to be made here is not that the complexity literature is explicitly against government participation in the making of socioeconomic systems. The central assumption of complexity economics, also sustained by this research, is that economies are non-equilibrium systems, which do not exist in isolation. As already stated, this literature acknowledges the institutional and ever-changing complexity of the economic activities, and recognizes (almost always implicitly) that state institutions (and their evolution) are part of this ecology.

However, there have been few explicit attempts to establish a theoretical link between government as industrial policy designer on the one side; and the notion of complex economic systems on the other. In contrast, much emphasis has been given to the notion of self-organization, to the detriment of other relevant elements. This absence ignores the strong body of evidence that shows that, in actual fact, the role of the state has gone far beyond of the *shaper* in the Hayekian sense. Nor there is any attempt to cope with this evidence theoretically.

Notice that we are not intending to deliver a theory of the state in the fashion of political theorists such as Max Weber, Charles Tilly, Michael Mann, Antonio Gramsci, Nicos Poulanzas, Theda Skocpol, Bob Jessop or the traditional Marxist School (a detailed discussion on these approaches can be found in Skocpol 1979; Evans et al. 1985, 1999, pp. 3–44; Jessop in Bryson et al. 2001; Jessop 2003b). Although this analysis instinctively and indirectly relies on insights of these sociological and political perspectives, our objective is more modest, namely to try to conceptualize on the position of the state in a complex economy. Another important conceptual source is the program of Institutionalist Political Economy (IPE)[2] proposed by Chang (2002, 2003b).

3.2 Anti-interventionist theories

As Millward (2005) argues, even before the Great Depression, most governments in continental Europe owned large utilities and had equity in large commercial banks. Already in the nineteenth century, western European municipal and state governments were owners of utilities companies before socialist parties even existed. However, paradoxically, in most of the nineteenth century, particularly the late nineteenth century, the laissez faire position dominated the economic profession; and while this view waned in the first (and part of the second) half of the twentieth century, it has resurfaced in the present period. Actually, the nineteenth (Western) century represents a battlefield between what Henry (2008) calls "soft" and "hard" laissez faire theories.

In the first group we have a more utilitarian based liberalism represented by Jeremy Bentham,[3] his disciple John Stuart Mills[4] and their predecessor Adam Smith. These three economists, while proponents of the individualist tradition; were also strong advocates of the intervention of the state in many areas of the economy. Some authors argue that the Victorian era was anything but a pure laissez-faire period. Although more linked to a natural rights based liberalism, it is also stated that Smith took a clear proto-utilitarian approach when analyzing the role of the state in diverse realms of the economy.

Authors such as Viner (1927), Frankel Paul (1980) and Henry (2008) reveal a less known dimension of the Smithian liberalism, which could be compatible not only with the standard exceptions surrounding defence, the provisioning of justice, and the construction of public works. In actual fact, he proposed so many exceptions to a generally laissez faire program in market relations themselves that it is unseemly to cast him as a forerunner of modern Chicago[School].

(Henry 2008, p. 311)

For example he also was an advocate of

a government-imposed ceiling on interest rates, government programs to direct capital toward beneficial investment, export restrictions on agricultural products, subsidies to business firms to assist them in reaching an economically viable size (a primitive 'infant industry' argument), and so on.

(ibid.)

Commenting about his praise of England's policy of high tariffs in the Navigation Acts, and its trade-off with free trade, Reinert (2007) goes further while arguing that Adam Smith might be seen as a "misunderstood mercantilist" (p. 133).

Indeed, in the chapter I of book IV of the *Wealth of the Nations* he understands and acknowledges the arguments made by his predecessor, Thomas Mun's *England Treasure by Foreign Trade*. Thomas Mun is known as one of the most sophisticated mercantilist thinkers of the seventeenth century and the one that introduced the argument of positive trade balance (over the hoarding of gold and silver) as the basis of the economic surplus. In addition, Smithian liberalism took a lot of the Physiocratic School, which coined the original term *laissez faire* with a more holistic perspective in mind (Gerlach 2002).

The second group, i.e. the hard laissez-faire theories could be traced to the statements contained by journals such as

the *Economist* during the years 1843–1854 under the editorship of James Wilson […]. It was the *Economist* which nurtured the budding antistatist, evolutionist, Herbert Spencer. In such journals, one could find consistent and principled arguments that condemned such statist proposals as the sanitary laws, compulsory vaccinations, and state grants to schools.[5]

Among the most important proponents of hard laissez-faire theories we should also mention those which could be somewhat inaccurately[6] labeled as rooted in a natural rights-based tradition: this is the tradition of Jean Baptiste Say,[7] Richard Cobden,[8] Thomas Mackay[9] and Frédéric Bastiat.[10] These authors played a pivotal role in the birth of the Austrian School, represented in its first generation by authors like Menger, von Böhm-Bawerk and von Wieser.

However, the origins of real articulated anti-interventionist theories in the Austrian School are to be found in its second generation, which initiated in the twenty century the case against central planning and public ownership; that was part of the calculation debate[11] started by Mises in 1921. Mises defined intervention as "a limited order by a social authority forcing the owners of the means of production and entrepreneurs to employ their means in a different manner than they otherwise would" (von Mises 1929, p. 20).

He claimed that without private property, a functional price system would not be possible because market exchanges could not take place and without them rational valuation would cease, resulting in economic chaos (von Mises 1922). Hayek, another important exponent of the Austrian school (along Menger and Mises), subsequently elaborated these arguments and became one of the most articulated advocates of the anti-interventionist school. Conversely, phenomena such as the Keynessian revolution, the success of the first stage of central planning in the Soviet Union; and the success of the state in advanced capitalist economies after World War II overshadowed the anti-interventionist trend until the 1970s, when adverse outcomes in advanced economies led to a revival (until the present day) of anti-interventionist theories.[12] In this context, Hayek's insights on the necessity to keep state activity to the lowest level possible played a determinant role in shaping the new anti-interventionist consensus and they still find great resonance in both orthodox and many heterodox scholars.

In his writings Hayek contrasts two traditions of liberalism. The first, and inseparable from the institution of private property, related to the legacy of Adam Smith, Edmund Burke or John Locke. The second, linked to the continental tradition of Rousseau and Voltaire, more prone to subordinate the freedom of individuals to certain political and normative goals, in line with the French Revolution and socialism. He built his anti-interventionist notions by favoring the first tradition over the second one. In his view, even when both traditions became ingrained into the Western democratic discourse, the second one aligned with increasing government control, which he saw as conflicting with the main liberal tenets and therefore rejected (Hayek 1966). He even accepted the hypothetical possibility of a liberal but not necessarily democratic order. Hayek's views in this topic are very much in line with the views of many classical liberal thinkers, which saw democracy as a potential danger for proprietary interests.

Still, on this basis, he developed enlightened and sophisticated notions of individual liberty and economy evolution, whose central insight rests in the assumption of the overwhelming complexity of a socioeconomic system (Hayek 1944, 1960). In the 1930s Hayek also attacked the feasibility of socialism, drawing on arguments such as the inability of the planners to interpret all the knowledge dispersed among the individual economic agents (Hayek 1944; Caldwell 1997). The collapse of Soviet-based socialism confirmed the insight of his theories. According to Henry (2008), in particular through the work of von Hayek, "the libertarian wing" of economics has exerted a strong influence in the recrudescence of the hard laissez faire doctrine in the current period (ibid., p. 210) (although, of course, the promotion of the laissez-faire program should not be confined to this discourse).

Nevertheless, as briefly mentioned in Chapter 2, Hayek recognized the need for state regulation in certain areas; and that its existence could be "at least in principle reconcilable with a free system" (Hayek 1960, p. 202). It needs also to be recalled that Hayek was not necessarily against a large state. As he pointed out, "it is the character rather than the volume of government activity that is important" (Hayek 1960, Chapter 5, p. 194). He acknowledges that "to Adam Smith and his immediate successors the enforcement of ordinary rules of common law would certainly not have appeared as government interference" (ibid.).

However, essentially, he believed that "there is good reason why all governmental concern with economic matters is suspect." He delimitated the scope of state action to certain activities that were "compatible with the functioning of the market" (ibid.). According to Hayek, state enterprises, control of prices (ibid., Chapter 15); and distributive and social policies (ibid., Chapter 19) were among the most important elements to be avoided by any good functioning society.

On the one hand, he recognized that the coercive power of the state would be justified if it serves to "general and timeless purposes" (ibid., p. 198). He assumed the existence of general rules arising from tradition, which have to be legitimated by the law. State coercion will be warranted, as long as it continues to enforce these rules. To accept such rules will enable each member of the society to shape his "protected sphere" and to differentiate between "what belongs to [this] sphere and what does not" (p. 123). This is, the state capacity to let the individual decide upon his property and action, lies at the heart of the Hayekian role of the state within complex social systems.

However, on the other hand, he undermines the institutional dimension of the rules and emphasizes its normative role. He acknowledges that "human imperfection" will lead to the need for interpretation and implementation by stating that "an independent judge" should be able to create legislation in order to solve specific situations. In doing this, the courts assure that the new specific legislation enhances the allocation efficiency of the spontaneous social order, while correcting things towards the general rules embodied by law.

But, as Vasconcelos (2010) points out, "from the moment in which Courts are allowed to correct Parliaments and Governments, the nature of the rules from spontaneous order and organizations cannot be assumed *statically* and *a priori*" (p. 61). Hayek's conception highlights the existence of a "bottom-up process of legal development, while statutory legislation typically ratifies customary precedents" (Hodgson 2009, p. 144). He insists in classifying certain "kinds of governmental measures which the rule of law excludes in principle" (Hayek 1960, p. 199). According to this conception, these measures could not be "achieved by merely enforcing general rules because they cannot be achieved" (ibid.). For him, general rules have always been there, as they respond to the very nature of individuals. However, it is not possible to continue considering the spontaneous order of law as a set of a-historical higher rules given the facts that legislation[13] now predates law and that "judicial neutrality has been empirically and theoretically rejected by different disciplines" (Vasconcelos 2010, p. 58; see also Chang 2011, p. 601).

On the other hand, this is not to say that the motivations of the enforcing third parties are always shaped by self-interest. As several authors have convincingly shown, human motivations are far more complex than what is already believed (Shengxiang et al. 2017; Beaussart et al. 2013; Kamenica 2012; Clithero et al. 2008; Thaler and Sunstein 2008; Cacioppo 2002; Fehr and Gächter 2000; Frey 1997, 2007; Kahneman et al. 1982). If we take this seriously, then we can no longer assume that government officials will necessarily act following selfish motives. Nor can we longer see legislation on government prerogatives as something already that simply deviate from the normal rules. Rather, the point being made is that a true understanding of the functioning of complex social systems requires a dynamic analysis of the co-evolution of institutional systems.

Hayek offers a sound evolutionary explanation of a spontaneous order based on the fact that all knowledge is dispersed and that any individual or organization is unable to possess it all. But this explanation is exclusively based on the interaction between individuals. According to him, complex systems are dependent on their impact on individuals. However, in actual fact, it cannot be said that a decentralized social order emerges from individual actions alone. Not only are individuals repositories of knowledge but also organizations (which Hayek sees as inimical to the spontaneous order) which are much bigger than individuals. An entity's social properties do not always depend on that entity's individual properties.

Reality actually consists of multi-leveled hierarchies that cannot be analyzed by reducing it to its isolated constituents. In fact, one of the core notions of complexity economics is that social systems are made of several interacting and overlapping levels, whose emergent properties cannot be explained in terms of just one level (Hodgson 2000). If we take the emergence story seriously, then it is necessary to accept that a two-way causation between individual and institutions is at play here (Chang 2002; Hodgson 2006). Individuals both constitute and are constituted by society. This means that the state as institution (and other institutions) can also affect the behavior of both individuals and other institutions.

3.3 Industrial policy as a recurrent theme

Economic development is activity-dependent. New technologies create scope for new innovative activities, increasing returns and therefore productivity, which ultimately leads to structural change in the long term, together with an improvement in living standards. Basically, increasing returns refers to mechanisms of positive feedback that manifest themselves when output increases by more than that proportional change in inputs. Growth in economic output requires either to increase the number of inputs that go into the productive process or to devise ways to obtain more output from the same number of inputs. The latter has been the main cause of economic growth and prosperity, which usually crystallizes as the result of the purposeful introduction of new technologies. Historically, there has been some sort of non-linear causal relation between the public hand and the development of industrial activities that show the highest increasing returns. This has been explored by contemporary researchers, who have found strong causal connections between the proportion of investments in high technologies manufactures (as share of the national product) and the increase in the national product percapita (De Long, 1992). There have also been found that targeting skilled workers in the tradable sector, particularly high-tech industries, generates a multiplier effect in the economy due to higher demand of the non-tradables, and possibly of other tradables too, provided the latter are complementary, or prone to be integrated, to the targeted industry (Moretti 2010; Moretti and Thulin 2013). The resulting virtuous cycle contributes to a more sophisticated occupational and economic structure, which allows a nation or region to pay its way in the world by producing unique innovations or better and cheaper versions of existing products.

This causality had already been intuitively understood not only by proponents of the infant industry argument such as Alexander Hamilton or Friedrich List, but also by some pre-Smithian political economists as well, e.g. Giovanni Botero and Antonio Serra (Reinert 2016). Adam Smith's *Wealth of the Nations* sketched important insights in this direction (although opposing government's activity in this point) in chapter XI of Book I, but these ideas were temporarily overturned by Ricardo's decreasing return views, which eventually became the trademark of classical and later neoclassical economics. It is worth mentioning other important figures of the classical period such as Charles Babbage, the computer pioneer and Andrew Ure, the encyclopedic Scottish physician, geologist and earlier business theorist, whose remarkables *On the Economy of Machinery and Manufactures* (1833) and *The Philosophy of Manufactures* (1835), respectively, strongly influenced Stuart Mill's views on increasing returns and Karl Marx's views, who was also well aware of the importance of technological innovation in economic evolution. At the end of nineteenth century, Alfred Marshall devoted some pages in the now famous Book IV of his *Principles* to this subject.

However, it is in the twentieth century where this notion began to be properly conceptualized: starting with the seminal paper *"Increasing returns and economic progress,"* written in 1928 by the celebrated American economist Allyn Young. Subsequently, during the 1940s and the 50s, his ideas began to be assimilated by his student Nicholas Kaldor, whose insights on the causation of growth led him to call attention to the positive feedback mechanisms that exist between manufacturing, productivity and structural change (Kaldor's growth laws, also known as Verdoom's law) (Kaldor 1967). It is not a coincidence that the views of economists such as Kaldor, and also Gunnar Myrdal, were developed in the context of what they denominated the circular cumulative causation approach. Basically, this approach emphasizes the multicausal and non-linear nature of the links between core economic variables.

A critical element that Kaldor's approach relies on is the evolutionary notion of cumulative causation advanced by the American institutionalist Thorstein

Veblen, which, combined with Young's insights, provides a dynamic, alternative framework to study the causal patterns that lead to innovation and economic development. Its emphasis in elements such as heterogeneity, interdependence and non-equilibriums represents a fundamental antithesis to the static neoclassical view of economic systems. Some scholars see a conceptual connection in the notions of all the above-mentioned authors in terms of their ideas about a disequilibrium theory of endogenous growth, which opens many possibilities for this dynamic theory of economic development to be interpreted in terms of complex systems (Lavezzi 2001).

The above-mentioned insights build part of the intellectual foundation of post-war heterodox economic thinking, which includes schools such as development and innovation economics, and the emphasis of some of these schools in the need for industrial and technology policies that help economic development. Indeed, the path towards increasing-returns activities based on state-of-the-art technologies is fraught with barriers of entry and uncertainty, which makes it difficult for firms to follow this path without deliberate policy intervention. This has become rather uncontroversial a statement, which finds renewed evidence in the resurgence of several initiatives in the aftermath of the financial crisis. However, the debate about both extent and nature of the intervention remains controversial and polarized until the present day (for a comprehensive analysis of the industrial policy debate in historical perspective see Andreoni and Chang 2019).

Hayek rightly argued that the fully centralized coordination of activities in a complex and continuously evolving modern economy would require gathering and processing information on a magnitude outside of the capabilities available to any present or future state. The power of this argument is now widely accepted even by many who favor an interventionist state. But, as earlier mentioned, Austrian and neo-Austrian school's rejection of state enterprises, control of prices and distributive and social policies was definitive. However, the historical evidence questions these assumptions given that these elements have actually *co-existed* with many successful development experiences.

In contrast to the above-mentioned views, historical evidence shows that industrial policy was the most employed instrument by today's industrialized nations, not only after World War II but also several centuries before (Reinert 1999, 2007). As several scholars point out, the development of new technologies demands more than private entrepreneurship; particularly in the early product development stages (Mazzucato 2011; Ruttan 2006; Chang 2002; Reinert 1999). This requires several decades of financial support to reach commercial viability and the "decision makers in the private sector rarely have access to the patient capital implied by a twenty year or even a ten year time horizon" (Ruttan 2006, p. 23).

Among these new technologies, the so-called *general purpose technologies* are the ones that show the highest increasing returns and thus create the greatest scope for innovation and economic prosperity. As Arthur (2009) rightly argues, "the value of technology lies not merely in what can be done with it but also in what further possibilities it will lead to" (p. 170). Understanding that economic development is activity-specific implies the uses of certain policies to introduce (and to diffuse) the right technologies in a country. Precisely, one of the consequences of the mainstream assumptions of no differences between economic activities, decreasing returns, perfect information and equilibrium was that orthodox (neoclassical) economists get used to model "a world where a coordinating nation-state was no longer needed" (Reinert 2012, p. 23).

Nevertheless, the existence of "a strong State, leading a nation into increasing return activities, historically has been an obligatory passage point in the development of any nation" (Reinert 1999, p. 317). The same author argues that "as economic agents, States exist for fundamentally the same reasons that firms exist, both of them for reasons not well captured by today's economic theory, which focuses on barter and atomism" (ibid.). This is what several scholars define as *developmental state* (Johnson 1982; Woo-Cumings 1999; Lazonick 2011). Other more or less equivalent definitions, although sometimes with substantial differences from each other, can be found in the *embedded autonomy* provided by (Evans 1995), *developmental bureaucratic state (DBS) vs. developmental network state (DNS)* (Block 2008) and in the *public-sector entrepreneurship* (for a historical review see Hayter et al. 2018, pp. 676–682). These definitions have led to recent fashionable notions of intervention, some more ambiguous than others, which reflect the new revival of industrial policy after the global financial crisis of 2008. Even with their limitations, partly influenced by the still strong "smartness" neoliberal ethos, these approaches bear witness of the need to talk about industrial policy, beyond the usual detractors [e.g. *entrepreneurial state* (Mazzucato 2011), and *entrepeneurial ecosystems* (Brown and Mawson 2019 for a critical assessment)

As Reinert (2007) points out, "if we insists in abandoning industrial policy because moving away from perfect competition" (p. 255) then we would have totally misunderstood the dynamics of the business world. He continues by affirming that "economic development is caused by structural changes, which brakes the equilibrium creating rents" (ibid.). In fact, demanding no rents means to remain forever in a steady stationary situation. Actually, economic development and innovation are about correlating public interest with the interests of the potential producers and other stakeholders. It is actually hard to separate economic policy from politics and certain interests, and this has been true even for the so-called two historical bastions of liberalism. Historically, "dynamic imperfect competition" has been the force behind economic growth, rent-seeking and `cronyism` being part of it (ibid.).

For instance, Jäntti and Vartiainen (2009) indicate how a pragmatic cooperation between business officials and government officials created the foundation of the successful Finnish corporatist growth model, which played a key role in enhancing the economic growth in that country. The model was not restricted to Finland, but also in countries such as South Korea, Taiwan, Japan and Austria (see Woo-Cumings 1999). Chang (2010b) points out how the Korean government prohibited LG Group to enter the textile industry and was forced to enter the cable industry, which became the foundation of its electronic business. He also mentions how the Hyundai Group was also forced by the Korean government to enter the shipbuilding business (one of the most successful of the group), under the threat of getting its subsidies cut. Reinert (1999) observes how this government also "coerced" Samsung from trading activities into the manufacturing of semiconductors in the early 1980s (p. 297).

Ruttan (2006) notes how the US military procurement policy of "second sourcing" and subsidies encouraged the diffusion of knowledge and the entry of new firms; and pushed semiconductor technology rapidly down the design and production learning curve. He remarks that by the mid-1950s the Army Signal Corps was funding about 50 percent of transistor development at Bell Laboratories as well as subsidizing facility construction by General Electric, Ratheon, RCA and Sylvania. The same applies for the computer and the internet industries. Similarly, the US government role in the development of the biotechnology industry has been extensively documented (Lazonick and Tulum 2011).

Daniel Defoe describes in his now almost forgotten book *A Plan of the English Commerce* (1728) how the King Henry VII started an import substitution policy in the fifteenth century to cover the technological gap in the wool industry (the high tech of the time) with the Low Countries (Chang 2003a, 2008). Reinert (2007) mentions how woolworkers employed their connections to King to influence the state to give them subsidies and to impose an export duty on raw wool. Brisco (1907) and Chang (2003a) also tell us how Whig politician Robert Walpole, the first British Prime Minister, is said to be the first person to initiate a comprehensive infant industry program in 1721 in order to promote manufacturing industries.[14] That included export subsidies, the lowering of tariffs on industrial inputs; import tariff rebates on inputs used for exporting or export quality controlled by the state. This set of events strongly influenced Alexander Hamilton; the first Treasury Secretary of the US, who first developed the theory of infant industry protection in his *Report on the Manufacturers* of 1791.

It was the Hamilton and Daniel Raymond (early nineteenth century) works that inspired the then free trade advocate Friedrich List[15] to embrace the infant industry argument after his exile in the USA (1825–30). Hamilton's proposals were introduced in subsequent periods (with varying degree) after the war of 1812 with England, which led to the introduction of the "American System," strongly promoted by Henry Clay.[16] This system, which consisted basically of infant industry protection, standardization and infrastructural development, was a definitive entrance of the US in the industrialization period.

Apart from setting important precedents such as the issuance of Treasury Notes, the aftermath of the war of 1812 gave a significant impulse to the development of manufacturing in the United States. Even if this was a somewhat unintended outcome of the war, it played an important role in the future debates on industrialization. The impossibility to import British products due to British restrictions and to the otherwise disastrous American embargo of 1807, and subsequent legislations,[17] prompted the creation of manufacturing facilities for cotton goods, woollen cloths, iron, glass, pottery and other articles. The emerging class of manufacturers formed the basis for a movement toward more protection, which found expression in the Tariff Act of 1816. This piece of legislation, initially supported by Southern states during the Era of Good Feelings, was the initial step into the construction of the American System.

Abraham Lincoln, was an ardent advocate of this System, which is reflected, for example in his protection of the "steel cronies" (Reinert 2007, p. 255). By paying a little more for steel, the US created a huge steel industry with well-paid jobs, which provided a base for government taxation. In 1877, steel producers used their political power to impose a 100 percent duty on steel rails (ibid.). This is a period that led the economic historian Paul Bairoch to call the US "the mother country and bastion of modern protectionism" (p. 32). Late-nineteenth-century economists such as Frank Taussig and Richard T. Ely commented on and agreed, although to different degrees, with this sort of policy.

Until the first decades of the twentieth century, the US was the most protectionist country in the world, with an average industrial tariff rate of 40 to 55 percent, while at the same time it was the fastest growing economy in the world (Chang 2002). The period after the American Civil War, specifically after the end of the Reconstruction period in 1877 until the beginning of the twentieth century, also known as the Gilded Age,[18] was probable the period where the US economy achieved the fastest growth and industrial development rates in its history (see also Cohen and DeLong 2016).

As Reinert (2007) points out, the problem with rent-seeking is whether this rent spreads through the economy in form of higher profits, higher wages and higher taxable income, or not. He mentions how Swedish industrialist Marcus Wallenberg used his political contacts during the 1950s and 60s to win support for the Swedish companies Volvo and Electrolux. Together with nineteenth-century United States, the targeted protections that Germany and Sweden provided to their nascent heavy industries in the late nineteenth and the early twentieth centuries are well known. But even Belgium, one of the less protected economies, provided targeted protection (Chang 2003a).

Germany and the US forged ahead of England in electromechanical engineering, consumer durables, and synthetic chemistry thanks to a set of very well calibrated intervention policies. As Di Maio (in Cimoli et al. 2009) and Freeman (2004) point out, the government provision of incentives for innovators was essential here. Friedewald (2000) observes how the political and military interests German Reich led to the creation of Telefunken Company, which succeeded internationally with its quenched spark system on the eve of the First World War. In his classical *Made in Germany* of 1896, Ernest Williams exposed how the German tariff system (first rigid under Bismarck and then more selective and sophisticated) was hurting the English manufacturers. This included sectors such as transportation, chemicals, steel and iron. He also praises the comprehensive (and then innovative) research and education policy carried out by the state of Imperial Germany; as well as the ingenuity of Germans manufactures (tolerated and often encouraged by the state) to overcome English regulations.[19] It is happening today with Chinese industrialization.

For another example, Chang (2007) argues that it seems very unlikely that the Finnish firm Nokia would have become a leader in mobile telecommunications if this firm had followed "rational decisions" and not been protected by the government. Nokia's electronic business, whose mobile phone business forms the core of the company's business today, was set up in 1960. Even until 1967, when the merger between Nokia, Finnish Rubber Works Ltd and Finnish Cable Works took place, electronics generated only 3 percent of the Nokia group's net sales. The electronics sector lost money for the first 17 years, only making its first profit in 1977 (Chang 2007).

On the other hand, powerful interest influencing domestic policies do not circumscribe to business and industries, but also include civil society groups of diverse tendencies. For instance, none of the aforementioned denies the fact that policies aiming at the protection of infant industries have often, although not universally, come together with some moral narrative that put natives against foreign citizens (which changes to reciprocity as the context changes). This has been particularly, but by no means exclusively, the case in the United States, where nativist movements that have emerged along the country's history (pro-black slavery, anti-Irish, anti-Chinese, anti-Italian, anti-German, anti-Mexican, anti-Muslim etc.) were at times coopted by political forces favoring protectionism, sometimes tacitly, sometimes consciously, and sometimes even inadvertently.

For example, in a fervent defense of protectionist policies, Congressman William McKinley, future president of the United States, speaks of "[...] defence to our own productions, as a discrimination in favor of our own and against the foreign[...]."[20] The us and them distinction has often played a significant role within protectionist policies. This applies to a wide range of politicians in all ideological persuasions, famous or infamous: from Henry Clay to current US president Donald Trump.

However, the implantation of multilateral agreements such as the General Agreement on Tariffs and Trade (GATT) after World War II showed that there is a way to promote trade between nations, while recognizing at the same time the specific needs of the nations. Previously, the U.S (due to lack of approval by the Congress after repeated submissions by President Truman) had, regrettably, rejected the Havana Charter, signed in 1948 in Havana by 56 countries. Among other things, the Havana Charter contained the ITO Charter, intended to create the "International Trade Organisation (ITO)," which was a project that "attempted to establish a mutually compatible set of policies blending free-trade objectives with recognition of state intervention in the domestic sphere and sectoral aspects of international trade" (Graz 2016, p. 282). The singular scenario after the World War II showed a commitment to restore the liberal economy but, this time, in the background of a new state legitimacy that rested on tools such as the welfare state, development planning and Keynessian policies. Contrary to the current World Trade Organization, there was the need and a real chance to find an effective balance between both aspects (more on the subject, see Graz 2016). The withdrawal of the U.S. in 1950 forced other nations, as no nation wanted to be in an agreement without the U.S., to resort to the only set of agreements available to coordinate trade, namely GATT, which had been signed by twenty-three countries in 1947. In contrast, only eight of the twenty-three signatory parties (United States, United Kingdom, Canada, Australia, France, Belgium, Luxemburg and the Netherlands) signed a "Protocol of Provisional Application of the General Agreement on Tariffs and Trade (PPA)," which was soon agreed by the rest of the fifteen parties (Bossche 2005, p. 81).

Although its overall purpose was to promote international trade by reducing or eliminating trade barriers such as tariff and quotas, it allowed a high number of special preferences that allowed less-developed, and developed as well, nations to engage in more favorable terms of trade. For example, the PPA, provided a "legislation exception" that allowed the contracting parties to retain any provision of their legislation which was inconsistent with the original GATT. This explains why no country never really adopted the original GATT signed in 1947 (Bossche 2005). It was not a perfect instrument because it was dominated by the most powerful nations but it showed nevertheless how multilateralism can be practiced without ignoring differences in levels of industrial development. It is also an irony that those who defended those exceptions in the PPA are the same who today, and until very recently completely blindly, affiliated themselves to the most ferocious application of unrestrained free trade principles in countries of different level of development.

As the international balance grew more precarious and economic philosophies shifted, this system of cooperation grew instable and discriminating. The World Trade Organization, a successor to GATT, represents, somehow, a departure from past efforts in term of balance. If well allowing some forms of preferential agreements and protections, the WTO has substantially reduced the ability of less developed nations to acquire and develop new technologies. China, whose industrial power has grown in this era, achieved its technological might by strategically opening some portions of the economy to WTO´s rules, while at the same time selectively protecting others based on clever interpretations of the same rules. To which extent this case provides a template for other, particularly smaller countries, is still a matter of discussion (for a discussion see Chang 2016).

Overall, the case for protection of infant industries illustrates the complexity of dealing with open systems. If, as the complexity perspective asserts, the economy is permanently open and in a constant condition of flux, then we should accept the possibility of exploitative behavior by well-positioned agents (as the Wall Street meltdown of 2008 showed). For all its faults, phenomena such as over-politicization and abuse of the state by powerful interest groups are an integral part of a complex economy. On the other hand, the fact that these aspects are, indeed, undesired, and the fact that they can lead to failed economic policies, does not necessarily preclude the effectiveness and convenience of an activist state involved in the implementation of more explicit long-run developmental goals.

The point is that, historically (and probably beyond the western world[21]) government intervention carefully conceived industrial policies that have been behind the industrialization efforts of most of the today leading economies. The Austrian and neo-Austrian argument of the state being pernicious to economic development does not match the historical evidence. The fact that the *government agency* has traditionally possessed hierarchical and other control advantages within a socioeconomic system does not seem to necessarily affect the process of economic development.

The present study defends the notion that, even if a direct causality cannot be assured (at least in traditional statistical variable-based terms, and, for the same reason, not completely rejected), it is plausible to say that at least both things (strong interventionist government and economic development) can coexist. But if we actually take into account the *purposeful* existence of industrial policy, then it is hard to deny the fact that it must have played some positive role in this process. Evidence seems to tip the balance in favor of this kind of explanation.

3.4 The ownership issue: States enterprises

The state has not only been a decisive agent when inducing the development of increasing returns activities by introducing protectionist measures, by directly subsidizing private sector, by being a supplier of high-quality demand for national production, or by creating the whole research and education system in which private business rests, but also has played the role of what Reinert (1999) calls "entrepreneur of last resort" (p. 282). In fact, there is no reason to assume a "sufficient supply of entrepreneurship at any point in time and in any culture – the poorer the nation, the less so" (ibid., 284). Of course, the Austrian school suspiciousness of state enterprises is profound. Hayek saw strong "justification for the distrust with which business looks on all state enterprise" (Hayek 1960, p. 196).

To be sure, that is neither to say that state ownership is an automatic solution nor that private property or other type of properties do not work,[22] but rather that this element is not critical for determining innovative behavior. Much more relevant are, for example, the abilities and incentives of those managers who exercise strategic control. As Chang (2010a) points out, there are many examples of state-owned enterprises (SOEs) in countries such as Singapore, Italy, France, Finland, Norway and Taiwan that were not just efficient in the narrow allocative sense but also led their country's economic growth process through technological dynamism and export successes (p. 8). The fact that SOEs are an enduring feature of economic landscape appears to be uncontroversial even for commentators and economic agents quintessentially related to the private sector (PwC 2015).

Private ownership has been traditionally considered by many economists as the only workable ownership type. However, there are a wide variety of property rights not fitting into this public and private dichotomy. For example, communal property rights over common-pool resources (Ostrom 2010), hybrid forms of property rights such as the cooperative or the so-called township and village enterprise (TVE) in China (Chang 2010a), copyleft licensing etc. It should not be asserted that a stronger protection of private property rights will necessarily lead to higher investment and thus higher growth. It will depend on the kinds of property rights that are being protected.

For example, historic evidence has shown that strong protection of landlord property rights has proven harmful for economic development in many countries. For example, the land reforms in Japan, Taiwan and South Korea after World War II represented a violation of the existing property rights of landlords; and even though they did not result in a voluntary agreement, these measures contributed decisively to the development of these nations. It could also be said that an excessive protection of the holders of company shares and other liquid assets can actually reduce real investment and thus growth, by putting short-term pressures on the managers, who have to cater to the impatience of highly mobile asset owners (Chang 2010a, 2010b). This became evident during the financial crisis that began in 2008. There is also strong evidence pointing to the fact that longer data exclusivity has not increased the development of new, beneficial drugs in the biopharmaceutical industry (Kesselheim 2010; Light et al. 2011).

In fact, several concrete examples support the idea the workability of SOEs mentioned above. Some of the most well known cases come from the East Asian economies, especially from Taiwan. For example, Taiwan had one of the biggest SOE sectors in the world until part of it was privatized in 1996. Public firms are still legally regarded as an important part of the state structure, with annual budgets, critical investment plans, high level personnel nomination, personnel management, financial auditing and even day-to-day matters all being under strict regulation and supervision by the relevant government organizations and processes (Chiu-Pu 2005). Although in 1996 some of the SOE firms were privatized, the Taiwanese government still held a controlling stake (averaging 35.5 percent) and appointed 60 percent of the directors (Chang 2008). The Chinese government has used an analogous strategy during the last three decades.

Successful SOE cases can also be found in South Korea. One of the most representative examples is the Pohang Iron Steel company (now privatized). This company was created in a time when South Korea only exported fish and various low value items. Against the recommendations of the World Bank (as in the most developmental steps of this country) South Korea invested strongly in heavy industry. While it is true that the resulting indebtedness[23] was assumed for its geopolitical partners (Japan and USA), this does not undermine the case that if correctly managed, SOEs can equal or even exceed the success of private firms.

Another good example is the Temasek Holdings investment company, which is owned by the by the government of Singapore. Temasek manages a portfolio of about $185 billion, or more than US$127 billion, focused primarily in Asia. It is an active shareholder and investor in such sectors as banking and financial services, real estate, transportation, infrastructure, telecommunications and media, bioscience and healthcare, education, engineering and technology, as well as energy and resources.

In addition, the Government of Singapore owns the Government Investment Corporation (GIC), which invests primarily the country's foreign reserves. In 2008, The Economist[24] reported that Morgan Stanley had estimated the fund's assets at US$330 billion, making it the world's third largest sovereign wealth fund.[25]

The case of France (as well as Italy, Austria and Norway) is also a representative one. Following World War II the French government managed several enterprises, in order to make them more efficient. Although many of these firms have since been (1996–2000) privatized, it was under state ownership that they flourished and contributed to their respective country's technological modernization. Firms such as Renault (automobile), Alcatel (telecommunication equipment), Thomson (electronics), Rhone-Poulecn (pharmaceutical), Thales (electronics), Usinor (steel, merged into Arcelor-Mittal, the biggest steelmaker in the world) and St Gobain (glass and building materials) are part of the extensive list of French SOEs. The state still remains the biggest stakeholder in Renault (Chang 2008).

In Latin America the Brazilian EMBRAER (short-range jet planes) became a world-class firm under government ownership. This firm is the world's biggest producer of regional jets and the third largest aircraft manufacturer after Airbus and Boeing. Although privatized in 1994, the state still holds the veto rights regarding technology transfer and military aircraft (Chang 2008).

Despite some privatization, public enterprises still provide a large proportion of the network services across the EU. Water, for example, remains a largely public function, despite all the pressures for privatization in recent years; a high proportion of energy services also remain in public hands. Partial state ownership is also practiced. For example 18.6 percent of German Volkswagen is owned by the state. This and many other examples illustrate that public ownership is not synonymous with inefficient local monopoly.

It is true that there have been many cases of SOE failures around the world. We can mention the case of the Indonesian aircraft industry, the success of Nissan without having been taken over by Honda (which was the initial objective of the Japanese government), the Korean aluminum-smelting industry, the French-English Concorde, etc. However, as Chang (2010b) argues, failure is the "very nature of risk-taking entrepreneurial decision in this uncertain world…" (p. 135). As a matter of fact, this kind of thing applies to both private and government enterprises, as well as for other types of properties.

The point to be made here is that to improve performance does not necessarily mean private property rights. In fact, as already suggested, even if it works, private property right can be really harmful for economic development. But even when a certain private business could be good for economic development, they can also fail (Chang 2008). Again, risk is the very nature of any business venture, private or not, and entrepreneurship is a collective rather than an individual activity. This is, private or not, neither firms nor individuals do innovate alone. But the point of this section is to point out that historic evidence shows that SOEs are not incompatible with innovation and economic development. In actual fact, SOEs are often more practical solutions for developing countries (as once today's developed countries were) that lack developed capital markets and tax and regulatory capabilities.

3.5 The usual neglect: Shaper but not selector

As already seen, historical evidence (if not absolutely conclusive) is at least reasonably persuasive about the crucial role of the government in the processes of innovation and economic growth. This role goes definitely far beyond the role of protector of property rights and provider of law. It also goes definitely beyond the *shaper* function attributed to it by most of contemporary economic and political commentators, including many heterodox economists. Given the fact that it is the neo-Austrian economists who have been the heterodox group most open to the complex system perspective, it is hardly surprising to find Hayekian notions across the whole complexity economics literature.

For example, let's consider Beinhocker (2006) and Colander and Kupers (2014) approaches represents, to the extent of our knowledge, some of the few deliberate attempts to cope frontally with the issue from a complexity economics view, proposing theoretical reflections that, as Witt (2003) recognized few years earlier, "[have] so far only rarely been addressed as an own object of in evolutionary economics." The notions proposed by Colander and Kuper were discussed above, therefore we focused in Beinhocker (2006), which was a book directed at broader audiences but which retains conceptual rigor and distinguished by its clarity. When arguing about the role of the state, Beinhocker (2006) points out that the complexity perspective distinguishes between two types of government action: (1) Policies that get the government involved in differentiating, *selecting* and *amplifying* Business Plans and (2) the government that *shapes the fitness environment*, while leaving Business Plan selection and amplification to market mechanisms.

The first group comprises experiences such as the Japanese industrial policy and the French interventionist state, i.e. the notion of developmental state as expressed by many development economists. The second group of policies is illustrated by Beinhocker (2006) with the example of hypothetic government actions to favor environmentally friendly Business Plans over environmentally unfriendly plans, without being selective or interventionist. Examples of such actions would include a carbon tax, emissions trading, or mandatory industry recycling requirements. In this second function the government would not actively select sectors or activities but it would be "rather shaping the fitness environment in which plans will succeed or fail" (pp. 426–7). In other words, it means making the conditions for the competition to occur without any interference.

Beinhocker (2006) argues that "as long as markets provide the mechanism for selecting and amplifying Business Plans, then the economic evolutionary process will innovate and adapt in response to those regulations." Therefore he sees the second (shaper) function as the legitimate economic function for a government to pursue under a complexity economics framework, mainly because "notions of efficiency in evolutionary systems are ephemeral" (p. 425). While the latter is right and there would be in principle nothing wrong with the government assuming this shaper function, one could ask the question about where should be placed the large historical evidence showing successful selective governments (in terms of Beinhocker).

As already mentioned (see above State enterprises), the state has not only helped to shape the environment for business to be able to flourish, but has also been selective and interventionist. Instruments such as, e.g., long term subsidies, tariff protections from imports, direct pressure to business (South Korea is an emblematic case), but also the deliberate action of government-based *non-firm organizations* (such as MITI in Japan, IRI in Italy and NIH in the US) and state-owned enterprises are among the most employed means.

While Beinhocker (2006) makes a very interesting, profound and truly evolutionary analysis of the economy as a complex adaptive system, he does not deliver, in our view, a convincing vision of the function of the government in a complex economy. In fact, by reviewing Beinhocker's (2006) position in regard of the state role in a complex economy, Gintis (2006) asserts that, of all the subjects treated in the book, Beinhocker's position in this regard "is probably closest to that of the neoclassical economics view" (p. 10).

Of course, this definition also displays some elements of other interpretations of the state's role and place in a complex economy. Even when this conception resembles more the Hayekian and neoclassical notions, that is, the market should be left alone to select the fittest projects within the economy (spontaneous order), it is possible to see neo-Schumpeterian traces in this analysis (see Chapter 4 for a detailed examination of neo-Schumpeterian theories). Indeed, the distinction is not trivial, because it is not the same the neoclassical interpretation as the Austrian or the neo-Schumpeterian ones. However the point is that this notion still relies on the (more or less) traditional dichotomy of the market and state which, deliberately or not, excludes an overwhelming body of evidence that is at odds with the phenomena it is supposed to capture. In Section 3.7 an alternative conceptualization will be proposed.

3.6 Market/government dichotomy

As already mentioned, the neo-Austrian school is one of the groups which have embraced the complexity perspective most seriously. This includes their perception of the market as the opposite of the government. As Foster (2005) argues

Modern neo-Austrians see the economy as a complex system of individuals who, because of this complexity, face uncertainty, which is to be reduced by adhering to behavioural rules that result in mutual benefits. These rules are an outcome of a process of "spontaneous order," whereby the best rules are selected and, ultimately, gain legitimacy in laws and constitutions.

(p. 880)

The notion of spontaneous order leads us to the dichotomy market and state. Foster (2005) continue by stating that for neo-Austrians "Knowledge and action are not optimized givens but emergent phenomena; it is argued that they must not be interfered with by entities such as governments, that are regarded as political entities 'outside' the economic system" (p. 880).

Precisely the irreconcilable notions about the role of "constrained optimization in making any convincing connection with history was one of the main reasons for the ontological split between neoclassical and neo-Austrian economists that emerged in the twentieth century" (ibid.). This clash of ideals happened despite mutual consensus on the point that "the individual is the appropriate level inquiry in economic analysis and that markets offer the best institutional rules for the promotion of economic activity"[26] (ibid.). Nevertheless, it is no exaggeration to say; that the dichotomy market and state championed by the neo-Austrian school is one of the major conceptual obstacles for advancing notions of self-organization that include a better understanding of the economic function of the state from a complexity perspective.

Even if agreeing with the proposition of letting the market select the fittest, it should not be ignored that, in practice, it is hard (if not impossible) to define what a free market economy should look like. This reflects the fact that governments have traditionally defined the rights and obligations involved in the functioning of markets (Chang 2002). The legitimacy and contestability of market structures will therefore be politically determined. At the same time, they will shape and constrain the behavior of economic agents toward customers, government officials, competitors, suppliers, employees and so on. Consequently, markets, as a political construct, are compatible with a great variety of societal ends, means and rationalities (ibid.).

If markets had evolved in natural ways, then many ex-communist countries would not have experienced the traumatic consequences following the decision to open their markets to foreign investment and to privatize the majority of their productive assets. Moreover the developmental crisis experienced by most developing countries in the last 30 years clearly demonstrates how naïve it is to believe that markets emerge naturally and grow conveniently beyond any government interference. Market rationality can only be insightful when related to an institutional structure.

Earlier we mentioned in more detail how the US and UK intervention stories are defining the market. These two countries precisely represent the model of non-interventionist economies according to mainstream scholars. However, we have seen that successive US administrations historically provided support through physical infrastructure, funding agricultural research and high import tariffs intended to protect emerging industries. In the 1949 classic *The Economic Mind in American Civilization,* Joseph Dorfman observes how as the "new economic problems grew to threatening proportions, the practice of going to the government for help intensified" (p. X, prologue). He continues by asserting that "small business wished the government to curb large business, and many interests clamored for high tariffs" (ibid.).

We have also already referred to the roles played by King Henry VII in the sixteenth century and Robert Walpole in the eighteenth century in England's industrial strategy. Polanyi (1944) explains in *The Great Transformation* how the government was critical in the decommonalization of the land and for the success of the wool manufacturing industry in England.

To say that the state defines the system of rights and obligations required for the market to exist is equivalent to saying that the market is a political construct (Chang 2002, 2011). The institutional arrangements that many economists take for granted have actually been the result of strong political debates. Right to self-ownership, right to vote, right to education and medical assistance, right to organize and an eight-hour working day are vivid paradigms. This is even more evident if we consider the recent legislations referring to gender, race or environmental issues. For instance, a few decades ago it would have been unthinkable in many places to talk about corporate environmental responsibility.

In general, discussions on economic policy within an evolutionary framework (from sometimes different perspectives) tend to elude this evidence (Witt 2003; Pelikan and Wegner 2003; Dopfer 2005; Dopfer and Potts 2008; Beinhocker 2006). Within this literature, much more emphasis has been made in elements such as self-organization and emergence; with no critical and historically sound reflections on the role of an interventionist state within these phenomena. However, as Witt (2003) acknowledges; "policy interventions are so pervasive in all modern economies that they cannot be ignored" (p. 78).

In actual fact, as discussed above, the state has always been a relevant agent in the economy. How can the complexity perspective come to terms with this overwhelming historic and contemporary evidence provided by the literatures on innovation and economic development? All this is telling us that instead of sustaining the ill-warranted dichotomy market and government (or private and public), it could be more useful to acknowledge the complex nature of production and exchange in the economy. A more realistic analysis of the role of markets in the innovation process should start by accepting its political nature.

3.7 The state as crucial hub within the complex economic network

There seems to be a consensus within all the above mentioned literature about the fact that innovation and development processes are the result of a collective learning-oriented and open-ended process. Therefore it requires coordination, interaction and risk-taking. For instance, Dopfer and Potts (2008) recognize that support for innovation, when it is done best, will necessarily be wasteful and is improperly measured if it seeks to eliminate all such waste. From the neo-Schumpeterian side, Lazonick (2006) argues that

> anyone who contends that, when committing resources to an innovative investment strategy, one can foresee the stream of future earnings that are required for the calculation of net present value knows nothing about the innovation process, maximisers can not actually be innovators because of the uncertainty involving the process.
>
> (p. 10)

The question is who assume those risks. As already mentioned there is nothing wrong with the role of the state as shaper of the conditions for firms to compete but it is quite unrealistic to assume that the private sector entrepreneurship be relied on as a source of major new general purpose technologies (Ruttan, 2006). Even catch-up efforts carried out by developing countries represent real entrepreneurial undertakings (Cimoli et al. 2009; Chang 2009). In any case, fact is that when new technologies or organizational practices are radically different from actual ones and the gains are so diffuse that they are difficult to capture by the firms, "private firms have only weak incentives to invest in scientific research or technology development" (Ruttan 2006, p. 22).

This kind of uncertainty has been also reflected in the literature of strategic management. As Lazonick and O'Sullivan (2000) argue,

> in general, the incumbent firms have been seen as unable to invest in new technology because the organisational capabilities they had developed to establish a dominant technological and market position may be unsuited to organising the transformations in technologies and markets that the new competition requires.
>
> (p. 99)

Christensen (1997) argues that established firms are successful by developing products for a known customer base (incremental change), but they fail to innovate for unknown customer-bases. This is explained by the fact that developing new technologies or opening new markets is an unpredictable endeavor, to which no incumbent is able to be exposed.

"Discovering markets for emerging technologies inherently involves failure, and most individual decision makers find it very difficult to risk backing a project that might fail because the market is not there" (ibid., 160). Instead, most established businesses play the card of optimization, which is not bad itself, but could end up by preventing the company from remaining competitive in the future. This represents a major dilemma for innovators.

Faced with this dilemma, Lazonick and O'Sullivan (2000) pose the question of who should decide about the allocation of corporate resources within an enterprise. They conclude that this decision is not the result of top manager deliberation alone, but actually the outcome of the integration of all the elements of the firm. Through this process, by definition, cumulative and collective, new productive resources are created. From this perspective, "the process of strategic decision making needs to be embedded within the organization, where participants in the process can understand how the existing capabilities of the enterprise can be developed and utilized to generate innovation" (ibid., p. 11). The process demands openness and autonomy for business units to explore and experiment their own portfolios; and to exchange experiences with other units. As a result, and expressed in dynamic systems terminology, these arrangements reduce entropy in that they allow the system to dissipates energy and make room for easier adaptability and integration.

However, even assuming that a firm decided to invest in developing new resources and exploring new markets, the historical evidence continues telling us that, seldom, a company (even the bigger ones) does it alone. What other actors are there, sharing the Knightian uncertainty during the process of new resources development?

As Lazonick and O'Sullivan (2000) acknowledge, to understand this process "a theory of innovative enterprise [...] must be imbedded in a theory of an innovative economy" (p. 121). This would require economists to free themselves from the myth of the market economy and accepting innovation as an organizational phenomenon; and

> business academics to see business organizations in the light of the economies and societies to which they are central – so that they can consider how organizational learning and strategic management might be the effects and causes of processes that can generate innovation.
>
> (ibid.)

In Chapter 4 we will go into more detail on the theory of innovative enterprise.

If we accept contemplating firms in terms of the economies and societies that contain them, and as effects and causes of the innovation process, then it would not be a problem to theoretically integrate the *government agency*, along with other firms and institutions, as a central piece into the process of *organizational integration* required by firms to accomplish organizational learning (more on this in Chapter 4). In fact, the history of economic development is the history of cooperation between firms (private or public) and government, the latter being the one who takes great part of the risks in radical innovation, makes connections between unrelated, but complementary groups; and develops platform standards for firms to be able to communicate. As Jessop (2003a) argues "the state operates as a power connector, i.e., as a nodal or network state within a broader system as well as a power container."

Therefore, it is not surprising that Block (2008) refers to *Developmental Network State* (DNS) to characterize the role of the state in Western Europe and the United States.[27] This entity "help firms develop product and process innovations that do not yet exist, such as new software applications, new biotech medications, or new medical instruments" (p. 4).The roles attributed by him go far beyond the *shaper function* since DNS (1) targets important technological challenges, whose solution would open up important economic possibilities, (2) puts together already existing technologies in new ways (technology brokering); and helps a group of technologists who are trying to commercialize a new product to make the business connections that they need to create an effective organization, to acquire the required funding, and to find potential customers for the product (business brokering) and (3) creates standards.All the functions include, of course, the long-term necessary financing of the innovative activity.

3.7.1 The risk taking function: Standards formally set vs. informally emerged

In our view, the design of standards is crucial for the rest of the activities mentioned by Block (2008) because they create the language for innovation to take place. Innovation and economic development do not only need new knowledge to be generated, but also require that knowledge to be diffused across the system, as fast and efficiently as possible for synergies to be able to take place.

It is also the better way to deal with uncertainty since the innovation costs are shared. Indeed, standardization helps by "breaking up a complex system into discrete pieces which can then communicate with one another only through standardised interfaces within a standardised architecture" (Langlois 2002, p. 19). In other words, standardization helps to both better and bigger work division and to specialization.This has not only technological, but also organizational implications when we consider the increased complexity of modern technology.

The aforementioned is particularly true in complex industries since they are made of a huge diversity of (often inevitably unrelated but at the same time) complementary pieces of knowledge. The trend of specialization has become obvious in the experiences of the IT and semiconductor industries, but also in the computer and software; as well as in the biopharmaceutical industries.The markets of these industries show the high levels of input and demand heterogeneity, which makes them the perfect candidates for modular organization. Heterogeneity in these industry inputs will increase the value to be obtained through modular product configurations.

According to Schilling (2000) the function of a *standard interfaces* is to make assets *non-specific* possible, thereby facilitating the adoption of modular structures. Modularity enables compatibility between disparate technologies, lowering the risk to the firm of gambling on a particular technology. Multiple technologies can coexist more peacefully (politically speaking) and the prospects for innovation improve hugely.

But in order to use these advantages under such an inevitably uncertain context as the innovation context, there must be someone that creates the standards.

Increasingly modularity, particularly in complex industries, demands the exist-ence of certain agents with the technological and organizational capabilities required to integrate the rest of network's agents into an innovative activity. This, in turn, requires these integrating organizations to increase (rather than to decrease) their knowledge base, in order to be able to coordinate diverse learning trajectories embodied in independent but complementary agents (Dosi et al. 2003).

AT&T's emergence as a national monopoly is a classical case of this kind of agent. The history of American telecommunications during a significant part of the twentieth century is indistinguishable from the history of the Bell System. Bell engineers established and maintained the efficiency and quality of their entire system by deploying standardized equipment throughout it (Russell 2005). However we should not forget the role played by the government's deci-sion to agree with the Kingsbury Commitment.[28] At the same time, as demand heterogeneity and value-chains fragmentation became apparent, and AT&T began to employ its monopoly power to slow (instead to boost) innovation, the government intervened by breaking-up the monopoly in 1982.[29]

Increased fragmentation in the value-chains and organizational flexibility is condemned to fail when no organization is able or willing to deal with the demands of organizational (or technological) integration (for example exces-sive emphasis in certain kind of intellectual property rights, lack of cooperation with government institutions, short term financial incentives etc.).[30] On the other hand, evolutionary literature on system integration (e.g. Prencipe et al. 2005) contains empirical evidence that provide a rationale for the critical role of vertical integrated firms in the design of certain partial standards within their industries (more on this in the next chapter). Therefore, the problem is not integration itself, but to change the rules of integration (when required) by the creation of standards.

The IEEE defines standardization as "the process that encompasses the ini-tiation, development and application of standards documents. It's the process of merging scientific research with application experience to determine the pre-cise, optimum technical requirements for an aspect of technology. The output of this merger is an authoritative document called a 'standard'"[31] (for compre-hensive and critical discussions see Libicki 1994; Cargill 2002; Russell 2005). To be sure, standards do not only embody technological capabilities, but also social capabilities in the sense described by Abramovitz (1986).

Reinert (2007) argues that technological change needs increasing returns created by standardization, from the weights and measures of the medieval city to the technical standards for mobile telephones and ISO standards. Economies of scope and scale, as well as network effects all depend on synergies created in networked systems (pp. 103–4). While some types of standards may be sector specific, others may be generic, and may vary in different geographical and insti-tutional contexts. The latter may reflect the influence of the national dimension in the governance structures of an industry or sector.

From an institutional perspective, standards are institutions that contain a considerable (but not the whole) amount of technological knowledge in codified form. Institutions co-evolve through processes of complex informal but also formal coordination that create common cultures, reputation mechanisms and mutually adapting expectations. In other words, they "may take different, stronger or weaker forms, e.g. enforceable rules or less binding codes of conduct" (Coe et al. 2008, p. 281). That is, standards may be both the result of consensus and evolution and may also be created. In Chapter 2 we discussed how the repetition of certain shared habits can led to the emergence of rule-following behaviors. This process of habituation makes it possible the institution to emerge. But it does not follow that habituation cannot result from top-down regulation.

Of course, standards do not need to be a government matter. Patents, for instance, can be seen as an institutional instrument used by the government in order to standardize the distribution of an invention's property rights. However, although useful under certain circumstances, this kind of standard has not always been of benefit for innovation, often being even detrimental, and sometimes inexistent (Moser 2013; Caplan 2003; Schiff 1971). On the other hand, sectoral or other sort of bottom-up standards have proven to be in many occasions a better device for new knowledge to be created. Allen (1983) and many since then have made a good case of innovation as a result of the diffusion of technical standards through non-government organizations (see, for instance, Bessen and Nuvolari 2016). Allen (1983) coins the term "collective invention" and points out that a close reading of the engineering literature of the nineteenth century indicates that most of the important innovations in the iron industry, particularly England's Cleveland districts, were the result of the free availability of technical information. New "technical knowledge was a by-product of normal business operation- and the technical information produced was exploited by agents other than the firms that discovered it" (p. 2).

Likewise Merges and Sonsini (2004) refer to the important role played, since medieval times, by non-government standard-setting institutions in the process of generating and diffusing new techniques and information. The fact of a group of experts coming together to define protocols and other common technical features to be shared by industry members is consistent with Moser (2013), which analyzed the rich archival technological information provided by historical events such as the nineteenth-century world fairs (since 1851) to conclude that most of the innovations of the period were made outside the patent system, which brings attention to other forms of collaborative innovation.

However, there exists evidence about the extent to which those free producers associations lobbied the government to achieve their goals, and the extent to which certain governmental regulations and bodies might have enabled their endeavors. For example, industrial and commercial fairs were spaces developed by governments with the explicit intention of diffusing new techniques and inventions in order to stimulate emulation, industrial prowess and economic development. France was a pioneer in this sort of events and they proved to be influential in the long term. The first national industry exhibition in France was launched by the Directory in 1798, at initiative of the statesman François de Neufchâteau, and the example was followed by the brilliant Jean-Antonie Chaptal during the Napoleonic and Bourbon era; the explicit goal being that of encouraging the French industrial landscape.

Chaptal believed in the government's role in the advancement of industry, in the introduction of new technologies and in the provision of public prizes for innovators and business leaders (Chaptal 1893). Following the British model set by the Society for the Encouragement of Arts, Manufactures and Commerce he created in 1801 the *Société d'encouragement pour l'industrie nationale* (Society for Encouraging National Industry), which went much further than the former. Chaptal's society, the epitome of the strong French tradition of industrial policy in the country (with the exception of the Cobden-Chevalier period of 1860– 92), was formed by a conglomerate of scientists, industrialists, bankers etc., who agreed in the goal of modernizing the French industry.

The Society was open by subscriptions but Chaptal's ministry (he was one of the best Napoleon's ministers) gave substantial subsidies. This organization offered prizes for many branches of industry, published a bulletin to encourage discoveries useful to industry and new products. In addition, the society sponsored transfer of technology from foreign industrial companies and improvements to business processes made by French innovators. Many inventors, researchers and companies received support. Prominent examples are L. J. M. Daguerre (1786–1851) for his work on the daguerreotype technique and Joseph Jacquard for his Jacquard's loom, which automated part of the process of running the loom by using punched cards.[32]

Last but not least, this non-firm government organization promoted the foundation of specialized schools and the exhibitions and industrial fairs carried out by successive French governments since 1801, even after Chaptal's death in 1831.[33] During the third industrial fair, Chaptal invited, for first time, foreign visitors, including Charles Fox, one of the most powerful statesmen of the day, who was sent by the British government to Paris in order to inspect the goods on display at the exposition. By the 11th exhibition in 1849, there were a number of national fairs taking place across Europe. This was the antecedent of what it is known as the first universal fair, held in the Crystal Palace in Hyde Park, London, in 1851, and followed, although with different character, until the present time.

Apart from the industrial exhibitions, there are also examples of other forms of interactions that led to the diffusion and standardization of technical knowledge. For example between 1688 and 1718 important innovations were taking place in London's clock and instrument-making industry. But, during the same period, the London Clockmakers Company lobbied intensively in order to abolish a number of specific patents related to their trades (Bessen and Nuvolari 2016). Merges and Sonsini (2004) mention, on the one hand, the marvelous innovativeness that resulted from bottom-up (non-state imposed) norms of knowledge sharing in the guild system-based Venice Glassmaking industry during the fifteenth century. But on the other side the authors also make it clear how the effective enforcement of these norms strongly relied on the government of Venice, which through a body called Council of Ten was involved at the highest level in maintaining the Venetian monopoly over high-value and prestige of glass production.

The removal of the patent system or its targeted introduction may be considered an important government action in order to support the domestic industry. In any case, it is useful to remember that, even when the state was not as interventionist as it became later after World War II, it still relied on different methods to protect its industries (see Chang 2003a).

In addition, historical evidence shows that when it comes to radical innovation, firms (even big integrated ones) tend to play safe (Christensen 1997; Ruttan 2006; Block 2008; Mazzucato 2011; Lee et al. 2012). Many established firms, which at some point in their growth history confronted and overcame this uncertainty; often continue to grow by following the less risky path of upgrading their product offerings for their current customer bases, but in the process fail to pursue strategies to innovate for customer bases that are emerging for which high levels of uncertainty exist.

When uncertainty is that big, the state has very often stepped in and stayed at least until the new innovative projects showed some commercial prospects. That is what the history of most of the big technological breakthroughs tells us. In such a case, we cannot say that the standard has emerged, but actually is being created to disrupt a given path and establish a new one. This is a very risky process, but if successful, might pave the way for the emergence (not the deliberate creation) of further (formal and informal) industry standards.

Of course, these disruptive ideas and the demand for new standards never come exclusively from the state, but are always the result of the complex and interdependent nature of the innovation process. In fact, there are always a lot of disruptive agents with good disruptive ideas outside the government, and within and outside of the corporate world. But it is not obvious that they are always able to successfully reach the movers and shakers. If they do, then disruptive new standards may be said to have emerged from the interaction between government and (still a minority of) disruptive agents. However, from the perspective of established (and most of the) agents, these new rules are still going to look disruptive, in the bad sense, and even coercive. At the same time, the more open and relatively decentralized (i.e. the less assortative[34]) government agencies are, the higher the probability that the integration of new ideas become part of the next innovation path. This does not mean that to dismantle hierarchy is the solution, but rather, as we shall see below, means that there is a complex trade-off between hierarchy and interdependency.

There has always been a tension between *de jure* and *de facto standards*. The core of the conflicts is whether industry standards[35] should be promulgated from a government body or, instead to emerge from a voluntary consensus process (Russell 2005). However, if we accept the phenomenon of the constitutive role of institutions, then we could interpret this contradiction as the two sides of the same coin. As above-mentioned, institutions can develop as the result of a semiconscious process of interaction and adaptation. Thereafter this process will be institutionalized through rules and sanctions for defection.

But, again, if this were the whole story, then we would have to accept that lock-ins can be "locked out" through the same process, which, as history shows, is not always the case. This offers a good rationale for *de facto* standards, as some agent needs to introduce a rupture in the system. After that, institutions may be internalized (or not) by the agents and serve as a point of departure for new consensual standards. Socioeconomic networks possess the property of social and individual agency, which means the ability of nodes to build and maintain ties for overlapping explorative and exploitative ties.

For example Abate (1999) and Ruttan (2006) show how non-proprietary Internet standards emerged and were developed by government-based, non-firm organization (a mix of academic and defense research). The Advanced Research Projects Agency (ARPA) of the US Department of Defense had begun to work together with scientists of the Stanford University on ARPANET during the1960s.[36] As early as 1972, following the demonstration of the technical feasibility of an ARPANET, the ARPA began exploring the possibility of transferring ARPANET management to a commercial carrier or another government agency.[37]

In 1982 the ARPANET TCP/IP protocols were adopted as the common language for the new Defense Data Network. At the same time, with the aim of supporting the commercialization of internet technology, the Defense Communication Agency (DCA) established a $20 million fund to subsidize the installation by computer manufacturers of TCP/IP on their machines. All the major computer manufacturers took advantage of the opportunity and by 1990 TCP/IP was available for virtually every computer in the American market.[38]

How could we conciliate the traditional notion of self-organization as the foundation of innovation with the available historical evidence? We simply can't. True, complex economic systems are autonomous in the sense that they define and defend their own boundaries and follow their own logic. But the state as institution must be part of this, instead of being seen as an external entity. Generally, orthodox (and sometimes unorthodox) economics tend to exclude the very properties that make the economy a dynamic system. Things such as technological change, political changes, etc., are considered exogenous or highly rationalized into dubious stylized facts, like the one denying significant role of the state in the economy.

However, instead of denying so blatantly the historical evidence available, it would be more interesting to analyze how such dynamic behavior might be endogenously generated, as a result of the structure of the economy itself. Indeed, history shows that the state decisively participates in the development and evolution of the distinctive operational codes that allow the system to "self-organize" itself. This more sophisticated notion of self-organization (note we are explicitly avoiding to use the term here in that sophisticated sense, see

Chapter 2) takes into consideration the fact that state agencies are expected to carry out a set of specific activities, which other agents, because of their functions and their position in the economic network, are unlikely to carry out.

We already saw that SOEs and private business enterprises may engage successfully in the same type of commercial activities. But government NFOs and business enterprises (private or not) do not necessarily engage in the same kind of investment activities. It is not only a matter of the presence of the profit motivation in the latter and its absence in the former, but actually a matter of the extent of the risk both entities are willing to run. It is wrong to assume that the business enterprises have the willingness to invest from the first stages of the development of an industry, "and all government had to do was to create the right 'framework condition'" (Lazonick and Mazzucato 2012, p. 7). If the latter was the case, then it would make sense to see standards solely as emerging institutions developed within the industry, the state being an external agent only responsible to codify them in order to ensure that the business world continue with business as usual.

However, the example mentioned above (and many others) actually tell us that the state "put its capital at risk at a time when the business sector was not willing to engage" (ibid.). Therefore, the state does not only fix markets but also makes them. While Keynes saw the state as an important demand enhancer in the downside of the business cycle, the reality is that the state is needed even in periods of growth, in order for the next (and still unknown) innovation story to be able to happen.

From a standards perspective, the *risk taking* function of the state has to do with both the ability and the willingness to invest in the creation of a set of technological and organizational standards for technologies and industries which have not been developed within the national economy, or have not been developed at all. These kinds of standards cannot be said to simply have emerged or developed along time and they usually tend to be received with reluctance by a good part of the business community. Block (2008) calls it a *facilitator* role of the state. In his words, "standards are often an issue, since purchasers need to know that a new product actually does what is promised and will work effectively in combination with existing infrastructure" (p. 5).

> Some technologies also require creating new regulatory frameworks that make it safe for firms to invest and overcome consumer concerns. Sometimes considerable coordination is required because a new technology depends on multiple firms making investments in the same time frame.
>
> (ibid.)

The case of the biopharmaceutical industry is an example of this, given the high level of diversity and uncertainty that is involved in the process of the development of biopharmaceutical products. This is the reason why the quality of regulation institutions determines so much in this industry (our case study confirms this, see Chapter 7).

The state as designer of standards interfaces contains not only the shaper role of the state described above, which most of the complexity literature refers to, but also includes, the *selector role* attributed to the interventionist state. When creating standards, this risk-taking function is compatible with the "pivotal role" given to *hubs* in complex non-random networks (see Chapter 2). The more a hub organization contributes to the creation of communication standards (in terms of degree, betweenness or closeness), other things being equal, the greater its contribution to the process of organizational integration. They are precisely hubs because most connections are routed through; and generate massive economic returns not because of internal capabilities alone, but generally because of their position within the network (Foster 2005, p. 888).

As already seen, many complex networks in the real world (including socio-economic networks) do not follow a random formation, which means that the nodes that compose them tend to link with nodes that already have a large number of connections (Barabási and Albert. 1999; Foster 2005). Foster (2005) argues that there are clear parallels between the "neo-Schumpeterian process and the evolution of hub-dominated networks" or national system of innovations. Recall that in Chapter 2 we mentioned that the economic system can be conceptualized as a hub dominated network, where mostly decentralized *government-based non-firm organizations* play an essential *networking* and *standardizing* role.

A somewhat singular example of standard setting comes from the non-compete agreements in the US state of California. Firms use non-competes to protect their interests: to prevent the disclosure of trade secrets, to respect customer confidentiality, and to prevent competitors from appropriating the specialized skills of its employees. Preventing an ex-employee from joining a competitor via a non-compete decreases the likelihood that an employee will violate the corresponding non-disclosure agreement at a new job. These clauses represent a legitimate right of firms to protect their proprietary information.

However, although the law of trade secrets is fairly similar across US states, the enforcement of non-competes varies significantly from state to state. California has chosen not to enforce them since 1865 (Marx et al. 2007). Stuart and Sorenson (2003) found out that proportionally more biotech firms were founded in states that proscribe enforcement of non-competes. Another American state with a flourishing biotech industry is Boston, which happens to be another state with unclear trade secret laws.[39] Moreover, according to Lazonick et al. (2007), the Boston area is the leading recipient of federal funding (NIH) that supports the biotech industry considering the years 1996, 1999, 2002 and 2005. At the same time, Lazonick et al. (2007) show that California ranks first among the states when it comes to the top 50 organizations that received funding from the NIH during the same years. At the same time Fallick et al. (2006) found an industry-specific increase in intraregional employee mobility for the California computer industry vs. other states.[40]

Summarizing, standards introduced by non-firm organizations can create intra-firm and inter-firm efficiencies: they facilitate economies of scale in manufacturing and promote interoperability between complementary products. This standardizing function includes the brokering role of the state, i.e. the role of creating knowledge (through national labs and universities), creating the institutional and organizational capabilities for new technologies and information to be acquired and diffused across sectors and the economy (Cimoli et al. 2009; Freeman 2008; Dosi et al. 1994). Foundation of economic development is the acquisition of more productive knowledge and that happens to be intrinsically related to the country's ability to build socially accepted institutions which help to absorb, use and develop technological and organizational knowledge (ibid.). If we take this seriously, then it would be plausible to assume *the government is the most important hub (or systems of hubs) within the economy.*

3.7.2 Hub diversity and hierarchy

Of course, as just mentioned, to argue that government plays a pivotal role in the economy is not to say that the government is the only *hub* that exists in an economy or the only agent deciding for everybody. The failure of the European Communism experience is very symptomatic in this regard. Actually, a large number of private and public multinationals and decentralized governmental as well as non-governmental organizations show simultaneously high degrees of centrality within the economic system.

As Dopfer and Potts (2008) argue,

> the quality of an innovation system is the ability of it to maintain the complexity of the system and an innovation system fails when it results in a reduction of diversity (i.e. degrees of freedom or the space of opportunity).

Socioeconomic systems need diversity. That is, diversity offers more chances to combine technologies and to foster synergies and complementarities between sectors and activities (Arthur 2009; Reinert 2007). This is because, as Simon, Hayek and others have suggested, economy is a non-linear and dynamic system, where all information cannot be collected or administered by just one centralized entity. This applies to all complex systems.

However, as we saw in Chapter 2, Russell Ackoff argued that social systems also are purposeful systems, whose parts are also purposeful systems that behave at "sub-purposeful level," i.e. following a common purpose in larger systems (Ackoff and Emery 1972, p. 220). The same idea can be found in Herbert Simon's hierarchy notion (see below in this section). Against this background, this study argues that serious innovative and developmental efforts involve levels of uncertainty, which prevents most non-government agents (mainly private firms) from deliberately assuming them in the long term, at least in their early, most risky, and thus genuine entrepreneurial phases. The fact that nodes (organizations and individuals) with high betweenness centrality (see Annexes) are quintessentially entrepreneurs because they have the ability to bridge non-redundant sources of information (Burt 2005). It is not a coincidence that authors such as Mazzucato (2011) use the term of *entrepreneurial state* to refer to the role of the state in the process of innovation. As already mentioned, innovation arises precisely from the combination of previously unrelated elements.

Innovation also requires the ability to deal with the technological and market uncertainties arising from the process. To deal with these uncertainties means to have the ability, in the long term, to organizationally integrate all the participants engaged in the hierarchical and functional division of labor within the innovation system. This allows the process of organizational learning within firms and industries to take place. As Lazonick and O'Sullivan (2000) put it, "[…] organizational learning is thus a problem of creating structures that encourage collective learning" (p. 73). These structures have been, for example in the case of United States, a wide group of decentralized government agencies taking funding decisions, linking technologies and people and creating standards (Block 2008).

From a network perspective, Burt (2005) defines the existing bridging possibilities within a network as *structural holes*, which create a competitive and informational advantage for the node that bridges the hole. Structural holes are an opportunity to broker the flow of information between people or organizations, and control the projects that bring together organizations from opposite sides of the hole. As Block (2008) acknowledges when referring to the structures of the developmental network state, "[e]ffective technology brokering that links scientists and engineers to others who have the ideas and techniques that they need to solve their problems is probably the most central developmental task […]" (p. 24).

He also recommends that "it is desirable to have some redundancy built into this structure" for "brokerage to be most effective." He argues that "with multiple windows and multiple potential brokers, an idea might be able to survive and ultimately flourish despite initial negative responses" (p. 8). This could be interpreted as a source of diversity in the system. That is, even when it is argued that the *government agency* disposes of top decisional powers within the hierarchy of sub-networks of an innovation system, it should not be thought of as a rigid centralized structure. The state role as hub can be disaggregated into several non-firm organizations (themselves separately to be understood as hubs in their own right) with similar and sometimes overlapping decisional powers.

The fact that redundant information has some logic from the perspective of a complex economic system (but might also end up in unwarranted waste of resources) has been stressed by several authors. For instance, Burt (2005) argues that even when network closure (high density of connection) exists, it allows everybody to be connected with everybody and reduces the risks involved in cooperation. But, at the same time, he also sees the existence of structural holes as the real opportunity for brokers and other nodes.

Foster (2005) argues that completely interconnected systems lack a sufficient degree of openness, in the sense of potential connectivity. This poses a major dilemma because "[e]volution can only occur when systems can change structurally, both in their internal order and in their relations with the external environment" (ibid., p. 876). In the same line of analysis, Beinhocker (2006) points out that this kind of situation leads to less adaptability since too many "interdependencies create conflicting constraints, and conflicting constraints create slow decision making […]" (p. 152). For this same reason he argues that *hierarchies* within the network are unavoidable. Scholarly work in the field of preferential attachment in complex networks has arrived to the same conclusions (Hébert-Dufresne 2015; Valverde and Solé 2006; Ravasz and Barabasí 2003)

The interplay between hierarchy and diversity does not go unnoticed by Block (2008), who recognizes, based on the experience of the US, that some centralization is critical for the DNS to be able to coordinate effectively. He acknowledges that some duplication of efforts is only desirable if different groups are able to learn from each other's successes and failures. State agencies that can be seen as hubs by virtue of their caliber as a non-firm organization should still interact with each other, precisely because of the possibility of duplication, to prevent the possibility of ineffective brokering. But too much interaction may lead us to the absence of structural holes, and to the conflicting constraints mentioned above. That's the reason why, in order not to incur some kind of vicious circle, Beinhocker (2006), relying on the insights of Stuart Kaufmann,[41] argues that "organizing the network into hierarchies is critical in enabling networks to reach larger sizes and to be organisationally more effective." This is especially useful for environments with unpredictable outcomes, such as innovative endeavors.

The idea is that a hierarchical organization of the network would improve, rather than reduce, adaptability in an unpredictable complex environment. In actual fact, "hierarchy can serve to increase adaptability by reducing interdependencies and enabling [the network] to reach a larger size[…]" (ibid., p. 154). The idea may look counterintuitive at first sight. The conventional wisdom is that hierarchy is a feature of bureaucracy that reduces adaptability but actually when a system is too sensible to change, a small change would affect the whole system. If the change were negative, then there would not be time to adapt to the new situation. By making the system less sensible, there would be at least a chance to save something, because the transmission would not be immediate. This improves the decision-making process because it reduces the scope of problems to deal with during the process, which allow us to be able to make a decision at all. By deliberately restricting our span of choices (even some good ones), we allow us to deal better with complexity. This is one of the reasons why some regulations are innovation enhancing.

For example, some government regulations can help business to become sustainable in the long term by restricting their interests in the short term (compulsory training requirements, restriction to import of obsolete technologies etc.), or to contribute to the creation and preservation of common pools of resources that all firms share etc. (Chang 2010b). That is, regulation as form of hierarchy need not necessarily conduce more bureaucracy, inefficiency or poor innovation; actually performance depends on some kind of regulation. As Beinhocker (2006) argues, this is a cautionary tale of the dangers of interpreting complexity theory at a purely symbolic level. In actual fact, there is a clear trade-off between the benefits of scale and the coordination costs and constraints created by complexity. This tension between interdependencies and adaptability is a deep property of complex networks and profoundly affects many types of systems.

This insight is rooted, among others, in the pioneering ideas of Herbert Simon on complex systems (more scholarly references in Langlois 2002). He argued that "[h]ierarchy[...], is one of the central structural schemes that the architect of complexity uses" (Simon 1962, p. 468). In fact, this study is assuming the Simon's definition of hierarchy as embedded in complexity. He defines hierarchic system, or hierarchy, as "a system that is composed of interrelated subsystems, each of the latter being, in turn, hierarchic in structure until we reach some lowest level of elementary subsystem" (ibid.). By defining hierarchy he acknowledges that, etymologically, the term has been used to refer to strictly subordinated subsystems.

He accepts that notion, but also proposes to expand it by considering "systems in which the relations among subsystems are more complex than in the formal organizational hierarchy" (ibid.). In fact, he argues that "even in human organizations, the formal hierarchy exists only on paper; the real flesh-and-blood organization has many inter-part relations other than the lines of formal authority" (ibid.). He establishes a distinction between this expanded notion of "hierarchy" and the traditional narrower definition, which he coins as "formal hierarchy." We employ the former because, in our view, it represents a more sophisticated and truly complex definition of hierarchy. In this kind of hierarchy the interdependency is so complex and sophisticated that subsystems cannot be completely discomposed.

When assuming hierarchy in Simon's fashion, it is easier to accept the proposition of *government non-firm organizations at the top of the socioeconomic network hierarchy*. This position would not indicate necessarily a strict relation of subordination among subsystems, but only a functional necessity, as other scholars have already suggested. For instance, even when Jessop (2003a, 2003b) avoids referring to the state as an entity with hierarchical control in complex systems, his sophisticated insights seem to tacitly recognize the critical; and singular role of the state in these systems. He recognizes this paradoxical position of the *government agency* when he argues that the state is an institutional subsystem which is simultaneously merely part of a wider, more complex society (and thus unable to control the latter from above) and also a part normatively charged with securing the institutional integration and social cohesion of that society.

The above-mentioned becomes apparent when one, for instance, considers the evolution of IT technologies in the American industry. Even while the US government-based Advanced Research Projects Agency (ARPA)[42] played a major hub role in the technology policy of the United States after World War

II, and in fact literally conceived many of the today's high technologies, many other big integrated private firms, supposedly hierarchically subordinated, also represented important hubs in the system. For instance, reduced-instruction-set computing (RISC) processors, widely used today in mobile phones and other applications (e.g. Apple iPhone and iPad, Nintendo, Playstation etc.[43]), were originally developed by IBM in early 1970s as part of its 801 computer, but they do not commercialized the technology because they were too uncertain about the results.

It was DARPA which funded additional research at the University of California, Berkeley, and at Stanford University as part of its Very Large Scale Integrated Circuit (VLSI) program in the late 1970s and early 1980s. The newly formed Sun Microsystems, Inc. licensed the RISC II architecture from the University of California and developed a RISC-based design that it subsequently incorporated into its workstations. RISC has since become commercially significant in a wide range of successful products from supercomputers to mobile phones.

We have seen in this section that, in order to make sense of the historical evidence available illustrating the decisive role of the government the existence of some kind of hierarchy within the complex socioeconomic network seems to be unavoidable. Given this evidence it is plausible to argue that organizational learning (even at firm level) is not possible without the action of the state. Of course, this is not to say that it always succeeds; only that it is indispensable. While complex economic systems are adaptive and are composed of adaptive entities, not all their composing entities are equally adaptive. Therefore it is necessary to differentiate between types of adaptiveness according to their function within the system.

3.7.3 Dynamically coherent agents (DCA)

The notions of diversity and hierarchy discussed above reveal that agents within complex system display different types of dynamics rather than just one type. For example, one of the preconditions for complex adaptive systems to experience a truly open-ended evolution is that their agents display what Rocha (2000) calls a *strong sense of agency*. He distinguishes between the later and the *weak sense of agency*.

Self-organizing agents with a weak sense of agency follow passive evolutionary trends, by coherently adapting to the changes of the environment. That is, they evolve by following external signals. This sort of agent is referred to by Rocha (2000) as *dynamically coherent (situated) agents (DCA)* and they are dependent of the environment's *distributed memory*. In semiotic terms, it could be said that its semantic[44] is also its pragmatic,[45] in the sense that "meaning is not private to the agent but can only be understood in the context of the agent's situation in an environment with its specific selective pressures" (ibid., p. 4). These sorts of agents would be just another indistinguishable dynamical component of a network of many components. It corresponds to the kind of adaptiveness which Ackoff defined as "other-self adaptation" in a 1971 pioneering paper, i.e. an entity[46] that responds to "an external change by modifying itself" (Ackoff 1971, p. 668).

In economic terms, the description of DCA fits very well with the typical actors of the mainstream (neoclassical) economic theories. Meaning a world populated by individual entities unable to influence to each other, and subject to the approval of market forces beyond their control. The main activity of these kinds of actors would be to focus on optimizing their functions in order to adapt to the environment, for equilibrium to be restored in the system. Several other (neoclassic and non-neoclassic) theories of the firm follow the same idea. The kind of network built by this sort of DCA match the "decentralised system of fully informed and fully connected perfectly competitive firms" (Foster 2005, p. 887). Mainstream theories start with the "presumption that a system is in a high state of order, or is capable of attaining such a state of stable equilibrium" (ibid., p. 875). This can therefore be "represented in sets of mathematical functions from which equilibrium solutions can be deduced" (ibid., p. 876).

However, from a complex economics perspective, constraint optimization, even if important, applies only "when there is a known set of future outcomes and known probabilities associated with each occurrence" (Foster 2005, p. 881). Even if this sort of certainty in the short term is made possible because of that the phenomenon of path-dependency, optimization does not need to result in economically beneficial outcomes, not to say innovation. As Ackoff (1971) suggested, this kind of agent is prepared to set short-term "goals," but not long term "objectives," which are the most necessary quality of purposeful entities (pp. 666–7). Innovation will in fact depend upon the opportunities and threats that systems face.

However, as already stated, such a fully connected system is unlikely to evolve because it lacks a sufficient degree of openness. If we necessarily need to acknowledge the existence of DCA in a complex socioeconomic system (most of the firms in an economy fall into this characterization), we need also to recognize that that these kinds of agents do play a very marginal role in structural change. Neither is our goal to disqualify firms as purposeful systems, because they are purposeful (since they have the ability to set ends). Rather our contention is that this kind of agent belongs more to the sub-purposeful level of the whole economy rather than to the level of those entities with the ability to set common purpose.

3.7.4 Dynamic incoherent agents (DIA): The true agents of change

On the other side, there exist agents that rely more on some kind of *local memory*, rather than the distributed memory of the first type of described agent. This kind of agent is referred to as *dynamic incoherent agents (DIA)*, in the sense that these entities possess an element of dynamical incoherence with the environment in which they are embedded (*strong sense of agency*). These agents are the cause of structural ruptures and truly open-ended evolution (the innovation process is per definition a dynamical incoherent process). They are truly autonomous entities that display a sense of unity (expressed in common purpose, concerted action) and emergent properties that reveal crucial causal powers within the system.

Rocha (2000) argues that the local memory of DIA is the result of the recombination of the symbols provided by what he, relying on von Newman, calls an "inert structure or code" or "*autonomic syntax*" (p. 10), which is defined as "components with many dynamically equivalent states which can be used to set up an arbitrary semantic relation with the environment" (Rocha 2000, p. 5). In other words, this code provides the material for DIA to construct their own *local memory* (different from the environment memory), which truly justifies and better explains its autonomy (ibid.).

The notion of DIA displays the kind of adaptation that Ackoff (1971) defined as "Other-other adaptation"; i.e. an entity that responds to "external change by modifying the environment" (p. 668). Of course, DIA can also show "Self-other" adaptation, which means reacting to internal change by changing the environment (ibid.). On the other hand, the idea of a local memory and inert structure seem to have strong links to Ackoff's idea of "learning how to adapt" (p. 668). In this notion an entity can "learn to increase [its] efficiency in the pursuit of a goal" (ibid., p. 669) if it has the "ability to modify [its] behaviour" (ibid.). But that an entity is able to modify behavior means that it is capable to make choices between different alternatives, thus displaying the ability to *memorize* a menu of different alternatives. In our view, what Ackoff (1971) calls "different alternatives" is similar to what Rocha (2000) calls "inert structure."

The word "inert," which Rocha himself put between quotation marks, refers to codes or structures that are, to some extent, independent from the entities they help create. Agents that share this code can recombine into new, unexpected entities and are said to form "semiotic closures" that exclude other agents (ibid.). For example the genetic code in biological systems exclude non-biological agents, a programming language in computing systems exclude non-computing systems, etc. But while Rocha (2000) focuses more on biologic or computational systems, Ackoff (1971) establishes a clear parallel with social systems. Either way, what is important here is that the "memory" of DIA is not the result of purely self-organization, but the result of their role in a *relational* system of networked agents. *Their position in the network forces them to learn to internally adapt themselves in a way that others do not need to.*

In terms of the theoretical discussion being held in this chapter, the "inert code" can be read, for example, as the set of activities in an economic system that could facilitate the creation of synergies among other economic agents. Depending on the hubs learning and reaction abilities to internal and external changes, and on their long-term objectives, some activities will be preferred over others. This will shape the environment of other actors in a given direction. However this does not mean that they are condemned to fail if they make the wrong choice. As the work of Ackoff (1971) reminds us, purposeful systems are precisely purposeful because they have the ability to change their goals in order to accomplish a long-term objective.

This, of course, could be also be interpreted for different levels. For instance, organizations within a country can differ among themselves, but they all share allegiance to the same legal system (code). It is also possible to find even tighter semiotic closures amongst entities of the same subsystem. For instance, companies within an industry dramatically differ from each other but they all share certain (if not necessarily all) standards, which define the kind of goods they produce, and which do not apply to the goods produced by other industries. However, as already suggested, to share a standard does not mean to be necessarily a dynamic incoherent agent.

At least in economic systems, DIA have the ability to set and change standards for the system to be able to better function. The point is that, even when dynamic incoherent agents won't be able to use all the memorized "different alternatives" at once because of Simon's bounded rationality; they will always have the chance to change their goals while using their memory to recombine choices or select new choices in order to achieve their long-term objective.

3.7.5 Government agency as a DIA

When considering the ideas discussed above, we can argue that it is possible to further conceptualize on the *government agency* as a *DIA* within the innovation system; because it has the potential (if not the actuality, see Chapter 2. Section 2.1) to lead to and to deal with structural ruptures. Its strong sense of agency becomes apparent in its role as, e.g., standard settler for the system. As historical evidence shows, an adequate supply of standards may not be "forthcoming through individual private enterprises [alone], as it may not be worthwhile for any single firm to undertake the cost of designing a reference standard that would be useful for the industry as a whole and redistributed freely" (Hughes et al. 1999, p. 43). Governmental support for the collaborative development of reference standards provided by state agencies, including such as national standards institutes that undertake such work, constitutes a mechanism to promote innovation.

Seen from this perspective, DIA (or nodes or actors) are also the hubs of the network. Of course, again, this is not to say that only the government agencies possess this kind of property. The growing (and to some extent historically evidenced) complexity of economic systems allows many other entities (e.g. big corporations) to play critical roles within the structure. Not even all government agencies play a pivotal role. However, the point is that, as already stated, it is plausible to assume complex economic networks as structures of hierarchically interrelated elements, which justifies not only the notion of different kinds of agents within a system, but also the notion of different kinds of hubs. In other words, a certain hub in a sub-network may be subordinated to other hubs within the same network. Not even a multinational corporation does the job alone. Some hubs can be (and in fact are) more hubs than others (so to speak), which justifies their theoretical differentiation. To differentiate is also important because in reality we can find all types of agents.

This differentiation, however, should not be taken as something static. We already saw in Chapter 2 that hierarchical non-random networks remain incomplete, even when connectivity increases. In this kind of networks nodes can evolve into hubs that most connections are routed through. Foster (2005) see non-random networks as a fair representation of economic systems when he argues that "people are not random in making connections—people have agendas (aspirations and preferences) in making connections. We do not have random conversations nor do we enter into binding contracts with random individuals" (p. 887). Indeed, since all type of agents co-exist (and co-evolve) within evolutionary systems; it is also plausible to argue that some agents can become hubs and that some hubs can escalate within the network hierarchy. Notice also that when we refer to government agency, we do not necessarily refer to one centralized entity, but more to a system of hub organizations across the system with the ability to interact with other hubs (including primarily big companies).

For instance, in 1956, at the request of the Air Force, the Massachusetts Institute of Technology (MIT) created Project Lincoln, now known as the Lincoln Laboratory, which oversaw the construction of the Semi-Automatic Ground Environment (SAGE) air-defense system. The project also involved several private firms such as IBM, RAND, Systems Development Corporation (the spin-off from RAND), Burroughs, Western Electric, RCA, and AT&T. Eventually, SAGE technologies worked their way into commercial products and helped establish the industry leaders.

SAGE was a driving force behind the formation of the American computer and electronics industry. IBM built 56 computers for SAGE, earning over $500 million, which helped contribute to its becoming the world's largest computer manufacturer. At its peak, between 7000 and 8000 IBM employees worked on the project. It became large enough to conduct its in-house research. IBM's Thomas J. Watson Research Center[47] figured not only in basic research but also supplied a source of applied research that allowed or, conversely, pushed federal support to focus increasingly on the longest-term, riskiest ideas. All this also contributed to the emergence of the software industry, where IBM played the role of a standard-setting organization. The same could be said of Bell Labs,[48] the long-time R&D division of AT&T.

Again, notice that we refer to the concept of hierarchy in the Simon's sense. That is to say, hierarchical position would not reflect necessarily a strict relation of subordination among subsystems, but only a functional necessity. In the next chapter we will explore in more detail the mechanisms that allow these integrating synergies to take place (organizational integration). We will also discuss the theoretical feasibility and practical functionality of conceiving this process within the national system of innovation framework.

Notes

1 An example can be extracted from the Herbert Gintis's review of the 2006 book of Eric D. Beinhocker, The Origins of Wealth: Evolution, Complexity, and the Radical Remaking of Economics. In referring to the position of complexity economics in regard to the state role in a complex economy, Gintis asserts that, of all the subjects treated in the book, Beinhocker's position in this regard "is probably closest to that of the Neoclassical economics view" (see H Gintis, The economy as a complex adaptive system, review of Beinhocker's The Origins of Wealth: Evolution, Complexity, and the Radical Remaking of Economics, *Journal of Economic Literature* XLIV, December, 2006, p. 1023).

2 There are important differences between IPE and the New Institutional Economics in their treatment of markets, state and politics. This study is not institutionalist in the sense of NIE, but in the sense of IPE. Chang (2002) places the intellectual traditions of IPE in the classic works of authors such as Karl Marx, Thorstein Veblen, Joseph Schumpeter, Karl Polanyi, Herbert Simon and more recent authors such as William Lazonick, Geoffrey Hodgson, Peter Evans, etc. This tradition, which is sometimes called Old Institutional Economics (OIE), differs in many aspects of the NIE. One of the most important aspects is that OIE does not conceive institutions only as constraints on the pre-formed behavior of individuals, but also as shapers of the individuals themselves (for a detailed discussion see HJ Chang, Breaking the mould: an institutionalist political economy alternative to the neo-liberal theory of the market, *Cambridge Journal of Economics* 26(5), 2002: 539–59).

3 Although Bentham was a decided individualist, his utilitarian stance led him to support things such as Poor Laws, hospitals for the indigent, workhouses for the unemployed; to levy taxes for redistribution purposes and to decrease the need for direct taxes; to recompense victims of crime when the perpetrator is indigent; to safeguard national security and establish courts and internal police; to disseminate useful information to industry; to label poisonous substances; to guarantee marks for quality and quantity on goods; to set a maximum price for corn; to provide security of subsistence by stock-piling grain or granary bounties to producers; to encourage investment in times of unemployment; to grant patents to inventors; to regulate banks and stockbrokers; to promote government annuities and a voluntary government insurance plan; to establish government banks; to establish and enforce a government monopoly on the issuance of paper currency; to engage in public works to put the unemployed to work; and, finally, to establish institutes, boards, and universities (see E Franken Paul, Laissez faire in nineteenth-century Britain: Fact or myth?, *Literature of Liberty* iii(4), 1980: 10–11).

4 Even when he was a decided opponent of industrial policies, Mill's Principles of Political Economy went further than Bentham in his ideas on state intervention in that he established a distinction between those laws of production, which were held to be immutable on the one side, and those laws of production that could be manipulated at the discretion of legislators on the other side. The purpose behind this distinction was to underscore the flexibility of distributing wealth. Social arrangements regarding distribution, rather than being immutable, as previous economists implied, ought to succumb to redistributive schemes, particularly those concerning private property. Not only did he endorse land nationalization, aid for the unemployed, the curtailment of inheritance, the granting of a *right* to relief, the enforcement of legal restraints against those among the poor who procreated,

compulsory education, regulation of child labor, government housing schemes, but also the regulation or, if necessary, the nationalization of monopolistic or large scale industries. Austrian authors such as Franken Paul see this as an undoubtable evidence of Mill's sympathetic stance toward socialism (ibid., p. 12).

5 Ibid., p. 15.

6 This definition of Lionel Robbins is criticized by Frankel Paul who states that even if undoubtedly perceptive, Robbins taxonomy failed in acknowledging the fact the Classical economists after Smith held nothing but contempt for either a natural law, deistic conception of the universe and man's place in it or for a moral philosophy buttressed by natural rights (pp. 8–9)/

7 In his *Treatise on Political Economy* of 1803, Jean-Baptiste Say leaves clear his notion on state intervention. Although he does not deny the existence of the state as such, he did definitely leave out the possibility of the state intervening in the economy.

8 An English manufacturer, representative of the Manchester School, known by his strong opposition to the Corn Laws. The Anti-Corn Law league was founded in September 1838 in Manchester as a pressure group of manufacturers. Paul Bairoch calls Cobden a "true apostle of free trade."

9 His *Plea for Liberty*, edited by MacKay and published 1891, is a critique to any intervention of the state in the economy. This book (chapter I and IV) advance many arguments against socialism, which were later employed by Mises and Hayek in their calculation debate.

10 Bastiat was a very influential popularizer of Say's theories (see e.g. Frédéric Bastiat, *Economic Sophisms*, trans. Arthur Goddard, introduction by Henry Hazlitt (Irvingtonon-Hudson: Foundation for Economic Education, [1845], 1996), available at http://oll.libertyfund.org

11 Oskar Lange gave a neoclassical solution to this problem, which was theoretically – from a neoclassical point of view – sound, but practically proved to be flawed.

12 Apart from the Austrian School, we could also mention the Monetarist School represented by Milton Friedman. The Keynesians had, since the synthesis of Hicks, been relying in the neoclassical tools to explain the microeconomic phenomena. In this constellation, the state had been naively assumed to correct all market failures that arose from microeconomic activity, and politicians were also believed to always respond to public interest. But the intense distributional conflicts resulting from the structural change and the deceleration of economic growth, not to mention the phenomenon of stagflation, made room for a massive Monetarist critique of the Keynesian welfare state (the best known attack on the theoretical Keynesian consensus). By relying on the adaptive rational expectations and on the Walrasian clearing market, the Monetarist rejected the effectiveness of the macroeconomic management by the state. This critique revealed serious flaws in the Keynesian discourse. Under the new constellation, the state was "confined to regulating the macroeconomic aggregates, leaving the allocation of resources to the neoclassical doctrine of free markets" (HJ Chang, Globalisation, Economic *Development* and the *Role* of the *State*, Zed Books, London, 2003, p. 25). Other important critiques to the state came from the New Contractarian School, rent-seeking theories, etc.

13 Legislation here is referring to the additional amendments that legal systems experience as the result of constant political deliberation.

14 Between this period and the repeal of the Corn Law in 1846, Britain implemented a most aggressive infant industry promotion program. The period 1846–1860 showed an increase in continental exports (1.9 percent between 1837/39 and 1845/46

to 6.1 percent between 1845/47 and 1857/59, which encouraged many Europe supporters of free trade (P Beiroch, Economics & World History: Myths and *Paradoxes*, University of Chicago Press, Chicago, 1995, p. 22). English efforts focused on France because it was the country with which Britain had the highest trade deficit. After secret negotiations in 1846 between Richard Cobden and Michel Chevalier, a former disciple of Saint-Simon, a free trade agreement (Anglo-French trade treaty) was signed in 1860. Between 1861 and 1866 almost all European countries engaged in so-called "network of Cobden treaties" (ibid.). However Bismarck's Realpolitik of strong protectionism since 1878 marked the end of the liberalism in the Continent and the beginning of a gradual return to protectionism in the nineteenth century, except England. Already by 1880 some British manufacturers were asking for protection, which was reintroduced in the early twentieth century.

15 Nineteenth-century German economist who is today commonly – but mistakenly – known as the father of infant industry protection argument. His masterpiece *The National Systems of Political Economy* (1841) was a condemnation of the British advocacy of free trade in the nineteenth century as an act equivalent to "kicking away the ladder," with which they climbed to the top. Other influences in List's work were, according to Bairoch, the works of German Adam Müller (1809) and of the Frenchmen Jean-Antonie Chaptal (1819) and Charles Dupin (1827). In a harsh critique of List's main work, Karl Marx accused him (among other things) of copying the book *Du gouvernement considéré dans ses rapports avec le commerce* (1805) written by François-Louis-Auguste Ferrier, Napoleon's Customs Inspector, in defense of the Continental System. This critique could also be seen as a result of the contrast between List's right-wing political views, which defended a bourgeois and aristocratic form of government and Marx's left-wing views, which defended a worker-based form of government.

However, despite the critique, history has shown that List can be considered a major figure in industrial policy history. Contemporary development economists such as Chang and Reinert cite his work explicitly when referring to appropriate economic policies for developing countries.

16 See H Clay, In Defense of the American System, Classic Senate Speeches February 2, 3, and 6, 1832 Available in: www.senate.gov/artandhistory/history/common/generic/Speeches_ClayAmericanSystem.htm

17 During the Napoleonic Wars the United States continue, as a neutral party, to trade with France and Great Britain. This sparked strong opposition from the British, who started to size American ships and to imprison British-American seamen. Jefferson responded with several Embargo legislations that sought to impose economic hardship on the British and to force them to end the violation of American shipping. The expected results never happened, causing instead devastating hardship in the American economy. See D Irving, The welfare cost of autarky: Evidence from the Jeffersonian trade embargo, 1807–09, *Review International Economics* 13(4): 631–45, 2005. See also JA Frankel, The 1807–1809 embargo against Great Britain, *Journal of Economic History* 42(2): 291–308, 1982.

18 Paradoxically, this period was also conspicuous by its rampant corruption and political patronage. In fact, the term "Gilded Age" was coined by Mark Twain and Charles D. Warner in their satirical novel *The Gilded Age: A Tale of Today*, in which they make critical observations about the social and political life of the period. This and other examples highlight the fact that the economic consequences of corruption are not always as straightforward as we may wish, however harmful it

may be for the rest of society. In fact, it has been more or less a normal phenom-enon in developing economies that suffer from chronic lack of administrative and regulative resources. For a very enlightened discussion on the subject, see HJ Chang, Bad Samaritans: The Myth of Free Trade and the Secret History of Capitalism, Bloomsbury Press, New York, 2008, pp. 160–81.

19 Made in Germany was a label introduced by the English Merchandise Marks Act of 1887, which was intended to prevent the forging of trade-marks, the label-ling of false quantities, and similar methods of commercial thievery by foreign (especially German) manufacturers. Famous examples of this were the stamping of a Sheffield name and address on a knife made in Saxony and Solingen or the exports to England by German firms of large numbers of sewing-machines, con-spicuously labelled "Singers," and "North-British Sewing Machines," with the Made in Germany stamp being placed in small letters underneath the treadle. Just as with some Chinese products today, there was the widespread popular belief in the English public, partially confirmed by Williams, that German products were "cheap and nasty." At the same time he recognizes that behind the German industrial tactics there is a very clever and well calibrated government strategy.

20 William McKinley, The value of protection, *The North American Review*, vol. 150, p. 742, 1890.

21 The debate about the role of the state in the technological development of ancient civilizations has often been biased. At the same time, to take a millennial perspec-tive meets the difficulty of finding reliable figures, which adds to the inexactness of the discussion. However, it seems to be undeniable the fact that the state played a significant role in the socio-economic life of ancient and pre-modern time China, India, Japan and the medieval Islamic world (all of them with their ups and downs). For example, some authors argue that the Meiji reforms were merely the endpoint of a long process of "rational state formation undertaken during the Tokugawa period" (see J Hobson, The Eastern Origins of Western Civilization, Cambridge University Press, Cambridge, 2004, p. 90). Modern scholars such as Andrew Watson acknowledged the pioneering role played by the Abbasid caliphate in sponsoring secular learning, as well as its systematic effort to collect and diffuse knowledge.

François Bernier, a French traveler in the late seventeenth century noticed the richness of the karkhanas in the Mughal empire. Karkhana were state sponsored and state-controlled manufacturing centers aimed at supplying the royal household and departments of government with provisions, stores and equipment. Karkhanas were later expanded into centers of vocational training as well. These organizations were involved in different sectors, such as metallurgy, mining, mint, textile, weap-onry, jeweler and so on. Central government also empowered local governments to engage in manufacturing and commerce. The result was a system called the Domestic Industry System, which consisted of various kinds of merchant-princes or Mahajans that supplied the capital and acted as intermediaries between the actual makers in the workshops and the final purchasers in the country and abroad. The undisputed primacy of the pre-modern Indian cotton industry is a classical example of this system. When British commerce was established with Asia in the seventeenth century, India was the unrivalled center of cotton manufactures in the whole world.

In the same line, Han and Sung China operated under a system in which the central government collected revenues from land taxes, imposed monopolies on certain commodities such as salt, iron and tea; and introduced controls in the grain trade in order to equalize grain prices. However, none of these elements prevented

China from introducing an unprecedented number of technological innovations, to achieve high agricultural productivity and to develop a remarkable industrial sector during the Han and Sung dynasties. For example, Chinese output of iron (per capita) achieved by the end of the eleventh century was only matched by Britain seven centuries later. In fact, in 1750 China produced 33 percent of world manufacturing output or 1600 percent that of Britain, which only in 1860 equaled that of the Chinese.

Great ancient scholars such as Kautilya (370–283 BCE), Wang Anshi (1021–1086), Al-Ghazali (1058–1111) and many others contributed to the theoretical debate on these issues. A comprehensive study needs to be carried out that organically integrates both Western and non-Western discourses and evidences into the field of innovation economics.

22 For example Korea, Sweden, Taiwan and Finland show that pragmatic cooperation between organized private agents (bankers and business leaders), on the one hand, and government officials and civil servants, on the other, have played a key role in enhancing economic growth.

23 In 1983 Korea filled the fourth place in the list of debtor countries with 43 billion $. More in E. Toussaint, The *World* Bank: A Critical Primer, Pluto Press, London, 2008.

24 Asset-backed insecurity. The Economist. 2008-01-17. www.economist.com/finance/displaystory.cfm?story_id=10533428

25 Sovereign Wealth Funds: Shrek or White Knight? The Economic Observer. 2008-02-27. www.eeo.com.cn/ens/feature/2008/02/27/92907.html

26 Even when the neo-liberal notion arising from the alliance of the Austrian and neoclassical school displays a common vision on issues related to state intervention, these two notions should be by no means taken as similar notions. There is a growing body of literature addressing the differences between the two (e.g. see HJ Chang, *Breaking Away*... 2002, J Foster, *From Simplistic*... 2005.

27 Even when this definition is more intended to describe process involving radical new technologies, I would argue that it also could apply to catch up experiences as well. In the next chapter we will add further arguments to this subject.

28 AT&T settled its first federal anti-trust suit with a document known as the Kingsbury Commitment, which established AT&T as a government-sanctioned monopoly. In return, AT&T agreed to divest the controlling interest it had acquired in the Western Union telegraph company, and to allow non-competing independent telephone companies to interconnect with the AT&T long-distance network. This allowed AT&T to use standards to create efficiencies on the supply side, which came to be known as the Bell System. Based on strategies for horizontal and vertical integration that largely depended on these standards AT&T became a global leader in telecommunications and – with over 1 million employees by the 1970s – the largest company in the world (see www.corp.att.com/history/milestones.html). Even when some Austrian critics argue that it killed competition (for an Austrian critique see www.cato.org/sites/cato.org/files/serials/files/cato-journal/1994/11/cj14n2-6.pdf) the innovations and economies of scale created by the Bell system are difficult to deny.

29 In 1968 Bell System tried to prevent Carterfone connected directly to the AT&T network. Carterfone was a device designed to be connected to a two-way radio at the base station serving a mobile radio system. The same year the US Federal Communications Commision allowed Carterfone to connect to the facilities of

AT&T (see the original text of the law in www.uiowa.edu/~cyberlaw/FCCOps/ 1968/13F2-420.html). During the 1970s, other emerging firms were also denied the connection, which eventually led to the government antitrust legislation against AT&T in 1982, after which Bell System ceased to exist. Particularly the ruling of 1968 has been said to have promoted innovations such as computer modems, fax machines, answering machines and to the advent of internet see KP Grattan, The Cellular Empire, Dominion *to* Democracy: A Policy Analysis *of* Open Access *on* Innovation, UMI Dissertation Publishing, Ann Arbor-MI, p. 26, 2008, see also www.historyofcomputercommunications.info/Book/1/ 1.10CarterfoneComputerInquiryDeregulation67-68.html#_ftn91)

30   The point is illustrated perfectly by the start-up movement developed in the US and Western Europe in high-tech industries. These are generally small (usually too small), high specialized firms, which have become a symbol of entrepreneurship, and risk-taking attitude among policymakers and traditional companies and managers in business such as IT. However, startups do not usually engage in research. "Notwithstanding the popular labeling of start-ups as 'high-tech' they apply the fruits of past research rather than generating more. In both respects, government funding plays a critical role in building the foundations for these innovative commercial investments." See P Lee et al. (2012), Continuing Innovation in Information Technology, National Academy Press, Washington D.C, 2012, p. 14.

31   www.thinkstandards.net/what.html

32   The punched cards introduced by Jacquard's loom were inspired by the French engineer and artist Jacques de Vaucanson (1709–1782), which had been working as government inspector of the silk manufactures, during the period of Louis XV, in order to save the industry from the decadence relative to England and Scotland. Vaucanson not only left impressive automata (e.g. the Digesting Duck) but was also, relying on the works of Basile Bouchon and his assistance Jean-Baptiste Falcon, the creator of the world's first completely automated loom by using punch cards. While Bouchon is seen as the creator of the world's first semi-automated industrial application (by applying the principle of a perforated paper to a drawloom, the antecedent of the punch card) and Vaucanson as the first to introduce a completely automated loom, it was Jacquard, however, the one who sophisticated the technical process which turn out to be highly productive and innovative. Jacquard use of punch card highly influenced Charles Babbage, which conceived the punched cards as a good devise to store programs in his Analytical Engine. This in turn influenced the American engineer Herman Hollerith, who used punched cards to store information in a tabulating machine which he used to input data for the 1890 US Census. Hollerith went on to create the tabulatin Machine Company in 1896, which became IBM in 1911 after merging with other three companies.

33   The organization still exists today and has played a central role in France's industrial and technological development.

34   Assortative mixing is a concept of the network theory that describes the tendency for vertices in networks to be connected to other vertices that are like (or unlike) them in some way. The term "assortative" usually refers to highly connected nodes (hubs) that have been proven to tend to link to other hubs. In contrast, dissasortative mixing could show the tendency of hubs to link with small nodes (see http://arxiv. org/pdf/condmat/0209450.pdf). Even when many social networks has shown a tendency to assortative mixing, and therefore to lock-in, we should also consider the existence of social and individual agency in the societal realm.

35 An exemplar case is the American Standards Association (ASA). There are a number of historical accounts of the nascent engineering associations in the United States, which made dedicated efforts by engineers to establish industry consensus for standards (e.g. railroads). However, after World War I, the "big five" engineering societies joined with the U.S. Departments of Commerce, Navy, and War in 1918 to found the American Engineering Standards Committee. By 1928, this group had reorganized and renamed itself the American Standards Association (ASA). The ASA and National Bureau of Standards both cooperated and overlapped in many areas, and jurisdictional conflicts were common.

36 The stated purpose was to enable smaller research laboratories to access large-scale computers at large research centers, without the necessity of ARPA supplying every laboratory with a multimillion dollar machine. See www.sandv.com/downloads/0701bera1.pdf

37 See http://faculty.apec.umn.edu/vruttan/documents/Chap6-Internet.pdf

38 Ibid.

39 See http://faircompetitionlaw.com/2011/06/19/massachusetts-trade-secrets-statute-still-uncertain

40 Even if there is no direct evidence relating this to the absence of enforceable noncompete agreements, it is very symptomatic that the Californian semiconductor industry and the biotech industry are the most representative within their respective sectors in the United States and worldwide.

41 American biologist and complex system researcher who proposed in 1993 a model of selection dynamics in the biological domain with heterogeneous interdependent traits, which have found broad applicability beyond biology.

42 Created in 1958 as ARPA, then the name was changed to Defense Advanced Research Projects Agency (DARPA) in 1972; and later renamed ARPA in 1983. ARPA was a particular office of the Pentagon; initially created in the aftermath of the Soviet success with Sputnik to push the technological frontier of Pentagon procurement efforts. The intention was to provide funding for "beyond the horizon" technologies, since the rest of the Pentagon's budget for research and development was linked to immediate procurement of weapons for the various military services. ARPA initiatives occurred across a range of technologies, but it was the office that supported technological advance in the computer field that established a new paradigm for technology policy. ARPA's computer offices carefully cultivated a model that was quite distinct from the standard practice of other government agencies that fund research. F Block, Swimming against the current: The rise of a hidden developmental state in the United States, *Politics & Society*, June, vol. 36 no. 2, 2008, p. 7)

43 See S Dandamudi, Guide to RISC Processors for Programmers and Engineers, Springer Science, New York, 2005.

44 Semantic is a branch of linguistics and logic concerned with **meaning**.

45 Pragmatics is the branch of linguistics dealing with language in use and the **contexts** in which it is used.

46 For Ackoff all purposeful entities and sub-entities are correctly defined as systems. We differentiate here only on definitional grounds. But we agree with the system view of Ackoff.

47 Its contribution, particularly during the period 1960–1984, has been acknowledged by IEEE, see www.ieeeghn.org/wiki/index.php/Milestones:IBM_Thomas_J._Watson_Research_Center,_1960_-_1984

48 The invention of the first transistor at Bell Labs was called an IEEE milestone, see www.ieeeghn.org/wiki/index.php/Milestones:Invention_of_the_First_ Transistor_at_Bell_Telephone_Laboratories,_Inc.,_1947. Bell labs is now the R&D subsidiary of the French-owned Alcatel–Lucent.

References

Abate J (1999), *Inventing the Internet*. MIT Press.

Ackoff R (1971), Toward a system of systems concepts, *Management Science* 17(11): 661–71.

Ackoff R and Emery F [1972] (2006), *On Purposeful Systems*. Aldine-Transaction, Fourth Paperback printing.

Allen R (1983), Collective invention, *Journal of Economic Behavior and Organization* 4: 1–24.

Amsden AH (1989), *Asia's Next Giant: South Korea and Late Industrialization*. Oxford: Oxford University Press.

Andreoni A and Chang HJ (2019), The political economy of industrial policy: Structural interdependencies, policy alignment and conflict management, Structural Change and Economic Dynamics 48 (March): 136–50.

Andrew R et al. (2011), Dimensions of publicness and organizational performance: A review of the evidence, *Journal of Public Administration Research and Theory* 21(3i): 301–19.

Arthur B (2009), *The Nature of Technology: What It Is and How It Evolves*. New York: Free Press,

Babbage C [1832] (2010), *On the Economy of Machinery and Manufactures*. Cambridge: Cambridge University Press.

Bairoch P (1995), *Economics and World History: Myths and Paradoxes*. Chicago: University of Chicago Press.

Barabási A and Albert R (1999), Emergence of scaling in random networks, Science 286 (5439) (October): 509–12.

Bastiat F [1845] (1996), *Economic Sophisms, Foundation for Economic Education*, trans. A Goddard, Irvington-on-Hudson, available at The Online Library of Liberty, http:// oll.libertyfund.org, last accessed in July 2018.

Beaussart ML et al. (2013), Creative liars: The relationship between creativity and integrity, *Thinking Skills and Creativity* 9 (August): 129–34.

Beinhocker E (2006), *The Origin of Wealth: Evolution, Complexity, and the Radical Remaking of Economics*. Boston, MA: Harvard Business School Press.

Bessen J and Nuvolari A (2016), Knowledge sharing among inventors: Some historical perspectives. In: D Harhoff and K Lakhani (eds.), *Revolutionizing Innovation: Users, Communities and Open Innovation*. Cambridge, MA: MIT Press, pp. 135–55.

Bessen J and Nuvolari A (2017), Diffusing new technology without dissipating rents: some historical case studies of knowledge sharing, LED *Working Paper Series*, 2017/28, November.

Block F (2008), Swimming against the current: The rise of a hidden developmental state in the United States, *Politics & Society* 36(2) (June): 169–206.

Bossche P (2005), The Origins of the WTO, The Law and Policy of the World Trade Organization: Text, Cases and Materials. New York: Cambridge University Press.

Brisco N (1907), The Economic Policy of Robert Walpole. New York: Columbia University Press.

Brown R and Mawson S (2019), Entrepreneurial ecosystems and public policy in action: a critique of the latest industrial policy blockbuster, Cambridge Journal of Regions, Economy and Society 12: 347–68.

Bryson J et al. (eds.) (2001), *Knowledge, Space, Economy*. London: Routledge.

Buchanan J and Tullock G [1962] (1990), *The Calculus of Consent*. Ann Arbor: University of Michigan Press.

Buchanan J et al. (1980), *Toward a Theory of the Rent-Seeking Society*. College Station, Texas: A&M University Press.

Burt R (2005), The social capital of structural holes. In: M Guillén (ed.), *The New Economic Sociology: Developments in an Emerging Field*. New York: Russell Sage Foundation, pp. 148–93.

Cacioppo JT (2002), Social neuroscience: Understanding the pieces fosters understanding the whole and vice versa, *American Psychologist* 57(11) (December): 831–4.

Caldwell B (1997), Hayek and socialism, *Journal of Economic Literature* XXXV: 1856–90, December

Caplan P (2003), Patents and open standards, A white paper for the National Information Standards. *NISO Press*, Bethesda, Maryland, Originally published in *Information Standards Quarterly* 4(4), (October).

Cargill C (2002), Intellectual property rights and standards settings organizations: An overview of failed evolution, Submitted to the Department of Justice and the Federal Trade Commission, Version 2.

Chang HJ (1999), The economic theory of the developmental state. In: M Woo-Cumings (ed.), *The Developmental State*. Ithaca and London: Cornell University Press, pp. 182–99.

Chang HJ (2002), Breaking the mould: An institutionalist political economy alternative to the neo-liberal theory of the market, *Cambridge Journal of Economics* 26(5): 539–59.

Chang HJ (2003a), *Kicking Away the Ladder*. London: Anthem Press.

Chang HJ (2003b), *Globalisation, Economic Development and the Role of the State*. London: Zed Books.

Chang HJ (2007) (ed.), *Institutional Change and Economic Development*. London: Anthem Press.

Chang HJ (2008), *Bad Samaritans: The Myth of Free Trade and the Secret History of Capitalism*. New York: Bloomsbury Press.

Chang HJ (2010a), Institutions and economic development: Theory, policy and history, *Journal of Institutional Economics*, 7(4) 1–26 (pre-publication copy).

Chang HJ (2010b), *23 Things They Don't Tell You about Capitalism*. London: Penguin Group.

Chang HJ (2011), Reply to the comments on "Institutions and Economic Development: Theory, Policy and History," *Journal of Institutional Economics* 7(4): 595–613.

Chang HJ (2016), *Transformative Industrial Policy for Africa*, United Nations, Economic Commission for Africa, Addis Ababa, Ethiopia.

Chaptal JA (1893), *Mes souvenirs sur Napoléon*. Paris: Librairie Plon.

Chiu-Pu C (2005), Ownership and management issues in Taiwanese public enterprises, *The Asia Pacific Journal of Public Administration* 27(2) (December): 163–80.

Christensen CM (1997), *The Innovator's Dilemma: When New Technologies Cause Great Firms to Fail*. Cambridge, MA: Harvard Business School Press.

Cimoli M et al. (eds.) (2009), *The Political Economy of Capabilities Accumulation: The Past and Future of Policies for Industrial Development*. New York: Oxford University Press.

Clay H (1832), In Defense of the American System, Classic Senate Speeches, February 2, 3, and 6, available at www.senate.gov/artandhistory/history/common/generic/Speeches_ClayAmericanSystem.htm

Clithero JA et al. (2008), Foundations of neuroeconomics: From philosophy to practice. *PLoS Biology* 6(11): e298.

Coan RW (2017), *A History of American State and Local Economic Development*. Cheltenham UK, Northampton, US: Edward Elgar.

Coe N et al. (2008), Global production networks: Realizing the potential, *Journal of Economic Geography* 8(3): 271–95.

Cohen S and DeLong JB (2016), *Concrete Economics: The Hamilton Approach to Economic Growth and Policy*. Cambridge, MA and London: Harvard Business Review Press.

Colander D (ed.) (1984), *Neoclassical Political Economy: An Analysis of Rent-Seeking and DUP Activities*. Cambridge, MA: Ballinger.

Colander D and Kupers R (2014), *Complexity and the Art of Public Policy: Solving Society's Problems from the Bottom Up*. Princeton and Oxford: Princeton University Press.

Colclough C and Manor J (1991), *States or Markets: Neo-Liberalism and the Development Policy Debate*. Oxford: Clarendon Press.

Dandamudi SP (2005), *Guide to RISC Processors for Programmers and Engineers*. New York: Springer Science.

DeLong JB (1992), Productivity and machinery investment: A long run look 1870–1980, Journal of Economic History 53(2) (June): 307–24.

Denhardt J and Denhardt R (2007), *The New Public Service: Serving, Not Steering*. New York, London: M.E. Sharp Armonk.

Di Maio M (2009), Industrial policies in developing countries. In: M Cimoli et al. (eds.), *The Political Economy of Capabilities Accumulation: The Past and Future of Policies for Industrial Development*. Oxford: Oxford University Press, pp. 107–44.

Dopfer K (2005), *Economics, Evolution and the State: The Governance of Complexity*. Cheltenham, UK: Edward Elgar.

Dopfer K and Potts J (2008), *The General Theory of Economic Evolution*. London and New York: Routledge.

Dorfman J (1949), *The Economic Mind in American Civilization*, Part III, 1865–1918, New York: Viking Press.

Dosi G et al. (1994), The process of economic development: introducing some stylized facts and theories on technologies, firms and institutions, Industrial and Corporate Change 1(1): 1–45.

Dosi G et al. (2003), The economics of systems integration: Towards an evolutionary interpretation. In: A Prencipe et al. (2003), *The Business of Systems Integration*. Oxford: Oxford University Press

Drechsler W and Randma-Liiv T (2014), The new public management then and now: Lessons from the transition in Central and Eastern Europe, *Working papers on Technology Governance and Economic Dynamics* 57, May.

Evans P (1995), *Embedded Autonomy: States and Industrial Transformation*. Princeton, NJ: Princeton University Press.

Evans P and Rauch J E (1999), Bureaucracy and growth: A cross-national analysis of the effects of "Weberian" State structures on economic growth, *American Sociological Review* 64(5) (October): 748–65.

Evans P et al. (eds.) [1985] (1999), *Bringing the State Back In*. Cambridge: Cambridge University Press.

Fallick B et al. (2006). Job-hopping in Silicon Valley: Some evidence concerning the micro-foundations of a high technology cluster, *Review of Economics and Statistics* 88(3): 472–81.

Fehr E and Gächter S (2000), Fairness and retaliation: The economics of reciprocity, *Journal of Economic Perspectives* 14(3): 159–81, Summer.

Ferlie E (2017), The new public management and public management studies. *Oxford Research Encyclopedia of Business and Management,* March 29, Retrieved June 26, 2019, from https://oxfordre.com/business/view/10.1093/acrefore/9780190224851.001.0001/acrefore-9780190224851-e-129.

Foster J (2005), From simplistic to complex systems in economics, *Cambridge Journal of Economics* 29(6): 873–92.

Frankel JA (1982), The 1807–1809 embargo against Great Britain, *Journal of Economic History* 42(2): 291–308.

Frankel PE (1980), Laissez faire in nineteenth-century Britain: Fact or myth? *Literature of Liberty* iii(4): 5–38.

Freeman C (2004), Technological infrastructure and international competitiveness, *Industrial and Corporate Change* 13(3): 541–69.

Freeman C (2008), System of Innovation. Cheltenham, UK; Northampton, USA: Edward Elgar.

Frey B (1997), *Not Just for the Money: An Economic Theory of Personal Motivation.* Cheltenham, UK: Edward Elgar.

Frey B (2007), Awards as compensation, *European Management Review* 4: 6–14.

Friedewald M (2000), The beginnings of radio communication in Germany, 1897–1918, *Journal of Radio Studies* 7(2): 441–63.

Gerlach C (2002), *Wu-Wei* in Europe. A Study of Eurasian Economic Thought, Department of Economic History, London School of Economics, Working Paper No. 12/05.

Gindis D (2009), From fictions and aggregates to real entities in the theory of the firm, *Journal of Institutional Economics* 5(1) (April): 25–46.

Gintis H (2006), The economy as a complex adaptive system, Review of the 2006 book of Eric D. Beinhocker: The Origins of Wealth: Evolution, Complexity, and the Radical Remaking of Economics, *Journal of Economic Literature* XLIV (December): 1018–31.

Grattan KP (2008), *The Cellular Empire, Dominion To Democracy: A Policy Analysis Of Open Access on Innovation.* Ann Arbor, MI: UMI Dissertation Publishing.

Graz J Ch (2016), The Havana Charter: when state and market shake hands. In Reinert E et al., Handbook of Alternative Theories of Economic Development. Cheltenham, UK, Northampton, MA, USA: Edward Elgar, pp. 281–90.

Hall D (1998), Public Enterprise in Europa, Paper presented at: IPPR Conference November 24, 1997 "What Future for Public Enterprise?" London, Institute for Public Policy Research (IPPR).

Alexander Hamilton's Final Version of the Report on the Subject of Manufactures (5 December 1791), *Founders Online*, National Archives, available at: https://founders.archives.gov/documents/Hamilton/01-10-02-0001-0007. [Original source: Syrett H (1966), *The Papers of Alexander Hamilton*, vol. 10, *December 1791–January 1792*, New York: Columbia University Press, 1966, pp. 230–340.]

Hayek FA [1944] (2007), *The Road to Serfdom: Text and Documents*, The Definitive Edition. Routledge: The University of Chicago Press.

Hayek FA [1960] (2008), *The Constitution of Liberty.* London: Routledge Classics.

Hayek FA (1966), The principles of a liberal social order, *Il Politico* 31(4): 601–18.

Hayter CS et al. (2018), Public-sector entrepeneurship, Oxford Review of Economic Policy 34(4): 676–94.

Hébert-Dufresne L et al (2015), Complex networks as an emerging property of hierarchical preferential attachment, Physical Review E 92, 062809.

Henry J (2008), The ideology of the laissez faire program, *Journal Economic Issues* XLII(1) (March): 209–24.

Hobson J (2004), *The Eastern Origins of Western Civilization*. Cambridge: Cambridge University Press.

Hodgson G (2000), Form micro to macro: the concept of emergence and the role of institutions. In: L Burlamaqui et al. (eds.), *Institutions and the Role of the State*. Cheltenham UK; Northampton USA: Edward Elgar, pp. 103–28.

Hodgson G (2006), What are institutions?, *Journal of Economic Issues* XL(1): 1–25.

Hodgson G (2009), On the institutional foundation of law: The insufficiency of custom and private ordering, *Journal of Economic Issues* XLIII(1): 143–66.

Hughes T et al. (1999), *Funding a Revolution: Government Support for Computing Research*. Washington, D.C.: National Academy Press.

Irving D (2005), The welfare cost of autarky: Evidence from the Jeffersonian trade embargo, 1807–09, *Review International Economics* 13(4) (September): 631–45.

Jäntti M and Vartiainen J (2009), The Finnish Developmental State and its Growth Regime, UNU-WIDER, United Nations University, Helsinki, *Research Paper* No. 2009/35.

Jessop B (2003a), Globalization: It's About Time Too!, *Political Science Series,* Institute for Advanced Studies, 85, Vienna.

Jessop B (2003b), Capitalism and the state. In: S Buckel et al. (eds.), *Formen und Felder politischer Intervention, Zur Relevanz von Staat und Steuerung*, Munster, Germany: Westfälischer Dampfboot, pp. 30–49.

Johnson C (1982*), MITI and the Japanese Miracle: The Growth of Industrial Policy, 1925– 1975*. Redwood City, CA: Stanford University Press.

Kaldor N (1967), *Strategic Factors in Economic Development*. New York, Ithaca: Cornell University.

Kahneman D et al. (1982), *Judgment under Uncertainty: Heuristics and Biases*. New York: Cambridge University Press.

Kamenica E (2012), Behavioral economics and psychology of incentives, *Annual Review of Economics* 4: 13.1–13.26.

Kesselheim A (2010), Using market-exclusivity incentives to promote pharmaceutical innovation, *The New England Journal of Medicine* 363(19) (November): 1855–63.

Kirman A (2011), *Complex Economics: Individual and Collective Rationality*. London and New York: Routledge.

Krueger A (1974), The political economy of the rent-seeking society, *American Economic Review* 64: 291–303.

Langlois R (2002), Modularity in technology and organization, *Journal of Economic Behavior & Organization* 49: 19–37.

Lavezzi A (2001), Division of Labor and Economic Growth: from Adam Smith to Paul Romer and Beyond. Paper prepared for the Conference: Old and New Growth Theories: an Assessment. Pisa, October 5–7, 2001.

Lazonick W (2006), Corporate Governance, Innovative Enterprise, and Economic Development, UNU WIDER, *Research Paper* No. 2006/71, July.

Lazonick W (2011), The Innovative Enterprise and the Developmental State: Toward an Economics of "Organizational Success." Paper prepared for: Institute for New Economic Thinking Annual 2011 Conference Crisis and Renewal: International Political Economy at the Crossroads Mount Washington Hotel Bretton Woods, NH, April 8–11, 2011.

Lazonick W and Mazzucato M (2012), The Risk–Reward Nexus. *Discussion Paper*. Policy Network.

Lazonick W and O'Sullivan M (2000), Perspectives on corporate governance, innovation, and economic performance. The European Institute of Business Administration, Fontainebleau Cedex, France.

Lazonick W and Tulum Ö (2011), The US biopharmaceutical finance and the sustainability of the biotech business model, *Research Policy* 40(9) (November): 1170–87.

Lazonick W et al. (2007), Boston's Biotech Boom: A "New Massachusetts Miracle"?, Research Paper, Center for Industrial Competitiveness University of Massachusetts Lowell, May.

Lee P et al. (2012), *Continuing Innovation in Information Technology*. Washington, D.C.: National Academy Press.

Libicki M (1994), Standards: The Rough Road to the Common Byte, Harvard University, Center for Information Policy Research, P-94–6.

Light D et al. (2011), Longer exclusivity does not guarantee better drugs, *Health Affairs* 30(4): 798.

List F (1856), *National System of Political Economy*. Philadelphia: J.B. Lippincott & Co.

MacKay T [1891](1981), *A Plea for Liberty: An Argument against Socialism and Socialistic Legislation*, Liberty Classics, Indianapolis. Available at http://oll.libertyfund.org/titles/313, last accessed July 2018

Marshall A (1927) [1890], *Principles of Economics*. London: Macmillan, Reprint.

Marx M (2007), Noncompetes and inventor mobility: Specialists, stars, and the Michigan experiment, *Management Science* 55(6): 875–89.

Mazzucato M (2011), *The Entrepreneurial State*. London: Demos.

McKinley W (1890), The value of protection, *The North American Review* 150.

Merges R and Sonsini W (2004), From Medieval Guilds to Open Source Software: Informal Norms, Appropriability Institutions, and Innovation, Conference on the Legal History of Intellectual Property, November 13, Madison Wisconsin

Mill JS [1848] (1871), *Principles of Political Economy*. London: Longmans, Green, Reader and Dyer, available at https://archive.org/details/principleseconom01milluoft, last accessed in July 2018

Millward R (2005), *Private and Public Enterprise in Europe: Energy, Telecommunications and Transport, 1830–1990*. Cambridge: Cambridge University Press.

Moretti E (2010), Local multipliers, American Economic Review: Papers & Proceedings, 100 (May): 1–7.

Moretti E and Thulin P (2013), Local multipliers and human capital in the United States and Sweden, Industrial and Corporate Change 22(1): 339–62.

Moser P (2013), Patents and innovation: Evidence from economic history, *Journal of Economic Perspectives* 27(1), Winter: 23–44.

Mun T [1664] (1895), *England Treasure by Foraign Trade*. Norwood, MA: Norwood Press.

Ostrom E (2010), Beyond markets and states: Polycentric governance of complex Economic systems, *American Economic Review* 100 (June): 1–33.

Pelikan P and Wegner G (eds.) (2003), *The Evolutionary Analysis of Economic Policy.* Cheltenham, UK: Edward Elgar.

Polanyi K [1944] (2001), *The Great Transformation: The Political and Economic Origin of Our Time.* Boston: Beacon Press.

Prencipe A et al. (eds.) (2005), *The Business of Systems Integration.* Oxford: Oxford University Press.

PwC (2015), State-Owned Enterprises Catalysts for public value creation?, www.psrc. pwc.com

Ravasz E and Barabási A-L (2003), Hierarchical organization in complex networks, Physical Review E 67, 026112.

Reinert E (1999), The role of the state in economic growth, *Journal of Economic Studies* 26(4/5): 268–326.

Reinert E (2007), *How Rich Countries Got Rich...and Why Poor Countries Stay Poor.* London: Constable.

Reinert E (2012), Economics and the Public Sphere, Working Papers in Technology Governance and Economic Dynamics, no. 40.

Reinert E (2016), Giovanni Botero (1588) and Antonio Serra (1613): Italy and the birth of development economics. In: E Reinert et al. (eds.), Handbook of Alternative Theories of Economic Development, Cheltenham, UK, Northampton, MA, USA: Edward Elgar, pp. 3–41.

Ritchie F (2014), Resistance to change in government: risk, inertia and incentives, Economics Working Paper Series 1412, University of the West of England, Bristol.

Rocha L (2000), Syntactic autonomy, cellular automata, and RNA editing: Or why self-organization needs symbols to evolve and how it might evolve them. In: J Chandler and G Van de Vijver (eds.), *Closure: Emergent Organizations and Their Dynamics.* Annals of the New York Academy of Sciences, Vol. 901, New York, pp. 207–23.

Russell A (2005), Standardization in history: A review essay with an eye to the future. In: S Bolin (ed.), *The Standards Edge: Future Generations.* Ann Arbor, MI: Sheridan Books, available in: www.arussell.org/papers/futuregeneration-russell.pdf

Ruttan V (2006), Is War Necessary for Economic Growth?, Historically Speaking-Issues (merged papers), Clemons Lecture, University of Minnesota, October 9.

Schiff E (1971), *Industrialization without National Patents – the Netherlands 1869–1912; Switzerland 1850–1907.* Princeton, NJ: Princeton University Press.

Schilling M (2000), Toward a general modular systems theory & its application to interfirm product modularity, *Academy of Management Review* 25(2): 312–34.

Shengxiang S et al. (2017), Fear, anger, and risk preference reversals: An experimental study on a Chinese sample, *Frontiers in Psychology* 8: 1371.

Simon H (1962), The architecture of complexity, *Proceedings of the American Philosophical Society* 106(6) (December 12): 467–82.

Skocpol T (1979), State and revolution: Old regimes and revolutionary crises in France, Russia, and China, *Theory and Society* 7(½), Special Double Issue on State and Revolution (January–March): 7–95.

Slembeck P (2003), Ideologies, beliefs, and economic advice: A cognitive–evolutionary view on economic policy-making. In P Pelikan and G Wegner (eds.), *The Evolutionary Analysis of Economic Policy.* Cheltenham, UK: Edward Elgar, pp. 121–68.

Smith A [1776] (2005), *Wealth of the Nation.* The Pennsylvania State University, Electronic Classics Series

Stuart T and Sorenson O (2003), Liquidity events and the geographic distribution of entrepreneurial activity, *Administrative Science Quarterly* 48: 175–201, Temasek Review 2008.

Thaler RH and Sunstein CR (2008), *Nudge: Improving Decisions about Health, Wealth, and Happiness*. New Haven, CO: Yale University Press.

Toussaint E (2007), *The World Bank: A Critical Primer*. London: Pluto Press.

Ure A (1835), The Philosophy of Manufactures: or, An Exposition of the Scientific, Moral, and Commercial Economy of the Factory System of Great Britain. London: Charles Knight.

Valverde S and Solé R (2006), Self-organization and Hierarchy in Open Source Social Networks, SFI Working Paper: 2006-12-053.

Vasconcelos G (2010), From Hayek's spontaneous orders to Luhmann's autopoietic systems. *Studies in Emergent Order* 3: 50–81.

Viner J (1927), Adam Smith and laissez faire, *Journal of Political Economy* 35(2) (April): 198–232.

von Mises L [1922] (1981), *Socialism: An Economic and Sociological Analysis.*, Indianapolis: Yale University Press. Full text from Yale University edition, English Edition (1951).

von Mises L [1929] (2011), *Critique of Interventionism*. Alabama: Ludwig von Mises Institute.

Wade R [1990] (2003), *Governing the Market: Economic Theory and the Role of Government in East Asia's Industrialization*. Princeton, NJ: Princeton University Press.

Witt U (2003), Economic policy making in evolutionary perspective, *Journal of Evolutionary Economics* 13: 77–94.

Woo-Cumings M (ed.) (1999), *The Developmental State*. Ithaca: Cornell University Press.

Young A (1928), Increasing returns and economic progress, *The Economic Journal* 38(152): 527–42.

Further reading

Abramovitz M (1986), Catching up, forging ahead and falling behind, *Journal of Economic History* 66: 385–406.

Amaral L and Ottino J (2004), Complex networks: Augmenting the framework for the study of complex systems, *European Physical Journal B* 38: 147–62.

Anderson G (2001), To change China: A tale of three reformers, *Asia Pacific: Perspectives* 1(1) (May): 1–19.

Barabási L et al. (1999), Emergence of scaling in random networks, *Science* 286(5439): 509–12.

Bernier F (1891), *Travels in the Mogul Empire: A.D 1656–1668*. London: Constable. Electronic reproduction, New York, N.Y., Columbia University Libraries, 2006, available at www.columbia.edu/cu/lweb/digital/collections/cul/texts/ldpd_6093710_000/index.html.

Bolin S (ed.) (2002), *The Standard Edge*. Ann Arbor, MI: Sheridan Books.

Brusoni S et al. (2001), Knowledge specialisation and the boundaries of the firm: Why firms know more than they make, *Administrative Science Quarterly* 46: 597–621.

Buchanan J (1979), *What Should Economists Do?*, Indianapolis, Liberty Press

Buchanan J (1986), *Liberty, Market and State*. Brighton, UK: Wheatsheaf Books Ltd.

Burlamaqui L et al. (eds.) (2000), *Institution and the Role of State*. Massachusetts, USA, Cheltenham, UK: Edward Elgar.

Chang HJ (2009), Industrial Policy: Can We Go Beyond an Unproductive Confrontation?, APlenary Paper for ABCDE (Annual World Bank Conference on Development Economics) Seoul, South Korea, June 22–24.

Dosi G et al. (1994), The process of economic development: Introducing some stylized facts and theories on technologies, firms and institutions, *Industrial and Corporate Change* 3(1): 1–45.

Fallick B et al. (2005). Job hopping in Silicon Valley: Some evidence concerning the micro-foundations of a high technology cluster (October 2005). IZA *Discussion Paper* No. 1799.

Festré A and Garrouste P (2009), The economic analysis of social norms: A reappraisal of Hayek's legacy, *Review of Austrian Economics* 22(3): 259–79.

Friedman M [1962] (2002), *Capitalism and Freedom*. Chicago: The University Chicago Press.

Gandhi M (1930), *The Indian Cotton Textile Industry: Its Past, Present and Future*, The Book Company Limited, available at http://archive.org/details/indian cottontext031792mbp

Hauknes J and Smith K (2003), Corporate Governance and Innovation in Mobile Telecommunications: How did the Nordic Area Become a World Leader?, STEP Report, Oslo, R-12.

Hawkins R et al. (eds.) (1995), *Standards, Innovation and Competitiveness: Politics and Economics of Standards in Natural and Technical Environments*. Cheltenham, UK: Edward Elgar.

Holland S (1972), *The State as Entrepreneur: New Dimensions for Public Enterprise: The IRI State Shareholding*. London: Weidenfeld and Nicolson.

Kauffman S (1993), *Origins of Order: Self-Organization and Selection in Evolution*. Oxford: Oxford University Press.

Lakhwinder, S (2006), Globalization, national innovation systems and response of public policy, *MPRA Paper* No. 641, November.

Lall S (2000), Export performance, technological upgrading and foreign direct investment strategies in the Asian newly industrializing economies: With special reference to Singapur, Investment and Corporate Strategies, *Desarrollo Productivo 88,* CEPAL.

Lazonick W (2002), Innovative enterprise and historical transformation, *Enterprise & Society* (March): 3–47.

Maddison A (2007), *Contours of the World Economy, I-2030 AD: Essays in Macro-economic History*. Oxford: Oxford University Press.

Mako W and Zhang C (2003), *Management of China's State-Owned Enterprises Portfolio*, World Bank, Beijing, available at: www.thepresidency.gov.za/ElectronicReport/ downloads/volume_4/business_case_viability/BC1_Research_Material/302500_ CHAO_Management_enterprises.pdf

Metcalfe JS (1994), Evolutionary economics and technology policy, *Economic Journal* 104: 931–94.

Mookerji R (2013), *Local Government in Ancient India*. Hong Kong: Forgotten Books. (Original work published by Oxford University Press, 1920.)

Newman M (2003), The structure and function of complex networks, *SIAM Review* 45: 167–256.

Nozick R (1974), *Anarchy, State, and Utopia*. New York: Basic Books.

Schilling M and Steensma K (2001), The use of modular organizational forms: an industry-level analysis, *Academy of Management Journal* 44(5): 1149–68.

Schweitzer F et al. (2009), Economic networks: The new challenges, *Science* 325: 422–5, July 24.

Shih S et al. (2006), Building global competitiveness in a turbulent environment: Acer's journey of transformation. In: W Mobley and E Weldon (eds.), *Advances in Global Leadership, Volume 4*. Bingley, UK: Emerald, Wagon Lane, pp. 201–17.

Shipman A (1999), *The Market Revolution and Its Limits: A Price for Everything*. New York: Routledge.

Simon H (1981), *The Sciences of the Artificial*. Cambridge, MA: MIT Press.

Simon H (1991), Organizations and markets, *Journal of Economic Perspectives* 5: 25–44.

Smith A [1776] (2005), *Wealth of Nations*. The Pennsylvania State University, Electronic Classics Series.

Steele D (1987), Hayek's theory of cultural group selection, *The Journal of Libertarian Studies* III(2): 171–95.

Stuart T and Sorenson O (2003), Liquidity events, noncompete covenants and the geographic distribution of entrepreneurial activity, *Administrative Science Quarterly* 48(2): 175–201.

Sudgen R (1993), Normative judgments and spontaneous order: The contractarian element in Hayek's thought, *Constitutional Political Economy* 4(3): 393–424.

Sunita K and Aishetu K (2006), State enterprises what remains? *The World Bank Group*, Number 304, February.

Thomas P (1926), *Mercantilism and East Indian Trade: An Early Phase of the Protection vs. Free Trade Controversy*. London: P.S King & Son Ltd.

Usselman S (2002), *Regulating Railroad Innovation: Business, Technology and Politics in America, 1840–1920*. New York: Cambridge University Press.

Veblen T [1899] (1994), *The Theory of the Leisure Class*. New York: Dover Publications.

von Neumann J (1966), *The Theory of Self-Reproducing Automata*. Champaign, IL: University of Illinois Press.

Zywicki T (2004), Reconciling Group Selection and Methodological Individualism. *Research Paper*, George Mason Law & Economics, No. 04-12. April. Available at SSRN: http://ssrn.com/abstract=524402 or http://dx.doi.org/10.2139/ssrn.524402

4   National systems of innovation

State-based non-firm organizations (NFOs) as integrators

4.1 The origin of growth

The works of Abramowitz and Solow revealed the importance of technological change in economic development. In 1956, economist Moses Abramowitz showed that capital accumulation only accounted for 10–20 percent of US economic growth, whereas Solow in 1957 estimated that, in the United States, approximately 90 percent of the output per labor hour in the period 1909–49 was attributable to reasons other than capital accumulation. This "residual" was assumed as the recipe of *growth causes* other than tangible capital (Solow 1957, p. 319). It was later called technological change and identified as the major cause of innovation.

Until this period, and a great deal of time thereafter, technical change was treated as an exogenous element by economic analysts. The most important forerunner of these models can be found in the Harrod-Domar model, which was intended to explain economic development in terms of savings rates and capital productivity. Solow`s model was in fact an extension of Harrod–Domar's, whose principal contribution was the term "residual." Notwithstanding the variations, neoclassical notions such as perfect equilibrium or fully informed and isolated economic agents prevailed in the discussion on the constitutive of innovation and growth; decreasing returns of production factors being the most basic assumption. In presence of decreasing returns, in Solow's model, more production per capita cannot explain increasing labor productivity in the long term or major variations in the growth rates of GDP per capita in individual countries.

In this view, when output per unit of labor added (marginal product of labor in neoclassical jargon) inevitably falls, then gross investment become increasingly less capable to cover the existing stock of physical capital per employee.[1] In these circumstances there is only a certain level of investments that can maintain capital to labor ratio at the same level, given that depreciation and growing workforce work towards the reduction of capital per worker in the economy. Therefore, there are no more incentives for manufacturers to increase the level of capital per employee; i.e. growth stalls. The exogenous residual added by Solow explains why this does not happen in the long term.

In addition, in these models all firms can operate on the technological frontier because they have complete access to the stock of technological knowledge. In other words, the stock of knowledge is like an open book, and all firms will tend to adopt the best-practice techniques because they are considered to be absolutely informed and thus to act rationally. As technological knowledge was considered completely available and codified, early growth models placed the main emphasis on accumulating tangible capital through investment and an increased labor.

Later, also from a neoclassical view, Arrow (1962) tried to rectify this by demonstrating why the resource allocation in innovative activities[2] cannot be optimal. He emphasized the fact that the cost of producing innovation is mainly fixed, but the cost of reproducing it is very low. Moreover the innovative firm cannot appropriate all the returns of its investments because information can be non-excludable and not-rival, thus showing characteristics of a public good. This is the typical "market failure" argument that builds a rationale for government R&D investments in basic science. An additional aspect stressed by Arrow was the fact that these innovations could serve as input for other innovations. That is, they can provide increasing returns by using them. This would further reduce the current return prospects for the individual innovator in the long run.[3]

The above-mentioned insights plus the increasing awareness of the critical role played by technology in the economic growth gave rise to the New Growth Theory, which started seeing technology as an endogenous, [linear] outcome of an R&D investment function, and as investment in human capital formation. These models of innovation included for first time in the neoclassical models the category *increasing returns to scale* as the real engine of growth. It also indirectly provided a rationale for government investment (education, R&D etc.).[4] This element would increase the growth rate by raising the incentive to innovate. Models of this type, the second group of models in this theory, were pioneered by Romer (1990) and Aghion and Howitt (1992).

A first stream of these models conceived accumulation of knowledge as a by-product of company decisions to invest in physical capital (Romer 1986). Even if each individual firm faces diminishing returns and perfect competition, the collective investments in physical capital assure that each company, through spill-over effects, can benefit from new technologies, therefore contributing to overall increasing returns. An important assumption here is that knowledge cannot be kept a secret and therefore cannot be completely protected. When each company generates knowledge in the process of learning through work, it instantly becomes available to all and completely free.

Based on Schumpeter's insights the second group of models recognizes the implausibility of both free diffusion of knowledge (at least under current conditions) and its theorization as an incidental result of the firm activity. Consequently, elements such as imperfect competition (monopolies structures, power) and the existence of an independent research and development system (R&D) are introduced (for a discussion see Sredojević et al. 2016).

The growing emphasis given by these models (and economics in general) to innovation in the growth process has substantially contributed to policymakers (and many academics as well) to focus their attention to variables such as public and firm R&D as a major proxy for innovation. However, as further theoretical and historical evidence has shown, R&D, while consubstantial to innovation, does not induce necessarily innovation alone. It is a necessary, but not a sufficient, condition for innovation to emerge.

4.2 The necessity of a systemic approach to innovation: The neo-Schumpeterian approach

The major critique of the emphasis in R&D given by new growth models came from neo-Schumpeterian economists. Among the most conspicuous, Freeman (1995) argues for a more systemic rather than linear notion of both the innovation and development processes, in which not only interacting firms, but also, and fundamentally, their interaction with *non-firm organizations* defines the scope of the innovation process. Even if the form and nature of these network relationships necessarily differs among developing countries and high industrialized countries, they are to be found either in catch-up processes (in developing countries) or in radical innovation efforts (industrialized countries). To focus exclusively on R&D investments would be to ignore the diverse amount of networking mechanisms at work in the innovation process.

The most important element of the critique is based on the idea that these models assume that the innovation process follows a straightforward sequence (linear) from basic research, through large-scale R&D, to the introduction of the innovation into the economy. However, Freeman (1995) shows that the causation is a non-linear one, because there exist "feedback loops" from market and non-market institutions, as well as from production into the R&D system, which have not been taken into consideration. In his words,

> technical change [does] not depend just on R&D but on many other related activities, such as education, training, production engineering, design, quality control, etc. etc., nevertheless R&D measures [have been in the past] very frequently used as a surrogate for all these activities which helped to promote new and improved products and processes.
>
> (ibid., p. 10)

In this context, Freeman (1995, 2008) cites the failure of the Soviet Union as an example. As he states, the Soviet system was based on separate research institutes within the Academy system, whose links to enterprise-level R&D remained rather weak despite successive attempts to reform and improve the system in the 1960s and 1970s. The magnitude of the waste of potential was such that, when compared to the Japanese economy during the 1970s, the proportion of gross domestic expenditure on research and development (GERD) as a fraction of GNP was of 4 percent in the Soviet economy and 2.5 percent in the Japanese economy (Freeman 1995, 2008). Yet Japan grew faster because it used R&D in a more intensive way, thanks to the central role played in its industrial policy by several non-firm organizations; with MITI (Ministry of International Trade and Industry) the most representative (the example is also cited by Mazzucato 2011).

Likewise, Demirel and Mazzucato (2012) argue that even when policymakers tend to assume a direct causal link between R&D and growth, there is, surprisingly, little empirical evidence on the subject. They carried out a study of the role of R&D in the firm growth in the US pharmaceutical industry between 1950 and 2008, which seems to support the arguments made in Freeman (1995). Their econometric evidence suggests that the relationship seems far from being a simple one, since the criteria for a firm to grow are a mix between firm size and other different aspects of the firm's innovative activity. According to these authors, there is no clear-cut trade-off between R&D and firm output. They argue that it is necessary to have a more sophisticated understanding of the conditions under which R&D can lead to growth, and how these conditions reflect in different industries.

This last point is very important because, for instance, focusing on GERD can lead to the omission of the huge variation in R&D investment across industries, and even across firms within an industry. This can also lead to missing out on the variety of complementary levels of R&D spending by firms and governments. A relevant example at firm level is shown by Apple's R&D/sales ratio during the period 2007–12 in comparison to other smartphone producers.[5] Even when Apple's absolute R&D expenses grew at an annual rate of 33 percent they did not match the far higher sales growth rate. In fact, among 13 of its top competitors, Apple was positioned at the bottom three in terms of the amount of R&D per dollar sold. Still, Apple's sales were larger than those of its rivals (including the top three Microsoft, Google and Nokia, with impressive R&D growth).

Freeman (2008) argues, however, that it is no surprise that the measurable R&D system was seen as *the* source of innovations, given the fact that in-house R&D departments had become a very important institution in the most innovative firms since the beginning of the second industrial revolution in Western Europe and North America (specially the United States) at the end of the nineteenth century. Freeman (1995) establishes the inception of in-house R&D as a major institutional innovation initiated in Germany around 1870.[6] The prestige of the institution (in its public variant) was reinforced during and after World War II, as many innovative technologies arose from large government R&D projects.[7] A similar trend followed in all industrial countries in the 1950s and 1960s, but also in several developing nations (e.g. Argentina, India, Brazil, Israel) as they began to establish research councils, national R&D labs, and other scientific institutions.

These elements make it easier to understand why the R&D system was perceived by policymakers and many researchers as the very source of innovation. In this particular, Freeman (1995) states that the emphasis in knowledge accumulation provided by "the so-called 'New' Growth Theory has in fact only belatedly incorporated into neoclassical models the realistic assumptions which had become commonplace among economic historians and neo-Schumpeterian economists" (p. 6).

Indeed, the brief chronological account illustrated above shows us that general R&D has been a large contributor to basic research for a long time. But to assume that R&D alone is responsible for innovation rests on the further assumption that technology as information is perfectly and unmistakably codifiable. However, we know today that it is important to distinguish between sheer information and knowledge.

While information refers to well-defined blueprints and procedures, technological knowledge involves procedures of a much more tacit nature, often embodied in organizational practices and specific to each technological paradigm (Marengo et al. 2009; Nonaka and Krogh 2009; Dosi 1988; Nelson and Winter 1982; Polanyi 1962). The evolutionary theory argues that each organization has its own way to cope with this tacitness, which offers a rationale to explain why some succeed and others fail, while it also justifies the existence of a high organizational heterogeneity within an economy. It is not possible to define an optimal size firm or a neoclassical representative agent.[8] This is very relevant from the point of view of technology policy, because its focus of attention switches from promoting optimizing behavior in firms and industries to the need for promoting creativity and diversity of behavior as brilliantly described by Metcalfe (1995).

A firm may invest a lot in R&D, but it can fail to create the coordination mechanisms needed to advance a successful product. This is fundamentally true for high-tech industries, which are characterized by a high degree of compatibility between components and diverse pieces of knowledge. Innovation is far from being an individual and linear process. Strong historical evidence suggests that the innovator is not alone in its task (Lazonick 2011; Lazonick and O'Sullivan 2000; Cimoli et al. 2009; Dosi et al. 2003; Chang 2003a; Lundvall 2002, Freeman 1995, 2008). In fact, innovative firms often do not have all the necessary knowledge to introduce innovative process or products. In order to be able to innovate, they have to interact with suppliers and other sub-contractors (von Hippel 2005) but mostly with government non-firm institutions such as universities, regulatory bodies, etc. (Cimoli et al. 2009; Malerba 2002).

Even if we might rely on the concept of market failure to explain government-based R&D investments in basic research, it would not be appropriate to understand government R&D investments targeted to support specific industries or technologies. This is true because, as already suggested, innovative behavior, although usually introduced at the company level, actually results from a wider and highly heterogeneous institutional structure that is, in turn, embedded in a unique sociohistorical context. Each sector has its own dynamic, and each nation has its own set of institutions to rely on. Therefore, it is not realistic to define one type of market failure, neither to legitimize only one-size-fit-all types of government intervention (as the neoclassic economics does) (Metcalfe 1995). All these elements make processes such as technological and institutional change cumulative, highly interdependent (relational) and very uncertain. For that reason, a systemic (network) approach would be more useful to understand both innovation and economic development.

4.3 Systems of innovation as networks

The very emphasis of a relational approach to innovation rests on the fact that it is not necessarily the stock of R&D but the ability of certain institutions of circulating and diffusing knowledge throughout the economy what defines the success of the technical/organizational change. The system approach bases on the role of uncertainty and cognitive limits to firms' or individuals' ability to gather and process information for their decision-making, known as "bounded rationality" (Simon 1991). Additionally, as already mentioned, there is a strong tacit component in every production process, given that not all technological knowledge can be easily codifiable. This kind of knowledge, which is highly complementary to codified information, is considered to be an immanent feature of every practical business activity (Lundvall 2002; Dosi 1988; Cimoli et al. 2009).

This systemic ability to deal with the uncertainty created by the growing division of labor created by specialization is what the neo-Schumpeterian literature on innovation calls *System or innovation approach*. Even if there is no canonical definition of innovation systems there is some consensus among several authors on the fact that the definition can be found in Freeman (1987, 1995); Lundvall (2002); Nelson (1993). For instance, Mazzucato (2011, p. 63) and Godin (2007) cites Freeman's definition of systems of innovation as "the network of institutions in the public and private sectors whose activities and interactions initiate, import, modify and diffuse new technologies." Godin (2007) cites Lundvall's definition of "the elements and relationships which interact in the production, diffusion and use of new, and economically useful, knowledge." (p. 7) A more straightforward definition is given by Nelson (1993) as a set of institutions whose interactions determine the innovative performance of national firms (p. 4).

To take a systemic approach to understand innovation means to conceive innovation systems as a relational concept that, as Freeman's definition states, can be understood and represented as a networked structure. Mazzucato (2011) argues that innovation requires a highly networked economy that enables knowledge to be shared. In Chapters 2 and 3 we referred to the parallels between the notion of hub-dominated networks and the neo-Schumpeterian theory.

An innovation system can be regional, sectoral or national (Lundvall 2002). These concepts do not actually need to be (and are not in fact) incompatible given that, within a national innovation system, there are specializations zones (innovative clusters, industrial districts, productive networks), which are directly or indirectly related to the national level (Lundvall 2007). However, given the available historical evidence, it is plausible to assume that the national dimension of the system of innovation plays the most crucial role in the shaping of new organizational and productive structures. Its influence in the causality of the process of technological change must not be linear, but it is nevertheless essential. We have commented on this in detail in the previous chapter when referring to the role of the state as designer of the industrial policy.

4.4 Defining NFOs

In the previous chapter, several examples and insights have been advanced about the ubiquitous presence of government-based *non-firm organizations* (NFOs) in most of the development efforts (particularly) since the nineteenth century (and even earlier). This section is aimed at both briefly defining the scope of the definition and contextualizing it in terms of the concepts related to it.

This study relies on the NFO notion advanced by Malerba (1999, 2002, 2006), who defines NFOs as a kind of agent which "support in various ways innovation, diffusion of new technologies and production of firms within a sectoral system"; and whose role "greatly differs among sectors" (Malerba 2002, p. 255). NFOs are not to be confused with non-governmental organizations (NGOs); as most of the NFOs involved in the process are government agencies or other public bodies. Neither should NFOs be confused with non-profit-organizations (NPOs) as some of the NFOs could actually be for-profit organizations. Both NGOs and NPOs could be part of the system, but are not, by far, the exclusive part of it. Typical examples of NFOs include universities, research centers, government agencies, regulatory bodies, financial institutions, venture capitals, technical associations, trade-unions, etc.

On the other hand, we have also seen that not all kinds of NFOs play a central role in the economy. As stated in Chapter 3, even when some private firms (or NFOs[9]) play a very important role in the innovation process, the evidence points specifically to (of course not all with the same intensity) government-based NFOs as a crucial element in determining the way an economy acquires, develops, modifies and diffuses new technologies and organizational methods throughout an economy (Cimoli et al. 2009; Block 2008; Freeman 2008; Chang 2003a, 2003b; Lundvall 2002) (below the point is developed in further detail). In this study it is argued that the role of private NFOs (e.g. financial institutions) has been more effective when combined with, or embedded in, a well-articulated technology policy.

That applies particularly to the case of private for-profits NFO during the last decades. For instance, Lazonick (2008, 2011) observes how the growing financialization of the New Economy in the United States may have become a real threat to the sustainability and stability of the system. In particular, Lazonick and Tulum (2011) argue that this also applies to the business model of the US American biotech industry. Pisano (2006) reaches similar conclusions from a different perspective.

Well-known example of private NFOs are venture capitalists. They were said to be the crucial element by financing innovative risky projects in young companies with growth potential. However, when we see their record, at least in the biotechnology industry, we see that they actually hinder innovation in its current form. Indeed, the ability to do an initial public[10] offering (IPO), even without a product, is the major inducement for venture capital to fund the biotech industry, since it does not have to wait until revenues are generated from a product to get returns on its investments (exit option). For example, during the period 1991–2004, 88 percent of biotechnology companies were making IPOs, but only 20 percent had any product on the market. The vast majority were still in pre-clinical and discovery phases (Pisano 2006, pp. 139, 155). In most of the industries, venture capitalists focus on areas of low technological complexity and low capital investments (Mazzucato 2011). Similarly to private venture capital, other supposedly *dynamically incoherent hubs* within the biopharma network of innovation, such as the private big pharma companies, actually focused on less risky variations of existing drugs (Light et al. 2011; Boldrin and Levine D 2008).

In contrast, a government-based NFO such as the US National Institutes of Health (NIH) has been, according to Lazonick and Tulum (2011) the nation's most important investor in knowledge creation in the medical field. The authors emphasize that without it, venture capital and public equity funds would not have entered into the industry. Between 1993 and 2004, 75 percent of new molecular entities were financed by public NFOs such as NIH in the USA or MRC in the UK (Mazzucato 2011). These NFOs satisfy the condition of being a *hub* within the system, in network terms; a highly connected node, or an organization; with links to many other organizations.

The importance of context embedded NFOs in the innovation process has been particularly stressed in the literature of both *national and sectoral systems of innovations.* For example, from a sectoral perspective, non-firm organizations are given a lot of importance. In fact, one core insight of this theoretical framework is that "the relationship between countries' international performance and sectoral systems may be mediated by national institutions and non-firm organizations that form national systems of innovation and production" (Malerba 1999, p. 27).

Conversely, more traditional approaches on innovation tend to ignore the role of NFOs. For instance, while acknowledging the tremendous progress made by more traditional industrial economics approaches, Malerba (2002) has also stressed that "in most of these studies, however, not much emphasis has been paid to the role of non-firm organizations [...]" (p. 247). As more traditional notions he refers to, for example, "the transaction costs approach, sunk cost models, game theoretic models of strategic interaction and cooperation, and econometric industry studies" (ibid.). In the same line, Mazzoleni and Nelson (in Cimoli et al. 2009) admit that

> there has been a tendency of many economists writing about innovation to write as if firms are the full story, neglecting other kinds of institutions

that are involved in the process that support and mold innovation in many modern industries.

(p. 385)

Further recognition of the subject can be found in Coe et al. (2008), which acknowledge that "[a]lthough the material economic processes of production, distribution and consumption are at the core" of a production network (they originally refer to global production network, but the analysis is similar for other levels) "these processes are not simply driven by 'firms'" (p. 280). In our previous discussion on the network approach in Chapter 2, we already cited Coe et al. (2008) stating that thinking the innovation system in terms of the networked approach allows us to identify a wide range of "non-firm actors" involved in the system.

In the next sections we will explore in greater detail a possible theoretical framework, in which the role of NFOs can be situated, as well as the importance of including government-based NFOs in the theoretical discourse on innovation. Likewise, we will refer to several other examples of the centrality of these organizations in the innovation process.

4.5 The national dimension of the systems of innovation: The role of state's NFOs

As stated previously, a system of innovation can be subdivided into several levels, existing usually interplay between these levels (Freeman 2004; Lundvall 2002). But, as suggested in Chapter 3, historically, government institutions and policies have directly or indirectly always been behind almost all forms of emulation and technological change. Relying on that kind of evidence, in the present study it is argued that it is the *national level* of the system the entity that determines the learning capabilities of the rest of the innovation system.

The notion of national is made here with an emphasis put in the role of the government. Private firms or any other type of institution could reach national importance, but it is difficult to find technological-frontier-based innovative firms or industries within a country whose government has failed to encourage in some form. That is the reason why this dimension has special significance as a conceptual tool. This conceptual tool has been referred in the innovation literature as the *national system of innovation approach*. Within this context, the present study stresses the central role played by government-based NFOs in the process of innovation.

The above mentioned general definition of system of innovation was actually developed originally for the national framework (Freeman 1987; Nelson 1993; Lundvall 2002). For example, the interacting elements referred to by Lundvall (2002) in his definition "are either located within or rooted inside the borders of a nation state" (p. 4). Cimoli et al. (2009) argues that "institutions and policies addressing technological learning have to do with the construction of *national system of production and innovation* [emphasis original]" (p. 22).

Freeman (1995) places the antecedents of the concept in the Friedrich List's *The National System of Political Economy* (1841). As already mentioned in Chapter 3, List was strongly influenced by Hamilton's ideas as well as by Daniel Raymond's notions on the American System. These notions helped him to develop a very influential view on industrial upgrading and innovation. "Not only did List anticipate these essential features of current work on national systems of innovation, he also recognized the interdependence of the import of foreign technology and domestic technical development" (p. 6). In addition, by targeting Jean Baptiste Say (but also Adam Smith) in his arguments, he also put great emphasis on the role of the state in coordinating and carrying through long-term policies for industry and the economy (ibid.).

The current notion of national system of innovation addresses major new developments in the world economy which deeply affect the whole concept, and were not present at List's time (ibid.). These elements include the rise of in-house professionalized R&D in industry, and the rise of multinational (or transnational) corporations (TNCs), operating production establishments in many different countries and increasingly also setting up R&D outside their original base. In particular, the problem of how the globalization affects the role on the nation-state has led to new accommodation of the concept. However, in principle, the Listian notion of a strong nation state remains the core element.

For instance, Coe et al. (2008) observes that "systems of governance and regulation are now more multiscalar, but national states retain a *critical role* within them" (p. 279). All the elements present in global innovation systems are regulated within some kind of political structure whose basic unit is the national state. International institutions exist only because they are legitimated by national states; subnational institutions are commonly subservient to the national level (although, of course, the situation could be more complex in federal political systems[11]) (Coe et al. 2008; Malerba 2002).

In this context, the object of a good industrial policy would be precisely to improve the country's ability to absorb or generate new knowledge as much as possible, so it can bring its capabilities as close to the frontier of the technological regime of the sector as possible and integrate them into the economy. Reinert (2012) argues that "productivity increases must take place inside the synergies of a finely woven web of diversified economic activities, all subject to increasing returns (a 'National Innovation System')" (p. 6).

In fact, the centrality of the *national level* the of innovation systems has been theoretically worked out, from different and sometimes conflicting perspectives, by a growing number of literature in the fields of both development (Cimoli et al. 2009; Chang 2002, 2009; Hirschman 1958; Abramovitz 1986, Reinert 1999, 2007) and (specially neo-Schumpeterian) innovation economics (Freeman 1995, 2008; Lundvall 2002; Cimoli et al. 2006; Lazonick 2002, 2006, 2011; Nelson 1993. This body of literature is further complemented by a convincing amount of historical evidence composed of both country-based and cross-country cases, which strongly suggest the notion of innovative firms and industries generally emerging as a result of explicit national government developmental efforts.

4.6 The sectoral systems of innovation

Systems of innovation can also be defined sectorally. They are delimited to specific groups of technologies or products and can be, but are not automatically, restricted to one sector or industry. A working definition of sectoral innovation system is given by Malerba (2002) as "a set of new and established products for specific uses and the set of agents carrying out market and non-market interactions for the creation, production and sale of those products" (Malerba 2002, p. 250).

In contrast to traditional industrial economics, the literature on sectoral systems pays much more attention to the role of NFOs and their role within the complex interdependencies created by agents' heterogeneity and complementarities, as well as to both the knowledge base and the learning process within firms and industries. Since each sector has its own basic technologies, learning regimes, inputs and demand compositions, it is important to know which institutions contribute to the innovative performance of a given sector.

Both national (patent system, business law, etc.) and sectoral institutions (labor market, sector specific financial organizations, disclosure agreements in software sector or regulation in biopharmaceutical sector) may affect sectoral systems of innovation (Malerba 1999, 2002, 2006). The idea of differences among sectors is today present in the whole literatures on development economics and innovation (from an evolutionary point of view see e.g. Marengo et al. 2009; Cimoli et al. 2009; Dosi et al. 2006).

According to Malerba (2002), the literature on sectoral innovation systems does not only provide empirical evidence of "the existence of differences across sectoral systems in the patterns of innovative activities,"[12] but also, "for each sectoral system, of similarities across countries" (e.g Malerba 2002, p. 253; Malerba and Orsenigo 1996, cited in Malerba 2002; Malerba 2006; Nelson and Rosenberg 1993; and Mowery and Nelson 1999). This means that technological regimes within an industry across countries will be more or less the same. The notion of technological regime can be found in Nelson and Winter (1982) and refers to the environment in which a firm operates, i.e., the specific learning requirements of the industrial sector and the way firms innovate technologies and access to markets.

However, at the same time, it does not mean that any country engaged in developing a given industry will develop the same set of institutions. This is the reason why the interplay between sectoral systems and national systems is a key aspect of this approach. Indeed, this interplay might be interpreted in terms of studying "the role of national institutions in affecting some basic cross-country 'invariant' features of the structure and dynamics of a sectoral system" (Malerba 1999, p. 27).

The last-mentioned element brings light to the discussion on the functionality of institutions; led by scholars of the Institutionalist Political Economy approach. For example, Chang (in Chang 2007) argues that "the big problem of the orthodox literature on institutions and development is its inability to clearly distinguish between forms and the functions of institution" (p. 19). He speaks of a "form-fetish" that had led to a dangerous denial of institutional diversity (p. 20). However, in actual fact, growing empirical evidence on such a diversity; and on the failures of institutional transplantation promoted by the "one size fit all" vision, is telling us that the same function (e.g. coordination, learning and innovation, income distribution and social cohesion, ibid., p. 18) can be performed by different institutional forms (see also Malerba 2006; Cimoli et al. 2009).This is why it is important to have knowledge of real-life institutions (the historic-comparative methodology proposed by Lazonick 2002) to be able to theorize on their role in innovation and economic development. This discussion is quite relevant in the analysis of sectoral systems.

> Sectoral systems have their own specificities in terms of technology, demand, knowledge, complementarities, firms, networks, institutions and dynamics. So differences across sectoral systems may be high. However, in a country, sectoral systems may be greatly affected by the national organisations and institutions, such as the national financial system, education, labor markets, intellectual property rights, and so on. As a consequence, some similarities among sectoral systems within a country may exist and those similarities may be different from the ones of another country.
>
> (Malerba 1999, p. 26)

Even when, according to this approach, sectoral features tend to remain invariant across countries, national innovation systems affect the absolute values of innovative variables (such as entry, concentration, turbulence and so on).

At the same time sectoral systems can also influence national systems of innovations. Certain sectoral organizations that had played a central role in a given sector may become national by contributing to develop new sectors, which in turn may lead to the creation of new institutions aimed to enhance the development of the latter. In other words, there is a two-way interaction between new technologies and institutions (Chang 2010; Reinert 2007). This interdependent and *re-constitutive* relationship is inherent to complex systems.

Within the sectoral system framework, "innovation is considered to be a process that involves systematic interactions among a wide variety of actors for the generation and exchange of knowledge relevant to innovation and its commercialization" (Malerba 2006, p. 14). Because all these elements are closely connected, it follows that their change over time results in co-evolutionary processes and this in turn implies the existence of path-dependency, which may lock sectoral systems into inferior technologies (Arthur 1989).This is, "the cumulative and collective character of the learning that generates innovation can pose barriers to further innovation when such innovation requires a new cumulation path and a new collective process" (Lazonick and O'Sullivan 2000).

However, when discussing the famous example of QWERTY,[13] Lazonick and O'Sullivan (2000) also argue that "it does not appear that, in the transitions from mechanical to electromechanical to electronic word-processing technologies, the QWERTY path dependency has posed any barriers whatsoever to *organizational* learning" (p. 98). This path dependency may well have survived over a century of technological change because the skills involved in typing were successfully segmented from the organizational learning involved in producing innovations in the machines that typists use. The fact that no business organizations came along to break the QWERTY path dependency is because of the limits to cumulative and collective learning in this particular activity (ibid.). The implication is that

> if one wants to look at the problem of the relation between learning and innovation that is raised by the literature on path dependency, one must take some care in identifying the critical sources and locations of organizational learning that have enabled major corporations to become dominant in the first place and that, in a changed competitive environment, block the innovation process.
>
> (ibid., p. 98)

These elements bring us to the question, "How do established companies react to a competitive threat from the appearance of technological change?" A closer look reveals that, as mentioned in the previous chapter, established companies find it difficult to deal with new disrupting technologies "because the organizational capabilities they had developed to establish a dominant technological and market position may be unsuited to organizing the transformations in technologies and markets that the new competition requires" (ibid., p. 99). The process is so uncertain and potentially expensive, that no one wants to afford it alone. On the other side, new entrants with new technologies are very often spin-offs of government-based NFOs. It seems to be that only (mostly government-based) sectoral and national organizations are able to deal in the long term with the uncertain new market and technological conditions (we will get into details about this point later in this chapter).

Further perspectives from which the notion of sectoral systems of innovation can be explored derive from the analysis of the composition of government allocation on R&D. As already mentioned, to focus on GERD, as proxy for knowledge accumulation; can be misleading because it can conceal important differences across industries and even among firms within a given industry. This phenomenon was also pointed out early on by Malerba (1992), who argued; in accordance with Nelson and Winter (1982), that learning by firms lies at the root of *incremental* change in industry. He also argues that "a variety of learning processes" (not only by doing in clear reference to Arrow's notion) is present within firms; each of them being linked to a specific source of technological and organizational knowledge (p. 857). Similar arguments were made in the pioneering works of Pavitt (1984) and Dosi (1988). Relying on empirical evidence extracted from a number of industries, they advanced sophisticated ideas on technological change and innovation. Among other things, two elements are recurrent in this literature: limits of total R&D constraints and collective character of the innovation process.

For example, Pavitt (1984) developed taxonomy of firms according to the activity they carry out and the sector they belong to. He advanced the existence of strong sectoral diversity and the need for a better knowledge of the "technological opportunities and constraints" that govern the behavior of the firm (p. 368). In identifying some sectoral patterns of technological change, Pavitt (1984) also suggested the inappropriateness of establishing a linear relationship between total R&D and innovation (he speaks of output diversification). He rather referred to a messy relationship between variables, non-linearity, etc. This will be especially true in science-based industries, because these industries provide many possible path of technological diversification.

In the same line of argumentation, and relying on the figures of six industrial economies[14] at that time, Dosi (1988) argued that "within the broad picture of national R&D investments, one observes stark intersectoral differences in the allocation of resources to research" (p. 1123). For example he cites figures of the US-based National Science Foundation on the composition of the US R&D expenditures and observes that about one tenth was devoted to basic research (80 percent financed by government), while one-quarter (50 percent financed by government) went to applied research, and the rest to development.

Also based in the Statistics of the National Science Foundation; Mazzucato (2011) provides figures for 2008 in the US and confirms the just mentioned trend. She observes that while government expenditures on R&D made only 26 percent of GERD (private sector 67 percent), it provided 57 percent of basic research when considering this indicator separately (private sector 18 percent). The rest is provided by universities and colleges; and other NFOs. The differences are more striking when the GERD is disaggregated in sectoral patterns (ibid.).

In short, the notion of *Sectoral systems…* brings important suggestions to theoreticians and policymakers. From a theoretical point of view it draws attention to the institutional variety that underlies the development of similar sectors in different national systems of innovation. This is relevant for example when considering the external sources of knowledge that support the learning processes in firm and industries. The fact that external sources must be considered was early argued by Malerba (1992). At the same time it is telling us that a variety of learning processes can be found across the different sectors. In terms of policymaking, the concept is also suggesting that governments that want to support technological change are required to invest not only in a certain industry and then leave things to the market, but also to selectively target the specific learning processes that might better fit their endeavor.

Additionally, the notion of *Sectoral systems…* is also suggesting that there is no point in copying mimetically the institutions of other sectoral systems.

According to Malerba (1999) "there is no way to identify an 'optimal' and 'coherent' sectoral system. So countries may differ in the role played by some sectoral elements as a result of past history and coevolutionary processes" (p. 27). In order for a country to achieve international performance in a given sector, it would be more important to see how their own national system of innovation can contribute to foster the new sector (see Malerba 2006 for further discussion, specifically referred to catching-up countries).

Similarly, it is not enough to know how to develop the sector, but also to know how the sector can contribute to international performance. According to the Other Canon School (see Reinert 2007), economic development is activity-specific because not all industries and technologies offer the same windows of innovation. In this sense, to look for the most close-to-the-frontier technologies will improve the future chances of economic growth. In one way or another, to understand the sectoral differences and their relation to the national institutions and to international performance is crucial for economic development.

4.7 A network within networks: The theory of the innovative business enterprise

As Freeman (1995) states, the production process takes place within firms. This means it is important to know how to make firms more innovative and to investigate their nature and internal processes as economic institutions, because they are the main container of technology. To deal with this subject has been in the central agenda of several approaches in fields such as industrial organization economics, strategic management, evolutionary economics and innovation economics. However most of the theories of the firm, even if they deviate from the unattainable neoclassical paradigm, tend to downplay the relevance of the factors external to the firm. More importantly, most of the firm conceptualizations in these fields have been made from an individual methodological perspective, which has prevented researchers from understanding the relational nature of innovation.

Nevertheless, it has become gradually more common place for business scholars and economists to accept the fact that firms need to interact with other firms to be able to innovate, even when most of them insist in affirming that to develop radically innovative capabilities remains a key managerial role (Teece 2007; Teece et al. 1997; Nonaka and Takeuchi 1995; Nonaka and Krogh 2009). In the field of innovation economics, the sectoral and national approaches have extended the analysis boundaries by including non-firm organizations as critical agents within the system (Malerba 1999, 2002; Freeman 1995, 2008; Pavitt 1984).

Recently; and somewhat as a sort of symbiosis between the firm-based approach and the systemic approach, new and more encompassing theories have begun to accept the role of other (private, public, private-public etc.) non-firm actors in the innovative performance of firms and in the creation of both cutting-edge technologies and their respective markets. In particular, *the theory of the innovative business enterprise* proposed by Lazonick (2002) represents a very interesting heterodox approach to firm theory, which pursues to integrate history and theory in the analysis of the innovative firms (see also Lazonick 2011 2008; Lazonick and O'Sullivan 2000).

According to Lazonick (2002, 2006, 2008, 2011) the firm's ability to innovate is mediated by three important social conditions: *Strategic control* is meant to transform strategy into innovation and is defined as a set of relations giving decision-makers the power to allocate the firm's resources in innovative strategies. The *financial commitment* is meant to transform finance into innovation and is defined as the ability to ensure the allocation of funds to sustain long–term projects, i.e. patient capital; and *Organizational integration*, which is described as "a set of relations that creates incentives for people to apply their skills and efforts to organizational objectives." This last condition will be further developed in the next section.

The theory of innovative business enterprise suggests taking a closer look at the social conditions strategic, financial and organizational related to the institutions under which innovative outcomes occur. This perspective pursues to understand how societies can create a corporate governance system that ensures strategic decision makers to have the abilities and incentives to make investments in innovative strategies (Lazonick and O'Sullivan 2000).

The theories of the optimizing firm take technologies and markets as given entities, and support the strategy of companies adapting themselves to given conditions. This is what Lazonick (2002) and Foster (2005) call *constrained-optimization methodology*, the neoclassic firm being the most obvious example of this methodology. However, other supposedly non–neoclassical approaches of the firm also fail to get rid of this way of thinking, namely of assuming given technological and market conditions in a perfect market.

For example Lazonick (2002) argues that in the Coasian-Williansonian notion, the most important task consists of optimizing firm performance by reducing transaction costs arising from asymmetric information between agents, without actually engaging in the real causes of innovation (see Lazonick 2002 for a detailed discussion). He also states that the Williamsonian notion of *asset specifity*,[15] while useful under different assumptions, is not represented here as a social-relational property of the system but in the terms of the neoclassical methodological tradition, i.e. as a "given constraint on the behaviour and performance of the firm" (ibid., p. 13).

A similar limitation is found in the resource-based approach, which also relies on the idea of asset specificity. Even when this perspective points out the importance of "knowledge alongside other costly to-imitate resources for competitive advantage" (Nonaka and Krogh 2009, p. 636), it takes as given the fact that firms have heterogeneous resource endowments (Rumelt 1984; Wernerfelt 2002; Barney 1991; Conner and Prahalad 1996; Dierickx and Cool 1989). Consequently, It does not provide a theory of the organizational success that explains how a particular firm (o group of firms) reached and maintains an advantageous position within an industry[16] (a very detailed critical discussion in Lazonick 2002, pp. 28–34, see also Teece et al. 1997, pp. 513–15).

In contrast to the above-mentioned, the theory of the innovative firm suggests that innovative firms cannot behave as optimizing firms, because innovation is an uncertain process, where relevant information is not just hidden or asymmetric (as the agency theory proposes) but unknown to the participants in the process. Therefore it would not be possible for a firm to follow "market" signals closely in order to enter or remain in an industry, and it cannot be done in isolation. As previously discussed, the idea of "markets" as crucial devices of resource allocation; "undermines the ability of particular economic actors to exercise extraordinary control over the resource allocation process" (Lazonick 2002, p. 5). In fact, "the existence in advanced economies of not only strong governments but also powerful business enterprises raises questions about the role of organizations and markets in generating superior economic performance" (ibid., p. 6).

We already cited Lazonick and O'Sullivan (2000) when stating that a theory of innovative enterprise must be embedded within a theory of an innovative economy, which may reveal that organizational learning and strategic management (at firm level) can be not only the cause, but more probably the effect of external processes that can generate innovation. Lazonick (2006) argues that to understand the way in which the technological trajectory of national industries requires a theory of economic development which includes the social conditions enabling innovating firms to exist. Therefore, the social conditions for an innovative firm to exist are not only "social" because they are part of a corporate culture internal to a given company,[17] but also because they are embedded in a network of relations external to the firm, which includes firm and (predominantly government-based) non-firm organizations that are essential for the development of an economy. Seen from this perspective, these social conditions could be an equivalent of the "social capabilities" of Abramovitz (1986, p. 387).

Lazonick and O'Sullivan (2000) observe that the actual dynamic of the innovation process rests on the "*interaction* between cumulative and collective learning *within* enterprises and cumulative and collective learning *across* enterprises" (p. 92). As already mentioned in Chapter 2, Coe (2008) argues that firms need to be conceptualized as relational networks embedded within wider networks of social actors, with varying degrees of imbrications and interconnection among them. Firm's boundaries are legally defined, but functionally diffuse. To accept that they are part of a broader ecology of agents shows promising fruitful prospects for bringing together *system-specific* and firm-*specific* categories and for exploring the creation of new relational concepts, which help to better explain the dynamic of innovation. We argue that one of these concepts is *organizational integration*. Hereafter we will engage in a more detailed theoretical and evidence-based discussion on this concept.

4.8 The concept of organizational integration

Although the just mentioned conditions are far from being the only conditions for an innovative business enterprise to exist, they pose in any case a realistic point of departure for our analysis. For example, it is plausible to assume that firms need to overcome high degrees of, and several types of, uncertainties (e.g. market, technology and competitive uncertainties) to become innovative. According to the theory of the innovative business enterprise, to face uncertainty in a more proper way requires the integration of all the activities involved in the innovation practice. Lazonick (2002) intends to capture this process in the concept of *organizational integration*.

The organizational integration (OI) has been chosen as the condition to analyze because, to a degree, it includes the other two. OI implies the existence of both financial commitment and strategic control.[18] According to Lazonick (2002) OI is "[t]he critical determinant of the success of an innovative strategy" (ibid., p. 14). OI is defined as "a set of social relations that provides participants in a complex division of labor with the incentives to cooperate in contributing their skills and efforts toward the achievement of a common goal" (ibid., p. 14). According to Lazonick (2011), it can be said an organizational success is when an economy shows good performance, because governments, businesses and other organizations are all working together to develop and utilize a society's productive resources.

The theory of the innovative business enterprise, and specifically the concept of OI, has been built relying, but also reflecting critically, on several theoretical approaches on the nature of the firm and on their respective articulations of the notion of organizational learning (e.g. Penrose 1959; Chandler 1977; Williamson 1975; Teece et al. 1997). Lazonick (2002) argues that OI is an essential social condition for an industry to engage in organizational learning. The notion of organizational learning stems from the evolutionary-based management literature (Teece et al. 1997; Senge 1990; Nonaka and Takeuchi 1995; Nonaka and Krogh 2009) and it basically refers to the ability of business organizations to absorb and create new knowledge and capabilities.

According to the theory of innovative business enterprise, organizational learning can be achieved by combining two important components of OI, one functional and another hierarchical. Functional integration refers to the process of developing new capabilities resulting from the combination of different activities, while hierarchical integration refers to ability to bring differently positioned activities into the learning process. Functional integration may not involve hierarchical integration. It can be the case of functional integration being carried out between components, whose relationship is neither formally nor dynamically hierarchical (e.g. research consortia, some mergers and alliances etc.). However, the point stressed by Lazonick and O'Sullivan (2000) is precisely that, when a hierarchy exists, sustainable and much more effective functional integration should be preceded or accompanied by hierarchical integration.

The term of hierarchical integration is being used in the dynamic sense stressed by Simon (1962), i.e. as a set of hierarchically yet interdependent subsystems, whose functioning needs to be modularized in order to reduce complexity, but only to the extent allowed by interdependency (nearly decomposable systems). In social systems (such as organizations or sectoral and national economies) this means hierarchical systems, which can be separated into subsystems, but whose interaction between them remains far from negligible (pp. 473–5). As discussed in the previous chapter, this notion differs from the notion of "formal hierarchy" which is typically associated with the term hierarchy. In our view, the component of hierarchical integration proposed by the theory of innovative enterprise could be interpreted as an evolution from a more decomposable hierarchy (formal) to a more dynamic and less decomposable one. When this occurs, it can be said that a hierarchical integration has taken place.

The classic example cited by Lazonick and O'Sullivan (2000) describes how in post-war Japan "hierarchical integration of traditional blue-collar workers into the development and utilization of manufacturing technology laid the basis for functional integration as technology became more and more complex" (p. 89). This applies for intra and inter-firm relationships as well. For example they make reference to how during the 1980s, among other industries, the Japanese automobile industry became well known for its ability to generate organizational learning through their supplier relations.

They make reference to Sako (1998) [updated version as Sako (2004)], which uses this example to suggest how different supplier relations across core companies operating in the same national environment may reveal differences in the internal organization of the learning processes in those companies. Indeed, recalling the terminology introduced in the previous chapter, we are referring here to agents with *strong sense of agency*, even if from a purely firm point of view. Later we will argue whether firms are the only (or the central) agents of change in this story. For now, however, it could be said that, at least from the firm and inter-firm levels, the Japanese hierarchical integration contrasts with the functional integration in US-American product systems, which was achieved by leaving shop-floor workers and manufacturing engineers (usually seen as second-class engineers) out of the learning process (Lazonick and Sullivan 2000).

As a result, during the 1970s and 1980s, Japanese firms challenged US firms in the "very industrial sectors in which even as late as the 1960s US corporations seemed to have held insurmountable competitive advantage[19]" (Lazonick 2006, p. 39).

> The unique ability of Japanese companies to transform technology acquired from abroad to generate new standards of quality and cost depended on not only the abilities of their engineers but also on the integration of shop-floor workers into organizational learning processes.
>
> (ibid., p. 43)

A building process of learning capabilities was developed over the last two decades. Institutional innovations such as cross-shareholding arrangements[20] and lifetime employment[21] allowed the emergence of a long-term learning culture and *organizational integration*.

While acknowledging that the organizational learning literature conceives organizational learning as a "dynamic and dialectical process," Lazonick and Sullivan (2000) also argues that most of this literature tends to ignore "the functional and hierarchical divisions of labour that exist within a company [...], and the ways in which these interactions must be changed to yield innovation in a particular industrial activity" (p. 77). The example of the US–Japanese comparison shows how critical is to understand that the influence of functional integration on innovation and international commercial prowess results from "the integration of product and process development, and the skill-base strategy that such integration entails" (ibid., p. 91).

It is further argued that to really grasp the scope of the concept of OI requires necessarily an analysis of functional integration in relation to the legacy of hierarchical integration or segmentation. By generally focusing on organizational behavior (e.g. core competencies), however, the typical strategic management-based literature on organizational learning tends to ignore that the transformation of technological and market conditions demands certain integration abilities, which is found only in certain organizations within an industry. A significant part of the strategic management and innovation literatures have focused on segmentation and outsourcing.

4.9 System integrators

To distinguish these functional and hierarchical divisions of labor in the learning process becomes much more important when we consider this phenomenon in the light of the complex product industries (Marengo et al. 2009), also called complex products systems in Dosi et al. 2003). In contrast to mass-produced goods, complex products are composed of multiple components and technologies, which make it unlikely to develop them in only one firm. As already mentioned in Chapter 2, to develop these kinds of products requires the participation of several technological fields, which involve the implementation of different forms of project collaboration (firm alliances, joint ventures partnerships, cross-licensing etc.).

This phenomenon has led to the emergence of a literature that has excessively focused in the benefits of vertical disintegration (modularity) within high-tech industries (Sanchez and Mahoney 1996; Schilling 2000; Langlois 2002). However, the literature on evolutionary systems integration argues, based on evidence from the complex industries, that actually increasing modularity tends to go "hand-in-hand with the increasing need of knowledge integration embodied in certain organisations or *system integrators*"[22] (Brusoni et al. 2001). Dosi et al. (2002) define system integrator as the agents that preserve interdependence, or in their words, as the agents who retain the knowledge about the "major overlappings and interfaces" within the complex product system. These integrating organizations are required to have the ability to move selectively, and simultaneously, up- and downstream to gain advantages in the marketplace, while integrating other small and medium size firms into the innovation process.

This literature provides abundant sectoral evidence which shows that, even in industries with well developed standards interfaces and a great deal of existing codified knowledge, system integrators have preserved a great deal of vertical integrated activities in order to maintain essential in-house capabilities. For example Brusoni (2001) finds this kind of evidence in a study about the UK-based chemical industry. Prencipe (2000) and Acha et al. (2007) shows the same for the aircraft engine industry and for the civil aircraft industry respectively. From a resource-based perspective, Hobday (in Prencipe et al. 2005, Chapter 4) argues that system integration has become the most important core capability of the modern high-technology firm. He provides evidence from the car industry (Sako 2004 and from the hard disc drive (HDD) industry (both cited from Prencipe et al. 2005),

In the same line can be mentioned the 1964 introduction of the IBM System/360 computer family, which unified the operating system software of the IBM product line.[23] This system provided the first instance of a broad "installed base" of computers with a single operating system and gave independent software vendors the opportunity to market the same product to a variety of users for the first time in the industry's history. The decision in 1969 of stepping down from the software business would have caused a disaster if IBM had not announced that it would continue to provide system software and previously produced applications and development tool software to both new and established users.[24]

The main argument behind this literature is that the nature of complex products usually differs from the nature of the knowledge which underlies their production. In other words, the boundaries of both products and knowledge do not match with each other. To outsource an activity does not necessarily mean to get rid of the capabilities behind it. In fact, the evidence shows that the more complex the system, the more important it is for leading firms to master interfaces and capabilities across different nodes of the network of specialized suppliers. To have developed in-house competences in most of the technological knowledge of the specific markets they compete in, puts them in a better position to design communication standards with the rest of the participants.

The notion of *system integration* is consistent with the idea of hub dominated networks discussed earlier in the study (see Chapter 2) and it also expresses the spirit and intention of Lazonick's concept of *organizational integration*. In fact, Lazonick and O'Sullivan (2000) argue that, instead of looking at (downstream or upstream) integration as a way to monopolistic control (neoclassic vision[25]) or as an optimal response to market failure (transaction cost theory[26]) one should analyze the roles of horizontal and vertical relations among enterprises within a particular industry by promoting collective and cumulative learning. That is, in order to generate higher quality, lower cost products, "one must also ask how the organizational integration of the activities *across* firms that participate in a specialized division of labour relates to the organizational integration of activities *within* these firms to generate organizational learning" (ibid., p. 92).

Referring to the vertical relation between suppliers and system integrators, Lazonick and O'Sullivan (2000) further argue that

> [t]he organizational integration of the component supplier into the organizational learning process of the systems integrator typically entails functional integration as well; the component supplier may provide distinct functional capabilities to the organizational learning process. But the relationship occurs within a well-defined hierarchical structure.
>
> (p. 95)

They also argue however, that emphasis in modularization in complex industries should not ignore that "[i]t is the system integrators that [develop a 'dominant design']" and "determine the allocation of knowledge between 'hidden information' that is proprietary and 'visible information' that is widely available to other companies" (p. 96).

They mention how IBM's strategy of outsourcing the development of key components (the microprocessor to Intel and the operating system to Microsoft) was critical to the development of modularization in the microcomputer industry (ibid.). Both Microsoft and Intel retained the right to sell their products to other companies (Lazonick 2008). Having gained strategic control over the development of software and hardware, both firms became system integrators in their own right.

However, the literature on system integration focuses on hidden information rather than uncertainty. That is, it does not provide an explanation on how new (disruptive) technological paths are created. To be sure, this literature, similar to the evolutionary-based dynamic capabilities perspective (Teece et al. 1997), provides profound evolutionary insights on the nature of knowledge and its management within an industry. The system integration perspective sees firms (and not the markets) as actual repositories of capabilities and competences "shaped by the firm's assets (positions) and its evolutionary path" (ibid., 524). Likewise, it concedes crucial importance to the notion of learning process as a collective phenomena and accepts inter-organizational learning as a way of taking advantage of technological opportunities created by "new scientific breakthroughs" (p. 523).

Yet, and also similar to the dynamic capabilities perspective (but also the resource-based, the neoclassical or the transaction costs perspectives), the system integration perspective "has nothing to say about how and whether changes in the national institutions of corporate governance support or proscribe strategies to develop and utilize 'dynamic capabilities'" (Lazonick and O'Sullivan 2000, p. 117; see also Lazonick 2006, 2008). They concede that

[r]esearch on organizational learning and strategic management has much to contribute to our understanding of the innovation process. But, ultimately, to say anything about economic performance – be it in terms of economic growth, income distribution, and/or financial stability – at either the microlevel of the enterprise or the macrolevel of the economy, this research must be linked explicitly to a theory of innovative enterprise, which in turn must be imbedded in a theory of an innovative economy.

(ibid., pp. 120–1)

As suggested above when discussing sectoral systems, Mazzoleni and Nelson (in Cimoli et al. 2009, pp. 378–408) point out that standard, but also most of evolutionary-based economic approaches are "mostly blind to[…] the important functions that public institutions are likely to play" (p. 385). Above was also discussed that the point has also been stressed by other Innovation System theorists such as Freeman (1995, 2008), Lundvall 2002, Malerba (2002) or Perez and Soete (1988) and Bell and Pavitt (1993). But even in this field, the treatment has been, with some exceptions, ambiguous, elusive, and non-committal. As Edquist (2001), a leading theorist of this tradition argues, a noteworthy

deficiency of the SI [System of Innovation] approach is that it lacks a component ("theory") about the role of the state. This is an important neglect, since the state and its agencies are important determinants of innovation in any SI.

(p. 17)

Indeed, the historical evidence shows that (usually government-based) NFOs play a crucial role in the way firms strategically allocate corporate resources, and in the way firms interact.

4.10 NFOs as locus of organizational integration

As subtly suggested above, the notion of system integration is consistent with the categorization advanced in Chapter 3. However, in our view, the concept of system integrator mixes the role of dynamically coherent agent with the role of dynamically incoherent ones (see Sections 3.7.3 and 3.7.4). Of course, in the context described by this literature, the system integrator actually plays the role of a dynamically incoherent agent, since, in contrast to other smaller specialized firms, the big integrated firms have the ability to influence the environment. But this mostly applies as long as firms engage in incremental innovation. As also commented on in the previous chapter, when exploring the risk-taking function of the state, firms are usually more efficient as incremental rather than as radical innovators. The level of "incrementality" varies, but in most cases the underlying principles of a given technology are known (e.g. Apple and Microsoft). Even if the most interesting part of the management literature acknowledges this, they still see the firm as a central repository of path-breaking innovation (Teece et al. 1997; Levinthal 2006; Teece 2007).

Indeed, there is a lot that firms can do to advance the development on radical technology. However, when we bring NFOs into the analysis, we realize that the organizational success of big corporations cannot be fully understood without the role of government NFOs. An excellent example comes from the development of the computing industry in the United States: specifically, the entrance of IBM in the computing market. There is no doubt that IBM has represented (and still[27]) represents an important system integrator within this industry; capable of integrating broad-based research efforts to rival those of universities and government laboratories.[28] But can it be identified as a *dynamically incoherent hub* (see Chapter 3) when it comes to the development of a radical new technology, even when it was capable of developing some within its own R&D laboratories? Some evidence shows that, even as a hub agent, they were hierarchically subordinated to government NFOs within the network of relations in the industry.

When leading American firms such as IBM[29] recognized that electronic computers posed a threat to their conventional electromechanical punched-card business back in the late 1940s, they began to build an industrial base for the new, promising business. Trusting both its leading position in electronic computing capabilities[30] and its own market power in electromechanical devices (90 percent of the domestic market), IBM had decided to build its electronic computer business employing its in-house R&D resources, thus avoiding government contracts (Hughes et al. 1999). However, by 1950 the company made a dramatic policy change because it realized that its capabilities were not enough to compete with the countrywide effort the government was carrying out. Government could commit to financially supporting the most risky and commercially and technologically unexplored projects in the long term.

On the other hand, scholars of the evolutionary traditions rightly argue that technological change (incremental or radical) arises from the recombination of already existing technologies; and therefore, firms could afford simultaneously non-incremental and relatively conservative changes (Arthur 2009; Levinthal 1998, 2006). New technologies tend to cover the needs of certain market niches, which in turn may provide the building blocks for the development of a new technology (or not). If the technology proves to be useful in other sectoral systems, then we have what the literature calls a *general purpose technology* (Rosenberg 1976; Levinthal 1998; Ruttan 2006). This is the kind of technologies that leads to broad economic growth and provides the very source of increasing returns in the economy.

However there are very good economic reasons to argue that not even a big integrated firm, with well developed in-house R&D capabilities, can afford the development of such technologies alone, by simply following existing market signals or focusing on an already known customer base. True, internal R&D departments had become the most salient and successful organizational innovation of the second industrial revolution (Chandler 1977; Freeman 1995, 2008).

On the other hand, these entire success stories would fall into the category of "market failure" seen from a traditional perspective. As Lazonick (2002) states, seen under the light of the innovative enterprise, modern corporations could be described as an organizational success rather than as market failures. A result of what he defines as *organizational integration* "rather than a response to a market imperfection," (ibid., p. 14). The more dynamic economies become, the more obvious appear to be the supposed market failures within them.

But even when we leave the market rhetoric aside, and embrace a more dynamic view of firms (e.g. Teece 2007), innovation is not a cost-free process either. New technologies bring costs. For example, when technologies and skills become obsolete, it usually leads to long learning costs. Even when today "most of the firms [...] pursue innovations through partnerships rather than primarily through their own laboratories, most innovation occurs among networks of collaborators that cross the public-private divide" (Block 2008, p. 19), playing NFOs the larger role at their development.[31]

In reality, products and processes require the organizational, hierarchical, functional and strategic integration of people with different hierarchies and functional specialties into the learning process. This is not only a long, but also uncertain process, which demands high fixed cost (given the size) and needs to be spread over large quantities of sold output. Therefore, a company pursuing an innovative strategy has to necessarily rely on scale and scope (Lazonick 2002). Even when new radical technologies can be created at firm level, they need to be combined and nurtured.

But to achieve that kind of coordination, a company would need to use standardized technical and organizational procedures that make it possible for individuals and other firms in the network to work together (i.e., become interoperable). This compatibility enables interacting components of different systems to achieve greater functionality. In fact, this is, according to the system integration literature, what the system integrators are supposed to do in a predominantly inter-firm environment. Any firm using standards would have all incentives to spread them within the production network, as they acquire economic value for their possessors only when being freely disclosed and jointly used.

However, as just mentioned, it may not be worthwhile for any single firm (not even a big one) to undertake the cost of designing a reference standard for things they do not even know. This is particularly true for disrupting technologies, whose general prospects are uncertain and long-term oriented. Some firms can take the risk, but historical evidence shows that most of them remain faithful to the path-dependency. But if some firms succeed, then they might have to charge such a very high price for the standard use, that it would deprive even those who pay the charges from enjoying the added benefits that would accrue to all users from enlarging the user community.

One example is the disproportionate use of intellectual property right protection. As a result the commodification (but also commoditization) of knowledge has become one of the major impediments to innovation in the present high-tech era, especially in the biotech business (see Pisano 2006; Lazonick and Tulum

2011; further general discussion on the subject from both historical and other industries' perspectives can be found in Kortum and Lerner 1999; Heller 1998; Heller and Eisenberg 1998; Cohen et al. 2000; Hall and Ham. 2001; Cargill 2002; Boldrin and Levine 2008). The fact is that a large cooperation between government and firms (being government agencies the larger risk takers) has been the case behind the development of most complex technologies.

For example, in Chapter 3 we mentioned that several authors argue that the widespread diffusion of internet took place because standards and protocols, such as TCP/IP and HTTP/HTML, were placed in the public domain (see Abbate 1999; Mowery and Simcoe 2002; Ruttan 2006; Block 2008).

> This relatively weak IPR regime reflected the network's academic origins, the US Defense Department's support for placing research in the public domain, and the inability of proprietary standards [such as the ones of IBM and IT&T, which refused to work with the government in the making of a internet standard] to compete with the open TCP/IP standard. The resulting widespread diffusion of the Internet's core technological innovations lowered barriers to entry by networking firms in hardware, software and services.
>
> (Mowery and Simcoe 2002, p. 1384)

Indeed, the use of patent pools (and other platforms) in this and other industries have been an important instrument employed by government-based non-firm organizations to influence the way firms allocate resources in order to achieve organizational integration; while reducing anxieties within the innovation ecosystem and contributing to diffuse and conserve a certain pool of resources within the economy (Sung and Pelto 1998; Clark et al. 2000; Gilbert 2004; Shapiro 2004; Lerner et al. 2005).

As already suggested, this is not only an internet story. Historically, these sorts of uncertainties have been faced by the government-based NFOs in other industries as well. The development of the personal computer (PC) is also illustrative of the symbiosis between government and industry in the evolving computer industry (Hughes et al. 1999). In the 1960s, the Advanced Research Projects Agency (ARPA or DARPA) and the National Aeronautics and Space Administration provided funding to create a new research program at the Stanford Research Institute to work on improving human–computer interactions. In 1968, the research group developed a computerized office system, which was the first system to use a mouse and the first to use windows. The use of a mouse and graphical user interface began the trend to make computers usable by anyone.[32]

Some time later, between 1973 and 1978, the company Xerox Palo Alto Research Center (PARC)[33] developed the first Alto Computer based on research financed by ARPA. They decided to include the Stanford's concept into a graphical user interface for Xerox's Alto computer. Even while Xerox was never able to market the Alto successfully its influence is noticeable in most business and home computers in use today. For example, Apple[34] incorporated many aspects of the Alto into the Apple Lisa, first produced in 1983, and its successor, the Macintosh. The popularity of graphical user interfaces grew rapidly. Eventually Microsoft introduced Windows, beginning the conversion of x86 PCs from the command-line operating system DOS to the operating systems prevalent today (Hughes et al. 1999).

After Xerox built its Alto computers, it donated 10 machines to Stanford's Computer Science Department. Then the Stanford University Network (SUN),[35] relying on DARPA's Very Large Scale Integrated Circuit (VLSI) program, developed new desktop computers with Ethernet networking and high resolution, high-speed graphics, which led to the creation in 1982 of Sun Microsystems Inc. (ibid.). In addition, most of the technology developed and improved with the help of these programs served as point of departure for the creation in 1984 of Cisco Systems.[36]

According to Lazonick (2006, 2001) analysis of the history of economic development in the twentieth century shows that, in terms of investment in new knowledge in terms of industry, the United States, the supposedly Mecca of free market and free enterprise, is actually the world's foremost developmental state. In fact, the role of US decentralized government-based NFOs in the role in invention, diffusion and commercialization of radical new technologies is behind the success of virtually all high tech industries during the Cold War (semiconductors, computers, computer software and biotechnology).

We have already mentioned ARPA (or DARPA) ((Defence) Advanced Projects Research Agency) as a central piece in this story, but the list include several others such as the well-known National Science Foundation (NSF),[37] the National Aeronautics and Space Administration (NASA) the National Institutes of Health (NIH),[38] and other less known such as the National Bureau of Standards (NBS)[39] or the Office of Naval Research (ONR).[40] Mazzucato (2013) documents how the 12 major technologies integrated in Apple's smart products,[41] including the iPhone and iPad, that differentiate these products from their rivals in the market were funded, developed and made commercially viable largely thanks to government-based NFOs.

On the other side, the failure or loss of competitiveness has been often linked to the lack of government integrative ability. For example, political changes during the 1970s (Vietnam War) led to a change of policy toward the role of government and science in the development of new technologies. The Nixon administration severely reduced the funds provided to NSF and ARPA (renamed DARPA) for the development of computing technologies. These activities began to see regarded as a solely private firms issue. However, at the same time, Japan's Ministry of Trade and International Development continued to play a key role in sponsoring and bringing Japanese companies together to cooperate in targeting new markets and technologies.

This may have been one of the reasons why the Japanese integrated circuit companies first captured a dominant percentage of the dynamic random access memory (DRAM) industry. The American world market share of the semiconductor equipment industry fell from 75 percent to 40 percent during the 1980s. This led to the creation of new federal initiatives, such as SEMATECH and high-performance computing, which began to dominate the research and policy agenda. As Hughes et al. (1999) observe "[i]n the United States—amid calls for government action—joint ventures, cooperative agreements, university–industry collaborations, and industry consortia began to emerge to fight the Japanese threat" (p. 113).

However, as they also state "[g]overnment support for science and technology [...] would never again enjoy the same prominence it had in the previous decade," what they call "the golden age of research support was over." This is also affirmed by Lee et al. (2012), which observe that "the period from 1995 to the present has been a turbulent one for the U.S. IT R&D ecosystem" (p. 11). They further add that as a result of a mix of external competitive pressures and lack of federal support,

> the United States risks ceding IT leadership [...] within a generation unless it recommits to providing the resources needed to fuel U.S. IT innovation, to removing important roadblocks that reduce the ecosystem's effectiveness in generating innovation and the fruits of innovation, and to remaining a lead innovator and user of IT.
>
> (ibid.)

In these particular contexts, past US experiences have already showed the way in which government reticence can affect the development of new technologies. For example, the public archives of the NASA,[42] point out how the reticence of the US government at the beginning of the twentieth century led the US to fall far behind other European nations in aeronautical development. While European governments, as well as industrial firms, tended to be more supportive of applied research in this field,[43] American government agencies remained unsupportive.[44] It was the war that led to the US Congress in 1915 to approve a five-year lease on life for a small advisory and coordinating body, whose purpose was modeled on that of the British Advisory Committee for Aeronautics and whose goal seems to have been that of keeping up with the Europeans.

This was the beginning of the National Advisory Committee for Aeronautics (NACA) which had a major impact on aircraft design and performance. As "[m]ost of the early advances that resulted from NACA research and development were 'dual use' – applicable to both military and commercial aircraft" (Ruttan 2006, p. 6). When the Soviet Union launched Sputnik in 1957, NACA was absorbed in 1958 "into a new agency, the National Aeronautics and Space Administration (NASA)" (ibid.). The examples can go on, but the point is that government-based NFOs have played a crucial role by the initial exploration and commercial deployment of technologies with long, unpredictable incubation periods, which requires steady work and funding.

Of course, private firms play a huge role too. In general, the genius, energy and creativity of non-state sector entrepreneurs (private, cooperative etc.) is the necessary complement of a visionary government. However, if we take a look to the NSF statistics, we will find out that in early periods, the government funding surpassed that of industry. For example during the period 1956–68 the US federal government provided more development resources to the industry than the industry itself.[45] If we look at the US applied research expenditures for the same period, we can see that the federal government provided most of the funding for universities research and, at least until the late 1970s, also a good part of the industry applied research.[46]

The same applies to the basic research, except when considering industry funded basic research for the industry, where the industry provided most of the funds across the whole period. However, as Mowery and Simcoe (2002) argue when referring to internet development, "though private investments were indispensable [...], their effects were mediated by the constellation of institutions and policies within the US national innovation system"[47] (p. 1383). The point has been also emphasized by Lee et al. (2012) and Hughes et al. (1999) for other industries.

4.11 Organizational integration from a network perspective

As already seen, the period from the 1950s until well into the mid 1990s (with some fluctuation in the middle), these agencies (by means of military contracts through the US Department of Defense, DoD) represented the very *dynamically incoherent hubs* (in our terminology see Chapter 3) of the US national innovation system. This decentralized system of agencies played the role of mobilizing the specialized capabilities of different groups of agents (e.g. university teams, industry R&D departments etc.) into a single integrated (while always incomplete, see Foster 2005) network and, on the other hand, displayed the necessary financial commitment that could sustain the innovation process until it generated returns. They provided the complementarities and necessary synergies within the system, so that organizational learning could happen.

In fact, it is them and not big firms, the kind of institutions who have historically played the role of system integrators when it comes to develop radical new technologies. They were the major (most central) contributors to *organizational integration* within the network and; it would be not far-fetched to suppose, that, if represented as a complex network, these government based non-firm agencies would achieve the highest scores of *centrality* (see Chapter 2, specifically Section 2.7).

In Chapter 2 we observed that the concept of centrality of individuals and/or organizations in their social networks is also one of the earliest notions employed by social network analysts. It basically refers to an actor or node which is "central" to a number of other connections. That is, a node with many direct contacts to other nodes and which can be seen as a major source of information and control. This multidimensional concept has been formally developed into different proxies with the aim to capture most of its characteristics (total degree centrality, betweeness centrality, closeness centrality, etc., see Annexes).

It is in this context that this research extends the proposition that the concept *organizational integration* (Lazonick 2002) can be effectively (if necessarily partially) captured by the notion of *centrality* discussed in Chapter 2. Being conceived as a *social condition,* this concept encompasses the idea of business enterprises as social structures that are in turn embedded in larger (typically national) organizational /institutional environments.

Successful organizational integration has to do with the ability of certain organizations to mobilize resources and allowing (both contextual and explicit) knowledge and innovation to disseminate across a company, industry, technological sector, or economy. These organizations, sometimes as users or producers of knowledge, voluntarily (or not) give up or "freely reveal" all intellectual property rights over that knowledge, and all interested parties are given access to it (von Hippel and von Krogh 2006, p. 295). As a production system becomes increasingly complex and its industrial base begins to emerge, it becomes necessary for the products, processes and procedures of the system to fit together and interoperate. From a social network perspective, organizations that provide this *interoperability* are structurally "central" to the sector or to the economy since they possess the property of integrating other organizations into the process of organizational learning.

The theory of innovative enterprise acknowledges that organizational learning is *collective* and *cumulative* (Lazonick 2002, 2011; Malerba 2002; Freeman 1995, 2008). It is cumulative because those tacit and context-dependent capabilities are accumulated over time and are crucial to build the new capabilities necessarily to the innovation process. This is, "what has already been learned [builds] a foundation for what can be learned" (Lazonick and O'Sullivan 2000, p. 96). It is collective because it depends on the integration on many different agents with specific (and idiosyncratic) organizational and technological capabilities. That is, "large numbers of people in the functional and hierarchical divisions of labour must interact in the learning process" (ibid.). "That such an industrial-organization perspective on the innovation process is needed has been explicitly recognized by economists working within the national [and sectoral] systems of innovation" (p. 92).

Therefore, "if one accepts that business enterprises are social structures that are in turn embedded in larger (typically national) institutional environments" or as Coe et al. (2008) argue, as relational networks embedded within wider networks of social actors, with varying degrees of imbrications and interconnection among them, [then] (1) "a theory of innovative enterprise must itself be embedded in a model of the relations" (Lazonick 2011 p. 5) among firms and other (non-firm) organizations that is able to encourage innovative strategies in an uncertain environment and (2) we can accept the workability of the definition of OI within the framework of the national (sectoral) system of innovation approach. Therefore, and consistent with this framework, *it is plausible to conceive economic growth and innovation as collective phenomena, which should be understood and explained in terms of relational categories; like the ones advanced by the network analysis.*

If heterogeneity across firms is likely to be a permanent feature of national (sectoral) systems of innovation; and we accept the idea of defining these systems as *systems of complex networks dominated by a group of diverse and hierarchically structured hubs,* then it is reasonable to assume that these hubs will have high scores of centrality when represented as a networked system.

Again, why precisely centrality? Because, as we already mentioned in Chapter 2, our network analysis focuses on describing graph-theoretic properties at the node level of analysis, mostly expressed by this notion. That is, the study explores the behavior of individual nodes based on their position within a network (system of social relations). In other words, *we explore the behavior of organizations in terms of their contribution to the organizational learning, being this contribution quantitatively expressed in the concept of OI.* The more dimensions of centrality in which an organization shows high degrees, the larger its contribution to organizational integration; and the closer it is to the definition of *dynamically incoherent agent* as defined in Chapter 3. In the Annexes we will explore a tentative quantification of OI for the case of the Cuban biopharmaceutical industry.

Note that the concept of organizational integration is not being represented in this research as an attribute that can be captured by a single measure; but as a notion expressed in several measures of centrality. This multidimensionality is consistent with the methodological approach being employed here, which relies on non-comparable observations. This study rejects the notion of individual agents being explained by their individual attributes alone.[48] Being conceived as a *social condition,* this concept encompasses the idea of business enterprises as relational structures that are in turn embedded in larger (typically national) organizational and institutional environments. This means that the relevant theoretical concepts and data are to be conceived relationally.

Last, but not least, even when it could be surprising to see a methodological tool (network theory) being employed as a theorization instrument, there is a good rationale behind this. In essence, as one of the leading studies in the field suggest, "[many] of the key structural measures and notions of social network analysis grew out of keen insights of researchers seeking to describe empirical phenomena and are motivated by central concepts in social theory." At the same time methods had to be developed to test specific hypotheses about these structural properties. "The result of this symbiotic relationship between theory and method [builds the foundation] of network analytic techniques in both application and theory" (Wasserman and Faust 1994, p. 3). Our intention here is to express a relationally defined theoretical concept by providing formal definitions, measures and descriptions (ibid.).

4.12 NFOs in leading and in catch-up economies

The phenomenon of NFOs as locus of organizational integration needs not only to apply to developed economies or technological leaders. In fact, as List suggested in his ideas on national system of innovations, Germany was a collection of independent developing countries. True, there are differences in the way resources are created or diffused.

Some experts on the pivotal role of the state in developed economies tend to assume that imitation involve less risk and therefore the idea of an entrepreneurial or networking state would not apply to developing (or more general catch-up) countries. For instance, Mazzucatto (2011) argues that "[u]nlike in a developing country, where technology is already available elsewhere in the world, an entrepreneurial state does not yet knows what the details of the innovation are…" (p. 68). Likewise, Block (2008) contends that "[t]he types of developmental policies being pursued in both Europe and the United States are quite distinct from the more familiar form of developmentalism that was deployed in East Asia in the decades after World War II" (p. 3).

He uses the example of MITI in Japan to argue that this case was a

> centralised form of state policy designed to help domestic firms catch up and challenge foreign competitors in particular product markets. As practiced in Japan and South Korea, it worked by government planners providing a series of economic incentives and subsidies to established firms to compete in markets that they would otherwise have considered too risky to enter.
>
> (ibid., p. 4)

Block (2008) further argues that Europe and the United States have created is something very different called a Developmental Network State (see Chapter 3), whose main focus is to "help firms develop product and process innovations that do not yet exist" (ibid.). While in Chapter 3 we briefly mentioned this definition, along with others, in order to generally refer to the importance of industrial policy (see Section 3.3 above), in this section we are going to go into details about the way in which these definitions differ from each other, and about how they are usually employed to establish a differentiation between catch-up and leading countries. We are also going to give a more detailed description of the specific roles played by NFOs in the developmental efforts that have taken place in catch-up countries; and to contrast these roles to the roles they are supposed to play in leading countries.

According to his definition, Block (2008) argues the MITI model no longer applies as a Developmental Network State because European and US American firms have "no international leader that firms can imitate" and they have already "strong incentives to innovate so the addition of government subsidies or incentives is unlikely to have any additional impact" (ibid., p. 4).

It is certainly true that catching-up countries have usually employed more centralized models to encourage emulation, being the case of the Ministry of International Trade and Industry MITI[49] a paradigmatic example. This agency was set up in 1949 in order to provide government leadership and assistance for the restoration of industrial productivity and employment in post-war

Japan. MITI served as an architect of industrial policy, an arbiter on industrial problems and disputes, and as a regulator.[50]

Since it encompassed a huge span of activities, MITI was able to integrate conflicting policies to minimize the negative impact in the domestic manufacturing sector and export industries (Johnson 1982). As suggested above, MITI was behind the early development of nearly all major industries by providing protection from import competition, technological intelligence, help in licensing foreign technology, access to foreign exchange, and assistance in mergers.[51] However, even when it provided guidance, technology and investments in new plants and equipments, it did not manage Japanese industry along the lines of a centralized economy. For example, Nissan and Honda explicitly denied any guidance from the Japanese government, although they may have benefited from the overall policy environment.

In addition, if the MITI model was created only to catch up by imitating leading countries (as Block 2008 suggests), how did several of the sectors encouraged by MITI manage to become leading innovators themselves (not only in design or other incremental innovations, but also in new technologies)? As already mentioned, by the 1970s and the 1980s Japanese products and processes began to out-perform those of United States and Europe in many industries. Similar cases are to be found in government based non-firm organizations such as KIST,[52] KAIS,[53] STDC[54] and ETRI[55] in South Korea[56] and ITRI[57] and ERSO[58] in Taiwan.

For example Kim (1997) observes how ETRI served as coordinator and diffuser of knowledge in the development of 4M DRAM (Dynamic random access memory). As a result, the *chaebol* Samsung passed from being six years behind the world leaders in terms development and four years behind in terms of DRAM at the early 1980s to developing the first world 256M DRAM in 1994.

True, the last decade has been less innovative for Japan in other modern industries (see e.g. Eyo 2011). However, the fact remains that it was able to develop new products with higher quality and "to more rapid diffusion of such [frontier] technologies as robotics,"[59] relying on the very structure that is said to have been created only for imitation (Freeman 1995; Lazonick and O'Sullivan 2000). Confirming this, in 2011 some business observers placed eight Japanese companies among the most innovative of all times (based on the number of patents).[60]

It seems to be more common that the functions of government NFOs co-evolve with technologies and institutions, rather than that a certain type of institutional form fits better than another (see above, Section 4.6). Granted, certain learning regimes and demand compositions are linked to more or less specific institutional forms, but as essential as this is, and perhaps more essential than a fixed formal requirement, it is whether the *developmental function* has been exercised. In fact, the same institution can exert different functions; and different institutions can carry out the same function in different countries (Chang 2007, pp. 16–33).

154 Theory and conceptualization

On the other side, if, as Block (2008) argues, European and American firms have already strong incentives to innovate then, for example, why are most of the giant pharmaceutical firms, the biggest integrators within the biopharmaceutical sector, investing most of the resources supposedly to be employed in innovation in me-too drugs and other low risk (from innovation point of view) medical products? Or why do they (this includes other industries as well) prefer investing in financial products rather than in innovative products? Actually, firm investment capabilities and incentives to innovate are multi-causal and complex phenomena, which do not only depend on the company's current technological state, but also, and we would argue most importantly, on the linkage capabilities, e.g.

> the skills needed to transmit information, skills and technology to, and receive them from, component or raw material suppliers, subcontractors, consultants, service firms, and technology institutions. Such linkages affect not only the productive efficiency of the enterprise (allowing it to specialise more fully) but also the diffusion of technology through the economy and the deepening of the industrial structure, both essential to industrial development.
>
> (Lall 1992)

Given the above mentioned, in the present study it is argued that government-based NFOs have played a pivotal role in both leading and catch up countries when it comes to dealing with radical uncertainty in order to foster industrial development. We argue that even when the differentiation between the kind of activity carried out by NFOs in each group of countries it is essential their roles actually overlap with the role played by these organizations in catch-up countries.

For the sake of the argument being made here, the kind of differences between, say, developing and advanced economies, do not prevent the government-based NFOs from playing the pivotal (even if different) networking role in both cases. While NFOs in advanced economies focus on the generation of new scientific and technological knowledge, as well as creating a market for them, their role in developing economies focuses more on sparking imitation, adaptation and emulation mechanisms when designing targeted catch-up policies for technologies that already exist.

However, this is not to say that developing countries catch-up attempts are less risky that the completely new adventure of looking radical new technologies. Even when the technology trying to be upgraded or acquired is already available in the world, "the process of catch-up involves [radical] innovation in an essential way"(Cimoli et al. 2009, p. 22). The difference is that much of the required innovation is organizational and institutional. It represents a major structural transformation in that it breaks from familiar practices, uncertainty about how to make new practice effective, and need of a sophisticated learning process. Gerschenkron's (1962) account of the policies and new institutions used in Continental Europe to enable catch-up with Britain illustrates the point. This also matches such success stories as Japan, Taiwan, South Korea and more recently China.

Similar to what occurs in the case of radical technological innovation in the advanced economies, developing countries have to confront high risk of failure during the catch-up process. In fact, there are many examples of aborted or failed catch-up and developmental processes. For example, the Latin-American experience shows that there is nothing automatic in an emulation process (Cimoli et al. 2009). This should not be taken as a rejection of the state role in the economy, as the neoliberal theories do, but as an invitation to a more careful reflection on the mechanisms that lead to a success or failure in any case. In this sense, the notions of *organizational integration as centrality* advanced here are meant to apply to developed and developing countries as well. Important here is to historically trace the role played by each institution in a given country, rather than to automatically assume them unable to carry out these functions.

Notes

1 In this scenario net investments (gross investments-depreciation) falls to zero because gross investments is only enough to counter the effect of depreciation of physical capital and growing labor force on decrease in capital to labor ratio.
2 Technology is still treated as information equally available to all firms. Production cost implications of the information involved are evidently fully known to the innovator ex ante; and its use can be easily regulated through a perfect property right, which can be interpreted as an ideal patent – unambiguous, costlessly enforceable, and of infinite duration, see S Winter, The logic of appropriability: From Schumpeter to Arrow to Teece, *Research Policy*, Vol. 35, Issue 8, October, 2006, pp. 1100–6.
3 These sorts of arguments contributed to build a rationale for the relatively recent sharp increase and sophistication of the patent system (mostly between the 1970s and 80s) However, as other authors argue, this does not have to be the case, as competition in high innovative industries is not a winner-takes-all process, but mainly a never-ending creation of new sub-markets. See L Marengo et al., Appropriability, Patents, and Rates of Innovation in Complex Products Industries, LEM, *Working Paper Series*, No. 5, April 2009.
4 In this framework, it was ideas that were endogenous and not the institutional framework required to transform ideas into products. Moreover, Arrow had introduced the notion of *learning by doing,* which was subsequently used by endogenous growth models. In these models, the experience with production or investment contributes to productivity. Moreover, the learning by one producer may raise the productivity of others through a process of spillovers of knowledge from one producer to another. Therefore, a larger economy-wide capital stock (or a greater cumulation of the aggregate of past production) improves the level of the technology for each producer. Consequently, diminishing returns to capital may not apply in the aggregate, and increasing returns are even possible.
5 See HDD Schmidt, You can not buy innovation, January 30, 2012, available at www. asymco.com/2012/01/30/you-cannot-buy-innovation/

6 It was in the German dyestuffs industry researching for new products and development of new chemical processes were introduced on a regular, systematic and professional basis. The in-house R&D lab soon emerged in other countries and industries (other than the chemical industry). The electrical industries of the United States and Germany introduced it sometime in the 1880s. Chemical firms in Switzerland also started to develop in-house R&D. At the end of the nineteenth century, these specialized R&D labs became an essential feature of the largest firm in the manufacturing industry and the most conspicuous institutional innovation of the second industrial revolution. The impact of this organizational innovation becomes apparent when we consider the fact that at its inception, the dye industry was a French–British business, German companies being marginal a player. In 1862 British firms controlled about 50 percent of the world market, and French firms another 40 percent, By 1873 German companies had 50 percent of the market, while French, Swiss and British firms controlled between 13 percent and 17 percent each. In 1913 German firms had a market share of more than 80 percent, Swiss had about 8 percent and French and British firms had disappeared from the market.

7 See V Bush, Science, the Endless Frontier, A Report to the President by the Director of the Office of Scientific Research and Development, United States Government Printing Office, Washington, July 1945.

8 The evolutionary approach developed by Richard Nelson and Sydney Winter, relying on the seminal contributions of Veblen and Schumpeter, also argues that the production function framework is the wrong way to understand technological change. They proposed an evolutionary theory of production and economic change outside the optimizing view of the production function that acknowledges the constant differentiation process that firms underwent in order to remain competitive.

9 By way of example, one of the most known private NFOs in the US during the last period is SEMATECH. SEMATECH began as a consortium of 12 semiconductor firms and was initially financed with $100 million per year of government-based NFO ARPA money that was combined with contributions from the consortium members. Sematech became self-supporting, relying on industry contributions alone, although ARPA continued to fund key academic work in chip design (see F Block, Swimming against the current: The rise of a hidden developmental state in the United States, *Politics & Society*, June, vol. 36 no. 2, 2008, p. 14).

10 In the context of this concept the word "public" is employed to indicate the purchase by different investors of a company's stocks. The term is widely used in financial economics. Note, however that in this study the word public is being employed in a different sense, namely to identify government activities.

11 Germany and the United States are two representative examples of federal political systems. In both countries, federal states dispose of large autonomy and policies can vary widely from one jurisdiction to another. Regional economic policies can certainly encourage the development of industry. However, there seems to be little evidence of regional industrial agglomerations emerging without strong central support (e.g. the biotech industry in Germany and in the United States, or the Silicon Valley phenomenon in the United States).

12 Franco Malerba offers some insights in this direction. For instance, according to him, in biopharmaceuticals, national health systems and regulations have played a major role in affecting the direction of technical change, in some cases even blocking or retarding innovation (see F Malerba et al., Catch up in different sectoral

systems: some introductory remarks, *Globelics India,* Innovation systems for competitiveness and shared prosperity in developing countries, Trivandrum, Kerala, 4–7 October, 2006, p. 11, note 5). The knowledge base and the learning processes have greatly affected innovation and the organization of innovative activities. In the early stages (1850–1945), the industry was close to chemicals, with little formal research until the 1930s and a major use of licenses. The following period (1945 to early 1980s) was characterized by the introduction of random screening of natural and chemically derived compounds. This led to an explosion of R&D. Few blockbusters were discovered every period: each one had high growth. The advent of molecular biology in the 1980s led to a new learning regime based on molecular genetics and rDNA technology. Innovation increasingly depends on strong scientific capabilities and on the ability to interact with science and scientific institutions in order to explore the search space (ibid., p. 13, note 7). In machine tools, internal and regional labor markets and local institutions (e.g. local banks) have played a major role in influencing international advantages of specific areas (ibid., p. 11 note 5). Products have increasingly being modularized and standardized and innovation has been mainly incremental and now is increasingly systemic (ibid., p. 13, note 7). In telecommunications, the role of regulation, liberalization/privatization, and standards have played a key role in the organization and performance of the sector (p. 11, note 5). In semiconductors, the industry has been characterized by a quite different set of actors, ranging from merchant semiconductor manufacturers to vertically integrated producers. The types of actors have been quite different from period to period and from country to country during the evolution of the industry. In chemicals, the structure of the sectoral system has been centered around large firms, which have been the major source of innovation over a long period of time (ibid.). In software, specialization of both global players and local producers is present. In addition, the changing knowledge base has created an evolving division of labor among users, "platform" developers, and specialized software vendors (ibid., p. 13, note 7). Standards and standard setting organizations are also important (ibid., p. 11, note 5).

13 In the case of the QWERTY typewriter keyboard, made famous by Paul David, millions of individual learners became adept at using a configuration of the alphabet that was originally intended to reduce the probability of type hammers interfering with one another on mechanical typewriters. With the elimination of the type hammer technology on, first, electric typewriters equipped with ball fonts, and, then, electronic computer technology, the QWERTY keyboard system remained in place because the manufacturers of these products had neither the incentive nor the ability to retrain the countless number of typists to use a straightforward ABCDEF keyboard (W Lazonick and MO'Sullivan, Perspectives on Corporate Governance, Innovation, and Economic Performance, The European Institute of Business Administration, Fontainebleau Cedex, France, 2000, p. 97). See also P David, Clio and the economics of QWERTY, *The American Economic Review,* Vol. 75, No. 2, Papers and Proceedings of the Ninety-Seventh Annual Meeting of the American Economic Association, May 1985, pp. 332–7.

14 The analyzed relation are expenditure on R&D development as a percentage of value added by sector and by country and sectoral ratios of R&D use to expenditure. The countries are USA, France, Western Germany, Japan, United Kingdom, Italy. See G Dosi, Sources, procedures and microeconomics effects of innovation, *Journal of Economic Literature,* Vol XXVI,, p. 1124, 1988.

15 When following the assumption of a given asset specificity one is led to think that the firm is not in a position to devise a corporate strategy in interaction with other non-firm agents. But this contradicts the historical evidence; because in reality, firms do not innovate in isolation. Government, firm and non firm organizations, have been an important constituent of innovation and economic development. (To understand the real sources of these assets' specificity it is necessary to engage in a comparative-historical analysis where history and theory can come together.)

16 A very important critique of this approach is directed to the assumption that the specific resources of the firms need to be non-tradable, in order to assure barriers of entry to other firms. However, at the same time, this perspective argues that firms' profit come from the rents extracted to the resources. But, as the theory of innovative business enterprise argues, if the specific resources are non-tradable, then why do they generate any residual (surplus revenues)? The theory also criticizes the use of the concept of rent in this approach. See W Lazonick, Innovative enterprise and historical transformation, *Enterprise & Society* 3 (March), 2002, pp. 32–3.

17 While acknowledging the broader nature of innovation, uses the term to refer to the corporate environment:

> "There is a recognition, therefore, in some (but, as we shall see, by no means all) of the organizational learning literature that the transformation of individual learning into organizational learning is a dynamic and dialectical process, where individuals must continually be confronted with the limitations of their own particular capabilities, and, perhaps of more importance, their beliefs. In a word, the learning company is treated as a 'social' organization".
>
> (W Lazonick and MO Sullivan, Perspectives on
> Corporate Governance... p. 77)

18 Organizational integration degenerates into organizational (and knowledge) segmentation when participants, particularly those in charge of the strategic control, "become prisoners of the bounded rationality." This is they "use accumulated assets as if they were general sources of revenues rather than [the result of] the historical accumulations of organizational learning" (see W Lazonick, Innovative enterprise and historical transformation..., 2002, p. 16). When this happens, the ones with the strategic control will financially commit to an optimizing and self-reinforcing (rather to an innovative) strategy with disregard of the long-term prospects for the organization. No matter how many financial resources an agent disposes of; and how much control it can have over the destinies of these resources, the lack of cumulative learning (caused by knowledge segmentation) will surely hinder innovation.

19 The fact of the rising Japanese productivity during the 1950–70s and innovativeness during the 1970–90s is by now a stylized fact. This has been shown in such industries as automobile, consumer electronic, semiconductors, etc. Consider, for instance, the Japanese rise to DRAM (Random Access Memory Chips) production. From the late 1970s, the Japanese became a competitive challenge to US producers, forcing most US companies, including Intel, to withdraw from the market after 1985. Also during the 1980s, Japanese companies such as Fujitsu, Hitachi, and NEC were able to achieve yields 40 percent higher than the best US companies. Essential to this advantage was the development of advanced semiconductor manufacturing technology, which emerged from the organizational integration of engineers into manufacturing activities, and interactive learning with equipment suppliers.

20 This is defined as a form of partnership or partial merger between companies that agree to buy a significant percentage of each other's stock. Cross-shareholding continues to provide implicit relational contracts that play a role in Japanese business society. This element highlights the importance of paying adequate attention to historical and institutional factors in analyses of development (for a detailed discussion, see M Scher, Bank-firm Cross shareholding in Japan: What is it, why does it matter, is it winding down? United Nations' Department of Economic and Social Affairs (DESA), *Discussion Paper*, No. 15, 2001.

21 Unlike the United States, Japanese companies of the decades following World War II overcame the sharp segmentation between salaried managers and hourly workers by extending permanent employment to both white-collar and blue-collar personnel, thus providing a foundation for the hierarchical integration of "shop-floor" workers into a company-wide process of organizational learning. Lifetime employment in particular, while not contractually guaranteed, still gave white-collar and blue-collar workers employment security to a certain retirement age. This won the enterprise the commitment of the workers, and gave companies an incentive to develop the productive capabilities of its employees.

22 The term was originally proposed by Roy Rothwell in 1992. See R Rothwell, Successful industrial innovation: critical factors for the 1990s, *R&D Management*, vol. 22, pp. 221–39, 1992.

23 See Steinmueller W.E, The U.S. software industry: An analysis and interpretive history, In: MERIT Research Memoranda, UNU-MERIT, No. 006, 1995, p. 17.

24 Ibid.

25 All integration attempts are seen in this theory as an effort to raise the prices in order to prevent non-integrated competitors facing "restricted supplies of and higher prices for that factor compared with the factor market conditions that would prevail under perfectly competitive conditions." Even when this may be the case, the theory does not explain why, under perfect technological and market conditions, some firms become monopolies and others do not.

26 In this literature, choices about integration are seen as a matter of markets vs. hierarchies. Hierarchical (i.e. vertical) relations are seen as a way to solve a market failure that may emerge under specific conditions in a given time, in order to enhance the optimizing capabilities of the firm, rather than its innovating capabilities (see W Lazonick, Innovative enterprise and historical transformation..., pp. 8–12). This dichotomy has been inherited by a good part of the literature in production networks and value chains. Vertical, hierarchical, linear are taken usually as synonyms. However, several authors suggest that a central factor explaining the vertical scope of firms is not to cover some market failure, but instead the process of accumulation of capabilities at the firm and industry levels (see F Malerba et al., Catch up in different sectoral systems...)

27 For instance, IBM has become a leading supporter of Open Source Initiatives. IBM is the only company to provide complete solutions of hardware, software and technical support for Linux. See http://web.archive.org/web/19991110114228/www.ibm.com/news/1999/03/02.phtml, see also http://lwn.net/Articles/185602/ and www.ibm.com/developerworks/university/opensource/

28 In 1984, for example, IBM still conducted 50 percent of the R&D (by dollar value) in the computer industry as a whole (see T Hughes et al., Funding a Revolution: Government Support for Computing Research, National Academy Press, 1999, p. 111).

29 Other firms include Remington Rand, also in the same business as IBM; and several other in business related to electrical components such as RCA, General Electric, NCR, Honeywell, Raytheon, Philco, etc. (ibid., p. 29).

30

"Using electronic circuits developed in its Endicott Laboratory as the country was entering World War II, IBM in 1946 introduced its 603 Electronic Multiplier, the first commercial product to incorporate electronic arithmetic circuits. Two years later in the fall of 1948, shipments of the IBM 604 began. Containing over 1,400 vacuum tubes, its electronic circuits performed addition, subtraction, multiplication, and division, and could execute up to 60 plugboard-controlled program steps between reading data from a card and punching out the result".

(ibid., p. 29)

31

"In 1975, forty-seven out of eighty-six domestic innovations were produced by Fortune 500 companies, and forty of these involved no outside partners. By 2006, the big firms were responsible for only six out eighty-eight innovations, and in most cases, they had partners. In 2006, fifty of these innovations were the products of researchers at US government laboratories, universities, or other public agencies, working alone or in collaboration with private firms. Another thirteen innovations came from 'supported spin-offs,' relatively new firms started by scientists or technologists that had received considerable Federal funding both before and after the firm's founding. Of the remaining twenty-five innovations that belonged to private sector organizations, at least another fourteen involved Federal dollars. In short, all but eleven of the prize winning innovations in 2006 depended on some public financing. Since these recognized innovations ranged over every sector of the economy, there is reason to believe that the pattern revealed in the awards reflects the broader trends in innovation in the U.S. economy".

(F Block, Swimming Against the Current… 2008, p. 19)

32 The invention of the mouse and its use as part of a graphical user interface represented a dramatic change from the standard command-line operation of computers. Most mainframe and timesharing systems at the time relied on typed commands that computer novices found cryptic and difficult to use. Text on the screen could often be edited only by referencing the line number as opposed to changing the text in place (T Hughes et al., Funding a Revolution… 1999, p. 109).

33 At that time it was a division of Xerox Corporation. After three decades as part of Xerox this research center was transformed in 2002 into an independent, fully owned subsidiary with the name of PARC (Palo Alto Research Center Incorporated). Its main goal consists of developing innovative science-based and business concepts with the help of commercial partners. Xerox remains the company's largest customer.

34 In 1979, Steve Jobs was invited to tour Xerox PARC. Jobs realized the potential for the Alto system. He told the demonstrator of the system, Larry Tesler, "Why isn't Xerox marketing this? …You could blow everything away" (ibid., p. 110).

35 This is the campus computer network for Stanford University. It was the site of one of the four original ARPANET nodes.

36 "A start-up's true tale." Often-told story of Cisco's launch leaves out the drama, intrigue, Mercury News, Dez 2001, available at http://pdp10.nocrew.org/docs/cisco.html

37 "Google emerged out of academic research at Stanford that was funded by the National Science Foundation" (see F Block, Swimming Against the Current... 2008, p. 29)

38 This NFO is behind the genetic engineering revolution. In the aftermath of the discovery of the structure of DNA in 1953, substantial funding from NIH made possible rapid advances in molecular biology by US scientists. Their achievements included understanding the genetic code and figuring out how DNA replicates itself. These breakthroughs paved the way for the creation of new organisms by combining DNA from different sources. NIH officials rapidly grasped the disease fighting possibility of genetic engineering and began to invest aggressively in advancing the technology, both with the grants they provided and with the research going on within their own labs. While in 1975, NIH supported only two recombinant DNA research projects in 1976, this rose to 123 projects with $15 million dollars of support. By 1980, this had increased to 1061 projects funded with $131 million of funding. when the UCSF (University of California, San Francisco) scientist Herbert Boyer helped found Genentech in 1976 (together with venture capitalist Robert Swanson), the first of the biotech startups specifically created to commercialize genetic engineering. NIH raised no objections when Boyer continued to use his NIH-funded lab at UCSF for Genentech's first commercial project – the development of a bacteria that would synthesize human insulin (ibid., pp. 8–10). Lazonick and Tulum (2011) provide further evidence on the ubiquity of government-based NFOs support in the biopharma industry. This support went beyond financing and covered regulatory framework, commercial incentives and a number of legislations.

39 Through its National Applied Mathematics Laboratory, [NBS] acted as a kind of expert agent for other government agencies, selecting suppliers and overseeing construction and delivery of new computers. For example, NBS contracted for the three initial Univac machines – the first commercial, electronic, digital, stored-program computers – one for the Census Bureau and two for the Air Materiel Command.

NBS also got into the business of building machines. When the Univac order was plagued by technical delays, NBS built its own computer in-house. The Standards Eastern Automatic Computer (SEAC) was built for the Air Force and dedicated in 1950, the first operational, electronic, stored-program computer in [the US]. NBS, in the person of Harry Huskey, built a similar machine, the Standards Western Automatic Computer (SWAC) for the Navy on the West Coast. Numerous problems were run on SEAC, and the computer also served as a central facility for diffusing expertise in programming to other government agencies (T Hughes et al., Funding a Revolution...1999, p. 89).

40 "ONR supported Whirlwind, MIT's first digital computer and progenitor of real-time command and- control systems" (ibid.). MIT refers to the Massachusetts Institute of Technology.

41 The technologies are (1) Microprocessor or central processing units (CPU), which are made of miniaturized integrate circuits whose development was largely thanks to the efforts of the US Air Force and NASA during the 1950s and the 60s; (2) Dynamic random access memory (DRAM), which was the offspring of research funded by the US government during the 1950s and the 60s; (3) the hard drive disk (HDD) was possible due to Spintronics technology, which was developed by DARPA and the Department of Defence (DoD) relying on other countries scientific

achievements (Germany, France); (4) different touch-screen systems developed by the British government NFO Royal Radar Establishment (RRE) during the 60s, by the European Organization for Nuclear Research (CERN) in the early 70s and by scientists at the University of Kentucky in the late 60s and early 70s. Based on these early touch-screen technologies; a PhD student and a post-doctoral fellow, funded by the NSF and the Central Intelligence Agency (CIA), developed the multi-touch concept on fully glass LCD display and commercialized it after creating the FingerWork company. Apple bought the firm in 2005 prior to launch the first iPhone's generation in 2007 (5) the Liquid-crystal displays (LCD) was created as thin-film transistor (TFT) at the laboratory of Westinghouse and funded almost entirely by the DoD, which wanted to develop an alternative to the Japanese flat panel display. When Westinghouse decided to end the project during the mid-70s, DARPA offered a $7.8 million contract in 1988 to its main developed (Peter Brody) after top computer and electronic companies including Apple, XEROX, IBM, Compaq and DEC had refused to take the risk. Brody founded Magnascreen in order to develop the TFT-LCD technology. In order to retain the technology in the US a research consortium was created by major display manufacturers with initial funding of NIST. In addition contracts were provided by other military and civilian government-based NFOs; (6) Lithium-polymer (Li-pol) and lithium-ion (Li-ion) batteries, both being developed with the support of the Department of Energy and the NSF. This technology was successfully launched by the Japanese Sony in 1991 and has become a manufacturing comparative advantage for several Asian and European countries; (7) the digital signal processing based on fast Fourier Transform algorithms (FFT) is very useful for data compression. This research is currently supported by NSF and DARPA (see http://groups.csail.mit.edu/netmit/sFFT/); (8) the internet (see Chapter 3, Section 3.7.1); (9) the Hypertext Transfer Protocol (HTTP), uniform resource locators (URL) and Hypertext Markup language (HTLM) first developed and implemented by CERN. The two scientists responsible redacted a document in 1989 describing the creation of a World Wide Web, which eventually became an international standard (10) cellular technology. Its antecedents are found in developed during the 50s; (11) global positioning systems (GPS) developed by DoD (the further development of the technology cost the US government $705 million annually). iPhone NAVSTAR GPS system consists of a complex of 24 satellite; a technology and an infrastructure which could not have been developed without the government's financial commitment; (12) artificial intelligence with a voice user interface program (last iPhone's virtual personal assistant, SIRI): in 2000 DARPA started to fund a program that included 20 universities and which was coordinated by the Stanford Research Institute (SRI). The program pursued the aim of developing a virtual office assistant. After iPhone was launched in 2007, SRI formed a SIRI (a venture-backed start-up) in order to commercialize the technology. In 2010 SIRI was acquired by Apple for an undisclosed amount. See M Mazzucato, The *Entrepeneurial State: Debuking Public* vs. *Private Sector Myths*, London, New York, Anthem Press, 2013, pp. 87–110. The description of the context and content of the technologies provided by this note have not been extracted from Mazzucato's book (which has only been employed to cite the technologies) but from the author's own research. It might be the case that some of the things described in this note are not present in Mazzucato's book or vice versa.

42 The National Aeronautics and Space Administration (NASA). Although primarily devoted to the space exploration and aeronautic research, is one of the US

government non-firm organizations that most supported the development of new technologies in the American system of innovation. Funded in 1958 to replace its predecessor NACA, the NASA "have supported high-performance computing, networking, human-computer interaction, software engineering, embedded and realtime systems, and other kinds of research" (P Lee et al., Continuing Innovation in Information Technology, National Academy Press, Washington, D.C., 2012, p. 9).

43 In 1909, the internationally known British physicist, Lord Rayleigh, was appointed head of the Advisory Committee for Aeronautics; in Germany, Ludwig Prandtl and others were beginning the sort of investigations that soon made the University of Gottingen a center of theoretical aerodynamics. In France the Office National d'Études et de Recherches Aéronautiques had been created in 1877 see http://history.nasa.gov/SP-4103/ch1.htm and http://history.nasa.gov/SP-4406/chap1.html

44 Aware of European activity, Charles D. Walcott, secretary of the Smithsonian Institution, was able to find funds to dispatch two Americans on a fact-finding tour overseas. Dr. Albert F. Zahm taught physics and experimented in aeronautics at Catholic University in Washington, D.C.; Dr. Jerome C. Hunsaker, a graduate of the Massachusetts Institute of Technology, was developing a curriculum in aeronautical engineering at the institute. Their report, issued in 1914, emphasized the galling disparity between European progress and American inertia. See http://history.nasa.gov/SP-4406/chap1.html

45 US development expenditures, by performing sector and source of funds: 1953–2009, www.nsf.gov/statistics/nsf12321/content.cfm?pub_id=4185&id=2

46 Ibid.

47 Indeed, as already stated, the most important role of NFOs is not only to be found in the long term funding, but in the bridging role played by them. For example, consider the indirect effects of government sponsored research, which consists of, e.g. (1) guiding private R&D programs toward potentially more productive areas of inquiry and assistance in training researchers, (2) exploratory science and academic engineering research activities to support commercially oriented and mission-directed research that generates new production technologies and products, (3) assistance in form of time- and cost-saving guidance as to how best to proceed in searching for ways to achieve some pre-specified technical objectives, which raise the expected rates of return and reduce the riskiness of investing in applied R&D, (4) under sufficiently strong incentives it becomes more likely to express more of the tacit component of the technical and research knowledge in forms that would make it easier to transmit, and eventually that is likely to happen (T Hughes et al., Funding a Revolution… 1999, pp. 49–50).

48 We take a more holistic approach, in contrast to the methodological individualistic one.

49 In 2001 MITI was reorganized as the Ministry of Economy, Trade and Industry (METI). See www.meti.go.jp/english/index.html.

50 Further details see the already classics in the Western literature on development; e.g., Chalmer Johnson, MITI and the Japanese Miracle: The Growth of Industrial Policy, 1925–1975, Stanford University Press, 1982 and Robert Wade, Governing the Market Economic Theory and the Role of Government in East Asian Industrialization, Princeton University Press, 1990. From a Japanese perspective see Miyohei Shinohara, MITI´s industrial policy and Japanese industrial organization, IDE-RETRO, Volume 14, Issue 4, 319–487, December 1976. For an Austrian-based critique on the MITI literature see www.econlib.org/library/Enc/Japan.html

51 www.fas.org/irp/world/japan/miti.htm
52 The Korea Institute of Science and Technology was the first South Korean contract research institute, created in the mid 1960s. Its main role was to develop industrial technologies. At that time it was organized into 31 independently managed laboratories, focused on food technology, mechanical and chemical engineering, material science, and electronics. It served as broker for technology transfer as well as in reverse engineering projects to promote the development of indigenous capabilities in the country. It was also responsible for the development of several technologies in the above-mentioned fields. Until the late 1970s, this organization essentially focused on developed technologies which were in the declining stage or mature stage in advanced countries. But as private R&D capabilities increased, it redefined its role by focusing on the development of frontier technologies (see Dal Hwan Lee et al. Performance and adaptive roles of the government supported research institutes in South Korea, pp. 1421–40, *World Development 19*(10), 1991, See R Mazzoleni and R Nelson, The role of research at universities and public labs in economic catch-up. In: Cimoli et al. Industrial *Policy* and *Development*, pp. 378–409, 200.
53 The Korea Advanced Institute for Science was created during the 1970s and it focused on providing graduate level in science and engineering to specifically cover the needs of firms such as Samsung, Goldstar and local affiliates of foreign companies. In 1982 it merged with KIST and became KAIST (Korea Advanced Institute of Science and Technology). See R Mazzoleni and R Nelson, The role of research at niversities and public labs...
54 The Semiconductor Technology Development Centre was created in 1975 in order to carry out indigenous research on semiconductors. Its first collaboration was a reverse engineering project with Goldstar (bipolar IC). In 1977 it merged with a research department of KIST to create KIET (Korea Institute of Electronics Technology), which carried out many projects with firms such as Samsung, Daewoo, Goldstar, Hyundai to develop ICs for applications in consumer electronics and telecommunications (ibid.).
55 The Electronics and Telecommunications Research Institute was created in 1985. It has mostly worked with the chaebols – e.g. Samsung, LG and Hyundai – in applied research and has been strongly influenced by them in the allocation of public R&D funds to technology areas (ibid.).
56 The South Korean semiconductor industry is a successes story in innovation learning and catch-up. During the 1960s and 1970s, the South Korean government placed great importance on industrialization, and focused its economic development strategy on a handful of large domestic conglomerates, protecting them from competition, and assisting them financially. Samsung was one of these companies. The government banned several foreign companies from selling consumer electronics in South Korea in order to protect Samsung from foreign competition and nurture an electronics manufacturing sector that was in its infancy.
57 The Industrial Technology Research Institute was a research institution created by the Taiwanese government in 1973.
58 The Electronics Industrial and Research Center was a former laboratory of ITRI, which became a key government-based NFO for inward technology transfer, and for the accumulation of indigenous capabilities in industrial research. It usually licensed foreign technology. It developed a pilot plant to master the technology and gave training to the future local workforce in the use of the technologies. Then the technology was transferred to a spin-off firm. During the 1980s ERSO also

provided venture capital and technological assistance to researchers who intended to exploit technologies developed or acquired by ERSO (e.g. Taiwan Semiconductor Company) promoted the formation of private spin-offs.

59 www.time.com/time/world/article/0,8599,1913913,00.html#ixzz0j5ZxitJX
60 The names are CANON, Hitachi, Toshiba, Sony, Matsushita, NEC Corp., Fujitsu and Mitsubishi. See www.businessinsider.com/most-innovative-companies-of-all-time-2011–6?op=1

References

Abate J (1999), *Inventing the Internet.* MIT Press.

Abramovitz M (1986), Catching up, forging ahead and falling behind, *Journal of Economic History* 66: 385–406.

Abramovitz M (1989), *Thinking about Growth and Other Essays on Economic Growth and Welfare.* Cambridge: Cambridge University Press.

Acha V et al. (2007), Exploring the miracle: Strategy and the management of knowledge bases in the aeronautics industry, *International Journal of Innovation and Technology Management* 1(4): 1–25.

Aghion P and Howitt P (1992), A model of growth through creative destruction, *Econometrica* 60: 323–51.

Aoki M (1990), Toward an economic model of the Japanese firm, *Journal of Economic Literature* 28 (March): 1–27.

Aoki M (1999), Information and Governance in the Silicon Valley Model. *Discussion Paper* #99DOF31, Stanford University, July.

Arrow K (1962), The economic implications of learning by doing, *Review of Economic Studies* 29(3): 155–73.

Arthur B (1989), Competing technologies, increasing returns, and lock-in by historical events, *The Economic Journal* 99(394) (March): 116–31.

Arthur B (2009), *The Nature of Technology: What It Is and How It Evolves.* New York: Free Press.

Barney J (1991), Firm resources and sustained competitive advantage, *Journal of Management* 17(1) (March): 99–120

Barro R and Sala-i-Martin (2003), *Economic Growth.* Cambridge, MA and London: The MIT Press.

Bell M and Pavitt K (1993), Technological accumulation and industrial growth: Contrasts between developed and developing countries, *Industrial and Corporate Change* 2(2): 157–209.

Bessen J and Maskin E (2000), Sequential Innovation, Patents, and Imitation, MIT *Working Paper* No. 00-01, Revised March 2006.

Biotechnology and Intellectual Property: Reinventing the Commons Workshop Report, McGill Centre for Intellectual Property Policy Montreal, Canada, September 25–27, 2005.

Block F (2008), Swimming against the current: The rise of a hidden developmental state in the United States, *Politics & Society* 36(2) (June): 169–206.

Boldrin M and Levine D (2008), *Against Intellectual Monopoly.* Cambridge: Cambridge University Press.

Brusoni S et al. (2001), Knowledge specialisation and the boundaries of the firm: Why firms know more than they make, *Administrative Science Quarterly* 46: 597–621.

Brusoni S and Prencipe A (2001), Unpacking the black box of modularity: Technologies, products, organisations, *Industrial and Corporate Change* 10(1): 179–205.

Bush V (1945), Science the Endless Frontier, A Report to the President by the Director of the Office of Scientific Research and Development, United States Government Printing Office, Washington, July, available at https://nsf.gov/od/lpa/nsf50/vbush1945.htm, last accesed in August 2018.

Cargill C (2002), Intellectual Property Rights and standards settings organizations: An overview of failed evolution, Submitted to the Department of Justice and the Federal Trade Commission, Version 2.

Chandler A (1977), *The Visible Hand.* Cambridge, MA and London: The Belknap Press, Harvard University Press.

Chandler A (2004), *Scale and Scope: The Dynamics of Industrial Capitalism.* Cambridge, MA: Harvard University Press.

Chang HJ (2002), Breaking the mould: an institutionalist political economy alternative to the neo-liberal theory of the market, *Cambridge Journal of Economics* 26(5): 539–59.

Chang HJ (2003a), Kicking Away the Ladder. London: Anthem Press.

Chang HJ (2003b) Globalisation, Economic Development and the Role of the State. London: Zed Books.

Chang HJ (ed.) (2007), *Institutional Change and Economic Development.* London: Anthem Press.

Chang HJ (2009), Industrial Policy: Can We Go Beyond an Unproductive Confrontation?, A Plenary Paper for ABCDE (Annual World Bank Conference on Development Economics) Seoul, South Korea, June 22–24.

Chang HJ (2010), Institutions and economic development: Theory, policy and history, Journal of Institutional Economics, 7(4): 1–26, pre-published copy.

Cimoli M et al. (2006), Institutions and Policies Shaping Industrial Development: An Introductory Note, LEM, *Working Paper Series*, No. 2, January.

Cimoli M et al. (eds.) (2009), *The Political Economy of Capabilities Accumulation: the Past and Future of Policies for Industrial Development.* Oxford: Oxford University Press.

Clark J et al. (2000), Patent pools: A Solution to the problem of access in biotechnology patents?, UPSTO *Research Paper,* December.

Coe N et al. (2008), Global production networks: Realizing the potential, *Journal of Economic Geography* 8(3): 271–95.

Cohen M et al. (2000), Protecting Their Intellectual Assets: Appropriability Conditions and Why U.S. Manufacturing Firms Patent (or Not), NBER *Working Paper* No. 7552, February.

Conner KR and Prahalad CK (1996) A resource-based theory of the firm: Knowledge vs. opportunism. Organization Science 7(5): 477–501.

David P (1985), Clio and the economics of QWERTY, *The American Economic Review* 75(2), Papers and Proceedings of the Ninety-Seventh Annual Meeting of the American Economic Association, May 1985, pp. 332–7.

Demirel P and Mazzucato M (2012), Innovation and firm growth: Is R&D worth it?, *Industry & Innovation* 19(1): 45–62.

Dierickx I and Cool K (1989), Asset stock accumulation of competitive advantage, *Management Science* 35(12) (December): 1504–11.

Dosi G (1988), Sources, procedures and microeconomics effects of innovation, *Journal of Economic Literature* XXVI (September): 1120–71.

Dosi G et al. (2002), The Economics of Systems Integration: Towards an Evolutionary Interpretation, LEM *Working Paper Series*, 2002/16, Draft – June 2002.

Dosi G et al. (2003), The economics of systems integration: Towards an evolutionary interpretation. In: A Prencipe et al. (eds.), (2005), *The Business of Systems Integration*. Oxford: Oxford University Press, pp. 95–114.

Dosi G et al. (2006), The relationships between science, technologies and their industrial exploitation: An illustration through the myths and realities of the so-called "European Paradox," *Research Policy* 35: 1450–64.

Edquist C. (2001), The Systems of Innovation Approach and Innovation Policy: An account of the state of the art, Lead paper presented at the DRUID Conference, Aalborg, June 12–15, 2001, under theme F: National Systems of Innovation, Institutions and Public Policies, National Systems of Innovation, Institutions and Public Policies, Draft of 2001-06-01.

Eyo, S (2011), A Comparison of Biotechnology Industry in Japan and Other Developed Countries (April 23), Available at SSRN: http://ssrn.com/abstract=1878599 or http://dx.doi.org/10.2139/ssrn.1878599

Foster J (2005), From simplistic to complex systems in economics, *Cambridge Journal of Economics* 29(6): 873–92.

Freeman Ch (1987), *Technology Policy and Economic Performance: Lesson from Japan*. London: Pinter Publishers.

Freeman Ch (1995), National system of innovation in a historical perpective, *Cambridge Journal of Economics* 19: 5–24.

Freeman Ch (2004), Technological infrastructure and international competitiveness, Industrial and Corporate Change 13(3): 541–69.

Freeman Ch (2008), *System of Innovation*. UK, USA: Edward Elgar.

Gaulé, P (2006), Towards Patent Pools in Biotechnology?, CEMI-REPORT-2006–010, *Working Papers Series*, April.

Gerschenkron A (1962), *Economic Backwardness in Historical Perspective, a Book of Essays*. Cambridge, MA: Belknap Press of Harvard University Press.

Gilbert R (2004), Antitrust for patent pools: A century of policy evolution, Stanford Technology Law Review. 3. http://stlr.stanford.edu/STLR/Articles/04_STLR_3

Godin B (2007), National Innovation Systems: The system approach in historical perspective, Project on the History and Sociology of STI Statistics, *Working Paper* No. 36.

Hall B and Ham R (2001), The patent paradox revisited: an empirical study of patenting in the U.S. semiconductor industry, 1979–1995, *RAND Journal of Economics* 32(1), Spring: 101–28.

Heller M (1998), The tragedy of the anticommons: Property in the transition from Marx to markets, *Harvard Law Review* 111: 621.

Heller M and Eisenberg R (1998), Can patents deter innovation? The anticommons in biomedical research, *Science* 280(5364): 698–701.

Hirschman A (1958), *The Strategy of Economic Development*. New Haven, CO: Yale University Press.

Hughes T et al. (1999), *Funding a Revolution: Government Support for Computing Research*. Washington, D.C.: National Academy Press.

Johnson C (1982), *MITI and the Japanese Miracle: The Growth of Industrial Policy, 1925–1975*. Stanford: Stanford University Press

Kim L (1997), The dynamics of Samsung's technological learning in semiconductors, *California Management Review* 39(3), Spring; ABI/INFORM Global.

Kortum S and Lerner J (1999), What is behind the recent surge in patenting?, *Research Policy* 28: 1–22.

Lall S (1992), Technological capabilities and industrialization, *World Development* 20(2): 165–86.

Langlois R (2002), Modularity in technology and organization, *Journal of Economic Behavior & Organization* 49: 19–37.

Lazonick W (2002), Innovative enterprise and historical transformation, *Enterprise & Society* 3 (March): 3–47.

Lazonick W (2006), Corporate Governance, Innovative Enterprise, and Economic Development, UNU WIDER, *Research Paper* No. 2006/71, July.

Lazonick W (2008), *Sustainable Prosperity in the New Economy? Business Organization and High-Tech Employment in the United States.* Kalamazoo, MI: W.E. Upjohn Institute for Employment Research.

Lazonick W (2011), The Innovative Enterprise and the Developmental State: Toward an Economics of "Organizational Success," Paper prepared for: Institute for New Economic Thinking Annual 2011 conference Crisis and Renewal: International Political Economy at the Crossroads Mount Washington Hotel Bretton Woods, NH, April 8–11, 2011.

Lazonick W and O'Sullivan M (2000), Perspectives on Corporate Governance, Innovation, and Economic Performance, The European Institute of Business Administration, Fontainebleau Cedex, France.

Lazonick W and Tulum Ö (2011), The US biopharmaceutical finance and the sustainability of the biotech business model, *Research Policy* 40(9) (November): 1170–87.

Lee DH et al. (1991), Performance and adaptive roles of the government supported research institutes in South Korea. *World Development* 19(10): 1421–40.

Lee P et al. (2012), *Continuing Innovation in Information Technology.* Washington, D.C.: National Academy Press.

Lerner J et al. (2005), The design of patent pools: The determinants of licensing rules, *The RAND Journal of Economics* 38(3) (November): 610–25,.

Levinthal D (1998), The slow pace of rapid technological change: Gradualism and punctuation in technological change, *Industrial and Corporate Change* 7: 217–47.

Levinthal D (2006), The neo-Schumpeterian theory of the firm and the strategy field, *Industrial and Corporate Change* 15(2): 391–4.

Light D et al. (2011), Longer exclusivity does not guarantee better drugs, *Health Affairs* 30(4) (April): 798.

Lundvall B (2002), *Innovation, Growth and Social Cohesion.* Cheltenham, UK, Northampton; USA: Edward Elgar.

Lundvall B (2007), National Innovation System: Analytical Focusing Device and Policy Learning Tool, Swedish Institute for Growth Policy Studies, *Working paper* R2007:004.

Malerba F (1992), Learning by firms and incremental technical change, *The Economic Journal* 102(413) (July): 845–59.

Malerba F (1999), Sectoral systems of innovation and production, DRUID Conference on: National Innovation Systems, Industrial Dynamics and Innovation Policy Rebuild, June 9–12, 1999.

Malerba F (2002), Sectoral systems of innovation and production, *Research Policy* 31: 247–64.

Malerba F (2006), Catch up in different sectoral systems: Some introductory remarks, *Globelics India.* Innovation systems for competitiveness and shared prosperity in developing countries, Trivandrum, Kerala, October 4–7.

Marengo L et al. (2009), Appropriability, Patents, and Rates of Innovation in Complex Products Industries, LEM, *Working Paper Series*, No. 5, April.

Mazzucato M (2011), The Entrepreneurial State. London, Demos,

Mazzucato M (2013), *The Entrepeneurial State: Debuking Public vs. Private Sector Myths.* London, New York: Anthem Press.

Metcalfe JS (1995), Technology systems and technology policy in an evolutionary framework, Cambridge Journal of Economics 19: 25–46.

Mowery D and Nelson R (1999), *The Sources of Industrial Leadership.* Cambridge: Cambridge University Press,

Mowery D and Simcoe T (2002), Is the Internet a US invention? – an economic and technological history of computer networking, *Research Policy* 31: 1369–87.

National Science Foundation (2012), National Patterns of R&D Resources: 2009 Data Update, *NCSES*, NSF 12–321, Arlington, VA. Available at www.nsf.gov/statistics/nsf12321/.

Nelson R (1993), *National Innovation Systems: A Comparative Study.* Oxford: Oxford University Press.

Nelson R and Rosenberg N (1993), Technical innovation and national systems. In: R Nelson (ed.), *National Innovation Systems.* Oxford: Oxford University Press, pp. 3–23.

Nelson R and Winter S (1982), *An Evolutionary Theory of Economic Change.* Cambridge, MA: The Belknap Press.

Nonaka I and Krogh G (2009), Tacit knowledge and knowledge conversion: Controversy and advancement in organizational knowledge creation theory, *Organization Science* 20(3) (May–June): 635–52.

Nonaka I and Takeuchi H (1995), *The Knowledge-Creating Company: How Japanese Companies Create the Dynamics of Innovation.* Oxford: Oxford University Press.

Pavitt K (1984), Sectoral patterns of technical change: Towards a taxonomy and a theory, *Research Policy* 13: 343–73.

Penrose E (1959), *The Theory of the Growth of the Firm.* New York: Oxford University Press.

Perez C and Soete L (1988), Catching up in Technology: Entry barriers and windows of opportunities In: G Dosi et al. (eds.), *Technical Change and Economic Theory.* London: Pinter Publishers, pp. 458–479.

Pisano G (2006), *Sience Business: The Premise, the Reality, and the Future of Biotech.* Boston, MA: Harvard Business School Press.

Polanyi M [1962] (1983), *The Tacit Dimension.* Gloucester, MA: Peter Smith Publisher Inc. Anchor Books.

Prahalad CK and Hamel G (1990), The core competence of the corporation, *Harvard Business Review* 68: 79–91.

Prencipe A. (2000), Breadth and depth of technological capabilities in complex product systems: The case of the aircraft engine control system, *Research Policy* 29: 895–911.

Prencipe A et al. (eds.) (2005), *The Business of Systems Integration.* Oxford: Oxford University Press,

Reinert E (1999), The role of the state in economic growth, *Journal of Economic Studies* 26(4/5): 268–326.

Reinert E (2007), *How Rich Countries Got Rich… and Why Poor Countries Stay Poor*, London: Constable.

Reinert E (2012), Economics and the Public Sphere, *Working Papers in Technology Governance and Economic Dynamics*, no. 40.

Romer P (1986), Increasing returns and long-run growth, *The Journal of Political Economy* 94(5): 1002–37.

Romer P (1990), Endogenous technological change, *Journal of Political Economy* 98: 71–102.

Rosenberg N (1976), *Perspectives on Technology.* Cambridge: Cambridge University Press.

Rothwell R (1992), Successful industrial innovation: Critical factors for the 1990s, *R&D Management* 22: 221–39.

Rumelt RP (1984), Towards a strategic theory of the firm. In: RB Lamb (ed.), *Competitive Strategic Management.* Englewood Cliffs, NJ: Prentice Hall.

Ruttan V (2006), Is war necessary for economic growth?, Historically Speaking-Issues (merged papers), Clemons Lecture, University of Minnesota, October 9.

Sako M (1998), Supplier Development at Honda, Nissan and Toyota: A Historical Case Study of Organizational Capability Enhancement, Said Business School, University of Oxford.

Sako M (2004), Supplier development at Honda, Nissan and Toyota: A historical case study of organizational capability enhancement, *Industrial and Corporate Change* 13(2) (April): 281–308.

Sanchez R and Mahoney JT (1996), Modularity, flexibility, and knowledge management in product and organisation design, *Strategic Management Journal* 17, Winter Special Issue: 63–76.

Scher M (2001), Bank-firm cross shareholding in Japan: What is it, why does it matter, is it winding down? United Nations' Department of Economic and Social Affairs (DESA), Discussion Paper, No. 15.

Schilling M (2000), Toward a general modular systems theory & its application to interfirm product modularity, *Academy of Management Review* 25(2): 312–34.

Senge P (1990), *The Fifth Discipline: The Art and Practice of the Learning Organization.* New York: Doubleday.

Shapiro C (2004), *Navigating the Patent Thicket: Cross Licenses, Patent Pools, and Standard Settings.* Cambridge, MA and London: MIT Press.

Shinohara M (1976), MITI's industrial policy and Japanese industrial organization, *IDE-RETRO* 14(4) (December): 319–487.

Simon H (1962), The architecture of complexity, *Proceedings of the American Philosophical Society* 106(6) (Dec. 12): 467–82.

Simon H (1991), Organizations and markets, *Journal of Economic Perspectives* 5(2): 25–44.

Solow R (1957), Technical change and the aggregate production function, *The Review of Economics and Statistics* 39(3) (Aug.): 312–20.

Sredojević D et al. (2016), Technological changes in economic growth theory: Neoclassical, endogenous, and evolutionary- institutional approach, *Economic Themes* 54(2): 177–94.

Steinmueller W (1995), The U.S. software industry: An analysis and interpretive history, *MERIT Research Memoranda* 9(006), UNU-MERIT.

Steinmueller W (1996), The U.S. software industry: An analysis and interpretative history. In Mowery (ed.), *The International Computer Software Industry.* Oxford: Oxford University Press.

Sung L and Pelto D (1998), Greater predictability may result in patent pools; as the Federal Circuit refines scope of biotech claims, use of collective rights becomes likely, *The National Law Journal,* ISSN: 0162-7325.

Teece D (2007), Explicating dynamic capabilities: The nature and microfoundations of (sustainable) enterprise performance, *Strategic Management Journal* 28(13) (December): 1319–50.

Teece D et al. (1997), Dynamic capabilities and strategic management, *Strategic Management Journal* 18(7) (August): 509–33.

von Hippel E (2005), *Democratizing Innovation*, Cambridge: MIT Press.

von Hippel E and von Krogh G (2006), Free revealing and the private-collective model for innovation incentives, *R&D Management* 36: 295–306.

Wade R (1990), *Governing the Market Economic Theory and the Role of Government in East Asian Industrialization*. Princeton, NJ: Princeton University Press.

Wasserman S and Faust K (1994), *Social Network Analysis: Methods and Applications*. Cambridge: Cambridge University Press.

Wernerfelt B (2002), Why should the boss own the assets?, *Journal of Economics and Management Strategy* 11: 473–85.

Williamson O (1975), *Markets and Hierarchies*. New York: Free Press.

Winter S (2006), The logic of appropriability: From Schumpeter to Arrow to Teece, *Research Policy* 35(8) (October): 1100–6.

Part II

Contextualization and analysis of the case

5 Cuban institutions and industrial policy until 1989

5.1 Political change as institutional change

Political changes have quite often been the reason behind the institutional change within a political economy. Many of these changes include broad military campaigns such as the European religious wars between the sixteenth and the beginning of the eighteenth centuries, the Islamic expansion between the sixth and thirteenth centuries, the western colonization between the fifteenth and twentieth centuries, and World Wars I and II. Political changes have also taken the form of nationalist and social revolutions, which have taken place throughout modern age in many places around the globe. Cases such as the American Revolution, the Mexican Revolution, the French Revolution and the Chinese Revolution are some of many examples. It is within this historical framework that the Cuban Revolution should be understood.

Relying on the theoretical framework outlined in the previous chapters, we will argue, based on the Cuba during the years 1959–89, that the political experience of a country must be included as a relevant and dynamic factor when analyzing its development strategy. This seemingly obvious statement usually runs counter to the analyses made from the perspective of traditional frameworks, probably because they fail to engage in an accurate institutional analysis. This neglect stems in part from the notional distinction between specialized knowledge and ideology present in most of the literature, and it hinders more fruitful conceptualizations that openly embrace the political foundations of the economic science. It is also a reflection of how the economic science has been painfully disconnected, for far too long a time, from both its interdisciplinary origins and its nature as a social science.

Of course, there is always a moral foundation, and it seems to be the case that, in the traditional interpretation of the Cuban and other cases, dichotomies such as state/market, public/private, etc., have been employed much more as ideological biases rather than as explicative frameworks. However, historical evidence and economic theory have shown that those terms have never been clearly defined and that the relationship between them is more complex and interdependent than lineal and mutually exclusive.

There is no reason to take it for granted that the market solution proposed by the orthodox discourse is superior in any form to a more politicized management of the economy. Here it is argued that precisely the kind of bias mentioned above is the very obstacle to a better understanding of any development experience (whether successful or not). Such an experience must be understood as an ongoing process of improvement of the state's developmental capabilities[1] rather than as a systematic reduction of its capacity to act as an active agent of change. Of course, this also applies for the Asian, American and most of the European development experiences (Lazonick 2006; Chang 2008, 2009; Amsdsen 1989; Evans et al. 1999; Micheisen and Kuisma 1992; Jäntti and Vartiainen 2009). Successful development experiences have usually been linked to institutional adaptation and institutional innovation, which have been mostly carried out by the state in the form of industrial policy, and have traditionally been contained within a long-term oriented social contract.

This sort of consensus is not meant to necessarily be the result of a convergent decision-making process. In fact, institution building is an essentially uncertain process and its relation to economic development in terms of causality is complex and interdependent. Generally a change in the economic structure is needed in order to create new institutions more than the other way around, but in practice economic activities and institutions co-evolve. This very often leads to conflict situations, which are then managed (or not) by an efficient developmental state. This process frequently excludes "potentially relevant agents from the decision making process" (Chang in Woo-Cumings 1999 note 39, p. 195), giving form to a certain developmental vision that can fail or succeed. However, failure should not necessarily be corrected by dismissing the state (although it could be the case), but by reforming it.[2] It is not about whether the state should be involved in the development process, because "as the ultimate guarantor of property and other rights in the society, it is bound to be" (ibid., p. 196). It is more about how the state can deal with this issue in a useful manner.

It is intended to show that the Cuban experience in the years 1959–89[3] just confirms these patterns. During this period a certain industrial base and new manufacturing branches were created (see below in this chapter *Cuba in the socialist economic world*), including the one that led to the biotech industry. In addition, a highly qualified and relatively skilled workforce was formed. However, government-based non-firm organizations failed to create the necessary synergies among economic agents and to provide room for diversity within the economic system. The adopted vision of industrialization, although supported with guaranteed external financing, was based on importing outdated technology and maybe more relevant, inherited the strong Soviet anti-innovation bias.

We will argue that these shortcomings should not be attributed uncritically as a problem of too much state and too little market, or even be circumscribed within the framework socialism vs. capitalism, but rather be seen as the failure of a type of state intervention, which can be corrected within the politically legitimated socio-institutional structure established by the Cuban revolution.

Of course, as long as that political legitimacy applies, which seems to be the present case in the Cuban society. We propose that the developmental/anti-developmental distinction developed by proponents of the Institutional Political Economy (e.g. Chang in Woo-Cumings 1999) could be a more productive way to analyze the Cuban (or any other) development strategy.

5.2 Before 1959

Even though several commentators place Cuba among one of the most advanced countries in Latin America during the 1950s, the Caribbean island remained unable to diversify its economy and to expand its socioeconomic development throughout the entire country. While the most urbanized sector of the metro-politan area, which according to several scholars received 60 percent of the country's investments, hosted 66 percent of all industrial facilities and provided 75 percent of the island's non sugar industrial production,[4] enjoyed a well-developed system of social security and education facilities, these sorts of facilities remained nonexistent in rural areas (most of the country).

During the first half of twentieth century, large public hospitals emerged in the country and provided free services, but they were limited to major cities and were chronically underfunded prior to 1959. Mutual clinics were created by mutual societies of Spanish origin and functioned within a cooperative framework. In return for a monthly fee, members of these societies received high-quality medical services. At the same time in the first half of the twentieth century, a significant network of private clinics flourished. They also provided high-quality services, but mostly worked on the profit principle, excluding the millions of people who could not afford to pay.

In addition, "in 1953 the illiteracy rate in rural areas was 3.6 times higher than in urban areas (41.7 and 11.6 percent respectively)."[5] According to the data from a survey made in 1956 among agricultural wage laborers by the University's Catholic Group, housing and sanitary would put the Cuban farmer among those living under the most miserable conditions worldwide. For example, only 7.3 percent of houses had electric lighting.[6] A report on Cuba's education system comments that "half of Cuba's children did not attend school at all, 72 percent of 13 to 19 year olds failed to reach intermediate levels of schooling, and there were over one million illiterate."[7] Analogous disproportions existed in housing, access to potable water/sanitation, and infant mortality.

The need to put a remedy to many of these social ills was also agreed with by the Truslow mission,[8] which was a 1951 economic and technical mission organized by the International Bank of Reconstruction and Development (later World Bank) in collaboration with the Cuban government. The well-detailed mission report (more than 1000 pages including annex) acknowledged the social and economic backwardness of the country; for instance that between 80 and 90 percent of the children in rural areas were infested by intestinal parasites. Based on these and other elements such as lack of railroads, roads and high quality water supplies and the low levels of gross capital formation, excluding construction,[9] the report advanced several recommendations aimed at improving a number of key indicators in the country, the diversification of the economy away from sugar being one of the most prominent. It also warned that not taking any action would increase political instability.

One of the most interesting proposals of the mission was the creation of an organization for applied research in order to contribute to the development of agriculture and industry (particularly those of benefits for American investors, e.g., sugar and its byproducts, minerals, foodstuff). In this sense, the report reflected the growing awareness among Cuban progressive intellectuals about the need for technological and industrial research. The *Fundación Cubana para la investigación Technológica*,[10] the name suggested, was expected to function as a center of Cuban industrial technology, to stimulate interest in improved production, research and development. It should also provide practical training for selected Cuban technologists who could have become interested in applied research as a career, offering them an opportunity to work in this field in close association with experienced industrial research workers from all parts of the world. This institution was also expected to conduct confidential research programs for private companies, in which the individual company would pay the cost and received exclusive rights to the results; as well as to conduct research for entire industries and for the interest of the country.

Although this report, clearly responding to American interests, discouraged the development of certain industries, such as steel[11] or hydroelectric power generation, and focused on climate-, natural resources-based, less technologically sophisticated, recommendations for Cuba,[12] it was right in the need to overcome "misplaced patriotism"[13] in science by employing foreign specialists to assist this project or, for that case, any other scientific enterprise to be promoted in the country. Even so, this was sort of a contentious statement to make in a country which was completely controlled by the trained personnel of a foreign superpower, whose very economic domination went almost unnoticed by the report, but was nevertheless at the root of most of the problems described in it. Still, by asserting that "[s]cience is no respecter of nationalities"[14] the report acknowledged the importance of international cooperation in scientific matters, in addition to pursuing more practical goals such as overcoming the lack of Cuban personal properly qualified to do the task at the time.[15]

However, as well-intentioned as it may have been, some of the recommendations provided by the report, particularly for the sugar industry, clashed with the demands of Cuban unions and other intellectuals. For example, the demand for low wages and the relaxing of controls in order to make it easier for managers to fire workers, even in the sugar industry. The report openly saw the existence of organized labor in this industry as part of the "costs" to pay in terms of the social "adjustments" imposed by the industry.[16]

In addition, while the report recommended Cuba to expand its export markets for sugar in Europe and to renegotiate its quota with the United States, it could not satisfactorily explain (even if it tried) how to proceed with this recommendation within the framework of the overwhelming US influence in Cuban affairs. The report had to acknowledge that, even when Cuba's foreign trade at the time was under the provisions of the General Agreement on Tariffs and Trade (GATT), signed by the Cuban Government at Geneva on October 31, 1947, which gave the country the theoretical possibility to withdraw any tariff concession on a specific product without securing the previous agreement of the other country, the Agreement could not do away with the tariff preferentials introduced by the unequal treaty of 1902[17] and ratified in the reciprocity trade treaty of 1934.[18] The reality was that until 1948, when GATT became effective, the main framework for Cuban trade policy had been shaped by these bilateral treaties with the US, and it would continue to be that way until the US government decided otherwise, particularly in the sugar industry.

In fact, the dependency on sugar cane was absolute,[19] with the prices and the sugar quota being set by the United States. Crude sugar and sugar products made up more than 70 percent of Cuba's foreign trade (O'Connor 1970, p. 59). Both world market and US quotas for the island were set by presidential decree, which varied according to the vagaries of the United States Congress. This dependency, along with natural price fluctuations of sugar in the world market, provided little dynamism to the economy. Cuba's investments booms depended on sugar's export levels, which had invariably a seasonal character. Several authors have shown that the sugar quota had negative effects in the Cuban economy (Dye and Sicotte 2004).

Internally, the sugar industry was organized as cartel (for a detailed account O'Connor 1970, pp. 59–62). The Mill Owners' Association and the Sugar Stabilisation Institute were the two Cuba's key political economic agents to determine how most of the island economic resources were to be employed. Each cane grower was assigned a quota and each sugar mill was awarded with two export quotas; for the US market and world market respectively. Manufacturing, banking, transport and commerce were inescapably tied to the sugar production.[20] In this context, 16 percent of the labor force was "openly unemployed," and around 14 percent were underemployed in the period from 1956–57.[21] An additional open unemployment (twofold) emerged during "the annual slack period of the sugar sector (dead season) over the period of the harvest." All this occurred in a period, during which the US economy enjoyed almost full employment.[22]

Even when during the 1950s a National Economic Council was created in order to design economic policies, the acute dependency made it impossible for this institution to become an effective planning agency. It just lacked real executive power. In fact, almost every economic decision had to be consulted upon with the representatives of the US government in Cuba. Although formally independent, the country remained politically and economically dependent (O'Connor 1970, pp. 12–36). This picture was completed by the existence of a de facto military regime (1952–59) which completely submitted to the US interests, accentuating the socioeconomic stagnation and thus generating strong opposition within various (and sometimes conflicting) sectors of Cuban society.

Resuming this scenario in a speech to United Nations in September 1960, Cuban revolutionary leader Fidel Castro addressed the audience:

"What did the Revolution find when it came to power in Cuba?[...] First of all the Revolution found that 600,000 able Cubans were unemployed – as many, proportionately, as were unemployed in the United States at the time of the great depression which shook this country and which almost created a catastrophe in the United States. That was our permanent unemployment. [...] On the other hand, 85 per cent of the small farmers were paying rents for the use of land to the tune of almost 30 per cent of their income, while 1 1/2 percent of the landowners controlled 46 per cent of the total area of the nation [...]

Public utilities, electricity and telephone services all belonged to the United States monopolies. A major portion of the banking business, of the importing business and the oil refineries, the greater part of the sugar production, the best land in Cuba, and the most important industries in all fields belonged to American companies. The balance of payments in the last ten years, from 1950 to 1960, had been favorable to the United States with regard to Cuba to the extent of one thousand million dollars.[...] One thousand million dollars in ten years. This poor and underdeveloped Caribbean country, with 600,000 unemployed, was contributing greatly to the economic development of the most highly industrialized country in the world [...]

What was the state of our reserves when the tyrant Batista came to power. There was $500,000,000 in our national reserve, a goodly sum to have invested in the industrial development of the country. When the Revolution came to power there was only $70,000,000 in our reserves. Was there any concern for the industrial development of our country? No.[...]"[23]

Now consider the words of his adversary at the time, then Senator and future president John F. Kennedy, who, after criticizing in the strongest terms the Communist orientation of Fidel Castro's revolution at a democratic dinner in October 1960, admitted that:

"[...] we refused to help Cuba meet its desperate need for economic progress [...] [I]nstead of holding out a helping hand of friendship to the desperate people of Cuba, nearly all our aid was in the form of weapons assistance – assistance, which merely strengthened the Batista dictatorship – assistance which completely failed to advance the economic welfare of the Cuban people[...]

[I]n a manner certain to antagonize the Cuban people, we used the influence of our Government to advance the interests of and increase the profits of the private American companies, which dominated the island's economy. At the beginning of 1959 United States companies owned about 40 percent of the Cuban sugar lands – almost all the cattle ranches – 90 percent of the mines and mineral concessions – 80 percent of the utilities – and practically all the oil industry – and supplied two-thirds of Cuba's imports[...] The symbol of this shortsighted attitude is now on display in a Havana museum. It is a solid gold telephone presented to Batista by the American-owned Cuban telephone company. It is an expression of gratitude for the excessive telephone rate increase which the Cuban Dictator had granted at the urging of our Government [...] It is no wonder in short, that during these years of American indifference the Cuban people began to doubt the sincerity of our dedication to democracy. [...]"[24]

The Cuban Revolution of 1959 resulted from these antagonisms.

5.3 Brief remarks on Cuban socialism

5.3.1 *The beginning*

In our view, the Cuban socialism needs to be understood as a question of expediency rather than as a premeditated act, at least if we assume the *real existent* Soviet-style socialism as a point of comparison. As already mentioned, the Cuban revolution draws more on "national popular traditions combined with the sense of frustration and indignation against corruption, repression, and U.S. domination."[25] In any case, to provide a clear definition of socialism remains a task to be achieved. In fact, we can find a number of theories and concepts referring to the subject, some of them even providing conflicting notions and set of practices regarding to critical issues such as property ownership, economic coordination and the like. Therefore we need to be cautious when referring to socialism as an encompassing term.

Actually, many of the elements usually associated with the traditional conception of socialism (e.g., social ownership in its different forms) are to be found in capitalist (and pre-capitalist) economies as well. In this regard, it would be safe to acknowledge the complexity of the issue when assessing a given country's political and economic history. To be sure, the differences between socialism and capitalism are real and necessary to articulate. However, for known historical reasons, these differences are not easily circumscribable to the traditional definitions based on certain models of economic organization. One of the most important elements in this respect is the fact that what was seen as mainstream socialism at the time of the Russia's October revolution was very different from what was seen as such thereafter.

Lenin's Bolshevik faction was actually a right-wing minority of the socialist movement.[26] This faction, which advocated the need of a vanguard-party in order to be able to achieve socialism, was heavily criticized by the mainstream socialists of the time.[27] Ideas of council communism, which advocated workers councils and industrial democracy, represented the mainstream of socialist though at the time and among its key figures we find such names as Anton Pannekoek, Otto Rühle, Rosa Luxemburg, Sylvia Pankhurst and Herman Gorter. Workers' councils played an important role in the success of Russia's February revolution in 1917, from which the Bolshevik faction capitalized. However, as the Bolsheviks succeeded in the October Revolution, and the following civil war, these bodies were dismantled or assimilated into a one-party structure. It is a complex subject[28] that needs more development, but the point is that to exclusively focus on certain models of economic organization in order to define socialism might be misleading and slippery.

Socialism has been attempted to be defined attending to different criteria, and this multiplicity of criteria reflects the multidimensionality of the phenomenon being defined, as well as the many aspects after which the dichotomy socialism/capitalism could be assessed. In order to gain more clarity about what distinguishes one system from another we would also need to further investigate and articulate certain ideological and behavioral dimensions of the subject, which have been hitherto underestimated, if not completely unmentioned, in most analyses on the subject. For instance, the question about whether this differentiation is a matter of mere political inclination or a matter of sustainability. Should the omission or acceptance of certain moral rights be justifiable as a matter of preference? If it is, should any combination of rights and responsibilities within a society be considered as a satisfactory mix to obtain certain goals, and how different institutional arrangements are able to capture those goals?

This endeavor will certainly be explored in further contributions but it goes beyond the scope of the present manuscript. For now, let us focus on the importance of looking at both the specific facts and particular points of contention within a society that may have led to certain institutional transformations.

In the Cuban case there was certainly a strong determination to radically change the old country structures and serve popular interest, but no unequivocal ideological references to Marx or to the Soviet Union statement were made. There were, in fact, serious disagreements between the Cuban revolutionaries fighting the Batista regime and the Cuban Communist Party of the time, which was subordinated to the Communist International led by the Soviet Union and very much involved in parliamentary politics, with all the compromising inherent to it. But, again, socialism should not be exclusively linked to Marx (he was a powerful analyst of the capitalist system, who strongly advocated the need to overcome it, but he was not necessarily a theorist of socialism) nor to the Soviet-style. The latter was always criticized by other socialist tendencies (including certain streams of the Cuban one) and has been used as a starting point for most criticism to socialism, however misguided. In Cuba, the popular demand for self-determination and social justice combined with the structure of the Cuban economy and the inevitable confrontation with the US government made a socialist solution the only practical way forward from early 1960 onwards.

"The rejection of established parties and dogmas, the belief in direct action, the quest for new and original solutions: these were the characteristics of the creative ferment which swept Cuba in the early years of the revolution."[29] Consequently, it would be more accurate, to define the revolutionary movement of those years as a socially progressive and nationalistic movement with an eclectic ideological basis. When asked about the nature of the Cuban process at that time, revolutionary leaders refused to give any encompassing definition.[30] The old communists, who were more integrated in the traditional political system, had even distrusted them.

The general attitude towards the revolution in the early moments was evidenced by the broad support of different sectors of the population. Not only revolutionaries in the strict sense, but also moderates and even non-revolutionaries, shared pro-national economic development points of view and were well aware of the honest handling of public funds. Names not directly related to the fights against the previous dictatorship, such as the Cuban economist Felipe Pazos, National Bank head until November 1959 were given important positions within the revolutionary government.

But the romance was brief. By early 1961 nearly all appointed government officials with anti-communist leanings or moderates, particularly those in the Foreign Service, had either been removed or resigned. From 1962 on, in addition, the freshness of the Cuban project became compromised by the implementation of Soviet models because of the unavoidable alliance required in the context of the Cold War. However, the Cuban model has maintained important aspects of its autonomy and creativity along the years. The very survival of this process during the worst years of the "Special Period" in the mid-1990s cannot possibly be explained in any other way than by the continued vitality of the consensus reached by the Cuban revolution. "The scarcity and hardship was such that any other government would have collapsed in a matter of months."[31]

5.3.2 Social progress as a prerequisite

The idea of social justice as pertaining exclusively to the realm of socialist ways of organization does not pass the historical test. While assessing the behavioral dangers of the division of labor Adam Smith's Book V (Chapter I, Part III) of his masterpiece *Wealth of the Nations* makes a clear case for a universal provision of education. Smith states that, as important as division of labor is for economic development, a worker "confined to [the repetition of] a few simple operations [...] has no occasion to exert his understanding, or to exercise his invention." He further expresses that this state of affairs would also negatively affects workers' sense of judgment in matters important for their communities and families too. He states that workers' dexterity in their trades seems,

> in this manner, to be acquired at expense of his intellectual [and] social virtues. But in every improved and civilized society, this is the state into which the labouring poor, that is, the great body of the people, must necessarily fall, unless government takes some pains to prevent it.

In addition, by making a plea for more industrial and social justice, Smith asks business owners and industrialists to provide some mechanisms that avoid overworking of laborers. He even mentions the work of Bernardino Ramazzini, father of occupational medicine, in order to discuss the social and economic benefits of some leisure time. Even when these last measures were not expected to be provided by the government (he believed that government should not interfere in businessmen affairs) he leaves clear proof of his understanding about the importance of industrial and social justice in a good functioning industrial civilization. In this sense he states that

> [i]f masters would always listen to the dictates of reason and humanity, they have frequently occasion rather to moderate, than to animate the application of many of their workmen. It will be found, I believe, in every sort of trade, that the man who works so moderately, as to be able to work constantly, not only preserves his health the longest, but, in the course of the year, executes the greatest quantity of work.
>
> (Book I, Chapter VIII)

On the other hand, such well-known cases as Disraeli's One-nation conservatism in Great Britain and Bismarck's social welfare institutions in imperial Germany exemplify the kind of pragmatism behind many social welfare institutions. There are, of course, clear moral considerations to be acknowledged, but the introduction of welfare institutions has essentially been directed at reducing social tensions and enhancing the legitimacy of the political system, whatever kind it may be. It is also about providing a more stable environment for long-term investments and improving workers' productivity and loyalty. Recently, the scars left by the most recent crisis have sparked a profusion of literature confirming how equality-enhancing interventions can drive higher and more sustainable prosperity (see, e.g., Ostry 2014; Kleinknecht 2014).

The discussion on the workability of the Cuban economy has been traditionally circumscribed within the dichotomy state vs. market; with socialism inevitability being associated with "asphyxiating" Soviet-style government intervention, overcharged welfare states and obstruction of the market mechanisms. However, we argue that this kind of framework is the very obstacle to a better understanding not only of the Cuban post-revolutionary experience, but also of other development experiences such as the Asian experiences, the American and most of the European development experiences.

As already seen in previous chapters, the dichotomy state vs. market is far from being a real one as it is the state the institution which has historically built and regulated the markets (Lazonick 2006; Chang 2002, 2008, 2009; Amdsen 1989; Evans et al. 1999; Micheisen and Kuisma 1992; Jäntti and Vartiainen 2009). The fact that the Soviet model adopted in Cuba proved to be wrong does not imply that a socially progressive contract carried out by committed states should not be pursued, both for welfare and economic reasons.

Socially progressive elements have been found to be the very basis of many successful and sustainable development strategies. For instance, Micheisen and Kuisma (1992) explain how the victorious right-wing-oriented white government after the civil war (1918) in Finland[32] had to introduce a land reform in order to provide farming land to a politically unstable rural proletariat. Chang (2003) argues that, after the electoral victory of the Socialist Party in Sweden, a historical pact between the unions and the employers' association took place in 1936. Employers would finance a generous welfare state in exchange for wage moderation from the union.[33]

Much has been said about the pioneering role of the German conservative state in the introduction of "social welfare institutions[34] in an attempt to defuse revolutionary agitation and establish social peace" (ibid., p. 63). After World War II and until the 1970s, these institutions became a new paradigm and pre-requisite of governance typified in the West European welfare state.[35] In this case, it is worth mentioning post-war Japan, where long-term company-based welfare schemes contributed towards stabilizing the rather volatile political atmosphere during this period (Ebbinghaus and Manow 2001).

In the classic *Trade and Market in the Early Empires* of 1957, Karl Polanyi shows that various forms of reciprocity and redistribution are to be found in many ancient empires and societies, thereby mentioning the Soviet Union as "an extreme instance" in modern times. He continues by asserting that "price-making markets [...] were to all accounts non-existent before the first millennium of antiquity, and then only to be eclipsed by other forms of integration" (Polanyi et al. 1957, p. 257). In the same line of reasoning, he suggests that, to only take the "limited marketing definitions" resulting from the institutional setup which emerged in the nineteenth century, is by all means inadequate "for the purposes of the social scientist's study of the economic field" (ibid.).

While acknowledging that the implementation of social welfare institutions may bring unbearable costs if not carefully monitored and instituted, and depending on the country specificities, some evidence (although not conclusively) suggests that there has been a common need for them across countries and times (Zaman 1991; Naqvi 1994). They have actually been a prerequisite for long-term development, and have been present in almost all of today's industrialized countries as well. As Chang (2003) states,

> [c]ost effective public provision of health and education can bring about improvements in labour force quality that can, in turn, raise efficiency and accelerate productivity growth. Social welfare institutions reduce social tensions and enhance the legitimacy of the political system, thus providing a more stable environment for long term investments.
>
> (Chang 2003, p. 102)

In addition, it can also encourage people to make riskier decisions about their future (e.g. mobility).

5.3.3 Developmental vs. anti-developmental elements

Indeed, the excessive government centralization has been (and still is) one of the problems of the Cuban economy. The Soviet legacy has become an obstacle because it has shaped the motivations and raison d'être of many important decision-makers and institutions in Cuba. Some segments within the Communist leadership still think in very rigid and dogmatic ways. These sectors have blocked reforms, and persist in retaining anti-developmental institutional structures within the country. Even when the last years have shown a number of reforms in order to make the economy more diverse and efficient,[36] excessive centralization of decisions and institutional stagnation continue to be a major deterrent in today's Cuban society. However, this stagnation co-exists with sectors and social groups searching for new ideas and methods. They might represent the developmental side of the Cuban process, even when they completely deviate from the traditional right-wing libertarian stance.[37]

In contrast, the theoretical framework offered by the institutional political economy, and assertive historic evidence, suggests that neither the market nor the state can be held as opposing categories (Chang 2002; Lazonick 2006). As we already pointed out, to define "free market" would be very problematic since in almost every successful development strategy of modern times the government has been involved. The role of the state is not defined by market failure, but goes beyond that. It is not about reducing the government to the role of provider of law and order and protector of property rights.

In actual fact,

> depending on which rights and obligations are regarded as legitimate and what kind of hierarchy between these rights and obligations is (explicitly and implicitly) accepted by the members of the society, the same state action could be considered an intervention in one society and not in another.
>
> (Chang 2002, p. 553)

From the industrial revolution in England to the American and German experience at the end of the nineteenth century, including again the Japanese, Finnish and the Taiwanese development experiences, it has been shown that institutional changes are, generally, politically legitimated processes.

To talk about the Cuban social project only as a problem of too much state intervention and lack of market in classic sense, would be to ignore that, while still within the consensus, a huge variety of institutional alternatives can be brought into existence, precisely because the process is still widely supported. To reject all these possible institutional combinations would be more an exercise of ideological bias rather than reasoned argumentation.

5.4 Main institutional changes since 1959

5.4.1 Period 1959–1964

The first priorities of the new government can be summarized in two goals: import substitution industrialization and agricultural diversification (García-Molina 2005; Mesa-Lago 2000; Alvares 1998; O'Connor 1970). This was clearly intended to escape from the trap of the sugar-based comparative advantage, which was what many developing countries were (are) doing by diversifying the economy. In more technical terms, this approach could be defined as an attempt at technological upgrading, based on a comparative-advantage-defying strategy. During this period, fundamental changes in ownership and management style were experienced, which eventually materialized in form of land reforms and a nationalization process. These newly created institutions were supposed to display the required capabilities for importing modern technology and organizational forms developed elsewhere in order to fight poverty and backwardness. This was to be achieved and promoted from a socially progressive environment.

In February 1959, the revolutionary government issued a Fundamental Law which established the basic guidelines for a new political, social and economic regime, which the Cuban people had chosen in the exercise of their right to self-determination.[38] Similar to other historical processes which radically change a society's political institutions, the Cuban revolutionary process dismissed no-longer-valid institutions, but kept other socially legitimate and useful ones. For instance, the provisions set forth in the 1940 Constitution[39] regarding the regulation of land ownership were retained. These provisions had been jeopardized at that time by the effects of the latifundia system and the traditional view of property being firmly anchored in private interests.

The most important socioeconomic institutions of this first period are the National Land Reform Institute (INRA) and the Central Planning Board (JUCEPLAN). These institutions were envisioned to put into practice the new development strategy. The former was conceived to implement agricultural diversification, while the latter was to coordinate government policies.

5.4.2 The National Land Reform Institute

Agrarian reform and diversification

The agrarian reform of 1959 led to the expropriation of latifundia, whose land was to be distributed to the landless peasants.[40] This measure had also been practiced in countries such as Japan, South Korea and Taiwan, as well as in many regions of Eastern and Central Europe (Vaskela 1996), as well as in many African, Latin-American and Western European countries.[41] Its main goal had been to alleviate and eradicate poverty or food insecurity among the rural population, and to reorganize the agricultural production in a more efficient way.

In Cuban reforms around 200,000 peasants benefited from this measure, which was carried out by the National Land Reform Institute (INRA).[42] This institution was created in 1959 with the explicit goal of implementing the Agricultural reform and the nationalizations of several foreign firms. Given the lack of specialized governmental institutions at the time, the INRA became the most powerful institution in Cuba, comprising several other functions such as establishment of the sugar policy, setting up of prices and the payment of indemnities[43] resulting from the expropriation process.

A Second Agrarian Reform Law was enacted in 1963. In this reform, medium and large farms accounting for 11.4 million hectares of land were put under control of the INRA; small farmers owning 7.2 million hectares of land were organized within the ANAP association.[44] The Cuban government supported ANAP by providing interest-free loans to its members. The aim of transferring most of the expropriated lands to the state was to accelerate the adoption of advanced technologies and boost productivity, while maintaining a non-exploitative labor system based on a better distribution of wealth. This would be the starting point for the establishment of large agricultural enterprises. Between 1961 and 1963, Soviet loans and technical assistance were given in the form of irrigation facilities, fertilizer factories etc.

The overall objective was to reduce unemployment and the dependence on imported food and raw materials. Top priority was given to rice, oils and fats (pork production), cotton and beans, which accounted for nearly $100 million US of Cuba's $165 million US foreign exchange expenditure on agricultural commodities in 1958 (O'Connor 1970, p. 216). As part of the agricultural diversification strategy, influenced by the anti-sugar bias of these years, several large estates producing sugarcane were cleared and replanted with rice, fruits or vegetable. The total planted area of sugarcane was reduced by 25 percent between 1958 and 1963 (Mesa-Lago 2000, p. 186).

A state food collection and distribution agency (Acopio) was created in 1962 in order to eradicate intermediary trade in agricultural production, which was a source of exploitation for the producers and price-fixing for the consumers. This collection system was part of the INRA, and was supposed to purchase, transport and regulate part of the agricultural production resulting from cooperative and private farmer production. It was also expected to be able to design price structures which could be attractive for private farmers and cooperatives, thus stimulating production and increasing the sales of agricultural goods.

Causes of the failure

The outcome of this agricultural strategy was ultimately negative for a number of reasons. Firstly, most of the agricultural workforce was composed of cane cutters with little experience in other kinds of agricultural activities, which led to poor agricultural outcomes and generated an acute labor shortage in the sugar sector. The rejection of sugar was partly based on the assumption that the industrialization program would save financial resources by producing import-substitute commodities. However, these prospects proved to be unworkable; and the country reported an increased deficit in the balance of trade from 1961 to 1963 (Mesa-Lago 2000; O'Connor 1970). Moreover, no concrete steps were made to increase the cane yields, thus sharply reducing sugar harvest in 1962 and 1963, the central source of funds to finance the development strategy. In fact, most credits were oriented towards other crops.

Secondly, the deep social transformation led to a change in the labor distribution; many workers emigrated to the capital in search of better occupations and to take advantage of the increase in educational opportunities. Wage rates in the cane fields varied with the amount of cane cut and loaded daily, which depended on the cane yields. For instance, in 1963 it was expected that 50 percent of labor force would receive an extra daily payment of 32 cents for cutting a certain amount of cane. This percentage was actually 33 percent less (O'Connor 1970, p. 220). By 1962, 90,000 cane cutters had left their regular jobs, and approximately 70,000 found employment on state farms. The wages were higher, the employment steadier and the work less difficult (ibid.).

Thirdly, the assimilation of new technologies is not spontaneous, but rather a complex learning process. Agricultural diversification requires large-scale investments in technical education and training of the rural labor force. The new irrigation techniques brought by the Soviets could not possibly be efficiently applied in this short period and without the corresponding qualifications. Agricultural technology transfer requires the presence of agents who not only understand the technologies but also the local conditions, providing extension services (Chang 2009). Soviet specialists lacked knowledge about Cuban insular, monoculture, developing economy (Mesa-Lago 2000). On the other hand, sugar production depended mostly on US equipment, whose delivery had been stopped by the economic embargo imposed on the island.

Fourthly, the 130 food collection centers (acopio) created by the INRA failed to integrate private agriculture into the structure of the planned rural economy. Lack of trained personal and the inexperience of the planners made it impossible to differentiate products by quality, region or season, which led to a "highly irrational" price structure (O'Connor 1970, p. 227). Low acopio prices seem to have discouraged private farmers (30 percent of agriculture), who increased auto-consumption and sold their productions on the black market rather that to the state.

Additionally, the INRA agricultural policy led to a breakdown in the distribution system. Middlemen in the agricultural sector were eliminated by unnecessarily nationalizing thousand of smaller wholesalers and retailers. However, neither the INRA nor the Ministry of Internal Commerce officials were prepared to assume such a task. Some foreign advisers attempted to convince the INRA to allow some middlemen and establish a sort of public–private structure, but there was a strong bias against private property (Mesa-Lago 2000).

The result of the overall policy was negative. Agricultural output per capita decreased by 38 percent between 1961 and 1963.[45] The decline in the principal exports (sugar and tobacco) reduced the importing capacity. The state farms failed to elevate crops yields, and a new state distribution system was unable to rationalize the private sector. The consequence was a serious food shortage which eventually led to the introduction of a rationing system based on subsidized products.[46] The attempt to reduce sugar dependency was not a bad idea, however it was introduced too quickly, ultimately dismantling the most effective export line at that time.

Nationalization and industrialization

The industrial ambitions of the new government had little precedent in Cuban republican history. Even during the times previous to the independency from Spain, American industrial interests ensured advantage through a number of unequal treaties, so-called reciprocity treaties, that prevented any serious, although not inexistent, industrial base from being developed in Cuba (Le Riverend 1975; Parker-Willis 1903; Dye and Sicotte 1999; Marqués-Dolz 2006). The reciprocity treaty of 1903, following the infamous Platt Amendment, sealed this dependency.

However, in 1927 the sadly remembered president Gerardo Machado encouraged a Customs-Tariff Law in order to promote the development of a domestic light manufacturing industry and to neutralize the decline in sugar prices. Duties on agricultural products were raised while tariffs on raw materials and industrial machinery were reduced, which favored new small manufacturing industries such as such as clothing, shoes, glass, paint, paper, as well as vegetable oils, beer and canned foods. Although limited in its scope and impact,[47] this proto-industrial policy represented an innovative step in Cuban economic history because it relied on more contemporary ideas in terms of industrial development, which emphasized industrial protectionism and import substitution (Le Riverend 1975, p. 238; Kuczynski et al. 1973, p. 23).

Subsequently, other, albeit scattered, voices called for industrial development. For example, as mentioned above, the World Bank-sponsored Mission Truslow recommended natural resources-based industrial diversification within a labor-hostile framework. Cuban economists such as (Spanish-born) Julián Alienes and Felipe Pazos also advocated domestic industrial development. However the Keynesian-inspired policies of public expenditure carried out by the sadly remembered dictator Fulgencio Batista, encouraged by Alienes, did not accomplish that.

One of the most tenacious critics of these policies was Cuban economist (graduated as lawyer and journalist) Raúl Cepero Bonilla. He pointed out that, while Keynesian policies could theoretically work in Cuba, they were in practice problematic in a context that privileged the importation of industrial products, whose consumption is in fact subsidized by that policy. He also favored technological improvement against Alienes recommendation of freezing wages (along with the Truslow mission), particularly in the sugar industry, in order to increase efficiency. This elements together with the influence of the Latin American structuralist School built the policy notions of the Cuban revolution, which also reflecting on Fidel Castro's Moncada Program, intended to initiate the, until that moment, most ambitious industrial policy plan in Cuban history.

During the first phase (1959–60) of industrial planning, the Cuban government attempted to create a favorable climate for Cuban private manufacturers. A nationalistic trade policy agenda was put in practice. Instruments such as tariffs, import quotas and licenses, and tax reforms were advanced. Private associations and public agencies supported the slogan "buy Cuban," which was promoted in publicity campaigns (O'Connor 1970, p. 241). Mass domestic purchasing power had expanded, and this situation created a positive environment for an increase in the domestic production.

The government also continued to encourage private investments through the Tax Reform law of July 1959, and via control over foreign trade and foreign exchange. For example, in February 1959, the National Bank introduced a system of import licensing, which covered about 200 consumer commodities. In July, all matters relating to tariffs were centralized under government control, and in September, import tariffs ranging from 30 to 100 percent had been imposed. By early 1960, import quotas extended across nearly all farm commodities (ibid., p. 242).

The tax Reform Law simplified the tax structure by reducing the number of taxes from 150 to 20. Middle-class personal consumption was reduced by introducing new taxes for luxury goods and services (10 to 30 percent) (p. 247). Moreover, a flat income tax (3 percent) was introduced, as were increases in real estate, inheritance and personal property taxes. A profits tax of 40 percent was also set up, but discriminated on behalf of reinvested earnings. This tax was actually reduced to 25 percent for all businesses located outside Havana, all non-sugar manufacturing industries, and all fishing and mining and agricultural industries (ibid.).

The results of this first period were positive but limited. As a favorable response, Cuban business increased production in textiles, footwear, food processing and other industries. However, perhaps because the national bank failed to strongly enforce the new trade controls, and due to the growing capital flight and the decline in the sugar prices, the balance of payments worsened. Real reserves were only $35.4 million, "an all time low" record (O'Connor 1970, p. 242).

Increasing centralization

In 1960, the revolutionary government took over the National Bank and increased restrictions on imports and the use of foreign exchange. INRA's Foreign trade and Production Department was designated as the sole importer and exporter of several agricultural products. Controls were placed on the repatriation of dollars to the United States, and monopoly on foreign trade was gradually established.[48] More intense controls resulted in an increase in foreign reserves to $175 million in 1960,[49] but this became a growing source of friction between businessmen and the revolutionary government after it took over all agencies and private organizations.

Business classes had already become disenchanted with the agrarian reform. Both sides wanted industrialization, but the state officials had strong bias against private enterprise, as did many other developing-country leaders in the 1960s and the 1970s. Moreover, the deterioration of the relations with the US government, the elimination of class privileges and prerogatives, and the nationalization measures carried out by the INRA were also increased by the mutual distancing between the middle-class reformers and revolutionaries. By the end of 1960, most parts of the retail trade (50 percent), banking, foreign trade and most of transportation (82 percent), construction (80 percent) and industry (85 percent) had been nationalized (García-Molina 2005; Mesa-Lago 2000).

Contrary to the current orthodox opinion, nationalizations have been often carried out by many governments as pro-developmental instrument. The examples of Italia, South Korea, France, and Austria illustrate this point (Chang 2008; Katzestein in Evans et. al. 1999). As discussed in Chapter 3, successful state-owned companies (or firms where the state is a major participant) can also be found in countries like Taiwan, China, Singapore and Germany, among others (Chang 2008; Amsden in Evans et al. 1999). In the case of Cuba, the temporary takeover of financially troubled businesses was established practice in pre-revolutionary Cuba. Several decrees promulgated by pre-revolutionary governments (1934, 1938, 1942) empowered the Ministry of Labor to seize private firms in order to rehire illegally discharged workers or erasing financial deficits. But the permanent nationalizations after 1959 provoked the exodus of most of the qualified workforce. Most of the managers, technicians, university professors and professionals left the country. Half of the country's medical doctors (excluding students at that time) followed suit too.

This situation accentuated the need to develop an educational system capable of supporting the development efforts. The first step was the literacy campaign. In 1960, the government decided to wipe out illiteracy by recruiting 120,000 volunteer teachers, most of them young high school students. Within one year, Cuba's literacy rate rose to 97 percent. In 1961, the health and the education system were also nationalized. Government expenditure in social security, education, health and housing gradually increased. Education expenditures increased by 32.1 percent during the period 1960–65,[50] and health expenditures did so by 34.4 percent.[51]

Extreme income differences were tackled by reducing housing and electricity costs by as much as 50 percent, and by establishing a system of minimum wages and pensions. In 1960, an urban reform law gave renters the right to buy the house in which they were living by paying the rent to the state for a period ranging from 5 to 20 years (Álvares 1998; Mesa-Lago 2000). Expansion of social services was concentrated in rural areas, which led to a reduction in the gap in living standards compared to urban areas. These measures expanded the domestic purchasing power, which could not however be emulated due to production shortages.

5.4.3 The Central Planning Board

As already mentioned, industrialization and agricultural diversification were the main policy objectives during 1960–64. After the public-private crash, and in order to carry out the established development strategy, Cuba's first real planning authority was created. The Cuban central planning board (JUCEPLAN) was created in 1960 to coordinate and execute the government policies, and to direct private business. JUCEPLAN's authority extended to determining investment priorities, raw material needs, production goals and the overall economic needs of the country.

The designs for the 1962[52] annual plan were begun in 1961, as well as that for 1962–65 (Álvares 1998; Mesa-Lago 2000; O'Connor 1970). A long list of projects was compiled. In the short-term, machinery and metalworking industries were given high priority. Chemistry, electronics and shipbuilding were left to the long-term. Large-scale, integrated industrial construction was postponed until 1965–70. However, as we have just seen, the development strategy could not be accomplished; the failure of the planning efforts being the main reason for this. As already mentioned, rapid industrialization did not materialize.

There were several implementation problems which ultimately led to the failure of the planning in this period. Firstly, the lack of reliable performance indicators and sectorial studies made it impossible to define realistic targets. Planning targets were measured by gross output, omitting enterprise efficiency and product quality (Mesa-Lago 2000). JUCEPLAN knew little about the actual economic cost and benefits of investment projects. This is why, even though the investment share of the productive sector increased from 70.7 to 74.6 percent in 1962–63, and budget allocations to finance production rose from 32.9 to 41.6 percent, capital productivity remained poor (Mesa-Lago 2000, p. 185).

Secondly, there was little, if any, coordination between the newly created ministries and their enterprises. Different sectorial targets thus could not be consistently synchronized; and complementarities and linkages were not achieved, which led to bottlenecks and shortages, sometimes intensified by import delays. These mistakes were not rapidly acknowledged and transmitted and no corrections were made.

Thirdly, political leadership decisions were implemented without prior discussion with JUCEPLAN. For example, state budgets were prepared by the Ministry of Finance, but this budget was not always integrated within the plan. As a consequence, investment decisions were not coordinated, and this situation led to serious inconsistencies (Mesa-Lago 2000). Fourthly, most of the staff in the ministries and agencies lacked reliable economic data and the adequate qualification to use them. The problems with the data of this period are pervasive. Fifthly, the relationship between the state and other socioeconomic agents was one-sided. Mostly for ideological reasons and Realpolitik practicalities,[53] "the notion of a strict separation between 'state' agents and 'non-state' agents" (Jäntti and Vartiainen 2009, p. 8) was (and is) rigorously applied in the Cuban case.

However, even though the developmental state has been historically strong and encompassing, most success stories relating to the country's growth strategy have been characterized by a "pragmatic co-operation between organised private agents [...], on the one hand, and government officials and civil servants, on the other [...]" (ibid.). Korea, Taiwan and Finland are representative examples. Corporatist regimes of that kind were not practiced in Cuba. Instead, "the collectivisation was too widespread and too rapid," destroying many economic micro-relations, when the state was not ready to substitute them (Mesa–Lago 2000). It could also be argued that it was not politically feasible. On the other hand, cooperative ownership forms were until recently[54] confined to agriculture.

5.4.4 Period 1964–1975

Strategy change

The first unsuccessful attempt led to a redefinition of the development strategy. The import-substitute policy without any important export source meant an increase (rather than a decrease) in Cuba's dependency on imported capital goods. The new strategy pursued a return to the sugar industry. This turn was in part accelerated by the Soviet Union's decision to purchase large quantities of sugar at high, stable prices. In 1964, a six-year commercial agreement was signed with the Soviet Union, which committed to purchase 24.1 million tonnes of sugar (annual imports would increase from 2 to 5 millions) between 1965 and 1970 at 6.1 cents/pound, a price above the then world market price[55] (Álvares 1998, p. 11).

Cuba, in exchange, was provided with subsidized oil and preferential credits. The Soviet Union granted Cuba technical aid for $138 million US to expand and modernize the sugar industry, and later an additional $46 million US for geological prospecting. The government investment policy was reoriented by placing a strong emphasis on agricultural machinery, chemicals fertilizers, and sugar milling and irrigation equipment. The agricultural share of state investment increased from 24.3 to 40.5 percent in 1963–65, while the industrial share declined from 31.6 to 18.1 percent (Mesa–Lago 2000, p. 201). It was the beginning of the agro-industrial strategy. Sugar was expected to provide sufficient foreign exchange earnings to accomplish industrialization.

The idea of non-traditional industrial upgrading was not abandoned, but postponed. However, during this stage, some items were produced according the comparative advantages, while others not so much. Nickel belonged to the first group during this stage, while steel belonged to the second. Both registered output increases in the period 1965–70. Cuba became the fifth largest shipping industry in Latin America, although it only actually employed 6 percent in foreign trade.[56] In 1965, the National Centre for Scientific Research (CNIC) was also created.[57] This multi-disciplinary institution is considered to be the incubator of the most of Cuban scientific institutions today and was established to promote the development of research and training activities in fields such as bio-chemistry, computer sciences and microbiology. In 1970 the first Cuban micro-computer was manufactured by ICID (Institute for Digital Research, see Section ICID in Chapter 7).

Strong investments in medical schools and a comprehensive health system were made around the same period. By the end of the 1970s, Cuba had developed a well-integrated structure comprising higher education, biomedical science and the public health system. As we will see in subsequent chapters, this created a pool of trained specialists that became the very basis of the Cuban biotechnology industry (see Chapter 7).

Despite some good results, the overall economic performance was negative; production from non-sugar based agriculture declined by 20 percent during the period 1967–70.[58] A major cause was the huge and unorganized sugar production plan targeted for 1970. There was also a decline in the quality of goods, and a further breakdown in the coordination system. In 1968, the remaining 25 percent of retail trade was nationalized under the "Revolutionary Offensive."[59] It was replaced with managers who lacked both skills and knowledge. Output and productivity declined rapidly.

During this stage, a debate was held about how to finance the Cuban state enterprise. The debate remained unresolved in 1966, when both alternatives were rejected. Instead, the state budget disappeared for a decade (1967–77), and other accounting techniques also lost relevance. After 1970, a governmental reform, and the official inclusion of Cuba in the Council for mutual economic assistance in 1972, took place. Since 1975, Cuba adopted the more Soviet-based orthodox enterprise system.

Debate on state enterprise financing

From 1960 to 1966, two different ways of enterprise financing co-existed in the Cuban economy: Budgetary control and self-financing. This gave way to a controversy which "touched the core of the nature of the Cuban economic structure" (O'Connor 1970, p. 262). Both sides advocated central planning and the use of accounting instruments, but had different conceptions of how to design the economic system. This is considered to be the most important economic debate on enterprise organization after 1959 in Cuba.

Budgetary control was championed by Ernesto Guevara, the then Minister of Industry seeking to adapt the system of economic accounting normally utilized in a single enterprise to the whole economy. In 1960, nationalized firms were placed in a centralized fund under INRA's control, given that there was no alternative financing plan for them. 69 percent of the nation's enterprises worked under this system, and they mostly encompassed industrial activities. Budgetary control means that enterprises receive all funds for their expenditure from the state budget in the form of a non-repayable grant.

The logic of Guevara's view was the following: as companies own no capital (i.e. belong to the state), all their profits go automatically to the national budget. Planners decide how to invest the surplus regardless the firms' profitability. The main incentive for managers and workers is not of a material nature, but mostly of a moral and collective nature. Worker consciousness, i.e. a shared sense of working together towards a common goal, was to be the principal motivation for managers and workers. Enterprise coordination was very important, and was to be achieved through a good communication system supported by computer techniques. The enterprises should run according to a unified budget.

The profitability was to be removed as firm-criteria, which was to be replaced by the fulfilment of fixed physical targets. This would determine the physical exchange between companies. Transactions among enterprises would take the form of accounting transfers, and competition would not be allowed. Financial control was to be carried out by a sort of holdings companies (Empresas Consolidadas), whose task was to coordinate the accounts of the individual companies in a given sector. The bank would play a mere accounting role in the system. According to this view, Cuba is a micro-unit in the world economy, whose internal prices must be closely related to international prices, even at the expense of domestic price-building.

The opposing view, held by Carlos Rafael Rodriguez, a renowned Cuban economist and the Minister of Foreign Trade, thought Guevara's system was idealist. Although they both agreed on the need for modern accounting techniques in the economy, this opposing side favored the self-financing of enterprises. Loans would be made to the individual firms, and paid back with interest. Under this more decentralized system, firms belong to the state, but should be considered as juridical independent companies. They must cover their costs with their own revenue, or face closure. Material incentives are employed to motivate managers and workers, relating performance with firm profitability (bonuses, prizes or enterprise services such as vacations etc.). Competition is allowed and prices should be based essentially on market relationships.

The defenders of self-financing argued that, although the Cuban state is the owner of firms, they cannot exercise actual control because the economy is not a unique enterprise. According to this side, ownership confers control only when production is highly concentrated, as was then the case in the advanced capitalist economies. They also argued that the large-scale, integrated enterprise was not the dominant form of economic organization in Cuba. Self-financing worked in about 31 percent of Cuban enterprises, mostly agriculture and foreign and domestic trade.

The Rodriguez vision bears some resemblance to the reforms that were being initiated in the Soviet Union at that time.[60] The Kosigyn reforms were initiated by the Alexei Kosigyn, Premier at that time, and consisted basically of a number of reforms in economic management and planning in order to deal with the growing complexity of the Soviet economy, which had notably reduced the efficacy of central planning.[61]

The theoretical epicenter of this debate was the validity of the Marxist law of value[62] under the new conditions of the Cuban economy. Basically, the law of value states that the trading ratios of different types of products reflect the cost in producing them, which is an expression of the amount of human labor-time invested in them. This determines the price of the products. Marx further argued that the value of these products (i.e. value of exchange) dominates the type of goods produced and exchanged, irrespective of the human needs they might cover (use value). While the Rodriguez vision acknowledged that this law should continue to play a role in the Cuban socialism, Guevara believed that, under the new conditions, this law would be difficult to apply since the new society was consciously trying to cover the most important needs of the population.

Relevance of Guevara's insights

While Rodriguez's vision clearly represented a straightforward and pragmatic stance in many issues, Guevara's vision was a mix of different points of views, which resulted however, in a very eclectic, yet very innovative set of ideas. Many (if not all) of Guevara's insights reflects a more realistic understanding of such processes as innovation, firm organization and non-monetary incentives. For example, his emphasis on coordination and integration bears resemblance to modern insights on innovation economics, which acknowledge the complex and interrelated nature of high tech products, the need for economics of scale or the existence or even prevalence of many non-market forms of allocation in most industries (see Chapter 4). The ideas of collective entrepreneurship, and of organizations (rather than market forces), as the central locus of innovation can be found in most of the current non-neoclassic literature.

The idea of non-material incentives bears resemblance with modern management insights on the importance of non-financial forms of compensation. In fact, the notion of human beings as cooperative and not necessarily egoistic entities has been emphasized since the emergence of the Human Relation School in the 1930s. Further literature has emphasized the Toyota production system as a paramount example of this approach (see Chapter 4). In this system, even shop-floor workers were trusted as moral agents in that they were allowed to display high levels of goodwill and creativity as they are given considerable degree of control over the quality of the production lines (of course, provided they received a decent wage).

In actual fact, if workers only strictly followed the rules stipulated by the contract, then output would be reduced by 30–50 percent.[63] To be sure, material self-interest is crucial, in fact, Guevara himself introduced in 1964 a new salary scale with 24 different basic levels plus a 15 percent bonus for over-completion.[64] However, the point is that to highlight the idea of moral incentives does not need to be blamed on an idealistic slip, but is actually a way to say that human motivations are complex and that such non-selfish motives (loyalty, honesty, self-respect, sense of duty, patriotism, public-spiritedness, altruism etc.) are always as, or more important than self-seeking behavior[65] when explaining workforce productivity. To build an economic system under the self-seeking assumption will lead to low rather that high efficiency (Chang 2010, pp. 41–50).

Guevara's ideas about technology are similar to what many development and innovation economists say about absorptive capabilities. Recently, some of Guevara's unreleased speeches and writing were published, and they confirm these insights. In his view it was very important for managers and policymakers to have actualized knowledge of the technological advances in their sectors.

He criticized the then Communist world, particularly the Soviet Union, for ignoring modern knowledge for ideological reasons. His opinion in this subject favored acquiring the most advanced technologies in the country regardless their origin or their creator's ideology (Guevara 2006, 258–61). He saw technological development as the basis of any good future Cuba could have. His views, in this respect, were decidedly profound and worth of further study.

Last but not least, the idea that the law of value is not valid, and the necessity to administer prices in order for them to harmonize with international prices, creates a clear argument for the protection of infant industry, one of the key tools of industrial policy. More recently, some scholars have criticized the whole idea of using the Ricardian and Smithian value-labor theories to deal with innovation and economic development. For example, the Other Canon School led by Erik Reinert argues that the great, production-based analysis of capitalism made by Marx has the weakness of having relied on Ricardo's labor theory of value.

Reinert (2007) argues that Ricardo's theory reduces qualitatively different activities to similar activities, distinguished only by the number of hours invested in them. By doing this, it rules out elements such as knowledge, entrepreneurship, leadership, organizational capabilities. When we analyze the qualitative differences between economic activities, we realize that one hour devoted to produce computer ships and one hour devoted to produce shirts are not the same. Therefore, by denying the validity of the Marx's law of value under the Cuban conditions of the time, Guevara was opening new possibilities to include new methods and ways to boost innovation and growth. This is confirmable when we see the new initiatives he developed in his practical activity as minister.[66]

The debate lasted until 1966, when the two organizational models were eventually dismissed. Instead, the central plan virtually disappeared, and the lack of coordination among special sectoral plans prompted input shortages, bottlenecks and proliferation of incomplete projects. Moral incentives were set in an extreme and distorted manner, and state budget and accounting techniques were suspended. Decisions were made (until the 1970s) without coordination, and poor resource allocation resulted in inefficiency, leading to the failure of the development strategy of this period. The clear developmental elements provided by each side were not taken into consideration.

Sugar target

In 1964, the sugar sector was transferred from INRA to the new created Ministry of Sugar. The INRA remained in charge of non-sugar agriculture, and, in 1965, the Prime Minister assumed control of this institution, while JUCEPLAN was controlled by the State President. An overall plan was abandoned in favor of major sectoral plans, with sugar being the main target. Targeting is inevitable in an economic policy, as it allows easier monitoring of the process, and therefore gives the planning agency more advantages by revising the targets along the way (Chang 2009). However, coordination between the state and the other economic players is vital to minimize the eventual costs of a targeting policy. The fundamental lack of coordination and realistic targets was the major cause for the failure of the great sugar production plan carried out in 1970.

Until 1970, investments in sugar production reached 70 percent of total investments. The sectoral Sugar's Plan set an initial output target of 7.5 million tonnes, but it was later raised to 10 million tonnes without a prior technical feasibility study. It became a political goal promoted through the media, mass organizations, schools, and work centers. The harvest occupied the lives of the Cuban people for an entire year, and passed into history under the name of "The Ten Million Ton Sugar Harvest." Although the 1970 harvest set a historical record of 8.5 million tonnes, it was still 15 percent below the original target.

In addition to the lack of feasibility plan, massive mobilization of unskilled workers to the cane fields and lack of sober planning contributed to the failure of this harvest. It is estimated that at the end of the 1970 harvest, more than one million people had worked in the cutting, loading and transporting of sugar cane. Worse still, as result of mismanagement, there was an untold divestment of the resources of other sectors, which in turn suffered a significant decline in output. For example, only two-thirds of the cultivated land destined for non-sugar agriculture was utilized. With the exception of rice, fish and eggs, the rest of the agricultural production suffered negative output (Mesa-Lago 2000).

1971–1975

The goal of industrialization through sugar production was not abandoned. However, after the failure of the harvest, important institutional changes took place in order to correct the negative outcomes of past strategies. They were criticized as highly idealistic and lacking the minimal objective knowledge to function properly.

Firstly, the plan was reinstated as the principal economic tool, with other sectorial and special plans being subordinated to it. Annual macro-plans were drawn up after 1973, as well as a global economic model (1973–75). Also during this stage (1972), Cuba became a full member of the Council for mutual economic assistance (CMEA), receiving special member status as a developing country within the socialist international labor division. This status included preferential trade agreements and other concessions, such as the postposition, until 1986, of Cuban debt with the Soviet Union for the period 1960–72. A credit was granted to cover the trade deficit for the period 1973–75, and to modernize the sugar industry and initiate new production (e.g. TV sets).

Also created in 1972 was the Executive Committee of the Council of Ministers, which represented an important change in the governmental structure established in 1959. Before the creation of this body, economic decisions had been made by the Council of Ministers. This body, in practice personified by the figure of the Prime Minister, also had absolute administrative and legislative power in the country. However, the observed inefficiency of the administration system led to the creation of a more collegiate structure, in order to better coordinate the different economic sectors. This body was to be made up of seven deputy prime ministers.[67]

5.4.5 Period 1976–1989

Soviet-based institutionalization

As already mentioned, the failure of the policies based on industrialization through sugar production for the period 1964–70 led to a reconsideration of the institutional mechanisms employed during that stage. Two different company-financing models worked simultaneously until 1966, when both were rejected. Chaos and inefficiency distinguished the period after 1966, which culminated in the missed target of the sugar harvest of 1970. As a result, during the period 1972–75, changes in the government structure were introduced in order to improve the state coordination system. Cuba was also officially entered into the Soviet-based international economic cooperation system, adopting a preferential status.

Since 1960, most of Cuba's organizations had been managed in a some-what Soviet style. The JUCEPLAN, a translation of the soviet GOSPLAN, had been created from the very beginning, as many of the revolutionary leaders had shown a clear preference towards centralization (as was also a prevailing trend in the period). However, prior to 1972, as stated above, experiments other than, and sometimes overly divergent from, the Soviet practice were conducted. From 1959 to about 1970, Cuba was relatively autonomous from the Soviet Union, and often somewhat overtly critical of the Soviet model and Soviet policies.

After Cuba's entry into the CMEA, however, a more orthodox, Soviet-style of management was finally institutionalized. This model was named the System of Economic Direction and Planning (SDPE), and was introduced in 1976. Soviet influence became dominant in all spheres, with ineffective management styles being the model to be followed. On the other hand, Soviet help provided the necessary resources to develop some non-traditional industries within an import substitution strategy.

Also during this stage (1978–81), the government legalized and encouraged several forms of self-employment in the service. Under this system, state enterprises could contract self-employed persons, providing them with input in exchange for 30 percent of their profits. Also introduced in 1980 was the free peasant market, in which private farmers were allowed to sell their surpluses after complying with their compulsory deals with acopio (state food collection system). Both measures were dismissed after the Rectification process was initiated in 1986.

Sugar continued to be the most important industry, and five-year-plan schemes were again introduced as the Cuban role in the CMEA-based inter-governmental coordination system. Beyond the controversies among scholars and the existing discrepancies by estimating the Cuban growth rate during this period, there is a solid consensus on the fact that, during the 1980s (until 1985), the Cuban economy experienced high growth rates.[68]

However, the model was based on the extensive growth of capital and labor, and not on innovation-based productivity. Moreover, it was dependent on external mechanisms of compensation supported by the association with the Soviet Union (Monreal 2005). Up to 1985 (and even earlier), the model began to show its own limits, which led to a rectification process initiated in 1986. This process was aimed to correct the distortions observed mostly during the earlier period (1981–85), and to introduce new (in Cuba) experimental organizational and managerial forms.

The System of Economic Direction and Planning (SDPE)

One of the most important aspects of the encompassing process of institutional reorganization carried out in Cuba after the failure of several industrialization strategies was the introduction of the SDPE in 1976. As already suggested, this structure was an attempt to create an institutional structure which could fill the coordination gaps left by earlier strategies. Given Cuba's official entry into the socialist economic system, it was also an attempt to make the Cuban economic structure compatible with the rest of the CMEA countries. This integration was to be achieved by drawing up five-year plans (1976–80, 1981–85, 1986–90). In actual fact, the new model and its goals were very similar to the Soviet version, which in turn was analogous to the ideas proposed by the advocates of self-financing during the debate of the 1960s (see above debate on state enterprise financing).

The main goals of the SDPE were basically the decentralization of state enterprises, the transfer of many decisions from the planners to the managers, and the reinstatement of material incentives. The number of state firms expanded from 300 to 3000, wage scales and quotas were reintroduced, and a collective incentive fund was to be based on company performance (for a detailed description, see Mesa-Lago 2000). In 1977, statistical activity began functioning, and the use of informatics techniques was introduced in order to coordinate economic activity. The system was designed to be introduced gradually, and to be regulated by the JUCEPLAN. Indicators such as cost, output and profit were also introduced to ensure reasonable ways of measuring performance and productivity.

However, in practice, the system failed for a number of reasons. Firstly, as in other stages, aggregated targets and macroeconomic projections were, in many cases, disconnected from the firm realities. For instance, more than 500 directive indicators were not integrated in a unified system. Indicators were centrally defined without real coordination with managers. Secondly, physical output indicators were again prioritized over financial indicators, making it difficult to compare company performance at an international level and control financial flows to the company (the state was to cover losses).

Thirdly, investments were made by a central decision, regardless of the enterprise's profitability, but more importantly, without a learning strategy. Even while this period saw the emergence of sectors such as agricultural machinery and implements, boats, computer keyboards and terminals, digital integrated circuits, the mix between excessive centralization and lack of science-industry integration led to very poor results.[69] To achieve the plan rather than to complete existing projects was the overall goal of the managers. As a result, many contracts were not fulfilled, creating bottlenecks and unused inventories. Last but not least, the country lacked an encompassing quality control system. In 1980, 90 percent of products did not meet quality standards, and many wage premiums were introduced without taking this into account. In 1986, only 25 percent of work quotas were technically sound (ibid.).

Cuba in the socialist economic world

The expansion of most of the industries during this period was based on a mechanism of external compensation supported by easy access to loans and credit, and high import indexes, which would be unsustainable under the prevailing international conditions. Even while it cannot be said that the manufacturing industries developed during this period are only a result of Soviet aid,[70] the fact is that the dependence on only one market is significant enough. For example, some estimates indicate that 80–85 percent of the Cuban trade relations were based on the Soviet block (Álvares 1998). On the one hand, Cuba found a market for its production, and preferential conditions for its development. Conversely, as a result of this integration, Cuba inherited an inefficient production system focused on the exporting of primary products (sugar, minerals and citrus produce), and which was only sustained by the growth of capital and labor input rather than technical and organizational change.

Cuba had entered an international production network as a supplier of commodities, but this network's industrial products were not competitive on the international market. Nevertheless, when the agro-industry and other industries caught up slightly, they were condemned to remain within the limits of the socialist subsystem. In this context, the exporting of some industrial products was promoted. For example, from 1976–80, 115 new exportable[71] items were incorporated, but they formed a very small share of the total value exports[72] (Monreal 2005). The Cuba's non-traditional exports increased by 42 percent during 1981–85, with 111 new items being created.[73] Two fifths of non-traditional products were exported in the competitive world-market[74] (mostly less developed countries). However, more than half the non-sugar exports benefited from CMEA's protected market (Zimbalist 1989).

Although the major strategy goal was to increase the export of industrial-based manufacturing, the reality was different. A sort of import-substitute industrialization was carried out, in part financed by the exporting of primary commodities. Industries such as metal processing, electronics, textiles, construction supply materials, agro–machinery, naval construction and assembly of transportation equipment experienced the creation of new productive capacities (Monreal 2005; Álvares 1998). Also introduced into the same import-substitution model, the biopharmaceutical industry began to be developed at this time.

In regional comparison, the country did very well in terms of export of value added products. For example, during 1980–85 industrial products grew to an average annual growth rate of 18.8 percent, 8.2 percentage points above the growth rate of the Dominican Republic, the next best performer in the group.[75] However, the necessary science-industry integration was absent of strategy; science and production remained essentially two completely different worlds.

Rectification process 1986–1990

In 1986, the Rectification Process (RP), which was mostly intended to correct the distortions observed between 1976 and 1985, was launched. The SDPE system was criticized for being a textual copy of the Soviet model, which was not feasible for Cuba. It was argued that the system had brought widespread corruption, social inequalities and economic mismanagement, which needed to be corrected. Between 1986 and 1988, 60 percent of enterprise managers were replaced. Some twenty ministers as well as dozens of vice ministers, national and regional department heads, lost their jobs. As a result of a direct and secret ballot, about 60 percent of the leaders of local workers' assemblies were replaced, as well as nearly all national leaders.

This period saw a recentralization of the enterprise system through the vertical merging of state enterprises into conglomerates (uniones lineales). In 1989, there were 61 conglomerates, which produced 60 percent of the industrial, construction and agricultural output, and employed one-third of the labor force (Mesa-Lago 2000, p. 269). Bonuses and wage incentives were revised and also recentralized. With these changes, the government attempted to take action to increase labor productivity and the efficiency of the investment process, strengthen work discipline, complete some unfinished projects and try new organizational models.

In practice, most of the SDPE problems could not be solved. Corruption continued and, in 1989, 81 percent of the 2.5 million work quotas had not been revised (ibid.). A food program to replace the dismissed free peasant market was also introduced, but failed to achieve its goals. The system continued to be dependent on Soviet fuel transfers. This situation, together with the decline in sugar prices and the deterioration of the term of trade with the Soviet Union, as well as the eventual collapse of the latter, led in the 1990s to an economic recession and to the worst economic crisis since 1959. However, there were also some attempts to try new organizational models, which may be worth briefly brief mentioning.

New organizational attempts

In 1985, the government started trying a new system in the Army Enterprise System. This system was called the "integral system of enterprise improvement," and represented a new experience in Cuba.[76] It was to be extended gradually, depending on its results, to the rest of the economy. Under this system, managers were given strategy control over the enterprise, which is the power to make all decisions and allocate resources in effective strategies, and bear responsibility at a national level and for their interactions with global economic players. That is to say, these state enterprises were given the power to engage in international trade.

Equally important was the commitment by the state to support any project perceived as being innovative. The state retained control of these enterprises, but they were run as separable entities on a more competitive basis. Corporate directors owed a strong fiduciary duty to the enterprise's principal shareholder – the state. To support this experiment, a new training structure was created. In 1988 universities were given the task of creating specialized programs based on modern management techniques in their operations. The previous structure had been institutionally subordinated to the JUCEPLAN.

The tourism industry, the most rentable sector after the economic crisis of the 1990s, contains important military based-corporations. For instance GAESA, or Grupo de Administracion Empresarial S.A. (Enterprise Management Group Inc.), is the holding company for the Cuban Defence Ministry's vast economic interests. Among its more visible subsidiaries are Gaviota S.A., which directly controls 20–25 percent of Cuba's hotel rooms in partnership with foreign hoteliers, and Aerogaviota, a domestic airline that carries tourists on refurbished Soviet military aircraft flown by Cuban air force pilots. The Cuban military's diverse business ventures bring in an estimated $1 billion US a year.[77]

In 1988, Cubanacán was created as a vertically integrated holding company organized to exploit the tourism industry. Similar to the military-based firms, this government-owned enterprise was also allowed to control its own finances, import its supplies, keep foreign exchange, establish joint ventures and hire foreign managers. The first joint venture with foreign capital was with the Sol Meliá Group (Hotel Meliá Varadero) of Spain in 1990. Several joint ventures have been signed with Cubanacán since then, as well as with Gaviota.[78]

A somewhat similar experience was initiated in the biotechnology industry. This time it involved medical doctors and genetic engineers instead of soldiers. By the end of 1981, the first interferon had been obtained in Cuba. After a few successful pilot projects, the Centre for Genetic Engineering and Biotechnology (CIGB) was opened in 1986, which is the most important of all Cuban biotechnology centers. Innovative products such as meningitis and hepatitis vaccines were developed here and sold to the Soviet Union and Brazil. The Centre for Immunoassay (CIE), the National Centre for Bioproduction (BioCEN) and the National Centre for Production of Laboratory Animals (CENPALAB) were subsequently created in 1987 (see Chapter 7).

Most of these biotech centers were created around research groups in existing laboratories and research centers, which created a cluster of organizations owned by the state but were competitively oriented. Although initially incorporated into the import-substitution strategy, this industry soon revealed its export potential as a producer of innovative biomedical products. Another difference can be observed in the workforce training patterns. Most post-graduate training of the Cuban qualified workforce occurred within the socialist world, largely in the Soviet Union. In the case of biotechnology, bio-scientist were sent to complete post-graduate studies both in the Soviet Union and in other advanced, capitalist, countries, enabling a more adequate catch-up process for this industry. The biotechnological industry was created by following the highest competitive conditions. This partly explains the productivity of its R&D investments, and ultimately the success of the industry (see Chapter 7.

Similar to the military experience, they were also allowed to engage in international trade and form joint ventures with foreign investors. Managers were also given strategic control over the resources, while remaining faithful to the state as owner. During the 1990s and the 2000s, Cuban biotechnology has become a world-class industry and one of the most important players in the Cuban economy.

Notes

1 According to Chang (in Woo Cummings 1999) to reconstruct the developmental state implies reforming or creating mechanisms for the state to be able to build political consensus out of the different visions within the society, then to provide a long-term vision and to engage in institutional adaptation and innovation to achieve those goals (pp. 182–99).

2 For example, the failures to promote exports and to create a competitive technological base are some of the key reasons that the Latin American industrial policies were not as successful as those in East Asia. However the economic performance of Latin America was far better in this period than in the period thereafter, when the state was virtually eliminated from the industrialization agenda in these countries.

3 This period covers the time period that began with the implementation of a broad set of social and economic programs introduced by the new government in 1959, through the experimentation with different models during the 1960s, the definitive adoption of the Soviet economic organizational style during the 70s, and ends with the collapse of the Soviet Union.

4 See J Morales and S Nápoles, Cuba: el proceso de industrialización y su dimensión regional, *Problemas del Desarrollo* 22(85) (Apr.–June): 199–227, 1991, p. 204. To put this numbers into perspectiva: Havana hosted 22 percent of the island's population, while Oriente province (the second in importance) hosted 33 percent of the population and provided 13 percent of non-sugar industrial production; ibid.

5 C Mesa-Lago, Market, *Socialist*, and *Mixed Economies*, The Johns Hopkins University Press, Baltimore and London, 2000, p. 172).

6 Melchor W. Gastón, Oscar A. Echevarría y René F. de la Huerta. Por Qué Reforma Agraria, *Serie B-Apologética*, Folleto No. 23. La Habana: Buró de Información y Propaganda, Agrupación Católica Universitaria, 1957. The reproduction of this

document was provided by José Alvarez, professor at Everglades Research and Education Center of the University of Florida. The document was published EDIS, FE 292, a publication of the Department of Food and Resource Economics, Florida Cooperative Extension Service, Institute of Food and Agricultural Sciences, University of Florida, Gainesville, FL. Published September 2001.

7   L Gasperini, The Cuban Education System: Lessons and Dilemmas, World Bank: Country Studies. Education Reform and Management Publication Series, Vol. I, No. 5, July 2000.

8   FA Truslow et al. (ed.), Report on Cuba: Findings and Recommendations of an Economic and Technical Mission organised by the International Bank for Reconstruction and Development in collaboration with the Government of Cuba in 1950, I B R D Special Publication, Sales Number: I BR D. 1951.3, Washington, D. C., 1951.

9

> "Private construction – most of it residential construction for the well to-do – has represented roughly one quarter of gross capital formation by Cuban residents. This form of investments makes virtually no contribution to the growth of productivity in the Cuban economy,"
>
> (Ibid, p. 514)

10   Cuban Foundation for Technological Investigation, ibid., p. 227.

11   The report stated that given the lack of cheap local fuel, the development of a steel industry was not an option for Cuba (ibid., p. 15). But, even when the development of such an industry would have represented a huge effort, the case seems to be one of protection of American steel interests, which few years later were contributing substantial sums to the Moa Bay Mining Project in Eastern Cuba. American steel companies and major automobile makers may have contributed, according to some authors, up to $US25 million. In comparison to this number, Freeport Nickel, the mining company, a wholly owned Freepor Sulphur subsidiary, only provided $US19 million. See I Pérez-Diaz, Niquel + cobalto en Cuba: Lo que fui como ingeniero, Ciencias Sociales, La Habana 2010,, p. 42; see also L Pease, David Atlee Phillips, Clay Shaw and Freeport, Sulphur, *Probe Magazine* 3(3) (Mar.–Apr.), 1996.

12   In general terms, since Cuba at present has no domestic fuel supply, certain types of industrial development-such as steel production-which are dependent on cheap local fuel, are clearly not for Cuba. Major Cuban development must be related to her basic resources – soil and climate – and to her mineral deposits, although indus-tries processing imported raw materials may also play a useful role. FA Truslow et al., (ed.), Report on Cuba…, p. 15.

13   Ibid., p. 223.

14   Ibid., p. 224.

15   "In spite of the considerable number of Cubans who study scientific courses in leading universities abroad, there is virtually no real research in the Republic today except that being conducted with the aid of foreign technical personnel. This may be because, hitherto, an objective analytical approach has neither been taught nor rewarded in Cuba.

"To remedy the lack of Cuban research workers, Cuba should create her own institution in which objective study can be learned from trained foreign research personnel." (italics in original), ibid., 225.

16   Ibid., p. 195.

17 This US–Cuba trade preferential treaty was signed in 1902 and ratified by both countries in 1903. It basically reduced tariffs for Cuban sugar (it could produce little else at the time) by 20 percent while it provided reductions between 20–40 percent for all kind of American products, including sophisticated capital goods. It is seen, together with the Platt Amendment of 1901 (included in 1903 to the Cuban Constitution) imposed by the US government, as the piece of legislation that defined the Cuba–US unequal relationship as one of economic and political domination. The treaty had antecedents in the colonial era, as Spain (in the name of Cuba) provided the United States (focused in its effort of finding markets for its industrial products and of asserting the Monroe Doctrine) juicy commercial concessions expressed in the trade treaties of 1884 and 1891. The treaty of 1902 was, even in the middle of the Digley tariff (1897–1909, the longest in US history), a natural continuation of these affairs. Cuban sugar producers were the only ones exempt from paying the high sugar duties, which led to specialization in the sugar industry. By 1909 Cuban exports to the US had competed away all other foreign competition. During 1905–27 foreign investments in the sector grew significantly and modern technology was introduced during the period. During World War I the industry experienced unusual highs, which led to speculation followed by a banking crisis in the island (1919–20) that wiped out almost all non-American producers. But it was the crisis of 1929, together with the Hawley-Smoot tariff, the event that brought the most significant declines in the Cuban sugar production. Neither the sugar controls introduced by Cuban government and producers, nor other world market price's control mechanisms (such as the International Sugar agreement, a private cartel) could prevent that by 1933 the Cuba's sugar exports (basically equivalent to the US market) had fallen almost the half respect to 1929. During the 1930s foreign corporations and banks sold cane fields to Cuban nationals and repatriated profits fell in relation to total spending outside of Cuba, which stimulated local economic activity. The treaty of 1934 abrogated the one of 1903 and introduced the system of sugar quotas that reasserted US's political and economic domination prior to 1929, by other means. From then on, even when sugar stopped attracting American investor interests, which began to focus increasingly in mining, public services and manufactures, the quotas represented part of the means to keep the island politically and economically dependent. In addition, increasing US investment in other areas did not significantly improve this situation due to the preferential tariffs.

18 FA Truslow et al. (ed.), Report on Cuba... p. 754–5.

19 Although sugar production fluctuated, the fact remains that the dependency on this product was overwhelming and provided little dynamism to the economy. In the 1950s, sugar exports accounted for 81 percent of total exports, C Mesa-Lago, Markets..., p. 171.

20 Crude sugar manufacture was the most important industry; mill and growers were the railroads' biggest customers.

21 Ibid., p. 172.

22 The US unemployment rate in 1953 was 2.8 percent, J Kuczynki et al. (ed.), Monopolios norteamericanos en Cuba, Editorial Ciencias Sociales, La Habana, p. 270, 1973.

23 Fragments of the speech of Dr. Fidel Castro at U.N. General Assembly, September, 26, 1960.

24 Remarks of Senator John F. Kennedy at democratic dinner, Cincinnati, Ohio, October 6, 1960.

25 D Raby, Why Cuba still matters, Monthly Review 60(08), January, 2009, available in: www.monthlyreview.org/090105raby.php

26 V *Lenin*, "Left-Wing" Communism: an Infantile Disorder, *Collected Works*, Volume 31, Progress Publishers, USSR, pp. 17–118, 1964.

27 See A *Pannekoek, Lenin as Philosopher: A Critical Examination of the Philosophical Basis of Leninism*, Marquette University Press, 2003; see also H Gorter, S Pankhurst, O Rühle, Non-Leninist Marxism: Writings on the Workers Councils. St Petersburg, Florida: Red and Black Publishers, 2007.

28 Some libertarian socialists see Stalinism as the logical extension of Leninism. See N Chomsky, The Soviet Union versus socialism, *Our Generation*, Spring/Summer, 1986.

29 Ibid.

30 **A** Savioli A, L'Unita Interview with Fidel Castro: The nature of Cuban socialism, L'Unita, Rome, No. 32, February 1, 1961: 1–2.

31 D Raby, *Why Cuba...*

32 Similarly, regional governments were "encouraged to start social housing projects and employers to improve working conditions in factories" (K Micheisen and M Kuisma, Nationalism and Industrial. Development in Finland, *Business and Economic History*, Second Series, Volume 21, 1992, p. 345).

33 During the 1950s and 1960s efforts made by the centralized trade union led to the introduction of a solidarity wage policy aimed to equalize wages across industries for the same types of workers.

34 Instruments such as an industrial accident insurance (1871), health insurance (1883) and state pensions (1889) are paramount examples. By the second decade of the twentieth century, many European countries had created welfare institutions.

35 It is worth mentioning that elements of welfare state institutions are actually recorded since ancient times. Some evidence can be found in the economic writings and policies of such scholars as Kautilya (370–283 BCE), king Asoka the Great (304–232 BCE) during the Mauryan period in ancient India, king Akbar (1542–1605) during the Mughal period in India, Wang Anshi (1021–1086) during the Song dynasty in China or Abu Yusuf (731–798) during the Islamic Abbasid period.

36 Since Raul Castro came to power in 2008 until the present day (2019), which includes the new president Miguel Diaz-Canel.

37 Many scholars of the anti-socialist, libertarian tradition see the solution within the classic framework of a broad restriction of the state functions supported by large-scale privatizations and deregulations. A Cuban scholar wrote that, "In Cuba, privatisation means, essentially, returning confiscated property to their previous owners" (Jorge Sanguinetty, Comments on "Economic Reform in Latin America and the Caribbean and Possible Implications for Cuba," ASCE, November 1998, p. 22), thus seeking to re-edit the preceding state of affairs, which happens to be precisely that leading to the Cuban revolution. For a detailed discussion on the different schools of thought dealing with revolutionary Cuba see Emily Morris, Unexpected Cuba, *New Left Review* 88 (July–Aug. 2014): 5–45.

38 This right, a rule of International Public Law that cannot be dissociated from the existence itself of any politically organized people even prior to their constitution as a State, had already been sanctioned at the international level in the United Nations Charter in 1945 as an inalienable and imprescriptibly right.

39 The 1940 Constitution of Cuba was implemented during the presidency of Federico Laredo Brú. It was primarily influenced by the progressive ideas that inspired the Cuban Revolution of 1933. Widely considered one of the most progressive

constitutions in existence at the time, it created explicit legal frameworks for land reform, minimum wage and public education, among other progressive ideas (see www.latinamericanstudies.org/constitution-1940.htm)

40 The Agrarian Reform Law limited the size of farms to 3333 acres and real estate to 1000 acres. Any holdings over these limits were expropriated by the government and either redistributed to peasants in 67 acre parcels or held as state-run communes.

41 Further information can be found in P Groppo et al., Land reform: Land settlement and cooperatives, FAO Report, 2003/3 Special Edition.

42 Instituto nacional de la reforma agraria, in Spanish.

43 Article 24 of the fundamental Law in force at the time of the expropriations recognized the right of national or foreign assets holders to an indemnity in the event of expropriation. The only exception was the confiscation contemplated in the case of people directly related to the deposed regime. Further information in www.cubavsbloqueo.cu/Default.aspx?tabid=271

44 The National Association of Small Farmers (ANAP) (Spanish: *Asociación Nacional de Agricultores Pequeños*) is a cooperative federation dedicated to promoting the interests of small farmers in Cuba. ANAP was formed in 1961, and its membership was limited to farmers whose land holdings were less than 67 hectares.

45 The effects of Hurricane Flora in 1963 also contributed to this negative result.

46 During the 1970s and the 1980s, as the country was able to import bigger quantities of food and other basic products, the system was retained as a distribution measure in order to protect the low-income sectors of the population. However, no effective system was designed to reduce the import dependence on food.

47 The reciprocity treaty of 1934 and the Costigan Jones Act of the same year did away with most of the industrial production achieved by Machado´s Custon-Tariff Act. The former by increasing the number of American products allowed to receive preferential treatment in the Cuban market and thus making it more difficult to Cuban industrists to prosper. The latter by imposing a fixed quota to the Cuban sugar, which artificially reduced Cuban sugar´s participation in the American market (see J Le Reverent, Historia económica de Cuba, Editorial Pueblo y Educación, pp. 248–9, 1975).

48 In 1961, the complete monopoly of foreign trade was granted.

49 J O'Connor, The Origins… p. 243.

50 Oficina nacional de Estadisticas, República de Cuba, 2009.

51 Ibid.

52 In this year the South Korean government also launched the First Five-Year Economic Development Plan in order to meet effectively the technological requirements of the planned industrialization and economic modernization.

53 The US embargo and the alliance with the Soviet Union decidedly contributed towards shaping the Cuban strategy

54 As part of the updating of Cuba's socioeconomic model started by President Raul Castro, five new laws went into effect December 11, 2012, creating a legal framework for the gradual establishment of cooperatives for non-agricultural purposes, and providing provisional regulations which will govern the process. This represents one of the most unprecedented economic reforms introduced since 1959 (see www.granma.cu/ingles/cuba-i/20dic-cooperatives.htm)

55 The average global price of sugar had been 4.38 cents per pound between 1957 and 1964. It then declined from 5.87 to 1.86 in 1964–66 to increase again to 3.75 in 1969–70 (C Mesa-Lago, *Market….* 2000, p. 216).

56 Ibid. It was not possible for Cuba to trade within Latin America. In 1964, the Organization of American States (OAS, championed by the United States) also broke relations with Cuba (except Mexico). The country lost the possibility to increase its trade with Latin America. On the other hand, trading with farther regions implied more fuel, and subsequent higher costs/lower profits.

57 In 1966 the Korea Institute of Science and Technology (KIST) was created in South Korea. As already mentioned, it was, just like the Cuban CNIC, a multidisciplinary organization. However, while CNIC remained more basic research oriented, KIST was built as a contract research center, and quickly established contact with industry.

58 C Mesa-Lago, *Market...*, p. 220.

59 Ibid., p. 210.

60 This is perfectly logical since, unlike Guevara, Carlos Rafael Rodriguez was a strong admirer of the Soviet Union and was one of the Cuban economists in the Cuban government that most did in order to move Cuba closer to the Soviet Union after the disagreements of the 1960s.

61 The policy increased economic independence of enterprises and they became the main unit of the economic system. That is, profitability became the first criteria; and profits were to be employed in different company's matters such as funds, material incentives, housing, etc. Most of the ideas of this reform came from the Soviet economist Evsei Liberman, who was the architect of many Soviet economic projects. The reform ended in 1971 as conservative elements within the government advocated for a return to a more centralized form of economic management (see Glenn E. Curtis, ed. *Russia: A Country Study*. Washington: GPO for the Library of Congress, 1996, available at http://countrystudies.us/russia/14.htm). However, a mild version of these reforms was later applied in Cuba with the introduction of the System of Economic Direction and Planning during the 1970s in whose application Carlos Rafael Rodriguez played a leading role.

62 Marx's insights are basically the ones contained in the value-labor theories of Smith and Ricardo. His main concern was to understand how this law determines exchange. His main critique to them was that they were unable to reconcile the idea of the regulation of trade by the law of value; with the profit in proportion to capital employed (rather than in proportion to labor-time worked). A similar notion of value-labor had been developed by the Muslim author Ibn Khaldun in the fourteenth century.

63 This refers to the practice known as work-to-rule or Italian strike, which consists of workers doing exactly what the contract stipulate. As Chang argues, "not everything can be specified in employment contracts and therefore all production processes rely heavily on the workers good will to do extra things..." HJ Chang, *23 things...*, 2010, p. 46).

64 This scale strongly conditioned wages to qualification, which created an incentive for training of new workforce to substitute the emigrated workforce.

65 "... in a world populated by selfish individuals, the invisible reward/sanction mechanisms can not exist" because "rewarding and punishing others for their behaviours costs time and energy only to the individuals taking the action, while their benefits from improved behavioural standards accrue to everyone" HJ Chang, *23 Things...*, p. 49).

66 The figure of Ernesto "Che" Guevara has been usually linked to his political activities and his ideological beliefs. However during the time he was Minister of Industry he put in practice a number of sound programs aimed at stimulating training

and innovation, given the big exodus of qualified workforce experienced by the country at that period. One of the most known programs was the creation in 1961 of the Movement of Inventors and Innovators, aimed at finding practical solutions to problems originated in manufacturing activity. As economic historian Helen Yaffe tells in his acclaimed 2009 book *Che Guevara: The Economics of the Revolution*, "when the Department of Industrialisation was set up within INRA, dozens of inventors arrived at the office to show their creations" (p. 140). She further states that he gave personal attention to the "most promising projects submitted" (p. 141). This was the beginning of a movement that was further institutionalized in 1976 as the National Association of Inventors and Innovators. The Association still exists and has been responsible for a number of solutions to practical problems in day to day production. Likewise, while in the Ministry of Industry, he set up nine R&D institutes intended to "find substitutes for costly imports, increase the value added to raw material exports, particularly sugar and nickel, created a mechanical industry to exploit Cuba's metallurgy reserves, produce spare parts and lay the foundation for an automobile industry" (p. 197). In 1963, while Vice Minister of technical development; he created the office of Automation and Electronics. He encouraged voluntary work and consciousness as forms of increasing productivity.

67 www.osaarchivum.org/files/holdings/300/8/3/text/14-2-118.shtml
68 In comparison with Further analysis can be found in Mesa-Lago (2000), Pérez-López (1987), Zimbalist (1989).
69 Of course, this does not justify the later government decision of shooting down all these industries when the Soviet Union collapsed.
70 According to Andrew Zimbalist Soviet aid to Cuba during the period under analysis (in per capita terms or as a share of national income) was in line with the amount of Western aid to many Latin American countries. Therefore, it cannot be inferred that Cuban economic growth was only due to external assistance. He states that, even with the many deficiencies of the model up to 1989, there had been certain developmental elements in the government economic policy, see A Zimbalist, Cuba's revolutionary economy, *The Multinational Monitor* 10(4), 1989.
71 During the period 1976–89, Cuba also exported citrus fruit, fish products, steel products, recycled raw materials, scrap metals, gas stoves, paper products, soldering irons and electrodes, non-electrical machinery, transportation materials and machinery, fibreboard, radios, sulfuric acid, batteries, teletransmission and processing equipment, among others.
72 Most of Cuba's exports (1976–89) to the socialist world were 63 percent sugar, 73 percent nickel and 95 percent citrus fruits Cuba imported 63 percent of its food, 98 percent of fuel, 80 percent of machinery, 57 percent of chemicals and 70 percent of industrial manufactures, see EC Álvares, Cuba, un Modelo de desarrollo con justicia social, Instituto Nacional de Investigaciones Económicas, La Habana: paper presented at XI Congress of the Latin American Studies Association, The Palmer House Hilton Hotel, Chicago, Illinois, September 24–26, 2008.
73 Apart from the significant growth experienced by commodities such as citrus fruit and fish products, the country also experienced a growth exports in steel products, recycled raw materials, scrap metals, gas stoves, paper products, soldering irons and electrodes, non-electrical machinery, transportation materials and machinery, fiberboard, radios, sulfuric acid, batteries, teletransmission and processing equipment, among others (see A Zimbalist, Cuba's Revolutionary Economy...). During 1990 some of this production was partially maintained.

74 In 1974 Western countries accounted for 41 percent of Cuba's trade, up from a low
    of 17 percent in 1962. In 1979 Western countries accounted for over 40 percent
    of Cuba's foreign trade, when world sugar market prices and Western bank loans
    provided a window of opportunity. But the decline in world market sugar prices
    during the late 1970s and the soaring Western interest rates at the same period led
    to an increase in the cost of servicing Western debts. As a consequence, and having
    little else to sell, the island's hard-currency debt rose from $660 million in 1974 to
    over $5 billion in 1987. (See S Eckstein, Foreign aid Cuban style, *The Multinational
    Monitor* 10(4), Economics, April 1989.)

75 However, the source of these figures, suggests, the growth rates alone can be deceptive
    if Cuba begins from a much lower base. In fact, he continues, the Cuban base level
    in 1980 of $360.4 million (converted at the official 1980 rate of exchange) is consid-
    erably above that in Panama ($90.3 million), Dominican Republic ($105.3 million)
    and Jamaica ($106.5 million), about the same as in Honduras ($291.9 million), and
    below that only in Costa Rica ($441.9 million) and Guatemala ($707.7 million),
    A Zimbalist, Cuba´s Revolutionary Economy...

76 There are many similar historical cases around the world.

77 http://ctp.iccas.miami.edu/FOCUS_Web/Issue46.htm

78 See F Godínez, Cuba´s tourism industry: Sol Meliá as a case study, *Cuba in Transition*,
    ASCE, University of Miami, pp. 50–9, 1998.

References

Álvares EC (1998), Cuba, un Modelo De desarrollo con justicia social, Instituto Nacional
    de Investigaciones Económicas, La Habana. Paper presented at XI Congress of the
    Latin American Studies Association, The Palmer House Hilton Hotel, Chicago,
    Illinois, September 24–26.

Amsden AH (1989), *Asia's Next Giant: South Korea and Late Industrialization.* New York:
    Oxford University Press

Chang HJ (2002), Breaking the mould: An institutionalist political economy alternative
    to the neo-liberal theory of the market, *Cambridge Journal of Economics* 26: 539–59.

Chang HJ (2003), *Kicking Away the Ladder.* London: Anthem Press.

Chang HJ (2008), *Bad Samaritans: The Myth of Free Trade and the Secret History of
    Capitalism.* New York: Bloomsbury Press.

Chang HJ (2009), Industrial Policy: Can We Go Beyond an Unproductive
    Confrontation?, A Plenary Paper for ABCDE (Annual World Bank Conference on
    Development Economics) Seoul, South Korea 22–24 June.

Chang HJ (2010), *23 Things They Don't Tell You about Capitalism.* London: Penguin
    Group.

Chomsky N (1986), The Soviet Union versus socialism, *Our Generation*, Spring/Summer.

Curtis G (ed.) (1996), *Russia: A Country Study.* Washington, D.C.: GPO for the Library
    of Congress.

Dye AD and Sicotte R (1999), U.S.-Cuban trade cooperation and its unraveling,
    Business and Economic History 28(2), Winter.

Dye AD and Sicotte R (2004), The US sugar program and the Cuban revolution,
    Journal of Economic History 64(3): 673–704.

Ebbinghaus B and Manow P (eds.) (2001), *Comparing Welfare Capitalism: Social Policy and
    Political Economy in Europe.* Japan and New York: Routledge.

Eckstein S (1989), Foreign Aid Cuban Style, *The Multinational Monitor* 10(4): Economics, April.

Evans P et al. (eds.) (1999), *Bringing the State Back In*. Cambridge: Cambridge University Press.

García-Molina J (2005), La economía cubana desde el siglo XVI al XX: del colonialismo al socialismo con mercado, *Serie Estudios y perspectivas* 28, CEPAL, Mexico D.F.

Gasperini L (2000), The Cuban Education System: Lessons and Dilemmas, *Country Studies Education Reform and Management Publication Series* I(5) (July), 21752, World Bank.

Gastón MW et al. (1957) [2001], Por Qué Reforma Agraria, *Serie B-Apologética*, Folleto No. 23. La Habana: Buró de Información y Propaganda, Agrupación Católica Universitaria.

Godínez F (1998), Cuba's tourism industry: Sol Meliá as a case study, *Cuba in Transition*, ASCE, University of Miami, pp. 50–9.

Gorter H et al. (2007), *Non-Leninist Marxism: Writings on the Workers Councils.* St Petersburg, FL: Red and Black Publishers.

Groppo P et al. (2003), Land reform, Land settlement and cooperatives, FAO Report, 2003/3 Special Edition.

Guevara E (2006), *Apuntes críticos a la economía política*, Editorial Ciencias Sociales, La Habana.

Jäntti M and Vartiainen J (2009), The Finnish Developmental State and its Growth Regime, UNU-WIDER, *Research Paper* No. 2009/35, June.

Katzenstein P (1987), *Corporatism and Change: Austria, Switzerland and the Politics of Industry*. Ithaca: Cornell University Press.

Kleinknecht A et al. (2014), Is flexible labour good for innovation? Evidence from firm-level data, *Cambridge Journal of Economics* 38: 1207–19.

Kuczynski J et al. (ed.) (1973), *Monopolios norteamericanos en Cuba*. La Habana: Editorial Ciencias Sociales.

Lazonick W (2006), Corporate Governance, Innovative Enterprise, and Economic Development, UNU WIDER, *Research Paper* No. 2006/71, July.

Lee D et al. (1991), Performance and adaptive role of the government supported Research Institute in Korea, *World Development* 19(10): 1421–40.

Lenin V [1920] (1964) *"Left-Wing" Communism: an Infantile Disorder*, Collected Works, Volume 31, Progress Publishers, USSR, pp. 17–118.

Le Riverend J (1975), *Historia económica de Cuba*. La Habana: Editorial Pueblo y Educación.

Marqués-Dolz MA (2006), *Las industrias menores: empresarios y empresas en Cuba (1880–1920)*. La Habana: Editorial de Ciencias Sociales.

Marquetti H (2006), La restructuración del sistema empresarial en Cuba: Tendencias principales. In: Evenly O (ed.), *Reflexiones sobre economía cubana*, Ciencias Sociales. Ciudad de la Habana: Editorial de Ciencias sociales, pp. 297–338.

Mesa-Lago C (2000), *Market, Socialist, and Mixed Economies: Comparative Policy and Performance, Chile, Cuba, and Costa Rica*. Baltimore/London: The Johns Hopkins University Press.

Micheisen K and Kuisma M (1992), Nationalism and Industrial. Development in Finland, *Business and Economic History*, Second Series, Volume 21.

Monreal P (2005), The problem of development in contemporary Cuba, *Journal of the Faculty of International Studies*, 19, Japan: Utsunomiya University, pp. 59–71.

Morales J and Nápoles S (1991), Cuba: el proceso de industrialización y su dimensión regional, *Problemas del Desarrollo* 22(85) (April–June): 199–227.

Morris E (2014), Unexpected Cuba, *New Left Review* 88 (July-Aug.): 5–45.

Naqvi SN (1994), *Islam, Economics and Society.* London and New York: Kegan Paul International.

O'Connor J (1970), *The Origins of Socialism in Cuba.* Ithaca, London: Cornell University Press.

Oficina Nacional de Estadistica (2009), Republica de Cuba.

Open Society Archives (1973), The system of government in socialist Cuba, Online: www.osaarchivum.org/files/holdings/300/8/3/text/14-2-118.shtml, last accessed July 2019.

Ostry J et al. (2014) Redistribution, Inequality, and Growth, *IMF Staff Discussion Note,* February.

Pannekoek A [1938] (2003), *Lenin as Philosopher: A Critical Examination of the Philosophical Basis of Leninism.* Marquette University Press.

Parker-Willis H (1903), Reciprocity with Cuba, *Annals of the American Academy of Political and Social Science,* Vol. 22, The United States and Latin America (July), pp. 129–147

Pease L (1996), David Atlee Phillips, Clay Shaw and Freeport, Sulphur, *Probe Magazine* 3(3) (March–April): 16–24.

Pérez-Diaz I (2010), *Niquel + cobalto en Cuba: Lo que fui como ingeniero,* Ciencias Sociales, La Habana

Polanyi K, et al. (eds.) (1957), *Trade and Market in the Early Empires. Economies in History and theory,* The Free Press, Glencoe Illinois

Raby D (2009), Why Cuba still matters, *Monthly Review* 60(08) (January), available at https://monthlyreview.org/2009/01/01/why-cuba-still-matters/.

Reinert E (2007), *How Rich Countries Got Rich…and Why Poor Countries Stay Poor.* London: Constable.

Remarks of Senator John. F. Kennedy at democratic dinner, Cincinnati, Ohio, October 6, 1960, Source: Papers of John F. Kennedy. Pre-Presidential Papers. Senate Files. Series 12. Speeches and the Press. Box 912, Folder: "Democratic dinner, Cincinnati, Ohio, 6 October 1960," available at www.jfklibrary.org/archives/other-resources/john-f-kennedy-speeches/cincinnati-oh-19601006-democratic-dinner, last accessed 6/2019

Sanguinetti J (1998), Comments on "Economic Reform in Latin America and the Caribbean and Possible Implications for Cuba," *Cuba in Transition,* ASCE, November: 20–22.

Savioli A (1961), L'Unita interview with Fidel Castro: The nature of Cuban socialism, L'Unita, Rome, 32, February 1: 1–2.

Smith A [1776] (2005), *Wealth of the Nation,* the Pennsylvania State University, Electronic Classics Series, Pennsylvania, US.

Speech of Dr. Fidel Castro at U.N. General Assembly, September 26, 1960, Source: Embassy of Cuba, Report NBR-FBIS, Report Date: 19600926, available at http://lanic.utexas.edu/project/castro/db/1960/19600926.html, last accessed, June 13, 2019, Original text in Spanish available at www.cubadebate.cu/especiales/2018/09/23/texto-completo-del-historico-discurso-de-fidel-en-la-onu-el-26-de-setiembre-de-1960/, last accessed, June 13, 2019

Truslow FA et al. (ed.) (1951), *Report on Cuba,* IBRD Special Publication, Washington, D.C.

Vaskela G (1996). The Land Reform of 1919–1940: Lithuania and the Countries of East and Central Europe, *Lithuanian Historical Studies*, Lithuanian Institute of History, V.1.P. 116–32.

Woo-Cumings M (ed.) (1999), *The Developmental State*. Ithaca and London: Cornell University Press.

Yaffe H (2009), Che Guevara: *The Economics of the Revolution*, London: Palgrave Macmillan.

Yglesia Martinez T and Capote Nestor (1993), *The Americas*, The History of Cuba and its Interpreters, 1898–1935 49(3) (January): 369–85.

Zaman H (1991), *Economic Fuctions of an Islamic State: The Early Experience*. Markfield, UK: The Islamic Foundation.

Zimbalist A (1989), Cuba's revolutionary economy, *The Multinational Monitor* 10(4).

6 Cuban industrial policy from 1989 to the present

Beginning in 1990, at the time of the collapse of the Soviet system, Cuba was to face the biggest challenge to its economy since the first days of the Cuban revolution. Gross domestic product fell by one-third in just four years, and foreign trade contracted by almost 75 percent. In Cuba, a national emergency adjustment program[1] was enacted, which basically put the country on a wartime economy-style austerity agenda. To make matters worse, the US government went for the jugular by tightening the economic embargo to the point of cruelty.[2] To deal with this complex situation became a matter of survival.

In addition, the model of the first 30 years of the Cuban socialist socio-economic system had been based on an industrial structure rooted mostly in a national "agro-industrial complex," with guaranteed financing, technology and markets from the real existing socialist world (Monreal 2005, p. 59). But in actual fact, the country had not been able to competitively upgrade its technological capability. An impressive social (education and health) system had been created; however innovation-inhibiting management and business practices had been at the core of the industrial policy of the period. Particularly at the earlier stages of the new social project, the country's industrial policy failed to promote organizational integration within the economy. Government non-firm agencies (similar if not identical to MITI in Japan, IRI in Italy, ARPA in the US etc.) failed to create the necessary synergies that could lead to innovation and this prevented industrialization from taking place. The advent of the crisis of the 1990s imposed the need for a competitive upgrading of the industrial structure and a redesign of the development strategy.

But countries' assimilation of new technologies does not take place automatically; rather they require an appropriate system of national institutions, which create the adequate social conditions for enterprises and individuals to acquire and improve their skills (Freeman 2008; Lazonick 2002). In the Cuban case, several institutional innovations were carried out in order to reintroduce the country in the international markets. However, with exception of biotechnology, financial priority was given to sectors such as tourism and nickel extraction, which became the most important growth engines of the national economy.

Even as the country began to recover in 1994, the development pattern remained essentially based on primary products and tourist services. As these activities began to show signs of stagnation, the export of medical services entered the scene, reaching an annual growth average of 28 percent between 2004 and 2007. As a result, GDP increased at an average rate of 9.2 percent during those years; but it decreased again to 2.5 percent during the period 2008–10, when the export of medical services shrank to 3 percent. The absence of a long-term growth strategy became apparent. Competitive upgrading of the manufacturing industry was not in sight. In fact, the country experienced an acute de-industrialization. This shed some doubt on the sustainability of the strategy advanced during the last almost three decades.

Actually, what prevailed until 2011 was some sort of crisis management policy, which nominally kept the goals of development as paramount rhetoric but in practice was aimed at surviving the impact of the economic crisis together with the growing hostility of the US foreign policy. However, the Cuban Communist Party approved in April 2011 a new set of economic reforms for the period 2011–15. The new strategy was unveiled in November 2010 when the government outlined 291 proposals for "updating" Cuba's economic model. The so-called "Guidelines of the Economic and Social Policy of the Party and the Revolution" were then broadly discussed by the population and subsequently revised. After 60 percent of the proposal was changed or corrected, a new version with 311 points was approved at the 2011 Party Congress.

Since then, another Party Congress has taken place, a new constitution was approved, and several other actualizations and developments plans have already been launched with the goal of making Cuban socialism competitive and sustainable. The last actualization of the guidelines (to our knowledge) was published in 2017 and contains 274 point, of which 45 are devoted to technology and industrial policy. The fact that science, technology and industrial development were explicitly acknowledged as key aspects for a sustainable development of the country is sign of a good direction. However, up to the present time, most relevant indicators reveal that there is a long way to go in terms of learning and strategy sustainability.

In this chapter we will take a look at the newest reforms advanced in Cuba, but, for obvious reasons, we cannot discuss their impact (they are happening right now). Rather, we will make some comments on their possible relevance and about the reason that led the government to engage in them. The biggest part of the critical discussion, however, will be focused on the impact of the last 25 years of economic policies. In this sense, it will be argued that Cuban policymakers need to redirect future growth strategies toward the export of innovation-, technology-based manufactures, if the country is to move upward in the global production networks.

6.1 First measures after the collapse of the Soviet Union

As just mentioned, during this period the focus of the Cuban government was to assimilate the impact of the crisis by attempting to maintain the most important social standards, which constituted the basis for the political consensus. For instance, in contrast with the shock therapies applied in Eastern Europe, the Cuban government decided to increase budget expenditures. During those critical years (1990–93), the government cut expenditures in activities such as defense and internal security by 38 percent, and administration by 8 percent, in order to gain resources for an 83 percent of increase in subsidies to cover losses in state enterprises (Dominguez et al. 2004).

The share of subsidies in the budget expenditure rose from 26 to 42 percent. In the same policy line, public health expenses increased by 15 percent during this stage (ibid.). In order to distribute the adjustment costs, many jobs were kept (even with no real content), subsidies (70 percent of the salary) were issued for downsized workers. As Chang (1999) points out, the state role as conflict manager should not simply be seen as "social" or "human," as the orthodoxy defends. It should rather be seen as a provider of insurance not only for certain, but mostly for uncertain contingencies, which could improve productivity in the long run by encouraging risk taking and investments in assets with limited mobility. Of course, badly monitored insurance can be conducive to moral hazard, but this does not invalidate the fact that lacking a conflict management mechanism discourages industrial investment and therefore economic development.

6.2 Reforms aimed to the domestic economy

A new group of measures were introduced in 1993, with the aim of improving the functioning of the domestic economy, i.e. to extend the availability of some services and increase agricultural productivity. First, the use of foreign currency by Cuban citizens (basically US currency) was decriminalized. This measure was intended to stimulate hard currency remittances from Cubans living abroad and to stop the booming hard currency black market.[3] The government created special stores at which individuals holding hard currencies could shop for mostly imported items not available to Cubans holding *pesos*. In 1994 the government created foreign currency exchange houses (*Casas de Cambio*, CADECA) at which Cuban citizens could exchange hard currencies for pesos at rates close to those prevailing in the hard currency black market. This allowed collecting hard currency and later redistributing the generated income in other priorities. Additional measures included reforms in the labor market and in the agricultural production. These groups of reforms have been subsequently updated after Raúl Castro came to power.

6.2.1 Changes in the labor market

After the collapse of the communist world, the Cuban government authorized self-employment in over 100 occupations, subject to some restrictions. Most of them were small-scale retail activities, such as transportation and other personal services.[4] The number of businesses such as restaurants and taxi drivers, exploded. These legalizations helped to create jobs and absorb employees fired from unprofitable state enterprises. Self-employment rose from only 1.6 percent of all workers in 1981 to 4.1 percent in 1999. However just a few activities were allowed in the small manufacturing sector and in primary production. Additionally, hiring conditions were also severely restricted and networking with state firms was poorly encouraged. By the late 1990s, the Cuban government chose to halt and partially reverse the economic opening. Overall, the economy remained highly centralized, with the state employing over 80 percent of the workforce (for a general discussion on the period see Sanchez and Triana 2008, Rodriguez 2014).

As soon as Raúl Castro assumed the presidency, he announced his aim to facilitate the expansion of the self-employment sector along with greater hiring flexibility, allowing small proprietors to exploit labor for profit.[5] In 2008 new Decree-law 268 was passed, allowing multiple employment opportunities in the state sector and paid part-time positions for university students, with the aim of stimulating production, enabling income growth and addressing issues raised by the ageing of the population. In 2011, after a pilot period of 20 months, during which barbers and beauty workers were allowed to lease their premises from the state and work independently, government passed Resolution No 516/11, which extended this reform to 24 different types of activities. With this system, the government leases the businesses for ten years, giving priority to those who worked for the businesses when they were under state control. This measure has been aimed at increasing the quality of services and labor.

As a result, the number of self-employees has increased substantially since 2010 (Figure 6.1). Under the new framework, there were in 2011 181 types of activities in which practitioners could engage, and be at the same time state employees.[6] That is a very different concept when compared with the restrictive conditions of the early nineties. Other restrictions that were also relaxed or eliminated include the prohibition on employing non-family members, and the size restrictions, like one limiting private restaurants to 12 chairs and as well as the tax code (Law 113 and Decree 308 of 2012). In order to guarantee credit for these new ventures, the government enacted in 2011 Decree-law 289 (with three central bank resolutions), which authorized around 500 banks across the island to offer loans to the growing number of start-ups, the self-employed, as well as farmers and people building their own homes. In order to extend the scope of activities and business models available, in December 2012 the government enacted Decree-laws 305 and 306 allowing the formation of 200 (experimental) non-agricultural cooperatives. Decree-law 309 of the same year establishes the general rules for these institutions. Until today (2019), there is no general cooperative law, therefore the experimental nature of the current legislation continues.

Agricultural cooperatives have existed in Cuba for a long time, but non-agricultural cooperatives represent a real qualitative change in the composition of the labor market since 1959. Until mid-2011, 67 percent of self-employees were coming from unemployment, and only 7 percent were university graduates, but this could change as non-agricultural cooperatives face no obvious restriction

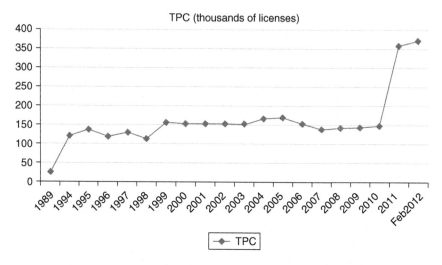

Figure 6.1 Number of self-employees, 1989–2012 (thousands of authorizations)
Source: Pineiro Hanecker C (2012) based on Cuba's national statistics office (ONE)
Available in http://thecubaneconomy.com/articles/tag/cooperatives/

in the kind of activities. Therefore, they are expected to play a crucial role in more substantial activities (in theory software design, high-tech professional services, construction materials, housing, light industry etc.). That is important because it is the type of activity (rather than the fact that it is a small business[7]) that determines the contribution of a firm to the average national productivity.[8] However, up to 2018 most of the non-agricultural cooperatives were to be found in the gastronomy sector (157 from 434). Also in 2018 the first wholesale markets were opened for these institutions, predominantly oriented to gastronomic activities. Likewise, in the same year, 13 percent of the country's working population[9] was involved in self-employment, mostly in low-end activities.

On the other hand, the fact that both the self-employed and cooperatives are allowed to contract with state enterprises, could open a lot of opportunities in this direction if more aggregate value activities received authorizing. We should remember the role played by the US government as demand enhancer in the development of the semiconductor, computer and software industries during the 1950s and 60s (see Chapters 3 and 4). The Cuban structure is completely different but the issue of the possible synergies that could emerge from the cooperation between high-tech cooperatives and the state is interesting to speculate about. However up to date, these measures are under study in Cuba. The growing emphasis in technology will probably cause in the near future many new developments to be implemented in this direction.

In tandem with these measures, and in order to reduce its inflated payrolls, the government had set up the plan to lay off up to a million state sector workers, or 20 percent of the workforce. In 2010 an initial plan to lay off 500,000 in just six months was indefinitely postponed because there was no place for them to go. An important part of the political capital of the government lies in its promise not to leave anyone behind in this significant economic shift. Therefore, concerns about the social dislocation and inequality were handled with care. Even when the rise of inequality and poverty has been significant, the government is still committed to maintaining the collective welfare system of which the revolution is most proud, including free and universal health care, education and social security.

Both self-employees and cooperative workers retain all their rights within the social security system. Special dispositions were created to fully include these workers in the pension systems, disability system, maternal care system etc. These are embodied in the above-mentioned Decree-law 306 for non-agricultural cooperatives and in the Decree-law 284 of 2011 (modifying earlier legislation). Let us remember that these measures are not only a moral, but an economic issue as well, because they encourage risk taking, entrepreneurship, and reduce the levels of social anxieties inherent to this kind of process. More importantly, work incentives are not solely made up of individually oriented financial rewards. An unstable society can become an obstacle to the creation of the collective institutions needed to encourage individual prowess. In actual fact, these measures act as a sort of collective incentive that allows the government to keep to its ideological path while at the same time, buy long-term stability and long lasting employee behavior. Non-financial incentives matter, and are even more relevant for the learning-based organizational integration needed in an innovative environment.[10]

6.2.2 Changes in the agricultural production

One of the most important measures of the period was the introduction of a new form of agricultural organization. The government approved terminating the existence of the majority of state farms, turning them into basic units of cooperative production (UBPCs in Spanish), a form of worker-owned enterprise or cooperative. The UBPCs allowed groups of workers to lease state farmlands rent free, in perpetuity. The state retained the property rights and the UBPCs would need to continue to meet production quotas for their key crops and to sell the rest. Each unit was free to choose its management scheme. This measure was complemented by the reopening of agricultural markets in 1994, which had been closed in 1986. These measures helped to reduce the excessive monetary liquidity and to increase government revenues.[11]

At this stage, the expansion of organic and urban agriculture played a crucial role, being an essential building block of the organizational innovations carried out during the 1990s in the sector.[12] For example, the production of vegetables typically produced by farmers fell drastically between 1988 and 1994, but by 2007 had rebounded to well over 1988 levels. Significant is the fact that this production was achieved despite using 72 percent fewer agricultural chemicals in 2007 than in 1988.[13] It is useful to remember that, after the collapse of the communist world, Cuba had lost 70 percent of its agrochemical and fuel imports and 50 percent of its livestock feed imports. Also as a result of the efforts to overcome this situation, total import dependency decreased considerably, and in 2003 was 16 percent. This percentage should not be confused with the import dependency on products that belong to the basic food basket, i.e. the food that is distributed through regulated government channels by means of a ration card, which shows alarming levels of import dependence.

However, in general, the institutional environment that allowed the purchasing of technology, access to financing and foreign investments, as well as the rigid and inefficient state controlled commercialization structure,[14] remained unchanged. Additionally, solid cooperation between local producers, government and national regional research centers and institutes, in order to create new production methods based on knowledge and technology (as was the case in the successful experiences in the US and Japan at the end of the nineteenth century) never materialized. Although the 1990s brought some stabilization to agricultural production, overall low productivity remained a central problem. For example, even if useful extension services and scientific management was available during the agro-ecological stage, the lack of scale keeps prices high, which makes it unable to cover the whole basic food basket. In addition, some problems such as viral crop diseases or drought tolerance have no agro-ecological solutions available yet. At the same time, the pace of high-tech (specially biotechnological) innovations to deal with the problem have been slow and not free from controversy.[15]

Food dependency rose in the 2000s, as imports from the United States grew and hurricanes devastated Cuba's agriculture. In 2008, the country imported 55 percent of its total food, equivalent to approximately $US 2.8 billion.[16] In order to increase agricultural production, the government enacted in 2008 Decree-law 259, which is intended to lease idle land,[17] or usufructs, to private individuals (renewable after 10 years) and agricultural cooperatives (25 years). The state also decentralized the distribution system so that local products could be sold locally, and adjusted the prices it pays to private farmers. By December 2009, 54 percent of this land had been already distributed. However, the results have been disappointing to date. For example, during 2010 agricultural production decreased by 2.8 percent.[18] In fact, the period 2002–10 showed a continued decline in the production of the 12 most important agricultural items, while at the same time food imports notably increased.[19] As of 2012, official sources indicated that the country still imported 70–80 percent of the items that comprised the basic food basket.[20]

Further legislation, such as the Decree-law 300 of 2012 and the Decree-law 311 of 2014, among others, continued creating space for the usufruct of idle state land for productive use. As of 2019 the state owned circa 80 percent of arable land while 70 percent was managed by agricultural cooperatives and private farmers. In 2019 the Decree-law 365 was enacted in order to actualize the legal norms in the agricultural cooperative sector. They are expected to provide new impulse to the badly needed food production in the island. However, the fact remains that, in 2019, according to official data, the country spent yearly $US 2 billion in food imports, of which $US 600–800 million could be produced domestically by improving land productivity. Circa 67 percent of arable land would produce mediocre results without being provided with water, fertilizers and so on. Again, the problem of lack of productive technologies arises. Recent news talked about significant investments in a water transfer system from the West to the East of the nation, where sub-optimal land needs to be improved for certain products to be cultivable. But the fact remains that without new technologies most of the land will yield poor results. The ongoing Covid-19 crisis has sparked a debate about how science could help mitigate food dependency.

Indeed, the country still has a long way to go in order to achieve food self-sufficiency. Because of the world food price crisis, the government has once again begun to emphasize the need (as it did during the 1990s) for food self-sufficiency. As a result, two food production models are fighting for relevance: the industrial and the agro-ecological. As the financial situation improved with the appearance of Venezuela as important oil providers, Cuban policymakers have at times begun to flirt with the idea of returning to more industrial schemes. This is important because to guarantee low prices, the country needs to increase the scale of production while boosting productivity.[21] However, at the same time, it is still debatable whether the government has chosen the right technological path (Altieri and Funes-Monzote 2012). To choose a technological path that does not consider the advantages of a more sustainable approach could be a mistake. After all, the idea of agricultural sustainability does not mean ruling out any technologies or practices on ideological grounds. If a technology works to improve productivity for farmers and does not cause undue harm to the environment, then it is likely to have some sustainability benefits (Pretty 2008, p. 451).

During the 2010s the country began to import fuel-based technologies instead of trying to invest the money in the development of non-fuel (or alternative-fuel) technologies and chemical substitutes, which can affect the economic long-term sustainability of the strategy. It also seems that Cuban officials are still betting for a lucrative strike that would prop up the economy, despite continuing disappointments.[22] However in a world that is (slowly but continuously) moving away from fuel-technologies (because of the high prices, the reduction of reserves, health-costs and other ideological reasons) it would be reasonable to invest in these new technologies as long as they are not completely controlled by powerful stakeholders.

It could be a good idea to explore the potentials (and downsides) of, e.g., 3D technologies in the creation of farm machinery and the environmental benefits of additive manufacturing compared to traditional manufacturing. 3D technologies show particularly great potential when employed in combination with participative forms of manufacturing, where the cooperative element created by the integration of producers and farmers may generate huge opportunities for economies of scope. It could be also useful to study the application of artificial intelligence-based technologies given its potential in providing tools for soil and crop monitoring as well as disease control without the need of employing pesticides. For example, in this sort of initiative farmers would feed algorithms with their experiences, which would contribute in turn to improve its ability of predicting the chance for a crop to perform well or to be infested by plagues.

Much of the knowledge with regard to these technologies is still concentrated in small start-ups, universities and research centers around the world. It may be cheaper for developing countries with the right scientific capabilities to absorb (and further develop and apply) this knowledge now (in form of scientific cooperation, pilot projects etc.) than later; when the basis technologies will be transferred to corporate stakeholders (which is already happening) and no longer available in the research centers. This would be an opportunity to innovate from the beginning, by catching up early (of course, a more risky move) instead of waiting and catching up later. It is not warranted to assume that in a world full of restricting and selective intellectual property rights, developing economies are going to have the chance to catch-up less expensively. After all, that is what historical evidence has continuously shown. The investments made in educating software engineers and the special emphasis made by the current Cuban president in the informatization of the Cuban society[23] may find a valuable task in the creation of a strategic programs intended for application to digital technologies in the agroecology.

At the same time, agro-ecological production represents the best example of organizational integration put in function of innovation in the Cuban agricultural sector. On the one hand, it is government regulation and control that helped ensure that new sustainable farming methods are adopted on a large scale. On the other hand, successful institutionalization of agro-ecology in both policy and practice was not a contribution of the highly inefficient government agricultural farms and enterprises, rather it was due to the coordinated, but decentralized, participation of non-firm organizations such as research institutes, the Ministry of Agriculture, agrarian universities and their networks, non-state agricultural organizations and the private independent producers.[24] A sustainable industrial agriculture should also include these experiences.

6.3 Reintegration of Cuba in the international economy

The institutional reforms of the first stage of the Cuban economic crisis were intended to manage the conflict that emerged from the dissolution of the socialist world. Then and thereafter, high priority was given to the reintroduction of the country into the international production chains worldwide. As a result, the government sought to create conditions for foreign investments to flow into the country and for introducing Cuba into the international production chains and technology markets. To achieve this goal, the government introduced a number of organizational transformations which were certainly innovative in the Cuban context.

6.3.1 Holding companies

The most relevant entrepreneurial innovation of the period was the creation of new holding companies ("corporations," corporaciones in Spanish), conceived to primarily operate in the dollar market economy, principally at national level but also abroad. A necessary complement, and also one of the most important institutional reforms, was the de-monopolization of the foreign trade through Article 18 of the previous Constitution. Until 1989, with few exceptions, the state accomplished the role of importer and exporter of all goods.

The corporations[25] were all owned by the state but they were also allowed to control their own finances, borrow on the international financial markets, import supplies, keep foreign exchange, establish joint ventures, and hire foreign managers. As long as managers reach their profit targets and operate with acceptable margins, they keep going. If they do not, then they are fired and a new management is inserted. Similar experiences, although by no means identical, can be found during the raising period of the East Asian economies (e.g. Chaebol in South Korea, vertical Zaibatsu and more horizontal Keiretsu in Japan) and more recently China; but also in Finland, Norway and Sweden with the telecommunication technologies (Jäntti and Vartiainen 2009; Hauknes and Smith 2003), and in Italy with aeronautic, car, steel and ship industries (Istituto per la Ricostruzione Industriale, IRI).[26]

Noteworthy is the fact that the military enterprise became the first experimental field for this kind of organizational form, which was subsequently extended to the rest of the economy. Today, many of the most rentable firms in the country belong to holding companies. Although some of the Cuban holdings had been created in the late 1970s (Cimex, Cubalse), it was during the 1990s, compelled by the crisis, that they took their current configuration. For example, the CIMEX Corporation, created in 1978 with legal representation in Panama in order to avoid embargo laws, is Cuba's largest trading company.[27] It comprises 94 firms, 61 of which are located abroad. According to official figures it is said (since the 1990s) to have annual sales above $1 billion US.

Other holdings include Copextel, a technology trading holding company; and Cubanacan, Habaguanex and Gaviota, which are devoted to tourism. A singular case is Cubalse, which was created in the 1960s and until its dissolution in 2009 the second largest Cuban holding company. Cubalse held chainstores, cafeterias, as well as car sales and apartment rentals offices. It also provided services to foreign firms and embassies. Given their prioritized status, most of these conglomerates have direct access to the Council of State, the highest government administrative body, and therefore the ability to expedite their strategies.

Between 2003 and 2005, the autonomy of companies operating with foreign currency was significantly reduced through the creation of the Committee of Foreign Exchange Approval (CAD in Spanish) and the Unique Income State Currency Account. The firms were compelled to ask for the authorization of the former to be able to purchase the necessary foreign currency for import, debt payments or foreign payments; and then profits were to be sent to the latter. The policy of President Raúl Castro replaced CAD with an approval system at ministry level, relaxing partially the company's loss of autonomy.

However, these efforts are not necessarily inconsistent with the historical evidence provided by cases such as Japan during the reconstruction phase after World War II (and thereafter under different conditions), when resources were centrally allocated in specific industries given their scarcity. Notwithstanding these distinctions, some questions could be asked: Are Cuban policymakers allocating resources in the right industries? Are the available monies being directed towards demand-dynamic sector products, e.g. R&D in the manufacturing sector?

In contrast to countries such as South Korea, Japan or Finland, Cuban conglomerates' development is closely linked to the expansion of non-manufacturing and non-tradable sectors like the Tourism industry, which were critical in the economic partial economic recovery of the Cuban economy (see *section below on Tourist services based growth*). This also served as a basis for the partial recovery experienced in some low-tech, non-competitive industries and non-tradable products. But they (the conglomerates) took a significant stake of the resources invested during the 1990s and thereafter. These businesses operate in the *mercado de frontera* or "export within borders" (Monreal 2005). These exports are originated by the growing domestic demand generated by firms (national, joint ventures or foreign) based in the country, which operate with foreign exchange where they have access to markets that are profitable and bring dollar revenues.

Many firms which belong to the biotechnology industry have also adopted some sort of holding structure, BioCubaFarma being the last great structure created in 2012. However, unlike the biotech industry, which is still an exception to date, most Cuban holdings have been net importers or service based companies with relatively little value-added and international competitive manufacturing capabilities to contribute. This aspect has been one of the fundamental flaws of Cuban development for the last 25 years.

6.3.2 Enterprise reform

At the beginning of the 1990s, modifications in the Article 16 of the previous Constitution had established changes in the country planning regime by shifting from a centralized to a more decentralized regime and substituting physical output for financial-based planning. These elements served as a basis for the organizational innovations of the 90s, which led Cuban policymakers to formally launch the enterprise reform process for the rest of the country in 1998. The so-called *Perfeccionamiento empresarial* (entrepreneurial improvement) seeks to establish a foundation and set specific guidelines for a process whose goal is to achieve more efficiency and productivity in Cuba's state-owned enterprises (for a general discussion on the period see Travieso-Díaz 2001, Peters 2001, Marquetti 2006).

In 1998 Law-decree No. 187 was enacted, which provides the framework for Cuba's enterprise reform program. Similar to the conglomerate experience, under this system the enterprises are given much more autonomy in several areas. For example, the decentralization of firm management, i.e., the state is to retain ownership but will allow the enterprise to manage its own affairs in a market environment. Salaries are not to be fixed, but pegged to productivity. After-tax earnings may, if authorized, be retained by the enterprise as capital reserves and so on.

To accomplish this purpose, enterprises must pass a rigorous examination process conducted by the Government Group of the Executive Committee of the Council of Ministers. This includes the adoption of modern management and accounting techniques. Upon approval, the enterprise formally enters the reform process and it is relieved of a series of regulatory requirements. However, like any process of institution building, this one is a complicated and sometimes contradictory process. By the time Raul Castro took office in 2006, less than a third of state enterprises had been reached by the reforms. In order to improve the quality of the process, in 2007 Law-decrees 252 and 281 were enacted, which attempted to further specify the reform rules. However, even when at the end of 2009 enterprises in this system contributed 65 percent of the country's income; excess control continued to obstruct the development of the most efficient enterprises.[28] Subsequently, in 2012 Law-decrees 295 and 302 were enacted in order to modify 252 and 281 respectively.

In 2017, and modifying the latter decree, new governance structures were introduced in the enterprise system with the aim of giving more autonomies to firms in different sectors. The Decrees 334, 335 and 336 introduced the figure of the Enterprise Management Central Organizations (OSDE), a sort of government non-firm organization that integrates companies, technologically related or nor, under one umbrella; this is with the aim of strategically assessing the process of enterprise reform, but without interfering in the autonomy of the companies. These organizations are expected to contribute to separate business activity from policymaking state functions in the predominantly state-owned Cuban business network, which should serve to encourage the performance of state-owned enterprises.

At the same time, Article 27 of the new Constitution, approved in the referendum in February, and which came into force in April 2019, ratified the state-owned enterprise as the main actor within the national economy (86 percent of income budget in 2018), with autonomy in its administration and management. OSDE are intended to be the mechanisms through which government will try to put this autonomy in function of the governmental goals. Actually, as above, and in Chapter 5, mentioned, there are antecedents for these merging and consolidation processes in the history of revolutionary Cuba.

The new legislation actually formalizes and standardizes the functions of many holdings that already existed and creates space for the creation of new ones. In general, business groups, related or unrelated, are very much part of the history of the twentieth century's economic and technological development, particularly in less-developed economies. They allow the integration of resources, otherwise scattered, critical for technological innovation and provide an effective way to overcome weak industrial bases and inadequate infrastructure, as well as to accelerate the growth of core sectors of the economy (Hobday and Colpan 2010).

In the Cuban case OSDE are to dictate the general strategy of the business group and are to be financed by the companies integrated to them. More emphasis is given to issues related to R&D, skills building and long-term development. They respond for their financial obligations but not for their integrated companies' obligations. Within this framework the managers of the individual companies have been given substantial freedom of action to direct their businesses and to make use of the firm's resources. According to the Decree 335 firms are not allowed to have losses. In that case they could be dissolved, merged or degraded to basic production unit, the latter being entities that provide goods or services to the companies they belong to, and therefore without legal personality. While in the past companies were created or dissolved by, and directly subordinated to, their ministries they now directly deal with OSDE. In turn, OSDE can be created, merged or dissolved by the Council of Ministers and are directly subordinate to the Council. In addition, single ministries and local government boards are also entitled to approve the creation of these organizations.

In general, the newest pieces of legislation are aimed at delegating more control over business decisions from central ministries to enterprise managers. However, while it is far too early to make any definitive assessment, some results show that OSDE, even when they have brought improvements in project execution capabilities, have also logically inherited many of the traditional shortcomings of the Cuban enterprise landscape. Recent government deliberations have acknowledged the existence of overstaffed bodies, increased expenses, too many meetings and procedures, and excessively centralized operations and approval processes among some of the problems of the new organizations.

Some policymakers recognize that many OSDE have become some sort of mini-ministries, which prevent companies from being more dynamic and their managers from the chance of achieving incremental innovation. Local government boards have also been criticized for failing to supervise the state enterprise system in their localities and only limiting to approve OSDE strategic development plans without any democratic scrutiny about their impact in the regions.

While all these problems, or versions of them, are part of any economic dynamic, it is important to emphasize that the most relevant outcome to evaluate here should be the ability to engage favorably in a technological learning process as a result of these integration efforts, which history has shown not to be always the case. In this sense, OSDE face similar challenges as the ones faced by other latecomers in the past. For instance, Asian business groups such as Samsung, Hyundai, Daewoo and Lucky Goldstar in South Korea and Teco, Sampo and Tatung in Taiwan needed to overcome their dislocation from main sources of technology and innovation. They also had to deal with the small size of local markets and difficulties in accessing advanced markets they needed to reach in order to gain foreign exchange (Hobday and Colpan 2010, p. 766).

The new context of updated guidelines, particularly the special attention to the development of new high-tech companies and sectors, and the insistence in making companies more productive and innovative, are signs of the right direction. Recently, in November 2019 the Decree-Law 363 was enacted, intended to promote the creation of Science and Technology Parks, which are expected to stimulate the integration of relevant societal agents (universities, research facilities, companies, etc.) in order to foster knowledge and technology transfer, generate R&D projects, incubate new businesses, provide added-value services to companies and other institutions, attracting foreign investment and encouraging domestic investments. Even more recently, in February of this year (2020) and clearly inspired by the vertical integrated model of the most important companies of the Cuban biotechnology industry (more on this model in Chapter 7), the Decree-Law 2 was enacted with the aim of defining the content and scope of high-technology enterprises and promoting their creation (seen, according to this Decree, as a legal figure). Companies that decide to introduce new technologies, to produce value-added products and are able to fulfill certain required criteria (e.g., net exports larger than 20 percent, less than 0.7 import-to-export ratio, value-added of more than 50,000 Cuban Pesos per employee, more than 25 percent of workforce with university degree and 15 percent of it with PhDs or similar postgraduate studies) will be granted for a three-year period the status of High-Technology Firm by the Council of Ministers. The would-be high-techs first need the approval of the OSDE, or any other government non-firm organization, they belong to, and then the latter will apply to the Council of Ministers, which will, with previous evaluation by the Ministry for Science and Technology (CITMA), approve/extend the status and may also revoke it if the company fails to fulfill the requirements. On their behalf, awarded companies will be given several fiscal exemptions and be allowed to distribute utilities in the way they see fit. Both pieces of legislation, to be assessed and supervised by CITMA, are inextricably related and represent an unambiguous acknowledgement of the need to develop indigenous innovation; and it could bring good results provided they are applied pragmatically. They may also help to complement the efforts of other recently created institutions, e.g., the Special Development Zone in the port of Mariel (see below).

On the other hand, the narrative of separation between business and state functions should not be taken too far given the blurred line between them in less developed, and even developed, environments. It is true that certain level of professionalization in business management is crucial for a successful industrial strategy, but successful strategies also require flexibility. Historical experiences in term of business group-government relations show that these relations are complex and messy, particularly, but not exclusively, in technological catch-up experiences.

For instance, sometimes a firm with losses justifies further subsidies and sometimes it does not. Historical evidence shows that even when "entrepreneurial failure" occurs the state has intervened with different sorts of policies in order to overcome the problems (ibid., p. 776). For example, one of the tasks of the Council of ministers respect to OSDE is that of making sure that technology transfer is carried out in a proper manner and according to the nation's development goals. But it could be the case that the companies doing R&D in an OSDE were not able to achieve certain transfer goal and are operating with losses. In that case some support would be needed provided that the needed technology has strategic value. As another example, recent experiences in the implementation of the OSDE show that some misinterpretations have occurred in dealing with the status of some companies, which were degraded to basic production units without a real justification, or without considering their strategic impact. There has also been the case of some basic production units, whose managers were prohibited from signing contracts and operating banking accounts.

All in all, the point is that organizational integration requires creativity and flexibility, particularly when it has to do with technology and industrial policy. The recent changes sketched above are part of an ongoing process, which will surely see further modifications. For that reason, this description should be taken only as an approximation of what is currently happening in the island's business fabric. More time will be needed to make an accurate assessment of these structures.

6.3.3 Foreign partnerships

Collaboration with foreign companies has been critical in the process of international reintroduction. As part of the first institutional reforms in 1992, several modifications were made to the 1976 Cuban Constitution to give incentives to foreign investors. State ownership was limited to the fundamental (instead of all) activities (e.g. land, waters, health education). Article 15 enabled the executive committee of the Council of Ministers to partially or totally transfer property rights in favor of foreign investors, provided they contribute to the economic development of the country and do not interfere with Cuban public institutions and goals.

During the same period, and as a complement of this measure, the creation of joint ventures of state-owned enterprises[29] with foreign firms (Article 23) was also allowed; and the existence of this kind of (mixed) ownership from inside Cuba was constitutionally permitted. Similar to other development experiences, the state remained the main partner in joint ventures and other associations, and foreign investments were to be approved by the government. The first joint venture with foreign capital had already taken place in 1990 in the tourism industry, as part of the pilot experience initiated with military enterprises during the mid-1980s.

In 1990 the number of partnerships with foreign companies was 20, while in 1993 it had grown to 112. This process provided a new way to obtain access to new technologies, management competencies and brand names, as well as access to established international networks. An important role was played here by the availability of a qualified labor force ready to assimilate new technologies, of an adequate infrastructure, and social stability, which offered a safe climate offered to foreign personnel.

Contrary to orthodox opinion, these elements have proven to be much more appreciated by foreign investors than the fact that strong regulation may or may not exist. Experiences such as those of the United States in the nineteenth century, China in the late twentieth century and other West European and South Asian nations built a strong historical case in this sense (Chang 2008, pp. 84–102).

In 1995 the Law of Foreign investments (Law 77) was enacted in order to further promote and regulate foreign direct investments beyond the framework previously established by the constitutional reform of 1992. For example, pursuant to the new law, 100 percent foreign ownership of investments would be permitted, up from the 49 percent allowed by the earlier statute. In the Cuban case, this regulation is expressed in the exclusive power to authorize foreign investments.[30] Investors are also required to observe the social security legislation and workforce is to be hired by a Cuban institution, created for these purposes.

To control the overall procedure, the Ministry of Foreign Investment and Economic Collaboration was created in 1994. In 2004, in order to make room for associations which do not enter in any of the categories described by the Law 77, Agreement 5290[31] was enacted. It specifically covers contracts of cooperated production and/or management of goods and services. Subsequent ancillary agreements and resolutions were enacted in order to continue modifying the law of 1997. As a result of these measures, the trend for partnerships with foreign actors, with some fluctuations, showed a steady increase since the 1990s. Its introduction within the institutional system contributed to the containment of the economic collapse. In 2014, a new Law of Foreign investments (Law 118) was enacted in order to adequate the mechanisms and incentives established by the law 77 to the new institutional changes.

After approval of the Law of Foreign investments of 1995, the Decree Law 165 was issued in 1996, allowing the creation of "Free Zones." Cuban legislation defined Free Zones as areas within the national territory, duly limited, without a residing population, of free import and export of goods, not linked to the customs boundaries. Industrial, trade, agriculture, technological and service activities would be allowed in this area under application of a special regime. The just mentioned resembles the Taiwanese and South Korean export-processing zones,[32] where investing foreign firms were rewarded with tax incentives (Chang 2008, p. 95).

However, even while Cuba's concessions to investors exceeded those of any other country in the region,[33] the Cuban Free Zones would not be able to fulfil their role as manufactured-based export promoters. Overall causes included poor institutional incentives to the importation of complex technologies, which require a highly skilled and qualified workforce, paradoxically the most valuable Cuban resource. Conversely, most activities within the free zones remained labor-intensive and low-end. In addition most of the firms were net importers, and only a few of them were producing a tangible product.

At the same time, the free zones were conceived of as enclaves, i.e. they were not introduced as part of a broader industrial policy. That is, networking between free zone- and inland-based firms was not encouraged, and neither development of support industries nor subcontracting to local firms took place. In order to correct these issues a huge new project has been on the making, with Brazilian help:[34] the Special Development Zone in the port of Mariel, 30 miles east of Havana, designated to promote exports and import substitution. The zone, allowing companies to benefit from simplified customs procedures, are part of a government effort to convince more foreign investors to produce high value-added goods and service exports in Cuba. Decree-law 313 of 2013 establishes a number of tax exemptions intended to attract them. Article 3 of the decree explicitly vows for ensuring the coordination of the Special Zone with the rest of the economy.

It is important to emphasize that the Special Development Zone, undoubtedly one of the most complex projects carried out in Cuba, is aggressively projecting the introduction and production of high technology in several areas of the economy. At the present time there are joint venture projects in areas such as the high-tech medical equipment, green technologies, biomaterials, etc. At the end of 2018 the Development Zone had 43 projects in its portfolio, 17 of which were ongoing projects.

On the other side, even while there was an upward trend in the number of joint ventures with FDI in Cuba up to 2002, there was a systematic decline in their total number due to the influence of several factors during 2003–2010 and beyond. The reasons for this decline are various, but it is clear that there was a stricter enforcement of the policy of government selectivity during the period.[35] This is perfectly consistent with the historical evidence, which shows that most countries have succeeded when they have actively regulated foreign investment, including FDI (Chang 2008, pp. 84–102). That becomes evident if we consider the fact that there were few businesses in the higher value-added or high technology areas (there were nine businesses in the biopharmaceutical industry).[36] In the rest of the (more low-tech merchandise and other services) sectors, dissolved companies did not make any significant contribution to the Cuban economy. In fact, seven established joint ventures represented over 80 percent of sales, and therefore, of exports. These businesses were involved in nickel, tobacco, citrus fruits, beverages, tourism and communications among others.

In any case, these years of economic opening have not been enough, by themselves, to make the Cuban economy more dynamic. Even if acknowledging that the usual political reasons stressed by most domestic commentators have definitely played a role here, there can also be structural reasons that are preventing the economy from making a quantum leap in moving toward sustainability. The introduction of the guidelines gave a new impulse to the idea of FDI as a crucial element in the development of the Cuban economy, given the lack of enough domestic savings. The creation of the Special Development Zone has made a valuable contribution, but the fact remains that the amount of needed investments remains under the government projected levels. According to José Luis Rodriguez, Cuban economist and former minister of economy, in 2018 FDI was 23.4 percent less than the expected amount.[37]

In these results a role has been played by factors such as the increased pressure of the American government, which has caused many international banks to pay huge fines for dealing with Cuba. And we should also take into account the great amount of resources devoted to pay the external debt after the renegotiations with several official and private creditors. According to Prof. Rodriguez, by 2017 82 percent of Cuban debt had been successfully canceled. However, in order to pay the rest amount, the government had to disburse $US23 billion in five years, equivalent to 12 times the trade surplus of 2013, which represents a colossal effort considering the cost of the American embargo (estimates of 2018, $US 130.2 billion). Even when there have been some discrepancies about the correct amount,[38] whereby the lack of official statistics play a great role, it is clear that any optimistic domestic investment plan should bring about justified skepticism.

According to the prevailing logic in Cuban policymaking circles, more investments are linked to more and better credit conditions, which would only be possible by paying the government debt obligations because this would improve the country's credit scores, which would in turn boost the confidence of foreign investors. Until the present day this has not happened. Until 2018 only 25 percent of the yearly projected of FDI levels had been reached. Certainly, the resources employed in external debt payments have prevented the country from relying more in its own resources and the American embargo plays its role in the difficulties with FDI (during 2019–2020 the Trump administration introduced the unprecedented amount of 130 punitive measures in order to destroy the Cuban economy).

However, without underestimating the abovementioned factors, it is also crucial for the government to be more efficient identifying its own assets. By focusing too much on the liability aspect, the policymakers inadvertently brought in the neoliberal mantra of avoiding increasing public deficit and debt. Of course, disproportionate deficit and debt are not desirable, but what is relevant here is the balance sheet in the long term and the ability to identify those resources that may represent a source of wealth in the future and spending on them, which is actually an investment instead of an expenditure.

Of course, let's face it, the process of identifying assets will necessarily depend on policymakers' judgments and worldviews and on how those judgments are accepted by the community. For example, in Cuba, policymakers' opinions on education, health and social spending have oscillated between being an ethically necessary expenditure and being a crucial investment. However, since the beginning of the economic actualization process in 2011, this view has oscillated in favor of the liability issue. Failing, at least partially, to see the distinctions, the Cuban government combined the payment of external debt with the reduction of public deficit and expenditure.

This situation has contributed to scenarios where investments have seldom reached the desired levels, and it has also reinforced the sensation of a rarefied financial environment. For instance, of the 167 domestic investment projects that were expected to be working in 2018 only 53 have been completed to date.[39] They were expected to grow 34 percent in that year but they only grew 13.2 percent. And it is fair to say that this modest increment was, among other causes, because in 2017 the government finally decided to increase budgetary expenditures.

Another issue is the fact that, in general, FDI record is mixed as a funding strategy. Countries like South Korea, Finland and Taiwan strongly distrusted FDI and strongly controlled or, most of the time, prohibited them as part of their highly successful industrial development strategies. But Singapore and China had a different stance; they made intelligent use of them which has also brought excellent results. The attitudes towards FDI can be diverse; however, the fact remains that, most of the time, FDI focuses in already existing facilities (brown field investments), which are less risky and cost-saving, usually involving little transference of technological content. On the other hand, green field investments, or investments where the foreign company builds facilities from scratch, are less common because they involve risks, technology transfer and long-term commitment. To decide for the latter, it must be clear that important gains can be made, which presuppose the existence of relevant capabilities in the country at the receiving end. That is, indigenous potential needs to be there.

However, one of the main problems with the FDI projects in Cuba up to date is precisely the lack of indigenous capabilities in the secure and stable supply of material and human resources, which creates bumps in the projects and prevents their realization. There is also the problem of feasibility studies that fail to make realistic assumptions about the conditions and variables affecting the project. In general, there is much faith about the possibilities of developing high-tech with FDI resources without having to invest in indigenous capabilities. This may be the case sometimes, but it may not happen in the way policymakers expect. Rather, indigenous capabilities developed with own resources have been shown to be the main FDI attractor. The introduction of Decree-Laws 363 in 2019 and Decree 2 in February of the present year (2020), mentioned above, may represent a step forward.

However, until very recently the focus of Cuba's policymakers was in the short term, natural resources and relatively low-end services, such as tourism. No wonder that, despite a significant number of tax-exemptions, relatively little investments in aggregate-value productions have been attracted. An economy with low levels of import substitution in value-added products, and without participation in the sophisticated high-tech value chains is very unlikely to produce the needed financial recourses for its development. During 2017 and 2018, according to Prof. Rodriguez, new short-term debts had accumulated.[40]

At the present time, and given the increasing hostility of Trump's administration, the government has begun to focus on import substitution of certain goods, support to national industry and on increasing and diversificating exports and services. Of course, it is too early to evaluate the impact of the newest reforms, but the pattern followed until the present, namely natural resource and service-based activity, can, and should be exposed to some critical analysis because of the path-dependency it has created, which is still affecting the way policymakers make their decisions. We argue in the next section that this very sectoral strategy, carried out by the government in the aftermath of the collapse of the communist world, has negatively affected the country's capacity to pay its way in the world.

6.4 Natural-resource and service-based export performance

There is an important difference between Cuba's international integration patterns during the period 1959–89 and the re-insertion strategy from the 1990s onward. While the former was based in the preferential compensation terms established by the Council for Mutual Economic Assistance (CMEA) in times of *real existent socialism,* the latter period of insertion in the capitalist world market had to be carried out on competitive terms. As already shown in this chapter, the Cuban government introduced a number of institutional innovations (from the point of view of the Cuban context) in order to adapt the economy to the new demands. However, the following section will argue that, even with the relative successes of both the tourism and the mining industries, such a competitive insertion has yet to be achieved. Not only by improving the performance of these industries, but also by radically changing the pace of development to a more sophisticated strategy that include more high-value industries. As discussed in Chapters 3 and 4, a proper notion of an innovative firm can only be conceived within a proper notion of economic development.

Just as with the pre-crisis period discussed in the previous chapter, a significant body of literature and comment has been written on the performance of the Cuban economy during the last thirty years, most of it focused on the dichotomy of the state-market. From this perspective, the over-centralized Cuban state has been systematically choking the development of free market forces, which are said to be the reason behind the poor performance of the economy. While there is some truth to this argument, we will argue that the main reason for the underperformance of the Cuban economy is not the existence of an interventionist state or the absence of free markets, but rather in the lack of economic policies promoting productive diversification and the development of high manufacturing industries, particularly those with export potential.

Until today, excluding some of the most recent policies, the fact remains that Cuban policymakers (with the exception of the biotech industry) have paid much more attention to low end products and services. And the extent to which this set of affairs has shaped the current policy is very significant. For instance, investment patterns continue to be biased against equipment, machinery and the like. The talk on innovation, long-term risk investments, high-tech production, science and discovery was virtually non-existent. Even in the aftermath of the widely publicized Sixth Congress of the Communist Party of Cuba,[41] and the subsequent edition in 2016, there were no clear signs of measures towards a profound reform in the productive structure. Instead, emphasis was given to increase productivity via the stimulus of small private business, fundamentally in non-tradable goods and services.[42] While these measures have a lot of value for the Cuban context, they may do little to really make the country internationally competitive.

Despite the abundance of historical evidence and economic arguments, provided supporting the notion of structural transformation as a prerequisite for economic development (Woo-Cumming 1999, Wade 2003, Rodrik 2004, Chang 2010, 2008; Reinert 2007; Cimoli et al. 2009) contemporary economic thinking on policy reforms has paid little attention to this argument during the last thirty years. The aftermath of the financial crisis in 2008 has led the international debate to move in this direction, but the prevailing view still continues to be that once the "economic fundamentals" – macroeconomic stability and well-functioning markets – are in place, structural transformation is an automatic process (Rodrik 2006, p. 2). This factor, together with the country's specialization according to the principle of comparative advantages, should complete the circle of measures proposed to developing countries during the last few decades.

As suggested above, Cuban policymakers have partially and perhaps unconsciously, also bought into this mantra. As Monreal (2005) states, the take-off during the 1990s only "represented an additional expansion of natural resource-based exports, rather than the emergence of a new ingredient for the country's development pattern that could be augmented with other assets, such as skilled labor, science or technology" (Monreal 2005, p. 62). However, historical evidence shows that nations which achieved economic development have always gone beyond the limits of their static comparative advantage and diversified into new activities that belong to the realm of wealthy countries.

For example, a comparison between the economic performance of Latin America and East Asia since the 1960s confirms that the composition of exports, rather than their volume, is the determining factor linked to the export's ability to generate sustained GDP growth (Palma in Cimoli et al. 2009, pp. 203–38; Rodrik 2006, pp. 5–6).

> If countries like China and India (and South Korea, Taiwan, Singapore, and Malaysia before them) have done so well, it is not primarily because their labor endowment advantage gave them the ability to compete in labor-intensive manufactures.[43] It is because they were able to quickly diversify into more sophisticated, technically-demanding activities that supported higher rates of economic growth.
>
> (Rodrik 2006, pp. 7–8)

The Cuban economy started to recover in 1994, with the GDP showing on average, a positive number during the period 1994–2008. And this recovery process has been one based on the intensive use of natural resources, with the biotechnology industry as an exception.[44] Low value added tourist services and nickel extraction industries have played the key role in the recovery process of the economy since the 1990s. Export diversification on behalf of value-added innovative manufactures was not systematically and articulately promoted in Cuba in the last thirty years.

The Cuban biotechnology industry remains the exception in Cuba's industrial landscape.[45] Cuban biotech has shown a very positive evolution during the last two decades and has shown the real potential of frontier technologies operating within the economy. However this industry still shows relatively few linkages within the domestic economy, which limits its developmental impact. In terms of developmental policy, the broader the manufacturing base, the better the opportunities to get into new economic activities with untapped productivity prospects.

6.4.1 On natural resources and raw materials

One of the quintessential challenges for Cuba's policymakers is to be able to increase the economy's productivity. However, it should be emphasized that productivity does not mean just any kind of productivity, but the right kind. That is, all economic activities are qualitatively different and offer dissimilar opportunities for innovation and industrial upgrading. To specialize in natural resources activities (such as *sun and sand* tourism and mining) and low-tech services do not generate much income for a developing country (Chang 2010; Palma in Cimoli et al. 2009, pp. 203–38; Reinert 2007).

There is nothing intrinsically wrong with a country using its stock of natural resources as an export item and as a source of short-term finance, so badly needed in early development stages. However, the history of economic development is the tale of countries trying to catch up with more technologically advanced nations, or as Malerba (2006) states, the history of countries "catching up in different sectoral systems" (pp. 16–21), in order to acquire higher technological capabilities. Historical evidence shows that almost no country has been able to develop into a sophisticated economy by relying solely on the export of raw materials or services (Chang 2007, 2008, 2010; Reinert 1999, 2007). To understand that, it is important to acknowledge the qualitative difference between economics activities.

Raw material activities are to be classified within the realm of decreasing returns activities (Reinert 1999, 2007). That is, while manufacturing activities present opportunities to achieve higher value-added products through innovation, raw materials-based activities are based on a limited stock of resources. For example the amount of productive exploitable land will gradually shrink, as the need of more production increases. Introducing technological innovation in these activities alone will tend to reduce the prices of raw materials (agricultural product, minerals etc.) in the international markets. This, the rest remaining equal, will tend to diminish export gains and national real wage averages. In order to remain profitable, these activities must be embedded in a successful industrial economy (ibid.). "A country with a broad-based manufacturing sector is more likely to take advantage of new opportunities than one which has specialized in a few primary based products" (Rodrik 2006, p. 12).

The same happens with services. These sorts of activities generally show low levels of both productivity and tradability (and therefore with low levels of scalability) (ibid.). Contrasting with domestic services, tradable economic activities provide scale opportunities for an economy (particularly a small one) in such a way that it can expand output without running into diminishing returns. No matter how productive a restaurant, a rental house or a barber can be, it won't be enough to raise the real wage levels or to increase international competitiveness.[46]

As William Baumol stated years ago, it takes four musicians as much playing time to perform a Beethoven string quartet today as it did in 1800 (Baumol and Bowen 1966). Domestic low-tech services do not provide much scope for innovation and therefore for productivity improvements. The conditions of production themselves preclude any substantial change in productivity. Therefore, increasing the share of low-tech services within the economy could lead to a decrease in the export earnings, which in turn means to become more dependent on external borrowing. To be sure, some services (engineering, consulting etc.) could provide the economy with new windows of innovation and more tradability opportunities; however they depend on the existence of a productive manufacturing sector. While manufacturing activities can increase productivity through mechanization and automation, traditional domestic services tend to remain more or less the same and have little chance of increasing overall productivity of the economy. However, Cuba's manufacturing landscape went in the opposite direction and in the present is barely non-existent, again, with exception of pharmaceuticals and related products, along with a couple of relatively low-end manufactures (furniture, beverages etc.) (Table 6.1).

As the case of pharmaceutical products indicates, investing in non-traditional tradable activities means that an economy is absorbing more sophisticated technologies and is increasing its chances of participation in the international market with more elaborated products of higher long-term productivity potentials. It also brings other opportunities such as trained workers and managers who can be employed in other firms, "and they provide inputs (and demand) for other activities which may not have started up otherwise. The social value of such investments greatly exceeds their private value" (Rodrik 2006, p. 2).

Cuba experienced a sudden decline in its foreign earnings during the last few years, which resulted from a very poor export performance. This, aggravated by other factors,[47] had an impact on economic growth and in the country's ability to honor its financial obligations to external creditors. External debt has increased since 2004, with the exception of 2018, according to CIA Factbook.[48] But the country was able to maintain this in-debt trend as long as the ratio of external solvency remained controlled by the growth of GDP. When the growth trend stopped, then the necessity for adjustment became apparent.

Even when many authors give much more meaning to the reduction of debt, which is of course a very important goal, some sort of intuitive sense is

Table 6.1 Changes in physical output in Cuba's manufacturing subsectors, 1989–2014

Sector	Percentage change
MANUFACTURES, TOTAL	–41.1
MANUFACTURES, TOTAL EXCLUDING SUGAR	–33–4
Sugar	–77–1
Food products	–19–0
Beverages	+17.5
Tobacco products	+8.5
Textiles	–85.3
Clothing	–80.0
Leather goods	–70.8
Wood products	–90.1
Paper and Paper products	–90.5
Petroleum products (2015)	–49.5
Pharmaceuticals (2014)	+1835.9
Chemical products	+2.9
Fertilizers	–92.0
Rubber and plastic products	–78.6
Construction materials	–69.8
Metal fabrication	–26.5
Metal products (excluding machinery and equipment)	–71.2
Machinery and equipment	–99.5
Electrical machinery and equipment	–70.4
Fabrication of TV sets, radio and communication equipment	–55.4
Medical/high precision optical equipment	+20.1
Transportation equipment	–97.6
Furniture	+96.5
Nonmetallic material products	–88.7

(Percentage change in physical production levels, 1989–2016) 1989 = 100
Source: Oficina Nacional de Estadísticas, Cuba (ONEi) (2019) Data available until 2016.

telling us that growth is more important. In the case of Cuba this means coming up with the necessary institutional transformation that allows creating higher capabilities in value added manufacturing activities. That's the reason why to promote innovation through related and unrelated diversification, and consequently, the formation of backwards and forward linkages within the domestic economy, should be part of the Cuban economic policy design. The actual challenge for Cuba is to be able to absorb more sophisticated technologies and to increase its participation in the international market with more elaborated products. Increasing the degree of value added manufacturing of resource-based exports helps build an export structure with higher long-term productivity potentials (Palma in Cimoli et al. 2009, pp. 203–38).

As already referred to above, the most recent version of the guidelines recognizes the need to engage in technology and industrial policy in order to boost productivity, diversify exports and substitute imports. The document mentions explicitly the goals of developing the nanotechnology, the electronic industry, metal transformation, etc. This is the right direction, but the fact is that up to date, except the biotech industry, the Cuban strategy has been based in low-ends. Still today policymakers insist in calling tourism industry as the locomotive of the economy, even when signals of the sector's relatively lack of dynamisms are apparent. The fact remains that during the period 2011–2016 the gross fixed capital formation amounts to (constant prices 1997) circa 14 percent, which is below the historical average for the group of upper middle income countries (circa 20–25 percent), to which Cuba belongs (according to the World Bank classification).

6.4.2 Nickel extraction

Nickel production, Cuba's principal export product, has experienced important increases during this period. Major national and foreign investments have been made in the sector since 1991.[49] This allowed production plants to be renovated, and the introduction of modern extraction technologies, which improved industry productivity and allowed Cuba to be ranked eighth in international nickel production in 2005.[50] The Joint Venture agreement, signed between the Canadian Sherritt and the Cuban SOE Compañía General de Níquel S.A., resulted in three jointly owned subsidiaries: (1) a processing plant in Moa, Cuba; (2) a refinery plant in Alberta, Canada; and (3) a sales and marketing company firm in the Bahamas. Cuban managers were trained in modern management techniques and in 1997 there were 30 Cuban professionals based at the Alberta plant in Canada. According to a study edited by the US based Geological Survey, in 2004 nickel accounted for about 61 percent of the country's total exports.[51]

Additionally, the increase in the world (mostly Chinese) nickel demand for the production of stainless steel led to a record increase in international market prices, reaching $24 US per pound in 2007.[52] This created earnings of approximately $2.33 billion US for Cuba in 2007.[53]

However, as is already known, depending on low value-added natural resources can leave a country open to vulnerabilities. One of them is the price volatility of these products, whose consequences for economic development are widely known.[54] This is exactly what has happened in Cuba, as nickel prices collapsed in 2008. The impact of the decline on export earnings was fully offset by a new revenue stream from oil processing ($800 million US) at the Cienfuegos (Cuban province at the center of the island) oil refinery.[55]

In 2009, however, earnings from both nickel and oil products were severely hit by falling international prices, reducing total goods exports revenues by 21.4 percent,[56] showing again the risk of relying on primary products. Nickel international prices experienced an overall reduction of 40 percent in 2009[57] and during that same period Cuba's unrefined nickel plus cobalt production oscillated between 60,000 and 65,000 tones, the lowest amount in a decade, giving an average of between 74,000 and 75,000 tones for most of that period.[58] This trend of decreasing production has continued until the present time. In 2017 and 2018 56,000 and 50,000 tones, respectively, were produced, which confirm the downward trend, among other causes. Beyond technical difficulties the downward tendency in international prices plays a role in the decisions made by producers. Between 2013 and 2018 international prices reduced 21 percent.

Cobalt, however, linked to Cuban Nickel, presents an opposite price tendency. The rise in demand of Cobalt in recent years, given its application in high-performance alloys and lately in lithium-ion batteries for mobile devices and electric cars, has boosted prices, which, even within the natural fluctuations,[59] are expected to remain high for a long time. However, as this line is redacted, no refining technology allows obtaining cobalt and nickel in their finished forms. This is even when Cuba, according to specialized sources, owns the third-largest global cobalt reserves in the world and ranks sixth in production. To put it in proportion, despite having just 1 percent of the land area of the United States, Cuba produces 550 percent more cobalt than the former.[60]

Although the joint ventures allowed the introduction of new mining technologies and the process has become somewhat a capital intensive one, Cuba's contribution to international supply chains continues to be basically the unrefined product, which has to be refined (as in Soviet times) outside the country; in Canada. In fact, the Cuban Nickel industry remains one with low domestic added value as there seems to be little evidence of the formation of strong domestic linkages that allow more sophisticated capabilities to be developed in this direction. This might also be a way to better deal with the vagaries of the American embargo. Indeed, as this lines are written (July 2019), Panasonic Corp, the Japanese multinational, informed that it was unable to determine how much of the cobalt used in batteries it makes for Tesla electric cars (models X and S) comes from Cuba and that it had suspended relations with a Canadian supplier, not explicitly mentioned but believed to be Sherritt, as a result of its concerns.[61]

But still without the sanctions, it would be worth creating value-added productions within the country. World's cobalt sources are not very abundant; in the north hemisphere only the US, with a tiny production, Canada and Cuba have some reserves. This poses a great risk for many car manufactures, especially Tesla, as the electric car's world contest has already begun. In this context, it is no surprise that Tesla has announced that it pursues the goal of eliminating as much as possible the cobalt as component of its batteries. They are probably investing strongly in R&D capabilities in order to find a substitute. Cuba should provide domestic linkages for its cobalt, and eventually find a substitute too.

On the other hand, even when the lack of strong domestic capabilities is a country-wide phenomenon, some modest and somewhat exceptional attempts should be mentioned. In 2003 a diversification attempt led the government to restructure the steel industry by creating six enterprises, which were to be part of ACINOX,[62] one of the most successful industrial groups in Cuban metallurgy, devoted to the commercialization of steel products in the domestic and foreign market.[63] The supply for the plant comes from steel scrap, industrial and naval equipment, old railways, imported ferroalloys and nickel sinter produced in Cuba. ACINOX controls several plants that produce billets, flat slabs and other unfinished long products, mainly for export to the Caribbean and Central America, and to a lesser extent to Colombia and Mexico.[64]

Some equipment is also domestically produced. However, its relevance in the country's overall exports and GDP is so far rather very modest.[65] There is neither a policy aimed to articulate a strategy for products with higher value added, nor domestic linkages capable of absorbing and disseminating new technology. As stated by Bateman and Chang (2012), as long as the circumstances are not transformed in opportunities for the formation of linkages within the local economy, i.e. the creation of a quality local structure of suppliers, new technology-intensive, innovation-driven local enterprises, with the technologies, market and scale requirements to benefit from cooperating with their counterparts, there will be little room for industrial upgrading and in turn for economic development.

6.4.3 A possible low-cost substitute of the Cuban nickel

Another danger of wealth based on natural resources is the creation of a more cost-effective, technologically advanced, synthetic alternative. It is happening with sugar substitutes such as high fructose corn syrup, and had already happened with crimson dye for Guatemala in the nineteenth century and with many other products during the twentieth century. The same has also begun to happen with nickel.

A substitute for refined nickel, described as "nickel pig iron" or "NPI," is already having a major impact on the nickel market and is causing reductions of the price of nickel. NPI is a low-cost and low-tech innovation in the production of stainless steel, developed and being increasingly used in China since 2006. It now accounts for about 10 percent of the world's $US21-billion-a-year nickel market and will have evident repercussions for countries such as Cuba, Canada, Russia and Australia. According to a report of the Toronto based Globe and Mail, the average Chinese producer of NPI can now be profitable at nickel prices of about $8.5 US per pound. Therefore "the days of $24 U.S. per pound nickel, last witnessed in 2007, are unlikely to ever return."[66]

Given this scenario, it would be a healthy policy for Cuba to create linkages and networks that create new opportunities for the production and export of technology-intensive products in this sector, which can move up the "value chain" in global networks. But this would require redirecting investments being made today into other sectors, which would necessarily represent a major structural shift in the current Cuban government policy conception.

Additional efforts to import technology could be made by encouraging the creation of foreign based networks within the Cuban diaspora.[67] The new law of foreign investment (118) opened many possibilities in this direction because it allows Cubans with residency outside the island to participate in the same FDI modalities which had been until that moment only reserved for non-Cubans. Of course, a more proactive role of the government would be necessary in order to make things work; for instance to improve abilities for capacity building through specialized assistance and guidance.

Apart from providing investment resources, the Cuban diaspora could provide important linkages to innovative technologies. Many member of this diaspora are qualified professionals that have managed to insert themselves into their host countries' labor markets. They have acquired experience, knowledge and connection that may prove useful for Cuba's industrialization efforts. China's success in manufacturing exports and India's in software can at least in part be explained by the position of these diasporas in global production networks (Kapur 2001). Also, higher income countries, such as Taiwan, Ireland and Israel, have been able to take the greatest advantage of technology transfers from their diasporas.[68]

6.4.4 Tourist-services based growth

Another characteristic of the period from the 1990s on has been the increasing reliance on the export of services. The most successful and sustained case is the tourism industry, and ultimately medical services (see next section). In fact, the tourism industry is the sector that has played the most important role in that process. Beginning in the 1990s, the tourist industry introduced new operational modes through diverse forms of association with foreign capital that led to a restructuring of that sector. In 1994 the Ministry of Tourism was created, with the aim to accomplish the priorities established by the government strategy.

As already mentioned, the organizational innovations in the tourism industry had already been introduced by the army enterprise system. The "integral system of enterprise improvement" had begun in 1985 and under it, managers were given a great deal of strategy control over the enterprise, which is the power to make all decisions and allocate resources in effective and innovative investment strategies. Similar to the military-based firms, the enterprises of the tourism industry remained under state control but they were run as separable entities on a more competitive basis (on SOE see e.g. Chang 2007; Cimoli et al. 2009; Evans et al. 1999; Pu 2005; Jäntti and Vartiainen 2009). Holding companies such as Cubanacan and Gaviota attracted many foreign firms, which later became official partners in joint ventures or other types of commercial agreements.[69]

In the specific case of tourism, new contract forms such as management contracts and cooperative production agreements were introduced. The management contracts have a validity of five to seven years but can be prolonged if the partners wish to do so (additionally, the contract conditions may also be modified). An important principle for the foreign partner is they have the right to appoint three key persons, namely the managing director, the market manager, and not least the chef de cuisine (Brundenius 2002, p. 4).

In the cooperative productive agreements, the company remains 100 percent Cuban. The foreign partner, "the investor," supplies the Cuban partner with raw material and/or technology and know-how, in exchange for a fixed sum per good produced. The foreign partner might also opt for purchasing the finished product for export. These are arrangements that tend to be of smaller size, for a limited period of time (ibid.).

The revenues from tourism were a crucial factor in the recovery experienced by the Cuban economy since 1994. In 1990, Cuba received 3 percent of the Caribbean area visitors and was 23rd in Latin America in the ranking of the most visited tourists' destinations.[70] By 2000, the former had risen to 10 percent, and the latter to 10th place. The number of hotel rooms increased from 12,900 in 1990 to 45,000 in 2007.[71] Its share in overall exports rose from 4.1 percent in 1990 to about 40 percent in 2000.[72] Gross earnings from tourism increased from $ 243 million US in 1990 to $2.4 billion US in 2005. Overall income figures from tourism surpassed $25 billion US during the period 1990–2007.[73]

While other sectors of the Cuban economy struggled in the early 1990s, the number of international tourist arrivals and tourism revenues increased steadily with the number of international tourists more than doubling, and revenues more than quadrupling, between 1990 and 1995. By 1994, tourism exports surpassed sugar industry[74] exports, making international tourism Cuba's top export industry (Figure 6.2). Gross revenues from tourism made up 66 percent

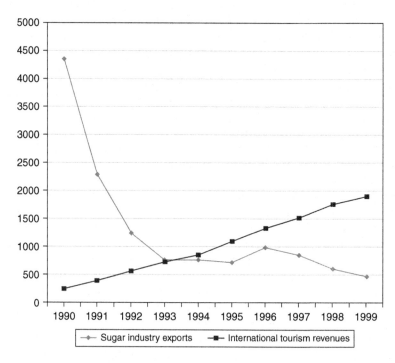

Figure 6.2 Sugar exports and tourism revenues, 1990–99 (million pesos)
Source: Perez-Lopez (2002).

Table 6.2 Tourism's interrelation with the local producers

	1990	2000
Total tourism income in the balance of payments	4%	41%
Purchases from local procedures out of total tourism entity purchases	12%	61%
Total employment in tourism enterprises (workers)	54,000	100,000
Indirect employment (workers producing goods for tourism)	30,000	200,000

Source: Figueras (2001)

of Cuba's service exports in 1998, which made tourism the most important source of service exports in the island.[75]

But the biggest significance of this industry as a leading sector did not come from foreign exchange and job opportunities provided. Much more important were the backward linkages established with other industrial activities of some technological sophistication. Tourism itself is a service of little technological complexity. This industry seems to have been promoted because of its potential to provide short-term earnings, given its status of static comparative advantage. The industry had to deal, however, with a high import component: Not only was management capacity scarce at the beginning of the 1990s, but complementary infrastructure and services were hard to find as well. In 1990, only 10–12 percent of the products and services demanded by tourism were available domestically.

That's the reason why the Cuban government encouraged the formation of domestic backward linkages in order to reduce the import component in the tourism sector. In doing so, the industry became a catalyst for other industries and services. Opportunities to supply the tourism sector created favorable conditions for the establishment of a considerable number of joint ventures in the agricultural, industrial and services sectors, which enjoyed an injection of foreign know-how.

Even when the data supporting this process are scarce, scattered and sometimes of anecdotal nature, some evidence of the relatively successful reanimation can be found in industries such as the textile industry, the furniture industry, the beverage industry and so on, as well as in more technologically intensive industries and services such as construction materials, transportation, telecommunication, IT and air transportation.[76] As shown in Table 6.2, in 2000 61 percent of the tourism demand was covered by local producers. This industry has been referred to as an engine of growth (Figueras 2001).

6.4.5 Shortcomings of the tourism industry as growth engine

In recent years, however, the industry has experienced a number of setbacks, leading to negative growth in tourist arrivals in 2006 and 2007. Although tourism reached record highs of 2.35 and 2.4 million tourists in 2008 and 2009 respectively, this falls far below the Cuban government's 2000 long-range forecast of 5–7 million annual tourists by 2010. During the four or five years previous to 2010, the recovery period deteriorated from eight years to 12–15 years.[77] International factors, such as 9/11, high oil prices and the American embargo,[78] as well as national factors such as maintenance difficulties in some hotels. Most of all the limited diversification of services and increasing prices has influenced a low rate of return. Probably with the exception of the Canadian market (at least until recently), all evidence indicates that Cuba's competitiveness in all major markets has been declining.[79] Cuba has been able to offset the low rate of return by attracting tourists from new markets, but the fact is that, even when 2008 showed some increases, this industry has entered a period of stagnation, aggravated by the current global economic conditions. Depending on the situation, the period 2008–18 has somehow confirmed this trend.

For example, while the period 2008–14 showed no important increases in revenues, the short-lived improvement in Cuba–US relations at the end of the Obama administration led to substantial increases in gross income during the period 2014–17.[80] The observed explosion in the visits of US citizens significantly boosted the industry and motivated further investments in the sector. In 2014 the number of visits surpassed 3 million tourists for the first time in history, and the same happened in 2016, where the number of visits surpassed 4 million tourists.

However, the aggressive measures taken by the Trump administration (the most important being the activation of title III of the Helms-Burton Act[81]) did away with whatever plans the Cuban state and other private stakeholders may have had. For instance, Trump's decision to stop American-based cruise tourism, which had started in 2015 and brought huge increases in the number of visitors, has left the sector in a very tight situation. Years 2017 and 2018 saw a marked reduction in both revenues, which created serious imbalances in the economy, as this industry is considered to be one of the main country's breadwinners. Nevertheless, this sort of sector's fluctuations are likely to continue, as long as the Cuba-American geopolitical scenario exists.

But beyond the geopolitical context, there is the fact that touristic activity has kept a rate of occupation of fifty percent during the period 2006-2018. Still, investments in the sector have kept growing at a faster pace, particularly after 2014, which raises serious concerns about the sustainability of a policy based on continuing building hotels and facilities for an activity which already has been working half its capacity for over a decade. This decline started even before the global financial crisis, the Trump hostility and the Covid-19 pandemic. During the period 2013-2018 the share of gross capital formation devoted to machinery and equipment remained stagnant, while that part dedicated to the construction sector exploded. At the time of this writing (2020) an acute sectoral imbalance is observed in the composition of investments, the tourist sector representing approximately one third of the total amount. It seems to be that Cuban policymakers continue to assume that the sector will stimulate the development of other industries, which seem very improbable.

Still, Cuban tourism industry will probably remain an important source of foreign exchange in the years to come, which is not undesirable in itself. This is the case, among other things, because almost any developing country which aspires to industrialize needs a source of income to be able to finance the process. And this source is frequently to be found in the exploitation of its natural resources. However, the question remains whether this industry should continue to be promoted in the way it has been, namely as the "locomotive for the Cuban economy" (Gutiérrez-Castillo and Gancedo-Gaspar 2002). And it is this point that this study disagrees with. Or in other words, should Cuban prosperity rely on the export of services such as tourism?

As already pointed out, the choice of tourism was a very circumstantial one. The country needed short-term cash after the outbreak of the crisis and took advantage of unquestionable resources in this area. However, as the sector began to create jobs and stimulate certain manufactures it started to be conceived as a development strategy. However, the reactivated industrial structure has been almost exclusively in low-tech manufacturing activities and has not allowed for the diversification of the tourist services or overcoming the consequences of de-industrialization in place since the 1990s (see Table 6.1 above).

In conjunction with the above-mentioned, many of the created jobs actually represented a backward step in terms of the structural composition of the Cuban workforce. Many experienced engineers and technicians migrated to the tourist sector as waiters or taxi drivers, which in fact was a loss for the economy. While, after a sharp decline, the country's labor productivity grew 42 percent during the period 2000–08, the overall indicator level does not reach the levels of 1989. In addition, the contribution of the sector to these increments is not clear. The most successful element of Cuban tourism remains to be one based on natural resources, i.e. sun and beaches and a limited number of more sophisticated services.

As suggested above, low-tech and natural-resource-based services, even if productive, are usually non-tradable and offer little room for high productivity gains. Low tradability means that they, unlike manufactured goods, cannot be shipped to the rest of the world. Tobacco, beverages and furnitures can, but, even when Cuban tobacco and rum have a special place in the world, they are not the sort of sectors that push in these times for higher overall productivity in the economy. Little productivity gains means that there are not too many chances to innovate and boost profits. In general, increasing the share of this sort of service economy will tend to bring low export gains (Chang 2010; Reinert 2007). This means deficit in the balance of payment and impossibility to access financial resources, which in turn means increasing dependence upon external loans. With no effort made to diversify into more high-tech services (e.g. highly tradable consulting, banking or engineering services), which demand in turn the existence of a strong and innovative manufacturing sector, the service branch finishes with decreasing returns.

This can explain, at least partially,[82] why even when the number of tourists increased during the period 1995–2000 (part of the best initial period of the industry), the income per tourist steadily declined year by year, and was in 2000 at the same level as in 1992, just when the tourist boom started. This indicator has remained (with few exceptions) in decline or stagnant during the period 2000–19. In 2017, while visits increased 16.5 percent (compared to the previous year), the income per tourist decreased from $US760 to $US722.[83] In addition, a number of efficiency problems have been hurting, since the beginning, the industry's ability to make more gains, even in the short term. For example, the high imported component within the sector, which in 2018 was 67 cents per monetary unit of gross income. Another one is, as just mentioned, the lack of diversification, whereby a number of potentially profitable choices are being severely underutilized. Alternatives such as health tourism and historic tourism,[84] commonly linked to high-tech, knowledge-based creative industries (only in the case of historic tourism) make up a very small share of the total revenues provided by the industry.

Cuba has been a popular health tourism destination for more than 20 years. This choice offers great potential in the case of Cuba, given its long-term investments in healthcare and biotechnology. Such unique Cuban treatments as the one for *retinitis pigmentosa*; often known as night blindness, have attracted many patients from Europe and North America. Cuba's medical tourism products and services provided care for a total of 19,670 tourist patients in 2006 and it is said to generate revenues of around $40 million US per year.[85] However, this number obviously makes up only a small fraction of the total revenues generated by the sector. In fact, until 2007 this segment represented only 2 percent of the services offered by the Cuban tourist industry.[86]

Interesting is the fact that Tourist Medical Services are provided by Servimed Cuba, which belongs to Cubanacan, the most important Cuban holding company in the tourism sector (in 2007 40 percent market share[87]). This means that cross-financing of more technology-based segments could be perfectly possible, had the policymakers and the executives of the industry the will to follow this strategy. This sort of strategy might not be delivering revenues in the short term, a time horizon which is discouraged even by the most mainstream approaches (see World Bank 2008, pp. 29–33), but it may become an alternative for the long term sustainability of the industry.

For example, historical evidence tells us how the long-term bets on a range of radical technologies in communications made by former government enterprises such as Telia, Telenor and Sonera, shaped the technologies which made Ericsson and Nokia world leaders (Hauknes and Smith 2003). Nokia's electronic subsidiary was allowed to register losses for 17 years before showing some profit, while it continued to be cross-subsided by the central division. Similar examples are found in Samsung and Toyota (Chang 2009).

However, notwithstanding the fact that some diversification in tourist activities could be found, services alone do not grant economic development. These circumstances do not create much incentive for value-added industrial exports to emerge, since tourism booms tend to increase demand for

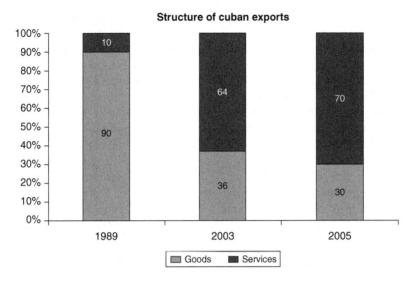

Figure 6.3 Structure of Cuban exports (in percentages)
Source: Molina 2009, Cuba: Economic Restructuring, Recent Trends and Major Challenges, The IDEA Working Paper Series 02/2009.

non-tradable resources, which could otherwise be employed in the tradable sector. Additionally, this scenario may lead to deindustrialization (see Table 6.1 above). In fact, a clear structural change has taken place in Cuba's balance of payments in the last decades. Services definitively displaced goods as the main cash earner, moving from just 10 percent of total revenues in 1989 to about 70 percent in 2005 (Figure 6.3).

Historical evidence shows that manufacturing has been, although not the only, the most important path to prosperity for nations. The single most relevant aspect that has historically distinguished rich countries from poor ones is their manufacturing capabilities. For Cuban policymakers it should not become an obsession to increase competitiveness in natural resource based services and industries, but to focus on an export-led strategy, which promotes innovation and product diversification in technology-intensive industries.

Unrelated diversification into technologically dynamic industries can bring the highest return, although after a long gestation period. For that reason it is important that profitability is defined from a long-term point of view. In developing countries, investment in capability building is a long but crucial process.

6.4.6 Professional services based growth

The increase of professional services exports confirms the above illustrated pattern of a service-based economy. However this new trend could (not necessarily) encourage the exports of medical equipment and other related value added manufactures. Still, the sustainability of this new path has yet to be achieved. As long as this circumstances are not transformed in opportunities for the formation of linkages within the local economy, i.e. the creation of a quality local structure of suppliers, new technology-intensive, innovation-driven local enterprises, with the technology, market and scale requirements to benefit from cooperating with their counterparts

The political alliance with Venezuela and the framework of the ALBA[88] evolved into various formal trade agreements. In 2000, an agreement was signed in which Venezuela agreed to provide Cuba with 53,000 barrels of oil a day at preferential prices from that country's extensive oil stock. In exchange, Cuba promised to supply Venezuela with 20,000 medical professionals and educators. At the beginning, trade agreements took the form of barter exchanges, but since 2003 payments for professional services have been made in cash.

In August 2004, the agreement was expanded: Venezuela was to provide over 90,000 barrels a day and Cuba increased the number of medical, public health officials and teachers to 40,000 in order to help staff the increasing number of health care and teaching centers it has in Venezuela.[89] In 2005 further agreements were signed on 192 joint projects worth $800 million US. Among these projects was the construction of 600 health clinics, 600 rehabilitation and physical therapy facilities, and 35 fully equipped medical centers in Venezuela with the assistance of Cuban medical personnel. Additional agreements with Venezuela have been signed on a yearly basis. Similar medical services have been provided in other third world countries on a much smaller scale. In July 2006, 28,664 Cuban health professionals were serving abroad in 68 countries.[90]

Even if the Cuban government does not offer disaggregated services statistics, thus making it more difficult to define the nature of service trade, rough estimates from several sources provide some evidence that seems to indicate that the numbers of professional services traded are truly significant, having even become the Cuban economy's biggest earner in the tertiary sector. For example, a US-based report states that the increase in non-tourism services exports between 2003 and 2005 was around $1.2 billion US for a total of $2.4 billion US, which puts non-tourism services ahead of gross tourism earnings (of $2.3 billion US) in 2005. Most of these are medical services.[91] Another US-based report based on statistics of the Economic Intelligence Unit (EIU 2007) estimated that in 2006 Cuba earned as much as $3 billion from professional services, mostly medical services; and that this revenue came almost exclusively from Venezuela (see also EIU 2010a).[92]

According to data from the World Trade Organization, non-travel commercial services[93] amounted to $5.1 billion US in 2006, compared to $ 2.1 billion US in travel services (Table 6.3). The increasing significance of non-tourist services, easily attributable to medical services mostly in Venezuela, can be easily observed during the period 2004–08. The creation in 2013 in Brazil of a similar program, *Mais Médicos* (more doctors), also contributed to these increments.

Table 6.3 Cuba services exports

Year	2000	2001	2002	2003	2004	2005	2006	2007	2008	2009
Commercial services	2643	2572	2450	2962	3789	7075	7201	8588	9252	8427
Tourist services	1876	1827	1764	1994	2068	2322	2127	2141	2267	2015

Source: ONE 2010 (Cuba), WTO Secretariat, United Nations Service Trade Statistics Database

Table 6.4 High-technology exports (percent of manufactured exports)

Year	2004	2005	2006
Cuba	11.8	18.3	33.5
OECD	17.4	19.5	18.5

Source: The World Bank

In this context, Cuban export of medical products and equipment may have received a significant push. According to data collected by the World Bank,[94] high technology exports, as a percentage of total manufactured exports, experienced an increase during the period 2004–06, growing at rates even larger than the ones of the OECD (Table 6.4). Of course, this seems to be a very circumstantial situation, whose analysis cannot be furthered because of lack of data. Before 2004, the levels used to be modest in comparison to the abrupt growth of 2004, probably linked to a favorable, but short-lived, conjuncture. After 2006, there is no information available. However, it is plausible to state that Cuba has a way to go in terms of having an articulated economic network that allows the country to achieve sustained levels of high-tech exports. More access to international markets is needed as well as more export diversification. Still, the fact of being able to achieve those numbers, albeit for a short period of time, makes the brief comparison useful because it shows the potential of Cuba's manufacturing fabric.

However, these services are based on preferential conditions. This means that the profitability of them depends on the political and economic conditions of the countries. Any situation, any external shock (for instance the 2008–09 crisis) could bring serious setbacks for the already fragile Cuban economy. For example, an agreement links the prices of Cuban exports of medical services with the price of imported oil from Venezuela.

This indexation would not be so risky had Cuba a more diversified export structure and partners, but in fact the opposite is happening, at least in the professional services sector. To be sure, the country's commercial relations have become far more diversified than in the Soviet era. Not only Venezuela, but also China and East Asian countries, and even Russia are also important partners. However, the weight of Venezuela's partnership plays a crucial role and while it has provided an important push to the Cuban economy, could be destabilizing in a crisis.

Cuba has already experienced the risks involved in the excessive dependence on these kinds of preferential bilateral treaties and should therefore avoid them as much as possible. Indeed, the recent political and economic instability in Venezuela resulted in fluctuation of the amount of professional services they can afford, which together with the new political forces in Brazil and in other Latin American countries led to a decline in the exports of professional services. In 2017 and 2018 there were substantial declines in the gained income from medical services. This sort of fluctuation makes professional services, at least in their current form, a very capricious source of income. It will be valuable as long as it comes with other sources.

However, much more important is the fact that these services are still not providing any significant backward linkages with the domestic industry. For example, the knowledge about new medical conditions or about specific unmet medical needs in other country could transform in new products, provided this is part of a strategy in which the government consciously keeps and encourages new communication channels between doctors and industry. On the other hand, it is true that the medical services could serve as a platform for the export of biotech products, medical equipment and the like. This could be an alternative since a growing biotech sector exists in Cuba, especially if a more effective market diversification strategy can be carried out.

Notes

1 The Special Period in Time of Peace (in Spanish: Periodo especial en tiempos de paz).
2 In 1992 the Cuban Democracy Act (Torricelli Act) was enacted, as was the Cuban Liberty and Democratic Solidarity Act of 1996 (Helms-Burton Bill), which extended the territorial application of the initial embargo to apply to foreign companies trading with Cuba, and penalized foreign companies allegedly "trafficking" in property formerly owned by US citizens but expropriated by Cuba after the Cuban revolution (see www.cubavsbloqueo.cu/Default.aspx?tabid=274).
3 This measure also introduced a double monetary circulation in the Cuban economy, which complicated entrepreneurial transaction and economic planning. After ten years (2003–05), most of the current accounts, transaction between state companies, retail stores and population save accounts were de-dollarized. US dollar functions were replaced by the convertible peso, a currency introduced in 1994 that was gaining gradually presence in the circulation. The duality that still persisted (Cuban peso-Convertible peso) aggravated by the duplicity of exchange rates between the two currencies, working 24:1 for the population and 1:1 for enterprises and other institutions. See P Vidal, Cuban economic policy under the Raúl Castro Government, Institute of Developing Economies of Japan's External Trade, 2010 (pp. 23–61) Organization in: www.ide.go.jp/Japanese/Publish/Download/Report/2009/pdf/2009_408_ch2.pdf
4 In 2010, some pilot projects were carried out by leasing some retail service-based businesses to individuals and cooperatives. These measures represented a significant

shift from the 1968 instituted state-based retail system, when all small businesses were nationalized without any economic consideration. Time will tell. See Cuba experiments with private retail enterprise, March 10, 2010, www.reuters.com/article/idUSTRE6294P020100310.

5 This measure was intended to alleviate the severe job cut reduction (1 million) in the state sector announced by the government. See: Government set to cut inflated payrolls, Patricia Grogg, IPS, August 2, 2010. In: http://ipsnews.net/news.asp?idnews=52355. See also: Raúl Castro's speech closing the first period of sessions of the National Assembly of the People's Power, August 1, 2010 (in Spanish). In: www.cubadebate. cu/noticias/2010/08/01/raul-castro-la-unidad-es-nuestra-arma-estrategica/

6 In mid-2011 the most common activities were cafeterias, restaurants, and food vendors (20 percent), transport services (10 percent), producers and vendors of house supplies (4 percent), street vendors (3 percent).

7 For example, while in the first quarter of 2010 labor productivity grew 4.3 percent the average salary saw a 0.9 percent decline in relation to the same period last year.

8 The purchasing power of most of the public sector's salaries is far from recovering from the crisis of the early 1990s (in 2009, 26,6 percent of the pre-crisis salary in 1989).

9 As of 2019, 31 percent of labor force, self-employed, cooperatives etc. worked in the non-state sector (www.cubadebate.cu/opinion/2019/03/25/balance-preliminar-de-la-economia-cubana-en-2018-y-algunas-perspectivas-para-el-2019-final/).

10 See for example Dewhurst et al., Motivating people: Getting beyond money, McKinsey Quarterly, November 2009, see also Shaw (1999), A Guide to Performance Measurements and Non-Financial Indicator, The Foundation for Performance Measurement, England.

11 From 1990 to 1993, monetary liquidity increased from 21.6 percent of GDP to 73.2 percent of GDP as citizens were not able to spend their cash holdings in consumption activities. In the same period fiscal deficit grew from 7.3 percent to 33.5 percent of GDP, as losses of state enterprises became larger and the government maintained social services expenditures close to pre-crisis levels. In May 1994, after a great national debate, the National Assembly of People's Power adopted a resolution calling to restore financial balance. The government reacted by increasing prices of non-essential products such as cigarettes and alcoholic beverages, and by reducing other unnecessary subsidies, particularly those covering enterprises losses. All these aspects were articulated in a new tax code in 1994 (Law 73) Macroeconomic stability was achieved without a significant shift from essential social programs.

12 Cuba became during the nineties a world reference in agro-ecological production. According to the UN's Food and Agriculture Organization (FAO), Cuba's average daily per capita dietary energy supply in 2007 (the last year available) was over 3200 kcal, the highest of all Latin American and Caribbean nations, cited from http://monthlyreview.org/2012/01/01/the-paradox-of-cuban-agriculture, see also www.guardian.co.uk/sustainable-business/agroecology-gaining-policy-support-food-shortage

13 http://monthlyreview.org/2012/01/01/the-paradox-of-cuban-agriculture

14 Producers had to sell up to 70 percent of production at excessively low prices to the national state company (Acopio in Spanish) responsible for gathering and marketing agricultural products, which left only 30 percent for them to freely commercialize.

15 http://monthlyreview.org/2012/01/01/the-paradox-of-cuban-agriculture

16 Ibid.

17 More than 50 percent of agricultural land had remained incomprehensibly in idle conditions.

18 See A Nova, Cuban agriculture and the current economic transformation process, From the *Island* 9, April 1, 2012, see also www.nodo50.org/cubasigloXXI/economia/nova_311211.pdf (Spanish), see also www.reuters.com/article/2012/08/31/cuba-food-idUSL2E8JVAUU20120831

19 Ibid.

20 http://monthlyreview.org/2012/01/01/the-paradox-of-cuban-agriculture

21 While advocates of the agro-ecological production in Cuba rightly say that there is still enough idle land to be sustainably exploited, mechanization is also important because not all the land has the same quality. At the same time, the country needs a high-tech sector that improves the national real wage average. This would allow the producers to keep attractive prices while simultaneously making it possible for more people to afford these prices.

22 see http://articles.sun-sentinel.com/2013-04-14/news/fl-cuban-oil-drilling-retreat-20130414_1_jorge-pi-north-coast-cuban-officials, see also www.cubastandard.com/2013/04/19/russian-offshore-drilling-to-end-earlier-than-anticipated/

23 https://caribreport.com/2019/01/16/cuba-diaz-canel-announces-national-workshop-on-computerization-of-society/

24 See Nelson E, Scott S, Cukier J and Galán Á (2009), Institutionalizing agroecology: Successes and challenges in Cuba. *Agriculture and Human Values 26*(3): 233–43. See also www.slate.com/articles/health_and_science/future_tense/2012/04/agro_ecology_lessons_from_cuba_on_agriculture_food_and_climate_change_.single.html; see also http://monthlyreview.org/2012/01/01/the-paradox-of-cuban-agriculture

25 Corporatism is usually depicted as counterpoised to democratic pluralism and free market forces. Indeed, the term was initially associated with Fascist governments during the 1930s. But in recent decades, corporatism has been used to describe a broad variety of political arrangements under governments both democratic and blatantly undemocratic, from Britain and Australia to Japan to Latin America, and even to describe certain aspects of Communist rule in Romania, Poland and the Soviet Union. Corporatist mechanisms, in short, do not define a political system. (citation from Unger and Chan (1994), China, corporatism, and the East Asian model. In: www.usc.cuhk.edu.hk/wk_wzdetails.asp?id=1544).

26 International Directory of Company Histories, Vol. 11. St. James Press, 1995.

27 Nationwide, the CIMEX S.A. corporation owns dozens of many large and small stores, 119 gasoline stations, 117 cafeterias, 47 photo services (digital and color), the tour operator HAVANATUR, finance and banking facilities, and real estate and duty-free zones businesses.

28 Visteme despacio…, Juventud Rebelde, July 3, 2010, In: www.juventudrebelde.cu/cuba/2010-07-03/visteme-despacio.

29 Cuban individuals were not allowed to participate either as private investors or as owners in the new corporate business system.

30 Further analysis; see English translation of the law online: www.cubaindustria.com/English/law_77.htm.

31 http://swisscuba.com/userfiles/file/Agreement5290english%282%29.pdf

32 Some authors state that the performance of this organization form in Asia has been mixed. However, they still recognize that the region has performed better than other developing regions. The cases of Taiwan, South Korea and Malaysia are confirmed to have been crucial in the development of the export-led industrialization strategy

carried out by these countries (see H Amirahmadi and W Wu, Export processing zones in Asia, Asian Survey XXXV(9) (Sep. 1995): 828–49).

33 For example, products that incorporated at least 50 percent Cuban added value were exempted from the payment of duty. No other country in the Caribbean Basin offered such incentives for export processing zones sales to the domestic market (see Decree-law of Free Zones and Industrial Parks, www.cuba.cu/negocios/DL165I. htm).

34 Brazil's Banco Nacional de Desenvolvimento Econômico e Social (BNDES) financed 85 percent of the $800 million port and infrastructure project, Cuba funded the remaining 15 percent, according to the former Brazilian government. Brazilian construction giant Grupo Odebrecht was in charge of the execution; Brazilian companies are provided practically all supplies and services for the project. See www. cubastandard.com/2012/08/31/brazil-offers-legal-assistance-for-free-trade-zone/

35 For a detailed analysis see Everleny (2010), The External Sector of the Cuban Economy, Woodrow Wilson Center Update on the Americas, October 2010, available at www.wilsoncenter.org/cuba

36 Ibid.

37 www.cubadebate.cu/opinion/2019/03/05/balance-economico-preliminar-del-2018-en-cuba-y-algunas-perspectivas-para-el-2019-parte-ii/

38 https://elestadocomotal.com/2018/01/30/el-pago-anual-por-la-deuda-externa-de-cuba-se-aceptan-apuestas/

39 http://en.granma.cu/cuba/2019-06-03/taking-advantage-of-national-industry-and-its-potential

40 www.cubadebate.cu/opinion/2019/03/05/balance-economico-preliminar-del-2018-en-cuba-y-algunas-perspectivas-para-el-2019-parte-ii/

41 The first congress held by the Cuban Communist Party in 14 years (which took place on April 16–19, 2011) was almost specifically aimed to introduce economic, social, and political reforms in order to modernize the country's economic system. Delegates approved about 300 economic proposals, including measures to legalize selling and buying of private property, decentralization of production, etc. For further details see www.cubanews.ain.cu/2011/0419sixth-congress-communist-party.htm, www.guardian.co.uk/world/2011/apr/19/cuba-castro-communist-congress, www. granma.cu/ingles/cuba-i/16-abril-central.html, www.bbc.co.uk/news/world-latin-america-13998167

42 See www.economist.com/node/21562954, see also www.cubastandard.com/2012/11/10/cuba-allows-private-management-of-state-owned-restaurants/

43 Even while China has done well by exporting labor intensive products (toys, garments, simple electronics) the fact is that China's export portfolio is much more sophisticated than what would be normally expected. According to development economist Dani Rodrik China is an outlier in terms of the overall sophistication of its exports: its export bundle is that of a country with an income per-capita level three times higher

44 Even though strong investments were made during the 1990s, the development of this industry actually began in the 1980s. These investments represented more a continuity (for good) rather than a rupture with earlier period.

45 See A Cárdenas, The Cuban Biotechnology Industry: Innovation and Universal Health Care (theAIRnet Working Paper # 2009-01, www.theairnet.org/files/research/cardenas/andres-cardenas_cubab_biotech_paper_2009.pdf) and E Lopez et al. (2006) Biotechnology in Cuba: 20 years of scientific, social and economic

progress, Journal of Commercial Biotechnology (2006) 13: 1–11, www.palgrave-journals.com/jcb/journal/v13/n1/full/3050038a.html

46 This has been a very flexible term, which has been employed simultaneously to both justify wage reduction and wage increase. This article refers to the later, being definition adopted by Reinert (2007, p. 227) of competitiveness as the degree of a country to produce goods and services "that meet the test of foreign competition while simultaneously maintaining and expanding domestic real income."

47 In 2008, three strong hurricanes hit the island provoking damages estimated in $9.7 billion; mainly in housing and food sectors. Another element is the global financial crisis.

48 www.indexmundi.com/g/g.aspx?c=cu&v=94

49 The formation of joint ventures with the Canada based Sherrit International allowed to improve the commercialization expertise and market shares for the Cuban Nickel (see Everleny 2002, Cuba: An Overview of Foreign Direct Investment, Carleton working papers, pp. 16–18, in: www2.carleton.ca/economics/ccms/wp-content/ccms-files/cep02-04.pdf).

50 www.indexmundi.com/minerals/?product=nickel&graph=production.

51 Minerals Yearbook, 2004, v. 3: Area Reports, International: Latin America and Canada, (pp. 91–4).

52 http://thecubaneconomy.com/articles/2010/06/bad-news-for-cuba%E2%80%99s-nickel-industry-and-sherritt/

53 Ibid.

54 See www.iisd.org/markets/policy/price.asp or http://siteresources.worldbank.org/INTPOVERTY/Resources/3356421210859591030/Food_Price_Watch_May2010.pdf

55 Cuba consumes a minimum of 150 000 barrels per day in petroleum products, of which up to 92 000 bpd comes from Venezuela. The rest is pumped from the Cuban northwest coast along with natural gas and power generation. However, in December 2007 a joint venture with the Venezuela's state run Petroleos de Venezuela S.A (PDVSA) was established in order to upgrade the Cuba's downstream operations. PDVSA reported in 2008 deliveries of 115,000 bpd of crude and refined products to Cuba, of which 93,300 bpd were sold to Cuban state-run Cubapetroleo (CUPET); and 27,500 bpd was PDVSA´s equity share. Revenues seem to represent CUPET´s share of the Cienfuegos joint-venture refinery exports. Based on data of the Cuban Foreign Trade Ministry, Reuters reports that nickel accounted for 39 percent of exports and oil for 22 percent, becoming the Cuba's second leading exports in merchandising sector, overtaking pharmaceuticals (9 percent). See Oil now second leading Cuban export-gov´t reports, June 10, 2009, in: www.reuters.com/article/idUSN1049707420090610

56 Economist Intelligence Unit, EIU Viewswire: Cuba economy: Structure of exports shifts, July 8, 2010.

57 Estudio económico de América Latina y el Caribe 2009–2010, Cuba, Economic commission for Latin America and the Caribbean (ECLAC).

58 Cuban nickel output seen lowest in a decade, in: www.reuters.com/article/idUSN3021507420091230?type=marketsNews

59 After soaring past $ US83,500 per metric ton (MT) in March 2018, cobalt prices began 2019 at $US55,000 per MT. Still, according to some analysts, cobalt as one of the most expensive metals on the market, and it could remain that way for the foreseeable future (see www.fool.com/investing/2019/01/20/2-top-cobalt-stocks-for-2019.aspx)

60 Ibid.
61 www.reuters.com/article/us-tesla-cuba-cobalt-exclusive-idUSKBN1K92Q9
62 ACINOX official website in: www.steels-net.cu/
63 Minerals Yearbook, 2004, v. 3: Area Reports, International: Latin America and Canada, (pp. 91–4). Additionally, ACINOX was prized with the exporter prize.
64 www.bnamericas.com/news/metals/Technology_improves_Acinox_exports
65 In 2007 the export of machinery and transport equipment, which identify metal-based value-added productions, made 4.6 percent of the total exports. This share actually represented a decrease in comparison with the 7.8 percent of 2006 (based on data ONE 2010).
66 A breakthrough in China, another blow for Sudbury, June 11, 2010. In: www. theglobeandmail.com/report-on-business/industry-news/energy-and-resources/ a-breakthrough-in-china-another-blow-for-sudbury/article1601530/   See   also Bad news for Cuba's Nickel industry and Sherrit, June 28, 2010. In: http:// thecubaneconomy.com/articles/2010/06/bad-news-for-cuba%E2%80%99s-nickel-industry-and-sherritt/.
67 The new updates in Cuban emigration policy announced by the Cuban government on October 17, 2012 and approved in February 2013 might open new spaces in this direction. However, it is too early to make any sensible analysis. Further details on the new regulations see www.granma.cu/ingles/cuba-i/17oct-EDITORIAL. html, see also www.nytimes.com/2012/10/17/world/americas/cuba-lifts-much-reviled-rule-the-exit-visa.html?pagewanted=all, see also www.washingtonpost. com/world/the_americas/cuba-to-ease-travel-abroad-for-many-citizens/2012/ 10/16/4f54607a-17a9-11e2-a346-f24efc680b8d_story.html
68 Lucas (2005).
69 For more details about the tourism industry in Cuba see Blanco (1998), Cuba's tourism industry: Sol Meliá as a case study, ASCE, Miami, pp. 50–9. See also Figueras (2006) El turismo internacional y la formación de cluster productivos en la economía cubana, In Everleny (ed.) (2006), Reflexiones sobre economía cubana, Editorial Ciencias Sociales, La Habana. See also Suddaby (1997), Cuba's *Tourism Industry*, ASCE, Miami, pp. 123–30. See also Espino (2000), Cuban tourism during the special period, ASCE, Miami,, p. 360–73 and Espino (2009), International tourism: An update, ASCE, Miami, 130–37. See also Brundenius C, Tourism as an Engine of Growth: Reflections on Cuba's New Development Strategy, Working Paper 02.10, Centre for Development Research, Copenhagen, 2002.
70 Figueras (2006).
71 Everleny (2009), The Cuban Economy: A current evaluation and proposals for necessary policy changes, Institute of developing economies, JETRO, Discussion paper No. 217, Japan.
72 Figueras (2006).
73 Everleny (2009), p. 13.
74 The constant decreasing and fluctuating nature of sugar prices and the termination of the preferential relations with the former Soviet Union led to the eventual dismantling of the industry in 2002 (for a more details see Nova (2006), Redimensionamiento y diversificación de la industria azucarera, in: Everleny (2009), pp. 108–57. See also Peters (2003), Cutting losses: Cuba downsize its sugar industry, Lexington Institute, December.
75 Since 1994, export earnings from tourism have been, on average, about 39 percent of total foreign exchange earnings; in 1998 the ratio of gross revenues to total goods

and services exports was 43 percent, compared to 22 percent in 1992. See Espino (2008).

76 For example, the manufacturing and furniture industries introduced new technologies and designed new products, which were able to compete with imports from different countries. For instance, the company Suchel-Camacho S.A now supplies all the hotels with mini bottles of shampoo, small soaps, body lotions and the like. In 2000, local breweries supplied 95 percent of the tourist market, with bottled water companies covering almost the entire market. New types of bottles, metal containers for beer and soft drinks were introduced, as well as new packaging technologies. In 2000, a joint venture was instituted with capital and technology from different countries in order to restart bus production. See MA Figueras, International Tourism and the Formation of Productive Clusters in the Cuban Economy, Paper presented to the Latin American Studies Association (LASA) XXII Congress, Washington, D.C., September 2001.

77 O Everleny, The External Sector of the Cuban Economy, Woodrow Wilson Center Update un the Americas, p. 15, October 2010, available at www.wilsoncenter.org/cuba

78 In 2002, following the terrorist attacks of 2001, the 2.7 percent decrease in international tourist arrivals to the Caribbean was cushioned to a large extent by a 7.1 percent increase in cruise passengers. But Cuba was unable to participate because the US embargo prohibits US-based cruises from including Cuba in their itineraries. Without this cushion, Cuba suffered a 5 percent decline in visitor arrivals, the first retreat since 1983 (see Espino (2008). Besides, US tourists account for 52 percent of all tourists in the Caribbean.

79 Ibid.

80 www.cubadebate.cu/noticias/2019/07/11/asamblea-nacional-ministerios-brindan-informacion-a-los-diputados-asiste-el-presidente-cubano/comentarios/pagina-2/#comment_content

81 www.bbc.com/news/world-us-canada-48113549

82 There is also the problem of the international tour operators. Most of the segments in a typical tourist package to Cuba are dominated by strong tour operators. It was estimated that in 2002 out of the total spending by a typical tourist on a package tour to Cuba, the tour operators (TO) get 20 percent, the airlines 40 percent and the remaining 40 percent are spent in Cuba (Brudenius 2002): Still another reason to diversify the industry and to improve marketing abilities.

83 www.cubadebate.cu/opinion/2018/03/17/cuba-y-su-economia-el-2017-recien-concluido-y-un-2018-que-apenas-comienza-iv/

84 For space reasons we cannot go into details here about this segment. But to have an idea, the Buena Vista Social Club phenomenon is, of course recognizing the imperialistic notion involved in that project, an example of the potential of this kind of tourism modality when the right marketing strategies are put in motion. According to Farley (2009), the project had sold up to that date 8 million copies, which made it a major recording industry success, all the more extraordinary when considering that their record company World Circuit (a non-Cuban label) was a small independent affair headed by one man, Nick Gold, in East London. See Farley (2009), The rejuvenating power of Buena Vista Social Club, Samples, Online-Publikationen des Arbeitskreis Studium Populärer Musik e.V. (ASPM). Cuban agencies specializing in tourism such as Paradiso S.A. could learn to emulate this success.

85 Cuba sells its medical expertise, in: http://news.bbc.co.uk/2/hi/business/3284995. stm

86 Evolución del turismo como locomotora de la economía cubana: Simposio, Desarrollo local y Turismo," 5–23 Julio, 2007, Universidad de Málaga, Espana. In: www.eumed.net/eve/resum/07-07/alb.htm

87 Ibid.

88 The Bolivarian Alliance for the Peoples of Our America (Spanish: *Alianza Bolivariana para los Pueblos de Nuestra América*, or ALBA) is an international cooperation organization based on the idea of social, political and economic integration between the countries of Latin America and the Caribbean.

89 For more details of the Cuba–Venezuela relationship see Perez et al. (2008), Cuba's new export commodity: A framework, in: A *Changing* Cuba in a *Changing World*, Bildner Center for Western Hemisphere Studies City University of New York, 2008, See also Romero (2009), South–South Cooperation between Venezuela and Cuba, Universidad Central de Venezuela, In: www.realityofaid.org/userfiles/ roareports/roareport_e48ca78931.pdf

90 Cuba and the global health workforce: Health professionals abroad. In: www. medicc.org/ns/index.php?s=12&p=0

91 Feinsilver (2006), Cuban medical diplomacy: When the left has got it right, Council of Hemispheric Affairs (COHA), Washington, in: www.coha.org/ cuban-medical-diplomacy-when-the-left-has-got-it-right/

92 Perez et al. 2008, p. 334.

93 According to WTO definition, the commercial services category is defined as being equal to services minus government services. Commercial services are further sub-divided into transportation services, travel, and other commercial services. See http://stat.wto.org/StatisticalProgram/WSDBStatProgramTechNotes. aspx?Language=E#Def_Meth_Services

On the other side, commercial services are defined as opposed to governmental services. "A service supplied in the exercise of governmental authority" means any service which is supplied neither on a commercial basis, nor in competition with one or more service suppliers. However, commercial services in Cuba as a result of governmental authority, are still of commercial nature and certainly compete with other suppliers. See www.wto.org/english/tratop_e/serv_e/1-scdef_e.htm

94 The World Bank defines high-technology products as products with high R&D intensity, such as in aerospace, computers, pharmaceuticals, scientific instruments and electrical machinery. See http://data.worldbank.org/indicator/TX.VAL. TECH.MF.ZS

References

Altieri M and Funes-Monzote F (2012), The paradox of Cuban agriculture, *Monthly Review* 63(8) (January).

Amirahmadi H and Wu W (1995), Export processing zones in Asia, *Asian Survey* 35(9): 828–49.

Bateman M and Chang H-J (2012), Microfinance and the illusion of development: From hubris to nemesis in thirty years, *World Economic Review* 1: 13–36.

Baumol W and Bowen W (1966), *Performing Arts: The Economic Dilemma: A Study of Problems Common to Theater, Opera, Music, and Dance.* Cambridge, MA: MIT Press.

Bermúdez-Lugo O (2004), Minerals Yearbook 2004. In: *Minerals Yearbook, Vol. 3: Area Reports, International: Latin America and Canada*. Geological Survey (USGS), pp. 91–4.

Brundenius, C (2002), Tourism as an Engine of Growth: Reflections on Cuba's New Development Strategy, Working Paper 02.10. Copenhagen: Centre for Development Research.

Cárdenas A (2009), The Cuban Biotechnology Industry: Innovation and Universal Health Care, the AirNet Working Paper # 2009-01. Available at www.theairnet.org/V2/healthcare-technology.php (last accessed December 6, 2012).

Chang HJ (1999), The developmental state. In: Woo-Cumings M (ed.). *The Developmental State*. Ithaca and London: Cornell University Press, pp. 182–99.

Chang HJ (2007). *State Owned Enterprise*. New York: United Nations DESA.

Chang HJ (2008) *Bad Samaritans: The Myth of Free Trade and Secret History of Capitalism*. New York: Bloomsbury.

Chang HJ (2009), Industrial Policy: Can we go beyond an unproductive confrontation? A plenary paper for ABCDE, Annual World Bank Conference on Development Economics, Seoul, South Korea, June 22–24.

Chang HJ (2010), *23 Things They Don't Tell You about Capitalism*. London: Penguin.

Cimoli M et al. (eds.) (2009), *The Political Economy of Capabilities Accumulation: The Past and Future of Policies for Industrial Development*. Oxford: Oxford University Press.

Dewhurst M et al. (2009), Motivating people: Getting beyond money, *McKinsey Quarterly*, November.

Dominguez J et al. (2004), *The Cuban Economy at the Start of the Twenty-First Century*. Cambridge, MA, London: Harvard University Press.

Economist Intelligence Unit (EUI) (2007), Cuba Country Report, Economist 1st-4th Quarter, Available at www.eiu.com (last accessed December 10, 2007).

Economist Intelligence Unit (EUI) (2010a), Country Report Cuba August 2010: Outlook for 2010–11: External Sector.

Economist Intelligence Unit (EUI) (2010b), *Cuba Economy: Structure of Exports Shifts*, July 8, 2010. New York, NY: Alacra Store (retrieved Dec 6, 2012 from www.alacrastore.com).

Espino M (2008), Internacional tourism in Cuba: An update, Cuba in Transition, ASCE, available at www.ascecuba.org/publications/ proceedings/volume18/pdfs/espino.pdf (last accessed December 6, 2012).

Estudio económico de América Latina y el Caribe 2009–2010: Cuba, Report Economic commission for Latin America and the Caribbean (ECLAC), available at www.one.cu/publicaciones/cepal/ Estudio%202009_2010/Nota%20de%20Cuba.pdf (last accessed December 6, 2012).

Evans P et al. (eds.) (1999), *Bringing the State Back In*. Cambridge: Cambridge University Press.

Everleny O (2002), Cuba: An Overview of Foreign Direct Investment. Carleton working papers. Carleton, Canada, 16–18. Available at www1.carleton.ca/economics/ccms/wp-content/ccms-files/ cep02-04.pdf (last accessed December 6, 2012).

Everleny O (ed.) (2006), *Reflexiones sobre economía cubana*. La Habana: Editorial ciencias sociales.

Everleny O (2009), The Cuban Economy: A Current Evaluation and Proposals for Necessary Policy Changes, Institute of Developing Economies – JETRO, Discussion paper 217, www.ide.go.jp/ English/Publish/Download/Dp/pdf/217.pdf, (last accessed at December 6, 2012).

Farley J (2009), *The Rejuvenating Power of Buena Vista Social Club*. Online-Publikationen des Arbeitskreis Studium Populärer Musik e.V. (ASPM).

Feinsilver J (2006), Cuban Medical Diplomacy: When the Left has Got it Right, Washington: Council of Hemispheric Affairs (COHA). Available at www.coha.org/cuban-medical-diplomacy-when-theleft-has-got-it-right/ (last accessed December 6, 2012).

Figueras MA (2001), International Tourism and the Formation of Productive Clusters in the Cuban Economy, Paper prepared to the Latin American Studies Association (LASA) 22nd Congress, Washington, DC, September 2001.

Freeman Ch (2008), *System of Innovation*. Cheltenham UK; Northampton USA Edward Elgar Publishing.

Gutiérrez-Castillo O and Gancedo-Gaspar N (2002), Tourism development: Locomotive for the Cuban economy, *ReVista*, Harvard Review for Latin America, Winter: 76–8.

Hauknes J and Smith K (2003), Corporate Governance and Innovation in Mobile Telecommunications: How Did the Nordic Area Become a World Leader? STEP Report R-12, Institute for New Technologies United Nations, University Maastricht, Oslo.

Hobday M and Colpan A (2010), Technological innovations and business groups. In: Colpan A et al. (eds.), *The Oxford Handbook of Business Groups*. New York: Oxford University Press, pp. 763–83.

Informe de Comercio Exterior Uruguay-Cuba: Exportaciones e Importaciones, Uruguay XXI, 2009, available at http://aplicaciones.uruguayxxi. gub.uy/innovaportal/file/523/1/uruguay_-_cuba.pdf (last accessed December 6, 2012).

Jäntti M and Vartiainen J (2009), The Finnish Developmental State and its Growth Regime, UNU-WIDER Research Paper 2009/35.

Kapur D (2001), Diasporas and Technology Transfer, *Journal of Human Development* 2(2): 265–86.

Lazonick W (2002), Innovative enterprise and historical transformation, *Enterprise & Society* 3: 3–47.

Lopez E et al. (2006), Biotechnology in Cuba: 20 years of scientific, social and economic progress, *Journal of Commercial Biotechnology* 13: 1–11.

Lucas R (2005), International migrations and economic development: Lessons from low-income countries. Stockholm, Sweden: Ministry of Foreign Affairs.

Molina E (2009), Cuba: Economic Restructuring, Recent Trends and Major Challenges, The IDEA *Working Paper Series* 02/2009.

Monreal P (2005), The problem of development in contemporary Cuba, *Journal of the Faculty of International Studies*, 19: 59–71.

Nova A (2006), Redimensionamiento y diversificación de la industria azucarera. In: Everleny O (ed.), *Reflexiones sobre economía cubana*. La Habana: Editorial Ciencias Sociales, pp. 108–57.

Oficina Nacional de Estadísticas (ONE) (2010), Anuario estadístico de Cuba 2010.

Oficina Nacional de Estadísticas (ONE) (2019), Cuentas Nacionales.

Palma J (2009), Flying Geese and waddling ducks: The different capabilities of East Asia and Latin America to "demand-adapt" and "supply-upgrade" their export productive capacity. In: Cimoli M et al. (eds.), *The Political Economy of Capabilities Accumulation: The Past and Future of Policies for Industrial Development*. Oxford: Oxford University Press, pp. 203–38.

Perez O et al. (2008), Cuba's new export commodity: A framework. In: Font M et al. (eds.), *A Changing Cuba in a Changing World*. New York: Bildner Center for Western Hemisphere Studies, City University of New York, pp. 327–44.

Perez-Lopez J (2002), *The Cuban Economy in an Unending Special Period*. ASCE: Miami.

Peters P (2001), State Enterprise Reform in Cuba: An Early Snapshot. Arlington, Virginia: Lexington Institute.

Peters P (2003), Cutting Losses: Cuba Downsize its Sugar Industry. Arlington, Virginia: Lexington Institute.

Pineiro Hanecker C (2012), Non-state enterprises in Cuba current situation and prospects. Paper presented at the Bildner Center, City University of New York, May 21.

Pretty J (2008), Agriculture sustainability: Concepts, principles and evidence, *Philosophical Transactions of the Royal Society B: Biological Sciences* 363: 447–65.

Pu C (2005), Ownership and management issues in Taiwanese public enterprises, *Asia Pacific Journal of Public Administration* 27(2): 163–80.

Reinert E (1999), The role of the state in economic growth, *Journal of Economic Studies* 26(4/5): 268–326.

Reinert E (2007), *How Rich Countries Got Rich and Why Poor Countries Stay Poor*. London: Constable.

Rodriguez JL (2014), The frontier of change in the Cuban economy, *Latin American Perspectives* 41(197/4) (July): 64–73.

Rodrik D (2004), Industrial Policy for the Twenty-First Century. Paper prepared for UNIDO, Harvard University.

Rodrik D (2006), What's So Special about China's Exports? Paper prepared for the project on "China and the Global Economy 2010" of the China Economic Research and Advisory Programme, Harvard University.

Romero C (2009), South-South Cooperation between Venezuela and Cuba, The Reality of Aid Network, pp. 107–14. Available at http:// realityofaid.org/userfiles/roareports/roareport_e48ca78931.pdf (last accessed December 6, 2012).

Sánchez J and Triana J (2008), Un panorama actual de la economía cubana, las transformaciones en curso y sus retos perspectivos, Instituto Real Instituto Elcano Documento de Trabajo 31, Madrid.

Travieso-Díaz M (2001), *Cuba's Perfeccionamiento Empresarial Law: A Step towards Privatization?* Miami: ASCE.

Vidal P (2010), Cuban Economic Policy under the Raúl Castro Government, Institute of Developing Economies of Japan's External Trade, available at www.ide.go.jp/Japanese/Publish/ Download/Report/2009/pdf/2009_408_ch2

Wade R (2003), *Governing the Market*. Princeton, NJ: Princeton University Press.

World Bank (2008) The Growth Report: Strategies for Sustained Growth and Inclusive Development, Commission on Growth and Development, Conference Edition (available at: www.ycsg.yale.edu/ center/forms/growthReport.pdf).

Woo-Cumings M (ed.) (1999), *The Developmental State*. Ithaca and London: Cornell University Press.

7   The Cuban biopharmaceutical industry

Case of developmental catch-up[1]

7.1 Introduction

In previous chapters, we have explored the positive role played by the state in the emergence and evolution of innovative firms and industries within a complex economy. We have seen that the debate on state intervention focused on the notion of market failure is problematic because it still relies on the idea of an "ideal free market" as a point of departure. Furthermore, we saw that this line of reasoning fails to acknowledge the institutional and political nature of the market; the state being the agent that actually designs the markets and their boundaries.

State intervention can be either bad or wrong depending on the kind of institutional incentives activated, but it has always been there. In fact, a great deal of historical evidence on the nature of innovation is telling us that government has been behind the emergence and further evolution of the most radical and disruptive forms of innovation. Depending on the historical background, issues of ownership may be relevant, but not necessarily in terms of the workability of an innovation strategy. More relevant is the question of what developmental factors determine the success of the later.

Chapter 4 showed that innovation may not be explained by the amounts of R&D spent on the economy alone (as important as it is), or by assuming a linear causation between this amount and innovation/economic growth (Freeman 2008). That is, a country with less R&D could display a better innovative performance than others with higher R&D spending.[2] Nor can innovation be understood as a process, where optimizing firms merely adapt to market and technological conditions, which have been taken for granted.

Rather, innovation is actually a non-linear, cumulative, uncertain process, which can be better captured by thinking of it as a system or as a *network* of organizations and institutions in constant organizational learning. This is broadly known in the literature as innovation systems. In this literature not only traditional firms, but also a much broader ecology that includes *non-firm organizations (NFOs)* (many of them government-based) and non-market institutions are taken into consideration as key elements of the innovation and production processes. Within this perspective, more emphasis is given to the systemic ability to make it possible that knowledge embodied in capabilities and technologies can be absorbed and disseminated through the economy.

Historical evidence suggests that well-situated NFOs have been able to facilitate cooperation by creating standards that allow other organizations to communicate, to share and to create knowledge within the economy. Particularly state NFOs, but by no means exclusively, have played an important role in the conception of successful technology and industry policies. By investing in incipient, and therefore still not well-designed, technologies this type of organizations assume a risk that few, if any, business companies are willing to take. If the strategy is successful, then new products and technologies will enter the economy, providing potential for productivity improvements, rise in real wages and positive structural changes within the economy.

This, notwithstanding the specificities, applies to developed as well as developing nations. Although the differences between both types of economies are apparent, poor countries might also be able to even take the lead in certain innovations, provided the right organizational synergy is there. While such a task would be hard to accomplish in established industries, dominated by high entry costs and patent-helmeted oligopolies hosted, predominantly, in rich countries, the story could be different with nascent technologies. Historical evidence suggests that patent policies that grant strong intellectual property rights to early generations of inventors may discourage innovation (Moser 2013).

Incipient technologies have not achieved the level of sophistication and acceptance that makes them a plausible alternative. In fact, they are usually less efficient than incumbent technologies, with which they co-habit for long periods of time (Arthur 2009; Bessen and Nuvolari 2017). Under those circumstances further innovation and improvement requires open ideas exchange and technology diffusion, which does not necessarily results in the loss of rents by incumbents (Bessen and Nuvolari 2017). And in this point there is an opportunity to be exploited by entrants that have invested in certain absorption capabilities, given that patents and other entry costs are still absent. At that time the technology is still in speculative phase, probable being debated more at universities and research centers than in companies. Provided a country has invested in research potential and other forms of "social capabilities" (as put in the widely cited classic Abramovitz 1986, p. 388), and is willing to take the risk to explore new ventures it might be that, in the future, this country will be in the position to be among the leaders in that technology, going from knowledge acquirer to knowledge creator.

We argue the above-mentioned may have been the case in the Cuba, which entered into the biotech world as the industry was still very incipient, and in many aspects, unable to block others because at the time it was not even clear what to patent or to hide. During that time NFOs were created that proved to be very effective acquiring, disseminating and ultimately creating the ground for novel technologies to be developed. However, we have also seen that this success needs not be the case.

While dealing with the historical features of the Cuban economy after 1959, in Chapters 5 and 6, we have seen a country whose forms of allocation and organizational framework have been shaped by and populated by government-based non-firms organizations and state owned enterprises (SOE). However, these chapters have also shown that, paradoxically, one of the most pervasive problems of this period was the lack of coordination between the state, research organizations and productive agents, making it impossible to maximize the flows of information among them, and impeding creative innovation policies from being set. Conceived from an evolutionary perspective we can say that the Cuban biotech sector, particularly some innovative firms within it, was able to differentiate enough from the rest of the economy.

The Cuban biotechnology industry results from the same constellation of non-firm organizations. However, this industry has managed to show more superior outcomes than the rest of the Cuban industries essentially because a better innovation-based coordination system has been set up. Creativity, cooperation, experimentation and even failure, as in the case of the electronic industry, have been allowed and profited from. In this chapter we intend to make the case for the Cuban biotechnology industry precisely as a networked structure that fits very well with the literature of innovation systems, especially within the notions of both *national and sectoral system of innovations.* Particularly, it is intended to explore the crucial role played by government-based non-firm organizations in the learning process – i.e. mobilizing resources and allowing knowledge and innovation to disseminate across the sector – within the Cuban biotech. Most attention will be given to the period until the year 2012, when the industry entered a new phase whose fully appreciation and evaluation is not yet fruitful in any way. It is the story of the formation of the industry that concerns us here.

In this chapter it will be argued that the development of the Cuban biotechnology industry must be understood in the context of a carefully conceived industrial policy, in which government-based non-firm entities are the greatest contributor to the high levels of *organizational integration* within the industry. As already shown in the chapter on national innovation systems, this concept stems from the *theory of the innovative enterprise* proposed by Lazonick (2002) and is defined as "a set of social relations that provides participants in a complex division of labor with the incentives to cooperate in contributing their skills and efforts toward the achievement of a common goal" (ibid., p. 14). Being conceived as a *social condition,* this concept explores the idea of business enterprises as social structures that are in turn embedded in larger (typically national) institutional environments.

In a nutshell, this chapter will be devoted to present the case of the Cuban biopharmaceutical industry and to analyze the causal chain of events, which led to the creation of its most important components. The analysis will proceed by describing the network according to its node subgroups. Here we will analyze in some detail the historic-institutional context, in which the most important organizations under study were developed; and the possible causal mechanisms behind the evolution and outcomes of the industry. These mechanisms will be contrasted with the great deal of historical evidence provided by a great variety of country and sector-specific cases.

Notice that we will not address the challenges of the industry in this text because we would need another book for it, but also because they are more apparent. It is clear that, as time passes, the industry will have to continuously develop and adapt in order to keep its capacity to deliver innovative products. Success is not a straightforward path, but also includes failure and decline. Technology constantly evolves and even once great innovative business enterprises, or whole oligopolistic structures, fall from grace in other times. It is in the nature of complex systems like the economy and this is the reason why the ability of business leaders and policymakers to constantly assess the state of new knowledge and allow stakeholders to be creative in their roles will remain very important.

Nobody expects to see a poor and small country like Cuba to succeed in such a venture. The financial limitations are obvious, political obstacles (which, as Abramovitz 1986 suggested, are particularly noxious in "scale-dependent" advanced technologies, p. 393) such as the American embargo limiting access to the most profitable markets worldwide are also obvious, and finally there are the evident rigidities and inadequacies of the Cuban system, which have been already discussed, magnified (and sometimes distorted) by a number of world commentators to the point of neurosis (therefore they do not need to be addressed any longer). In our view, a more interesting question would be: how on earth did this country manage, despite all these limitations, to develop such a decent industry (in 2009 hailed as the best biotech sector of the developing world according to the American journal *Nature*)? That is the question to be explored here.

7.2 The Cuban biotech industry

The pervasive lack of data makes it difficult to establish an accurate picture about the outcomes of Cuba's biotechnology industry. Official statistics do not provide, for example, disaggregated figures of patent registration, R&D expenditures or turnover of dedicated biotechnology companies. However, even if scattered and unsystematic, the available evidence of the Cuban biotechnology achievements seems to be unequivocal. As Pfeffer (in Burns 2005, p. 111) affirms, in clear recognition of the inherent difficulties of relying on financial measures to assess the achievements of the biotechnology, its impact in the healthcare system is perhaps the most obvious way to measure its success.

This is especially true if the biopharmaceutical industry is conceived as part of a highly interrelated and complex biomedical research ecosystem, which is composed of a broad variety of organizations, government being a crucial player, aimed at "harness innovation in health technology in an efficient and effective manner."[3] This has finally begun to be recognized by the movers and shakers of the pharmaceutical industry worldwide, which has experienced a set of gradual transformations in its business model.

Most pharmaceutical companies have been moving away from their monolithic blockbuster business model, dubbed "Pharma 1.0," to a more collaborative, global and value-driven model called "Pharma 2.0." However, new and sweeping trends have emerged that are shifting the industry towards Pharma 3.0 business model; focused on health outcomes. While Pharma 1.0 and Pharma 2.0 paid more attention to develop and market drugs; Pharma 3.0 is a reconfiguration of the model with a focus on health outcomes where the traditional product – a drug – is only one part of pharma's value proposition.[4] Seen from this perspective it cannot be overemphasized that the Cuban biopharmaceutical business model has actually been a (neglected) forerunner of Pharma 3.0.

7.2.1 From a health economics perspective

To begin with, the costs of the Cuban health system remain low compared to its health standards, even if health services have become recently more expensive in Cuba[5] (measured in terms of total expenditure as percent of GDP). To illustrate this, we rely on the definitions given by both the System of Health Account (SHA) of the OECD[6] and the National Health Accounts (NHA) of the WHO,[7] which term current health expenditure as "the sum of health care goods and services for final consumption of resident units" (OECD, Eurostat, WHO 2011). The most important here is that this definition includes the cost of the goods and services produced by a country and therefore gives a good idea of how expensive is its health system.

By taking a look at the per capita total expenditure on health of Cuba, it will be found that even while Cuba spends more than the average of upper middle income countries,[8] it spends substantially less than high income countries (in current US$).[9] However, the country has managed to achieve health outcomes far superior to those of its income group; and more importantly, comparable with those of the high income countries (Table 7.1). This could be interpreted as a comparative advantage in term of cost of the medical services and goods produced in Cuba.

The results are also significant at the regional level. For instance, according to the World Bank statistics, GDP per capita in 2008 in Latin America was $US7844.5 (in current US$) compared to $US5565.3 in Cuba (World Bank). Nevertheless, the country excelled in several indicators of mortality and disease prevention (Figures 7.1 and 7.2).

Considering the whole region of the Americas in 2008 (Canada and US included), according to the WHO the per capita expenditure on health was $US2902 compared to $US672 in Cuba. However infant mortality in the region was 15 per 1000 live births, compared to 5 per 1000 in Cuba. Using whatever measure, when health outcomes are correlated with GDP per capita, Cuba is clustered with high income countries such as Canada and the UK on the former scale and with upper middle income countries on the latter (Figure 7.3).

We could also look at Cuba's performance rates of reduction in infectious diseases or the proportion of the immunization programs;[10] or its contribution to fighting neglected diseases.[11] In the same line, we could also consider the diagnosis and treatment of chronic conditions,[12] particularly taking into

Table 7.1 Health indicators and health expenditures, 2009

	Infant mortality rate (per 1000 live births)	Life expectancy at birth	Under five mortality rate per 1000 live births	Per capita expenditure on health (current US$)	Total expenditure as % of GDP(2000)	Total expenditure as % of GDP(2008)
Cuba	5	78	6	672	6,7	12,1
High income average	6	80	7	4590	10	11,1
Upper middle income average	19	71	22	570	5,9	6,3
Global average	42	68	60	854	8,7	8,7

Source: Based on WHO 2011.

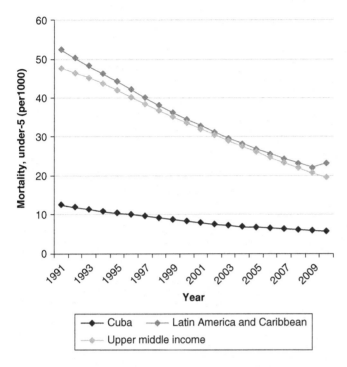

Figure 7.1 Mortality, under-five (per 1000), 1991–2009
Source: Based on World Bank Data.

account that, according a report of the WHO.[13] 80 percent of chronic disease deaths occur in low and middle income countries like Cuba.

Whatever the selected indicator, the point is that the Cuban health system has managed to achieve health outcomes at the level of high income countries while usually spending less. If the country had to acquire most of its needed medical products from foreign providers and at international prices, it would not have been able to achieve these standards at the same cost. Presumably, it would not have been able to afford the products at all, as it is the case in most of the developing world. The use of the vaccine against hepatitis B in Cuba is a good example. Before 1990, the vaccine had not been used systematically in the country because of its high cost. It had only been imported and used on high risk groups. When the country was able to manufacture its own vaccine, it started in 1992 a universal vaccination of newborn children, coincidentally the same year the United States started its campaign.

A study covering the results of both campaigns for the period 1995–2003[14] shows the huge progress made by Cuba in fighting the disease (see Figure 7.4). The reduction of incidence of this acute disease for all ages reached 95.6 percent in Cuba and 67 percent in the United States (years 2003 and 2002 respectively).

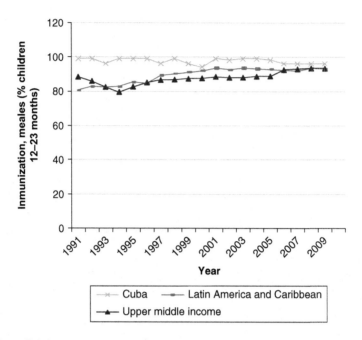

Figure 7.2 Immunization, measles, 1991–2009
Data source: Own estimates based on World Bank Data.

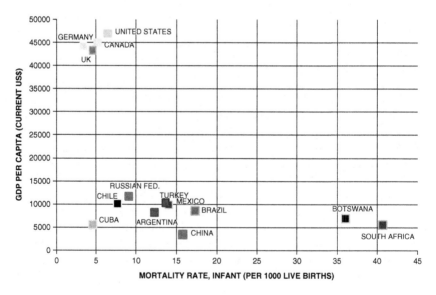

Figure 7.3 GDP/infant mortality, 2010

GDP figures correspond to 2008.
Infant mortality figures correspond to 2010.

Data source: Own estimates based on World Bank Data.

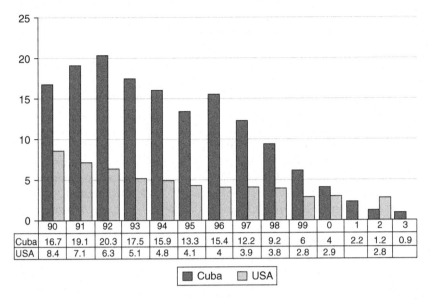

	90	91	92	93	94	95	96	97	98	99	0	1	2	3
Cuba	16.7	19.1	20.3	17.5	15.9	13.3	15.4	12.2	9.2	6	4	2.2	1.2	0.9
USA	8.4	7.1	6.3	5.1	4.8	4.1	4	3.9	3.8	2.8	2.9		2.8	

■ Cuba   □ USA

Figure 7.4 Incidence of acute hepatitis B. Cuba–USA, 1990–2003
Source: Delgado et al., 2003.

In fact, in 2001, Cuba reached the goals the United States set for 2010. In 2010, the country managed to eradicate the conditions in all children under 15.

In the adult population there were also huge improvements. If in 1992 there had been 2194 cases, the number of people affected had by 2010 decreased to 11 cases. There is no intention to highlight any political undertones in this comparison, but just to emphasize the fact that there is no way that Cuba achieved these outcomes without having wisely invested in some manufacturing and organizational capabilities. The comparison is also interesting because the United States and Cuba are the two producers of recombinant vaccines against hepatitis B recognized by the WHO in the Americas.

The role of the biotechnology industry becomes apparent when considering that, according to a World Bank report of 2002, "[…] at present, nearly 80 percent of finished pharmaceutical products used in Cuba are locally made."[15] An article published in *Scientific American Worldview* in 2012 confirms this by stating that "[l]ocally produced biopharmaceuticals supply 80 percent of domestic needs and the sector."[16]

A paper published by *The Lancet* in 2009 assured that the "local production of diagnostics and drugs" covers "85% of the needs, including antiretrovirals and cytostatics."[17] Likewise, the same *Scientific American* article of 2012 cites officials of the industry who affirm that these industries "produce 585 of the 868 essential medications registered for domestic use." This includes a dozen vaccines, generic antiretrovirals for people with AIDS and over 40 biopharmaceuticals.[18]

This is confirmed by *Business Monitor International*, which states that from the "basic medicine list released in 2009, a total of 562 drugs were Cuban, while 307 were imported"[19] (see Espicom's data in Annex 5.7 for period 2009–11). In addition, the fact that the domestic production increased during the period 1997–2008 may help to accept that, indeed, something has been happening in Cuba in terms of drug production (see Annex 5.8).

At the same time, international public opinion begins to realize the potential and achievements of this industry, notwithstanding the ideological biases. For instance, an editorial published in 2009 by the prestigious Nature spoke of the Cuban biotechnology as the "developing world's most established biotechnology industry, which has grown rapidly even though it eschewed the venture-capital funding model that rich countries consider a prerequisite."[20] A trilateral 2013 study carried out by the World Trade Organization (WTO), the World Intellectual Property Organization (WIPO) and the World Health Organization (WHO) states that "Cuba has a vibrant research-based biotechnology industry that has developed a number of innovative vaccines" and also "has numerous innovative products in the pipeline."[21]

Individuals such as Dr. James Larrick,[22] a US entrepreneur, were cited in 2004 by a Nature Biotechnology report about the good prospects of the Cuban biopharmaceutical industry[23] and he confirmed in 2011 his belief that Cuba's biotechnology is clearly world-class.[24] Also, Professor Hudson Freeze,[25] Director of the Genetic Research Program at the US-based UC San Diego, is of the opinion that Cuba has become world-class in this competitive arena.[26]

More skeptical voices, such as the German virologist and Nobel Prize winner (2008) in Physiology or Medicine, Harald zur Hausen, do not think that the Cuban biotechnology (specifically cancer research) has reached international standards. However, he acknowledges the huge progress made by the industry and believes that it has good prospects for the future.[27]

A similar skepticism is shared by the American molecular biologist and Nobel Prize winner (2003) in Chemistry, Peter Agre. Agre thinks that the question of reaching international standards is a difficult one because the prevailing trade embargo has isolated Cuba from the US, and clear evaluations have not been possible. He suspects that this lack of communication may have increased the skepticism that exists in the US concerning Cuban biotech programs (he mentions the therapeutic cancer vaccines). That said, he also recognizes that he has been impressed by the zeal with which Cuba has advanced public health in their country and in some of the poorer countries in Africa and Latin America.[28] At the same time, it is telling that even the US government follows with attention the development of some Cuban cancer products.[29]

7.2.2 Biopharmaceutical trade balance

The same 2002 World Bank report mentioned above also states that

> [...] the growth of the local pharmaceutical industry, which by the mid-1990s was bringing Cuba some 100 million dollars a year in export earnings,

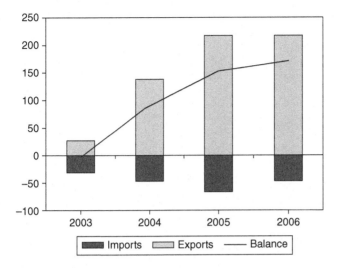

Figure 7.5 Cuba pharmaceutical trade balance (USmn)
Source: Business Monitor International (2010). Based on data from the UN Comtrade (public data).

has not only covered domestic demand for medicines, but has also led to the development of products that compete on the international market.

Likewise, Business Monitor International employed data from the UN Commodity Trade Statistics Database (UN Comtrade) to show that the Cuba Pharmaceutical Trade Balance during 2003–006 was improving (Figure 7.5). Even when some inaccuracies are revealed in the figure of 2006, the same trend is confirmed by the numbers of the Cuban Statistics Agency (ONE) for the period 2006–09 (Figure 7.6).

Most of the trade partners of Cuba are emerging countries that benefit from the low cost of the products (Figure 7.7). For example, "strategic alliances with Brazil, and importantly, China and India—in 2012 the source of 44 percent of Cuba's raw materials for biopharmaceutical products—contribute to enhance commercial relations."[30] At the same time Cuba maintains a huge number of cooperative projects with these countries, which have contributed to boost the prestige of the industry and have led to economies of scale, as many procedures are standardized in those countries, manufacturing plants are built and use Cuban medical doctors in cooperation programs made of the industry products. It is not surprising to see that the current biggest trade partner of Cuba (Venezuela) is the same country that hosts the largest number of Cuban health professionals.

In addition, the data given by a 2011 Espicom Business Intelligence Report shows that during the period 1995–2010, even with fluctuation, the Cuban pharmaceutical trade balance has been positive, except for four years (Table 7.2). This signals that during these years, something was happening in this industry.

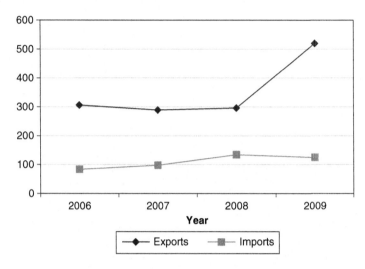

Figure 7.6 Cuba pharmaceuticals foreign trade (USmn)

Data source: Cuba's National Statistics Office (ONE) in accordance with sections and chapters of the Standards International Trade Classification (SITC).

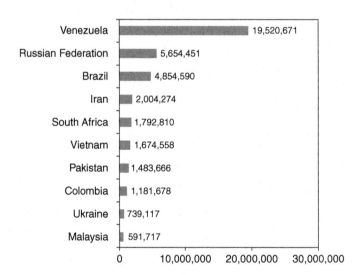

Figure 7.7 Cuba's top ten export countries of blood product for therapeutic uses (US$)

Source: Business Monitor International (2010) based on UN Comtrade, BMI Database.

Table 7.2 Balance of pharmaceutical trade, 1995–2020 (thousand US$)

Year	Raw material	Antisera and vaccines	Semi-finished medicaments	Retail medicaments	Total
1995	–765	29734	–655	–11135	17179
1996	–5695	34382	–1418	–7628	19640
1997	–5071	41200	–125	–3725	32278
1998	–8251	18965	143	–15552	–4695
1999	–4510	12376	4690	–4827	7728
2000	–6648	15975	4900	–6527	7700
2001	–6820	16109	626	–9029	887
2002	–7405	23654	1070	–5820	11499
2003	–7979	25475	841	–306	18031
2004	–10782	15333	1392	–8012	–2069
2005	–6926	16336	482	–22761	–12869
2006	6761	21524	–654	–25636	1995
2007	36127	19384	–420	–21880	33212
2008	–21723	2960	–1508	–25978	–46249
2009	18894	10263	–1276	176013	203895
2010	30606	21505	–824	150512	201878
2014	–	–	–	–	425190
2015	–	–	–	–	450060
2016	–	–	–	–	474510
2017	–	–	–	–	499040
2018	–	–	–	–	524170
2019	–	–	–	–	550220
2020	–	–	–	–	577580

Source: Espicom Business Intelligence (2011) based on data from the UN Comtrade.
Data from 2014–20 provided by BMI (2016). 2016–2020 figures are BMI's estimates based on Cuba's National Bureau of Statistics (Oficina Nacional de Estadísticas, ONE), UN Comtrade and BMI.

Significant is the fact that vaccines show positive balances in all the years, showing the potential reached by the industry during the period. In 2010, the surplus amounted to $US201.9 million, of which $US150.6 million was accountable to retail medicaments. Raw materials, antisera and vaccines recorded surpluses of $30.6 million US and $21.5 million US. The surplus in retail medicaments during 2009 and 2010 could be an outcome of the import substitution strategy initiated by the government during the 1990s.

It should be pointed out that the data offered by Espicom are reverse data (see Annex 5.9). As Cuba does not offer disaggregated data in relation to the pharmaceutical industry, data was obtained by looking at other countries' imports from Cuba, which give an indication of how much activity is taking place, but, as the Espicom report acknowledges, tends to underestimate the level of exports.

For example, a look at the figures of 2010, shows that the aggregated export figure given by the Cuban National Statistics Office ($US491,489)[31] is higher than the one obtained by Espicom ($US277,753). When looking at the trade balance figures of the year 2008, Espicom obtained a negative figure, while the figures of the Cuban Statistical office reflect a positive figure.

The point is that the numbers could be even better than the ones reflected by this report. In fact, the above-mentioned article in *Scientific American Worldview* states that "Cuba's exports of biopharmaceutical products increased fivefold between 1995 and 2010"[32] and confirms that the "sector is now the country's second largest export earner after nickel."

However, even if we do not possess detailed statistics on the performance of Cuban biotechnology, it is at least reasonable to assume, taking into account the above-mentioned, that this industry is going to deliver cost-effective products to the national health system when compared to other countries of similar and even higher income groups.

7.2.3 Innovative outcomes of the industry

At the same time, the picture becomes more intriguing when we acknowledge that several of the drugs produced and exported at lower cost by Cuba are not just generics but include a significant number of innovative drugs and vaccines. The evidence arises not only from the excellent results obtained by introducing these products into the domestic market, but also from internationally acknowledged bodies such as the WIPO Award schemes, of which Cuba makes systematic use as a means of giving public recognition to its creators and promoting the importance of innovation. This is a yearly award conceded by the United Nation's World intellectual property organization to the best innovations worldwide (WIPO awards). In this work, and for the sake of the argument being made here, we will only refer to the awards given in the field of health biotechnology and other medical technologies.

For instance, Cuba was (until 2013) the only country in the world that had come up with an effective vaccine against meningitis B. The product was developed by the Finlay Institute, which is an organization dedicated to vaccine research and production. It is being commercialized by the company Vacunas Finlay, the commercial arm of the Institute. This vaccine (VAMENGOC-BC®)[33] was awarded in 1989 with the WIPO's Gold Medal.[34] To date, more than 55 million vaccine doses have been administered in Cuba and 15 other countries, primarily in Latin America and the Caribbean. The product has also been patented in the European Union and in the US.[35]

PPG, polycosanol, is a pharmaceutical derived from sugarcane wax used to reduce patient morbidity and mortality due to atherosclerotic cardiovascular disease.[36] The product was developed by the National Center for Scientific Research (CNIC in Spanish), considered an incubator company within the industry,[37] and is being commercialized by Laboratios DALMER S.A., the commercial arm of CNIC. The product won a WIPO Gold Medal in 1996.[38]

Also important is the world's first synthetic vaccine (Quimi-Hib) against Haemophilus influenzae type b (or Hib). This particular bacterium causes nearly 50 percent of all infections, some of which lead to deafness and mental retardation, in children under the age of five worldwide.[39] The product was developed by the Laboratory of Synthetic Antigens,[40] a small lab which belongs to the faculty of Chemistry of the University of Havana, in close cooperation with several Cuban biotech organizations and the University of Ottawa in Canada.

According to a Chemical and Engineering News report,[41] this is the first commercial vaccine made from a synthetic carbohydrate, which is said to be cheaper than those based on natural carbohydrates. It makes it possible to envision a new generation of carbohydrate-based vaccines.[42] The product won the WIPO Gold Medal Award in 2005 and the same year was given the Agilent Technologies Foundation Health Award (Tech Award), awarded since the year 2000 by Technical Museum of San Jose, California.[43] Cuba is saving $2.5 million US yearly with this product.

The Cuban biopharma industry has also developed Surfacen, which is used to treat infant respiratory distress syndrome, a frequent cause of death in premature babies. The product was developed by the National Center for Animal and Plant Health (CENSA) and won the Silver Medal at the 26th International Fair of Inventions Geneva in 1998 and the Gold medal for best invention in the 2007 WIPO awards. This medicine allows the country to save $3 million US yearly. Before that, a foreign medicine would be imported and only employed in the most critical cases. Additionally, it had to be obtained at great expense in other countries due to the US embargo on the island. Other awards include a kit for quick diagnosis of vaginitis, which received the Bronze Medal at 27th International Fair of Inventions Geneva in 1999.

For another example, Heberprot-P is a novel and unique Cuban biomedicine for treating diabetic feet developed by the Center for Genetic Engineering and Biotechnology (CIGB). Administered locally into chronic wounds, the product reduces the risk of amputation in diabetic foot ulcer patients, as it accelerates healing with human recombinant epithermal growth factor (hr-EGF). The product was awarded with the WIPO Award for Best Young Inventor and a WIPO Gold Medal at the International Inventions Fair in April of 2011.[44] Heberprot-P is already used to treat over 20,000 patients in Cuba and other nations. It has been granted patents in 15 other countries, including the USA, China and Australia, and is in clinical trials for use in others.

Other innovative products include Nimotuzumab, which was developed by the Center of Molecular Immunology (CIM). It targets epidermal growth factor receptors, and is aimed at various epithelial cancer types, including non-small cell lung, glioma, oesophageal, brain metastasis, colorectal, pancreatic, prostate, cervical and breast cancers. The product is being commercialized by CIMAB, the commercial arm of CIM (Havana), and its partner YM BioSciences (Mississauga, Canada).[45] A more recent Cuban innovation is CimaVax-EGF, which was officially released for commercial use in September 2011 and is the world's first lung cancer vaccine. While current treatments may improve the survival rate when the cancer is caught in its early stages, the five-year survival rate for late-stage lung cancer can be less than 1 percent. The vaccine, called

CimaVax-EGF, has also been developed by the CIM and is intended for patients with lung cancer in stages three and four who have shown no positive response to other kinds of treatment, such as chemotherapy and radiotherapy. Although the vaccine doesn't cure the disease, it might turn the cancer into a manageable, chronic disease by generating antibodies against the proteins which triggered the uncontrolled cell proliferation.[46]

More than 1000 lung cancer patients have already undergone trials in Cuba, where the vaccine is now distributed free of charge.[47] In September 2012 Malaysian biopharma company Bioven, which has a unit in Aberdeen, Scotland, announced the start of its pivotal Phase III trial of CimaVax-EGF in the United Kingdom.[48] The vaccine has been approved in several Latin American countries and is currently being tested in Canada, China and Malaysia. Plans are under way to undertake trials in other countries in Europe and Thailand.[49]

In 2015, as part of the ephemeral rapprochement policy carried out by the Obama's administration, a New York state trade mission to Cuba made it possible for CIM and the New York-based Roswell Park Cancer Institute to sign a historical agreement that will allow the vaccine to undergo clinical trials in the United States. It remains to be seen whether the current Trump's administration wish the deal to continue. Still, even within that sort of uncertainty, in September 2018 the commercial subsidiaries of the two organizations decided to form the first US–Cuban biotech joint venture. Innovative Immunotherapy Alliance, S.A. will operate in the Cuba's newly created Mariel Special Development Zone in order to carry out research, development and marketing of CimaVax-EGF and other three innovative Cuban immunotherapies.[50] Despite of what might happen in the future with this project, it has established a milestone in the rocky relations between both countries and shown the international prestige gained by the Cuban biotech industry.

A recent innovative product is Racotumomab (Vaxira); which is CIM's second lung cancer vaccine.[51] Clinical trials carried out on some 1700 patients have shown that 24 percent of late-stage lung cancer sufferers lived for two years with Racotumomab, whereas the figure was only 8 percent on chemotherapy and radiotherapy. Phase III trials are continuing in seven countries and the drug is expected to be marketed in 25 countries. The product is currently commercialized together with an Argentinean company.[52]

Last but not least, WIPO's officials have confirmed that both CIGB and CIM received the WIPO Award for Innovative Enterprises in 2012.[53] That provides further proof of the innovative potential of Cuba's life sciences industry.

7.3 The international industry: The need for organizational integration

In the previous section it was shown that while we cannot compare disaggregated R&D investments or yearly revenues in the case of Cuban biotech, we know, however, that its capacity meets more than 60 percent of domestic demand (including a significant number of innovative, world unique products). This element has contributed to substantially reduce Cuba's reliance on pharmaceutical imports and; consequently, helped to maintain country's health standards comparable to those of high income countries at a much lower cost. In addition, highly qualified officials of the industry assure that Cuban biotech works with positive cash flow,[54] which, if true, would be a privilege within the biopharma industry.

The last assertion can sound far-fetched at first glance, but taking a closer look at the predominant business model in the worldwide industry, we can at least advance some plausible explanations for this phenomenon (see below Section 7.3.1). It could be said, for instance, that most of the decision makers in the worldwide industry (US, EU-15) have not been paying much attention to the "voice of the industry." From a sectoral perspective, the biopharmaceutical business presents some relevant features, which also happen to be its most conspicuous organizational challenges. These features can be captured in two elements: Persistent uncertainty and complex knowledge structures (Pisano 2006; McKelvey et al. 2004).

To develop an innovative drug takes years, heavy amounts of R&D, and has a significant chance of failure. As Pisano (2006) states, biopharmaceutical products are "components in a complex system" (p. 42), which is a sign of the challenges faced by R&D in this industry. The process of discovering and developing a drug has four major phases: Target identification and validation[55], Lead identification and optimization,[56] Preclinical phase,[57] Human clinical trials (1, 2, 3)[58] and Regulatory approval[59] (Pisano 2006, pp. 45–52).

Given the lack of causal knowledge in many areas of biomedicine and the absence of high-fidelity testing models,[60] drug development remains a highly "iterative and inductive process" with significant levels of uncertainty involved in (ibid., pp. 53–9). One of the implications is that this process requires the integration of knowledge arising from many different fields and business areas, which raises significant challenges in terms of both the financing and the organizational mechanisms to manage and reward risk taking; i.e. institutional arrangement to assure return from intellectual property, scope of the contractual arrangements (e.g., licensing), etc.

The above-mentioned has, in turn, implications for the innovation strategies and business models employed by the industry. For instance, the question of whether vertical integration or alliances fit better with the need of assuring both that information flows across organizational boundaries; and that specialists in different fields cooperate. But also the question of what mechanism is most appropriate to improve the process of organizational learning in the long term, precisely in an industry with high rates of failure, plays an important role in this context.

The demonstration that these challenges remain lies in the fact that, across the 35 years of existence of modern biotechnology, the overall cash flow of the industry has been negative.[61] Even worse, the innovation rate in the industry remains very low in relation to the amount of resources invested (E&Y 2011). Over its more than thirty of existence the biopharmaceutical industry has generated some 30 blockbusters (defined as at least $1 billion in sales in any one year), which reflects the relatively low overall returns in terms of drug development in relation to the huge amount of funds that have been invested in the industry (Lazonick and Mazzucato 2012, p. 15). The fact that small specialized biotech firms are exclusively licensing their government-funded discoveries and that most stakeholders of the industry are not being properly rewarded in relation to both the risk incurred and the amount of resources invested or that most investments are being allocated in marketing and me-too drugs on the one side and on product-less companies and stock- buyback on the other, raise important questions on the sustainability of the current set of institutional incentives in the industry.

Evidence arising from everywhere repeatedly and strongly suggests that the predominant worldwide business model is actually working against the tempo needed by the technological regime of the industry. This evidence ranges from industry reports (Ernst & Young 2008, 2009, 2010, 2011, 2012) through academics (e.g. Light et al. 2011; Light and Warburton 2011; Lazonick 2008, 2011; Lazonick and Tulum 2011; Pisano 2006; for papers exclusively on patenting issues see Bessen and Maskin 2000; Boldrin and Levine 2008; Clark et al. 2001; Shapiro 2004; Marengo et al. 2009; Cohen et al. 2000), to politicians.[62] But let us take a closer look at both history and current form of the biotech business model.

7.3.1 Business models of the biopharmaceutical industry: A story of wasteful strategies

The pharmaceutical industry has followed a vertically integrated business model for a long time.[63] However, the emergence of biotechnology[64] has made the drug business more complex due to the introduction of both a new set of participants and a new sectoral logic.[65] In the early 1980s the vertical integrated model became the blueprint for the first wave of biotech companies,[66] which came to be known as FIPCO model (fully integrated pharmaceutical company). This first generation of integrated startups was initially expected to compete on equal terms with pharmaceutical companies. However, investors' enthusiasm rapidly dried up when they realized that biotechnology was far from providing a low-risk approach to drug development. Companies of subsequent business models (e.g. technology-platform), abandoned vertical integration and became dependent on licensing their technologies to big pharmaceutical companies (R&D monetization). Consequently, today's differentiation between pharma and biotech has become fuzzy.

R&D monetizing strategies consist of the commercial exploitation of intellectual property; often in form of exclusive licenses agreements and/or strategic alliances. An intellectual property license is a contract by which permission is given by the licensor to the licensee to exploit the licensor's intellectual property.[67] In the pharmaceutical sector, most intellectual property licenses are granted on an exclusive basis, which means the right to exclude others (including the licensor[68]) from exploiting the intellectual property (Kesselheim 2010). A strategic alliance is a relationship where two parties contribute their different but complementary resources and capabilities to achieve a common objective.[69]

A strategic alliance will almost invariably involve a license. However, while a license is fundamentally a passive relationship in the sense that the licensor, having granted the license, is not required to do anything else, the granting of a license by one alliance partner to the other is likely to be only one of the contributions that one alliance partner makes to the alliance. Strategic alliances in the pharmaceutical sector will generally fall into one of two categories: Co-Development and Co-Marketing Agreements. In the biopharmaceutical sector the financial terms of both license and alliances are usually a combination of (1) up front payments, which are paid upon the signing of the contract (2) milestone payments, which are paid as particular milestones along the development, clinical and regulatory pathway are reached, and (3) royalties, once there is a product in the marketplace.[70]

These strategies found their momentum in 1980 when the Bay-Dole Act allowed federal funded research to be patented in the US.[71] The introduction of this Act served as an incentive for small specialized biotech firms, mostly stemming from universities, small public labs, etc., to patent their discoveries and to license them to big pharma companies after the proof of concept (phase II) was established. Big pharma companies, which have been finding it more difficult to develop innovative drugs[72] then take charge of large-scale phase III,[73] regulatory approval, distribution and marketing, and small biotechs receive royalties in exchange.

After exclusive marketing rights expire, copies (generic drugs) enter the market, and the price usually falls to as little as 20 percent of what it was. In order to extend this exclusivity, the Hatch-Waxman Act was enacted in 1984,[74] which provided longer and more frequent extensions for drug patents. Until 1984 US patent legislation had treated medical discoveries in the same way as other innovations, but the introduction of this law represented a real boost to the outsourcing strategy mentioned above. The main reason for this is that it allows pharmaceutical companies to focus on sales and marketing, while letting smaller firms to develop product for existing markets and existing treatment modalities.

According to Pisano (2006 pp. 176–8) this model has proven commercially successful (in the short term) for less novel products or me-too drugs. The development of these drugs require less investment in specialized downstream assets; i.e. clinical, marketing and distribution infrastructure, and they can be differentiated in the market through advertising. For instance, "although Pfizer lost market exclusivity for atorvastatin, venlafaxine, and other major sellers in 2011, revenues remained steady compared with 2010, and net income rose 21 percent" (Light and Lexchin 2012, p. 2). From 1960 to 1980, prescription drug sales were fairly static as a percent of US gross domestic product, but from 1980 to 2000, they tripled.[75] From the perspective of an established pharmaceutical company, it makes sense to focus most research on extending or replacing existing best-selling drugs, in order to expand its patent protection and to avoid competing with generics. However, broader and longer patents of minor variations of existing drugs forces pharmaceutical companies to waste precious resources for no good social reason.[76] The current ratio of basic research to marketing in 2012 was 1: 19 (ibid.).

Likewise, it could make sense from the point of view of a specialized small company to position itself into a small segment of the industry value-chain and to enter into strategic alliances with larger pharmaceutical companies. This became regular practice in the 1990s, when new technological advances related to the Human Genome Project created a new stream of biotech specialized entrepreneurs more focused on tool based/technology platform model.[77] They were supposedly to be able to generate faster revenues than the FIPCO model through royalties, milestone payments, licensing and services fees or subscriptions.

However, in practice, the typical contract duration for R&D alliances with established pharmaceutical firms is around four years, which is three times shorter than the typical product development cycle (Pisano 2006, 179). Companies under pressure from quarterly reports have difficulty justifying long searches for breakthrough drugs to investors (Light and Warburton 2011). Alliances deals are usually employed as a tool to signal good prospects to potential investors rather than to build long-term oriented collaboration. Indeed, the persistent low R&D productivity of the industry is proving that deals alone do not create value. More important is how the partnership uses the capital it raises and how well it creates value from its activities. Unfortunately, since the 1980s, companies have always found themselves to be more embedded in an institutional environment, where stock market valuation[78] plays the crucial role in the business model of the industry.

When the start-up does an IPO[79] the big pharmaceutical partner can get a return to its R&D investment by cashing in the equity stake it has as part of the R&D contract. Deals are focused on meeting specific short-term milestones in order to fulfil quarterly expectations. To fail meeting a milestone could mean the termination of the alliance. This kind of partnership management shows little commitment beyond a single project, which prevents partners from taking innovation-boosting, entrepreneurial risks, e.g. investing in specialized assets, learning jointly or sharing proprietary information.

In this context, the true commercial value for technology platform companies, universities, public research organizations and overall R&D entities resides in the ability to generate proprietary knowledge and to protect it via patents. These patents are exclusively licensed to existing firms or start-ups that try their luck with venture capitalist investors.[80] But the ability to do an IPO, even without a product, is the major inducement for venture capitals to fund the biotech industry, since it does not have to wait until revenues are generated from a product to get returns on its investments (Lazonick and Tulum 2011). Venture capitalists have a time frame of about three years (Pisano 2006, pp. 139,

155), while the product development time in the biotechnology industry is much longer.

The reason for this time-frame is that closed-end funds are raised from institutional investors for a ten-year period,[81] and the VCs are then under pressure to have the funds invested and return to the institutional investors within this time-frame. For example, during the period 1991–2004, 88 percent of biotechnology companies were making IPOs, but only 20 percent had any product on the market).The vast majority were still in pre-clinical and discovery phases (ibid., p. 143).This is highly problematic role of venture capitals, because it runs in opposite direction of what long-term product innovation need, especially in the biopharma industry. No wonder that the financial crisis started in 2008[82] significantly lowered prospects of returns from IPOs and almost erased venture capitals from the funding menu of the biopharmaceutical companies worldwide (E&Y 2011 and 2012).

Similar to the FIPCO companies, specialized firms raised quick expectations among stock and VC investors, and shortly thereafter, skepticism and disappointment.[83] In fact, platform technology companies such as Millennium and Celera vertically integrated into drug R&D and began to develop their own products. In this way, they adopted the same model of the first generation of entrants of the previous two decades. However, in actual fact, the map of the industry continues to be determined by the proliferation of a huge number of specialized small "expertise islands," which have been proved to be inadequate from both industry[84] and economy points of view.[85]

It is hard to overemphasize that this model has clearly proven counterproductive for more innovative drugs. One of the most important reasons being that the tacit nature of the knowledge being created in the industry and the extreme complexity and complementary character of the discovery process within the industry, makes it almost impossible for companies without integrated in-house (or long-term collaboration) capabilities to grow into a sustainable scale. The strong interdependence between a target (particularly if novel), the molecule's structure and its physical properties, the dosage form, the manufacturing/distribution process, the design of appropriate clinical trials and the patient population play a crucial role in the performance of a product. It is virtually impossible to isolate one component without considering the implication for the other elements.

In addition, the absence of codified standards platform (like in the semiconductor or software industry) does not simply allow a problem to be easily broken into a set of relative independent modules (the auto industry is a good example of modularity) (Pisano 2006, pp. 149–52).This is maybe one of the reasons why positive performance in the industry has been concentrated in few vertically integrated or FIPCO companies (Amgen,[86] Genentech,[87] Genzyme, Biogen,[88] Chiron,[89] Biovail etc.) (ibid., p. 116). In 2004 Amgen and Genentech accounted for more than the 53 percent of the cash generated by the sector (ibid., p. 115).

In this industry vertical integration has reduced the risk of operating under a regime of radical uncertainty, difficult-to-transfer tacit knowledge, specialized assets and unclear intellectual property issues. Likewise, it has allowed the rapid diffusion of knowledge and information; and has contributed to long-term cumulative learning. Indeed, as observed in Chapter 4 (Section 4.9), instead of looking at (downstream or upstream) integration only as way to monopolistic control (neoclassic vision) or as an optimal response to market failure (transaction cost theory) one should analyze the roles of horizontal and vertical relations among enterprises within a particular industry by promoting collective and cumulative learning.

However, it is important to point out that such an organizational integration requires firms to develop internal capabilities to integrate the complex pieces of the biopharmaceutical R&D; and this is not an automatic process. Vertical integrated firms may (and have) become containers of islands of expertise that operate isolated from each other. In addition, vertical integration in the bio-tech world makes it more difficult to pursue diversified R&D portfolio strategies, given the huge amount of investment required to fund downstream assets (Pisano 2006, p. 172). In order to hedge (but by no way eliminate) this risk, vertical integrated firms need to have at disposal a huge network of specialized collaborators (suppliers, distributors, subcontractors) and; most important, a committed source of funding that allow them to engage in the complex and uncertain process of cumulative search and experimentation that innovation entail, until they are able to generate higher quality, lower cost products. That is the kind of commitment shown by government agencies such as the US-National Institutes of Health (NIH).

7.3.2 NFOs as foundation of the biopharmaceutical industry

In fact, a good reason for FIPCO's good performance is to be found in the financial and institutional support provided by government-based NFOs. Indeed, unlike venture capital and stock market investments, which have fluctuated widely from year to year, funding provided by the NIH increased in nominal terms in every single year from 1970 to 2008, except for a small decline in 2006 (Lazonick and Tulum 2011). Since its inception in 1938 through 2012, NIH provided $840 billion in 2012 dollars to fund the knowledge base of the health care industry, with more than half of this funding since 1998. Between 1998 and 2003 the NIH budget doubled, increasing by 14.7 percent per year.[90] The annual average budget between 2009 and 2012 was of $31 billion, which is twice as much as in the early 1990s and three times in the mid-80s.

Since 1976, the year Genentech was founded as the first biotech company in life sciences, the NIH has funded approximately $726 billion[91] (in 2012 dollars). Through the NIH, the US government has long been the nation's (and the world's) most important investor in knowledge creation in the medical fields (see Lazonick and Tulum 2011). According to Mazzucato (2011), 75 percent of the new molecular entities (i.e. real innovative drugs) of the

American biopharma trace their research not to private companies but to the NIH (p. 55). According to Light and Warburton (2011), 84.2 percent of all funds for discovering new medicines come from public sources. The point is that the huge knowledge base which biopharmaceutical business is dependent on comes from government funds. Without NIH funding venture capital and public equity funds would not have flowed into the biotech business.

Not to mention the fact that in 1983 the introduction of the Orphan Drug Act encouraged biopharmaceutical companies to invest in the development of drugs for "rare" diseases in exchange for generous tax credits for R&D as well as market exclusivity (seven years from the time that a drug is approved for commercial sale by the FDA) (Lazonick and Tulum 2011). This law represented an important incentive to biotech investment. Indeed, orphan drugs were the most important source of revenue for biopharma companies in the earlier phases of enterprise growth. For example, we could mention leading therapeutic drugs such as Amgen's Epogen and Neupogen (for anemia) Genentech's Rituxan (for rheumatoid arthritis), Genzyme's Cerezyme (for Gaucher's disease), or Biogen Idec's Avonex (for multiple sclerosis) (Lazonick and Tulum 2011). Note that this and other laws apply exclusively to products conceived and manufactured within the United States (e.g Bayh-Dole Act section 24), which make them a de facto instrument of strategic industrial and trade policy (Cimoli et al. in Cimoli et al., p. 512).

However, as already discussed, huge amounts of government resources are being misallocated, in the best of the cases, in drugs with scarce innovative potential to exorbitant prices and/or in speculative transactions because it is often only the presence of speculative stock markets on which non-state financiers of these businesses can "exit" from their investment in innovative enterprise. Therefore, it may be the case that to sustain the innovation process at the enterprise level government should take an active role in the governance of companies that make use of this support. To expect that a speculative stock market[92] will enable them to secure returns investments long before the actual products in which they have invested generate substantial sales may serve to undermine the extent of the investments that companies make in generate innovative products (Lazonick and Tulum 2011).

The fact that "the business of biotech is driven by specialization and fragmentation [...] that impede the information flow" and put firms under market pressure "to optimize short-term perception of value" is seen by Pisano (2006, p. 159) as the partial outcome of "exogenous, institutional conditions" (government regulations, functioning of capital market etc.). However, historical evidence shows that this institutional environment has not been as exogenous as suggested. For example, the creation of venture capitals and NASDAQ as ideal liquid market is inextricably linked to the rise of the microelectronic industry; and later became the foundation of the biotech business.[93] The US government created firms and financiers, which later lobbied in the US congress in order to shape the current institutional conditions.[94] Actually, we should talk more about a co-evolution between companies and environment or "set of socially-devised institutions" (Lazonick and Mazzucato 2012, p. 13). The fact that most biotech firms remain product-less firms has not only to do with the firm strategy, but more with the speculative nature of the system of biopharmaceutical finance. The government has provided the funds for the industry but it has failed to create upfront standards to encourage integration and collaboration (e.g. standardization of clinical trials). There has been therefore little incentive within the industry to promote organizational learning and to build long-term capabilities.

As a result, important synergies, i.e. network effects and economies of scope, arising from organizational integration have being systematically ignored by decision makers, which may have led to proverbially wasteful and inefficient business models. Having said this, it is not hard to imagine that, even when the industry continues to be a resource-demanding one in financial terms,[95] it is possible for a poor country like Cuba to develop an innovative biotech industry by spending much less, provided the existence of both a sector-consistent business model and the stakeholders financial commitment.

For example, one of the important *specificities* of Cuban biotech is the absence of ownership fragmentation of complementary assets. This fragmentation, basically expressed in the mutual blocking of property rights through exclusive licensing of patents, is one of the most pervasive, perverse and inefficient mechanisms of the prevailing model in the industry worldwide. It may have prevented economies of scope from being realized because the cost of a set of resources or skills can not be spread over more than one product or company (for a pioneering discussion see Panzar/Willig 1980, Teece 1981). Had the Cuban industry companies worked under this prevailing model, they would have not been able to provide affordable medicaments, nor perhaps to develop an industry at all.

No wonder many of the world leading pharmaceutical companies are moving to the so-called "pharma 3.0" model, which gives priority to health outcomes and advancing a more holistic approach to health care, something Ernst & Young (2012) calls "holistic open learning networks" (p. 1). As the report acknowledges, "[t]he underlying inefficiency and redundancy of drug development have become particularly incongruous in the current financing climate – an extravagance we can no longer afford" (ibid.). This is something Cuban policymakers and industry insiders recognized from a long time ago. In fact, the Cuban biopharmaceutical industry can be said to be an early forerunner of this model.

In the following section the argument will be advanced that *government-based non-firm entities* are the most important agents of integration within the Cuban industry. They did not only finance the innovation process, but they also allowed the creation of a spin-off business model by serving as research incubator for most of the companies of the industry. Much more importantly for the sake of the argument being made here, *they have exerted a crucial brokering function by allowing open flows of knowledge and resources across the boundaries of otherwise competing companies. This connecting role demands the continuous creation of standard interfaces and protocols such as regulatory frameworks and other shared platforms; in order to encourage a less costly, long-term collaboration.*

This last element has been crucial when linking heterogeneous and complementary actors of the network, which has made it possible for small specialized firms to have a sustainable existence along with the core companies of the industry. This allows the system, in turn, to simultaneously profit from the advantages of the functional hierarchy provided by the vertical integration and the flexibility of the modular production system (*see below In-house modularity*).

7.4 Organizational analysis of the Cuban biopharmaceutical industry

7.4.1 NFOs in the Cuban biotech

The choice of non-firm organizations was made precisely because of their role within the Cuban economy. The organizational framework of the country is distinguished by the predominance (in some times absolute and overwhelming) of government-based non-firm organizations (ministries, associations, government bodies etc.) that have provided the most important component in Cuba's predominant non-market forms of allocation.

The Cuban biotechnology industry has not been an exception, but actually the confirmation of the rule. However, this industry has managed to show more superior outcomes than the rest of the Cuban industries.[96] This raises several questions: What did the government do right this time? What kinds of institutions are supporting this industry? How could a country like Cuba be able to develop an internationally competitive biotechnology industry? Are we talking about an exceptional case? What role do country-specific institutional innovations play in the process of technological change? *And most importantly, did government's non-firm organizations play a role here?* These are the kinds of questions that motivate this analysis.

There is almost universal consensus among Cuban scholars and practitioners on the fact that the most relevant underlying catalyst of this success is the high degree of integration between research organizations, universities, the health system and the governmental regulatory authorities. This kind of integration has been consciously fostered by the government since the very beginning of the industry; precisely pursuing the aim of ensuring organizational learning and social efficiency.[97] Of course, that is not to say that they knew exactly what they were doing; or the outcomes of their actions. Actually, innovation involves a complex process of cumulative search and experimentation in the presence of uncertainty. Indeed, many of the governmental decisions were a result of past experiences and mistakes, the most resounding being the failure of the electronic industry in Cuba. However, even in this case, government's ability to strategically allocate its resources allowed this failure to be (at least partially) compensated by redirecting these technologies into another successful branch within the biotech industry (see below Section 7.4.5).

It could be theorized that this process has not only created *social efficiency* in that it has activated cost-reducing mechanisms through networking effects and economies of scale and scope, but also cost-effective innovation-effects through user-innovation diffusion. "If user-innovators do not somehow also diffuse what they have done, multiple users with very similar needs will have to independently develop very similar innovations—a poor use of resources from the viewpoint of social welfare" (von Hippel 2005, p. 9). But what kind of organization is activating all this collaboration and integration mechanisms?

In the particular case of Cuba, several ministries and government bodies have introduced research programs for the promotion of indigenous technological capabilities. In fact, the development and production of pharmaceuticals in general – and biotechnological products in particular – is without doubt the most successful example of the Cuban R&D programs.[98] Over a period of 20 years or so, the Cuban government invested around $1 billion US to develop the country's first and most important science node – that of West Havana – composed of a significant number of facilities related to biotechnology.

However, as discussed above (and also in Chapters 3 and 4), the existence of this phenomenon, is not limited to a strongly government-controlled (or centrally planned) economy, but is instead common to almost all catch-up and technology policy experiences – not only in the biotech but in other high-tech industries as well.[99] For example, as already mentioned, the role played by the US government's National Institutes of Health (NIH) in supporting the creation of American biotech; as well as its contribution to maintaining the US lead in this industry has been crucial (Lazonick and Tulum 2011; Mazzucato 2011; Light and Warburton 2011; Chang 2003). Countries such as Germany,[100] France[101] and the UK[102] are also known for their government-funded research sectors (Senker in McKelvey et al. 2004, pp. 112–13). In actual fact, successful examples of innovation show that state-funded labs and other non-firm organizations have been involved in the most risky phases of the research (Lazonick and Tulum 2011; Mazzucato 2011; Light and Warburton 2011).

If we take all this historical evidence seriously, a somewhat striking similarity arises from the fact that there is nothing special with the Cuban state investing and being strongly involved in biotechnology (or any other frontier technology) because everybody else has done it. However we still have different performances. Why does the American biotech industry perform differently than the European one? Why has the Cuban biotech industry achieved a pretty interesting pipeline and several innovative (and much more affordable) products while investing less than other biotech industries in both the developed and the developing world as well? As already pointed out, we should not assume a linear link between R&D investment and innovation and economic development. The difference might rather be found in the strategy and in the specific institutional-organizational setting, i.e. which institution or organization carries out what function.

Policies following sectoral development have generally been dependent on the particularity of the underlying institutional settings. Therefore, to be able to advance reasonable policy measures, it is necessary to know the specific institutions and type of organizations that shape an innovation system. But, at the same time, it is necessary to acknowledge that the aim has always been that of activating sector-specific mechanisms. Sector specificity is determined by the predominant technological regime that embodies the developmental function within the industry; i.e. learning requirements of the industry, type of technology, product cycle, markets access, etc. In other words, from a cross-country point of view, what varies is the institutional and organizational form that carries out the *developmental function, not the function itself.* Usually, an organization carries out more than one function simultaneously, as will be seen below.

7.4.2 Cuban biotechnology: A story of functional integration

The Cuban biotechnology industry has a huge cross-sectoral institutional structure, whose affiliates are parts of different ministries. Its beginnings are to be found in the early 1980s. By the end of the 1970s Cuba had developed a well-integrated structure comprising higher education, biomedical science and the public health system. Strong investments in medical schools and in a comprehensive health system were made around the same period. This created the pool of trained specialists who became the very base of 1981's Biological Front (Lopez et al. 2007).

The Biological Front was an interdisciplinary scientific consultative body created to coordinate the interests of the different ministries and institutions, which were related to the development of the biology and biotechnology industries. This sort of scientific think-tank was characterized by a flexible, cooperative and collective work style, and the main idea behind its creation was to put high-quality researchers from different organizations together, in order to fill the gap between science and economy. During previous decades, the government had been able to create a critical mass of scientific, as well as number of other important institutions. However, a strong linear conception of technological development had been followed, which led to weak linkages between R&D and technological development. Practice showed that investment in R&D alone does not automatically lead to innovation. Government active policy was needed, concretely from the Council of State.

The first obtained product was Interferon *(IFN- α)*, in 1981. Six Cuban scientists were sent to Helsinki in order to be trained in the production of interferon as developed by the Finnish Serum Institute.[103] After they had obtained their training, a special laboratory was set up in a small house in Havana to see if they could reproduce the Finnish results and produce IFN-α in Cuba. By the end of 1981 the first interferon had been created in Cuba. In 1982, the Center for Biological Research was created, in order to continue this work.

In 1992, after several pilot projects, the West Havana Biocluster was officially inaugurated. In subsequent periods, new facilities have been gradually included in the industry, contributing to its growing organizational complexity. At the beginning of the 2010s the industry was comprised of over 300 biotechnology centers, ranging from large, modern facilities to small, modestly equipped labs, conducting research and developing pharmaceuticals and vaccines. Foremost among these new centers is the complex of around 60 (at that time) organizations, many of them located at the West Havana Biocluster,[104] employing approximately 10,000 workers and more than 7000 scientists and engineers. Among these actors, there is a relatively small group of firms that represent the core (strategic network) of the industry (see next section).

The industry can therefore be described as a set of organizations that join their efforts, cooperate and integrate, whenever it is necessary to cover national public health demands and exports. That is, "as a network of agents interacting in a specific industrial area under a particular institutional infrastructure" (Carlsson et al. 2002, p. 237). This system could be considered part of a large Cuban Medicine/Public Health sectoral innovation system, that is, "a group of firms (organisations)[105] involved in developing and making a sector's products and in generating and utilizing a sector's technologies" (Breschi and Malerba 1997, p. 131).

The notion of links among the firms brings us to that which this study considers the most important aspect of the organizational integration within the Cuban biotech industry: sustained and institutionalized inter- and intra-organizational collaboration. The strategy behind the Cuban biotech categorically excludes competition between individual firms (contrary to that of Silicon Valley) and focuses on collaboration.[106] The process of linking complementary capabilities (so needed for drug development) has been actively encouraged through both explicit *in-house modularity* (see below In-house modularity) and different forms of *cross-organizational cooperation*. The almost absolute absence of competition between firms may sound strange to many free-market (but also less orthodox) economists, but the fact is that historically dynamic entrepreneurship has increasingly become collectivistic (Chang 2010; Hobday and Perini in Cimoli et al. 2009).

Cross-organizational cooperation

The *strategic network* of the West Havana Biocluster is formed by a small group of in-house modular firms (e.g. CIGB, CIM etc.) which were until recently under the control of a specific office within the Council of State, which allowed them close ties with the country's central decision-making powers. In March 2009 the responsibility for Cuban biotechnology was transferred from the Council of State to the Ministry of Science, Technology, and Environmental Issues (CITMA). This change was in response to a governmental reorganization process initiated in 2009. More recently, in December 2012, with Decree 307 the Council of Ministers approved the creation of BioCubaFarma (Grupo de las Industrias Biotecnológica y Faramcéuticas), which represents the most significant reorganization of the industry in two decades.

BioCubaFarma is a state holding that consists of 38 companies, including the commercial branches of all research institutions of the Scientific Pole in western Havana and all companies within the Quimefa Group (see below, Section 7.4.10). As a result, the Quimefa group has disappeared as an independent legal entity. The Quimefa Group was a state holding that represented the Cuban traditional pharmaceutical industry and was devoted to producing small molecules (chemically based drugs) in order to save the cost of importing them into the country. It mostly produced generics and it was (so to speak) the non-biological side of the Cuban medical technologies. The biotechnological complex of western Havana and Quimefa, which formally belonged to different ministries, were located in different places in Havana (or outside Havana). Quimefa was supposed to follow a completely different logic.

However, in reality, it worked closely with the biotechnological part of the industry located in west Havana. Therefore, this integration, albeit noteworthy from the legal point of view, does not actually represent a significant shift in the functional conception of the industry.[107] At the time this research was being conceived, these entities were still separate legal entities, but already completely interrelated. Therefore they were represented as such.

Nor does this merge lead to any change in our analytic point of view. In fact, it corroborates the logic being followed by the present study, namely, the fact that the Cuban biopharmaceutical industry has its very foundation in a huge integration effort. While developing the visual representation, we were trying to make sense of the separation between the part of the industry devoted to small molecules (chemically based products produced in the traditional pharmaceutical industry) and the biotechnological sector. However, in our representation it is impossible to acknowledge such a functional separation. Notice that, we always refer to the biopharmaceutical industry as one industry, precisely because it made little sense to establish that distinction between the Cuban pharmaceutical and the Cuban biotechnological production. In fact, for similar reasons, it is a distinction that is presently becoming obsolete worldwide (see E&Y 2012, pp. 2–6).

The fact that the visualization was made by following relational data reveals the importance of relying on this type of information to better understand the significance of openness and long-term mutual expectation in the innovation process. This confirms the fact that micro learning dynamics, economy-wide accumulation of technological capabilities and industrial development are inextricably related (Cimoli et al. 2009). Even before the changes took place in the industry, the visualization was, somewhat semiconsciously, showing what this merge has made obvious: they have worked all together for a long time. Therefore, even though Quimefa Group no longer exists as a separate organization, we will continue with the same representation, because it was carried out assuming that this holding was already part of a huge, indivisible industry. Additionally, this organization is part of the development history of the industry and its outcomes until the present day.

At the time its creation, the new BioCubaFarma was planning to double exports of the Cuban bio-pharmaceutical industry to more than $1 billion per year within five years. That would total $5.076 billion, a huge difference with respect to the previous five years, with total exports of $2.779 billion. At the same time, the new changes are still in the process of legal accommodation. Whether the industry has achieved this goal is hard to say given the lack of data, so a reasonable assessment of BioCubaFarma's performance will need to wait. However, it should not be an obstacle for business to continue given the fact that, as already mentioned, this step toward more integration is like the ripe fruit that had to fall: a logical consequence of earlier moves.

In current times the organization has been dealing with punctual shortages which have come to be as dramatic as 100 generic drugs absent from the list of essential medicines for the population during the 2016–2017 (in 2018 the total amount of essential medicines was of 761 products, of them 486 nationally produced). In 2019 there was a shortfall of circa 40 generic medicines. This happens basically, but not exclusively, in the chemical side of the industry (former Quimefa), which usually manufactures all the generic drugs, both for exports and domestic consumption. Most important causes of these deficits are said to be shortages of raw material, of which the industry imports 90 percent. This can be seen as a weakness, which needs to be properly assessed. Recent efforts of import substitution seem to move in that direction but it is too early to make a solid assessment. On the one hand, the ongoing sanitary events related to the Covid-19 pandemic have been dealt with effectively by re-adapting already existing products (employed in Cuba and abroad) and developing new ones. Simultaneously, however, the collapse of international value chains as a result of the current pandemic (2020) has contributed to aggravate the shortages of raw materials. In any case, and beyond the current juncture, the industry, under its new configuration, still shows innovative potential and favorable prospects. Nonetheless, after only 8 years, we cannot talk of any significant impact yet. Having made this important digression, we can continue with the story of the strategic network.

At the beginning of the section we observed that the *strategic network* of the West Havana Biocluster is formed by a small group of in-house modular firms (e.g. CIGB, CIM etc.). These firms do what industry officials call the closed cycle; and it refers to the in-house completion of all products' development phases (in our view, another word for vertical integration). However, even when each of these companies is equipped to cover the complete product development process, collaborative projects among them (and with other non-strategic facilities) are also frequent. Informal knowledge sharing between individual researchers and the usual lending and borrowing of technical equipment in joint R&D projects, and in integrated manufacturing lines are characteristic features of the Cuban industry. Again, cooperation, rather than competition, is the motto of Cuban biotechnology.

In order to set up the framework of the industry, frequent meetings are held by the representatives of the companies, the government and governmental regulatory agencies. This body can be defined as the *Strategic Decision Body* of the Cuban biotechnology Industry; whose existence enables clear definition of the general objectives (e.g. group diseases to be combated in the country, risky social groups, contracts with international organizations etc.) and orientation of investments around the population's current needs and/or export niches.

Each sale or joint venture contract will be approved by the Strategic Decision Body on a case by case basis (Lopez et al. 2006). This body is also regularly informed about specific research proposals and projects' progress. Again, it does not mean that companies lack decision-making power; actually, they have a high degree of autonomy. In order to function properly as a knowledge producer, the biotechnology industry requires large amounts of horizontal communication and operational freedom. However, the close contact between companies and government officials is crucial for the making of adequate strategic and tactical choices within the industry. Strategic network managers can be defined as administrators, facilitators, and generators of knowledge and data to be used as input for the decisions made by the Strategic Decision Body. This enables coherent confrontation of the inherent technological, market, and competitive uncertainties of the innovation process.

As can be inferred from the above-mentioned, the Strategic Decision Body has the major say in the funding decision of the industry. Managers have the task of generating financial returns, but they do not alone control the generated cash flow. Instead, the export revenues go to a Council of State's account, then after deliberation of the Strategic Decision Body, are redistributed to the centers to cover operational costs[108] and investments. The new business and production targets are carefully expressed in a comprehensive budget, which is also regularly controlled or corrected according to the information brought by the managers. Whenever specific expertise is needed, temporal allocation of human resources can also be carried out from a center to another, which in turn increases the perception of common interest, collaboration and consensual culture among the employees.

The Annexes show a visual representation of the network of the most important organizations (and their connections) that shaped the biopharmaceutical industry up to 2012 (p. 420-421). The color of the nodes shown in the visualization indicates the function of the organization represented, as well as the flows of resources, with link color and direction included. (Please note that while the figures appear in greyscale in print, the Annexes will be available to view in full color online at: www.routledge.com/9781138558984.)

Note that many of the related organizations are not necessarily in regional proximity (although most of them are) to each other.[109] As Orsenigo (in Braunerhjelm and Feldman 2006) (at least partially) concedes, knowledge flows are heavily structured by a variety of economic and social factors which in many instances do not have any clear geographical connotation. Although he acknowledges the relative importance of agglomerations, he concludes that they represent more the outcome of certain processes rather than the automatic effect of specifics preconditions and agglomeration factors (p. 217). Actors may be tied together closely in one relational network but be quite distant from one another in a different relational network.

Therefore it is functional integration, rather than regional integration, under analysis here. This study of the Cuban biotech industry focuses on 54 organizations, which have been proven, according to the collected data; to be *functionally* (in terms of social distance) related one another. Note, however, that we are intentionally omitting a lot of incidental data in order to focus on the most important relations from the point of view of the biopharmaceutical industry.

We will make some reference to these supplementary organizations in subsequent sections. However, we will mostly refer to organizations that are included in the network visualization, as most of them have been chosen by following the periodical list elaborated by the Cuban Drug Control Agency (CECMED) which covers the organizations authorized to carry out the kind of activities they do. In addition to the CECMED's data bank, the study has employed public data offered by the companies and non-firm organizations featured in the visualization, as well as personal interviews and written communication with officials and employees, etc.

7.4.3 The central organizations

The *red* nodes represent the central organizations, which are non-firm organizations related to regulation, administration and legislation. (The red nodes refer to a group of nodes represented in a figure that used to be within the text, but now has been placed in the Visualizations section of the Annexes (see p420 onwards. Please note that while the figures appear in greyscale in print, the Annexes will be available to view in full color online at: www. routledge.com/9781138558984.) Among these organizations, we can find the different ministries, the State Council and the regulation authorities of the national health system. Ministries such as Agriculture, Basic Industry (Ministry of Energy and Mines since November 2012), Informatics and Communications (Ministry of Communications since March 2013), Science and Technology (CITMA) and Public Health are displayed here. However this section focuses on two more decentralized organizations, whose functions provide them with a very central position in the Cuban biopharma eco-system: The National Regulatory Agency (CECMED) and the National Clinical Trials Coordinating Center (CENCEC).

These two organizations not only offer the kind of expertise that contributes to value creation, but also directly participate in the decision-making process that shapes the strategic allocation of the resources. More important, for the sake of the argument being made here, is their role by establishing standard interfaces between organizations (or between activities within an organization), which allows reducing assets specifically and easily engage in long-term collaboration and organizational learning. Standards such as uniform employment policies, shared platforms and process protocols can be considered as shared standards that facilitate communication as well as knowledge transfers between heterogeneous organizations.

Shared standards and protocols make the way easier for organizational integration in that they allow organizations to efficiently exchange with multiple partners by reducing enforcement, search and monitoring costs. They provide important incentives to pursue the advantages of flexibility in an industry with a high degree of supply and demand heterogeneity, as with biotechnology. These mechanisms are at play fundamentally because of the existence of regulatory organizations of the health system (CECMED and CENCEC), which, not surprisingly, are related to almost all the organizations. These two organizations are dependencies of the Ministry for Public Health (MINSAP).

A few words about the Cuban health system

Cuba's medical history is populated by significant contributions and scientists. For instance, in 1804, not much longer after Edward Jenner in 1796, Dr Tomas Romay helped to introduce and widespread the at the time most modern inoculation method against smallpox. During the second half of the nineteenth century several renowned medical doctors made contributions to the healthcare in the island. In 1894, only months after Emile Roux in France, and probably simultaneously or before than William Hallock in the United States, Dr. Juan Nicolás Dávalos Betancourt, known as the father of Cuban bacteriology, developed a method to obtain the anti-diphtheria vaccine in the island. Also great scientists such as Dr. Nicolás Guiteras Gener, father of Cuban parasitology and the great ophthalmologist Juan Santos Hernández are part of the Cuban medicine of the second half of nineteenth century and beyond.

In addition, names such as Carlos J. Finlay and Joaquín Albarrán, both of them nominated several times for the Nobel Prize, and many other distinguished names (the list is long), are known for their important innovations in medical sciences.[110] The first half of the twentieth century also witnessed the creation of important health institutions. In 1902, as the US-controlled Cuban republic was formally inaugurated, the new government appointed Diego Tamayo Figueredo, a distinguished physician and disciple of Louis Pasteur, as Home Secretary. This institution, which was charged with the task of overseeing the country's sanitary affairs, chose Dr. Finlay for the role of National Health Supervisor.

The world had already known about the genius of Dr. Finlay, who spent his whole career defending his theory about the mosquito *Aedes aegypti* as transmitting agent of yellow fever.[111] He also made important contributions to the organization of communal healthcare and to the integration of public healthcare institutions into the first world's health ministry in 1909. He, along with the abovementioned names, which also included Aristides Agramonte, Enrique Barnet, Juan Le Roy and others, belong to what is called Cuban Hygienist School of the early twentieth century.

As already mentioned in Chapter 5, during the first half of twentieth century, large public hospitals emerged in the country and provided free services, but, despite the personal efforts of some Cuban medical doctors, they were limited to major cities and were chronically underfunded prior to 1959. Mutual clinics were created by mutual societies, mostly of Spanish origin, and functioned within a cooperative framework. But it was required to be part of these communities in order to be eligible for high-quality medical services. We also mentioned that in the first half of the twentieth century, a significant network of private clinics flourished. They also provided high-quality services, but mostly worked on the profit principle, excluding the millions of people who could not afford to pay.

Until the public health system absorbed the last non-public clinics in 1970, the Cuban healthcare system, as it did before the revolution, consisted of three types of healthcare services: public provision, mutual clinics and private provision. The government's new measures included a unified regulatory framework for all levels of the system – which prior to the revolution had been painfully fragmented – along with a 15 percent price reduction for home-grown medical products and a 20 percent cut for imports (Baldarraín-Chaple 2005). The changes provoked a strong reaction from foreign companies that dominated the Cuban market, which until that moment had been free to set prices for their products without government regulation, as well as the laboratories, retailers and medical personnel linked to them. The clash led to many closures and other actions, creating a supply crisis that resulted in the nationalization of the industry in 1960.

The Cuban Public health system after the revolution will not be detailed here because it has already been extensively discussed elsewhere (see e.g. Baldarraín-Chaple 2005; Herrera 2005, Navarro 1972; Hadad 2005; Christensen 2003; Keck and Reed 2012; Cooper et al. 2006; De Vos 2009; De Vos et al. 2008a, 2008b; Campion and Morrissey 2013). However, it would be useful to point out that the Cuban health system is highly centralized in plan preparation but highly decentralized in plan implementation. It can be conceived of as a huge and very complex network of organizations, of which the biotechnology industry is part.

The need to analize public health from a complex system perspective, and its many practical and theoretical possibilities, has only begun to be acknowledged very recently (Rusoja et al. 2018). In fact, at the time the present research on the Cuban biotechnology started (2008) the modest, but steady, surge in publications that the subject has experienced during the last decade had not yet occurred. However, even when there is nothing near a consensus on this approach and even when its key conceptual tools are still in their very infancy, the growing recognition of the need of such a line of enquiry is already unquestionable (for a review on this issue see Rusoja et al. 2018; Rutter 2017; Carey et al. 2015; Jackson and Sambo 2020).

This research is precisely defending the point that the Cuban Biotechnology achievements could not be explainable without considering this industry being part of a broader socioeconomic development strategy, aimed primarily at finding cost-effective solutions to local health. It is the success in accomplishing this goal that has made it possible for Cuban companies to further capitalize their achievements into commercial opportunities by entering the global market as a low-cost producer of high quality products.

Cuban health ideology has been based on the fundamental principle that health protection and care is a right of all and a responsibility for the state. The Ministry of Public Health (MINSAP) controls the national health care system, which is universal and free for all Cubans resident on the island.[112] MINSAP is in charge of carrying out the government health policy, the general regulation of the medical sector and the conduct of medical research is divided into six vice-ministries and has a further 22 national directorates. At a local level, healthcare provision is the responsibility of provincial and municipal health directorates.

Another important element of the Cuban health policy is its commitment to preventive care, which has led to the creation of a comprehensive community programs, aimed directly at neighborhoods. During the 1960s, the revolutionary government pursued the first set of strategies to transform the country's health care structures when it established a system of integrated community clinics (polyclinics); and moved to train more health personnel. The polyclinic-based system aimed at universal coverage within territorially defined districts and was the first program of the current community-based health care model. Medical care priorities were changed to the point that all graduates were expected to promote human welfare and preventative medicine, but also were expected not to engage in private practice and to perform rural service for three years.

The early municipal polyclinic model (1960s) had showed lack of integration of health care activities across disciplines, persistence of curative over preventive priorities, lack of teaching and research opportunities in primary care, and inadequate coordination of polyclinic relations with hospitals and emergency room. As a result, the polyclinic model of primary health care was corrected and expanded during the 1970s. The system focus shifted at this phase from expressed morbidity to prevention, which contributed to reduce hospitalization and emergency room utilization; and therefore to reduce the use of more expensive services and facilities. Simultaneously, professors and medical residents increased their collaboration in polyclinic activities; thus promoting opportunities for teaching and research in primary care. To further develop the focus on preventive medicine, a new holistic approach encompassing evaluation of social factors and preventive health care strategies was introduced in the 1980s: the family doctor program.

Specifically, the family doctor program was officially created in 1984. The program is based in neighborhood clinics (*consultorios*) staffed with a physician and a nurse. They are responsible for a number of families in the geographic area surrounding their *consultorio* (about 1000 patients per physician in urban areas in 2013), and are more or less integrated into the community they serve. Cuba's 29 medical faculties (Cuba Health Statistics Yearbook, Anuario Estadistico de Salud 2019 in original Spanish), remain steadily focused on primary care, with family medicine required as the first residency for all physicians. This factor provides continuity for patients and makes it easier to advance disease prevention, particularly in the realm of non-communicable chronic diseases, Cuba's number one health problem (Reed 2008, see also Anuario Estadistico de Salud 2019, p. 31).

The family doctor networks play an important role by collecting community-based information about specific clinical and epidemiological patterns affecting each region. This allows the creation of comprehensive national records that help determine which health issues pose the greatest risk to society. Virtual infrastructures such as INFOMED[113] have contributed to the extension of the family doctor-and-nurse model of primary care, increased interdisciplinary integration of the activities of diverse health care actors, and emphasized continuous data collection, analysis, and dissemination throughout the system (Séror 2006). This information, in turn, contributes to better allocation of resources to deal with risk and channel the sector's creativity in ways that lead to more socially productive innovation. This is astoundingly similar to the patient rapprochement mechanisms included in the new holistic approach envisioned by the new business model Pharma 3.0 (see above Section 7.3).

In fact, as the 2012 report Beyond Borders points out, future talks in the industry will be about the

> need to engage with patients by identifying relevant populations [...], developing ongoing relationships with them and collecting their data with their informed consent. This has the potential to enable better outcomes through an increased focus on prevention and health management....
>
> (E&Y 2012, p. 6)

In turn, to have databases with comprehensive patient information would allow for appropriate individuals to "quickly and easily be enrolled once a suitable [clinical] trial comes along," making it "possible to substantially speed up clinical trial enrolment [and thus to save money]" (ibid.). Nothing could be closer to the approach employed by the Cuban health system since the 1980s. The commitment of the Cuban government towards prevention, integration and collaboration is nothing else than the expression of its financial constraints.

In the 1960s, the government acquired private local producers, and foreign producers reduced imports and closed their plants. The domestic industry was underdeveloped. Foreign subsidiaries controlled 50 percent of the market, importers accounted for a further 20 percent and local production was accountable for the remaining 30 percent (Espicom Business Intelligence 2011). In the 1970s, and in order to minimize the impact of the US blockade, the first investments were made in pharmaceutical production plants. These efforts were complemented by purchasing drugs in both Western and Eastern Europe.

Following the collapse of the Soviet Union, East European supplies as well as the hard currency to purchase drugs in Western Europe dried up. Cuba's public health financing experienced a dramatic reduction, from over $250 million a year in the late 1980s to $65 million in 1993, only rising slowly to around $160 million in late 1990s. As a consequence, imported pharmaceuticals represented around 52 percent of Cuba's public health expenditure. As a result, the government implemented a program for import substitution and domestic production of drugs, encompassing a total of 422 pharmaceuticals at a cost of $75 million.[114] At the same time, further investment continued to be made in health biotechnology.

However, the foundation of innovation is not only to be found in R&D investments alone (see Chapter 4). In the Cuban case, it has been more important the openness underlying the government strategy; namely the intentionality to integrate national research and innovation policy. That is, the ability to recognize the need to create standards tools (such as the above-mentioned INFOMED) that foster inter-organizational exchange of research and ideas. Indeed, visions such as Pharma 3.0; or the experience of the biopharmaceutical industry worldwide are telling us that integration efforts will not be successful if industry and health system continue to be seen as separate entities (Olson and Downey 2013). In this respect, as several authors point out, it needs to be emphasized that Cuban organizational innovations such as the family doctor program "represents the first international effort to provide family medicine universally [...] as part of an integrated national health system" (Eckstein 2003, p. 131).

The Cuban health system – its universal access and coverage, as well as statistical records – has provided a formidable backbone for research, enabling massive informed-consent participation in clinical trials of new medications and vaccines, as well as longitudinal studies on conditions such as chronic vascular diseases and cancer. It helps explain why massive vaccine campaigns can be carried out effectively and rapidly. The case of the vaccine against meningitis B, developed by the Finlay Institute, is an example of this (see below Finlay Institute). In fact, we argue that the integration of biotech and health system has been the foundation of the success of the government's long-term strategy. This strategy has, so far, created the best (maybe the only) example in Cuba of a sectoral system that has proved capable of assimilating the best technology, improving upon it; and organizing the linkages between science, technology and markets necessary to generate higher quality, lower cost products; and necessary for the exploitation of new technological trajectories.

Of course, there is no room for romanticizing here. The Cuban healthcare system is not a perfect system. Particularly in the last decade some critics have tried to raise issues such as material shortages and inefficiencies, authoritarian methods in the doctor–patient relationship, ideological bias of the system, etc. Without completely undermining all the critiques,[115] it needs to be pointed out that the objective of this research is not to criticize the Cuban health system. Instead, our main point is to highlight the good performance of the system in relation to the economic conditions of the country.

In this respect, it is clear that given factors such as the developing country condition of Cuba (in terms of basic infrastructure such as roads, housing, plumbing and sanitation), the additional shortages imposed by the American embargo and the starting material conditions[116] of the Cuban health system, the performance of the country's health system should have been far worse than it is. The evidence is found in many countries of the region, which, even with more GDP/per capita and better starting conditions do not perform necessarily better. That is what we do want to explain. In addition, most of the critics (not all of them) tend to show the same ideological bias they are intended to criticize.[117]

National Regulatory Agency (CECMED)

The task of any drug regulatory agency is overseeing and regulating the medicines market place in order to ensure that manufacturing and distribution are to be made in compliance with international standards (GMP,[118] GCP,[119] GLP[120]). The Cuban National Drug Regulatory Agency (CECMED) was created in 1989 by Resolution No. 73 of the Ministry for Public Health as the as a project of the Science and Technique division of this ministry; and was subsequently upgraded as the Cuban National Regulatory Authority. Its main purpose was to centralize and develop all the procedures in relation to the control of medicaments and diagnostic kits. Cuba's medication regulatory agency guarantees protection of the public health through a sanitary control and regulatory system, ensuring that drugs and diagnostics, imported or locally manufactured, are safe, effective and of acceptable quality.[121] CECMED is also responsible for approving the Clinical Trials and authorizing marketing, post-marketing and licensing activities.

The effectiveness of these factors allowed the pre-qualification of the Hepatitis B vaccine by the World Health Organization (WHO).[122] In fact, the prestige won by CECMED has allowed it to cooperate with the WHO, pre-qualifying products for the treatment of AIDS, malaria and tuberculosis. It has also directly contributed as expert force to develop the regulatory systems of several countries in Asia, Africa and Latin America (Casanueva 2007). The performance of CECMED and its compliance to international standards is also regularly evaluated for the WHO.

CECMED's most important regulatory functions include drug registration (marketing authorizations), renewal and variation of registered products; and the lot release for vaccines and biological products. It also comprises authorization, inspections and regulatory control of clinical trials; as well as regulatory inspections and granting of licenses in such areas as manufacturing, distribution, imports and exports. That is, CECMED has the power to provide or withdraw the operation license (in case of not meeting the required standards) of virtually all the organizations involved in core activities of the industry (manufacturing, trading, domestic distribution), which, by virtue of the characteristics of the Cuban industry, are themselves well connected to each other. This function makes it probably the most influential organization within the industry.

In addition, this influence allows CECMED to spread and obtain information quickly. The regulatory function of CECMED makes it imperative for this organization to be able to constantly transmit, evaluate and retransmit the requirements for manufacturing permissions, certifications and marketing. The faster good quality information can be spread, the faster and the more productive the rest of the system will function. Likewise, CECMED's multifunctional nature imposes the obligation to constantly identify staff qualification necessities; or to integrate new regulatory capabilities. For example; in 2011, the National Control Center for Medical Devices (CCEEM) was integrated into CECMED.

At the same time, and responding to the institutionalized cooperation ethos within the industry, CECMED works to integrate approaches with several of the most important companies such as the Molecular Immunology Center (CIM) and the Genetic Engineering and Biotechnology Center (CIGB), in close collaboration with CENCEC, to conduct clinical trials in compliance with commonly established criteria and procedures, and to speed the registration process of the products.

Another important factor shaping the performance of CECMED is its emphasis on post-marketing surveillance, including Adverse Events Following Immunization (AEFI). This function became a central objective of CECMED in the year 2000; and particularly after 2005, when a WHO assessment on the Institutional Development of CECMED was completed. However, the most important element here is the cooperation of CECMED with other organizations in order to improve its regulatory performance. For example, there is a National Coordinating Pharmacovigilance Unit that coordinates the National Monitoring System of adverse reactions suspicions produced by drugs.

In addition, the internal organization of CECMED was modified in 2005; in conformity with the benchmark revisions made by a WHO's capacity building program (together with other international regulatory bodies) in order to strengthen the performance of the national regulatory agencies across the world (Pérez and Sanchez 2008). The organizational changes carried out by CECMED included the creation of a national laboratory in charge of physical-chemical-microbiological and biological analysis, as well as the creation of specialized departments in such fields as pharmaceutical inspection (see Annex 5.7).

There is also the Quality Division of the former Quimefa (this division has been now integrated into the state holding BioCubaFarma), which oversees the quality of the national industry products. Both CECMED and this division maintain surveillance systems. Every month, the data is analyzed and cross referenced based on the product, batch, manufacturer, place of report, etc., and, this way, the two systems feedback themselves. A monthly meeting is also held to check the results of the systems. All this information is sent to the post-marketing system of CECMED. These work division and collaboration process have allowed minimizing the amount of risky products in the domestic markets. It also gives strong credibility to the Cuban products overseas.

The lack of cooperation and compatibility in the surveillance process is one of the problems faced by the industry worldwide. Consider the example of the US Food and Drug Administration (FDA), by far the best known, and one of the most prestigious drug regulation agencies in the world. According to Light (ed.) (2010), the ability to assess the safety of products after marketing approval of this organization has been increasingly compromised as a result of the deregulation and the influence of pharmaceutical companies.

Despite the new safety initiatives of 2007,[123] serious problems remain. For instance, many agency information databases are incompatible with each other; and it has, as a result of the chronic under-funding,[124] too few inspectors to monitor the quality of active ingredients (ibid., pp. 57–9). Additionally, drug safety has not been given its own organizational division. In fact, the control of side effects "still rests with the division that approved the drug." Many decisions are taken without consulting epidemiology safety specialists. At the same time the agency remains partially funded by the industry it regulates.[125]

All these elements have, according to Light (2010), seriously affected the autonomy of FDA and its ability to access rigorous post-marketing surveillances. In fact, prescription drugs have become the fourth-leading cause of death in the US.[126]

Likewise, lack of standardization of the new drug application data submitted to FDA has serious implications for FDA reviewers. The applications have extremely variable and unpredictable formats and content, which limits reviewers' ability to address in-depth questions and late-emerging issues in a timely manner. It also impedes timely safety analysis to inform risk evaluation and mitigation strategy decisions, and limits the ability to transition to more standardized benefit–risk assessments (Olson and Downey 2013). In fact, when referring to these limitations, Ron Fitzmartin, senior advisor in the Office of

Planning and Informatics at FDA's Center for Drug Evaluation and Research (CDER) recognizes that "[i]t is unbelievable that in 2012 we are still saying that" (ibid., p. 55).

National Clinical Trials Coordinating Center (CENCEC)

The National Coordinating Center of Clinical Trials (**CENCEC**) was created in 1991, and it is the first Clinical Research Organization (CRO) created in Latin America. Its main objective is designing and executing clinical trials of Cuban products requiring evaluation before entering national and international markets.

The fulfilment of these functions demands frequent review and adaptation of the CENCEC to international trends in contractual clinical trial research; in order to help the Cuban organization(s) to keep up to date. This needs to be done as quickly and effectively as possible; for that reason, this organization possesses a coordinated network of clinical trials at the national level, supported by a specialized staff in each of the provinces of the country for the conduction of these studies.

The structure of CENCEC's site network reflects the non-rivalry ethos of the industry and represents an important organizational innovation, together with the fact that no other country has a national network for clinical trials (Pascual et al. 2011). Also, it should be recalled that the usual scenario in the worldwide industry is that of CROs and academic medical centers competing head to head for the opportunity to enroll patients in clinical trials.

Corporate sponsors have been able to dictate the terms of participation in the trial and academic researchers may have little or no input into trial design, no access to the raw data, and limited participation in data interpretation terms (Davidov et al. 2001; Light 2010, p. 16). The competition for scarce trial sites and the desperate need for product differentiation as a result of shrinking pipelines (expressed in trials with too many endpoints) raise the expenses for recruiting trial sites,[127] which in turn leads to more clinical trial work being outsourced.[128] The fact that there are a great number of sites worldwide, but not all with the adequate requirements for safety and data collection, has raised concern over product quality.[129]

The peculiarity of the Cuban CRO (CENCEC) is that it works together with academic medical centers. CENCEC's National Clinical Trial Sites Network is composed of hospitals throughout the country. This Network has functional units in the country's medical universities, with more than 30 professionals who divide their time between academic responsibilities and leadership of clinical trials. These clinical studies are conducted using the services of teaching hospitals attached to the medical universities in each territory.

To enhance the Network's effectiveness, sub-centers have been set up in three provinces and coordinating groups in nine provinces, all methodologically subordinated to the CENCEC. Each is responsible for coordination, quality assurance and training of clinical research personnel in its jurisdiction. This relatively high centralization makes possible economies of scale in administration when carrying out the clinical trials and multi-center trials.

For the multi-center trials network be able to work properly, CENCEC provides centralized protocol guidelines of clinical trials (particularly for Phase III) that are to be followed in multi-center trials by clinical sites across the country. The Sites Network helps speed patient recruitment, product development and subsequent approval; but also contributes to researchers' knowledge and skills in conducting clinical trials.

CENCEC also has to work closely with the drug regulatory agency CECMED and at the same time with the sponsoring firms, in order to have the clinical trials approved. A company (sponsor) presents its pre-clinical information to CENCEC, in order to prepare the clinical trial for a given product. Then the CENCEC prepares, together with the interested sponsor, a technical report, which is sent to CECMED for approval.

CECMED (just as FDA in the US and EMA in Europe, or other Drug regulatory agencies do) evaluates, then determines, if the clinical trial project is in compliance with good clinical practice guidelines (GCP). If the report gets approved, the clinical trial can be carried out. However, in order to increase the probabilities for this to happen, and in contrast with the current international practice, the CENCEC combines the efforts of both sponsoring companies and CECMED to review and refine trials designs. Additionally, it provides both advice on preparation of clinical reports for submission to the drug regulatory agency and guidance on clinical product evaluation strategies. Indeed, the CENCEC acts as knowledge bridge between different organizations, as well as between them and the Drug Regulatory agency. The resulting data are put to disposition of other companies through the health-system-based electronic network.

These elements pose the two government-based NFOs among the most influential organizations within the industry. By virtue of their functions, these two government entities are associated with many types of knowledge and resources. Both count on specialized departments and workforces in constant contact with themselves and with the industry (domestic and abroad) in order to stay up to date with the latest technical and procedural information.

This in turn makes it possible for the industry to count on the most actualized regulations and operational standards, for an effective *organizational integration* (in form of intra-industry and inter-sectoral collaboration) to be able to take place. These two NFOs are at the core of the industrial policy followed by the government. As above noted, they are organizationally subordinated to the Ministry for Public Health, which has a priority status for the Cuban government.

The fact that Cuban regulators are fully government-funded may also explain the good functioning of the industry. Light and Lexchin (2012) propose that the EMA and other regulatory agencies should be fully financed "with public funds, rather than relying on industry generated user fees, to end industry's capture of its regulator" (p. 4). Contrary to the conventional notions, recent research shows that countries with more stringent regulation have actually contributed to a more innovative and competitive pharmaceutical industry. "This is because exacting regulatory requirements force companies to be more selective in the compounds that they aim to bring to market" (Munos 2009, p. 964). By making research more demanding, stringent regulatory requirements "promote the emergence of an industry that is research intensive, innovative, dominated by few companies and profitable" (ibid.).

The crucial role of regulators as catalyzers of innovation has also been acknowledged by Pharma 3.0. The most important feature of this holistic approach is the capacity of a diverse set of stakeholders to be open and learn by connecting diverse data sets that allow the creation of common pools of information. These networks could bring together genetic data from patients, claims data from payers, data on failed clinical trials from life sciences companies, insights from disease foundations etc. (E&Y 2012, p. 6).

However, the pooling from data raises the question about standards because the absence of standards undermines the ability to collectively analyze the shared information. It is in this point where it becomes apparent the need of engaging regulators in the making of regulatory regimes that allow different assets and insights to be gathered in real time through more flexible approaches. That means that stakeholders and regulators will need to work together in order be able to encourage new approaches to R&D and clinical trial design. Developing standards will play a crucial role in accelerating the creation of promising R&D tools (e.g. biomarkers and disease models) and can help make drug R&D to be more productive and efficient across the breadth of the ecosystem (ibid.). As discussed above, this is something CENCEC and CECMED have been doing for a long time.

However, "aligning interests in the development of data standards and the sharing of data is not easy" (Olson and Downey 2013, p. 45). The search for common interests "requires identifying common values and integrating them into the research enterprise." Communication and transparency can help identify and spread these common values while also building public trust. It is our contention that in this point Cuba's life sciences industry has developed a truly comparative advantage. We argue that the story of Cuban biopharmaceutical industry provides a remarkable example of how openness and integration can save significant time and cost. While the lack of information on the Cuban biotech prevent us to provide more accurate data, it would be impossible, without relying in integration, to explain how a country with such constrained resources can produce a huge number of affordable drugs to tackle diseases that run rampant in low- and middle-income countries. According to the WHO,[130] the industry has "more than 90 new products are currently [2013] being investigated in more than 60 clinical trials" in several countries.

7.4.4 Firms as research spin-offs

The beginnings of the Cuban biotech industry are found in the early 80s. However, the foundation was laid much earlier. Most Cuban biotechnology research centers emerged from already existing centers, as the Cuban state had been investing in scientific research since the 1960s. The main organization created then was the National Center for Scientific Research (CNIC) in July 1965. Visualization 1 (see Annexes) shows that CNIC has reciprocal linkages with all organizations of the strategic network. This research-production firm was originally a non-firm entity staffed by a small group of physicians that had graduated just a few years ago, who answered the government call to dedicate themselves to biomedical research. The institution was also staffed by chemists and engineers of different specialties.[131] Many of today's "brains" in the industry received their first scientific training in this organization.

Just as with KAIS in South Korea, the main goal of CNIC in its first years was to increase knowledge of "basic sciences" (mathematics, physics, chemistry, biology) of young medical graduates, and initiate them into research tasks. It was a postgraduate school complementing existing universities and colleges, producing the high-level scientists. To that effect, a series of courses and practices taught by Cuban and foreign professors was organized. After taking these courses, several young researchers won graduate scholarships to study in Western and Eastern European countries.[132] However, an important difference is that KAIS (just as KIST) was much more mission-oriented than CNIC. The Korean organization interacted since the beginning with the industry; while CNIC remained more rooted in basic science and had little contact with industry.

In a few years, and thanks to huge investment in research equipment, CNIC turned out to be the national "center of excellence" for chemical and biological experimental research. In the biological field, special importance was attained by the microbiology, micro-organism genetics and neurophysiology laboratories but also by bio-chemistry and computer sciences, from where important working teams and research centers arose in the eighties. Similar to other countries' experiences,[133] this multi-disciplinary organization is considered to be the *incubator*[134] for the rest of Cuban scientific institutions today; and was established to promote the development of research and training activities in frontier fields.

The success of this spin-off business model was based on elements such as the provision of a costless physical environment to the new firms, which were subsequently helped to grow by sharing support services, such as the availability of secretarial help, a receptionist, and access to copiers and professional services, including acquisition of financial resources, business planning, and legal and accounting ties to international research partners and marketing support.

CNIC functioned as a focal point for access to the broad spectrum of available business services and provided the point of contact for entry into various technology programs. The good results are consistent with the international practice that asserts that incubated companies have a dramatically higher rate of survival than the average spin-off.[135] Even when the incubator model has experienced transformation in some countries (such as the US) that made it more expensive for small firms to grow,[136] the Cuban industry remain to the sharing model as a basic paramount. However, the focal role of CNIC has been gradually assumed by other organizations within the industry. From its beginnings as an essentially non-firm organization between the 1960s and the 80s, it has thereafter adopted the form and function of a typical company of the strategic network, by focusing on developing products and integrating a trading arm into its structure.

7.4.5 Strategic network organizations

As already suggested, most of the firms of the strategic network of the Cuban biotech industry were former departments or divisions of CNIC. This strategic network is formed by a small group of *in-house modular* firms (see below in-house modularity), which were until 2009 under the control of the Council of State, then work under supervision of CITMA for a short period and now are part of BioCubaFarma, a state holding created in December 2012 as part of the economic reforms carried out by Raúl Castro.

This nodes group also includes the Center for Medical Research and Development (CIDEM), which does not directly belong to the strategic network, but offers services (e.g. microbiologic, biologic and toxicological studies) to the centers of the strategic network and to the medical-pharmaceutical (small drugs) sub-network. It main establishments can carry out processes such as Chemical & Microbiological Control, Chemical Research or the manufacturing of Cytostatic medicaments.

However, this organization plays a more important role in the chemical-pharmaceutical branch by producing and commercializing mostly generics and synthetic products.[137] Its main function is still conducting research aimed at supporting different national or sectoral programs directed at import substitution. Founded under Resolution No. 148/1992, CIDEM (Spanish: Centro de Investigación y Desarrollo de Medicamentos) is Ministry for Public Health's (MINSAP) scientific and technical arm.

By taking a look at the ego network or (sphere of influence) arising from the subgroup formed by the in-house modular facilities of the industry (see Visualization 2 in the Annexes) one can see that it covers a big portion of the network. This is consistent with the fact that these facilities represent the core of the industry and exchanges resources with most of the network actors and with almost all the actor of their subgroup.[138]

Visualization 3 shows that even suppressing the rest of the subgroups, the linking level within the strategic network is very significant. One reason for this could be that many of these organizations were created from the same incubator, which makes it more probable that those scientists that worked together previously will tend to keep collaborating. However, had an encouraging institutional setting not been there, this close collaboration would hardly have taken place.

Indeed, it is the government decision of creating expedited channels of cooperation (e.g. through absence of exclusive licensing, regular meetings, state ownership of the patents and facilities, no competition ethos of the industry, etc.) among the in-house integrated firms the reason of the high level of linkages among them. Nevertheless, the fact remains that having belonged to the same incubator (CNIC) provided an environment of dynamism and flexibility, which improves the prospects for knowledge sharing and learning.

In-house modularity

In-house modularity is a definition[139] employed here to describe the governance structure of the core firms (strategic network) of Cuban biotech and it should not be confused with our variable under study, namely organizational integration.[140] The companies of the strategic network of the Cuban biotech industry are *in-house modular* because they are *vertically* integrated firms working under a *horizontal* and non-linear regime (not to confuse with horizontal integration). This concept applies to both intra- and inter-organizational levels and conceives the core firms within the Cuban biotech industry as networks integrated within a wider network of organizations, even when subjected to formal hierarchical control.[141]

As already discussed, vertical integration means that companies of the strategic network are organized so that research, development, production, marketing, and follow-up evaluations for a given product are carried out within the same administrative unit. Cuban industry officials call this structure the *closed cycle,* which could, in fact, be identified with the notion of a *vertical integrated firm,* in that it refers to the in-house completion of all the product's development phases. However, the term could also be associated synonymously with vertical/hierarchical/linear, which is employed by a good part of the literature on production networks and value chains (see e.g Gerefi 2005; Thompson 2003; Williamson 1975).

However, practical evidence shows that vertical and horizontal relations are interlinked in a much more complex way (Coe et al. 2008). That also strongly applies to Cuban biotech. For example, research, pharmaceutical development, pre-clinical and clinical studies, regulatory and intellectual property issues, manufacturing, negotiations, and commercial tasks for the development of Heberprot-P ® (treatment of diabetic's foot) were coordinated by the Heberprot-P ® task force. The task force belonged to a product management team, directly subordinated to the General Direction of CIGB (see CIGB in the next section) with constant intensive interventions of all institutional directions (research, development, regulatory affairs etc.). That is why the term "closed cycle" is being substituted with a more encompassing one.[142]

Closed cycle as vertical integration could also be associated with the traditional purpose that Williamson (1975) reserves for this kind of structure, namely the reduction of transaction costs. However, other authors suggest that in addition to the cost factor, the *accumulation of capabilities* at the firm and industry levels, essentially expressed in form of shared languages, routines and coordination, is a central element that explains the vertical scope of firms (Malerba et al. 2006; Schilling 2000. In order to avoid confusion between the common definition of vertically integrated companies on the one hand and the actual non-linear and dynamic nature of vertical integration, in-house modularity will be used instead.

On the other hand, the notion of horizontal regimes has been usually linked to the flexibility given by modular forms of production (modularity) as opposed to hierarchies (see e.g. Miles et al. 1997). In management science modularity basically refers to the property of some production/organizational systems to be decomposed into independent modules and then further recombined (Schilling 2000; Schilling and Steensma 2001). This process increases the flexibility in the end product by allowing a variety of possible configurations to be assembled, thus increasing the opportunity costs of those producers that stay in a single configuration. Products can be made increasingly modular by adopting a standardized interface that makes the product compatible with other firms' components.[143] This process is influenced by factors such as heterogeneity of inputs and demand[144] and is utilized by the semiconductor industry, as well as the automobile, computer and software industries.

However, the very notions of market and hierarchy as distinct and clearly distinguishable categories is problematic because it tends to obscure the fact, that in practice, the configuration of the system of production and distribution is far more complex and dynamic than is usually assumed (for further discussion see Coe et al. 2008). There are industries, with high heterogeneity in inputs and demand, whose characteristics, however, make it very difficult for them to work under a modular regime, because most of their underlying technologies are hard to codify. As above discussed, this is the case of biotechnology, where to develop a product requires constant interaction between the agents involved in the process, thus making a shared experience a critical asset (Pisano 2006, 149–52). This element might at least partly explain why the most successful companies in the industry have been integrated under the FIPCO model (see above, Section 7.3.1).

At the same time, the high levels of input and demand heterogeneity shown by the biopharmaceutical sector signal the possibilities of knowledge recombination (and thus innovation) that could be obtained if the system were able to exploit the potential offered by modularity. In fact, in the worldwide industry certain institutional incentives have made R&D companies, universities and public research organizations within the industry more prone to try to profit from these conditions by generating proprietary knowledge and exclusively licensing it via short-term based alliances. However, the output of this trend toward industry disintegration has so far been very disappointing as a business model, perhaps, precisely because the need for integration has not been sufficiently addressed.

In this context, the Cuban biotech industry has been organized in such a way that the components of its vertically integrated (and most important) companies also have the ability to take advantage of the gains of modularity while successfully dealing with the strong pressures for integration of the industry. For example, the product Heberkinasa®, employed in emergency rooms in case of acute myocardial infarction, was produced by CIGB's facilities for more than 15 years. After effectiveness was demonstrated; and emergency departments became more acquainted with the product, it was decided to transfer the technology package to BIOCEN (see below, Section 7.4.6). However, CIGB does not have to worry about losing the capabilities acquired during those 15 years because there is no mutual blocking between these organizations. That is, openness and collaboration are constantly encouraged.

Through the existence of NFO-based technical and organizational *standard interfaces,* vertically integrated firms (such as CIGB, CIM, Finlay Institute etc. see below) do not become knowledge fortresses unable to interact with the rest of the industry. Rather, they have become the most important innovation agents within the Cuban biopharmaceutical complex. That is consistent with the role played by systems integrators discussed in Chapter 4. Indeed, these companies have developed in-house competences in most of the technological knowledge of the specific markets they compete in, which puts them in a better position to design communication standards with the rest of the participants. NFO-based standard interfaces allow specific assets to become less specific thus facilitating knowledge exchanges between heterogeneous organizations.

Indeed, as pointed out in Chapter 3, when it comes to disruptive innovation, some industry standards usually precede the existence of voluntary and consensual standards (see Section 3.7.1). That applies more than ever to the biomedical sector, where, among a number of other issues, many researchers and practitioners also stress the important role of regulators by creating the standards that will allow clinical trial data to be shared. Shared clinical data is expected to contribute to innovation by allowing available data to be reused at no cost, thus increasing the chances for new drugs to be developed (Olson and Downey 2013). However, standardization of such complex data as those produced by clinical trials is needed upfront. The rules for collaborative expert input and consensus need to be established by regulators along with standard development organizations (usually NFOs). This, in turn, requires political will.

For example the European Medicines Agency (EMA), the NFO which regulates drugs and biologicals in Europe, has very recently taken the position that clinical trial data will no longer be considered commercial confidential information (ibid., p. 58). EMA's officials recognize that this measure puts many people from industry "outside their comfort zones" (ibid., p. 58). However, they also acknowledge that it has to be done because the industry is moving toward a new model of openness in which data are made available for others to reanalyze and combine with other data. In fact, Light and Lexchin (2012) observed that EMA "does Europe a disservice by approving 74 percent of all new applications based on trials designed by the companies, while keeping data about efficacy and safety secret" (p. 2). Consensual standards make it much easier to engage in broad-based cooperative projects, but people and organizations need the right incentives to contribute (if not always voluntarily) their data. This context demands for regulators to issue the corresponding upfront standard.

These standards can take the form of technological interfaces and organizational interfaces such as process protocols, uniform employment policies, and shared platforms such as regular meetings of institutional directors, the creation of inter-institutional task teams for specific projects, non-exclusivity licensing[145] within the industry and other forms of cross-organizational cooperation. Most of the products of Cuban biotech have been developed as a result of the cooperation between several organizations.

Notice that the term *vertically integrated* will continue to be used when referring to cases others than Cuban biotech. Among other reasons in order to show that very often what is meant as "vertical integrated" in traditional sense (hierarchical, resulting from market failure) could actually be defined as "in-house modular." Even if organized as a formal hierarchies, Cuban biotech firms cannot be understood as hierarchical and linear structures only designed as a result of market failure, but as in-house modular structures which are crucial for product and process innovation. Below is a summary of the role of these organizations in the existence of the Cuban biotech industry.

Center for Genetic Engineering and Biotechnology (CIGB)

The CIGB is the Cuba's biotechnology leading research-production organization. This in-house modular company has 20 years of experience in the production of recombinant biopharmaceutical molecules such as interferon, Hepatitis B vaccine, Synthetic Haemophilus influenza type b vaccine, Tetra- and Penta-valent combined vaccines, streptokinase, epidermal growth factor formulated in different forms, monoclonal antibodies and other products, which are already producing a positive impact on public health in Cuba and a positive cash flow from sales to more than 50 countries[146] (see additional information, including selected product portfolio, in Annex 5). Many of these products have been certified by the World Health Organization (WTO), e.g. the Hepatitis B vaccine. This is by far the most innovative company of the industry (see Annex 7 for a list of the most relevant biotechnology-based active pharmaceutical ingredients (APIs) developed by CIGB). CIGB operates 12 manufacturing plants and as of 2011, had six operational licenses.

The beginnings of the genetic engineering in Cuba date back to 1977. At that time, researchers of the Microorganism Genetic Department (MGD)[147] of the CNIC were working on the genetics of microorganisms and molecular biology. In 1981 the Biological Front was created, in order to obtain leukocytes interferon (a group of proteins with antiviral properties). As early as 1978, researchers at the MGD knew about the possibility of recombination.[148]

Production of interferon (IFN) obtained from human leukocytes began to take place as early as 1981 in a small lab staffed with a group of workers of the CNIC. But at the same time, there was increasing interest in obtaining the recombinant IFN because it had soon become evident that the demand for the product couldn't be met with the leukocytes obtained from the country's blood banks. Consequently, it was decided to produce it by genetic engineering, which would provide in the long term a much cheaper method; since it allowed mass cultivation and purification from bacterial cultures.[149]

Then, parallel to the production of IFN leukocytes, which was being created in a separated lab, a lab for obtaining IFN recombinant was set up. Afterwards, both groups started to work together forming the Genetic Engineering group. After learning that the recombinant IFN had been already obtained by Tamaguchi in Japan and Weissman at Hoffman-La Roche labs, the Center for Biological Research (CIB) in 1982 was created and the group began to work in that direction. The IFN beta (1983), alpha (1986) and gamma (1988) were created shortly after the pioneers in the field. Further government investment led to the creation of the CIGB.

In 1981, UNIDO (United Nations Industrial Development Organization) decided to create a center of excellence for the transfer of biotechnology to developing countries. Cuba applied for the vacancy, but it was awarded to India.[150] The Cuban Government then decided to create its own center. On July 1, 1986, the (CIGB) was inaugurated, and CIB became a division of it.

This vast research-productive complex has about 1400 staff workers, including 550 scientists and engineers work in more than 50 research and development projects. It is staffed with state of the art equipment in several fields including the most recent technologies (genomics, proteomics etc.). The project portfolio of CIGB is covered by more than 70 inventions intellectually protected by more than 1900 patent application worldwide. CIGB has published 680 peer-reviewed papers in scientific journals, (from 1986 to 2006) and they have been cited in more than 3000 papers.[151]

The hepatitis B vaccine manufactured at the CIGB has reduced the incidence of this infectious disease in Cuba from 376 cases in 1991 to eradication in 2000, it has been on the WHO's list of vaccines purchased by UNO from 2001. $220 million worth of vaccine were sold in 10 years and 100 million doses have been used.[152] This vaccine was first obtained in 1986 by employing recombinant methods, quite avant-garde at the time.[153] CIGB's manufacturing plant N° 1 is devoted to the production process of the recombinant Hepatitis B surface antigen, which is also the API for the vaccines Heberbiovac-HB®, Trivac-HB®, and Heberpenta®.

In Visualization 4 we can see that, as is the case with most of the in-house modular facilities, the CIGB engages in reciprocal resource exchange with the rest of the organizations of its subgroup. For example, the manufacturing plant N° 4 has to do with the production of new pharmaceutical products derived from the results of the CIGB's biomedical research activity. The first lots for clinical trials are manufactured in this facility, operating under clean room conditions. It is also intended and designed to perform contract manufacturing operations, according to commercial agreements with partners. At the same time, lots of APIs for clinical trials of CIM's lung cancer vaccine have been also manufactured in this production facility. In turn, plant N° 10 is a review and packaging facility for products manufactured in Plant N° 4 and other products that can been process in this productive area.

On the other side, a relatively exclusive relation arises with organizations outside the subgroup. This is obviously due to the fact that the CIGB is the research-production organization that most exploits economies of scale and scope by collaborating with other facilities (within and outside the strategic network).

A relative recent example is the collaborative relation established with the small Laboratory of Synthetic Antigens (LAGS), which belong to the University of Havana and had no manufacturing capabilities to scale-up the first world-wide synthetic vaccine anti-*Haemophilus influenzae* type b Quimi-Hib® for clinical trials; developed by them. Large-scale production was made possible by the CIGB's staff, a few months after the vaccine discovery. The pharmaceutical facility Plant N° 3 is devoted to the manufacture of the API of the vaccine in accordance with regulatory requirements of CECMED. The vaccine's API is from two primary raw materials, supplied to the CIGB by Vacunas Finlay, S.A, the trade arm of Finlay Institute).

Center for Neurosciences

Another example of research spin-off resulting from CNIC is Cuba's Center for Neurosciences (CNC). The origins of the organization date back to 1966, when a small neurophysiology unit was created in CNIC in order to introduce the application of quantitative and automated methods for the analysis of the brain's electric activity. Concretely, the objective was to develop computerized equipments to analyze electrical brain signals, and eventually create instruments for early diagnosis of neurological, psychiatric, and development disorders.[154]

In 1969 Neurophysiology Unit's researchers had access for first time to a CAT-400C[155] computer, donated by US scientists, for computerized evaluation of brain disorders. During the early 1970s, Cuban brain's researchers also collaborated with US colleagues on developing one of the earliest methods for computerized (also called quantitative) electroencephalogram (qEEG) analysis or neurometrics.[156] At the same time, the development of the first Cuban midrange[157]computer in 1970 (see below ICID) allowed both experimenting with and exploring the potential of endogenous technology. This made it possible for Neurophysiology Unit's researchers to develop in 1972, in close collaboration with the Ministry of Public Health, the first prototype of the MEDICID-01, the first Cuban computerized EEG system (see Annex 6).

The research activity of this small division took a different level when MEDICID-03, the first Cuban digital diagnosis equipment and the first exportable item (to Mexico) was developed in 1982, which led to the creation of a full department of computational Neurosciences,[158] still subordinated to CNIC. The main purpose of the department was to improve this technology, made mostly of Cuban-designed and Cuban-manufactured hardware,[159] and to introduce it into the national health system. This laid the foundation for the development of a national neuroscience diagnostic network in the 1980s, which, in turn, enabled the center to launch in 1991 one of the world's first national programs for early detection of hearing loss (Valdés and Obrador 2009). In 1992 Cuba became the world's first country to systematically introduce the use of quantitative electroencephalogram (qEEG) in a public health system. In 1990 MEDICID-3E had become the first Cuban qEEG equipment registered in France and Switzerland (ibid.).

Since the 1980s, five generations of this equipment have been designed and produced, expanding functional capabilities along different lines under the Neuronic trademark. In 1990 the Council of State created the Center for Neurosciences as a Research-production facility, but still as a department of the CNIC. Structurally, the CNC was composed by a mixture of the previous department and a division of the Institute for Digital Research (ICID). In 2005 CNC was registered officially as an autonomous Research-Production-Trading facility.

Cuba's Center for Neurosciences electroencephalography and electromyography equipments is being exported to over 20 countries in North America, Asia, Africa, Europe and Latin America under the Neuronic trademark.[160] The Spanish subsidiary (located at Saragossa) of this Cuban company has earned the European Union's certification for sale in Europe and won in 2009 the National Exporter Award for the volume of goods commercialized.[161]

Institute for Digital Research (ICID)

It is worth mentioning that the existence of a branch within the Cuban biotech industry devoted to medical equipments is closely related to the attempt to develop an electronic industry. The electronic industry in Cuba dates back to the 60s when the CNIC was created. In 1962 the Department of Automation and Electronics was created in the Cuban Ministry of Industry, which explicitly aimed at the development of electronics and computing in Cuba. In 1965, the University of Havana acquired a second generation[162] computer Elliott 803[163] for information processing. This equipment was purchased as part of the scientific equipment for CNIC, which, as above noted, was created in 1965. In 1968 an agreement with the French government was reached for the purchase of two SEA 400 second-generation computers that were destined to process the information for the population census of 1970. By virtue of the same agreement with the French government, near a dozen of IRIS10 third generation computers were purchased in 1972.[164]

The first Cuban mini (or midrange)-computer in 1970 was manufactured by ICID (Institute for Digital Research). This government owned company had been created in 1969 with the aim of developing an electronic and computing industry in Cuba, precisely when the industry was emerging in the rest of the world.[165] This was about the same time the first generation of biomedical researchers was being trained at CNIC. The muster equipment, from which the Cuban computer was developed, was provided as a donation by Dr Erwin Roy John of New York University[166] (a PDP-8 L/I model[167]), which was surprised to see how the Cubans had managed to reverse engineering the computer in 18 months.[168] This computer (second generation) was developed under the name of CID 201 A[169] and in 1971 was started its serial production.

Having no access to US system (because of the US embargo) and facing software incompatibilities (with French computers) was a real challenge for the developers of the first Cuban computers. For that reason the first domestic software (LEAL 201) was created in 1971 employing as reference the French Auto-code Elliot 803-Mark III.

In 1972 the first line of Cuban video terminals, CID 702, was developed. In 1973 the CID 300, the first Cuban third generation minicomputer, was developed, compatible with the operating system of the PDP-11 model (the successor of PDP-8), which began serial production in 1978. However, the Cuban overall hardware production fell behind shortly thereafter, when Cuba introduced the Soviet-based labor division system.

According to some scholars, the main reason high-tech development during the 1970s fell behind was to be found in the obsolescence of devices built in the former Soviet bloc and a strong dependence on components from the same market, which hindered Cuba's national hardware production (Pons et al. 2007). After the development of CID 300, Cuba became part of the Intergovernmental Council Committee, which was the CMEA[170] body aimed at the computing development. The purchase of French computers stopped and Cuba specialized in video-terminals and keyboards, which were exported mostly to Soviet Union. Training programs and methodologies were changed as a result of this situation, with catastrophic consequences for the Cuban industry. The biotechnology industry did not suffer the same fate because it remained catching-up to keep abreast of the countries that were at the technological frontier. A lesson to be learned for future industrial policies programs.

Nevertheless, and thanks to the brokering function played by CNIC, an important stage was reached in 1982, when the computerized system for brain research MEDICID was developed. As mentioned above, since the 1970s, research on advanced medical equipment and applications was taking place within the CNIC. The current ICID and the Center of Neurosciences were actually integrated into one department within the CNIC. Afterward, the development of complex medical equipment and automated systems became the specialization of ICID. Subsequently, a number of medical applications have been developed by ICID for the Cuban Health System. Some of them are being currently exported via COMBIOMED,[171] ICID's trading agency. ICID is today part of the strategic network of the Cuban biotech industry.

However, even when the most important value contribution to ICID products proceed from the ability to combine high tech equipment in a new, creative way, the fact remains that, if a hardware industry had been developed, important value gains could have been made. In contrast, most of the high-tech components are being imported, which represents an outflow of resources.

Center for Immunoassay (CIE)

The cooperation between the biochemistry and micro-organism genetics divisions of CNIC accounted for the emergence of the first generation of Cuban molecular geneticists. During the 1980s CNIC developed the procedures needed to obtain polycosanol (known as PPG), the production of which became a small industrial branch in the country. CNIC carried out some synthesis works, though it focused on chemical analysis. For that purpose, it introduced in Cuba the techniques of mass spectrometry, nuclear magnetic resonance, atomic absorption, ultracentrifugation, automatic analysis, as well as many others.[172]

As a complement, CNIC also created repairing and manufacturing workshops and started to develop lab instrument manufacturing, including some equipment for medical use. This work line of CNIC was the starting point for creating, in the eighties, an institution specialized in designing and producing clinical diagnosing equipments: the Center for Immunoassay.[173]

In 1987 the Center for Immunoassay (CIE) was created as another of CNIC's research spin-offs. Its foremost purpose was to develop enzymatic tests (screening methods) for pregnant women, in order to timely detect birth malformations. The main motivation to develop this method started in 1975, when researchers of both the Clinical Diagnosis and the Biochemical Immunology divisions (Immunochemistry group) at CNIC and researchers of the Center for Medical Genetics[174] of the Ministry for Health (first separately and short thereafter as a team) became interested in the field of diagnostic methods. The Cuban Immunochemistry group knew that prenatal diagnosis by using radio-immunologic methods had been developed in England in 1979. However the expense and hazards of preparing and handling the radioactive antigen[175] influenced the decision to do it by using immunochemistry, a method with which they had been working since the mid 1970s[176] and which was considered avant-garde at the time.[177]

With the development of personal computers during the 1980s, experimentation with fully automated systems for micro-analytical methods using immunochemistry methods increased worldwide. During this period a method called ELISA[178] was being increasingly employed, but it had also proven too expensive to be used in large-scale screening.

Cuba's government objective was to be able to cover the whole population of pregnant women, or, in other words, to carry out mass screening. For that reason, a system using a smaller quantity of reagents was developed. Even while the principle was the same as ELISA, this new system required major changes in the kind of reagent and technology (new automated procedures) employed. The new reagent UMELISA AFP was introduced in 1982 in the National health System to develop an economical alpha-fetoprotein screening test for fetal malformations[179] (see Annex 5.5).

The resultant product packet of CIE has been called SUMA® (ultra-micro-analytic system) technology, which offers significant cost savings and other advantages. A decade after the creation of CIE, each analysis costs 30–50 percent less, making mass-screening possible. This leads to prevention, which is, in contrast to curative medicine, the principle of the Cuban health system. Other products affirming the same principle are e.g., a glucometer developed for diabetic patients and specially designed for tropical climates, which is being provided to the Cuban public health system at 60 percent of the international price. CIE stopped receiving a budget from the government at the beginning of the 1990s. Since then, it finances its own R&D, as well as production, through sales and exports.

SUMA is the CIE's product insignia and it is currently being commercialized by CIE's trading agency Tecnosuma Internacional S.A. International subsidiaries are to be found in Brazil, Mexico, Argentina and China. For several years Tecnosuma has been given the national award as the best exporter.[180]

SUMA technology applications cover the whole health system, comprising all the municipalities. It includes such country-wide programs as the maternal-infant program, the epidemiological surveillance program and blood control programs. Part of the export-profits obtained by Tecnosuma and Neuronic are employed to finance and coordinate a huge country-wide network of laboratories to carry out the diagnosis of prenatal and perinatal care malformations. For example, in 2008, CIE grossed US $22 million that were re-invested in new 42 laboratories in 2008 and another 64 in 2009. As a result, some municipalities now have three labs. This process moves the technology closer to the community, therefore creating more room for the innovative and cost-reducing potentials arising from the user-producer links[181] and economies of scale. This technology has played a significant role in the prevention and reduction of the infant mortality in the country.

In 2011, CIE's worker productivity was 22 times higher than the national average productivity. Its director was also Vice-President of BioCubaFarma.

National Center for Animal and Plant Health (CENSA)

Given the increasing necessity to find solutions to the problems of livestock in the country, the CNIC's Animal Health division was created in January 1969. In addition to the research in this field, this division also provided postgraduate training and highly specialized services to other companies in the country. For example, this division played a crucial role in during the epidemics of swine fever in 1971 and 1980.

In 1976 this division started to work as an independent administrative unit and on September 1, 1980, CENSA was officially inaugurated. On June 15, 1981, research objectives were expanded to the field of plant protection, fighting against diseases and pests from Cuba's main crops: sugar cane, citrus, coffee and tobacco. In 1991, the activity scope was extended to the production of drugs, vaccines and diagnostic kits for humans. These products, along with the ones devoted to animal and plant use, are to be commercialized under C-KURE trademark. Since 2007, CENSA works by annual objectives[182] in previously defined priority fields for the middle and long terms.

In contrast to the in-house modular companies, its commercialization unit does not have operation autonomy. That means, for example, the unit cannot engage as an independent entity in joint ventures with international partners. However the fact that it has an export–import license reveals a quality that differentiates it from other organizations within the industry, which also have internal commercialization departments, but no license. The other yellow node represents the Center of Isotopes (CENTIS). (*Editorial Note*: Please note that while the figures appear in greyscale in print, the Annexes will be available to view in full color online at: www.routledge.com/9781138558984.)

Center for Molecular Immunology (CIM)

Other non-firm organizations (besides the original CNIC) have incubated successful companies. This is the case for CIM, which is part, along with the CIGB, of the most innovative and leading exporter core of the Cuban biotech industry (see selected product portfolio in Annex 5). In 2011, CIM has three operational licenses for three manufacturing plants.

Although many of its leading researchers also received training in the CNIC, most of them were originally trained in 1970 at the Institute of Oncology and Radiobiology, which belonged to the Ministry of Health. Furthermore, many of the institute's graduates worked there, acquiring decisive experience in pioneering fields such as the production of monoclonal antibodies to combat different types of malignant tumors.

In 1989 the institute was considered a reference in monoclonal antibodies and started to receive further support from the government (specifically from Academy of Sciences). In 1990 it was decided to create an independent facility specialized in monoclonal antibodies. The CIM was completed and opened in 1994 as a spin-off of the Institute of Oncology. At the moment of its birth, CIM already had a lot of research and production experience[183] that accelerated its successful international engagement. To mention an example, in 2008 the Cuban cancer vaccine program was the largest outside of the USA, including eight therapeutic vaccines, six of which were already undergoing clinical testing (Lage 2008). During the period 2008–10, the number of clinical trials in the area of Oncology represented the 59.9 percent (106) of the overall trial number. The second therapeutic area was infectious diseases, at 10.7 percent (19).

The institute also introduced the production of recombinant Epidermal Growth Factor (EPG), when researchers had hypothesized that it could be useful in the diagnosis of breast cancer. Until the end of the 1980s and early 90s the institute had to rely on a very long process of obtaining EPG from the urine of pregnant women. For that reason, they contacted the CIGB; which by then had already been created, and discussed the possibility of producing a recombinant version of the product through genetic engineering. The effort was successful and today the CIGB continue to produce EPG for curing of burns and other wounds.

Visualization 5 (see Annexes) shows the immediate neighbors organizations of the CIM; excluding the members of its own group (the components of the strategic network are excluded to avoid repetition). The most important feature that arises from the visualization of the CIM is that its value creation structure is, obviously, related to other industrial and commercial facilities. However, the fact that the value structure of the firm depends also directly (not indirectly as it usually is assumed) on several non-firm central organizations (the red nodes) is representative of the role of this type of organization within the Cuban biotechnology value chain. As already noted, this is more or less the same for other companies of the strategic network.[184] (*Editorial Note*: Please note that while the figures appear in greyscale in print, the Annexes will be available to view in full color online at: www.routledge.com/9781138558984.)

Finlay Institute

The Finlay Institute, created officially in 1991, is along with the CIGB and CIM (with whom it regularly cooperates), among the most important: a research-production organization, dedicated to the development of vaccines (see selected product portfolio in Annex 5). It is a start-up company formed by workers of several organizations. Its antecedents are to be found in the early 1980s, when Cuba was hit by a severe epidemic of meningitis. While vaccines against the types A and C were already available in the world market, there was no vaccine for the type B, which rose frighteningly in Cuba during the period 1982–84. At that time, to solve this problem was considered the first priority of the health system.

To have an idea of the magnitude of the crisis, we need to point out that from 1916 to 1975 meningococcal disease took an endemic form, with 10 to 40 sporadic cases annually. However, in May 1976, an epidemic began as household outbreaks with general incidence increasing by 50 percent (from 0.4 to 0.8 per 10^5 population). In 1978, the incidence increased to 1.5 per 10^5 population, and in 1979 reached 5.6 per 10^5 population. During 1983 and 1984, meningococcal disease reached a general incidence of 14.4 per 10^5 population, but in specific age groups – such as infants under one year – it was extraordinarily high, surpassing 120 per 10^5 population (Sotolongo et al. 2007).

In order to seek a solution, the government created in 1983 a team of 15 researchers from members of different staffs. The group started to work in an ad-hoc department created in the National Center for Bioproduction (BIOCEN), another research-production organization of the strategic network (see visualizations). After nearly six years of basic research, as well as pharmacological, preclinical, and clinical trials, followed by phased scaling up of the manufacturing process, researchers and technicians produced a vaccine candidate.

After the safety and efficacy of the product was demonstrated, the national regulatory authority – CECMEC – licensed the vaccine for use in Cuba. It was introduced as a nationwide vaccination campaign in 1989–90 on 3 million infants, children and adolescents aged three months to 24 years. It is currently administered in a routine two-dose vaccination schedule at three months and five months of age, which resulted in a sharp and sustained decline in the incidence of the disease reaching 0.2 per 10^5 in 2006[185] and 0.08 per 10^5 population in 2008 (Sotolongo 2009). The same effects were shown in other countries (see Rodríguez et al. 1999 for the case of Brazil) VA-MENGOC-BC® is the first world's commercially available vaccine against serogroup B meningococcus, protected by three patents in 20 countries.[186]

An interesting thing is that the time it took to develop the vaccine was less than the average time for vaccine products (biological or synthetic), which is circa 10–15 years.[187] One possible explanation could be the close relationships between the different organizations of the industry. For example, the research team was composed of two workers[188] that belonged to the C.J.F Biological Products, a manufacturing company that belonged to the medical-pharmaceutical (currently the producer of injectable medicaments) and the rest belonged to the CNIC. Other organizations such as CIGB also collaborated. Last but not least, as the workers of the industry acknowledge, is the financial commitment showed by the government in these issues, especially for the process of scale-up required by the last stages of the trial. Likewise, the fact of having a very high rate of patient enrolment, made simple by the very inclusive and highly networked health system, is also mentioned.

The Finlay Institute had three operational licenses as of 2011.

7.4.6 Other research-production organizations

Other research-production organizations in the strategic network of the industry are the Kouri Institute (IPK), the National Center for Production of Laboratory Animals (CENPALAB), the National Center of Bioproduction (BIOCEN) and the Pharmaceutical Chemistry Center (CQF). The IPK Institute of Tropical Medicine is the successor of the one created in 1937, and was re-founded in 1979 by expanding its focus in order to protect the Cuban population from the so-called tropical diseases, cooperate with other developing countries in combating these diseases, and contribute to developing medical sciences in general, particularly microbiology, parasitology, epidemiology and tropical medicine. New laboratories and several other divisions have been subsequently included.[189] In 1993, IPK moved to new, enlarged and modernized facilities and was officially opened in 1994.

The IPK belongs to the Ministry of Public Health and it is basically dedicated to research and services. This includes the validation of vaccines or other products requiring clinical trials, field studies, among other similar activities. But it is also equipped for the production (at request) of cultures, biological reagents or raw materials needed by the industry. For example, this organization carried out the epidemiological assessment of the effectiveness of the antimeningococcal vaccine (see Finlay Institute) in 1991 and 2000. It also contributed to the commercial scale production and demonstration of the innocuousness and effectiveness of the recombinant vaccine against hepatitis B (see above, CIGB). The Institute also has developed a broad network of international collaboration and has become a world reference for infectious diseases.[190]

CENPALAB is an organization created in 1982 with the aim of producing and commercializing laboratory animals. Here are carried out experimental toxicology analyses that are part of the pre-clinical phase of the process of clinical trials. This is, before vaccines or medical products are to be tested in humans. CENPALAB covers the whole domestic demand and it develops research on diagnostic resources to assess the levels of pathogen agents in animals. Certainly, it also plays a very important role in the Cuban agricultural and veterinary sciences.

BIOCEN is another important research-production organization of the Cuban biotechnology industry, officially opened in August 1992. This institution, however, is much more focused on developing manufacturing capabilities for vaccines and medicaments developed by the industry. For example, the production and packing operations of the hepatitis B vaccine, developed at CIGB, were carried out in BIOCEN. However BIOCEN has also developed its own products and components. In recent years, the organization's researchers obtained a novel group of anti-anemia tonics of natural origin and high efficiency (Trofin[191] being the most successful). It has also developed and manufactured the active component of several cancer vaccines designed at the Center for Molecular Immunology.

The CQF belongs to the Ministry of Public Health and was developed to carry out scientific-technical research directed towards obtaining bioactive substances for the formulation of medicines for human use. It is a Teaching Unit of the Ministry of Public Health, the University of Havana and the University of Medical Sciences and it has built an impressive international (more than 40 institutes and organizations from 20 countries) and national collaboration network with almost all the research and health centers in the country.[192]

The CQF has developed several medicaments for the medical-pharmaceutical (small molecule) sector as well as software applications for the biotech industry.[193] According to the UNESCO Science report of 2010, this organization was the number one in the Cuba's top 20 S&T research organizations measured in terms of items such as the number of prizes awarded by the Cuban Academy of Sciences over 1997–2006, on the basis of the number of papers published and the socio-economic benefit of the research results (Table 7.3).

7.4.7 Manufacturing companies

Among production firms, i.e. organizations almost exclusively devoted to the manufacture of vaccines, medicaments and other products, we find a group of firms that are closely linked to the biopharma companies: The Novatec Lab,[194] the Llorad Lab,[195] the Aica Lab[196] and the Placental Histotherapy Center (PHC) products are commercialized throughout institutions of the strategic network (Visualization 10). The value of their contributions resides primarily on their specialization in the preparation and bottling of certain injectable medications. This process also includes technologies for the aseptic filling and packaging of the products. The rest of the value (R&D, commercializing, import of raw materials and laboratory reagents, quality assessment, clinical trials etc.) is distributed among other organizations.

An important distinction must be made in the case of the PHC, which, in addition to manufacturing, also carries out high quality research and is well known for R&D focused on searching for new medicines and other products

Table 7.3 Cuba's top 20 S&T research organizations

Center of Pharmaceutical Chemistry	www.cqf.sld.cu
Cuban Institute of Sugar Cane Derivatives	www.icidca.cu
Institute of Animal Science	www.ica.lnf.cu
University of Havana	www.uh.cu
Center of Genetic Engineering and Biotechnology	www.cigb3edu.cu
Institute of Tropical Medicine Pedro Kourí	www.ipk.sld.cu
Havana Technological University José A. Echevarría	www.cujae.edu.cu
Institute of Cybernetics, Mathematics and Physics	www.icmf.innf.cu
Center of Molecular Immunology	www.cim.sld.cu
Finlay Institute (vaccines R&D)	www.finlay.edu.cu
Las Villas Central University Marta Abreu	www.uclv.edu.cu
National Center for Plant and Animal Health	www.censa.edu.cu
National Center of Scientific Research	www.cnic.edu.cu
National Institute of Agricultural Science	www.inca.edu.cu
Bioplants Center – Ciego de Avila University	www.bioplantas.cu
Cuba Neuroscience Center	www.cnuero.co.cu
Institute of Plant Health Research	www.inisav.cu
National Institute of Economic Research	www.inie.cu
Institute of Ecology and Systematics	www.ecosis.cu
Institute of Meteorology	www.insmet.cu

Source: Clark (2010)

from human placenta.[197] This center provides also clinical services such as computerized clinical assessment and digital photography to estimate the duration of the treatment and the required amount of drugs, training on the use of placenta products for each case etc.

The rest of the green nodes are exclusively devoted to the production of generics and other medicaments (Visualization 11). (*Editorial Note*: Please note that while the figures appear in greyscale in print, the Annexes will be available to view in full color online at: www.routledge.com/9781138558984.) They are related to the medical-pharmaceutical side of the industry, which focuses mostly on the production of small molecules (rather than biologic) drugs. For instance, we could mention the Reinaldo Gutiérrez Lab (R.G. Lab.) which researches, produces and distributes pharmaceuticals. In 2011, the company had two operational licenses for the production of oral contraceptives and pressurized aerosols.

The MedSol Lab focuses on the production of solid forms. In 2011, the company had two operational licenses for the production of finished products. Around 90 percent of total production serves the domestic market, while the remainder is exported mainly to Latin America. Also worth mentioning is the Roberto Escudero Lab (R.E. Lab), which manufactures pharmaceutical semi-solid products and had in 2011 three operational licenses for the production of creams and ointments, suppositories and powders; and the 8 de Marzo Lab (8.M Lab), developed in collaboration with UNIDO and specialized in the production of beta lactamic antibiotics and penicillins and had in 2011 two operational licenses for the production of cephalosporins and penicillins and sterile cephalosporanic powder, respectively.

CECMED continuously re-evaluates the bioavailability and bioequivalence requirements of the domestically produced pharmaceuticals (mostly generics), in order for them to keep up to date with international requirements (WTO, FDA, EMA etc.). The most recent were published under Decree No. 18/2007 in February 2007.

Also within this area, we have included four organizations that do not classify in any specific group, but that are strongly related to the production units. It is essentially a group of organizations devoted to the national distribution of pharmaceutical products. These are the Wholesale Havana, the Import Medicament Unit, and ENCOMED.

ENCOMED is an umbrella organization that belongs to the Ministry of Basic Industry and contains 15 wholesale drugstores across the country (one per province). These drugstores are in charge of the domestic distribution chain of pharmaceuticals, and are represented in the visualization by Wholesale Havana, given that we are using Havana a reference point. Early in 2011, CECMED reported 26 wholesalers with an operational license across the country, and most of them were involved in the distribution of human pharmaceuticals. One of the few exceptions was CIMAB, the trading arm of CIM, which has also been given license for wholesaling biopharmaceuticals. The distributions will be carried out according to previous planning on the need of each province The Import Medicament Unit is in charge of distributing drugs and vaccines which have been imported and the ones imported that require especial temperature conditions.

7.4.8 High value service companies

There are organizations mostly devoted to providing sophisticated services to other companies in the industry. In this category there are two organizations: Biomundi[198] and CEADEN. The first one is a business intelligence consulting organization that belongs to the Ministry of Science, Technology and Environment (CITMA) and provides services on strategic profiles, market and tendency studies and carries out the implantation of intelligence systems. It is a useful tool for the biotechnology sector, mainly for technological surveying and prospective.

The second orange node represents the Center for Technological and Nuclear Applications (CEADEN), which also belongs to CITMA. (*Editorial Note:* Please note that while the figures appear in greyscale in print, the Annexes will be available to view in full color online at: www.routledge.com/9781138558984.) This organization was created in 1987 with the aim of providing engineering and technical consultancy to the biopharma complex and to other sectors in the country. The biggest share of its clientele is composed of organizations of Cuban biopharma. Most of the industry's equipments and system tools made of stainless steel are welded, assembled and further monitored by staff of CEADEN.

Although represented by yellow nodes, given its characteristics (see above CENSA), the Center of isotopes (CENTIS) also provides high value services to the industry. (*Editorial Note*: Please note that while the figures appear in greyscale in print, the Annexes will be available to view in full color online at: www.routledge.com/9781138558984.) For example, it provides phamaco-kinetics and bio-distribution studies with radio-labeled compounds to evaluate the absorption, distribution, metabolism and excretion of current and potential new drugs in biological models. It also provides service of calibration of specialized instruments and centralized measurements services for different radioimmunoassay reagents. CENTIS has also been given licenses to export medicaments and to import active pharmaceutical ingredients (APIs).

7.4.9 Trading companies

Trading organizations represent one of the most important groups of firms within the Cuban biotech. This group of companies is in charge of the domestic and international commercialization of the products created by the biopharmaceutical complex. The majority of the commercial arms (trading agencies of the strategic network's research-production centers) were created in order to complete the product production cycle, which integrates basic and applied research, experimental development, *engineering* design and production. The most relevant example is Heber Biotec, which is the most important trading company within Cuban biotech. This company has been given license to export pharmaceuticals, biologics and active pharmaceutical ingredients APIs, both biotechnology-based and chemically synthesized). It has been also given the exclusive marketing rights of to the Placental Histotherapy Center and to the pharmaceutical laboratories Novatec, Aica and Liorad.

CECMED also gave export licenses in 2011 to CIMAB (the trading arm of CIM) to export biopharmaceuticals and other medicaments for the treatment of cancer. Vacunas Finlay, the trading arm of Finlay Institute, was given license for biopharmaceuticals, especially vaccines and immunoglobulins. Laboratorios DALMER, the trading arm of CNIC, is allowed to export APIS and human pharmaceuticals.

One of the greatest contributions of these firms is realized by establishing partnership for joint development and out-licensing[199] around the world, which leaves a greater margin for scale-up, economies of scale, and cost-reduction of clinical trials. In a survey among developing countries engaged in South–North entrepreneurial collaboration in the health biotechnology,[200] published by Nature Biotechnology in 2009, it is shown that Cuba is engaged in the highest number of such collaborations (10.5 per firm in each region). It is the only country, of the surveyed list that has an equal percentage of firms involved in North and South collaboration (see Annex 3).

Other important trading organizations of the biopharma complex are Servicex 4 and FARMACUBA (Visualizations 15 and 16 respectively). Servicex is the import service office of the Cuban Council of State (legislative government). It is composed of several departments of which Servicex Department 4 is in charge of importing diagnostic kits and reagents exclusively for the biotechnology industry. FARMACUBA is in charge of the whole importing–exporting activities of the medical–pharmaceutical complex. In 2001 the national pharmaceutical industry (until then under MINSAP) was re-organized under the Ministry of Basic Industry (MINBAS and Ministry of Energy and Mines since November 2012) in order to increase pharmaceutical exports. Since then, FARMACUBA was solely responsible for importing and exporting for QUIMEFA (until its dissolution in December 2012). FARMACUBA's trading activity mainly has to do with the small molecules drugs and reagents of the national chemical and pharmaceutical consortium Quimefa Group (now part of BioCubaFarma), which is the holding covering the medical–pharmaceutical industry (see next section).

FARMACUBA also supports CENCEC's planning and distribution program of supplies across its entire national network of clinical sites. CENCEC projects availability and demand for medical resources and supplies at each clinical site. These are acquired centrally by the Center and distributed through the certified clinical trial supply distribution service of FARMACUBA's national distribution channel.[201]

7.4.10 Holding companies

The *gray* nodes represent the holding organizations of the industry. The creation of new holding companies (corporations), "corporaciones" during the 90s represented an entrepreneurial innovation in the Cuban context. The holdings are all owned by the state but they were also allowed to control their own finances, borrow on the international financial markets for their own account, import its supplies, keep foreign exchange, establish joint ventures, and hire foreign managers (only for the tourism industry). The economy began to take this configuration to face the crisis of the 1990s by giving more autonomy and at the same time keeping the organizational integration. In the visualization three of the most important holdings of the Cuban biopharma complex are represented.

The Labiofam Entrepreneurial Group, which belongs to the Ministry of Agriculture, maintains a broad product portfolio that ranges from biolarvicides, natural products and foodstuff, homeopathic medication, to household cleaning products. The Group has an industrial plant for the manufacture of plastic containers and it has several research laboratories where biopharmaceutical medicaments are developed in conjunction with other organizations such as CIGB. Labiofam products are commercialized in over 35 countries by its trading arm Labiofam S.A.[202]

The other holding company was the Quimefa Group (now part of BioCubaFarma), which belonged to the Ministry of Basic Industry (MINBAS). It was created essentially to improve exports and to substitute imports, a program begun in 1991. Until 2000 IMEFA (in Spanish *Industria Médico-Farmacéutica*), a division of the Ministry of Public Health (MINSAP) was in charge of producing the small molecules drugs needed by the National Health System, mostly of the generics. However in 2001 most generic pharmaceutical production was shifted to MINBAS, which had created the QUIMEFA group as part of the *Union Química*, a division of MINBAS end of 2000. QUIMEFA absorbed all operations of IMEFA aiming at operations efficiencies and increasing exports. According to official figures, during the period 2008–09, Quimefa has saved the Cuban economy over $2.5 million, when it began to manufacture 16 products that were previously imported.[203]

A careful national monitoring of demand is carried out in Cuba. According to the National Health Program, MINSAP is to gather information (through its extensive communal network) and to present an estimate of the possible national demand. Before producing a medicine, its therapeutic value and economic feasibility is tested, i.e. whether it is more expensive to produce or import it. This is carried out in close collaboration with ENCOMED, the distribution company of the QUIMEFA Group and QUIMEFA. From this the national demand and possible imports are determined. Imports and exports are carried out by FARMACUBA, the trading arm of QUIMEFA.

In actual fact, the frontiers between QUIMEFA and the Biotech-based Western Biocluster are hard to define, as they continuously work together. This was confirmed when in December 2012 both entities were officially merged into BioCubaFarma, a state holding that will continue with the work they were doing before.

However, as mentioned above, this does not alter the analytic point of view of this research whatsoever. On the contrary, it is a confirmation of the point being made by the present study, namely, the huge organizational integration on which the existence of this industry is based.

For example, according to a 2011 report of Espicom Business Intelligence,[204] QUIMEFA and the Biotech-based Western Biocluster were collaborating to renew a quarter of the national list of essential medicaments. QUIMEFA's 2007–12 production program included 73 products, 31 of which were going to replace imported products and 42 new products.

The last holding company is the Electronic Group (EG), which belongs to the Ministry of Informatics and Communications (MIC).[205] The holding is composed of 15 facilities focused in import substitution and exports. The main bond of the group is to be found in the Institute for Digital Research (ICID), which belong to EG.

Notes

1 Part of this chapter, a shorter and modified version of it, was published as A Cárdenas-O´Farrill, State and innovative enterprises: The case of the Cuban pharmaceutical industry, *Business and Economic History On-line (BEH)*, Vol. 12, 2014. The author is grateful to Roger Horowitz and Andrew Popp from the Business History Conference (BHC) for granting permission to reproduce it in this book.
2 Consider the case of Japan and the Soviet Union. During the 1970s the former spent 2.5 percent of its GDP on R&D, while the latter spent 4 percent. Yet Japan grew into a much more sophisticated and faster growing economy.

3 Biomedicine and health innovation: Synthesis report, OECD Innovation Strategy, November 2010.

4 See P Flochel and F Kumli, Pharma 3.0: delivering on health outcomes, *Journal of Business Chemistry*, 2011 available at www.businesschemistry.org/article/?article=125, see also Ernst &Young (2011), Progressions: building Pharma 3.0

5 This has become apparent since 2006 and can be at least partially explained by the increasing number of medical professionals on temporary foreign contracts. Although this practice has been a cornerstone of Cuban foreign policy since 1959, from the nineties on, however, and due to preferential commercial agreements with Venezuela and other countries, the number of doctors abroad has sharply increased. This has created tensions in the preventive concept of the Cuban health system and has contributed to increasing the role of curative medicine (which is more expensive), expressed in the increase in the use of first line emergency services. Another element is the demographic ageing process, which demands more day care homes for the aged and the technical upgrade of diagnostic and treatment capacities. For further details, see Vos et al. (2008), Commentary: Cuba's health system: challenges ahead, Health Policy and Planning (published by Oxford University Press in association with The London School of Hygiene and Tropical Medicine). See also. P De Vos et al., Uses of the first line emergency services in Cuba, Health Policy 85(1) (Jan.): 94–104, 2008.

6 See OECD, Eurostat, WHO, A System of Health Accounts, OECD Publishing, 2011.

7 The definition given by the *Indicator Code Book* of the WHO identifies total expenditure on health (THE) as the sum of all outlays for health maintenance, restoration or enhancement paid for in cash or supplied in kind.. It is the sum of General Government Expenditure on Health and Private Expenditure on Health (pp. 187–90).

8 According to the World Bank income group definition.

9 When we consider the PPP int. $, we have that in terms of its living standards Cuba spends even less than the upper middle income group in average. According to the WHO (2011) Cuba's per capita health expenditure in 2008 was of $495 in comparison with $830 spent in average by its income group and $4246 spent by upper income countries (representing countries such as the US an extreme in this list with $7164). We employ, however, the current figures given the tradable nature of the products and services considered.

10 See, for example A Pérez et al., Impact of antimeningococcal B vaccinacion, Mem Inst Oswaldo Cruz, Rio de Janeiro, 94(4): 433–40, 1999. See also G Delgado et al., Vaccination strategies against hepatitis B and their results: Cuba and the United States, *MEDICC Review* 2003; or G Abreu et al., Cuba's strategy for childhood tuberculosis control, 1995–2005, *MEDICC Review* 13(3): 29–34, 2011.

11 See C Morel et al. (2005) Health innovation networks to help developing countries address neglected diseases, *Science* 39 (July): 401–3, 2005.

12 See for example, R Herrera, Cuba's national program for chronic kidney disease, dialysis and renal transplantation, *MEDICC Review*, 2005. See also G Reed, Chronic vascular diseases in Cuba: Strategies for 2015, *MEDICC Review* 10(2) (Spring): 5–7, 2008; see also The success story of HIV and AIDS control in Cuba, In: http://prairiefirenewspaper.com/2009/02/success-story-of-hiv-and-aids-control-in-cuba; see also M Delfin et al. Epidemiology of hypertension in Cuba, *MEDICC Review*, 2000; see also Treatment to cure Psoriasis in Cuba, http://ntsa.wordpress.com/tratamientos-alternativos/treatment-to-cure-psoriasis-in-cuba/; see also G Giraldo, Interview with Pedro Ordunez, *MEDICC Review* 10(1): 15–17, 2008.

13 Preventing chronic diseases: A vital investment, WHO global report, available in: www.who.int/chp/chronic_disease_report/part1/en/index.html; see also J Dy et al. (2009), A comparative analysis on the healthcare systems of China and Cuba: Treatment of cancer patients, De La Salle-College of Saint Benilde, Manila, Philippines, available in: www.scribd.com/doc/55417998/Comparative-Analysis-on-Healthcare-Systems-Between-China-and-Cuba

14 G Delgado et al., Vaccination strategies against hepatitis B and their results...

15 W Kaplan and R Laing, Local Production of Pharmaceuticals: Industry Policy and Access to Medicines. Health, Nutrition and Population Discussion Paper, The World Bank, Jan. 16, 2005.

16 Conner Gorry, Biotech: The Magic Pill? Cuba's burgeoning biopharmaceutical sector helps keep the island economy afloat, Scientific American Worldview, available at www.saworldview.com/article/biotech-the-magic-pill

17 P De Vos, The right to health in times of economic crisis: Cuba's way, *The Lancet* 374 (Nov. 7): 1575–6, 2009.

18 Conner Gorry, Biotech: The Magic Pill? Cuba's burgeoning biopharmaceutical sector helps keep the island economy afloat, Scientific American Worldview, 2012, available at www.saworldview.com/article/biotech-the-magic-pill

19 Available at http://store.businessmonitor.com/article/346369

20 See Cuba's biotech boom, *Nature* 457(130), January 8, 2009, doi:10.1038/457130a, available at www.nature.com/nature/journal/v457/n7226/full/457130a.html

21 H Bartels et al., Promoting Access to Medical Technologies and Innovation: Intersections between public health, intellectual property and trade, WHO, WIPO and the WTO, Geneva, 2013, p. 113, available at www.wto.org/english/res_e/booksp_e/pamtiwhowipowtoweb13_e.pdf

22 See his profile here: http://investing.businessweek.com/research/stocks/private/person.asp?personId=1368445&privcapId=19713&previousCapId=142316&previousTitle=Sofinnova%20Ventures,%20Inc.

23 Thorsteinsdóttir H et al., Cuba-innovation through synergy, Nature Biotechnology 22, Supplement (Dec.): 19–24, 2004.

24 Electronic communication in 2011 with the author of the present study.

25 See his profile here: www.sanfordburnham.org/talent/Pages/HudsonFreeze.aspx

26 Electronic communication in 2012 with the author of the present study.

27 Electronic communication in 2011 with the author of the present study.

28 Electronic communication in 2013 with the author of the present study.

29 See http://clinicaltrials.gov/show/NCT01813253, see also http://clinicaltrials.gov/show/NCT00561990

30 Conner Gorry, Biotech: The Magic Pill? .... 2012.

31 The conversion is based on the official exchange rate given by the Cuban Central Bank for foreign currencies and Cuban convertible Peso (CUC), which is 1. The official rate of exchange of Banco Central de Cuba is published exclusively to be used by Cuban enterprises, when registering the operations made in foreign exchange. This rate of exchange is not valid for currency purchase and selling operations between financial institutions and the population or enterprises.

32 Conner Gorry, Biotech: The Magic Pill?... 2012.

33 A halal version of the vaccine is being currently developed. The initial markets would be Malaysia, Indonesia, Singapore and Brunei, see USM, Cuba's Finlay develop halal vaccine for meningitis, Business Times, 2010/03/01, Online: www.btimes.com.my/Current_News/BTIMES/articles/vacin/Article/. See also http://wsicubaproject.org/halalvaccine_1107.cfm

34   www.wipo.int/export/sites/www/ip-outreach/en/awards/women/pdf/cu.pdf
35   See F Sotolongo et al. (2009), Cuban meningococcal BC vaccine: Experiences and contributions from 20 years of application, MEDICC Review 9(1) (Fall): 16–22.
36   See www.purematters.com/herbs-supplements/p/policosanol-ppg
37   This is the first research center created after 1959 (in 1965) and is responsible for having provided professional education to many of the scientist, which were to be later the leaders of the current industry.
38   www.wipo.int/tools/en/gsearch.html?cx=00039556715131772I298%3Aaqrs59qtj b0&cof=FORID%3A11&q=wipo+awards+cuba&sa=Search#1128
39   www.globalexchange.org/countries/americas/cuba/foodAndMeds/1510.html.pf
40   This is a small but important research organization that belongs to the Faculty of Chemistry of the University of Havana. In order to have an idea of its innovative potential, it can be said that this synthetic vaccine costs 12 times less than the older version. Cuba currently produces around 10 million doses a year; domestic demand is fewer than one million annually; and it is expected to reach 50 million doses a year by scaling-up production, which will further reduce the price due to economies of scale. The organization is depicted in violet (Visualization 23), which represents organizations exclusively or mainly devoted to research. The other organization in violet is the Centre of Medical Genetics (a short reference to this center can be found in the section CIE below).
41   S Borman and C Washington, Carbohydrate vaccines: Novel chemical and enzymatic oligosaccharide synthesis techniques could lead to a new generation of carbohydrate-based vaccine agents, Chemical and Engineering News August 9, 82(32): 31–5, 2004, Online: http://pubs.acs.org/cen/coverstory/8232/8232vaccines.html
42   The breakthrough was not the development of the vaccine itself, which was already available, but the invention of a synthetic version of the vaccine, which is substantially cheaper and much easier to manufacture than the non-synthetic vaccine currently on the market. Pharmaceutical companies currently can produce just one-fifth of the 500 million doses needed a year. With the new synthetic vaccine, Cuba alone may be able to manufacture 50 million doses a year. In: C Juma and L Yee-Cheong, Innovation: Applying knowledge in development, UN Task Force, 2005, p. 23.
43   See article on website of the Santa Clara University of California, www.scu.edu/sts/nexus/fall2005/StephensArticle.cfm
44   See   www.woundsinternational.com/news/cuba-wins-awards-for-diabetic-foot-treatment, see also http://heberprot-p.cigb.edu.cu/index.php?option=com_content&view=article&id=23&Itemid=60&lang=en
45   To date, the consortium has tested Nimotuzumab in 9842 patients in Cuba, Argentina, Brazil, Canada, China, Colombia, Germany, India, Indonesia, Japan, Malaysia, Mexico, Singapore, South Africa, South Korea, Thailand and the Philippines. Trials are also being conducted in Europe, Japan and North America. See YM Biosciences, Inc. www.ymbiosciences.com/products/nimotuzumab/licensee_links.php
46   Some preliminary results of the phase II published in 2010 showed a mean of 18.53 months survival (median, 11.47 months) in those vaccinated under 60 years old. See www.cimab-sa.com/publicaciones/75649301.PDF
47   See   http://medicalxpress.com/news/2011-09-cuba-world-lung-cancer-vaccine.html

48 See www.ihs.com/products/global-insight/industry-economic-report.aspx?id=10 65971583

49 Ibid.

50 www.zedmariel.com/en/news/first-cuban-american-joint-venture-incorporated-biotech-sector

51 www.cim.co.cu/commercial_products.php

52 See www.cubacontemporanea.com/en/cuban-scientists-work-lung-cancer-vaccine/, see also www.vaxira.com/new-therapeutic-vaccine-against-lung-cancer. pdf and www.ft.com/intl/cms/s/0/b75510d4-cf96-11e2-a050-00144feab7de. html#axzz2WYKHolvb

53 This information has been confirmed in July 2013 by WIPO's official (email communication).

54 A Lage, Socialism and the knowledge economy: Cuban biotechnology, Monthly Review 58(7) (Dec.): 53–5, 2006. Originally published as "La economía y el socialismo," Cuba Socialista (November 2004). Dr. Lage Dávila is the General Director of the Centre of Molecular Immunology in Havana (CIM), which is among the top 3 Cuban biotech companies. CIM is the only Cuban center whose products have been so uniquely innovative that they have been allowed to enter clinical trials in the US territory, even with the US embargo against Cuba. Dr. Lage himself is one of the top international Cuba's scientists. He specialized in malignant transformation and cancer vaccines, fields in which he has more than 100 papers published. For these reasons, this research considers his statements as highly plausible. According to Dr. Lage, the Cuban biotech industry has been for several years providing more financial resources to the country than it consumes. He confirmed this in a national interview later (August 2011). You can find it here (only in Spanish) www.revolucionomuerte.org/index.php/entrevistas-2/3845-las-razones-del-desarrollo-cientifico-cubano. This assertion however, still needs to be confirmed with hard data. This has been to date impossible to carry out.

55 This phase is about finding the specific biochemical pathway, receptor, protein or gene that serves as suitable point of intervention in a disease process.

56 This phase is about finding a molecule – potential drug – that can inhibit the target.

57 Generating data on the effectiveness of the candidate compound before testing it in humans.

58 This phase is about evaluating effectiveness in humans. It is divided in three or four phases, involving a gradually larger patient population. From these phases, the phase II (proof of concept) is considered to be the most important because it gives a more precise idea about the cost and affectivity of the product.

59 A regulatory agency must analyze all the information regarding the drug candidate results in trials; and further approve or disapprove it marketing application. In well-developed innovation systems, a further post-marketing surveillance is carried out by the same or several other regulatory bodies, in order to prove the pharmacological effects of the drug in a huge population.

60 Having identified both the acting target behind some medical condition is no guarantee of success. Targets need to be validated and if a molecule that inhibits that target could be identified, the chance is 1–5000 that this molecule will become a commercially viable drug. However, recent advances in the field of artificial intelligence (AI) are expected to have the ability to help to improve this rate. AI technologies have already found application in healthcare; e.g., in the treatment of chronic

diseases and the interpretation of medical images (IBM's Watson) or in the detection of certain health risks through data collected via a mobile app and in treatment of eye condition (Google's DeepMind). The prospects for drug design are big. However the adoption has been slow for quite obvious reasons. One of them is that the industry has a past in terms of trying new technological platforms which resulted in hyperoptimistic biases. The other one is that these platforms are very capital-intensive and the industry is characterized by long product-development cycles, which means huge up-front investments. Another one is the complexity of the diseases targeted, even in the presence of high-powered computing systems, which implies significant regulatory and technical uncertainty (for additional insight see www.mckinsey.com/industries/pharmaceuticals-and-medical-products/our-insights/how-new-biomolecular-platforms-and-digital-technologies-are-changing-r-and-d)

61 Since the US accounts for a large majority of the industry's revenues, the US story is very similar to the global one. The industry experienced aggregate profits during the period 2008–10 for first time in its history; mainly because, since 2008, the American branch of the sector has attained positive cash flow. This was not because of the success of its commercial leaders," but because of steep cost cutting by a broad swath of companies" due to the financial crisis (E&Y 2012, p. 25). However, overall results remained negative in Europe, Canada and Australia. In 2011, American bio-tech net income fell, even after adjusting for the acquisitions of three large US-based companies: Genzyme Corp [acquired by Sanofi-Aventis (France) in 2011], Cephalon [acquired in 2011 by Tevas (Israel)] and Talecris Biotherapeutics [taken over by Grifols (Spain) in 2011] — which collectively had revenues of US$8.5 billion in 2010 (E&Y 2012, p. 25). As the E&Y Beyond Borders report states, in an industry that has been in the red for the vast majority of its history this "decline in profitability may simply be a sign that things are indeed starting to return to normal" (E&Y 2012, p. 26).

62 See: www.ncsl.org/IssuesResearch/Health/StateLegislaturesMagazineMarketing DrugsDeba/tabid/13788/Default.aspx;   see   also   http://keionline.org/timeline-bayh-dole

63 The raise of the pharmaceutical industry is strongly related to the raise of the managerial capitalism, which distinguished precisely by the vertical integrated companies. The modern pharmaceutical industry has its origins in the end of the nineteenth century in Germany, as already vertical integrated leading chemical companies (Hoescht, Bayer, BASF) used both the expertise gained by their in-house R&D labs and the overall professionalization of science in Germany, particularly chemistry, to expand into other areas such as pharmaceuticals. By 1913, Germany was the largest exporter of pharmaceuticals in the world, accounting for almost half of the share of world exports. A great deal of economies of scope were at play here, given that the acquired facilities to produce dyes, pharmaceuticals or photographic films used the same intermediate products and processes (see Chandler 2004, pp. 474–85). Many of these innovations were subsequently copied in the rest of Europe (particularly Switzerland) and by the United States.

64 The origin of the biotechnology as indirect manipulation of biological organism is as old as humanity. However modern biotechnology is linked to the advent of genetic engineering, which finds its earlier antecedents in the works of Luis Pasteur (1822–1895), Gregor Mendel (1822–1884) and Friedrich Miescher (1811–1887). In 1869 Miescher found microscopic substance in surgical bandages, which he

called nuclein. Subsequent experiments and conjectures carried out by several scientists led Nikolai Koltsov (1895–1940) to propose the earliest hypothesis of double-helical macromolecules that was confirmed in the model of Watson and Crick in 1953. The last two received the Nobel Prize in 1962 when their model was confirmed by several experiments (including the ones carried out by Maurice Wilkins, who shared the Nobel Prize of 1953). Previously, several experiments had decisively contributed to Watson and Crick findings. For example, we can mention the experiments of Friedrich Griffith (1877–1941) in 1928, Oswald Avery (1877–1955) and co-workers in 1943, Alfred Hershey (1908–1997) and Martha Chase (1927–2003) in 1952; as well as the experimental data provided by Rosalind Franklin (1920–1958) and Raymond Gosling (1926) in the same year. Then in 1968 Werner Arber (1929) discovered a type of enzymes capable of cutting (gene scissors) DNA, which paved the way for recombinant technologies. In 1973 the era of gene technology started when several renowned researchers independently developed DNA sequencing methods, which helped later to recombine in vitro pieces of DNA to another gene.

65 Traditional pharmaceutical industry produces what is known as small molecule drugs (SMD). These molecules have low molecular weight and are produced by chemical synthesis. The fact that they are the result of a stable and predictable chemical process makes it possible that identical copies can be made. SMD are simple, well defined and independent of the manufacturing process. In contrast, large molecules or biological drugs (LM) have high molecular weight and are produced in living cell cultures; and now also by genetic engineering (direct rather than indirect manipulation of organism genome). The result of genetic engineering are recombinant molecules, which are produced by bringing together genetic material from multiple sources, creating synthesized (recombinant) versions of substances that already exist in nature or creating sequences that would not otherwise be found in biological organisms. The first recombinant product was insulin, which had traditionally been obtained from animal sources (e.g. pigs and cattle). The fact that genetically engineered LM are complex and heterogeneous mixtures of genetic material means that their manufacturing process is more expensive and more challenging than for traditional SMD. Even minor changes in manufacturing process can cause significant changes in efficacy or immunogenicity. Therefore it is nearly impossible to ensure an identical copy of a LM (biosimilar), which makes its regulation very important, if more difficult. All this makes the overall process highly unstable if compared to the production of SMD. As an example aspirin, which is considered a small molecule drug, measures just 180 daltons and has 21 atoms (1mg≈ 6.0221366516752E+20 daltons). It has little ability to initiate an immune response and remains relatively stable over time. In contrast, a typical monoclonal antibody biological drug measures 150,000 daltons, contains 20,000 atoms, degrades over time, and has the ability to generate a significant immune response. Thus, the production of a biological is an inherently unstable situation requiring also special handling and storage (see www.gabionline.net/Biosimilars/Research/Small-molecule-versus-biological-drugs)

66 Recombinant DNA and monoclonal antibody (mAb) technologies formed the basis of the first biotechnology business model.

67 www.wipo.int/sme/en/documents/pharma_licensing.html#P510_29610

68 In contrast to the exclusive license, a sole license is one where the licensor retains the right to exploit the intellectual property itself. Likewise, a non exclusive license

allows the licensor to retain the right to exploit the intellectual property itself and, in addition, to license other licensees as well. However, both types of contracts are highly unusual in the biopharmaceutical industry as big pharma players (the usual licensees) often impose their negotiation muscle. Another form of contract is the assignment, which has the effect of permanently transferring the ownership of intellectual property from an organization (or person) to other. However the incidence of assignment is significantly smaller than licensing because, among other reasons, it does not involve performance obligations from the assignee (see www.wipo.int/sme/en/documents/pharma_licensing.html#P510_29610)

69 Ibid.

70 Ibid.

71 The Act did articulate taxpayer protection rights concerning non-exclusive licenses – if the action "is necessary to alleviate health or safety needs which are not reasonably satisfied," or the action "is necessary to meet public uses" (see www.law.cornell.edu/uscode/35/usc_sec_35_00000203----000-.html) See also www.keionline.org/bayh-dole. But a 1983 Executive Memo liberalized access to include coverage for large corporation (see www.presidency.ucsb.edu/ws/index.php?pid =40945&st=&st1=#axzz1eKsKUfhw. Subsequent amendments eliminated some remaining restriction on the terms of exclusive patent licenses. For a timeline of this Act, see http://keionline.org/timeline-bayh-dole

Germany and Japan have implemented similar rules, and even the University of Cambridge put a Bay–Dole type system into place in 2005. Developing industrial powers are also implementing patenting laws for publicly funded research, including China, Brazil, Malaysia and South Africa. Both advocates and opponents of the legislation agree with the fact that this piece of legislation is one of the most important institutional determinants of the industry. See S Loewenberg, The Bayh–Dole Act: A model for promoting research translation?, *Molecular Oncology* 3(2): 91–3, 2009 and T Siepmann, The global exportation of the U.S. Bay-Dole Act, University of Dayton Law Review 30(2): 210–43, 2005. See also AD So, Is Bayh-Dole good for developing countries? Lessons from the US experience. PLoS Biol 6(10), 2008: e262. doi:10.1371/journal.pbio.0060262

72 For instance, according to Gary Pisano, while R&D spending increased over the period 1980–2005, the rate of introduction of new applications fell. Other researchers have found that from 1950 to 2008, the US Food and Drug Administration (FDA) approved 1222 new drugs (new molecular entities (NMEs) or new biologics). However, although the level of investment in pharmaceutical research and development (R&D) increased dramatically during the same period (US$50 billion per year in 2009), the yearly rate of new drug introduction is no greater now than it was 50 years ago (see B Munos, Lessons from 60 years of pharmaceutical innovation, *Nature Reviews Drug Discovery* 8: 959–68, 2009, p. 959). More, as Light and Lexchin argue, most of these drugs have provided only minor clinical advantages over existing treatments. Indeed, according to the authors, out of 218 drugs approved by the FDA from 1978 to 1989, only 34 (15.6 percent) were judged as important therapeutic gains. They mention another report that covers a roughly similar time period (1974–94), which concluded that only 11 percent were therapeutically and pharmacologically innovative. They further make reference to a number of independent reviews carried out since the mid-1990s, which have also concluded that about 85–90 percent of all new drugs provide few or no clinical

advantages for patients (see D Light and J Lexchin, Pharmaceutical research and development: What do we get for all that money?, *BMJ* 2012: 345).

73 This view is confirmed by Light and Warburton. Here the argument of corporate risk is called into question, precisely because most of the trial costs are incurred in Phase III trials, when the risk of withdrawal is low, less than one in two.

74 The Hatch-Waxman Act, named for US Senator Orrin Hatch (R-Utah) and US Representative Henry Waxman (D-Calif.), was meant mainly to stimulate the foundering generic industry by short-circuiting some of the FDA requirements for bringing generic drugs to market. While successful in doing that, Hatch-Waxman also lengthened the patent life for brand-name drugs. Since then, industry lawyers have manipulated some of its provisions to extend patents far longer than the lawmakers intended

75 www.nybooks.com/articles/archives/2004/jul/15/the-truth-about-the-drug-companies/?pagination=false

76 It is not surprise at all that "[p]harmaceutical companies report that they invest around three times more in the combination of marketing, advertising, and administration than in research." See D Light and J Lexchin, Foreign free riders and the high price of US medicines. *BMJ* 2005, 331*(7522): 959.* Confirming this statement, Boldrin and Levine (2008 chapter 9) states that 30 top pharmaceutical firms concentrate on producing low-risk me-too drugs, which cost at twice as much in promotion and advertising they do in R&D. In actual fact, it is said that 50 percent of the R&D costs are spent on advertising drugs, which does not result from innovation.

77 The genomics and subsequently the proteomics era that began mid 90s led to new research paradigm based on high speed automation and the analysis of huge amounts of data. It was the time of combinatorial chemistry, virtual screening and computer aided drug design. In contrast to FIPCO companies, the wave of firms created during this period focused on one of these technology platforms, rather than on product technologies or therapeutic applications. Representatives firms following this model are Celera, Incyte and Millenium which specialized in developing proprietary genomic databases. More on the different biotech models see Pisano (2006, pp. 81–96) and Burns R (ed.), The Business of Healthcare Innovation, Cambridge University Press, 2005, pp. 103–90.

78 Stock option-based forms of compensation have become a major feature of the whole American economy. Business historian and organization theorist William Lazonick shows how the emergence of NASDAQ during the 1970s enhanced the prospect of an early and successful IPO boosted the New Economy explosion in the US, leading to a highly speculative, more insecure and probably unsustainable development model worldwide (see W Lazonick, Sustainable Prosperity in the New Economy? W.E. Upjohn Institute for Employement Research, Kalamazoo, Michigan, 2008). For example, by 2003 NASDAQ-like instruments such as the German Neuer Markt and Japan's JASDAQ had collapsed in scandals, while others were virtually moribund, e.g., France's Nouveau Marche, Italy's Nouvo Mercato, Hong Kong's GEM, and Malaysia's MESDAQ. In 2001 EuroNM Belgium had been closed and in 2004 NASDAQ Europe. Many of the new stock markets did not survive the avalanche of exits by bad firms. See G Giudici and P Roosenboom (eds.), The *Rise* and *Fall* of Europe's *New Stock Market*: Advances in *Financial Economics*, Elsevier, Vol. 10, 2004.

79 In financial economics an Initial Public Offering (IPO) or stock market launch is the first sale of stock (shares) by a private company to the public. The term "public" should not be confused with government policy. In finance, public enterprise refers to a company whose shares are available and traded on the stock market or other over-the-counter market. In order to avoid confusion, this study has used the term government-based firms or state owned enterprises (SOE).

80 That is, risk capital arrives not in the earliest (and most risky) phase of development, but when public investments have already taken the major risk in basic and trans-lational research. Contrary to conventional wisdom, they are not that risky. In the microelectronics industry, for which the Silicon Valley VC industry was developed, 3–5 years was adequate. They co-evolved with the industry and exercised a degree of strategic control. Nevertheless the development of the VC industry and related institutions such as NASDAQ made it possible to make use of VC for biotech, as long as the stock market remained sufficiently speculative.

81 Venture Impact: The Economic Importance of Venture Backed Companies to the U.S. Economy, www.nvca.org/index.php?option=com_content&view=article&id=255&Itemid=103

82 The amount of capital raised declined sharply in 2008. Companies in the Americas and Europe raised US$16 billion in 2008, a 46 percent decline from 2007. IPO funding fell 95 percent to US$116 million. Publicly traded biotechs have always achieved net losses globally. The global industry's net loss improved 53 percent, from US$3 billion in 2007 to US$1.4 billion in 2008 (Ernst & Young Report 2009).

83 It was soon realized that the number of genes is smaller than previously supposed, which means that most of diseases (and their drugs) are the result of unknown com-plex interaction between them and the proteins they produced. There is also little knowledge about the biologic and pharmacologic functions of these genes, which makes the search even more uncertain. This uncertainty was quickly reflected by the loss of enthusiasm of investors (see Pisano 2006).

84 The study Critical I (2006), when trying to make sense of the different venture cap-ital investment patterns in the biotechnology industry between Europe and the US, (according to age and size), concludes that for firms on both sides of the Atlantic, those with better growth prospects are more likely to be funded over older firms. Investors in Europe have put money into only 9 percent of the companies that were founded between 2002 and 2004 while US investors have backed 22 percent such companies. However, European investors put money in 19% of companies that, although very young, had nevertheless grown to more than 20 people. This com-parable US figure is 26 percent. Therefore, low proportions of European private companies attracting investment has to be attributed to company performance. In other words, the apparent reluctance of investors in Europe is due to relative paucity of opportunity – fewer European companies are investable (Critical I 2006, p. 15) available at www.bionova.gr/texnomesitia/critical.pdf .

85 Hobday and Perini (in M Cimoli et al. (ed.), The Political Economy of Capabilities Accumulation, OUP, 2009) discuss extensively the theory and policy implications of the assumption of SME´s being uncritically taken as agents of innovation, mostly (but not exclusively for developing countries (pp. 470–97). See also HJ Chang, 23 *Things They Don't Tell You* about *Capitalism*. London: Penguin, 2010 (pp. 157–67).

86 Applied Molecular Genetics (Amgen) was created in 1980 and is the world's largest independent biotechnology company.

87 Genetic EngineeringTechnology (Genentech) was created in 1976 and is considered to be the first biotech company that ever existed. It was taken over in 2009 by F. Hoffmann-La Roche Ltd (Switzerland).

88 Named Biogen-Idec after a merge with IDEC Pharmaceuticals in 2003 and renamed as Biogen Inc. in 2015 following shifts in research core areas. Biogen, founded in 1978 in Geneva, had been one of the oldest biotech companies.

89 The company was founded in 1981 and was acquired by Novartis (Switzerland) in 2006.

90 Data updated from Lazonick and Tulum, U.S. Biopharmaceutical Finance and the Sustainability of the U.S. Biotech Business Model, *Research Policy* 40(9), 2011: 1170–87, using http://officeofbudget.od.nih.gov/spending_hist.html

91 Ibid.

92 Over the past two decades, but especially in the 2000s, the executives of US business corporations, encouraged by Wall Street, have become committed to the practice of allocation substantial corporate resources to buy back their own corporate stock (see Lazonick and Tulum, U.S. Biopharmaceutical Finance... 2011).

93 However, for an ICT company it was possible to generate a commercial product within a few years after being created, while in the biopharmaceutical industry it takes at least a decade. Therefore US venture-capital model seems to have been ill-suited to the biotech industry from the very beginning.

94 As already mentioned in Chapters 3 and 4, the high-tech district known as Silicon Valley was either producing directly for the government or, increasingly from the 1960s, spinning off government-financed technology for commercial uses. In addition, in 1958 the US government launched a program to provide subsidies to the creation and growth of start-ups. Many of the firms of the emerging venture-capital industry of the 1960s received funds from this program. At the same time, in 1963 the US government (specifically the US Securities Exchange Commission) encouraged the National Association of Security Dealers (at the time a non-profit organization in charge of the regulation of the trading activities of its members) to use computer technology to create a national electronic quotation system for over-the-counter stocks (stocks traded without assistance of exchange trading facilities). The result was the formation in 1971 of the National Association of Securities Dealers Quotation System (NASDAQ), which, in contrast to the New York Stock Exchange (NYSE) has no stringent listing requirements. NASDAQ has made it possible for venture capitalist to engage in speculative investments. In 1973 was formed the US-based National Venture Capital Association, which along with the Silicon Valley-based American Electronic Association convinced the US Congress to reduce the capital-gains tax rates during the 1980s and to increase the amount of funding that pension-funds could invest in risky assets (see W Lazonick and M Mazzucato 2013, The risk-reward nexus, *Industrial and Corporate Change* 22(4) (Aug. 1, 2013): 1106–8).

95 A much more modest estimate of the cost of drug development has been offered by other sources than the estimate given by DiMasi et al. (2003) See Light and Warburton (2011).

96 For example, according to a report of the Economic Commission for Latin America and the Caribbean (ECLAE) the gross income per employee provided by the Cuban biotech industry is double that of the tourism industry; the latter seen by many as the engine of Cuban economy. See, Estudio económico de América Latina y el Caribe, 2009–2010, pp. 245–50.

97   Of course this is not to say that they knew exactly what they were doing or the outcomes of their actions. Actually, many of the governmental decisions were a result of past experiences and mistakes. The most resounding was the failure of the electronic industry in Cuba. However, being able to strategically allocate its resources, this failure was redirected into another (at least partially) successful branch within the biotechnology.

98   I Clark, UNESCO Science Report, pp. 123–31, 2010.

99   Consider the example of institutions such as MITI in Japan, KIST and KAIS in Korea, ITRI and ERSO in Taiwan, DARPA and the National Academy Foundation in the US and so on. As mentioned in previous chapters (3 and 4) most of the most today's successful firms in the industrialized world are strongly related to these government agencies.

100   Consider the programs of the Federal Ministry of Education and Research (BMBF: Bundesministerium für Bildung und Forschung) as executive arm of federal public R&D policies: At the moment of writing this note the most renowned of these policies programs are BioRegio and BioProfile.

101   Consider the Agence Nationale de la Recherche (ANR), pôle de compétitivités, Oséo and the creation of a specific status for young innovative enterprises. Moreover, it has been created a sort of task force for health care industries called Comité Stratégique des Industries de Santé (CSIS). And last but not least, regional administrations very often offer some form of public support to biotech, through incubators or subsidies. Since 2004 research policy tries to increase finance for public research and collaborations with private companies. Due to the multiplicity of sources of funding from public institutions (CIR, pôles de compétitivité, Oséo, regions, etc.) an estimation of total public support is difficult to perform. Yet the state is clearly investing to develop biotech and other innovative industries through different schemes.

102   Venture capital market tends avoid the early development phases. As a response to this, government money has been concentrated on seed and early stage funding, see: UK Biotechnology Industry, House of Commons Trade and Industry Committee, Twelfth Report of Session 2002–03, London, Published on September 3, 2003. In the UK the MRC, a public funded lab, receives annual `grant-in-aid` funding from Parliament through the Department for Business, Innovation and Skills (BIS). It works closely with the Department of Health, UK research councils, industry and others stakeholders to identify and respond to UK´s health need.

103   In 1980 oncologist Richard Lee Clark, president of MD Anderson Hospital in Houston, Texas (the first cancer hospital in the United States) travelled with a North American delegation to the island. There he met the then Cuban president, Fidel Castro, with whom he discussed his groundbreaking research on interferon, a "wonder drug" in the battle to cure cancer. Shortly after that, Clark hosted two Cuban scientists at his hospital in Houston, sharing his research and expertise. After Houston, the next stop for Cuban researchers was the Helsinki-based laboratories of Dr. Kari Cantell. Clark had visited Cantell in 1979, shortly before his trip to Cuba, and directed the Cuban scientists to seek Cantell´s expertise. Cantell was the first person to isolate interferon from human cells in the 1970s. In 1981 a group of Cuban scientists headed by Manuel Limonta spent a week working with Cantell and his colleagues learning the procedure to reproduce interferon in large quantities. See Cuba's Pharmaceutical Advantage, NACLA Report on the Americas,

July–Aug, 2011 available at: http://findarticles.com/p/articles/mi_go1653/is_201107/ai_n58256857/, See also E Bravo, Development within *Underdevelopment. New Trends* in Cuban Medicine, Editorial José Martí / Elfos Scientae, 1998.

104 On a lesser scale, but by no means with less success, biotechnology has been expanded to other provinces, mainly Camaguey, Sancti Spiritus, Villa Clara, and Santiago de Cuba.

105 The term "institutions" was added by the author.

106 This insistence on cooperation and planning instead competition may sound very socialistic for many observers; however it is not a Cuban unique feature at all. In fact, "depending on the estimate, between one third and one half of international trade consists of transfers among different units within transnational corporations" (see HJ Chang, 23 *Things They Don't Tell You* about *Capitalism*, Penguin, 2010, p. 208).

107 BioCubaFarma does not depend on any ministry; it is a completely (government-owned) autonomous entity. But the strategic network of the industry was already working under this schema.

108 However, the way in which these resources are used (e.g. salary incentives) are decided within the centers.

109 The geographical aspect (regional proximity) has played an important role in Cuban biotechnology, but is far from being the fundamental aspect behind innovation. Spatial clustering can be relevant, because it might create channels for transmitting tacit knowledge and creating beneficial interdependencies for all individual firms. However, this does not mean automatic absorption capacity.

110 For a comprehensive analysis of the history of Cuban medicine see the work of prestigious historian of Cuban healthcare, and medical doctor, Dr. Gregorio Delgado García.

111 Finlay's theory was, after working tirelessly during the 1870s in experiments and field tests, officially presented at the Havana's Royal Academy of Medical, Physical and Natural Sciences and at the 1881 International Sanitary Conference in Washington. It was generally poorly received, among other reasons, because at that time the germ theory was gaining recognition and his theory of the mosquito as an intermediate host of the parasite was seen as clumsy and outlandish. It was ridiculed in the Spanish and American press during two decades. Only the high level of infections within the American occupation army during the intervention campaign known as the Cuban-Hispano-American war forced Americans to consider Finlay theory, which was successfully confirmed in a field test during 1900 in Havana. The job was carried out by the Walter Reed Commission, composed of four brave physicians of the American army. One of them, Jesse Lazear, was fascinated by Finlay's theory and was given by the latter several eggs for his experiments. He deliberately allowed himself to be infected by the bite of a mosquito in order to explore the disease and died as a result. James Carroll, another physician of the group, survived an infection but eventually died, years later, as a result of complications linked to the infection. Aristides Agramonte, another member, was a Cuban pioneer of the bacteriology which made important contributions to the field in Cuba during the first three decades of the twentieth century. Walter Reed, the leading figure of the Commission, was also fascinated by Finlay theory and gave him credit in his articles. However, the credit was apparently not emphatic enough, which caused Reed to receive all the credit during

many decades. Finally, during the last six decades, the name of Finlay has been given the deserved credit as the real genius behind the discovery. This is still a source of sadness and content in the history of bacteriology. To be fair, there were other names that made notable previous contributions to the yellow fever research. The best known are the French physician Louis-Daniel Beauperthuy, the Scottish physician Patrick Manson and the American physician Josiah C. Nott, the last one also infamously known for his racist views and theories. But it was Finlay who gave the correct account on the disease. Until his death in 1915, he was nominated seven times for the Nobel Prize.

112   The government of Cuba decided that from May 1, 2010 and thereafter all foreign and also Cubans living abroad should have travel insurance which covers medical expenses or a policy for medical expenses with coverage in Cuba. No more free healthcare for Cubans living abroad. See www.cubaminrex.cu/english/LookCuba/Articles/Others/2010/06-04.html

113   The information requirements of the Cuban national health care system continued to increase in complexity with the emergence of institutional networks and continuing emphasis on education and research. All of these factors contributed to further development of telecommunications infrastructures to support health care information, communication, and service delivery. These infrastructures reduced institutional health care costs in difficult economic conditions. INFOMED was founded in 1992 as the Cuban National Health Care Telecommunications Network and Information Portal. The virtual infrastructure maintained through INFOMED includes the Virtual Library (Biblioteca Virtual en Salud, BVS) and Virtual University (Universidad Virtual), the Health Information Observatory (Vigilancia en Salud), and key ministerial structures accessible through the portal. Specialized networks connect provincial information centers, research institutes, hospitals and institutions of higher education (including community level), but also foster communication and interaction with the international scientific community. The Virtual Library integrates access to Cuban electronic publications in medicine and public health as well as important US, Latin American and international publication initiatives. Medline and the US National Library of Medicine offer subscribed English language bibliographic databases while SCIELO, the Latin American Scientific Electronic Library Online, initiated in Brazil, offers medical journals by country of publication (Brazil, Chile, Cuba, Costa Rica, Spain and Venezuela) in English, Spanish and Portuguese. Technical personnel at both the national and provincial network nodes are specialized in network management, the Linux operating system and system security. While MINSAP is largely responsible for hierarchical control, INFOMED is the vehicle for horizontal communication and coordination throughout the health care system. In 2002, INFOMED was awarded the Stockholm Challenge Prize in the health category for life-improving information technologies (see A Séror, A case analysis of INFOMED: The Cuban National Health Care Telecommunications Network and Portal, *J Med Internet Res* 8(1) (Jan.–Mar.): e1, doi: 10.2196/jmir.8.1.e1, 2006); see also www.stockholmchallenge.org/project/data/infomed-health-information-network-cuba)

114   www.pugwash.org/reports/ees/ees8e.htm

115   Several problem of the Cuban health system have become apparent in the two last decades: the physical deterioration of facilities and the serious supply shortages caused by the economic crisis in Cuba in the early 1990s, the growing public dissatisfaction related to service instability, wait times, physician absence because of

administrative duties, new teaching responsibilities or international cooperation abroad, or the growing costs of the health care. In order to address these issues, a general reorganization of primary care was launched in 2008, followed by a complete reform (currently under way) of the health system in 2010, mainly but by no means exclusively for economic reasons. For example, according to official figures, during the first decade of the new millennium, the health care budget did not decrease. Another delicate problem to be addressed is the material living and working conditions of health professionals. It is well known that the majority of Cuban physicians who have neither served internationally nor have the benefit of supplementary income sources – such as family assistance or remittances – generally experience economic constraints similar to those of other workers in the country (professional or otherwise). These situations, although not exclusive to Cuba, are infrequent in other countries, where professions with significant social recognition – medicine, nursing and rehabilitation specialists, among others – frequently constitute a strata with an income advantage. See L Iniguez (2013), Overview of evolving changes in Cuba's health services, MEDICC Review 15(2) (Apr.): 45–51.

116 Cuban physicians were highly trained and well respected, but nearly half of them left for the United States when the new government set about drastically reforming the health sector. Thus, from 1959 through 1967, when accumulated expertise was most needed, the island of six million people lost 3000 of its 6300 physicians and found itself with just 16 professors of medicine and a single medical school.

117 For example see www.miscelaneasdecuba.net/media/pdf/Article-Hirschfeld-Press.pdf . In this critique, the American anthropologist Katherine Hirschfeld makes a libertarian (and quasi postmodernistic) critique of the system in that she blames the centralized system of all the problems without engaging in any serious debate in this direction. For example, if the centralized system and Marxist ideology are the problem, why do the countries of the region do not perform better? She cites the examples of the Soviet Union and communist China (and suggests that Cuba also does it) as countries that systematically manipulate statistics in order to advance a political agenda. However, apart from the fact that, in the case of Cuba, the contrary has been proven by specialized articles in prestigious journal the author do not even mention (see www.thelancet.com/journals/lancet/article/PIIS0140673606684225/fulltext doi:10.1016/S0140-6736(06)68422–5) is this only true for socialist countries? Could we say for example that China is manipulating something when they affirm they are growing economically? Without denying that some manipulation can exist, the facts speak for themselves. The collapse of the Soviet Union speaks for itself. Last but not least, she too does not engage in any serious discussion of the real impact of the American embargo on the island.

While these sorts of one-size-fits-all critiques do not stand by themselves, it needs to be acknowledged that problems exist and that a debate about them should be welcomed (see for example the harsh critique contained in a letter to President Raul Castro; written by a team of medical surgeons of a Havana hospital, www.cubainformacion.tv/index.php/manipulacion-mediatica/45829-medios-tergiversan-y-anaden-parrafos-a-carta-de-medicos-del-hospital-calixto-garcia-al-gobierno-cubano-leer-verdadera-carta (original letter Spanish). However, to highlight the point of the ideological bias of many of the critics, here you can see a manipulated version of the letter, which was evidently made following political objectives rather than objectivity (www.elmundo.es/blogs/elmundo/habaname/ 2012/09/25/sos-del-servicio-de-cirugia-general-del.html) (manipulated version in Spanish).

118 Good manufacturing practices (GMP) is a system for ensuring that products are consistently produced and controlled according to quality standards. It is designed to minimize the risks involved in any pharmaceutical production that cannot be eliminated through testing the final product. The main risks are: (1) unexpected contamination of products, causing damage to health or even death, (2) wrong labels on containers, leading to the patient getting the wrong medicine, (3) not enough or too much active ingredient, resulting in ineffective treatment or adverse effects. See http://apps.who.int/medicinedocs/en/d/Js6160e/11.html

119 Good clinical practices (GCP) refers to a standard for clinical studies which encompasses the design, conduct, monitoring, termination, audit, analyses, reporting and documentation of the studies and which ensures that the studies are scientifically and ethically sound and that the clinical properties of the pharmaceutical product (diagnostic, therapeutic or prophylactic) under investigation are properly documented. See http://apps.who.int/medicinedocs/pdf/whozip13e/ whozip13e.pdf

120 The notion of Good Laboratory Practices (GLP) is defined in the OECD Principles as *"a quality system concerned with the organisational process and the conditions under which non-clinical health and environmental safety studies are planned, performed, monitored, recorded, archived and reported."* The purpose of the Principles of Good Laboratory Practice is to promote the development of quality test data and provide a tool to ensure a sound approach to the management of laboratory studies, including conduct, reporting and archiving.

   The position of GLP studies within the drug development process is specific to the second stage. See www.who.int/tdr/publications/documents/glp-handbook. pdf

121 Equivalent of the American FDA.

122 O Jacobo, Role of the National Regulatory Authority in Prequalification of Vaccines. Experience of CECMED, Developing Countries Vaccine Manufactures Network (DCVMN) mimeo, 2007, available at www.fiocruz.br/bio/media/ DCVMN%202007/apresentacoes%20dia%2012/Table%201/Olga%20Jacobo%20 Casanueva%20CUBA/2_olga.pdf;   see   also   www.who.int/immunization_ standards/vaccine_quality/pq_suppliers/en/

123 We are referring to the Food and Drug Administration Amendment Act passed by the US Congress in 2007. This Act gave the agency new regulatory power, more money and more safety-related mandates (Light ed. 2010, p. 57).

124 According to several experts, budget cuts of FDA started under President Carter. President Reagan increased the trend by issuing an Executive Anti-regulation Order. In many aspects, industry was left to regulate itself (see D Light (ed.), The *Risks of Prescription Drugs*, New York: Columbia University Press, 2010, pp. 52–3). Other institutional changes, such as the weakening of the once-legendary federal pension system, has made it more difficult to retain well-trained regulatory scientists, which flow continuously to the industry (ibid.).

125 Industry financing became law in 1992 under the Prescription Drug User Fee Act, which allowed companies to pay for each new drug application. These fees would provide funds to the FDA. In return, the industry required that 90 percent

of reviews be completed in less time. It also prohibited the use of fees for any post-marketing drug safety activities. An estimated 20 million US citizens were exposed to drugs approved under this Act, that were then withdrawn soon after for their severe adverse effects. Corporate fees went from one-tenth of total FDA funding to more than half (ibid., pp. 54–6).

126 See www.fda.gov/Drugs/DevelopmentApprovalProcess/DevelopmentResources/DrugInteractionsLabeling/ucm110632.htm

127 An article quoting data of a Cutting Edge Information survey states that the average per-patient trial costs across all therapeutic areas rose in Phase I from $15,023 in 2008 to $21,883 in 2011. In Phase II, the cost rose from $21,009 to $36,070. In Phase IIIa, the cost increased from $25,280 to $47,523 and in Phase IIIb, cost jumped from $25,707 to $47,095. Finally, Phase IV expenses rose from $13,011 to $17,042. The article can be found in www.pharmalot.com/2011/07/clinical-trial-costs-for-each-patient-rose-rapidly/. According to the article The Cutting Edge surveyed 21 drugmakers, 12 biotech companies, nine device makers and 23 contract research organizations. The survey can be found in www.cuttingedgeinfo.com/research/clinical-development/trial-operations/

128 For Phase I trials, 58 percent are now outsourced, compared with 35 percent in 2008. In Phase II, the figure is 63 percent, up from 36 percent. In Phase IIIb, 54 percent are outsourced versus 46 percent, and in Phase IV, 51 percent are now outsourced, compared with 43 percent three years ago (ibid.).

Risk proliferation syndrome have been said to have made prescription drugs the fourth-leading cause of death in the US (see D Light ed., The risks of prescription drugs... 2010).

129 See http://ipsnews.net/news.asp?idnews=40472

130 See www.who.int/features/2013/cuba_biotechnology/en/

131 http://resultados.redciencia.cu/historia/periodo_5_4_en.php

132 International linkages played a central role in building expertise in the Cuban bio-technology. Cuban specialists were sent abroad to obtain PhDs in pioneering life science organizations in Western Europe and the United States, including the Curie Institute (Paris), the Pasteur Institute (Paris), Heidelberg University (Heidelberg, Germany) and Harvard University (Cambridge, MA, USA) (Thorsteinsdóttir et al. 2004). However, substantial learning capabilities and in-house research effort were required to absorb and translate the acquired knowledge into innovative world-class products. This is quite consistent with many other catch-up experiences where foreign students, apprentices or broker agents played a central role. Mazzoleni and Nelson mention the cases of Taiwan, South Korea and Japan and Brazil (see Mazzoleni and Nelson in: M Cimoli et al. (eds.), The *Political Economy* of Capabilities... 2009, pp. 378–408). We could also add the case of China and India (ibid.). This is nothing different from the industrial, trade and technology policies on behalf of the wool manufacturing industry carried out by Britain from XVI century on (see HJ Chang, Kicking *Away*... 2003, pp. 19–24). We could also mention the role played by Samuel Slater in the development of the textile industry in the United States (see www.woonsocket.org/slaterhist.htm) or the role played by Peter Beuth as head of the department of trade and industry in the Prussian Ministry of Finance when setting up the *Gewerbeinstitut* (Craft Institute) in 1820 (see HJ Chang, Kicking Away... 2003, pp. 32–5). When going back in the timeline, we find the role played by the French Jesuits priest Francois Xavier d'Entrecolles by revealing the Chinese technique of manufacturing porcelain

(W Rowe and T Brook, China's Last Empire: The Great Qing. Cambridge, MA: The Belknap Press of Harvard University Press, 2009, p. 368), and mercury (see L. Barnes, Needles, Herbs, Gods, and Ghosts: China, Healing, and the West to 1848. Cambridge: Harvard University Press, 2005, p. 101). Many other examples of this kind can be found in these and other countries, but the point is that technology transfer, be it in the form of licensing, joint ventures or reverse engineering, has always been part of a good emulation strategy.

133 KIST during the 1970s in Korea, IRI in Italy.

134 Finland, for instance, is typical of countries that locate incubators to nurture startup firms near universities that host biotechnology centers of excellence. See: J Senker et al. (2000), European exploitation of biotechnology—do government policies help?, Nature Biotechnology18(6) (June): 605–8.

135 In recent decades, US-based incubator managers have reported that somewhere between 80 and 90 percent of companies that have incubated with them are still in existence after five years. This figure vividly contrasts with the Small Business Administration (SBA) statistic that finds that only 50 percent of start-ups survive their first five years. These figures are less surprising when one considers that nine of ten companies fail because of management deficiencies, and that 90 percent of these deficiencies could have been foreseen. See EM Zablocki in A Krattiger et al. (eds.) (2007), Intellectual Property Management in Health and Agricultural Innovation: A Handbook of Best Practices, p. 1307).

136 Today, however, most incubators prefer the company-centered approach, charging market rates for rent and offering services as the value-added benefit of locating in the incubator (ibid.).

137 CIDEM develops antiretrovirals, cytostatic medicines, immunosuppressants such as oral cyclosporines, homeopathic medicines, bacterial endotoxins marketed under the ENDORETO brand, pharmaceutical forms of aloe vera and Plectranthus amboinicus, and antihistamines and antiasthmatics.

138 Note that the node(s) selected in the visualization will be represented (and henceforth) within a circle.

139 In Cárdenas-O´Farrill (2009) the same concept was introduced as "in-house integration." Henceforth it will be used as in-house modularity.

140 The concept will not be fully developed here. It is merely employed in order to define the kind of functioning of a group of firms within the Cuban biotech which might be applicable to other cases. In-house modularity should not be confused with organizational integration (OI), which is the generic concept being employed here. Actually in-house modularity could be considered a concrete case of OI.

141 For example, while Heber Biotec is the trading arm of the Center of Genetic Engineering and Biotechnology (CIGB), it is also involved in the commercialization of products of other organizations without marketing capabilities. That is, Heber Biotec has not only specialized in CIGB products (although vertically integrated within CIGB), but it is also flexible enough to go beyond CIGB product configuration. In contrast to the typical alliances and other short term contracts that take place in the worldwide biotech industry, Heber Biotech has an institutionalized long-term commitment to other companies that lack in-house capabilities, which allows more flexibility (modular-like behavior) while at the same time strengthening mutual commitment (more characteristic of vertical integration). This also allows employees to develop firm-specific knowledge (but

still highly combinable with other firms' knowledge stock) and loyalty sense, so important in industries such as the biotechnology.

142 That is also considering that many industry officials (and academic experts) tend to use the term, partly unaware of its possible theoretical implications, while ironically trying to express the same notion covered by the term in-house modularity.

143 Visible consequences of this process are phenomena such as large-scale downsizing and outsourcing, which have conquered the industrial landscape of the last three decades in both developed and developing countries. A very detailed discussion on the subject can be found in W Lazonick, Sustainable Prosperity... 2008.

144 The inputs into a product system include both the technological options available to achieve particular functions and the resources and capabilities of the firms involved in the production process. Heterogeneity in these inputs will increase the value to be obtained through modular product configurations (see M Schilling (2000), Toward a general modular systems theory and its application to interfirm product modularity, *Academy of Management Review* 25(2): 323).

145 The firms still retain their proprietary technologies (patents, secrecy etc.) but these technologies work within an open standards-based production system, so that companies can reap the gains of compatibility with a wide range of complementary knowledge while still retaining the rent-generating potential of their proprietary component. Different technologies can coexist more peacefully because they are made compatible.

146 http://gndp.cigb.edu.cu/index.html# A complete list of the product in which CIGB has been involved can be found in www.heber-biotec.com/Ingles/default.htm

147 A significant part of the work was actually being doing by Dr Luis Herrera, the then head of the department and current president of CIGB. According to Bravo (1998), there was actually a different group working molecular biology, but the book also acknowledges that Herrera was also an expert in this field.

148 Recombinant technology was discovered by Cohen and Boyer around 1975 (1972–3 first papers and 1974 application for patents). The first drug using recombinant technology was insulin, manufactured by Genentech (which had been founded by Boyer and the venture capitalist Swanson) and licensed by Elli Lilly.

149 The difference is that the leukocyte IFN contains different types of IFN's. The recombinant version allows obtaining a purified IFN type, which makes its production more economical. The possibility of recombinant IFN had been expressed by Sid Pestka, of Roche Institue, in 1978. Genentech labs and several other were simultaneously trying to be the first obtaining it, but it was finally obtained first by Taniguchi, a Japanese researcher and then by Weissman Lab at Biogen, the competitor of Genentech. A couple of months later, the Pestka lab cloned interferon cDNA for both IFN-a and -b on the same plate and then contracted with Genentech. After that, Genentech did not expand the deal with Hoffmann-La Roche and the IFN gamma was obtained in collaboration with Boeringer Ingelheim and other Japanese partners. See David V. Goeddel, Ph.D., "Scientist at Genentech, CEO at Tularik," an oral history conducted in 2001 and 2002 by Sally Smith Hughes for the Regional Oral History Office, The Bancroft Library, University of California, Berkeley, 2003, see also P Fitzgerald- Bocarsly (1997), The history of interferon: An interview with Sid Pestka, at: www.isicr.org/newsletter/isicr4.2.pdf

150   To be clear, this sentence is not intended as an indictment of UNIDO, but as an idea of the proportion of the risk taken by the Cuban government when it decided to invest in this facility, in which UNIDO did not participate. However, the Cuban government has always been involved in cooperation projects with UNIDO since the very creation of this UN agency in 1966. Up to date (2018), Cuba, as a founding member, has participated in about 180 projects involving circa US$ 31 million, including technical assistance and quality management systems for projects related to the production of paper, glass and latter renewables etc. Also as a result of this cooperation was inaugurated in 1978 a pharmaceutical Lab (8 M Lab, see Visualization) (see www.granma.cu/cuba/2018-08-31/onudi-cuba-desarrollo-de-una-estrategia-sustentable-y-sostenible-31-08-2018-14-08-24, see also https://50.unido.org/impact/index.html#home/1978-cuba)

151   http://gndp.cigb.edu.cu/index.html#

152   Ibid.

153   The hepatitis B virus was discovered in 1965 by Nobel Prize winner Barauch Blumberg. Four years after discovering the hepatitis B virus, the first hepatitis B vaccine was developed, which was initially a heat-treated form of the virus. In 1981, the FDA approved a more sophisticated plasma-derived hepatitis B vaccine for human use. Merck Pharmaceuticals manufactured this plasma vaccine as "Heptavax," which was the first commercial hepatitis B virus vaccine. Dr Saul Krugman played a significant role in this research. See www.hepb.org/professionals/hepatitis_b_vaccine.htm, See also http://library.med.nyu.edu/library/eresources/featuredcollections/krugman/index.html.In 1986, Chiron developed the technology to obtain genetically engineered (or DNA recombinant) hepatitis B, which was licensed to Merck (according to an article in the New York Times, www.nytimes.com/1986/10/13/business/biotechnology-spotlight-now-shines-on-chiron.html). The Cuban recombinant vaccine was also developed in 1986 at CIGB, which illustrates how the biotech industry of Cuba was right at the forefront of the technological frontier.

154   At the time, there were only five research groups in the world who shared those same objectives. See G Reed and J Torres (2008), Riding the brainwaves of Cuban science: Interview with Pedro Valdés Sosa, Vice Director for Research and Director of Neuroinformatics Cuban Neuroscience Centre, Havana, *MEDICC Review* 10(2) (Spring): 11–13.

155   The Computer of Average Transients (CAT) was invented in 1960 by the Austrian-born musician, scientist and inventor Manfred Clynes with the objective of measuring brain electrical activity. This machine, one of the first special purpose digital computers, was used around the world and greatly furthered brain research.

156   Neurometrics is the science of measuring and interpreting brainwave frequencies. The term was coined after a homonymous foundational paper was published in 1977 by Science. This paper happened to be the result of the close collaboration between Dr. Erwin Roy John (1924–2009), a world-renowned American neuroscientist and pioneer in the field of Neurometrics; and other scientists, including Dr Pedro Valdés-Sosa, pioneer of the field in Cuba and founder (and current director general) of the Cuban Neuroscience Centre. In fact Dr Valdés is registered as co-author of this foundational paper, which, as in the case of other disciplines within the Cuban biopharma, gives an idea of how cutting edge was the knowledge that many Cuban scientists were dealing with at that time. Actually, they were not only catching up, but co-pioneers in many fields (see the paper ER John

et al., Neurometrics, *Science* 24 June 1977, 196 (4297): 1393–1410, doi:10.1126/science.867036, available under www.sciencemag.org/content/196/4297/1393. citation). At the same time, the mentoring role and long-term collaboration of Dr John with young Cuban scientists at that time (and thereafter) has gained recognition among Cuba's neuroscientists and policymakers (see www.ecnsweb.com/roy-john.html).

157 A contemporary term for "minicomputer," which is the kind of computer developed during the 1960s, whose size ranges between the big mainframe and the microcomputers. The Americans recognized UM1-NX, produced at the Leningrad Electromechanical Plant (LEMZ) from 1963, as the world's first minicomputer. In a review of Soviet computers published in *Control Engineering* (no. 5, 1966) with the title "Desktop Model," the UM1-NX was described as "remarkable" for its size and low energy consumption (see http://web.archive.org/web/20080804025916/http://sovietcomputing.com/node/49). However they were unable to keep the pace after the microprocessor revolution.

158 The takeoff of the Cuban neuroscience is inextricably linked to the design and building of the country's first micro-computer (PC) in 1970 – when it was very difficult for Cuba to access this kind of technology (ibid.).

159 During the 80s, applications of these devices to the biological sciences were frequent and several computer programs were written or adapted to allow such applications. See T Pons et al. (2007), Computational biology in Cuba: An opportunity to promote science in a developing country, Plos Computational Biology 3(11) (Nov.), e277: 2047–51.

160 G Reed and J Torres, Riding the brainwaves.... 2008.

161 Cuba's Neuronic company doing well in the World Market, www.cubaheadlines.com/2009/11/09/18557/cuba%E2%80%99s_neuronic_company_doing_well_world_market.html

162 The second computer generation is based on transistors and diodes, which substituted the vacuum tubes of the first generation. The third is based on integrated circuits (miniaturized transistors placed on silicon chips called semiconductors) and the fourth is based on microprocessors (thousands of integrate circuits built on a single silicon chip). A fifth generation based on artificial intelligence (human intelligence being simulated by a machine was started by the MITI in Japan during the 1980s without success.

163 This was a small, medium speed digital computer manufactured by the British company Elliott Brothers in the 1960s. See www.ourcomputerheritage.org/wp/upload/CCS-E3X1.pdf

164 See T Lopez et al. in J Impagliazzo (ed.) (2008), History of Computing and Education, Springer, pp. 57–74.

165 During the academic period 1970–71, the University of Havana introduced undergraduate programs in Computing Science and computing engineering, only five years after the creation of the first world's computing science department at Stanford University (ibid., p. 68).

166 See G Reed and J Torres, 2008.

167 PDP-8 was the first commercially successful Western minicomputer manufactured by Digital Equipment Corporation DEC in the 1960s and introduced in 1965. It is generally recognized as the most important small computer of the 1960s. It was the least expensive parallel general purpose computer on the market, the first computer sold on a retail basis, and the first parallel general purpose digital computer

sold in a table-top configuration (see www.pdp8.net/). After the advent of the microprocessor, minicomputer leading manufacturers (except IBM) collapsed or merged. DEC was sold to Compaq in 1998.

168 This is nothing different from the kind of emulation strategy which led, for example, to Brazilian engineers, trained at both Instituto Tecnologico da Aeronautica and MIT, to develop the Brazilian aircraft industry in 1969 under the roof of Embraer, a government-owned company. The Korean semiconductor industry developed in 1975 in collaboration with the Semiconductor Technology Development Centre (STDC) and Goldstar to produce bipolar integrated circuit (IC) through reverse engineering. The case of the Taiwan's semiconductor industry is also illustrative. Companies such as Taiwan Semiconductor Manufacturing Corp, which resulted from a joint venture with Phillips, were created to produce VLSI chips (see R Mazzoleni and R Nelson in M Cimoli et al. eds. 2009).

169 The computer was designed by the talented engineer Orlando Ramos, head of the Centre. The prototype was called CID 301. The letter "A" was included to identify the serial model.

170 The Council of mutual economic assistance (also called Comecon, 1949–1991), was an economic organization under hegemony of Soviet Union comprising the countries of the Eastern bloc along with several others countries of socialist orientation elsewhere in the world. Cuba was accepted in 1972 as a full member. The Comecon was the Eastern Bloc's reply to the formation of the OECD in Western Europe. See Library of the US Congress Country Study: Appendix B, the Council for Mutual Economic Assistance available in: http://memory.loc.gov/frd/cs/germany_east/gx_appnb.html

171 Currently, COMBIOMED commercializes ICID products to Angola, Algeria, Bolivia, Brazil, Colombia, Chile, Ecuador, Spain, France, Ghana, Mexico, Peru, Ukraine, R. Dominican Rep., Russia, Venezuela and Vietnam See www.combiomed.sld.cu/

172 http://resultados.redciencia.cu/historia/periodo_5_5_en.php

173 Immunoassay is a biochemical test to identify the concentration of a certain substance within a mixture of substances.

174 This is basically a basic/applied research organization, which is also devoted to human resources training, and health services in the area of medical genetics. The National Medical Genetics Center was created in 2003 and it belongs to the Higher Institute of Medical Sciences of Havana and the Western Havana Scientific Pole. As the National Reference Center for Medical Genetics, it also coordinates the National Medical Genetics Network that operates at all levels of care, beginning in the community polyclinic, where patients are referred by their family doctor, in order to detect, study and keep registries of genetic diseases and congenital malformations in their coverage areas. Genetic risk detection, community-level follow-up of screening and diagnostic programs genetic counseling, and research on the causes and prevalence of genetic diseases and/or the role of genetic risk factors in common diseases are very important tools for prevention. These programs include neonatal screening and prenatal screening for maternal serum alpha-fetoprotein (MSAFP), sickle cell anemia risk, and fetal chromosome abnormalities. A national registry of families with multiple members affected by common diseases – such as asthma, high blood pressure, ischemic heart disease, diabetes mellitus, dementia, depression, schizophrenia, bipolar disorder, cancer, alcohol addiction, and mental retardation – has been kept since 2004 as part of a

study on the role of genetic factors in the origin of these conditions. In 2009, over 43,000 families had been included in this registry. These services are voluntary and free of charge. The National Medical Genetics Center is also responsible for undergraduate and postgraduate training, research, and introduction of new technologies in the field (see B Marcheco (2009), Cuba's National Medical Genetics Program, *MEDICC Review* 11(1) (Winter): 11–13).

175 This does not mean that radio-immunoassay (RIA) had not been developed in Cuba. In 1988 the Centre of Isotopes (CENTIS) was created (its current facilities in 1995) with the aim of developing, manufacturing and commercializing products such as radiopharmaceuticals, radioisotopic generators and; conventional and radioisotopic diagnostic reagents, which are suitable for medical and agricultural purposes, as well as for genetic engineering and biotechnology.

176 See E Bravo, Development within…1998.

177 Evolution of diagnostic tests began in the 1940s with colorimetric measurements of the enzymes and metabolites found in biological fluids using classical chemistry methods and agglutination reactions. In the 1950s, the radio-immunoassay (RIA) was developed by Rosalyn Yalow and Solomon Berson. This group was later awarded the Nobel Prize in 1977 for developing an RIA to detect and measure blood glucose levels in diabetic patients. In the 1960s, immunoassay technology was enhanced by replacing radioisotopes with enzymes for color generation. The use of enzymes eliminates the use of radioactive materials; and has faster reaction times, higher specificity to the target molecule, and longer shelf-lives compared to RIAs. Although immunoassay techniques were first described in the 1950s, they were not readily applied outside of clinical laboratories until the advent of economical automated plate-reading systems and personal computers to analyze data. See www.immunochemistry.com/what-history-immunoassays

178 Enzyme-linked immunosorbent assay. Engvall and Perlmann of at Stockholm University in Sweden, and Anton Schuurs and Bauke van Weemen in the Netherlands independently published their first paper on ELISA in 1971. Among the first commercial manufacturers of fully automated systems are firms such as Boehringer-Mannheim (Germany), Abbott (United States), and Organon Teknika (The Netherlands). Across the years Enzyme immunoassay (EIA) and enzyme-linked immunosorbent assay (ELISA), as non-radioactive variants of immunoassays, have become household names for medical laboratories, manufacturers of in vitro diagnostic products, regulatory bodies, and external quality assessment and proficiency-testing organizations. See Lequin (2005).

179 Since then, 28 diagnostic tests have been developed, as well as 16 generations of equipment to screen for conditions ranging from congenital hypothyroidism and phenylketonuria (PKU) in newborns, to HIV, hepatitis and dengue. See G Reed, Generating Appropriate Technologies for Health …2009.

180 See website of Centre for the Promotion of Cuba Foreign Trade and Investments (CEPEC) www.cepec.cu/premioexportador.php

181 The user-centered innovation process is in sharp contrast to the traditional model, in which products and services are developed by manufacturers in a closed way, the manufacturers using patents, copyrights and other protections to prevent imitators from free riding on their innovation investments. In this traditional model, a user's only role is to have needs, which manufacturers then identify and fill by designing and producing new products (see E Von Hippel, Democratizing *Innovation*, MIT Press, 2005). A vivid example of this is the CIE, which dispose of a network of 181

laboratories located in all the country's municipalities, in order to receive accurate information about genetic and environmental factors. This information will be then used as start point for the development of new products. Another 55 laboratories are located in research institutions and armed forces health facilities. See G Reed, Generating Appropiate *Technologies*... 2009.

182 In 1995, a process of organization change started; based on the adoption of the Strategic Planning and Direction by Objectives. In 1996 the main strategic document up to 2000 was written and adopted, reviewed and adapted later up to 2007 (see website of CENSA: www.censa.edu.cu/index.php).

183 See www.cimab-sa.com/index.php?action=desarrollo

184 The exclusion of the rest of the components of the strategic network has been deliberated; in order to show more clearly both the high level of integration in this industry and the level of dispersion of the value chain. Visualization 5 will be taken as a representation of the rest of the individual firms that belong to the strategic network.

185 www.who.int/vaccine_research/diseases/soa_bacterial/en/index1. html#Vaccines%20against%20group%20B%20meningococci

186 In January 2013 Novartis received approval from the European Union to market its Bexsero against meningitis B. However, Reuter wrongly stated that this vaccine is the first against the condition, which is not strictly true. See www.reuters.com/ article/2013/01/22/us-novartis-europe-meningitis-idUSBRE90L07D20130122. In fact, the Cuban vaccine has been employed for more than two decades in Cuba and other countries with impressive results. In 1999 the Cuban vaccine caught the attention of the pharmaceutical company, SmithKline Beecham (now Glaxo SmithKline), which subsequently reached an agreement with the Finlay Institute to market the vaccine globally. Given the size of the US market, there was obvious interest in being able to market the vaccine in the US. Although the initial US government response was negative, SmithKline Beecham managed to galvanize enough scientific and medical support to demonstrate that the Finlay vaccine was the only option available on the market. After two years of negotiations, SmithKline Beecham received a license from the US Treasury Department allowing them to finalize the deal with Finlay and bring the vaccine to the US market, providing these vaccines were produced in SmithKline Beecham facilities. However, the political confrontation between Cuba and the US has prevented the vaccine to be given a widespread use in the US.

187 www.historyofvaccines.org/content/articles/vaccine-development-testing-and-regulation

188 One of these two workers was in fact Concepción Campa, who was later elected the head of the group and is today one of the most internationally acclaimed Cuban scientists. After getting her biochemistry degree, she started work in CJF Biological products in the department of quality control. See E Bravo...1998.

189 www.ipk.sld.cu/indice1.htm

190 See www.ipk.sld.cu/indice1.htm, see also www.paho.org/english/dd/pin/ Number17_article4_4.htm; see also M Guzmán (2005), Deciphering dengue: The Cuban experience, *Science* 309(5740) (Sep. 2): 1495–7.

191 www.biocen.cu/producto/trofin/indicetr.htm

192 www.cqf.sld.cu/ingles/relaciones/relaciones.htm

193 www.cqf.sld.cu/ingles/productos/productos.htm

194 Laboratorios NOVATEC produces oral solid products in tablet and capsule presentations. The company supplies about 38 products to the. In 2011, NOVATEC was processing its operational license for the production of tablets, coated tablets and capsules.

195 In 2011, LIORAD lab had two operational licenses for the production of dental anesthetic products and liquid injectables, respectively.

196 In 2011, AICA Lab had an operational license for the production of injectables.

197 The director, Professor Dr. Carlos Miyares Cao, has a well-known international prestige for having discovered the only medicines in the world for the effective and innocuous treatment of Vitiligo, Psoriasis and Alopecia See website www. histoterapia-placentaria.cu/ingles.htm

198 For the sake of simplicity; the visualization only displays the links of Biomundi to the Ministry of Technology (CITMA) and to the holding QUIMEFA, which represent the relation of this center to both the biotech and chemical firms respectively.

199 This strategy is part of a coordinated and targeted alliance-building policy, in which the Cuban firms remain with the strategic control of their R&D assets. Consequently, neither equity purchase nor sharing of Cuban tangible asset property will be included in any agreement. In contrast, a highly financiarized form of exclusive IP-based, R&D outsourcing has become the dominant practice among biotech firms worldwide See e.g. CIGB's Negotiation Policy at http://gndp.cigb. edu.cu/index.html#

200 The surveyed firms worked in the health biotech sector in six developing countries – Brazil, China, Cuba, Egypt, India and South Africa. These countries were selected on the basis of their position as southern leaders in the field, as identified through previous research on health biotech in developing countries. The survey followed a broad definition of "collaboration," considering it to be any work jointly undertaken by firms and organizations in developed and developing countries that contributes to the production of knowledge, products or services in health biotech. See CC Melon at al. (2009), A survey of South–North health biotech collaboration, Nature Biotechnology 27: 229–32.

201 See Pascual et al. (2011).

202 www.labiofamcuba.com/en

203 www.cubaminrex.cu/english/LookCuba/Articles/Economy/2009/0810.html

204 www.espicom.com/Prodcat2.nsf/Product_ID_Lookup/00000336? OpenDocument

205 Since March 2013, Ministry for Communications (Decree Law 308).

References

Abramovitz M (1986), Catching up, forging ahead and falling behind, *Journal of Economic History* 66: 385–406.

Abreu G et al. (2011), Cuba's strategy for childhood tuberculosis control, 1995–2005, *MEDICC Review* 13(3): 29–34.

Arthur B (2009), *The Nature of Technology: What It Is and How It Evolves.* New York: Free Press.

Baldarraín-Chaple E (2005), Cambio y Revolución: El surgimiento del Sistema Nacional Único de Salud en Cuba, 1959–1970, *Acta Hispanica ad Medicinae Scientiarumque Historiam Illustrandam* 25: 257–78.

Barnes L (2005), *Needles, Herbs, Gods, and Ghosts: China, Healing, and the West to 1848.* Cambridge MA: Harvard University Press.

Bartels H et al. (2013), *Promoting Access to Medical Technologies and Innovation: Intersections between Public Health, Intellectual Property and Trade.* Geneva: WHO, WIPO and the WTO.

Bessen J and Maskin E (2000), Sequential Innovation, Patents, and Imitation, MIT, *Working Paper* No. 00-01, Revised March 2006.

Bessen J and Nuvolari A (2017), Diffusing new technology without dissipating rents: Some historical case studies of knowledge sharing, LED, *Working Paper Series,* 2017/28, November.

Biomedicine and health innovation: Synthesis report, OECD Innovation Strategy, November 2010.

BMI Research Group (2016), Cuba's Pharmaceutical & Healthcare Report Q4 2016, Part of BMI's *Industry Report & Forecast Series,* BMI Research, London.

Boldrin M and Levine D (2008), *Against Intellectual Monopoly.* Cambridge: Cambridge University Press.

Borman S and Washington C (2004), Carbohydrate vaccines: Novel chemical and enzymatic oligosaccharide synthesis techniques could lead to a new generation of carbohydrate-based vaccine agents, *Chemical & Engineering News* 82(32) (Aug. 9): 31–5.

Braunerhjelm P and Feldman M (eds.) (2006) *Cluster Genesis: Technology Based Industrial Development.* New York: Oxford University Press.

Bravo E (1998), *Development within Underdevelopment. New Trends in Cuban Medicine.* La Habana: Editorial José Martí/Elfos Scientae.

Breschi S and Malerba F (1997), Sectoral systems of innovation: Technological regimes, Schumpeterian dynamics and spatial boundaries. In: Edquist C (ed.), *Systems of Innovation.* London: Frances Pinter.

Burns R (ed.) (2005), *The Business of Healthcare Innovation.* Cambridge: Cambridge University Press.

Campion E and Morrissey S (2013), A different model – medical care in Cuba, *New England Journal of Medicine* 368: 297–9.

Cárdenas-O'Farrill A (2009), The Cuban Biotechnology Industry: Innovation and Universal Health Care, *the AIRnet Working Paper* # 2009-01.

Cárdenas-O'Farrill A (2014), State and innovative enterprises: The case of the Cuban pharmaceutical industry, *Business and Economic History On-line (BEH),* 12: 1–76.

Carey G et al. (2015), Systems science and systems thinking for public health: a systematic review of the field, *BMJ Open* 5: e009002. doi:10.1136/bmjopen-2015-009002.

Carlsson, B et al. (2002), Innovation systems: Analytical and methodological issues, *Research Policy* 31(2): 233–45.

Casanueva J (2007), Role of the National Regulatory Authority in Prequalification of Vaccines. Experience of CECMED, Developing Countries Vaccine Manufactures Network (DCVMN) mimeo.

Chandler A (2004), *Scale and Scope: The Dynamics of Industrial Capitalism.* Cambridge, MA: Belknap Press of Harvard University Press.

Chang HJ (2003), Kicking *Away* the *Ladder.* London: Anthem Press.

Chang HJ (2010), 23 *Things They Don't Tell You* about *Capitalism.* London: Penguin Group.

Christensen A (2003), Cuba's jewel of tropical medicine, *Perspectives in Health Magazine,* The Magazine of the Pan American Health Organisation 8(2): 22–5.

Cimoli M et al. (eds.) (2009), *The Political Economy of Capabilities Accumulation: The Past and Future of Policies for Industrial Development*. Oxford: Oxford University Press.

Clark I (2010), UNESCO Science Report, pp. 123–31.

Clark J et al. (2000), Patent Pools: A Solution to the Problem of Access in Biotechnology Patents, United States Patent and Trademark Office, Research Paper, December.

Coe N et al. (2008), Global production networks: Realizing the potential, *Journal of Economic Geography* 8(3): 271–95.

Cohen M et al. (2000), Protecting Their Intellectual Assets: Appropriability Conditions and Why U.S. Manufacturing Firms Patent (or Not), NBER *Working Paper* No. 7552, February.

Cooper R et al. (2006), Health in Cuba, *International Journal of Epidemiology* 35: 817–24.

Cuba Health Statistics Yearbook, Anuario Estadistico de Salud 2019 in original Spanish.

Cuba's Biotech Boom (2009), *Nature* 457: 130.

Curtis G (ed.) (1996), *Russia: A Country Study*. Washington: GPO for the Library of Congress.

Davidov F et al. (2001), Sponsorship, authorship and accountability, *Canadian Medical Association Journal* 165(6), September 18, 786–88.

Delfin M et al. (2000), Epidemiology of hypertension in Cuba, *MEDICC Review*, II(2), available at: https://www.medicc.org/publications/medicc_review/II/heart/html/epidemiology.html (last accessed October 2020).

Delgado G et al. (2003), Vaccination strategies against hepatitis B and their results: Cuba and the United States, *MEDICC Review* V(1), available at https://www.medicc.org/publications/medicc_review/1004/pages/cuban_medical_literature.html (last accessed October 2020).

De Vos P et al. (2008a), Commentary: Cuba's health system: Challenges ahead, *Health Policy and Planning* 23(4): 288–90.

De Vos P et al. (2008b), Uses of the first line emergency services in Cuba, *Health Policy* 85(1) (Jan.) 94–104.

De Vos P (2009), The right to health in times of economic crisis: Cuba's way, *The Lancet* 374 (Nov. 7): 1575–6.

DiMasi J et al. (2003), The price of innovation: New estimates of drug development costs, *Journal of Health Economics* 22: 151–85.

Dy J et al. (2009), A Comparative Analysis on the Healthcare Systems of China and Cuba: Treatment of Cancer Patients, De La Salle-College of Saint Benilde, Manila, Philippines, available in: www.scribd.com/doc/55417998/Comparative-Analysis-on-Healthcare-Systems-Between-China-and-Cuba, last accessed Sep. 2018.

Eckstein S (2003), *Back from the Future: Cuba under Castro,* Second edition. New York: Routledge.

Ernst and Young (2008), Beyond Borders: Global Biotechnology Report.

Ernst and Young (2009), Beyond Borders: Global Biotechnology Report.

Ernst and Young (2010), Beyond borders: Global Biotechnology Report.

Ernst and Young (2011), Beyond Borders: Global Biotechnology Report.

Ernst and Young (2012), Beyond Borders: Global Biotechnology Report.

Espicom Business Intelligence (2011), Cuba: A World Pharmaceutical Market Report, Q4 2011.

Fitzgerald- Bocarsly P (1997), The History of Interferon: An Interview with Sid Pestka, ISICR, Issue 4:2, available at: www.isicr.org/newsletter/isicr4.2.pdf (last accessed July 2019).

Flochel P and Kumli F (2011), Pharma 3.0: Delivering on health outcomes, *Journal of Business Chemistry* 7(3): 155–63.

Gereffi G (2005), The global economy: Organization, governance and development. In: Smelser N and Swedberg R (eds.), *Handbook of Economic Sociology.* Princeton: Princeton University Press, pp. 160–82.

Giraldo G (2008), Interview with Pedro Ordúñez, *MEDICC Review* 10(1), Winter: 15–17.

Giudici G and Roosenboom P (2004), *The Rise and Fall of Europe's New Stock Market,* Series: Advances in Financial Economics, Vol. 10, Emerald Group Publishing Limited.

Gorry C (2007), Interview with Vicente Vérez Bencomo. Director of the Center for the Study of Synthetic Antigens, University of Havana, *MEDICC Review* 9(1), Fall: 14–15.

Gorry C (2012), Biotech: The magic pill? Cuba's burgeoning biopharmaceutical sector helps keep the island economy afloat, *Scientific American Worldview,* 68–9.

Guzmán M (2005), Deciphering dengue: The Cuban experience, *Science* 309 (5740) (Sep. 2): 1495–7.

Hadad J (2005), International Workshop on Epidemic Neuropathy in Cuba: Report summary. *MEDICC Review* VII(7): 27–30.

Herrera R (2005), Cuba's National Program for Chronic Kidney Disease, Dialysis and Renal Transplantation, *MEDICC Review* VII(5): 2–5.

Hughes S (2003), Scientist at Genentech, CEO at Tularik, Program in the History of the Biological Sciences and Biotechnology, Regional Oral History Office, The Bancroft Library, University of California, Berkeley.

Impagliazzo J and Lee J (eds.) (2008), *History of Computing and Education.* Dordrecht, The Netherlands: Kuwer Academic Publishers.

Iniguez L (2013), Overview of evolving changes in Cuba's health services, *MEDICC Review* 15(2) (Apr.): 45–51.

Jackson M and Sambo L (2020), Health systems research and critical systems thinking: the case for partnership, *System Research and Behavioral Sciences* 37: 3–22.

Jacobo O (2007), Role of the National Regulatory Authority in Prequalification of Vaccines. Experience of CECMED, Developing Countries Vaccine Manufactures Network (DCVMN) mimeo.

Juma C and Yee-Cheong L (2005), Innovation: Applying knowledge in development, UN Millenium Project Task Force on Science, Technology and Innovation.

Kaplan W and Laing R (2005), Local Production of Pharmaceuticals: Industry Policy and Access to Medicines. Health, Nutrition and Population, Discussion Paper, The World Bank, Jan. 16.

Keck C and Reed G (2012), The curious case of Cuba, *American Journal of Public Health* 102(8) (Aug.): 13–e22.

Kesselheim AS (2010), Using market-exclusivity incentives to promote pharmaceutical innovation, *The New England Journal of Medicine* 363(19): 1855–62.

Lage A (2006), Socialism and the knowledge economy: Cuban biotechnology, *Monthly Review* 58(7) (Dec.): 53–5.

Lage A (2008), Connecting immunology research to public health: Cuban biotechnology. *Nature Immunology* 9(2) (Feb.): 109–12.

Lazonick W (2002), Innovative enterprise and historical transformation, *Enterprise & Society,* 3: 3–47.

Lazonick W (2008), *Sustainable Prosperity in the New Economy? Business Organization and High-Tech Employment in the United States,* W.E. Upjohn Institute for Employment Research, Kalamazoo, Michigan.

Lazonick W (2011), The Innovative Enterprise and the Developmental State: Toward an Economics of "Organizational Success" Paper prepared for: Institute for New Economic Thinking Annual 2011 Conference Crisis and Renewal: International Political Economy at the Crossroads Mount Washington Hotel Bretton Woods, NH April 8–11, 2011.

Lazonick W and Mazzucato M (2012), The risk-reward nexus, pre-print copy, later published in *Industrial and Corporate Change* 22(4) (August 2013): 1093–128.

Lazonick W and Tulum Ö (2011), US biopharmaceutical finance and the sustainability of the biotech boom, *Research Policy Journal* 40: 1170–87.

Lequin R (2005), Enzyme Immunoassay (EIA)/Enzyme-Linked Immunosorbent Assay (ELISA), *Clinical Chemistry* 51(12) (Dec.): 2415–18.

Light D (ed.) (2010), *The Risks of Prescription Drugs.* New York: Columbia University Press.

Light D et al. (2011), Longer exclusivity does not guarantee better drugs, *Health Affairs* 30(4) (Apr.): 798.

Light D and Lexchin J (2005), Foreign free riders and the high price of US medicines. *The BMJ* 331(7522): 958–60.

Light D and Lexchin J (2012), Pharmaceutical research and development: What do we get for all that money? *The BMJ* 345: e4348.

Light D and Warburton R (2011), Demythologizing the high costs of pharmaceutical research, *BioSocieties* 6: 34–50.

Loewenberg S (2009), The Bayh–Dole Act: A model for promoting research translation? *Molecular Oncology* 3(2): 91–3.

Lopez E (2002), Development of Cuban biotechnology, *Journal of Commercial Biotechnology* 9(2) (Dec.): 1–5.

Lopez E et al. (2006), Biotechnology in Cuba: 20 years of scientific, social and economic progress, *Journal of Commercial Biotechnology*, 13(1): 1–11.

Lopez E et al. (2007), Taking stock of Cuban biotech, *Nature Biotechnology* 25(11): 1215–16.

Lopez T et al. (2008), Cuban experience on computing and education. In: Impagliazzo J (ed.), *History of Computing and Education.* New York: Springer, pp. 57–74.

Malerba F et al. (2006), Vertical Integration and Dis-integration of Computer Firms: A History Friendly Model of the Co-evolution of the Computer and Semiconductor Industries, CESPRI *Working Paper* No. 191.

Marcheco B (2009), Cuba's National Medical Genetics Program, *MEDICC Review* 11(1), Winter: 11–13.

Marengo L et al. (2009), Appropriability, Patents, and Rates of Innovation in Complex Products Industries, LEM, *Working Paper Series*, No. 5, April.

Mazzucato M (2011), *The Entrepreneurial State.* London: Demos.

McKelvey M et al. (eds.) (2004), *The Economic Dynamics of Modern Biotechnology.* Cheltenham, UK, Northhampton, MA, USA: Edward Elgar.

Melon CC et al. (2009), A survey of South-North health biotech collaboration, *Nature Biotechnology* 27: 229–32.

Miles RE et al. (1997), Organizing in the knowledge era: Anticpating the cellular form, *Academy of Management Executive* 11(4): 7–20.

Morel C et al. (2005), Health innovation networks to help developing countries address neglected diseases, *Science* 39 (July): 401–3.

Moser P (2013), Patents and innovation: Evidence from economic history, *Journal of Economic Perspectives* 27(1) (Winter): 23–44.

Munos B (2009), Lessons from 60 years of pharmaceutical innovation, *Nature Reviews Drug Discovery* 8 (Dec.): 959–68.

Navarro V (1972), Health, health services, and health planning in Cuba, *International Journal of Health Services* 2(3): 397–432.

OECD, Eurostat, WHO (2011), *A System of Health Accounts.* OECD Publishing.

Olson S and Downey A (2013) (eds.), *Sharing Clinical Research Data: Workshop Summary.* Washington, DC: The National Academy Press.

Panzar J and Willig R (1981), Economies of scope, *American Economic Review* 71(2): 268–72.

Pascual M et al. (2011), Cuba's National Clinical Trials Coordinating Center: Emergence, evolution, and main results, *MEDICC Review* 13(1) (Jan.): 46–51.

Pérez A et al. (1999), Impact of antimeningococcal B vaccination, *Mem Inst Oswaldo Cruz* 94(4): 433–40.

Pérez R and Sanchez C (2008), Capacity building: NRA assessment/benchmark system and institutional development plan: Experience of the Cuban National Regulatory Authority, *XIII International Conference of Regulatory Authorities,* September 16–19, 2008, Bern.

Pisano G (2006), *Science Business: The Premise, the Reality, and the Future of Biotech.* Boston, MA: Harvard Business School Press.

Pons T et al. (2007), Computational biology in Cuba: An opportunity to promote science in a developing country, *Plos Computational Biology* 3(11), e277 (Nov.): 2047–51.

Reed G (2008), Chronic vascular diseases in Cuba: Strategies for 2015, *MEDICC Review* 10(2) (Spring): 5–7.

Reed G (2009), Generating appropriate technologies for health equity: Interview with José Luis Fernández Yero, Director of the Immunoassay Center, Havana, *MEDICC Review* 11(1) (Winter): 14–17.

Reed G and Torres J (2008), Riding the brainwaves of Cuban science: Interview with Pedro Valdés Sosa, Vice Director for Research and Director of Neuroinformatics Cuban Neuroscience Center, Havana, *MEDICC Review* 10(2) (Spring): 11–13.

Rodríguez A et al. (1999), Impact of antimeningococcal B vaccination, *Mem Inst Oswaldo Cruz,* Rio de Janeiro, 94(4): 433–40.

Rowe W and Brook T (2009), *China's Last Empire: The Great Qing.* Cambridge, MA: The Belknap Press of Harvard University Press.

Rusoja E et al. (2018), Thinking about complexity in health: A systematic review of the key systems thinking and complexity ideas in health. *Journal of Evaluation in Clinical Practice,* 24(3): 600–606.

Rutter HR et al. (2017), The need for a complex systems model of evidence for public health, *The Lancet* 390(10112) (Dec. 9): 2602–4.

Schilling M (2000), Toward a general modular systems theory and its application to interfirm product modularity, *Academy of Management Review* 25(2): 312–34.

Schilling M and Steensma K (2001), The use of modular organizational forms: An industry-level analysis, *Academy of Management Journal* 44(6) (Dec.): 1149–68.

Senker J et al. (2000), European exploitation of biotechnology: Do government policies help? *Nature Biotechnology* 18(6) (June): 605–8.

Séror A (2006), A case analysis of INFOMED: The Cuban National Health Care Telecommunications Network and Portal, *Journal of Medical Internet Research* 8(1) (Jan.–Mar.): e1.

Shapiro C (2004), *Navigating the Patent Thicket: Cross Licenses, Patent Pools, and Standard Settings.* Cambridge, MM, London: The MIT Press.

Shaw A (1999), *A Guide to Performance Measurements and Non-Financial Indicator.* The Foundation for Performance Measurement, Mattison Public Relations, available at www.scribd.com/doc/50964226/A-Guide-to-Performance-Measurement-and-Non, (last accessed July 17, 2013).

Siepmann T (2005), The global exportation of the U.S. Bay-Dole Act, *University of Dayton Law Review* 30(2): 210–43.

So AD et al. (2008), Is Bayh-Dole good for developing countries? Lessons from the US experience. *PLoS Biol* 6(10): e262.

Sotolongo F (2009), Meningococcal Vaccine Production and Vaccine Research in Cuba, Presentation at the 4th Conference on Global Health on Vaccination Research, Oslo, 2009.

Sotolongo F et al. (2007), Cuban meningococcal BC vaccine: Experiences and contributions from 20 years of application, *MEDICC Review* 9(1) (Fall): 16–22.

Teece D (1980), Economies of scope and the scope of the enterprise, *Journal of Economic Behavior & Organization* 1(3): 223–47. Reprinted in D Faulkner, ed. (2002), *Strategy: Critical Perspectives on Business and Management.* New York: Routledge.

Thompson G (2003), *Between Hierarchies and Markets: The Logic and Limits of Network Forms of Organization.* Oxford: Oxford University Press.

Thorsteinsdóttir H et al. (2004), Cuba-innovation through synergy, *Nature Biotechnology* 22, Supplement (Dec.): 19–24.

Valdés P and Obrador A (2009), Stratified active screening: Where neurotechnology meets public health, *MEDICC Review* 11(1) (Winter): 7–10.

von Hippel E (2005), *Democratizing Innovation.* Cambridge: MIT Press.

WHO (2010), Indicator Code Book.

WHO (2011), Global Health Indicators.

WHO Global Report (year unavailable), Preventing chronic diseases: A vital investment, available in: www.who.int/chp/chronic_disease_report/part1/en/index.html (last accessed Sep. 2018).

Williamson O (1975), *Markets and Hierarchies.* New York World Bank Data: Free Press.

Zablocki EM (2007), Formation of a business incubator. In Krattiger A et al. (eds.), *Intellectual Property Management in Health and Agricultural Innovation: A Handbook of Best Practices.* Oxford, UK: MIHR and PIPRA, Davis, USA, pp. 1305–14.

Conclusions

The story of the Cuban biopharmaceutical industry can be told along different, even conflicting, narratives. Two of them are relevant in this study. On the one hand, the neoliberal narrative advances that the excessive government role in the making of this industry has been made at expense of the participation of the private sector, which, if left alone, might have brought many more developments like this one, and faster than otherwise. This narrative also claims this success has been made at expense of the sector employees, which have been paid extremely low wages that contribute to the low cost of the products. The conclusion is, according to the neoliberal lecture, that the country would have been better off had the state just focused in general conditions and infrastructure and had let the market do its ways.

However, even when historical counterfactuals are difficult to conceive, a cursory view throughout the evidence provided by many examples of industrial development, reveals a more complex picture than the one advanced by the neoliberal canon, which makes the claim above highly unlikely. Firstly, the private sector, if a legitimate actor in an economy, does not need to be a locus of innovation, particularly if left on its own. Secondly, any developmental experience has often required some sort of trade-off between current and future consumption and income, whose participants accept, or not, according to how legitimate are seen the goals involved. While the question about low wages is a valid one, we would also need to ask why the workers in the industry did not take the streets to overthrow the government instead of agreeing to cooperate with its goals. But understanding this process involves politics, culture, morals, psychology, history and many other "extra-economic" arguments that go beyond the discouraging notional distinctions made by neoliberal pundits and beyond what they are ready to discuss without falling into simplistic and Manichaeistic explanations.

On the other hand, the industrial policy narrative asserts that no country has achieved a dynamic transformation in its economic structure without resorting to some kind of targeted government policy. This action would help to upgrade the technological landscape, realizing increasing returns by innovation and increasing life standards in a sustainable way. This process has been, and remains, challenging for many developing and developed nation as well. While dealing with innovations and economic development's intrinsic uncertainties inevitable mistakes have been committed, which has caused a number of resonating failures. The critics of this sort of policy turned it into a black sheep and put it as the evidence of government failure.

However, industrial policy is no longer a black sheep. When the field of development economics emerged shortly after World War II, the need of state intervention in the industrial development was somehow assumed as a logical consequence of the structural inadequacies of developing nations. Of course, historical evidence leaves clear that this involvement is far from being exclusive to developing nations. Later, the neoliberal period put forward its anti-state bias, at least in word. And now the crisis of 2008 plus its aftermath have brought the subject under fresh discussion again, forcing us to rethink the intellectual foundations of the previous orthodoxy.

In this context it would be high time for different interpretations to certain events to be tried, which from an orthodox point of view, had hitherto been seen, at the very best, as aberrations of the norm. However, the contrary seems to still be the case. Even when a growing number of dissenting voices have begun to be heard, the role of the state remains one of the most contentious issues to be addressed by contemporary economists and political economists. Still today, a significant number of policymakers and academics around the world persist in dismissing the notion of the state as a crucial economic agent. The unfortunate results are inequality, political instability and decreasing productivity, even in presence of buoyant technological advancement.

In the middle of all this great denial, it is no surprise that Cuba, the remote Caribbean socialist island remains to be read along the same neoliberal lines, be it due to strong ideological resistance, or simply because of sheer lack of imagination. In any case, no matter the circumstances, the discussion on the failures and achievements of the Cuban socialism continues to be circumscribed to the state-market dichotomy. The poor economic performance of the Cuban economy, it is argued, results from the rejection of market mechanisms and from the overall intervention of the state.

The argument advanced in this book suggests, though, that this framework may be the very obstacle to a better understanding of the Cuban (or any other) experience. Indeed, on the one hand, excessive centralized government decision-making has been, until recent times, the dominating feature of Cuba's economic landscape, and it has had an impact in the dynamicity of the economy. But, on the other hand, without considering the highly government-controlled Cuban context, it would have been impossible to understand how such a poor country, economically besieged and embattled by the most powerful nation on earth, has been able to develop such a resource-intensive industry, as the biotechnology, successfully.

One important element in this discussion is the fact that this dichotomy does not help in assessing the dynamic and complex nature of industrial development and the high probability of failures in this respect. Failure is part of any entrepreneurial undertaking, public or private, and variability and differentiation are aspects that constitute accepted part of the evolutionary approach. From this perspective, there is nothing extraordinary in the fact that some sectors or firms perform better than others, even if they belong to the same institutional constellation. Creativity, absorptive capacity, ability to adapt and overall strategy play a role in this differentiation process. This is what separates, in terms of output and innovativeness, the Cuban biotechnology from other sectors in Cuba, not necessarily the extent of government intervention, which has been as huge, although of a different nature, as in any other sector of the Cuban economy after 1959, the year the revolutionary government came to power.

So, what about that "different nature" of intervention that made the Cuban biotech sector a juggernaut in the developing, and at times the developed, world? In this book it is argued that in this case the state exerted its influence as agent of change, as a central hub in a complex network of institutions. This role is quite consistent with the history of innovation and economic development, where government bodies, we call them government non-firm organizations (NFOs) to distinguish them from state owned enterprises, have been the conveying belt of resources, information and knowledge within an economy. In the particular case of the Cuban biopharmaceutical sectors it means that, in contrast with other sectors, the state played a developmental role by accomplishing structural transformation while contributing to introduce and disseminate new technologies and innovative products throughout the economy. Doing this implies the ability to bring all the stakeholders to cooperate, i.e. networking them, and to make them feel comfortable and secure when taking risks and facing uncertainty.

This is particularly relevant in modern high-tech industries, whose products are made of different underlying bodies of technological knowledge, which usually involves the participation of many different companies in their production. But similar needs for connecting with others are far from being the exception along the history of technological and economic development. However, technology evolution has made the process more complex and interdependent in current times, which in turn demands more specialized forms of institutional governance. To be successful in this task, policymaking will increasingly have to play a dual scientific and policy advisory role and will need better sectoral knowledge and closer interaction with technologists; but will also need more generalists that do not lose the big picture and always reflect on how sustainable societal goals can be achieved (think of the role played by US National Academy of Sciences). In an international context where ethical issues related to, e.g., artificial intelligence and biomedical technologies become gradually the norm, future trends will probably show a growing participation of more diverse society stakeholders in the making and design of new products and technologies.

In general, cooperation is important because innovation requires knowledge recombination and experimentation, which is easier to accomplish in an environment that encourages open flows of knowledge and resources across the boundaries of heterogeneous organizations. Openness helps to reduce the inherent uncertainty in the innovation process and to build long-term expectations among the diverse agents involved in the system. This process creates an opportunity to build collective pools of knowledge that contribute, among other things, to gain interoperability within the system and to reduce the cost of innovation by creating economics of scope and scale.

The above-mentioned perfectly applies to a branch such as the biopharmaceuticals, where, in addition, much of these collective pools are governed by a strong tacit component needed to be learned and not easily movable. When complementarity demands emerge then the resulting asset specificity needs to be lessened by making the specific knowledge to become available. This type of knowledge is acquired largely through association with other people, which means also the integration of different disciplines and learning cultures. This requires the continuous creation of standard interfaces and protocols and long-term commitment that encourage and help these people to engage in that kind of learning. The lack of integration (given the lack of government involvement) may lead to higher costs and to a halt in the innovation process, which are some of the big challenges that the conventional innovation model in medical technologies is facing today.

At the sector level, NFOs continue to have an impact on early-stage drug development worldwide (although this has often been neglected). However they also play an important role in subsequent stages of the innovation process within the industry. For example, government regulatory agencies (such as CECMED and CENCEC in the Cuban case) control the quality of health products, which determine whether a product is ready to be marketed and, if so, how quickly. The Cuban case has shown that regulatory agencies are of particularly importance within the biopharma industry. For example, they need the ability to rapidly transmit information and knowledge to others (structurally) directly tied to them, either simultaneously or not. But they are also expected to communicate as fast as possible with those organizations which are not directly tied to them

At the same time, the Cuban case shows that regulatory agencies within the biopharma sector also require the capacity to monitor knowledge flows and have a better picture of what is happening in the industry because they have been given the power to grant or to withdraw the operation license (in case of not meeting the required standards) of virtually any organization involved in core activities of the industry (manufacturing, trading, wholesaling/retailing, domestic/international distribution). Consequently, they are also required to be proficient in many types of knowledge and resources and to be able of being part of the dynamic of different subgroups within the network. This may help to explain why the recognition of regulatory agencies' ability to set standard interfaces, which can in turn be shared by the whole network of organizations, is seen as a crucial aspect within the biopharma, and healthcare sectors worldwide. It also helps to explain why, beyond the traditional functions of safety, efficacy and quality of new medical products, a growing number of industry reports make the case for the inseparable links between these regulation bodies and the innovation process in the biopharmaceutical industry.

In this study it is argued that the Cuban biopharmaceutical industry, in comparison to many of their homologous industries in the rest of the world, has developed certain comparative advantages in achieving integration. In fact, the Cuban biotech is embedded in an institutional system that encourages collaboration, and as a paramount rule, excludes rivalry. This element makes it easier for small specialized firms to have a sustainable existence along with the core companies of the industry. In other words, it builds a mechanism to assure good ideas not to be lost, no matter where they come from. This, in turn, allows the system to simultaneously profit from the advantages of the functional hierarchy provided by the vertical integration and the flexibility of the modular production system (this study calls this combination of elements *in-house modularity*). These sectoral and organizational properties provide interesting suggestions for future research and they are revealed as an essential part of successful policy-making in this particular technological realm.

All the above-mentioned issues, however, apply not only at one sectoral level, but also at a technology-policy level. The fact that we engage specifically with the biopharma industry should not obscure the fact there is a huge amount of historical evidence pointing to the central role of the state as a technologist. The case of the Cuban biotechnology industry shows that the government was able to create, bring together and harmonize the activity of a highly heterogeneous set of socio-economic agents, which then interacted in creative but task-oriented ways in order to fulfil certain technological and societal goals. It could be said that it was successful in creating the agents and then achieving organizational integration among then. It can be talked of as an organizational success when an economy or industry shows a good performance, because governments, businesses and other organizations are all working together to develop and utilize a society's productive resources. But we know from experience, recent and past, that this is easily said but difficult to accomplish.

As the evolution of Cuban industrial efforts since 1959 has shown, even when genuine attempts were made to industrialize the country, a strong anti-developmental side of the Cuban project played a protagonist role, namely lack of organizational integration. Even while a powerful cooperation ethos was present in Cuba from the beginning of the revolution, i.e. the exhortation to engage in a long-term, cooperative, organizational competence building process; and therefore in innovation-based activities, most important government based-non-firm organizations failed to achieve the necessary synergies and diversity among the agents involved in the process. This lack of coordination between the state and productive agents has been pervasive during most of the revolutionary period, making it impossible to activate targeted flows of information among them, and preventing policy targets from being accomplished.

In particular the crisis brought by the collapse of the communist world during the 1990s imposed the need for a competitive upgrading of the industrial structure and a redesign of the development strategy in Cuba. Several institutional innovations were introduced that helped the country partially recover from the impact of the crisis and to increase its participation in the global market. These changes, however, did not represent a significant shift towards a more technology-oriented organizational integration within the economy. In some ways, these changes even represented a regression with respect to the way of thinking about development that had prevailed in previous periods. The earlier (even if not export-based) strides toward industrialization were partially abandoned and replaced by a more natural resources, service-based mindset.

The switch to a more service-based economy was partly caused by the necessity, partly because of the influence of the service-hype of the nineties, when everybody thought manufacturing to be a thing of the past. Opposing this trend, historical evidence shows that manufacturing has been, albeit not the only, the most important path to prosperity for nations. The most relevant feature that has distinguished rich countries from poor ones is their high-tech manufacturing capabilities (with their high-tech based services), which open more possibilities for increasing returns and therefore generally provide higher productivity prospects.

The Cuban experience, along with many other experiences in the developing and developed worlds, confirms, however, that a service-based economy without industrial linkages is not enough to build a sustainable development strategy. Instead, worrisome structural weakness, evidenced in the overall tertiarization and deindustrialization experienced during the last decades have become entrenched in the Cuban society. This has affected attitudes towards technology and innovation, employment structure and policy expectations, within and outside the government.

On the other hand, this is the time that saw the biotechnology industry to become established in the industrial landscape. Millions were invested during the 1980s and 1990s in order to build the biopharma complex. And the experience of Cuban biotechnology could be very helpful for future industrialization endeavors in the country, because it shows a way in which national stakeholders can be successfully integrated. Of course, it does not mean that the same constellation of institutions that contributed to the development of the biopharmaceutical sector will fit the development of other sectors. Rather, it means that a well-organized body of sectoral and national organizations already exists with the potential ability to capture new technological opportunities for the development of new industries.

For example, the success and needs created by genetic engineering have led Cuban policymakers to involve themselves with the development of the nanotechnology, which in turn may lead the country to invest in the material science, and so on. However, one of the most important challenges that Cuban policymakers will need to overcome for the future is that of encouraging multi-disciplinary and multi-organizational cooperation required to develop modern, and increasing returns-laden high-tech sectors. The over-centralized Cuban environment has very often not allowed enough autonomous government-based NFOs to be developed. To develop one industry can be done in a centralized way, but to develop several interesting and innovative technologies within an industry, or in several related industries, it is necessary to develop a network of organizations, in whose creation, government based NFOs should play a major role.

Even if resource constrains play always a major role in the performance of the Cuban economy, significant savings could be made by using the right organizational strategy, as the biotech shows. For example to step in cutting-age, not yet fully developed sectors, where the enforcement of IPR is still preliminary and less invasive. Also by targeting the use of the abundant indigenous qualified workforce, in Cuba or abroad, in order to absorb new knowledge to be later reengineered in pilot projects. The new reforms being carried out in the country could help in these endeavors. The most recent economic guidelines outlined by the government, with the participation of the population, are looking in the right direction in terms of technological development. On the other hand, no matter how much self-employed and cooperatives the country can have, they are not going to be able to contribute to innovation if they devote themselves to low-end activities. In order to step in more sophisticated and innovative activities they will need to be integrated into a development strategy encouraged by government NFOs. Maybe the structure created by Cuban biotech can serve as template for future Cuban industries.

In view of all these contrasting features one may ask: how comes that different, and conflicting, attitudes towards innovation coexist within the same policymaking body be conceptualized? Or does the Cuban biotech need a separated, independent theory? Above we mention the evolutionary approach as a point of departure for the analysis. However we need to be more specific about the role of the state because this is an aspect in which ideological bias still plays a big role.

An orthodox analysis of the Cuban case would conclude that the Cuban case is a sort of freak instance (not necessarily meant in a positive tone) or an unusual event because the state has never played a role in economic development. However, again, the results of Cuban biotech are actually quite consistent with the historical evidence on the role of NFOs in industrial and economic development. This would be clearer for history-sensitive scholars, but even many economists sympathetic to using history (such as many complexity economists) prefer to deemphasize, albeit not ignore, the pervasive role played by the government in the industrial history.

For instance, the development of American biotech would have not been possible without the role played by the US government's National Institutes of Health. The networking and developmental role played by DARPA and the National Academy Foundation in the creation of the American software, semiconductor and IT industries is also a matter of fact. But government-based NFOs such as MITI in Japan, KIST and KAIST in Korea, ITRI and ERSO in Taiwan and IRI in Italy, Telia and Sonera in the Nordic countries, have also been mainly responsible for the development of successful industries in their countries. There is nothing necessarily similar in Cuba but the creation of the

National Center for Scientific Research in 1965 and then the specific sectoral roles played by CECMED and CENCEC have been shown to be crucial in the development of the Cuban biopharma.

Of course, it would be inane to try either to equate such a heterogeneous bunch or to try to compare its components. Rather, the point being made is that behind almost all success stories of industrial development, there are certain (usually government-based) non-firm organizations playing the roles of funders, customers, incubators, business/technology brokers, targeted resourcing, or synergies creators. The fact that the forms of government involvement have been widely diverse calls for a framework that acknowledges that ideological preferences exist. Economic systems are embedded very much in cultural and political environments, which exert an important influence in the shape of their institutional settings. To understand the way in which they function, we need to acknowledge that the analysis of economic outcomes involves the interaction of a wide diversity of entities.

In this sense, the delineated theoretical framework has been built on the assumption of the economy as a complex system, in which government-based non-firm organizations can be defined as the most central hubs within the system, given their historically crucial role in the process of innovation. In network theory hubs are highly connected nodes, which play the important role of bridging many small communities of nodes (or isolated nodes) into a single, integrated network. The idea of a hub dominated network helps to better conceive economies and innovation systems as structures with high degrees of heterogeneity and complementarities.

To conceptualize the state as hub within the economy highlights the fact that this entity is not independent from the rest of the system, but co-evolves with it. As network theory suggests, hubs are the natural outcome of the evolution of non-random networks in the real world. In fact, as evidences shows, the state as an agent cannot be taken as a monolith but as a multi-functional entity inserted in the society. The state is an ensemble of capacities that offer unequal chances to different forces within and outside the state. The realization of these capacities depends on complex interdependencies between the state, the political system; and the rest of the society. The fact that a government fulfils a developmental function in a sector does not mean that it is developmental in others. In most cases, the *government agency* actually expresses itself in a variety of non-firm organizations, whose weight varies according to their position in the socioeconomic system. Sometimes, some non-state institutions, e.g. big corporations might emulate the influence of some NFOs. What history shows is a story of reciprocal interdependence, strategic coordination, and structural coupling.

However, while there exists a variety of hubs in the economy, it is also true that complex economic activities respond to a functional hierarchy. The real world shows that when the technologies being explored are new and with unpredictable commercial prospects (i.e. unknown customers and markets), not even big private players make the necessary steps to develop them fully. Usually, the government has had to step in and assume the development of these technologies in the long term. Even when the technology has been developed, the state has stayed to diffuse the results in the economy and to encourage the (subsidized) cooperation between non-government actors for new prototypes to able to be developed and new markets to be explored. In the end, it has been critical in developing the hitherto inexistent markets for the new products. In many cases, even SOEs have been created to fill the gap.

For this reason we propose to acknowledge the existence of different kinds of hubs organized in a hierarchy structure. Within this structure, government-based non-firm organizations (of course, not all of them) are conceived as dynamic incoherent agents (DIA) of the system. According to the literature on complex systems, dynamic incoherent agents have the ability not only to adapt to the environment, but most importantly, to differentiate from the environment and change it. They rely on a different kind of autonomy when compared to dynamic coherent agents (DCA), which only adapt to the environmental memory (see Chapter 3). In contrast, dynamic incoherent agents are able to develop a local memory which allows them to make their own interpretation of the environmental rules. It is DIA, the kind of agents (hubs in this case) that reflect a strong sense of agency and therefore represent real agents of change.

This distinction helps to clarify the hierarchical relations not only between normal agents and strong agents (hubs), but also among hubs. A big corporation is not the same as a big state non-firm organization. While the former disposes of hierarchical causal powers in its sub-network, it could not compete with the latter at other levels of the network. Some hubs are more hubs than others as the world consists of functional hierarchies of different sorts, within companies and institutions and between them.

To accept that NFOs are crucial in helping firms face technological change in an uncertain and complex economic system, requires conceiving the latter as social structures that are in turn embedded in larger (typically, but not exclusively, national) institutional environments. In other words, firms are to be conceived as relational networks embedded within wider networks of social actors, with varying degrees of imbrications and interconnection among them. By acknowledging the wide degree of connection possibilities available in society, promising prospects for the creation of new relational concepts to study innovation could be opened.

We proposed that one of these relational concepts could be that of *organizational integration* as defined in the context of the theory of innovative business enterprise innovative (Chapter 4). The concept of organizational integration is meant to uncover the set of social relations that provides participants in a complex division of labor with the incentives to face uncertainty and to cooperate in contributing their skills and efforts in order for the process of organizational learning to be as encompassing as possible. As suggested above, NFOs are said to be the greatest contributor to organizational integration within an innovation system, and this helps to explain how the Cuban biotech case is related to the wide range of historical evidence conveyed in this study.

This contrasts with the kind of capabilities developed by the neo-liberal state, which have been shown by the historical and contemporary evidence to be a failure everywhere. Evidence also shows that even this sort of state is not necessarily incompatible with technological innovation; however the question is how sustainable can be an order that has had the tendency to encourage institutions that disrupt the very ability of most stakeholders to commit their resources in certain investments because its advocates fail to understand the implications of the collective and cumulative nature of innovation. Dismantling societal insurance mechanisms, institutionalizing job and income instability and outsourcing useful government capabilities are positions not likely to make the innovation process sustainable or even possible because they do not promote organizational integration and therefore no long-term expectations among the agent involved in the process.

In addition, the neo-liberal state has made it easier for certain powerful non-state agents to position along the chain of innovation without any welfare justification. The result is that these agents systematically extract rather to add value to the economy, making the process even more conflict-prone. However to dismiss the state is not an option, but to reform it. It is important to start a worldwide debate about the role that governments should play in order to boost innovation and economic development in a sustainable manner. So far, the case seems to be clear that providing long-term employment opportunities, solid social security systems and affordable educational opportunities and healthcare are not only moral issues but also profoundly economic ones.

Seen under this light, the case of Cuban biotech seems to be the confirmation of a robust body of cross-country historic evidence which shows that to ignore the role of government could be part of the innovation sustainability problem that a good part of the world faces today.

Annexes

Annex 1

Intellectual Property

Another important factor affecting integration and knowledge-sharing in this industry is the form in which intellectual property is negotiated. As already noted, exclusive licenses of government-funded inventions are issued for private firms on the assumption that exclusive licensing creates incentives to commercialize these inventions. A broader hope of Bayle-Dole Act, and the initiatives emulating it, was that patenting and licensing of public sector research would spur science-based economic growth as well as national competitiveness (So et al. 2008). However, there is an increasing body of literature addressing the inconvenience of individual patenting in complex product industries in general; and in the biotech industry specifically (Boldrin and Levine 2008; Clark et al. 2000; Shapiro 2004; Cohen et al. 2000). The main argument is that too many isolated patents in complementary assets in a common technology system inhibit innovation by increasing licensing and transaction costs;[1] thus slowing or stopping the knowledge-sharing and the development of new products.

The process of ownership fragmentation of complementary assets and high transaction costs has increased the innovation costs and uncertainty in a field like biotechnology, whose very innovative force resides precisely in the ability to build long-term knowledge-sharing of tacit information. This mutual blocking of property rights has been described by Michael Heller as the *Tragedy of the Anticommons* (Heller 1998). This phenomenon is a pervasive element of most alliances and licensing agreements in the biotechnology industry (Pisano 2006; Heller 1998; Shapiro 2004). Consequently, a big lag between R&D spending and R&D output has emerged. While R&D spending has increased over the last 15 years,[2] the rate of introduction of new applications has fallen (Pisano 2006, p. 118). To stimulate innovative products, many pharmaceutical companies focus more on redundant products, whose expensive patent protection incurs added costs for the consumer for no good reason.[3]

Historical evidence suggests that learning activities by catching-up countries and the development of innovative industries has taken place in environments with lax conditions regarding patent enforcement. Boldrin and Levine (2008, pp. 214–25) show the case of the pharmaceutical industry in Europe, Italy, Switzerland, France and Germany being well known. It is also suggested that, even after the Bay-Dole Act of 1980, which authorized the results of federal funded research to be patented no "major scientific discoveries have been pouring out of American universities' laboratories at an unprecedented rate" (ibid., p. 228). On the contrary, this institution, together with others, is said to have helped to increase litigation costs and the possibility to use intellectual property to as an instrument to pressure competitors. The 1995's World Trade Organization's (Geneva) Agreement on Trade-Related Aspects of Intellectual Property Rights (TRIPS) and its subsequent provisions (TRIP plus) pose even more entry barriers for the biopharmaceutical industry, especially for developing countries. Thought the 2002 Doha Declaration has allowed for some flexibilities, the fact remains that most developing countries cannot make use of them, either because of the existence of extra provisions or because, in many cases, the very applicability of these flexibilities presupposes the existence of an infrastructure which the very core of TRIPS precludes. Cuba, as a signatory of this agreement, had to find some IP strategy to overcome this disadvantage.

Annex 2

International alliances of Cuban biotech

The Cuban biotech industry also pursues a clear global oriented commercial strategy. Different organizations work together on the introduction of novel products into the most regulated markets such as US, Europe, Canada and Japan, by promoting early stage partnerships for joint development and sharing commercial opportunities with partners. Corporate partnership for joint development and out-licensing to other countries is also part of the strategy of the industry.

However, this strategy is part of a coordinated and targeted alliance-building policy, in which the Cuban firms remain with the strategic control of their R&D assets. Consequently, neither equity purchase nor sharing of Cuban tangible asset property will be included in any agreement[4]. In contrast, a highly financiarized form of exclusive IP-based, R&D outsourcing has become the dominant practice among biotech firms worldwide (acquired through alliances, development agreements and licensing).

The effectiveness of the Cuban strategy is reflected by a survey among developing countries engaged in biotechnology, published by Nature Biotechnology in 2009, which presents data on South–North entrepreneurial collaboration in health biotechnology.[5] Here it is shown that Cuba is actively collaborating with the North and South and engaging in a relatively high number of such collaborations (10.5 per firm). It is the only country of those

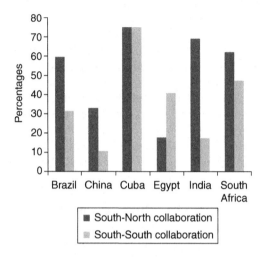

Figure A2.1 Percentage of firms in international health biotech collaboration, 2009
Source: Melon et al. (2009).

surveyed that has an equal percentage of firms involved in North and South collaboration (Figure A2.1).

As already mentioned, HeberBiotec has also excelled in the creation of a solid international network of partners and distributors.[6] To mention a few examples of how this works in practice, in 2000 the Indian company Panacea Biotec entered in a joint venture with Heber Biotec in order to manufacture Hepatitis-B in bulk form. A new company – Pan Heber Biotec Ltd – was formed, in which the two partners hold equal stakes.[7] Another example; the leading Brazilian pharmaceutical company EMS entered into a $100 million US agreement with Heber Biotec for a joint drug development venture.[8] Under the terms of the agreement, Heber Biotech will transfer technology and provide marketing rights for products developed by the Center for Genetic Engineering and Biotechnology of Cuba.

EMS should provide infrastructure and logistic support for the global distribution of Heber's products. EMS is present not only in Brazil, but in more than 15 other foreign markets, including European destinations.[9] HeberBiotec also has partnerships with the Biovac Institute[10] and the Litha Healthcare Group Ltd[11] in South Africa and with Bioven Holdings[12] in Malaysia.

Other important commercializing firms of Cuban biotech are CIMAB S.A and Vacunas Finlay S.A. CIMAB is the trading arm of the Center for Molecular Immunology (CIM), and specializes in the commercialization in the national market and abroad of biopharmaceutical products employed as cancer therapeutics, specially monoclonal antibodies and other recombinant proteins, for the diagnosis and treatment of cancer.[13] CIMAB S.A. has established commercial associations (for distribution or R&D) with more than 25 pharma-ceutical companies in several countries, including the United States, which is relevant if we consider the troubled relationship between both countries because the American embargo.

For example, before the landmark agreement of 2015 with Roswell Park Institute, an agreement between CIMAB (the commercial arm of the Center for Molecular Immunology) and CancerVax, of Carlsbad, California was signed in 2004 in order to undertake joint development and licensing of Cuban cancer vaccines. The deal was approved by the US Treasury Department, des-pite the US trade embargo against Cuba.[14] CIMAB also established a joint venture, called CIMYM (a joint venture between CIM and the Canadian firm YMBiosciences, to develop and market monoclonal antibodies-based cancer therapeutics. To accomplish this purpose, YMBiosciences usually should finance the R&D costs, the clinical trials in Cuba and abroad and the patent protection fees. It would also share development costs according to a structure of up-front fees, R&D funding and milestone payments previously discussed. CIM would retain manufacturing rights and obtain royalties from the sales of the products. In 2009, Cancer product Nimotuzumab was approved to be used in clinical trials in the US under application from YMBiosciences, which showed hope for another exemption to the American embargo.[15]

Annex 3

Cuba: Country-based patent pool

The way in which IP is employed within the Cuban biotech network represents another form of collaboration very particular to the Cuban model. It encourages cooperation between scientists of different firms by speeding the knowledge transfer process. Within Cuba, no organization has exclusive licensing rights in relation to one another.

The patents generated by the Cuban industry are individually acknowledged but owned by the government, given that the patents are issued by state owned firms. This mechanism avoids the problem of mutual blocking and patent war within Cuba. The whole process functions as a kind of patent pool, where every firm has the possibility of using complementary knowledge to advance new products. This may also resemble, although is not the same, some sort of *internal* open source of innovation, which is no surprise at all, as the notion of "cooperation instead of competition" is one of the most promoted values in the industry at a national level.

Cuba belongs to the World Intellectual Property Organization (WIPO) and therefore offers and has the right to receive protection for foreign and Cuban patents respectively. Patents are granted by the Cuban Intellectual Property Office (OCPI – Oficina Cubana de la Propiedad Industrial), and applications to other countries are carried out depending on the specific needs of the industry.

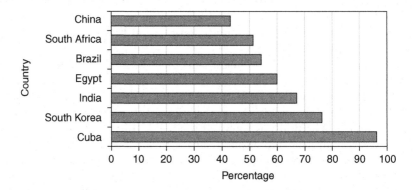

Figure A3.1 Percentage of total patents assigned nationally, 1990–2003
Source: Quach et al. (2006). Inderscience retains the copyright of this figure and the article from which it has been taken.

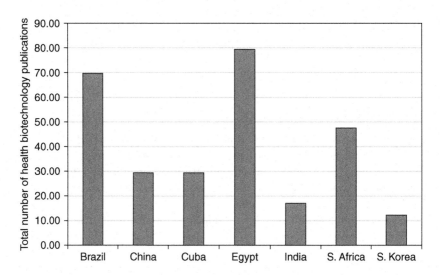

Figure A3.2 Ratio of health biotech papers for every one health biotech patent, 1991–2002
Source: Ibid. Inderscience retains the copyright of this figure and the article from which it has been taken.

Another important issue in relation to patenting is the nationality of the owner. According to an explorative study conducted by Quach et al. (2006) on the patenting behavior of a group of developing countries for the period 1992–2003,[16] Cuba has the highest level of national assignees, with almost all of their inventions assigned to their nationals (Figure A3.1). This puts the country in a relatively strong position to capitalize on their inventions and allow it to develop its industrial sector while at the same time making their patenting laws compatible with the choking restrictions imposed by TRIPS.[17] This is reflected by the fact that even while the number of health biotechnology patents is much lower in Cuba than in almost all the countries included in the study, Cuba shows in the period under study the lowest ratio of health biotechnology papers to health biotechnology patents (Figure A3.2).

Annex 4

Network analysis of Cuban biotech

The role of non-firm organizations (NFOs) finds its theoretical expression in the concept of national (sectoral) innovation systems, where generally these kinds of organizations are placed at the center of the innovation process, the state being an important actor in this process. Within this literature individual firms are conceived as part of a broader network of organizations where the competences for innovation are distributed throughout the nodes and links of the network. The relevance of state policy (and government based non-firm organizations) is not to be solely confined to its ability to provide a large amount of R&D, because the causation of the innovation process is not linear from R&D to innovation. Much more important is its ability to create standard interfaces between organizations, which allow the coordination of intra-industrial change through the creation of inter-firm and inter-sectoral linkages. This process would make it possible for growth and innovation to develop into a more holistic targeted form.

A4.1 Research objective

The general objective of this case study is to analyze *the set of institutions and organizations which have determined the existence of the biotechnology industry in Cuba.* The analysis focuses on the West Havana Biocluster because that is where the most important organizations of the industry are hosted. We will only refer to health biotechnology, given both the preponderance of this branch in Cuba and its central role in establishing the reputation of the industry.

When we refer to set of institutions, we do not only mean formal institutions (including organizations) but also the informal institutions that prevail in the Cuban innovation system. This is important because, as discussed in Chapter 4, sectoral systems can be greatly affected by the system of national institutions. The system of national institutions is expected to provide codified (or institutionalized) standards that allow sectoral agents to embrace openness as a principle.

As already discussed, openness reduces the inherent uncertainty in the innovation process and helps to build foreseeable expectations among the heterogeneous ecology of agents involved in the system. This process creates an opportunity to build collective pools of knowledge that contribute to reduce the cost of innovation and therefore to encourage risk taking; knowledge recombination and experimentation. Many of these collective pools are governed by a strong tacit component. This kind of knowledge, which is highly complementary to codified information, is considered to be an immanent feature of every practical business activity. Therefore, not to provide a platform for these informal institutions to further develop may end up disrupting the innovation process.

In order to make the general research question operational, the following causal hypothesis has been established: government-based NFOs play a crucial role in the process of organizational integration (OI) within the Cuban biotech industry. Within the national and sectoral systems there are certain types of agents that generally display the larger ability to contribute to the processes of circulation and diffusion of knowledge throughout the economy. Historical evidence suggests that government agencies have played a very important role in this direction. In this chapter we will try to corroborate this for the Cuban biopharmaceutical industry. The concept of OI is defined as "a set of social relations that provides participants in a complex division of labour with the incentives to cooperate in contributing their skills and efforts toward the achievement of a common goal" (Lazonick 2002).

According to Lazonick (2011), "the need of organizational integration derives from the developmental complexity of the innovation process – that is, the need for organizational learning – combined with the imperative to secure high levels of utilization of innovative investments if the high fixed costs of these developmental investments are to be transformed into low unit costs." The notion of organizational learning stems from the evolutionary-based organization science school (Teece 1997; Nonaka and Takeuchi 1995; Nonaka and Krogh 2009) and it basically refers to the ability of business organizations to make their processes more efficient by absorbing and creating new knowledge and capabilities.

Subsequently, this notion has also been assimilated by the literature on both innovation (Freeman 2008; Lundvall 2002) and development economics (Chang 2002). While the organization literature focuses primarily, although not exclusively, on the firm (or group of firms) as unit of analysis, the system of innovation and the development literatures place the firm within a network of (firm and non-firm) actors, in which government non-firm organizations are central in shaping the way in which business enterprises operate (Malerba 2002). Relying on this framework, the theory of the innovative firm (Lazonick 2002) proposes the concept of *organizational integration* as a causal mechanism behind the process of organizational learning.

A4.2 On the network method

Network analyze has been widely employed to assess industry and technology environments. Particularly in the biotech industry there are antecedents such as Powell et al. (1996/2005) or Porter et al. (2005). Also the general issue of dealing with public health issues as complex systems is embedded in the current discussion on health policy (Rutter et al. 2017). Reflecting on those and many other applications of the method (see Chapter 2) the present study employs the network analysis in order to find out how central are government-based non-firm organizations (NFO) in the Cuban biotech network.

Statistical methods and social network methods

While mainstream statistical methods[18] demand independent units of analysis, network methods deal directly with the patterned, relational nature of social structures.

Statistical methods of analysis – be it cross-tabulation, correlation, or more complex multivariate techniques – proceed by categorizing individual entities possessing similar combinations of attributes into similar analytic cells. Each attribute is treated as an independent unit of analysis and lumped into social categories with others possessing similar attribute profiles. Social structures and processes are treated as the sum of individual actors' individual attributes (Wellman 1988; Borgatti et al. 2009).

In contrast, the network analysis seeks explanations in the regularities of how people and collectives actually behave, rather than in the regularities of their beliefs about how they ought to behave, individual attributes being less relevant. For example, the causal variable selected for our analysis (organizational integration) does not classify as an individual attribute, but as a relational variable, i.e. a combination of different causal factors expressed in different *centrality* measures. This is pretty consistent with the fact that, in social phenomena, effects can also be causes.

These differences become apparent when considering, for example, the type of data required by each method. Conventional social science data consists of a rectangular array of measurements. The rows of the array are the cases, or subjects, or observations. The columns consist of scores (quantitative or qualitative) of attributes, or variables, or measures.

The conventional data structure is one that leads us to compare how actors are similar or dissimilar to each other across attributes (by comparing rows). Or, perhaps more commonly, we examine how variables are similar or dissimilar to each other in their distributions across actors (by comparing or correlating columns). Rather, network analysts look at the data in fundamentally different ways. Actors (nodes) are described by their relations, not by their attributes. Also, the relationships themselves are just as fundamental as the actors that they connect.

Additionally, common statistical procedures estimate standard errors based on observations from independent random sampling. The very assumption of statistical independence, which makes these methods appropriate for a powerful categorical analysis, detaches individuals from social structures and forces analysts to treat them as parts of a disconnected mass. Researchers following this tack can only measure social structure indirectly, by organizing and summarizing numerous individual covariations. They are forced to neglect social properties that are more than the sum of individual acts (Wellman 1988, p. 38).

In contrast, network observations are non-independent (by definition) and they are all relevant, although not equally, to the central argument being made (they are not random). Consequently, conventional inferential formulas do not apply to network data (though formulas developed for other types of dependent sampling may apply). It would be deceitful to assume that such formulas do apply, because the non-independence of network observations will usually result in under-estimates of true sampling variability – and hence, too much confidence in our results.

Moreover, the data of this network analysis proceeds from different types of levels and it is essentially non-comparable. This case study (and most case studies and their observations) is based on pieces of evidence that (even if quantitative) arise from different populations. That is, much of the information is not coded in a way that conforms to standardized variables. Hence, they cannot be handled within a dataset format, usually referred to as a sample.

A brief definition

As already discussed in Chapter 2, a social network is a set of actors (or points, or nodes, or agents) that may have relationships (or edges, or ties) with one another. Networks can have few or many actors (individuals, organizations, nations, groups etc.) and one or more kinds of relations between pairs of actors (resources, beliefs, friendship ties etc.) (see also Borgatti et al. 2009; Wasserman and Faust, 1994; Freeman 1979; Wellman 1988).

To manage the amount of data involved even in network systems (particularly but not exclusively in social networks) can be complicated. That is the reason why it is helpful to use mathematical and graphical techniques[19] in social network methods to describe the pattern of social relationships that connect the agents involved. Formal representations ensure that all the necessary information is systematically represented, and provides rules for doing so in ways that are much more efficient than lists. In other words, it provides methods and concepts that can be used to characterize networks and the positions of nodes within them.

As a necessary starting point, we need to know that the relationship between each pair of actors in a population, rather than the individual attributes of the agents is the element to be considered in a network analysis. This is consistent with the fact that network data in social sciences are often not probability samples, and the observations of individual nodes are not independent. This reveals important differences between the network analysis and conventional statistical analysis.

Each tie or relation may be *directed* (i.e. originates in a source actor and reaches a target agent, e.g. the relation "to be a parent of"), or it may be a tie that represents cooccurrence, co-presence, or a bonded-tie between the pair of actors (*undirected*, e.g. the relation "to be a sibling of"). Directed ties are represented with arrows and bonded-tie relations are represented with line segments. These ties may be reciprocated (A links to B and B links to A), which can be represented with a double-headed arrow.

The ties may have different strengths or weights. These strengths may be binary (representing presence or absence of a tie), signed (representing a negative tie, a positive tie, or no tie); ordinal (representing whether the tie is the strongest, next strongest etc.); or numerically valued (measured on an interval or ratio scale).

In undirected data, actors differ from one another only in how many connections they have. With directed data, however, it is important to distinguish between *in-degree centrality* and *out-degree centrality*. If an actor receives many ties, it is often said to be *prominent*, or to have *high prestige*. That is, many other actors seek to direct ties towards that particular actor, and this may be an indicator of importance. On the other hand, actors with unusually high out-degree may be able to influence others, or make others aware of their views. Thus, actors with high out-degree centrality are often called *influential* actors.

Last but not least, it is important to point out that the network method being employed here serves as a complement to the evidence provided by both historical narrative and other comparative historical studies, upon which most of this study relies (see Chapter 1). One of the main criticisms made to the social network analysis is that most of the work done by analysts has focused on the consequences of networks rather than the antecedents (e.g. how ties formed).

That is one of the reasons why this research employs such qualitative tools as *process-tracing* and *cross-level reasoning (*see Chapter 1*)*. By using these tools, an effort was made to construct causality within the case[20] and to build a theory-based explanation by *re-contextualizing* the contextual evidence (abductive logic). Of course, the network analysis is also appropriate for advancing new explanations for existing problems, but only when understanding the phenomenon under study. Hence, it should not be seen, at least within this research, as a sole provider of causal explanation, or as causal explanation in itself, but rather as an additional, rather modest and necessarily incomplete, effort to explore the relational nature of innovation within a historic and institutional constrained phenomenon.

That is also the reason why, even when employing a quantitative tool, this case study is being considered as one of an essentially qualitative nature. As Wellman (1988), one of the major contributors to the theory of social network analysis states, if networking techniques can be integrated with more strictly historical work by tracing the conditions under which system members behave, the combination should improve our understanding of social relationships and large-scale structural change (Wellman 1988, p. 47). Bearing these cautionary words in mind may help the reader to have a better sense of the boundaries and benefits of the approaches been employed in this research.

A4.3 Network data collection

This study of the Cuban biotech industry focuses on 54 organizations, which have been proved, according to the collected data; to be *functionally* (in terms of social distance) related one another (see Chapter 7, Figure 7.8). Note, however, that we are intentionally omitting a lot of incidental data in order to focus in the most important relations from the point of view of the biopharmaceutical industry. On the other side, it was not always possible to confirm some plausible assumptions in terms of the relevance of some organizations.

Most of the relational data was collected relying in two fundamental public sources. The first is the periodical list elaborated by the Cuban Drug Control Agency (CECMED) which covers the organizations authorized to carry out the kind of activities they do (year 2012, before December). In addition to the CECMED's data bank, the study employed public data offered by the companies and non-firm organizations featured in the visualization (available predominantly in their websites), as well as personal interviews and written communication with officials and employees. Notice that these relationships belong to the period prior the creation of BioCubafarma (see Section 7.4.2) and therefore represent only an approximation of what exists today (2019) as the industry is still in a process of restructuring and accommodation.[21]

Even when the creation of BioCubaFarma confirms many of results of the analysis, at the time this investigation began (2008) many components that belong today to the holding were located in different sector and were supposed to work under different logic. For example, the industry's large and small molecules parts were only merged as part of the new holding. However the fact that policymakers saw this as a functional necessity confirms the insights advanced by this analysis.

The study has made use of the best known data collection methods in social network analysis, namely the *Full network* method. The method consists basically of collecting information about each actor's ties with all other actors. Full network data is necessary to properly define and measure many of the structural concepts of network analysis (e.g. betweenness).

The obvious difficulty of collecting data from every member of a population is made more manageable by complementing this method with others, such as *Snowball* methods and *Ego-centric networks* (with alter connections). The former begins with a focal actor or set of actors. Each of these actors is asked to name some or all of their ties to other actors. Then, all the actors named (who were not part of the original list) are tracked down and asked for some or all of their ties.

In many cases it will not be possible (or necessary) to track down the full networks beginning with focal nodes (as in the snowball method). Then it is recommended to employ the later approach, which is to begin with a selection of focal nodes (egos), and identify the nodes to which they are connected. Then, we determine which of the nodes identified in the first stage are connected to one another. This can be done by contacting each of the nodes; sometimes we can ask ego to report to which of the nodes it is tied (Hanneman and Riddle 2005).

In order for these two last approaches to work properly, it is necessary to determine how to select the initial nodes. Starting in the wrong place or places could lead to missing whole sub-sets of actors who are connected – but not attached to the starting points. In this study, the natural starting points are the nodes that belong to the strategic network; because the whole story of Cuban biotech turns around these organizations. This does not necessarily mean that these companies always play the major role in the process of organizational learning, just that they are the starting point of the relational network.

A4.4 Basic assumptions

The visualization and analysis has been carried out with the software ORA 2.0 (Organizational Risk Analizer),[22] developed by an interdisciplinary group led by Dr Kathleen M. Carley at the Center for Computational Analysis of Social and Organizational Systems Carnegie Mellon University in Pennsylvania, United States. ORA is a dynamic meta-network assessment and analysis tool which contains hundreds of social network metrics that can be applied to the study of different intra- and inter-organizational structures. However, the way in which we conceive nodes and links does play a role in the metrics` results. For that reason, we will briefly refer here to the basic assumptions underlying our analysis.

As already mentioned in Chapter 7, the nodes are classified according to the type of activity they are involved in. However, given the high degree of multi-functionality and integration within Cuban biotech, no exact resource will be identified to any organization. Therefore, even when the type of resource may be clearer in some cases than in others (e.g. a bank), links usually correspond to more than one resource. One organization can bring different resources into a partnership, e.g. technology, manufacturing capabilities, marketing expertise, scientists, proprietary knowledge, etc. For this reason, links in the visualizations (see Visualization section below) are generically identified as resources or knowledge, rather than as the specific resource that a given organization is supposed to more frequently provide. This is more consistent with the organizational structure of the Cuban industry and offers a more realistic view of the relations within the industry.[23]

Also consistent with the organizational structure of the industry is the type of links being represented. It is worth noting that the flows of resources are represented in the whole network as binary links, which can go in both directions (see Visualizations section below). However, this links are not given any weight. One of the reasons we do not include weighted links[24] in this study is because it is assumed that relationships among agents find in practice few obstacles within the Cuban biotech industry.[25] This aspect plays a role in the calculation of the metrics.

A4.5 Organizational integration conceived as centrality

The kind of network analysis proposed for the Cuban biotech industry makes most of the emphasis in the nodes and their network positions.[26] This is, we fundamentally explore node-level properties relating to the structural importance or prominence of a node in the network (Borgatti et al. 2009). As already mentioned in Chapter 2, within this level of analysis, the most widely studied property is *centrality*. This notion has become widely accepted as a very important structural attribute of networked systems in a wide range of branches, including social systems.

The concept of centrality of individuals and/or organizations in their social networks is also one of the earliest notions employed by social network analysts. It basically refers to an actor or node which is `central` to a number of other connections. This means, a node with many direct contacts to other nodes and which can be seen as a major source of information and control (Freeman 1979; Wasserman and Faust 1994; Borgatti 2009; Opsahl 2010). This multidimensional concept has been formally developed into different proxies with the aim to capture the most of its characteristics (total degree centrality, betweeness centrality, closeness centrality etc.).

As already discussed in Chapter 4, in this research the notion of centrality will be related to the concept of *organizational integration* (Lazonick 2002). This is the causal variable chosen for the analysis of Cuban biotechnology. This concept is defined as "a set of social relations that provides participants in a complex division of labor with the incentives to cooperate in contributing their skills and efforts toward the achievement of a common goal" (ibid., p. 14).

Being conceived of as a *social condition,* this concept encompasses the idea of business enterprises as social structures that are in turn embedded in larger (typically national) organizational/institutional environments, which should be understood and explained in terms of relational categories, like the ones advanced by the network analysis.

In addition, successful organizational integration has to do with the ability of certain organizations to mobilize resources and allowing knowledge and innovation to disseminate across a company, industrial or technological sector. From a social network perspective, they are structurally "central" to the sector and possess the property of integrating other organizations into the process of organizational learning. Without them, the innovation process could not possibly take place. They play a crucial role by encouraging innovative strategies in the typically uncertain environment of high tech industries such as the biotechnology. In this study, we want to explore the importance of non-firm organizations within the context of the Cuban biotechnology.

The following section will quantitatively explore the kind of organizations that have the major stake in the just mentioned process. This will be done by measuring different types or node (unit) centrality indices obtained from a standard network analysis. The analysis will look for supporting the established hypothesis that *non-firm organizations are essential to the process of organizational integration.* As noted above, the current study is intended to particularly explore the role played by these kind of entities, given their critical importance in the innovation process within the Cuban biotech industry (and in other high tech industries around the world in many different periods).

However, it does not mean that other organizations are not considered. Given the open nature of the Cuban industry, it is not surprising at all, that other organizations also play an essential role in the organizational learning process. As will be seen, this is the case of the firms that belong to the strategic network of the industry, which represent the selling and exporting core of the Cuban biotechnology.

The indicators to be considered are degree centrality, eigenvector centrality, closeness centrality, betweenness centrality, in-degree-centrality and out-degree centrality. These are among the most commonly employed measures within network analysis.

Following this set of measures, other derivations of the six mentioned indicators will be considered in order to cover as many as possible different centrality dimensions in the study. However the six above mentioned indicators are the main ones to be considered and deeply explored.

A4.6 Core notions of centrality

This section will focus on three measures, which are somewhat the pivotal point of many others that have been subsequently developed. The section of results and discussion will be devoted to the network analysis of the case under study; several other measures will be presented.

Degree centrality

Based on other authors' previous research, Freeman synthesizes three properties to calculate the centrality of a node: based on the maximum possible *degree*, on *closeness*, and on *betweenness*. *Degree centrality* is based on the idea that having more ties (and hence higher degree) means being more important. As already suggested, degree of a node pj is defined as the count of other nodes, pj (i≠j), that are adjacent to it (two nodes directly connected by a link) (Freeman 1979). Freeman defined degree centrality *C'D (Pk)* as

$$C'_\mathrm{D}(\mathrm{p}_k) = \frac{\sum_{i=1}^{n} a(\mathrm{p}_i, \mathrm{p}_k)}{n-1}$$

where $\sum_{i=1}^{n} a(\mathrm{p}_i, \mathrm{p}_k)$ is the number of adjacent point to the node *Pk* (degree of Pk) and *n* is the total number of nodes in the network. This measure is also the normalized measure of degree centrality.

Newman (2010) acknowledges that although degree centrality is a simple centrality measure, it can be very helpful because it seems reasonable to suppose that social actors who have connections to many others might have more influence, more access to information,[27] or more prestige than those who have fewer connections.

The straightforwardness of the mechanisms described by this index makes it easier to understand its significance for innovation and economic development. The literature on innovation and development economics gives enough evidence on the importance of direct ties between economic agents. It also reveals the central role played by government non-firm organizations in the development of innovative products, technologies and organizational practices (Chang 2002, 2010; Reinert 2007; Cimoli et al. 2009).

Betweenness centrality

Another centrality measure illustrated by Freeman (1979) is *betwennness* centrality, which is "based upon the frequency with which a [node] falls between pairs of other [nodes] on the shortest path (geodesic) connecting them" (p. 221). Borgatti (2005) described this measure as the number of times that any actor needs a given actor to reach any other actor. This indicator may be useful for example as an index of the potential of a node for control communication in the network. Freeman (1977, 1979) defined betweeness centrality *C(B)* of a point P(k) as:

$$C_B(p_k) = \sum_{i<j}^{n}\sum^{n} b_{ij}(p_k)$$

where $i \neq j \neq k$ $b_{ij}(p_k) = \left(\dfrac{1}{g_{ij}}\right)(g_{ij}(p_k))$ is the probability that point *Pk* falls on a randomly selected geodesic connecting *Pi* and *Pj*, *gij (Pk)* is the number of geodesic linking *Pi* and *Pj* that contain *Pk*, and *1/gij* is the probability that any particular geodesic connects Pi and Pj. *A normalized index is also provided.*

Betweenness is a very important feature in economic and innovation systems. Social actors with a high degree of betweenness are ideal brokers that build relationships among previously unrelated actors.

Closeness centrality

The third measure of centrality developed by Freeman (1979) is one based on *closeness. Closeness centrality* assumes that actors who are able to reach other actors at shorter path lengths, or who are more reachable by others at shorter path lengths, are in favored positions. In contrast to degree centrality, this includes also non-adjacent nodes. If degree centrality reflects the level of direct connections; and betweeness reflects the ability of intermediary, closeness has more to do with the quality of efficiency and independence. Freeman (1979) defines closeness centrality as:

$$C_C(\mathrm{p}_k)^{-1} = \sum_{i=1}^{n} d(\mathrm{p}_i, \mathrm{p}_k)$$

This is the inverse of geodesic of each node to every other node in the network, where *d (Pi, Pk)* is the number of edges in the geodesic linking *Pi* and *Pk*. A normalized measure for closeness centrality is also provided.

A4.7 Results and discussion

A4.7.1 Total Degree centrality

We start by showing in Table A4.1 the results of degree centrality. The total degree centrality (or degree centrality) of a node is the normalized sum[28] of the number of nodes that are adjacent to it and therefore, in direct contact (the

Table A4.1 Total degree centrality

Rank	Nodes	Value	Unscaled
1	Regulation agency (CECMED)	0.387	41.000
2	Center for Genetic Engineering and Biotechnology (CIGB)	0.349	37.000
3	Pharmaceutical Chemistry Center (COF)	0.349	37.000
4	Finlay Institute	0.330	35.000
5	Center for Molecular Immunology (CIM)	0.311	33.000
6	National Center for Scientific Research (CNIC)	0.302	32.000
7	Center for Immunoessays (CIE)	0.302	32.000
8	National Coordinating Center for Clinical Trials (CENCEC)	0.283	30.000
9	National Center for Bioproduction (BIOCEN)	0.283	30.000
10	Institute for Digital Research (ICID)	0.283	30.000

foundational mathematical definition can be found in Freeman 1979; see also Wasserman and Faust 1994; Newman 2008). The degree of a vertex (also called indistinctive node or agent) in a network is the number of edges attached to it. This index (as well as the rest of the indexes) is normalized to get measure in interval from 0 to 1, where 0 means the smallest possible and value 1 the highest possible centrality. Organizations with a high degree centrality are those who are linked to many others and so, by virtue of their position have access to the ideas and resources of many others. The table shows the first ten nodes but the analysis focuses in the top three nodes.

The results of this index show that CECMED is the most central organization within the network. Equally relevant are the CIGB and the CQF, second and third in the score respectively, which is coherent with the fact that they are the first two strategic network organizations to be found in the list among the Cuba's top 20 R&D organizations, according to research achievements, national prizes and their economic contribution (they rank first and fifth respectively).

This index could be interpreted as a measure of immediate effects of what happens at time $t + 1$ only; or in other words, as a measure of immediate influence, which at the same time could involve different kinds of flow processes.[29] Borgatti (2005) establish a typology of flow process and analyses how different centrality measures fit to the study of each of them.

In the specific case of the Cuban biotech industry it could be telling us that these organizations possess the best ability to rapidly transmit information to others directly tied to them. One of CQF's and CIGB's (through Heberbiotec) most significant features is their impressive domestic (and international) collaboration network. Given that most of the projects within the Cuban biopharmaceutical complex involve more than one organization, it is easy to understand why these organizations rank among the top three when measuring degree centrality. However, it is not a surprise to find that companies of the strategic network of the Cuban biopharmaceutical complex[30] have a central position.

Noteworthy is the fact that a non-firm organization (NFO henceforth) surpasses them, which gives an idea of the central role played by NFOs in Cuban biotechnology. Indeed, the national drug regulation agency CECMED ranks as the most central entity according to degree centrality. This element could be related to the ability of transmitting information at once to others, which is highly relevant for systems based on parallel duplication flow processes. The Freeman degree centrality (the one being calculated here) could be employed to evaluate processes that involve walks, trails or paths (Borgatti 2005). The case of CECMED involves the existence of walks where information needs to be diffused simultaneously, which also applies to this measure since in those cases the probability of receiving – in the next time period – something that is randomly distributed in the network, will be entirely a function of the number of ties that a give node has (ibid.). In these processes, similarly to a radio broadcast, information can be diffused and replicated simultaneously throughout the system, which contributes to the joint learning.

The centrality of CECMED consists of providing regulatory standards for the whole biopharmaceutical industry. This function is similar to that of the FDA or EMEA, but a difference is that CECMED belongs to the national health system, which has an explicit interest in allowing information to rapidly distribute across the system. As already mentioned, to ensure that manufacturing and distribution are in compliance with international standards is the main task of a drug regulation agency. In fact CECMED is much more directly involved in the process because it directly helps other organizations meet required international standards, such as good production and clinical practices, product labeling and post-marketing pharmacovigliance.

In addition, there is a national normative context, which consists of a highly complex system of routines and protocols (documentation, regular data monitoring, regular pharmacologic control etc.) for the national industry. It is in this set of particular standards where CECMED has developed a dynamic comparative advantage. This national institutional framework arises from the harmonization of the international criteria with the specific characteristics of the country (list of essential medicines, predominant medical conditions, health policy etc.). During this process, a high level of collaboration within the regulatory agency and the industry has been the rule of the Cuban biopharma system, which has allowed developing standards guidelines in agreement with all the national actors involved.

As already discussed in this study, the creation of standards facilitates communication and knowledge transfers between heterogeneous organizations within the industry and thus allows cost reduction. This allows CECMED to better fulfil its national regulatory needs, by issuing documents that can be used as reference to design research & development projects, also including regulatory requirements since the beginning of research to guarantee the proper development of new products. A concrete example can be found in the recent development of a regulatory framework for the development of pharmaceuticals obtained from transgenic plants in Cuba (Hechavarría-Nuñez et al., 2009)

Last but not least, degree centrality could be linked to the property of developing processes that involves no indirect links. This is, two nodes *i* and *j* co-construct something that is unique to them while engaging in a similar activity with others. The part of creating something common fits the three top ranking nodes being considered here. Particularly CIGB and CQF create products that are the result of the direct interaction with other organizations. But the case of CECMED also fits the part of "engaging in similar activity," in that similar sets of information result in very different products. To develop a certain product, a firm has to follow the procedures of CECMED, but at the same time CECMED needs specific knowledge about the product or procedure being approved. Therefore each firm has a unique relationship to CECMED even while assimilating a set of standards common to the rest of the firms.

A4.7.2 Closeness centrality

Although total degree centrality is a very powerful (and visibly simple) index, it only takes into consideration the immediate ties that an agent has, rather than indirect ties to all others. One agent might be tied to a large number of agents, but those others might be rather less connected to the network as a whole. This means that the agent could be quite central, but only in a local neighborhood. In a case like this, and in order to better capture functional distance among nodes, the index of closeness centrality is introduced (Table A4.2). (The foundational mathematical definition can be found in Freeman 1979; see also Borgatti 2005; Wasserman and Faust 1994; Newman 2008).

Closeness centrality approaches emphasize the distance of an agent to all others in the network (not only the immediate agents). It is defined as the inverse of the average distance in the network between the node and all other nodes.[31] Most central units, according to closeness centrality, have the shortest path and can quickly interact with all the others because they are close to them.

According to Borgatti (2005), shortest path is an important assumption when analyzing closeness because it defines the two kinds of flow processes that this measure is suitable for: those in which things flow along shortest paths, such as the package delivery process, and those in which things flow by parallel duplication. In the latter case, all possible paths are followed simultaneously, including the shortest path, and so the net effect is the same. It would be inappropriate to see closeness centrality as an index of reception speed for other flow processes than those in which traffic did not travel along shortest paths (ibid.).

This index shows how long it takes for an organization to spread knowledge to other organizations within the network. In the case of information flows, this index could be interpreted as the expected time until arrival of relevant information flowing through the network. For instance, in an R&D technology-sharing network, high scoring organizations will be well-positioned to obtain novel information earlier and able to develop products sooner than others. In a broader context, it also means the ability to monitor information flows and have a better picture of what is happening in the network as a whole.

The results show three NFOs with the highest closeness scores. Among them, the Center for Medical Research and Development (CIDEM), placed in third position, seems to be more relevant than it first appears. The particularity of CIDEM is that it offers services (e.g. microbiologic, biologic and toxicological studies as well as chemical research) to both the centers of the strategic network (biological producers) and to the medical–pharmaceutical (small drugs producers). That is, although it plays a more important role in the chemical–pharmaceutical branch by producing and commercializing mostly generics and synthetic products, CIDEM's high closeness score shows that it also effectively communicates with the biological-based part of the Cuban biopharmaceutical industry. That is the kind of organization with the potential to promote technology cross-fertilization and innovation. Indeed, when we scratch the surface, we find that CIDEM's main establishments carry out a number of complementary activities that contribute to accelerate the processes of both small and large drug development.

Again, and more interestingly, the results also reflect that the two regulators, CECMED with the highest score, followed by CENCEC, are among the top three organizations, if centrality is considered in terms of closeness. The observed outcome is consistent with the fact that these two organizations are explicitly designed for spreading information quickly and effectively throughout the system. The regulatory function of CECMED makes it imperative for this organization to be able to constantly transmit, evaluate and retransmit the requirements for manufacturing permissions, certifications and marketing. In order for this information to diffuse rapidly and efficiently, a system called *Operation Normalized Procedures* has been implemented, which consists of a methodology that establish the steps to follow in order to evaluate the information received for the clinical trials. This methodology is part of the system of particular regulations created as guide for the domestic industry. An incomplete guide will lead to a poor and belated evaluation.

Table A4.2 Closeness centrality

Rank	Nodes	Value	Unscaled
1	Regulation agency (CECMED)	0.757	0.014
2	National Coordinating Center for Clinical Trials (CENCEC)	0.654	0.012
3	Center of Medical Research and Development (CIDEM)	0.530	0.010
4	CLEADEN	0.525	0.010
5	Ministry for Public Health	0.486	0.009
6	Pharmaceutical Chemistry Center (COF)	0.486	0.009
7	Biomundi	0.465	0.009
8	LABIOFAM Group	0.457	0.009
9	Center for Genetic Engineering and Biotechnology (CIGB)	0.449	0.008
10	Finlay Institute	0.449	0.008

For example, when a product is under scrutiny, CECMED needs to contact experts regarding the condition that the vaccine or drug under probation is meant to relieve. For this, there are certain routines and procedures with a pre-establish format that cover the way in which they will be recruited, and how the evaluation and post-evaluation will take place, as well as ethical and social aspects (depending on the kind of product). After the trial or the commercialization has begun, a periodical security report has to be sent to CECMED as per a defined chronogram. The faster good quality information can be spread, the faster and the more productive the rest of the system will function. The fact that CECMED has the highest degree of closeness centrality is a signal of good function and is part of the explanation for the relatively good performance of the Cuban biopharmaceutical industry.

Likewise, the results reflect that CENCEC functions as a contract research organization (CRO), namely designing and executing clinical trials of Cuban products requiring evaluation before entering national and international markets. The fulfilment of these functions demands frequent review and adaptation of the CENCEC to international trends in contractual clinical trial research in order to help the Cuban organization(s) to keep up to date. This needs to be done as quickly and effective as possible; and for that reason, this organization has designed a multicenter trials network across the country that applies a single protocol. This is a very important organizational innovation in the Cuban case, given that no country disposes of a national network for clinical trials, which means that every time a trial needs to be done, different and potentially conflicting procedural views (sponsoring company and the private CRO) are minimized.

The criteria uniformity provided by CENCEC allows patients to be more quickly enrolled, to carry out simultaneous clinical trials and reduces the costs of clinical sites. Greater efficiency leads to cost- and time-savings that could mean the difference in the international market and adding time to a drug's lifecycle.

A4.7.3 Eigenvector centrality

A more sophisticated version of the notion of degree centrality is the index eigenvector centrality. While degree centrality gives a simple count of the number of connections a vertex has, eigenvector centrality acknowledges that not all connections are equal. The fact that an agent is linked to agents that are themselves well connected, will provide it with more influence than less linked agents. This index is defined as the extent to which the centrality of a node is proportional to the average of the centralities of its neighbors.[32]

In the scores showed in Table A4.3, NFOs are confirmed to be central agents in the network. The singularity in the result is that CECMED has obtained the maximum score (followed by CENCEC). In other words it means that all the organizations directly related to the Drug regulatory agency are themselves well connected within the network. Of course, the visualized representation

Table A4.3 Eigenvector centrality

Rank	Nodes	Value	Context*
1	Regulation agency (CECMED)	1.000	1.885
2	National Coordinating Center for Clinical Trials (CENCEC)	0.951	1.694
3	Center for Genetic Engineering and Biotechnology (CIGB)	0.948	1.685
4	Finlay Institute	0.945	1.673
5	Center for Immunoessays (CIE)	0.921	1.578
6	National Center for Scientific Research (CNIC)	0.905	1.519
7	Center for Molecular Immunology (CIM)	0.897	1.488
8	National Center for Bioproduction (BIOCEN)	0.880	1.419
9	National Center for Animal and Plant Health (CENSA)	0.819	1.182
10	Pharmaceutical Chemistry Center (COF)	0.810	1.149

necessarily omits several other facilities and organizations that could influence this score. However, the result would not be of such a difference since many of the most important agents of the industry are represented. Furthermore, it is consistent with the functions of CECMED as a Drug regulatory agency. CECMED has the power to provide or withdraw the operation license (in case of not meeting the required standards) of virtually all the organizations involved in core activities of the industry (manufacturing, trading, domestic distribution), which, by virtue of the characteristics of the Cuban industry, are themselves well connected to each other.

The fact that the same top three organizations (and in the same order) of the closeness centrality are the ones that obtained the highest degrees of eigenvector centrality is a signal of the level of influence these organizations have within the network. Even when both measures can be viewed as indicators of influence, this sort of coincidence does not necessarily follow. Closeness takes into account only the shortest-path distance among vertexes and eigenvector centrality considers all kind of distances. This becomes clear when we compare the rest of the scoring organizations in both measures (Tables A4.2 and A4.3).

A4.7.4 Betweenness centrality

As important as the distance from a node to another one, is the notion of which node lies on the shortest path among pairs of other nodes. This property is called *betweenness* centrality and is defined as the normalized sum of the probabilities that a certain node fall on a randomly selected geodesic (shortest-path) linking two other nodes.[33] The betweenness of a vertex measures how much flow will pass through that particular vertex. Such agents have control over the flow of information in the network because they link pair of nodes. (The foundational definition is to be found in Freeman 1977; see also Freeman 1979; Newman 2008; Wasserman and Faust 1994.)

Betweenness is said to work better for the kind of processes characterized by indivisible traffic (e.g. package delivery process,) that transfers from node to node along shortest paths until it reaches a pre-determined target.[34]

This does not only apply to goods, but to certain kinds of information as well. In many social contexts an agent with high betweenness will exert substantial influence not because of its being in the middle of the network (although it may be) but of lying "between" other agents in this way. They could play a brokering role between groups by bringing the influence of one group on another or serve as a gatekeeper between them. Table A4.4 shows the results of this index for the Cuban biotech network.

First of all, it is no surprise that CQF is placed among the top three scorers in betweenness centrality. As mentioned in Chapter 7 (Section 7.4.6), this core organization has built one of the most impressive (both national and international) collaboration networks within the industry. This network includes almost all the research and health centers in the country.

The results also reflect the significance of trading organizations. In fact, even if FARMACUBA does not show direct links to the core firms of the industry, it represents a crucial transfer point. Through its link to CIDEM it connects with the core firms of the industry; and, at the same time, it directly connects to the manufacturing companies of the chemical side of the industry (small drugs). The fact that FARMACUBA shows the highest betweenness score reflects the importance of foreign trade for the Cuban biopharmaceutical complex. In fact, although the industry produces more than 60 percent of the local needs, it imports about 90 percent of all raw materials used in domestic production.

The score also shows, again, the relevance of non-firm organizations within the industry. This time CENCEC, the organization in charge of carrying out the clinical trials is placed among the top three nodes (second). As noted above, the most central agent in terms of distance does not necessarily have to be the most central agent in terms of control or betweenness. The most important feature in terms of betweenness is not how fast knowledge will be transferred (although it matters a lot) but it has actually to do with the role of organizations as coordinators of knowledge or information essential for the solution of a problem.

Table A4.4 Betweenness centrality

Rank	Nodes	Value	Unscaled
1	FARMACUBA	0.194	535.885
2	National Coordinating Center for Clinical Trials (CENCEC)	0.184	508.079
3	Pharmaceutical Chemistry Center (COF)	0.172	472.927
4	Banco Exterior de Cuba	0.110	302.480
5	Quimefa Group	0.108	298.860
6	Ministry for Science and Technology (CITMA)	0.103	284.981
7	Institute for Digital Research (ICID)	0.095	261.403
8	Center for Medical Research and Development (CIDEM)	0.083	228.869
9	Ministry for Public Health	0.083	227.820
10	Regulation agency (CECMED)	0.071	195.241

As noted above, CENCEC provides centralized protocol guidelines of clinical trials (particularly for Phase III) that are to be followed in multicenter trials of clinical sites across the country. But it also has to work closely with the drug regulatory agency CECMED and at the same time with the firms, in order to have the clinical trials approved. A company (sponsor) presents its pre-clinical information to CENCEC, in order to prepare the clinical trial for a given product. Then CENCEC prepares, together with the interested sponsor, a technical report, which is sent to CECMED for approval. This technical report involves information which is primarily of interest of the company seeking to initiate the trial, CENCEC and CECMED, and therefore it does not need to be communicated to any other organization.

CECMED (just as FDA in the US and EMA in Europe, or other drug regulatory agencies do) evaluates if the clinical trial project is in compliance with good clinical practice guidelines (GCP). If the report gets approved, then the clinical trial can be carried out. If granted, then the information flows from CECMED to CENCEC again; and then to the sponsor. Indeed, the CENCEC acts as knowledge bridge between different organizations and between them and the Drug Regulatory agency during the trial. In addition, and in order to increase the probabilities for this to happen, and also in contrast with the current international practice, the CENCEC joins efforts with both sponsoring companies and CECMED to review and refine trials designs, it provides both advice on preparation of clinical reports for submission to the Drug Regulatory Agency (CECMED), and guidance on clinical product evaluation strategies.

A4.7.5 Out-degree centrality

The four indexes proposed until now are the most widely used in (especially social) network analysis, and they reflect in different ways how centrality can be conceived. However the relation between nodes has been analyzed only taking into consideration the amount of ties, but ignoring their direction. But, since the network being analyzed here is a directed one, it is also important to explore the directions in which knowledge and resources flow. In directed networks it is relevant to know who provides most of the resources and to whom. In the case of Cuban biotechnology it would complement the metrics shown above by finding out if the most linked organizations are also the organizations associated with the largest flow of resources within the network.

When considering the directed data, we need to distinguish centrality based on both in-degree and out-degree. In social network's analyst jargon, if an agent receives many ties, it is said to be *prominent*, or to have high *prestige*. That is, many other agents seek to direct ties to them, and this may indicate their importance. Agents who have unusually high out-degree are associated with more types of resources than others, and thus are able to exchange with many others, or make many others aware of their views. Actors who display high out-degree centrality are often said to be *influential* actors.

The first of the two indexes to be presented is the out-degree centrality (Wasserman and Faust 1994; Hanneman and Riddle 2005). In terms of matrix operations this index represents the sum of the directed ties that a row (source) sends to its related columns (targets).[35] In Table A4.5 we find that the pattern observed above continue to be confirmed when considering directed data. The drug regulation agency CECMED stands at the top of the ranking with an exceptionally high score, followed by CENCEC and then by the Center for Medical Research and Development (CIDEM), MINSAP's scientific and technical arm.

These results pose NFOs as the most influential organizations within the industry. This comes along with the fact that, by virtue of their functions, these two government entities are associated with many types of knowledge and resources. Both count on specialized departments and workforce in constant contact with themselves and with the industry (domestic and abroad) in order to stay up to date with the latest technical and procedural information. This in turn makes it possible for the industry to count on the most actualized regulations and operational standards, for an effective *organizational integration* (in form of intra-industry and inter-sectoral collaboration) to be able to take place.

Table A4.5 Out-degree centrality

Rank	Nodes	Value	Unscaled
1	Regulation agency (CECMED)	0.717	38.000
2	National Coordinating Center for Clinical Trials (CENCEC)	0.509	27.000
3	Center of Medical Research and Development (CIDEM)	0.377	20.000
4	Pharmaceutical Chemistry Center (COF)	0.321	17.000
5	CEADEN	0.302	16.000
6	Center for Genetic Engineering and Biotechnology (CIGB)	0.283	15.000
7	Finlay Institute	0.283	15.000
8	Servicex Department 4	0.264	14.000
9	Center for Molecular Immunology (CIM)	0.264	14.000
10	National Center for Scientific Research (CNIC)	0.264	14.000

These two NFOs are an important element of the industrial policy followed by the government. As noted above, they are organizationally subordinated to the Ministry for Public Health, which has a priority status for the Cuban government. These organizations were designed with the explicit objective of centralizing the regulatory functions within the biopharmaceutical industry. However, the regulation of the safety, efficacy and quality of new medical products is also inextricably linked to innovation, in large part because regulators determine the extent of clinical trials necessary for products to gain marketing authorization, the cost of which is a significant part of overall product development. The prevalence of poor quality or even harmful medicines in underdeveloped drug regulatory systems (as it is the case in most of the developing countries) is a waste of resources that undermines already overburdened health-care systems and puts public safety at risk.

Likewise it is interesting that the third organization in the ranking is one that is much more engaged in coordination than in manufacturing. Even if CIDEM has its own manufacturing facilities, its role has mostly to do with providing microbiologic, biologic and toxicological studies to the biopharmaceutical complex aimed fundamentally at import substitution. When taking a look at its score, one can see the high priority given by policymakers to the domestic manufactured drugs and medicaments.

A4.7.6 In-degree centrality

As stated above, in-degree has to do with the links an agent receives from other nodes within the network. In matrix operation terms it represents the directed links that a column (target) receives from its related rows (source).[36] The results are shown in the Table A4.6.

The in-degree scores show a different picture, which is still coherent with the functional distribution throughout the Cuban biopharmaceutical industry. The highest score belongs to the CIGB, followed by the Finlay institute and the CQF. There is no NFO in this list because they are actually value providers for the rest of the industry. The receivers of these resources (in form of regulatory information, technical assistance, quality control, etc.) are the organizations in charge of making use of and transforming them into innovative and affordable

Table A4.6 In-degree centrality

Rank	Nodes	Value	Unscaled
1	Center for Genetic Engineering and Biotechnology (CIGB)	0.415	22.000
2	Finlay Institute	0.377	20.000
3	Pharmaceutical Chemistry Center (COF)	0.377	20.000
4	Center for Molecular Immunology (CIM)	0.358	19.000
5	National Center for Scientific Research (CNIC)	0.340	18.000
6	Center for Immunoessays (CIE)	0.340	18.000
7	National Center for Bioproduction (BIOCEN)	0.340	18.000
8	Institute for Digital Research (ICID)	0.321	17.000
9	National Center for Animal and Plant Health (CENSA)	0.302	16.000
10	Center for Neurosciences (CNC)	0.283	15.000

products. It is no surprise that the first company among the receivers in the ranking is the most important *in-house modular* firm within the industry (CIGB). This company, along with the Finlay Institute and the CIM, are considered the top three innovative, successful and most prestigious organizations of the Cuban biopharmaceutical complex.

The explanation of the CIM not being among the top three in the in-degree scores, even while being a leading innovator in the industry, is perhaps to be found in the high level of specialization of this organization. As noted above, the CIM specializes in cancer therapeutics, causing it to rely on certain types of resources. It offers a huge palette of products, but all of them related to one area. This is not the case of other companies with higher scores in the index. For instance, even if the Finlay Institute also specializes in vaccines, it covers a broad scope of therapeutic areas, which makes its portfolio much more diversified. On the other side, the study does not take into account the international linkages of these organizations, in which CIM and its trading arm (CIMAB) have a remarkable presence, perhaps more substantial than CIGB.

These results could indicate that the biotech innovation system in Cuba tends to privilege organizations with a diversify product and project portfolio, which makes more room for economies of scope. Indeed, two organizations of the top three (the CIGB and CQF) are two of the entities whose research portfolios covers huge amounts of therapeutics areas. Most likely this is one of the reasons they are the two organizations from the health biotechnology sector that find a place among the top 20 R&D organizations in 2010 (see Chapter 7, Table 7.3).

Table A4.7 Key nodes

Rank	Betweenness centrality	Closeness centrality	Eigenvector centrality	In-degree centrality	Out-degree centrality	Total degree centrality
1	FARMACUBA	Regulation agency (CECMED)	Regulation agency (CECMED)	Center for Genetic Engineering and Biotechnology (CIGB)	Regulation agency (CECMED)	Regulation agency (CECMED)
2	National Coordinating Center for Clinical Trials (CENCEC)	National Coordinating Center for Clinical Trials (CENCEC)	National Coordinating Center for Clinical Trials (CENCEC)	Finlay Institute	National Coordinating Center for Clinical Trials (CENCEC)	Center for Genetic Engineering and Biotechnology (CIGB)
3	Pharmaceutical Chemistry Center (CQF)	Center for Medical Research and Development (CIDEM)	Center for Genetic Engineering and Biotechnology (CIGB)	Pharmaceutical Chemistry Center (CQF)	Center for Medical Research and Development (CIDEM)	Pharmaceutical Chemistry Center (CQF)
4	Banco Exterior de Cuba	CEADEN	Finlay Institute	Center for Molecular Immunology (CIM)	Pharmaceutical Chemistry Center (CQF)	Finlay Institute
5	Quimefa Group	Ministry for Public Health	Center for IImmunoessay	National Center for Scientific	CEADEN	Center for Molecular Immunology (CIM)

Table A4.7 Cont.

			s (CIE)	Research (CNIC)		
6	Ministry for Science and Technology (CITMA)	Pharmaceutical Chemistry Center (CQF)	National Center for Scientific Research (CNIC)	Center for Immunoessays (CIE)	Center for Genetic Engineering and Biotechnology (CIGB)	National Center for Scientific Research (CNIC)
7	Institute for Digital Research (ICID)	Biomundi	Center for Molecular Immunology (CIM)	National Center for Bioproduccion (BIOCEN)	Finlay Institute	Center for Immunoessays (CIE)
8	Center for Medical Research and Development (CIDEM)	LABIOFAM Group	National Center for Bioproduccion (BIOCEN)	Institute for Digital Research (ICID)	Servicex Department 4	National Coordinating center of clinical trials (CENCEC)
9	Ministry for public Health	Center for Genetic Engineering and Biotechnology (CIGB)	National Center for Animal and Plant Health (CENSA)	National Center for Animal and Plant Health (CENSA)	Center for Molecular Immunology (CIM)	National Center for Bioproduction (BIOCEN)
10	Regulation agency (CECMED)	Finlay Institute	Pharmaceutical Chemistry Center (CQF)	Center for Neurosciences (CNC)	National Center for Scientific Research (CNIC)	Institute for Digital Research (ICID)

A4.8 Complementary measures

In order to complement (and further test the validity of) the results observed in the selected centrality indexes, another six related measures will be taken into consideration. Most of them are derivations of the selected core indexes, in that they show complementary aspects and other dimensions of the centrality notion being considered above. The complementary indexes are *hub centrality, authority centrality, information centrality, clique membership count, simmelian ties and clustering coefficient.* As the study is fundamentally intended to cover the features of the Cuban biopharmaceutical complex through the indicators that we have already dealt with above, this section will only briefly refer to these additional indexes and mention their respective top scoring organizations. They are instead; a way of testing the validity of the conclusions arrived at in the preceding section. The complete scoring lists can be found in the annex.

A4.8.1 Hub and authority centrality

We start with hub and authority centrality. The primary objective of these measures is to strengthen the argument of the eigenvector centrality, by taking into account directed links. Hub and authority centrality are in fact two generalizations of eigenvector centrality. As above stated, this measure (eigenvector centrality) takes into account agents, which are connected to agents that are themselves well connected.

When considering hub and authority, a balance between in and out-links is made, in order to evaluate if the information or resources are being provided by relevant sources and being directed at the desired destinies. For example, an organization can have a high in–degree, in that it receives many links (information, resources etc.) from others, but it does not mean that all relevant information is being received. A closer look could reveal that much information is being sent by unrelated organizations that do not provide any real value to the organization.

A way to know that the links are provided by a relevant organization would be to know if the received links are from nodes that have many out-links providing information on a common topic to other related nodes. This property is called *authority centrality* and identifies organizations that are receiving information from a wide range of others, each of whom sends information to a large number of others. Additionally, *hub centrality* identifies organizations that are sending information to a wide range of others, each of whom has many others reporting to them. An agent is hub-central if its out-links are directed to agents that have many other agents sending links to them. Therefore, it could be inferred that these two properties have a mutually reinforcing relationship. A good *hub* points to many good authorities; a good *authority* is a node that is pointed at by many good hubs. The foundational concept of these two categories can be found in Kleinberg (1998). They were initially intended to improve the efficiency of the search in the hyperlinked environment of the World Wide Web.[37]

The scoring tables of these indicators confirm to a great extent the results stated above. The top three scoring agents in the authority centrality results (Table A4.8) are almost identical to the in-degree results. This indicates that the two first organizations are receiving resources from important providers. The exception is to be found with CQF, whose third place in the in-degree ranking is taken by the Center for Inmmunoessay (CIE) in the authority ranking. This could mean that even if CQF receives more information from different sources than CIE (as the in-degree scores shows), CIE sources are organizations that are sending information to more others than CQF's. As stated earlier, CIE began working to develop an economical alpha-fetoprotein screening test to detect fetal malformations and has by now developed 28 diagnostic tests and 16 generations of equipment to screen for conditions ranging from congenital hypothyroidism and phenylketonuria (PKU) in newborns, to HIV, hepatitis and dengue. Once again, a sign of how diversified product portfolios are encouraged more than product specialization.

Even when CQF has a diversified portfolio, it seems to emphasize research over product development and it depends much more on direct links rather than indirect links to other organizations. If we take a look to the eigenvector scores above, it will be found that CIE has a higher score than CQF, which is consistent with the results shown by authority centrality.

Table A4.8 Authority centrality

Rank	*Nodes*	*Value*
1	Center for Genetic Engineering and Biotechnology (CIGB)	1.000
2	Finlay Institute	0.964
3	Center for Immunoessays (CIE)	0.951
4	National Center for Bioproduction (BIOCEN)	0.934
5	Center for Molecular Immunology (CIM)	0.929
6	National Center for Scientific Research (CNIC)	0.911
7	National Center for Animal and Plant Health (CENSA)	0.855
8	National Center of production of laboratory animals (CENPALAB)	0.843
9	Institute for Digital Research (ICID)	0.817
10	Pharmaceutical Chemistry Center (CQF)	0.816

The top three in the hub centrality results (Table A4.9) show (as in the out-degree results) CECMED and CENCEC in the first and second place respectively. This result is consistent with the abovementioned and reaffirms the relevance of non-firm organizations (NFOs) when considering their contribution to organizational learning. The third in the score is again the Center for Immunoessay (CIE), which seems to play a very important role within firms that form the strategic network of the Cuban biopharmaceutical industry as a provider of resources. This is coherent with the fact that this organization specializes in a broad range of screening tests that are to be employed by a broad range of organizations. Most important, for the development of their technologies, it highly depends on the collaboration with high rated organizations (in term of in-links) such as CIGB and Finlay Institute. These elements could help to explain its high score as hub.

A4.8.2 Information centrality

Another complementary indicator being considered is the *Information centrality*. It complete name is Stephenson and Zelen information centrality and it is calculated as the harmonic mean of a node's distance to the others.

Table A4.9 Hub centrality

Rank	Nodes	Value
1	Regulation agency (CECMED)	1.000
2	National Coordinating Center for Clinical Trials (CENCEC)	0.903
3	Center for Immunoessays (CIE)	0.771
4	Center for Medical Research and Development (CIDEM)	0.730
5	Finlay Institute	0.727
6	Center for Genetic Engineering and Biotechnology (CIGB)	0.727
7	National Center for Scientific Research (CNIC)	0.710
8	Center for Molecular Immunology (CIM)	0.709
9	Pharmaceutical Chemistry Center (CQF)	0.682
10	LABIOFAM Group	0.673

Its foundational mathematical and conceptual definition can be found in Stephenson and Zelen (1989). This is another measure of closeness centrality that takes into account all paths in the networks instead of only the geodesic (shortest-path). As stated above, closeness centrality assumes that all communication occurs through the shortest path, and then all flow channels are by default geodesic. However, it can be that information takes a more indirect route (for example through random communication). Therefore, and in contrast to the shortest-path closeness centrality, the information centrality index assumes that all paths (not only the geodesics) can be relevant to the network.

This measure is conceived more for processes where the function and route of the information, knowledge or resources have not been previously defined. Notice, however, that the case of the Cuban biotech network corresponds to a system, which has been explicitly designed to minimize the information's time route. Therefore, it makes sense to use the shortest-path centrality for Cuban biotech. Notwithstanding this, the *information* measure could help test the overall efficiency of the different organizations if the geodesic assumption is assumed. In other words, it allows seeing how efficient the shortest-path winning nodes are under the new assumption.

Table A4.10 Information centrality

Rank	Nodes	Value	Unscaled
1	Regulation agency (CECMED)	0.030	2.044
2	National Coordinating Center for Clinical Trials (CENCEC)	0.030	2.007
3	Center for Medical Research and Development (CIDEM)	0.029	1.951
4	CEADEN	0.028	1.906
5	Servicex department 4	0.028	1.880
6	Pharmaceutical Chemistry Center (CQF)	0.027	1.862
7	LABIOFAM group	0.027	1.841
8	Finlay Institute	0.027	1.822
9	Center for Genetic Engineering and Biotechnology (CIGB)	0.027	1.804
10	Center for Molecular Immunology (CIM)	0.026	1.803

The results of the information centrality (Table A4.10) show; that the two non-firm organizations with the highest scores in the shortest-path measure are the same (and in the same order) high scoring organizations under the new assumption. Indeed, the national drug regulation agency CECMED and the National Clinical Trials Coordinating Center CENCEC are the two first organizations in the ranking. This could mean that these two NFOs are not only efficient by sending information to other through the pre-destined route, but are also able to spread information rapidly even if the *message* is not initially meant to take the shortest way.

For example, in the case of CECMED, consider the regular publication of information relating to the post-marketing phase of a given medical product. Even when this information is primarily intended to promptly reach the organizations involved in the development of one specific product, the information centrality measure could be telling us that this message might also spread to the rest of the network as fast as it has reached the initially desired organizations. This could apply in case of CENCEC, with the information of a certain clinical trial. Of course, this explanation excludes messages or information, which are not intended to be publicized. Otherwise, the measure could be telling us how fast confidential information spills over the system.

The third high scoring organization is the Center for Medical Research and Development (CIDEM) whose role is fundamentally (although not exclusively) providing microbiologic, biologic and toxicological studies to the biopharmaceutical complex aimed essentially at import substitution. CIDEM takes the place of CIGB, which is the third in the shortest-path closeness ranking. This could indicate that CIGB is not primarily intended to spread information through the network. Its high closeness score means that CIGB works better when it knows with whom it is working, which is consistent with its function of product developer. CIGB is good spreading information to the partners it has already found. In contrast, CIDEM is capable of spreading information more quickly than CIGB to the whole network; because it is less specific information and may be useful for several organizations. This element might reflect its high score in the information centrality.

A4.8.3 Clique count, clustering coefficient, simmelian ties

This last group of complementary indicators is intended to analyses sub-network structures according to the quality and quantity of nodes that form it. They are mostly complementary to measures such as total centrality degree in that they explore how adjacent (neighbor-based) and decentralized structures within the network favor information diffusion. Note that we are referring here to local structures, which means the relation between a node and its immediate neighbors rather than global measures (referred to the whole network).

Clique membership count

We begin with clique membership count, which is simply the number of distinct cliques to which each node belongs. A clique is defined as a group of three or more agents that have many connections to each other and relatively fewer connections to those in other groups. The foundational definition was provided by Duncan and Perry (1949) and proposes that a subset of a "certain group forms a clique provided that it consists of three or more members each in the symmetric relation to each other member of the subset, and provided further that there can be found no element outside the subset that is in the symmetric relation to each of the elements of the subset" (ibid., p. 97).

The Table A4.11 shows that CECMED and CENCEC are the first and the second in the top three ranking. The third place belongs to FARMACUBA, which shows, as in the betweenness measures, the weight of trade within the industry.

After having been shown in other indicators above that two NFOs (CECMED and CENCEC) are the main contributors to organizational

Table A4.11 Clique membership

Rank	Nodes	Value
1	Regulation agency (CECMED)	35.000
2	National Coordinating Center for Clinical Trials (CENCEC)	24.000
3	FARMACUBA	23.000
4	Center for Genetic Engineering and Biotechnology (CIGB)	19.000
5	Finlay Institute	19.000
6	National Center for Scientific Research (CNIC)	17.000
7	Center for Immunoessays (CIE)	15.000
8	Pharmaceutical Chemistry Center (CQF)	14.000
9	Center for Molecular Immunology (CIM)	13.000
10	Center for Medical Research and Development (CIDEM)	12.000

integration (expressed in different centrality indexes) within the industry, it makes sense to find these organizations being part of the most number of cliques within the network.[38] This could be interpreted as the ability of organizations to contribute to the specific dynamic of different subgroups within the network. Earlier (see total degree centrality), while exploring the degree centrality high rankings of these two NFOs, we referred to the capacity of two nodes i and j to co-construct something that is unique to them while engaging in a similar activity with others. The clique membership counts complements and confirms the just mentioned property by showing how CECMED and CENCEC are able to be part of different levels of local embeddeness.

Clustering coefficient

The second indicator being considered; which is strongly related to the concept of clique, is the indicator of clustering coefficient. This indicator measures the extent to which a node's neighbors are also connected with each other, or in other words, how close they are to being a clique (cliqueness) (foundational definition can be found in Watts and Strogatz 1998).

Table A4.12 Clustering coefficient

Rank	Nodes	Value
1	State Council	1.000
2	Center of Medical Genetics	0.967
3	Laboratory of Synthetic Antigens (LAGS)	0.700
4	Biomundi	0.659
5	LABIOFAM Group	0.624
6	National Center of Production of Laboratory Animals (CENPALAB)	0.621
7	Center for Neurosciences (CNC)	0.619
8	National Center for Animal and Plant Health (CENSA)	0.555
9	Center for Immunoessays (CIE)	0.545
10	Import Medicament Unit (UEBMI central freezing)	0.500

The Table A4.12 shows the Council of state, the Center of Medical Genetics and the Laboratory of antigens (LAGS) as the three top scoring organizations in the rank. Even if this result can look somewhat unexpected at first sight, a closer scrutiny shows that this indicator does not measure the extent to which the organizations belong to a clique, therefore it is not surprising to find three relatively isolated entities scoring the best points in the ranking.

On the other hand, the fact that entities with low degree show high clustering coefficients is a sign of hierarchical networks (see Chapter 2). According to Ravasz and Barabási (2003), the essential idea behind this sort of network is that the *clustering coefficient* of a node tends to decrease as the degree (number of connections to other nodes) increases. That's also the reason why, with respect to this indicator, we cannot find the biggest hubs of the system among the top scores. This is also a sign of the fact that the Cuban biotech sectoral system of innovation could formally[39] fit the definition of *hub dominated network* given by the authors.

The clustering coefficient might be stressing the high level of institutionalized inter- and intra-organizational collaboration within the industry. The Council of State had until recently the control of the strategic network of the industry. This was changed in 2009. However, as already mentioned; the Council still supervises the Servicex Department 4, which is in charge of importing diagnostic kits and reagents exclusively for the biotechnology industry. This facility is highly specialized in all the specific requirements of the biotechnology industry, which makes its services very essential. The fact that it belongs to the State Council is a sign of the kind of commitment that still remains in the central government to the biotech industry.

It is also interesting to point out, that the score "1" shows that the neighbors of this node, namely the companies of the strategic network, are totally connected to each other. That is, the strategic network shows no structural hole. In social network analysis, a structural hole is defined as the absence of a tie among a pair of nodes in the ego-network (Borgatti 2009). The lack of structural holes around a node means that the node's contacts are "bound" together – they can communicate and coordinate so as to act as one, creating a formidable "other" to negotiate with (ibid., p. 14). This is the basic principle behind the benefits of worker's unions and political alliances. In contrast, a node with many structural holes can play unconnected nodes against each other, dividing and conquering.

The second top scoring node is a relatively unknown organization (founded in 2003): The Center of Medical Genetic (also called National Medical Genetic Center). As briefly stated earlier, the National Medical Genetics Center is essentially a basic/applied research organization focused on high-tech diagnostic, research, human resource training and on the introduction of new technologies in the field. It belongs to the Higher Institute of Medical Sciences of Havana (which belongs to the Ministry of Health, MINSAP) and it closely works with all the core companies the Western Havana biotech complex. The Genetics Center has created a genetic registry that contributes to accelerate clinical trials, to focus medical research and to personalize medicine. The fact that it is linked to the most important actors in the industry speaks for itself.

The other organization among the top three (and the third in the score) is the Laboratory of Synthetic Antigens (LAGS), which is a vivid example of both the idea expressed in the previous paragraphs, and of the sense of the indicator being explored. The LAGS is a small lab, which belongs to the faculty of the Chemistry Department at the University of Havana, and had been working to make the process of chemical synthesis more efficient, in order to obtain a cheaper and more efficient vaccine.

In 1999 the vaccine was given top priority in the Cuban biotech industry when the Council of State instructed the CIGB to put its scientific and productive infrastructure at disposal of the development of the vaccine. The LAGS ended up leading a huge collaboration network (including important foreign partners) that made possible the development of the first synthetic vaccine for human use approved in the world, and the first major product of the Cuban biotech industry with origins in university laboratories. Large-scale production was made possible by the CIGB's staff, a few months after the vaccine discovery. The visualization of LAGS relationships (see below, Visualizations) focuses on three of the highly connected strategic network companies that played a major role in this cooperation.

However, in practice, at least ten organizations and over 300 people contributed their complementary capabilities to obtain this product. The fact that the neighbors of these three just mentioned organizations are strongly clustered (no structural holes), explains how organizations that are not embedded in strong cliques may find themselves in a particularly advantageous position. Expressly, the case of LAGS shows how relatively small, or at first glance, unrelated organizations that do not belong to the strategic network of the industry, can develop innovative products at a relatively low cost by relying on resources and knowledge of strong connected cliques.

On the other hand, the ability of creating cross-boundary knowledge should not be taken for granted. It should not be forgotten that this fluent interchange has been ultimately made possible by the fact that the Cuban biopharmaceutical industry works under an institutional regime that categorically excludes competition between individual firms and focuses on collaboration. Otherwise one could have an environment composed of organizations wary of disclosing information that would benefit their counterparts; where bargaining power (and its linked costs) would be favored over open knowledge exchange across organizational boundaries.

Simmelian ties

Also strongly related to the process of cross-boundary collaboration is the notion of simmelian ties, the last indicator being explored in this research. The central idea behind this concept is that of two agents (nodes), which are reciprocally tied to one other and, at the same time, each is reciprocally connected to a third agent (the foundational definition and the algorithm can be found in Krackhardt 1998, 1999; see also Dekker 2006).

This measure establishes a difference between the dyads (relation between two nodes) and dyads embedded in a clique. The latter tend to be more stable by facilitating cooperation and conflict resolution by reducing bargaining power of single agents, and by moderating the pursuit of individuals' self-interests. For example, in the case of disagreement between the parties, a normal dyad (or isolated bridge) experiences a larger threat of being dissolved than in simmelian structures, where a third party tends to reduce the dissent.

Simmelian ties are a good example for adaptation and binding mechanisms within a social network. These mechanisms can be used to explain how relational roles affect outcomes. For example, unlike the transmission mechanism (observed in the role of NFOs), adaptation is not transmitted from one node to another, but rather is similarly created in each node because of their similar relations to others. This mechanism is not present in isolated bridges.

As a typical example of isolated bridge, consider, for instance, the case of the alliances and manufacturing contract within the biotech industry worldwide. According to Pisano (2006), the typical contract duration is less than four years, which is three times shorter than the typical product development cycle, which invalidates any long-term perspective. This will disincentivize the investment in specific assets, sharing proprietary information, joint learning and risk taking by the fear that the relationship can be terminated at any moment. To add a third partner may help stabilize the collaboration by making the sharing of information imperative if the collaboration is expected to survive. In other words, it reduces the potential individualism of the agents, therefore making group behavior more predictable. These elements are critical in an industry like the biopharmaceutical, which depends *per se* on interdisciplinary communication. The emergence of Pharma 3 as new philosophy signals the increasing awareness among industry officials and policymakers about the importance of these mechanisms (see Chapter 7).

The three first scoring organizations in simmelian ties match the three most innovative firms of Cuban biotech. This is not surprise at all, given that these organizations are integrants of the strategic network of the industry, which is a very dense clique (total absent of structural holes) within the industry. This can be easily seen in the visualization of the strategic network.

The high level of interdependency observed in the strategic network of the industry explains the high level of innovation of these companies. Indeed, one of the critical implications of the existence of simmelian structures is that increased stability promotes the development of common language and shared understandings among the parties involved. This common knowledge is essential to overcome interpretive barriers and achieve the kind of successful cross-boundary knowledge integration which is conductive to innovation. The notion of in-house modularity (see above) proposed for the core companies of the Cuban biotech, is highly compatible with the notion of simmelian ties and could open an interesting research agenda for future undertakings.

However, when analyzing this indicator, a warranted question could arise: Why are the most cited NFOs (CECMED and CENCEC) not scoring high in an indicator that has to do with the ability to promote shared standards when, for the most part, these two organizations have been shown to play a critical role in the making of these types of standards within the industry? A possible answer could be that most of the links for these two non-firm organizations with the rest of the network are out-links, which causes them to be viewed more as sources, or top-nodes. They are much more relevant as givers of information and as shapers of organizational standards, which has been shown in the measures of out-degree and hub centralities. In fact, it could be said that this "shaper" role has created a common ground for other subgroups in the network to be able to develop their own cooperation subsystems.

On the other hand, companies such as CIGB and Finlay Institute can be seen among the top three scoring nodes in indicators such as in-degree and authority centrality. This is signaling the prominence of these organizations as receivers of resources, in contrast with the more influential role played by CECMED and CENCEC. However, if we take a look at the Cuban biotech network configured by type of activity, one can see that the nodes representing

Table A4.13 Simmelian ties

Rank	Nodes	Value	Unscaled
1	Center for Genetic Engineering and Biotechnology (CIGB)	0.245	13.000
2	Center for Molecular Immunology (CIM)	0.226	12.000
3	Finlay Institute	0.226	12.000
4	Center for Immunoessays (CIE)	0.226	12.000
5	National Center for Scientific Research (CNIC)	0.208	11.000
6	National Center for Bioproduction (BIOCEN)	0.208	11.000
7	Center for Neurosciences (CNC)	0.189	10.000
8	National Center for Animal and Plant Health (CENSA)	0.189	10.000
9	National Center of Production of Laboratory Animals (CENPALAB)	0.189	10.000
10	Institute for Digital Research (ICID)	0.189	10.000

research–production organizations type (the one covering organizations such as the three highest scores in the indicator simmelian ties) show a significant number of mutual linkages with other product-related activities, which explains their innovation potential (see Visualization 25).

CECMED and CENCEC show out-links to almost all the activities but receive little. Therefore, it can be concluded that while firms like CIGB and Finlay Institute contribute to direct product innovation, organizations like CECMED and CENCEC contribute to the creation of a significant part of the centralized regulatory standards and protocols that makes these innovations possible. For example, any company can claim to have developed an innovative drug, but the quality of this drug, the quality of the procedures under which it was produced, and its clinical effects, still needs to be carefully scrutinized before it reaches the buyer.

The ability to assess the safety of products after marketing approval of organizations such as US Food and Drug Administration (FDA), by far the best known and one of the most prestigious drug regulation agencies in the world, has been increasingly compromised as a result of the deregulation and the influence of pharmaceutical companies. According to Light (2010), prescription drugs have become the fourth-leading cause of death in the US. It is a sure sign that to have an industry with only potentially good innovators is not enough.

A4.9 Conclusion

The results of the network analysis above seem to confirm the previous historic-qualitative analysis carried out in the study, which is that government-based, NFOs are an essential factor contributing to *organizational integration* and therefore, to organizational learning, within the industry. The largest part of this contribution is carried by the two most important regulatory and coordinating bodies of the industry: The National Drug Regulatory Authority CECMED; and the National Coordinating Center of Clinical Trials CENCEC. Table A4.7 shows the top scoring nodes of the network side by side for the six selected measures and they are ranked among the top three high scoring organizations in four of the six considered measures.

In addition, a group of six complementary indexes has been included (*hub centrality, authority centrality, information centrality, clique membership count, simmelian ties and clustering coefficient*). Most of them are derivations of the selected core indexes, and show complementary aspects as well as new dimensions of the centrality notions being considered above, in addition to confirming the earlier conclusions.

This contribution of NFOs could be interpreted as the ability to provide shared standards to the whole network of organizations. These shared standards can take the form of uniform policies, protocols and group platforms etc. and they tend to reduce asset specificity and offer an embedded environment that helps to lessen search, enforcement and monitoring, and innovation costs. This could mean the existence of important cost and innovation effects resulting from economies of both scale and scope, as well as user-producer interactions along the value chain.

In Chapter 3 we discussed the possibilities that standards may emerge and can also be created. In many industries, day to day operational standards simply emerge. As institutions, standards can arise through the repetition of certain shared habits, which can eventually lead to the emergence of rule-following behaviors. This process of habituation makes it possible for the institution to emerge. These institutions can be further codified or not; the point is that they have the capacity to create long-term expectations for the participants involved in the process. In contrast, when it comes to the creation of new knowledge or cutting age innovations, firms (even big integrated ones) tend to play safe. In this case, disruptive new standards tend to emerge from the interaction between government NFOs and (still a minority of) disruptive agents. However, from the perspective of the rest of the agents, these new rules are going to look very disruptive and even coercive.

Consider the issue of the regulation of the financial industry. Should regulators to allow this highly deregulated and (from an internal point of view) efficient industry to continue with its upsetting practices just because the sector's standards have emerged? In this case, to impose regulations would actually create new standards, very disruptive for the industry, but necessary for the rest of the economy. In fact, the very advantage of being an incoherent hub within the system consists of having (at least the theoretical) capability to regulate from a different logic and therefore subvert what could seem very obvious and rational for other agents. From this perspective, as already discussed in Chapter 3, it may be said that standards both emerge and are imposed at the same time, depending of the point of reference. This interdependent and *re-constitutive* relationship is inherent to complex industrial systems and it is the very foundation for an evolutionary understanding of the processes of institutional change and innovation.

The just mentioned role of NFOs in creating effective regulatory standards can be clearly observed in our analysis of the Cuban biopharmaceutical industry. The fact that the two regulatory organizations mentioned above show high scores in most of the indicators could be inferred as a sign of how crucial the setting of *standard interfaces* is, when they are to be shared by the whole network of organizations. Indeed, government regulation of the industry influences manufacturing practices, biotechnology research choices, testing procedures, laboratory construction and practices, and marketing of new products.

A closer look from a network perspective reveals that important transmission and adaptation mechanisms are at play here. For example, these two NFOs are influential enough to shape, and therefore make, more predictable the behavior of other organizations. Or, in other words, to make the adaptation of other organizations more homogeneous. In the language of evolutionary-institutional economics it means that these organizations greatly contribute to the stabilization of expectations within a network of heterogeneous agents. In business organization, this means saving time and money. If two nodes have ties to the same (or equivalent) others, then they face the same environmental forces (in form of standard norms and regulations) and are likely to adapt by becoming increasingly similar, which makes cooperation easier and more likely to succeed.

Consider now the transmission mechanism, if knowledge is to flow properly across the industry, these two entities need to fulfil a number of inter and intra-organizational criteria that are in part dependent on their structural position within the industry network, which provides the conduits for the flow of information and norms. For example, they need the ability to rapidly transmitting information to others directly tied to them, whether simultaneously or not (total degree centrality). But they are also expected to communicate quickly to organizations which are not directly tied to them (closeness, eigenvector and information centrality).

They also require the capacity to monitor knowledge flows and have a better picture of what is happening in the industry (closeness centrality) because, as in the case of CECMED, they have been given the power to provide or withdraw the operation license (in case of not meeting the requirements) of virtually all the organizations involved in core activities of the industry (manufacturing, trading, domestic/international distribution). The monitoring need is also found in CENCEC, which is in charge of the national network of clinical sites. Consequently, they are also required to be proficient in many types of knowledge and resources and to be able to be part of the dynamic of different subgroups within the network (out-degree and hub centrality, clique membership).

Strong transmission and adaptation mechanisms can also be found in other subgroups of the network. While the non-firm organizations represent (in network jargon) the most influential entities within the industry, the most innovative firms of the industry are the most prominent entities of the network of organizations. The fact that the most innovative companies of the industry (in-house modular companies) are the ones that receive more knowledge and resources from other sources (in-degree centrality) and, at the same time, appear to provide an important contribution to the stability of inter-firm platforms (in terms of simmelian structures), is the confirmation of their relevance in the process of cross-boundary knowledge integration.

The clearest example of inter-firm cooperation within the Cuban industry is the *strategic network,* which represents a subgroup with*in the industry*. The strategic network is a relatively small group of firms among the actors of West Havana Biocluster, which represents the core of the industry. The existence of standards provided by NFOs to the system has made it easier for these companies to develop their own cooperation subsystem and to foster innovation. These efforts have taken the form of employment policies, IP sharing, or shared platforms in activities such as research, manufacturing or commercialization capabilities. Most of the products of the industry (innovative or generics) are the result of a collaboration between several organizations.

Last but not least, it should be remembered that the links between organizations within the Cuban biotech industry respond to a certain policy strategy aimed at covering national public health and export demands. The whole network of organizations is embedded in an institutional system that encourages collaboration and, as a paramount rule, excludes rivalry. All medical care is officially free and the national health system is controlled by the Ministry of Public Health (MINSAP). MINSAP is in charge of carrying out of government health policy, the general regulation of the medical sector and the conduct of medical research. The industry is a result of a government investment representing an explicit and the most successful attempt of industrial policy and technology upgrading in the Cuban soil up to date.

Annex 5

Table A5.1 Finished product portfolio of the three most important facilities of the Cuban biotech until 2011 (selection)

Finlay Institute Products Portfolio 2011 (Selection)

- Meningococcal BC vaccine, Va-Mengoc-BC
- Meningococcal AC vaccine, vax-MEN-AC
- Trivalent leptospiral vaccine, vax-SPIRAL
- Typhi Vi polysaccharide vaccine, vax-TyVi
- Tetanus vaccine, vax-TET
- Tetanus vaccine, vax-TET-5
- Diphtheria-tetanus vaccine for paediatric use, VA-DIFTET
- Diphtheria-tetanus vaccine for adults, dT
- Diphtheria-tetanus-pertussis vaccine, dTP

Source: Finlay Institute, www.finlay.sld.cu/english/products/products.htm

CIM product portfolio 2011 (selection)

- Anti CD3 monoclonal antibody: treatment of patients with organ transplant rejection
- Recombinant Human Erythropoietin r-HuEPO: treatment of anemia
- Recombinant Granulocyte Colony-Stimulating Factor, rgCSF: treatment of neutropenia
- "Humanized" Monoclonal Antibody Anti Epidermal Growth Factor Receptor: Recognizes the epidermal growth factor receptor for cancer treatment as well
- Tumor Imaging Products Specific imaging of tumors using freeze dried monoclonal antibody preparations for Tc-99m labeling
- in vitro diagnostic products
- Ondansetrone, $C_{18}H_{19}N_3O$ (293.37)
- Cytostatics

Source: CIM

CIGB most relevant APIs 2011 (selection)

- Recombinant hepatitis B surface antigen (rHBsAg)
- Synthetic antigen polirribosil ribitol phosphate for haemophilus influenza type b vaccine
- Recombinant μ 2b interferon (rIFN μ2b)
- Recombinant γ interferon (rIFN)
- Transfer Factor (FT)
- Recombinant human erythropoietin (rhEPO)
- Recombinant Granulocyte Colony Stimulating Factor (rG-SCF)
- Monoclonal antibody CB- Hep1 (CB-Hep1)
- Plantibody HB-01
- Recombinant protein p64k (rP64K)

- Human recombinant epidermal growth factor (rhEGF)
- rhEGF for parenteral use

A complete list of the product portfolio can be found at www.heber-biotec. com/Ingles/farmabio.htm

Source: CIGB.

Table A5.2 Historical development of CIGB products approved for commercialization

Year	Biotech product (generic name)	Indication(s)
1981–1990	Leuferon (human IFN)	Viral infections and cancer
	Hebertrans (leukocyte extract termed transfer factor)	Immune deficiencies, herpes and ataxia telangiectasia
	Heberon alfa R (recombinant IFN-α2b)	Hepatitis C and cancer
	Hebermin (recombinant EGF) produced in *Escherichia coli*)	Burns and ulcers
	Heberbiovac HB (recombinant HbsAg)	Hepatitis B
1991–2000	Heberkinasa (recombinant streptokinase)	Cardiovascular disease
	GAVAC (recombinant Bm86 protein vaccine)	Cattle tick (*Boophilus microplus*)
	Heberon Gamma R (recombinant IFN-γ)	Juvenile rheumatoid arthritis
2001–2007	Quimi-Hib (Hib vaccine)	Pneumonia and meningitis
	Bivalent 'HB-Hib' recombinant vaccine comprising HBsAg and Hib)	Hepatitis B, pneumonia and meningitis
	Trivac HB (tetravalent (DPT-HB) vaccine)	Diphtheria, tetanus, whooping cough and hepatitis B
	Heberpenta (pentavalent (DPT-HB+Hib) vaccine)	As above plus *Haemophilus influenzae* meningitis
	Heberviron (recombinant IFN-α2b and ribavirine)	Hepatitis C
	Hebervital (recombinant granulocyte colony stimulating factor)	Leukopenia, neutropenia
	Heberitro (recombinant erythropoietin-α)	Anemia
	HeberNem (*Corynebacterium paurometabolum* C924 strain)	Biological control of plant nematode infestation
	Acuabio I (invertebrate and fish nutritional supplement containing a defined combination of amino acids)	Prevention of white spot disease

[a] Table does not list new formulations of existing products, such as Heberbiovac HB, Heberon alfa R liquid without albumin, Heberon alfa R lyophilized without albumin, and Heberkinasa without albumin, Hebervis and Citoprot-P.

Source: Lopez et al. (2007).

Table A5.3 CIGB Biomedical Project Pipeline, 2012

PROJECT	AREA	DISCOVERY	PRECLINICAL	PHASE I	PHASE II	PHASE III	APPROVAL
Heberprot-P	Wound healing	■	■	■	■	■	■
SK suppository	Gastroenterology	■	■	■	■	■	
CIGB 230 (Anti HCV vaccine)	Infections	■	■	■	■		
CIGB 300 (antitumoral peptide)	Oncology	■	■	■	■		
CIGB 228 (anti HPV therapeutic vaccine)	Oncology	■	■	■	■		
Therapeutic vaccine anti HBV (NASVAC)	Infections	■	■	■	■		
Therapeutic vaccine against prostate cancer	Oncology	■	■	■			
CIGB 500 (cytoprotective agent)	Cardiovascular	■	■	■			
CIGB M3 (Rec. anti CEA antibody fragment)	Oncology	■	■	■			
CIGB 370 (antitumoral agent)	Oncology	■	■				
CIGB 166a–598a (anti VEGF antibodies)	Oncology	■	■				
CIGB 247 (anti VEGF vaccine)	Oncology	■	■				
Vaccine against haemorraghic dengue	Infections	■	■				
Anti viral molecules against dengue	Infections	■	■				
CIGB 845 (neuroprotective agent)	Autoimmunity	■	■				
CIGB 552 (antitumoral agent)	Oncology	■	■				
Therapy based in the combination of interferons alpha 2b and gamma	Oncology	■	■				
Therapy based in the combination of ifn alpha 2b and phycocianine against MS	Autoimmunity	■	■				
CIGB 814. Peptide against rheumatoid arthritis	Autoimmunity	■	■				
CIGB 50. Therapeutic vaccine against rheumatoid arthritis.	Autoimmunity	■	■				
CIGB 55. Peptide against rheumatoid arthritis.	Autoimmunity	■	■				

Source: CIGB, Business Portfolio 2012–13.

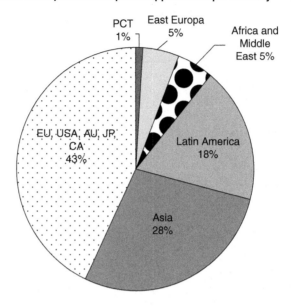

2009 CIGB patents and patent applications per territory

Numbers of patents

Total	1004
EU, USA, AU, JP, CA	427
Asia	284
Latin America	179
Africa and Middle East	56
East Europe	48
PCT	10

Legend:
- ■ Total
- ⬚ EU, USA, AU, JP, CA
- ■ Asia
- ▨ Latin America
- ◤ Africa and Midle East
- ▧ East Europe
- ■ PCT

Figure A5.4 CIGB patents, 2010.

Source: Author's interpretation of data available at CIGB–Heber Portfolio 2010.

Table A5.5 Cuban immunoassay technology in the national public health system

TEST	Year introduced	Number of tests performed and/or Universe	Cases detected (mass screenings only)	Technology
PREGNANT WOMEN				
Congenital malformations (Alfa-fetoprotein)	1982	3,364,151	7,536	UMELISA AFP
Ectopic pregnancy and trophoblastic disease (Human chorionic gonadotropin)	1992	Case-by-case basis (available nationwide)	n/a	UMELISA HCG
NEWBORNS				
Congenital hypothyroidism (Thyroid Stimulating hormone)	1986	2,917,438	754	UMELISA NEONATAL TSH
Phenylketonuria (phe)	2000	620,235	11	UMTEST PKU
Congenital adrenal hyperplasia (17-OH-Progesterone)	2005	343,551	11	UMELISA 17 OH NEONATAL PROGESTERONE
Biotinidase deficiency (Biotinidase)	2005	324,735	1	UMTEST BIOTINIDASE
Galactosemia (Galactose)	2005	288,626	2	UMTEST GAL
INFECTIOUS DISEASES				
HIV-AIDS (anti-HIV 1&2)	1988	24,616,148 (including blood donors, pregnant women, and for general epidemiological surveillance)	10,615 seropositive tests Of blood donors: 0.63%	UMELISA HIV 1+2 RECOMBINANT
Hepatitis B (HBsAg & other serological markers)	1986	15,770,641 (including blood donors, pregnant women, and for general epidemiological surveillance)	Non-specific reactivity among blood donors: 0.97% Confirmed cases among blood donors: 70,590 (0.74% of blood donors)	UMELISA HBsAg PLUS HBsAg CONFIRMATORY TEST UMELISA ANTI-HBsAg UMELISA ANTI-HBc UMELISA ANTI-HBc IgM
Hepatitis C (anti-HCV)	1992	8,586,826 (including blood donors and for general epidemiological surveillance)	Reactivity in blood donors: 0.85%	UMELISA HCV
Dengue (IgM antibodies)	1995	Suspected cases during outbreaks	n/a	UMELISA DENGUE IgM PLUS
Leprosy (IgM antibodies)	1993	Suspected cases	n/a	UMELISA HANSEN
Chagas (IgG antibodies)	1994	All travelers to Cuba from endemic countries or regions	n/a	UMELISA CHAGAS
Tetanus (IgG anti-toxin)	1996	Blood donors	Donations with required titers used for production of human tetanus immunoglobulin	UMELISA TETANUS
NON-COMMUNICABLE CHRONIC CONDITIONS				
Diabetes mellitus (blood glucose)	2008	Diabetic patients	Currently being rolled out through primary care services	SUMASensor (Glucometer)
Prostate cancer (Prostate-specific antigen)	2003	63,606	n/a	UMELISA PSA
Atopic diseases (Total IgE)	1987	Children with suspected allergies	n/a	UMELISA IgE

Source: Reed (2009). Based on data provided by the Centre for Immunoassay.

Table A5.6 Cuban neurotechnology timeline

1969	First use of a CAT-400C computer, donated by US scientists, for computerised evaluation of brain disorders
1970	First Cuban microcomputer used for electroencephalogram (EEG) analysis
1972	First prototype of the MEDICID-01 computerised EEG system
1977	Neurometrics Paper on computerised brain diagnosis published in *Science* by joint US-Cuban group[4]
1982	Industrial production begun of MEDICID-03 computerised EEG system, foundation of the national neuroscience diagnostic network
1983	Electric response audiometry screening initiated in Havana for infants aged 3 months at risk for hearing loss
1983	First Cuban video game released for learning assessment in school-age children
1990	MEDICID-3E: first Cuban computerised EEG equipment registered in France and Switzerland
1991	Early hearing screening program scaled up to national coverage
1992	First generalised use of Quantitative Electroencephalogram (qEEG) in a public health system[5]
1996	AUDIX system developed for early hearing loss detection
1997	Battery of tests designed for assessing learning disorders in children
1999	Video games introduced for learning disorder rehabilitation
2001–2003	National disability study carried out[6]
2004	National human brain mapping project initiated
2005	National cochlear implants program initiated neurodevelopmental disorder study carried out in cotorro municipality, havana city province
2006	National learning disability prevalence study carried out
2008	Software introduced for diagnosis and treatment of neurodevelopmental disorders

Source: Reed (2009).

Table A5.7 Strategic core of the biotechnology industry, 2011

Company	Creation date	Number of workers	Commercial branch	Creation date
CIGB	1986	1245	Heber Biotec	1991
CIM	1994	400	CIMAB	1992
Finlay Inst.	1991	920	Vacunas Finlay	1991
CENSA	1980	406		1980
CNIC	1965	1193	DALMER	1965
CIE	1987	244	Tecnosuma	1987
CENPALAB	1982	414		1982
BIOCEN	1992	800		1993
CNC★	1990		Neuronic	1990
IPK	1937(1979)			

Complete name of the Centers
CIGB: Center for Genetic Engineering and Biotechnology
CIM: Center for Molecular Immunology
Finlay Inst: Finlay Institute
CENSA: National Center for Animal and Plant Health
CNIC: National Center for Scientific Research
CIE: Center for Immunoassay
CENPALAB: National Center for Production of Laboratory Animals
BIOCEN: National Center for Bioproduction
CNC: Center for Neurosciences

Notes
★ The facilities of Neurosciences are still part of the CNIC. For this reason it has been difficult to localize the number of workers. New and independent facilities were under construction at the time this research was taking place.

Although these centers also do research and innovation, CENSA, BIOCEN and CENPALAB facilities are more specialized in product manufacturing. They constantly collaborate with other organizations in this endeavor. At the same time, their products are usually commercialized by Heber Biotec or any other commercial branch of the industry.

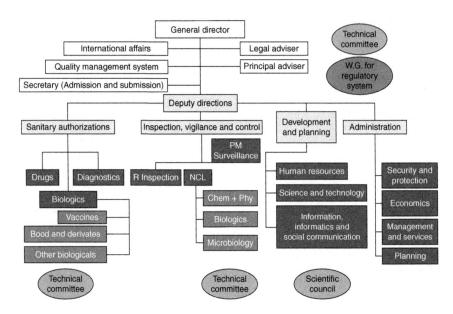

Figure A5.8 General organization chart (CECMED).
Source: Pérez and Sanchez (2008).

Domestic indicators

Table A5.9 List of essential medicines by sector and origin, 2009–11

	Total	Hospital	Pharmacy	FPM	ESP	COM	FVH
Imports	305	283	22	22	21	10	0
Local production	562	229	333	329	303	288	4
Total 2009	**867**	**512**	**355**	**351**	**324**	**298**	**4**
Imports	283	254	29	22	21	19	7
Local production	585	248	337	333	309	284	4
Total 2010	**868**	**502**	**366**	**355**	**330**	**303**	**11**
Imports	305	256	49	41	40	19	8
Local production	580	245	335	330	306	281	5
Total 2011	**885**	**501**	**384**	**371**	**346**	**300**	**13**

Source: Espicom Business International (2011). Based on data of Cuba's Ministry for Public Health (Spanish acronym MINSAP).

Table A5.10 Pharmaceutical production by type, 1997–2008 (million pesos)

	Human pharmaceuticals	Raw materials and medicinal plants	Total	%Change
1997	141.2	1.3	142.5	n/a
1998	120.9	1.2	122.1	–14.3
1999	125.6	1.6	127.2	4.2
2000	119.5	1.4	120.9	–5.0
2001	136.4	1.3	137.7	13.9
2002	170.4	1.6	172.0	24.9
2003	198.0	1.8	199.8	16.2
2004	218.4	8.1	226.5	13.4
2005	285.6	7.7	293.3	29.5
2006	353.2	11.2	364.4	24.2
2007	397.4	9.1	406.5	11.6
2008	607.5	8.2	615.7	51.5

Source: Espicom Business International (2011). Based on Cuba's National Statistics Office (ONE).

Trade

Table A5.11 Pharmaceutical exports by category, 1995–2010 (thousand US$)

	Raw materials	Antisera and vaccines	Semi-finished medicaments	Retail medicaments	Total	%Change
1995	6,962	30,119	283	5,731	43,096	n/a
1996	1,267	35,221	159	9,686	46,333	7.5
1997	1,499	42,085	356	6,606	50,546	9.1
1998	448	21,204	311	3,428	25,391	–49.8
1999	1,342	13,631	4,839	4,798	24,610	–3.1
2000	359	19,580	4,977	5,897	30,813	25.2
2001	523	19,189	1,081	7,464	28,256	–8.3
2002	334	26,119	1,483	8,842	36,778	30.2
2003	306	28,121	1,294	12,477	42,199	14.7
2004	109	17,207	1,841	13,240	32,397	–23.2
2005	5,088	20,069	1,223	4,718	31,098	–4.0
2006	17,877	27,046	235	13,586	58,745	88.9
2007	49,958	31,177	183	22,951	104,269	77.5
2008	30,315	14,067	402	25,476	70,260	–32.6
2009	35,298	18,120	775	235,767	289,959	312.7
2010	50,111	28,362	702	198,578	277,753	–4.2
%Total	18.0	10.2	0.3	71.5	100.0	~

Source: Espicom Business International (2011). Based on UN Comtrade, using reverse data.

Table A5.12 Pharmaceutical exports by country/region, 2010 (thousand US$)

	Raw materials	Antisera and vaccines	Semi-finished medicaments	Retail medicaments	Total	%Total
Venezuela	0	0	0	178,793	178,793	64.4
Brazil	50,006	9,478	0	0	59,484	21.4
Panama	0	383	8	10,840	11,231	4.0
Argentina	0	7,667	0	1	7,668	2.8
Colombia	0	2,011	0	0	2,011	0.7
Germany	0	0	0	1,926	1,926	0.7
Nicaragua	1	1,307	0	545	1,853	0.7
South Africa	0	1,114	0	541	1,656	0.6
Singapore	0	0	0	1,320	1,320	0.5
Dominican Rep.	0	29	0	1,205	1,234	0.4
Subtotal 1-10	*50,007*	*21,989*	*8*	*195,172*	*267,177*	*96.2*
Mexico	94	1,005	0	11	1,110	0.4
Algeria	0	742	0	322	1,064	0.4
Ukraine	0	943	0	83	1,026	0.4
Tunisia	0	505	451	0	956	0.3
Ecuador	0	907	0	40	947	0.3
Indonesia	0	0	0	793	793	0.3
Canada	0	6	0	659	665	0.2
Peru	0	617	0	9	626	0.2
Russia	0	390	0	230	620	0.2
Pakistan	0	586	0	0	586	0.2
Subtotal 11-20	*94*	*5,700*	*451*	*2,147*	*8,392*	*3.0*
Other	10	672	243	1,259	2,184	0.8
Total	**50,111**	**28,362**	**702**	**198,578**	**277,753**	**100.0**
EU-27	0	121	4	2,080	2,205	0.8
LATAM	50,105	23,575	8	191,881	265,570	95.6

Source: Espicom Business International (2011) Based on UN Comtrade, using reverse data.

Table A5.13 Pharmaceutical imports by category, 1995–2010 (thousand US$)

	Raw materials	Antisera and vaccines	Semi-finished medicaments	Retail medicaments	Total	%Change
1995	7,727	385	938	16,866	25,916	n/a
1996	6,962	840	1,577	17,313	26,692	3.0
1997	6,570	885	481	10,332	18,268	−31.6
1998	8,699	2,238	168	18,981	30,086	64.7
1999	5,852	1,256	149	9,626	16,882	−43.9
2000	7,007	3,605	77	12,424	23,114	36.9
2001	7,343	3,080	454	16,493	27,369	18.4
2002	7,739	2,465	413	14,662	25,279	−7.6
2003	8,285	2,647	453	12,784	24,169	−4.4
2004	10,891	1,874	449	21,252	34,466	42.6
2005	12,014	3,733	741	27,479	43,966	27.6
2006	11,117	5,522	889	39,222	56,750	29.1
2007	13,830	11,792	603	44,831	71,056	25.2
2008	52,039	11,107	1,910	51,453	116,509	64.0
2009	16,404	7,856	2,051	59,754	86,065	−26.1
2010	19,506	6,857	1,526	47,987	75,875	−11.8
%Total	25.7	9.0	2.0	63.2	100.0	~

Source: Espicom Business International (2011) Based on UN Comtrade, using reverse data.

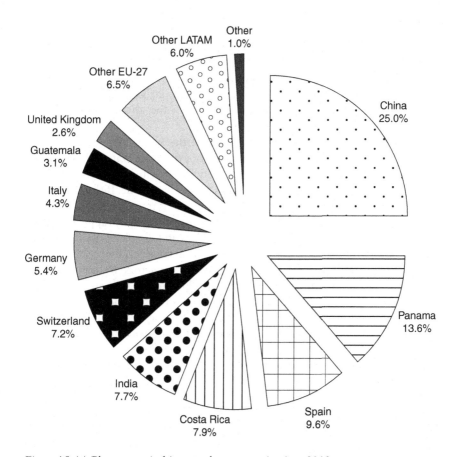

Figure A5.14 Pharmaceutical imports by country/region, 2010.

Source: Espicom Business International (2011). Based on UN Comtrade, using reverse data.

Visualizations

The following visualizations show the ego-networks of the most important actors of the Cuban biopharmaceutical complex. "Ego" is an individual "focal" node; and the ego-network is the collection of all nodes to whom ego has a connection at some path length. In social network analysis, the connection is usually one-step; that is, it includes only ego and actors that are directly adjacent. We follow the same approach here.

Focal nodes are depicted within a circle of the same color of the nodes. The color of the nodes indicates the function of the organization represented. The color and arrowhead of the links identify the origin and direction of the resource respectively (e.g. a blue link comes from a blue node. If the arrowhead is directed toward a green node, then the blue node is transferring resources to the green one). (*Editorial Note*: Please note that while the figures appear in grey-scale in print, the Annexes will be available to view in full color online at: www.routledge.com/9781138558984.) As mentioned in Annex 4 node relations are assumed to be taking the form of binary links (two actors are connected or they aren't), and the resources to flow in both directions. Links are generically identified as resources or knowledge, rather than as the specific resource that a given organization is supposed to more frequently provide. This is due to high degree of multi-functionality and integration within Cuban biopharmaceutical industry.

Before starting with the ego-networks we show the whole network illustration.

Cuban biotechnology – network illustration

Legend

green	production firms, i.e. organisations, almost exclusively devoted to the manufacture of vaccines, medicaments and other products
violet	organisations exclusively or mainly devoted to research.
orange	organisations mostly devoted to provide high-tech services to other companies
light blue	trading organisations (domestic and international commercialisation)
grey	holding organisations of the industry
red	central organisations (NFOs related to regulation, administration and legislation)
yellow	research – manufacturing organisation with trading licence but without an autonomous commercialisation unit
dark blue	strategic network

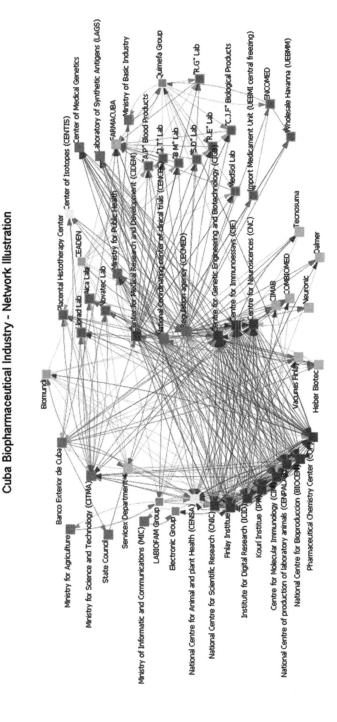

Cuba Biopharmaceutical Industry - Network Illustration

Recurring top ranked nodes – Cuban biotechnology

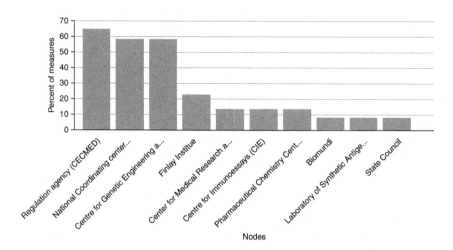

1. National Centre for Scientific Research (CNIC)

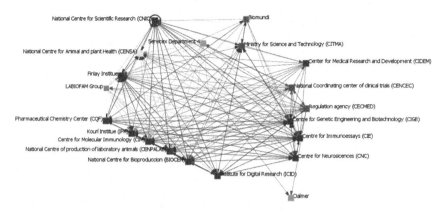

CNIC metrics

Total Degree	Closeness	Eigenvector	Betweenness	Outdegree	Indegree
0.302	------	0.905	------	0.264	0.340
Authority	Hub	Information	Clique membership	Clustering coefficient	Simmelian Ties
0.911	0.710	------	17.000	-----	0.208

------ Not among the top ten in the rank

2. Strategic network

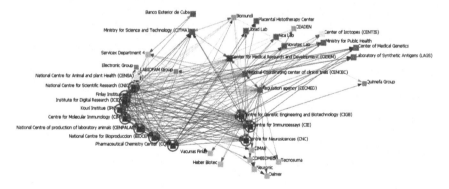

3. Strategic network (excluding other subgroups)

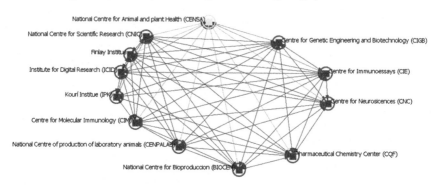

4. Centre for Genetic Engineering and Biotechnology (CIGB)

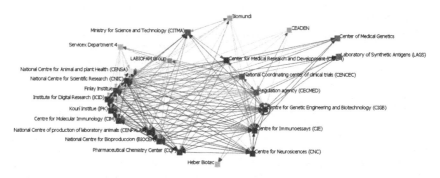

CIGB metrics

Total Degree	Closeness	Eigenvector	Betweenness	Outdegree	Indegree
0.349	0.449	0.948	-------	0.283	0.415
Authority	*Hub*	*Information*	*Clique membership*	*Clustering coefficient*	*Simmelian Ties*
1.000	0.727	0.027	19.000	-----	0.245

5. Centre of Molecular Immunology (CIM) (influences excluding the strategic network)

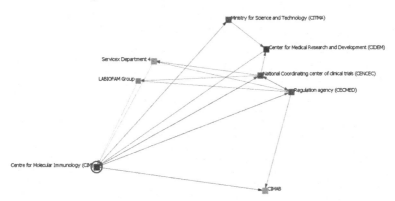

CIM metrics

Total Degree	Closeness	Eigenvector	Betweenness	Outdegree	Indegree
0.311	------	0.897	-------	0.264	0.358
Authority	Hub	Information	Clique membership	Clustering coefficient	Simmelian Ties
0.929	0.709	0.026	13.000	---------	0.226

6. Chemical Pharmaceutical Centre (CQF)

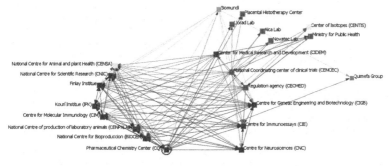

CQF metrics

Total Degree	Closeness	Eigenvector	Betweenness	Outdegree	Indegree
0.349	0.486	0.810	0.172	0.321	0.377
Authority	Hub	Information	Clique membership	Clustering coefficient	Simmelian Ties
0.816	0.682	0.027	14.000	-------	---------

7. Finlay Institute

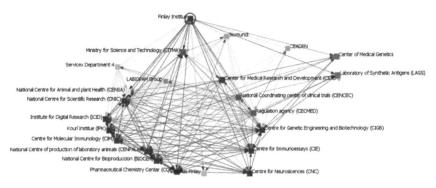

Finlay Institute metrics

Total Degree	Closeness	Eigenvector	Betweenness	Outdegree	Indegree
0.330	0.449	0.945	---------	0.283	0.377
Authority	*Hub*	*Information*	*Clique membership*	*Clustering coefficient*	*Simmelian Ties*
0.964	0.727	0.027	19.000	-------	0.226

8. Center for Immunoassay (CIE)

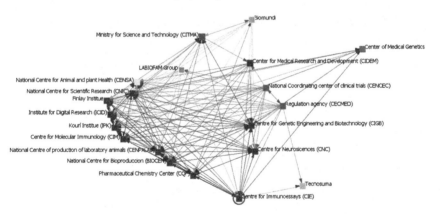

CIE metrics

Total Degree	Closeness	Eigenvector	Betweenness	Outdegree	Indegree
0.302	-------	0.921	---------	---------	0.340
Authority	*Hub*	*Information*	*Clique membership*	*Clustering coefficient*	*Simmelian Ties*
0.951	0.771	--------	15.000	0.545	0.226

9. Pharmaceutical Research & Development Centre (CIDEM)

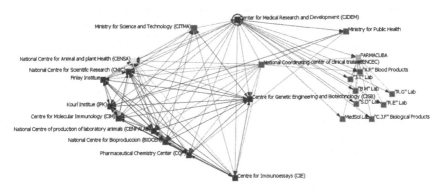

CIDEM metrics

Total Degree	Closeness	Eigenvector	Betweenness	Outdegree	Indegree
------	0.530	---------	0.083	0.377	---------

Authority	Hub	Information	Clique membership	Clustering coefficient	Simmelian Ties
-------	0.730	0.029	12.000	-------	-------

10. Aica, Novatec, Llorad Lab, PHC

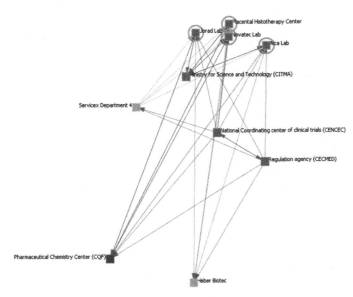

Aica, Novatec, Llorad Lab, PHC (the same for all organizations)

Total Degree	Closeness	Eigenvector	Betweenness	Outdegree	Indegree
-------	---------	--------	----------	--------	--------
Authority	Hub	Information	Clique membership	Clustering coefficient	Simmelian Ties
---------	-------	-------	-------	-------	-------

11. Manufacturing (chemically produced drugs)

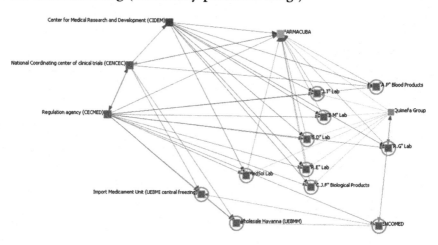

Manufacturing (chemically produced drugs) (the same for all organizations)

Total Degree	Closeness	Eigenvector	Betweenness	Outdegree	Indegree
-------	---------	--------	----------	--------	--------
Authority	Hub	Information	Clique membership	Clustering coefficient	Simmelian Ties
---------	-------	-------	-------	0.500★	-------

★ This score belongs to the Import Medicament Unit (UEBMI central freezing).
 No manufacturing unit scores among the top ten

12. Biomundi.

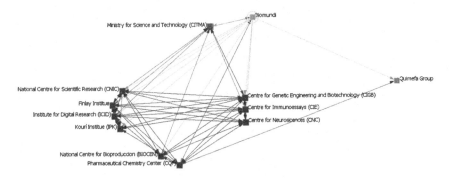

Biomundi metrics

Total Degree	Closeness	Eigenvector	Betweenness	Outdegree	Indegree
-------	0.465	--------	--------	--------	-------
Authority	Hub	Information	Clique membership	Clustering coefficient	Simmelian Ties
--------	-------	--------	-------	0.659	-------

13. CEADEN

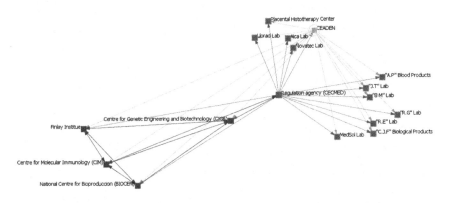

CEADEN metrics

Total Degree	Closeness	Eigenvector	Betweenness	Outdegree	Indegree
-------	0.525	--------	---------	0.302	--------
Authority	Hub	Information	Clique membership	Clustering coefficient	Simmelian Ties
--------	-------	0.028	--------	--------	-------

14. Trading agencies (strategic network)

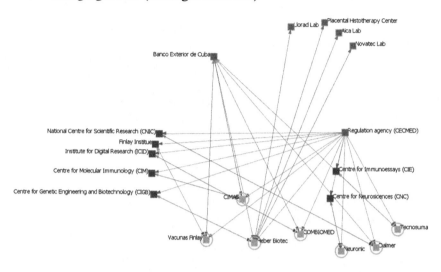

Trading agencies (strategic network) metrics (the same for all organizations)

Total Degree	Closeness	Eigenvector	Betweenness	Outdegree	Indegree
--------	---------	---------	----------	--------	--------
Authority	*Hub*	*Information*	*Clique membership*	*Clustering coefficient*	*Simmelian Ties*
--------	-------	---------	-------	-------	-------

15. Servicex 4

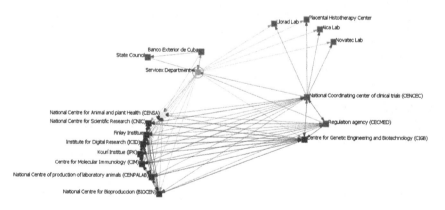

Servicex 4 metrics

Total Degree	Closeness	Eigenvector	Betweenness	Outdegree	Indegree
-------	--------	---------	----------	0.264	--------
Authority	Hub	Information	Clique membership	Clustering coefficient	Simmelian Ties
--------	-------	0.028	---------	--------	-------

16. FARMACUBA

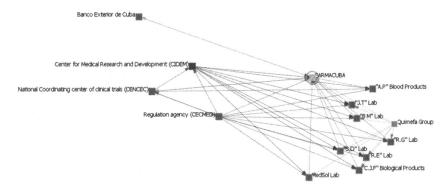

FARMACUBA metrics

Total Degree	Closeness	Eigenvector	Betweenness	Outdegree	Indegree
-------	--------	---------	0.194	---------	--------
Authority	Hub	Information	Clique membership	Clustering coefficient	Simmelian Ties
--------	-------	---------	23.000	--------	-------

17. LABIOFAM Group

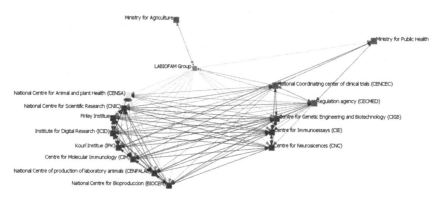

LABIOFAM metrics

Total Degree	Closeness	Eigenvector	Betweenness	Outdegree	Indegree
--------	0.457	----------	----------	----------	--------
Authority	*Hub*	*Information*	*Clique membership*	*Clustering coefficient*	*Simmelian Ties*
--------	0.673	0.027	----------	0.624	----------

18. QUIMEFA Group (now part of BioCubaFarma)

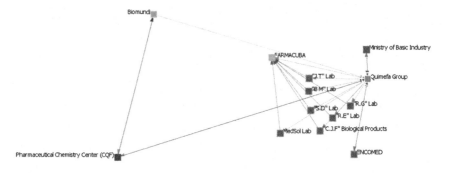

Quimefa metrics

Total Degree	Closeness	Eigenvector	Betweenness	Outdegree	Indegree
--------	--------	--------	0.108	-------	-------
Authority	*Hub*	*Information*	*Clique membership*	*Clustering coefficient*	*Simmelian Ties*
--------	------	--------	----------	----------	--------

19. National Drug Quality Control Centre (CECMED)

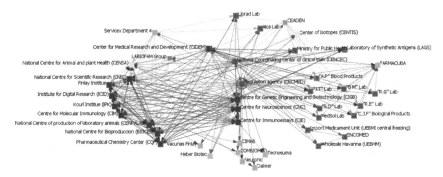

CECMED metrics

Total Degree	Closeness	Eigenvector	Betweenness	Outdegree	Indegree
0.387	0.757	1.000	0.071	0.717	-------
Authority	*Hub*	*Information*	*Clique membership*	*Clustering coefficient*	*Simmelian Ties*
-------	1.000	0.030	35.000	---------	---------

20. National Clinical Trials Coordinating Center (CENCEC)

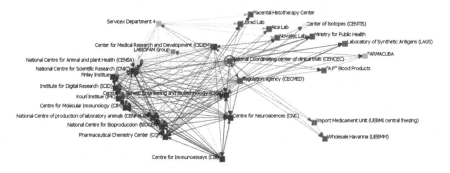

CENCEC metrics

Total Degree	Closeness	Eigenvector	Betweenness	Outdegree	Indegree
0.283	0.654	0.951	0.184	0.509	--------
Authority	*Hub*	*Information*	*Clique membership*	*Clustering coefficient*	*Simmelian Ties*
---------	0.903	0.030	24.000	---------	---------

21. Ministries of Science and Technology (CITMA)

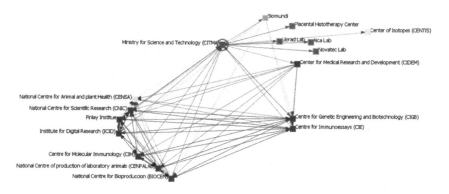

CITMA metrics

Total Degree	Closeness	Eigenvector	Betweenness	Outdegree	Indegree
--------	---------	---------	0.103	-------	-------
Authority	Hub	Information	Clique membership	Clustering coefficient	Simmelian Ties
--------	------	--------	---------	---------	---------

22. Banco Exterior de Cuba

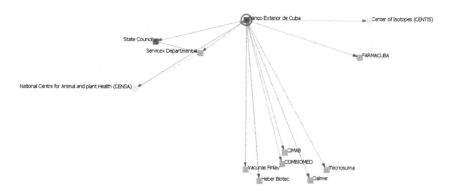

Banco Exterior de Cuba metrics

Total Degree	Closeness	Eigenvector	Betweenness	Outdegree	Indegree
-------	---------	---------	0.110	--------	---------
Authority	Hub	Information	Clique membership	Clustering coefficient	Simmelian Ties
--------	------	--------	---------	---------	---------

23. Laboratory of Synthetic Antigens (LAGS)

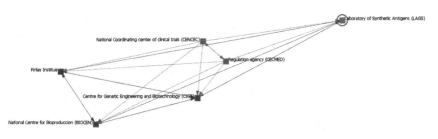

LAGS metrics

Total Degree	Closeness	Eigenvector	Betweenness	Outdegree	Indegree
-------	--------	----------	----------	----------	---------
Authority	*Hub*	*Information*	*Clique membership*	*Clustering coefficient*	*Simmelian Ties*
---------	-------	--------	---------	0.700	---------

24. State Council

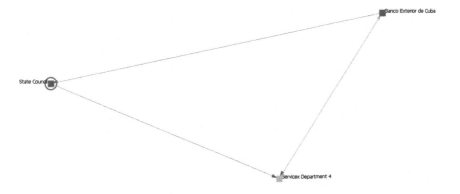

State Council metrics

Total Degree	Closeness	Eigenvector	Betweenness	Outdegree	Indegree
-------	--------	--------	--------	----------	--------
Authority	*Hub*	*Information*	*Clique membership*	*Clustering coefficient*	*Simmelian Ties*
---------	-------	---------	---------	1.000	---------

25. Cuban Biopharmaceutical Industry (by type of activity)

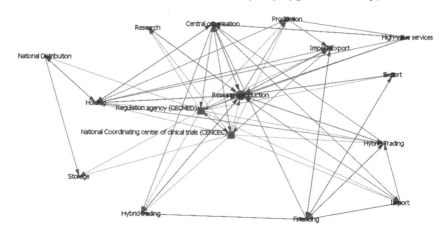

STANDARD NETWORK ANALYSIS (FULL REPORT)

Input data:	Cuban Biotechnology
Start time:	Sat, June 29 16:44:43 2013

Network level measures

Measure	Value
Row count	54.000
Column count	54.000
Link count	383.000
Density	0.134
Isolate count	0.000
Component count	1.000
Reciprocity	0.388
Characteristic path length	2.696
Clustering coefficient	0.319
Network levels (diameter)	7.000
Network fragmentation	0.000
Krackhardt connectedness	1.000
Krackhardt efficiency	0.838
Krackhardt hierarchy	0.073
Krackhardt upperboundedness	1.000
Degree centralization	0.263
Betweenness centralization	0.166
Closeness centralization	0.785
Reciprocal?	No (38% of the links are reciprocal)

Node level measures

Measure	Min	Max	Avg	Stddev
Total degree centrality	0.019	0.387	0.134	0.109
Total degree centrality [Unscaled]	2.000	41.000	14.185	11.549
In-degree centrality	0.019	0.415	0.134	0.118
In-degree centrality [Unscaled]	1.000	22.000	7.093	6.234
Out-degree centrality	0.000	0.717	0.134	0.144
Out-degree centrality [Unscaled]	0.000	38.000	7.093	7.621
Eigenvector centrality	0.003	1.000	0.391	0.324
Closeness centrality	0.019	0.757	0.375	0.115
Closeness centrality [Unscaled]	0.000	0.014	0.007	0.002
Betweenness centrality	0.000	0.194	0.031	0.049
Betweenness centrality [Unscaled]	0.000	535.885	86.611	134.343
Hub centrality	0.000	1.000	0.278	0.306
Authority centrality	0.004	1.000	0.323	0.312
Information centrality	0.000	0.030	0.019	0.008
Information centrality [Unscaled]	0.000	2.044	1.260	0.523
Clique membership count	0.000	35.000	6.185	7.239
Simmelian ties	0.000	0.245	0.049	0.083
Simmelian ties [Unscaled]	0.000	13.000	2.593	4.416
Clustering coefficient	0.000	1.000	0.319	0.235

Total degree centrality

Rank	Nodes	Value	Unscaled	Context*
1	Regulation agency (CECMED)	0.387	41.000	5.460
2	Centre for Genetic Engineering and Biotechnology	0.349	37.000	4.646
3	Pharmaceutical Chemistry Center (CQF)	0.349	37.000	4.646
4	Finlay Institute	0.330	35.000	4.238
5	Centre for Molecular Immunology (CIM)	0.311	33.000	3.831
6	National Centre for Scientific Research	0.302	32.000	3.627
7	Centre for Immunoessays (CIE)	0.302	32.000	3.627
8	National Coordinating Center of Clinical	0.283	30.000	3.220

9	National Centre for Bioproduccion (BIOCE)	0.283	30.000	3.220
10	Institute for Digital Research (ICID)	0.283	30.000	3.220
11	National Centre for Animal and Plant Health	0.264	28.000	2.813
12	Centre for Neurosciences (CNC)	0.245	26.000	2.406
13	National Centre of Production of Laboratory	0.245	26.000	2.406
14	Center for Medical Research and Development	0.217	23.000	1.795
15	Ministry for Science and Technology (CIT	0.208	22.000	1.591
16	Kourí Institute (IPK)	0.208	22.000	1.591
17	Banco Exterior de Cuba	0.189	20.000	1.184
18	Servicex Department 4	0.170	18.000	0.777
19	CEADEN	0.160	17.000	0.573
20	LABIOFAM Group	0.151	16.000	0.370
21	Quimefa Group	0.142	15.000	0.166
22	FARMACUBA	0.142	15.000	0.166
23	Biomundi	0.123	13.000	-0.241
24	Ministry for Public Health	0.104	11.000	-0.649
25	Center of Medical Genetics	0.094	10.000	-0.852
26	Heber Biotec	0.085	9.000	-1.056
27	Llorad Lab	0.075	8.000	-1.259
28	Novatec Lab	0.075	8.000	-1.259
29	Placental Histotherapy Center	0.075	8.000	-1.259
30	Laboratory of Synthetic Antigens (LAGS)	0.075	8.000	-1.259
31	Aica Lab	0.066	7.000	-1.463
32	Center of Isotopes (CENTIS)	0.066	7.000	-1.463
33	MedSol Lab	0.047	5.000	-1.870
34	"R.G" Lab	0.047	5.000	-1.870
35	"8 M" Lab	0.047	5.000	-1.870
36	"J.T" Lab	0.047	5.000	-1.870
37	"C.J.F" Biological Products	0.047	5.000	-1.870
38	"R.E" Lab	0.047	5.000	-1.870
39	ENCOMED	0.047	5.000	-1.870
40	"A.P" Blood Products	0.047	5.000	-1.870
41	CIMAB	0.047	5.000	-1.870
42	Tecnosuma	0.047	5.000	-1.870
43	Vacunas Finlay	0.047	5.000	-1.870
44	COMBIOMED	0.047	5.000	-1.870

45	Import Medicament Unit (UEBMI central fr	0.038	4.000	-2.074
46	Wholesale Havana (UEBMM)	0.038	4.000	-2.074
47	"S.D" Lab	0.038	4.000	-2.074
48	Electronic Group	0.038	4.000	-2.074
49	Dalmer	0.038	4.000	-2.074
50	Ministry of Basic Industry	0.028	3.000	-2.278
51	Neuronic	0.028	3.000	-2.278
52	Ministry for Agriculture	0.019	2.000	-2.481
53	Ministry of Informatic and Communication	0.019	2.000	-2.481
54	State Council	0.019	2.000	-2.481

* Number of standard deviations from the mean of a random network of the same size and density.

| Mean: | 0.134 | Mean in random network: | 0.134. |
| Std.dev: | 0.109 | Std.dev in random network: | 0.046. |

In-degree centrality

Rank	Nodes	Value	Unscaled
1	Centre for Genetic Engineering and Biotech 0.415	22.000	
2	Finlay Institute	0.377	20.000
3	Pharmaceutical Chemistry Center (CQF)	0.377	20.000
4	Centre for Molecular Immunology (CIM)	0.358	19.000
5	National Centre for Scientific Research	0.340	18.000
6	Centre for Immunoessays (CIE)	0.340	18.000
7	National Centre for Bioproduccion (BIOCE	0.340	18.000
8	Institute for Digital Research (ICID)	0.321	17.000
9	National Centre for Animal and Plant Health	0.302	16.000
10	Centre for Neurosciences (CNC)	0.283	15.000
11	National Centre of Production of Laboratory	0.283	15.000
12	Kourí Institue (IPK)	0.283	15.000
13	Ministry for Science and Technology (CIT	0.264	14.000
14	FARMACUBA	0.245	13.000
15	Banco Exterior de Cuba	0.170	9.000
16	Heber Biotec	0.132	7.000
17	Llorad Lab	0.094	5.000

18	Aica Lab	0.094	5.000
19	Novatec Lab	0.094	5.000
20	Placental Histotherapy Center	0.094	5.000
21	Center of Isotopes (CENTIS)	0.094	5.000
22	Ministry for Public Health	0.094	5.000
23	Laboratory of Synthetic Antigens (LAGS)	0.094	5.000
24	Center of Medical Genetics	0.094	5.000
25	Wholesale Havana (UEBMM)	0.075	4.000
26	Quimefa Group	0.075	4.000
27	MedSol Lab	0.075	4.000
28	"R.G" Lab	0.075	4.000
29	"8 M" Lab	0.075	4.000
30	"J.T" Lab	0.075	4.000
31	"C.J.F" Biological Products	0.075	4.000
32	"R.E" Lab	0.075	4.000
33	"A.P" Blood Products	0.075	4.000
34	Servicex Department 4	0.075	4.000
35	Center for Medical Research and Development 0.057	3.000	
36	Import Medicament Unit (UEBMI central fr	0.057	3.000
37	"S.D" Lab	0.057	3.000
38	Regulation Agency (CECMED)	0.057	3.000
39	National Coordinating Center of Clinical	0.057	3.000
40	LABIOFAM Group	0.057	3.000
41	CIMAB	0.057	3.000
42	Tecnosuma	0.057	3.000
43	Vacunas Finlay	0.057	3.000
44	COMBIOMED	0.057	3.000
45	Dalmer	0.057	3.000
46	Biomundi	0.038	2.000
47	Ministry of Basic Industry	0.038	2.000
48	ENCOMED	0.038	2.000
49	Electronic Group	0.038	2.000
50	Neuronic	0.038	2.000
51	CEADEN	0.019	1.000
52	Ministry for Agriculture	0.019	1.000
53	Ministry of Informatic and Communication	0.019	1.000
54	State Council	0.019	1.000

Out-degree centrality

Rank	Nodes	Value	Unscaled
1	Regulation Agency (CECMED)	0.717	38.000
2	National Coordinating Center of Clinical	0.509	27.000
3	Center for Medical Research and Development	0.377	20.000

4	Pharmaceutical Chemistry Center (CQF)	0.321	17.000
5	CEADEN	0.302	16.000
6	Centre for Genetic Engineering and Biotech	0.283	15.000
7	Finlay Institute	0.283	15.000
8	Servicex Department 4	0.264	14.000
9	Centre for Molecular Immunology (CIM)	0.264	14.000
10	National Centre for Scientific Research	0.264	14.000
11	Centre for Immunoessays (CIE)	0.264	14.000
12	LABIOFAM Group	0.245	13.000
13	Institute for Digital Research (ICID)	0.245	13.000
14	National Centre for Bioproduccion (BIOCE	0.226	12.000
15	National Centre for Animal and Plant Health	0.226	12.000
16	Biomundi	0.208	11.000
17	Quimefa Group	0.208	11.000
18	Banco Exterior de Cuba	0.208	11.000
19	Centre for Neurosicences (CNC)	0.208	11.000
20	National Centre of Production of Laboratory	0.208	11.000
21	Ministry for Science and Technology (CIT	0.151	8.000
22	Kourí Institute (IPK)	0.132	7.000
23	Ministry for Public Health	0.113	6.000
24	Center of Medical Genetics	0.094	5.000
25	Llorad Lab	0.057	3.000
26	Novatec Lab	0.057	3.000
27	Placental Histotherapy Center	0.057	3.000
28	ENCOMED	0.057	3.000
29	Laboratory of Synthetic Antigens (LAGS)	0.057	3.000
30	Aica Lab	0.038	2.000
31	Center of Isotopes (CENTIS)	0.038	2.000
32	Electronic Group	0.038	2.000
33	CIMAB	0.038	2.000
34	Tecnosuma	0.038	2.000
35	Vacunas Finlay	0.038	2.000
36	Heber Biotec	0.038	2.000
37	COMBIOMED	0.038	2.000
38	FARMACUBA	0.038	2.000
39	Import Medicament Unit (UEBMI central fr	0.019	1.000
40	Ministry of Basic Industry	0.019	1.000
41	MedSol Lab	0.019	1.000
42	"R.G" Lab	0.019	1.000
43	"8 M" Lab	0.019	1.000
44	"J.T" Lab	0.019	1.000
45	"C.J.F" Biological Products	0.019	1.000

46	"R.E" Lab	0.019	1.000
47	"S.D" Lab	0.019	1.000
48	"A.P" Blood Products	0.019	1.000
49	Ministry for Agriculture	0.019	1.000
50	Ministry of Informatic and Communication	0.019	1.000
51	State Council	0.019	1.000
52	Neuronic	0.019	1.000
53	Dalmer	0.019	1.000

Eigenvector centrality

Rank	Nodes	Value	Context*
1	Regulation Agency (CECMED)	1.000	1.885
2	National Coordinating Center of Clinical	0.951	1.694
3	Centre for Genetic Engineering and Biotech	0.948	1.685
4	Finlay Institute	0.945	1.673
5	Centre for Immunoessays (CIE)	0.921	1.578
6	National Centre for Scientific Research	0.905	1.519
7	Centre for Molecular Immunology (CIM)	0.897	1.488
8	National Centre for Bioproduccion (BIOCE)	0.880	1.419
9	National Centre for Animal and Plant Health	0.819	1.182
10	Pharmaceutical Chemistry Center (CQF)	0.810	1.149
11	National Centre of Production of Laboratory	0.809	1.145
12	Institute for Digital Research (ICID)	0.801	1.115
13	Centre for Neurosicences (CNC)	0.731	0.843
14	Center for Medical Research and Development	0.730	0.841
15	LABIOFAM Group	0.707	0.749
16	Kourí Institue (IPK)	0.694	0.700
17	Servicex Department 4	0.653	0.540
18	Ministry for Science and Technology (CIT	0.625	0.433
19	Biomundi	0.545	0.122
20	CEADEN	0.406	−0.415
21	Center of Medical Genetics	0.322	−0.739
22	Ministry for Public Health	0.299	−0.831
23	Laboratory of Synthetic Antigens (LAGS)	0.287	−0.878
24	FARMACUBA	0.260	−0.979
25	Llorad Lab	0.220	−1.136
26	Aica Lab	0.220	−1.136

27	Novatec Lab	0.220	-1.136
28	Placental Histotherapy Center	0.220	-1.136
29	Center of Isotopes (CENTIS)	0.216	-1.152
30	"A.P" Blood Products	0.203	-1.201
31	Heber Biotec	0.182	-1.283
32	Banco Exterior de Cuba	0.170	-1.328
33	Quimefa Group	0.170	-1.331
34	MedSol Lab	0.156	-1.385
35	"R.G" Lab	0.156	-1.385
36	"8 M" Lab	0.156	-1.385
37	"J.T" Lab	0.156	-1.385
38	"C.J.F" Biological Products	0.156	-1.385
39	"R.E" Lab	0.156	-1.385
40	Import Medicament Unit (UEBMI central fr	0.132	-1.478
41	Wholesale Havana (UEBMM)	0.132	-1.478
42	"S.D" Lab	0.131	-1.480
43	Vacunas Finlay	0.128	-1.491
44	Tecnosuma	0.127	-1.497
45	Dalmer	0.126	-1.500
46	CIMAB	0.126	-1.502
47	COMBIOMED	0.120	-1.525
48	Neuronic	0.105	-1.581
49	ENCOMED	0.087	-1.651
50	State Council	0.050	-1.795
51	Electronic Group	0.049	-1.799
52	Ministry for Agriculture	0.043	-1.822
53	Ministry of Basic Industry	0.028	-1.878
54	Ministry of Informatic and Communication	0.003	-1.977

Mean: 0.391   Mean in random network: 0.513
Std.dev: 0.324   Std.dev in random network: 0.258

Closeness centrality

Rank	Nodes	Value	Unscaled	Context*
1	Regulation agency (CECMED)	0.757	0.014	6.239
2	National Coordinating Center of Clinical	0.654	0.012	4.387
3	Center for Medical Research and Development	0.530	0.010	2.149
4	CEADEN	0.525	0.010	2.054
5	Ministry for Public Health	0.486	0.009	1.361
6	Pharmaceutical Chemistry Center (CQF)	0.486	0.009	1.361
7	Biomundi	0.465	0.009	0.977

8	LABIOFAM Group	0.457	0.009	0.832
9	Centre for Genetic Engineering and Biotech	0.449	0.008	0.693
10	Finlay Institute	0.449	0.008	0.693
11	Centre for Molecular Immunology (CIM)	0.445	0.008	0.625
12	National Centre for Scientific Research	0.445	0.008	0.625
13	Centre for Immunoessays (CIE)	0.445	0.008	0.625
14	National Centre for Animal and Plant Health	0.438	0.008	0.492
15	Institute for Digital Research (ICID)	0.438	0.008	0.492
16	Quimefa Group	0.434	0.008	0.428
17	Kourí Institue (IPK)	0.434	0.008	0.428
18	FARMACUBA	0.431	0.008	0.364
19	Ministry for Science and Technology (CIT	0.427	0.008	0.302
20	National Centre for Bioproduccion (BIOCE	0.417	0.008	0.120
21	National Centre of Production of Laboratory	0.414	0.008	0.061
22	Servicex Department 4	0.411	0.008	0.003
23	Centre for Neurosciences (CNC)	0.408	0.008	-0.054
24	Banco Exterior de Cuba	0.402	0.008	-0.165
25	Center of Isotopes (CENTIS)	0.371	0.007	-0.721
26	Llorad Lab	0.356	0.007	-0.990
27	Novatec Lab	0.356	0.007	-0.990
28	Placental Histotherapy Center	0.356	0.007	-0.990
29	Vacunas Finlay	0.351	0.007	-1.074
30	Heber Biotec	0.351	0.007	-1.074
31	CIMAB	0.349	0.007	-1.116
32	Tecnosuma	0.349	0.007	-1.116
33	Center of Medical Genetics	0.344	0.006	-1.198
34	COMBIOMED	0.344	0.006	-1.198
35	Aica Lab	0.319	0.006	-1.646
36	Laboratory of Synthetic Antigens (LAGS)	0.317	0.006	-1.680
37	Ministry for Agriculture	0.315	0.006	-1.714
38	ENCOMED	0.312	0.006	-1.781
39	Electronic Group	0.310	0.006	-1.814
40	Dalmer	0.310	0.006	-1.814
41	MedSol Lab	0.306	0.006	-1.878
42	"R.G" Lab	0.306	0.006	-1.878
43	"8 M" Lab	0.306	0.006	-1.878
44	"J.T" Lab	0.306	0.006	-1.878

45	"C.J.F" Biological Products	0.306	0.006	-1.878
46	"R.E" Lab	0.306	0.006	-1.878
47	"S.D" Lab	0.306	0.006	-1.878
48	Ministry of Basic Industry	0.305	0.006	-1.910
49	"A.P" Blood Products	0.305	0.006	-1.910
50	State Council	0.294	0.006	-2.093
51	Neuronic	0.291	0.005	-2.151
52	Ministry of Informatic and Communication	0.238	0.004	-3.115
53	Import Medicament Unit (UEBMI Central Fr	0.019	0.000	-7.055
54	Wholesale Havana (UEBMM)	0.019	0.000	-7.061

Mean: 0.375   Mean in random network: 0.411
Std.dev: 0.115   Std.dev in random network: 0.056

Betweenness centrality

Rank	Nodes	Value	Unscaled	Context*
1	FARMACUBA	0.194	535.885	7.797
2	National Coordinating Center of Clinical	0.184	508.079	7.318
3	Pharmaceutical Chemistry Center (CQF)	0.172	472.927	6.712
4	Banco Exterior de Cuba	0.110	302.480	3.774
5	Quimefa Group	0.108	298.860	3.711
6	Ministry for Science and Technology (CIT)	0.103	284.981	3.472
7	Institute for Digital Research (ICID)	0.095	261.403	3.065
8	Center for Medical Research and Development	0.083	228.869	2.505
9	Ministry for Public Health	0.083	227.820	2.487
10	Regulation Agency (CECMED)	0.071	195.241	1.925
11	Kourí Institute (IPK)	0.064	177.719	1.623
12	Centre for Genetic Engineering and Biotech	0.051	140.522	0.982
13	Finlay Institue	0.042	115.000	0.542
14	National Centre for Scientific Research	0.038	105.802	0.383
15	LABIOFAM Group	0.037	102.000	0.317
16	Electronic Group	0.037	102.000	0.317
17	Centre for Neurosciences (CNC)	0.036	98.341	0.254

18	Centre for Molecular Immunology (CIM)	0.034	93.449	0.170
19	Centre for Immunoessays (CIE)	0.031	86.652	0.053
20	National Centre for Animal and Plant Health	0.027	74.659	-0.154
21	Servicex Department 4	0.026	71.282	-0.212
22	Heber Biotec	0.016	43.116	-0.698
23	National Centre for Bioproduccion (BIOCE	0.013	35.046	-0.837
24	ENCOMED	0.011	30.368	-0.917
25	Biomundi	0.007	18.193	-1.127
26	Center of Isotopes (CENTIS)	0.004	11.499	-1.243
27	National Centre of Production of Laboratory	0.004	10.610	-1.258
28	COMBIOMED	0.003	7.484	-1.312
29	Llorad Lab	0.002	6.098	-1.336
30	Novatec Lab	0.002	6.098	-1.336
31	Placental Histotherapy Center	0.002	6.098	-1.336
32	Aica Lab	0.002	4.354	-1.366
33	Vacunas Finlay	0.001	3.800	-1.375
34	Tecnosuma	0.001	3.540	-1.380
35	CIMAB	0.001	3.259	-1.385
36	CEADEN	0.000	1.000	-1.424
37	Ministry of Basic Industry	0.000	0.667	-1.429
38	Dalmer	0.000	0.405	-1.434
39	MedSol Lab	0.000	0.199	-1.438
40	"R.G" Lab	0.000	0.199	-1.438
41	"8 M" Lab	0.000	0.199	-1.438
42	"J.T" Lab	0.000	0.199	-1.438
43	"C.J.F" Biological Products	0.000	0.199	-1.438
44	"R.E" Lab	0.000	0.199	-1.438
45	"A.P" Blood Products	0.000	0.199	-1.438

Mean:	0.031	Mean in random network:	0.030
Std.dev:	0.049	Std.dev in random network:	0.021

Hub centrality

Rank	Nodes	Value
1	Regulation Agency (CECMED)	1.000
2	National Coordinating Center of Clinical	0.903
3	Centre for Immunoessays (CIE)	0.771
4	Center for Medical Research and Development	0.730
5	Finlay Institute	0.727

6	Centre for Genetic Engineering and Biotech	0.727
7	National Centre for Scientific Research	0.710
8	Centre for Molecular Immunology (CIM)	0.709
9	Pharmaceutical Chemistry Center (CQF)	0.682
10	LABIOFAM Group	0.673
11	National Centre for Bioproduccion (BIOCE)	0.649
12	Institute for Digital Research (ICID)	0.646
13	National Centre for Animal and Plant Health	0.642
14	National Centre of Production of Laboratory	0.634
15	Centre for Neurosicences (CNC)	0.609
16	Servicex Department 4	0.600
17	Biomundi	0.581
18	CEADEN	0.407
19	Kourí Institute (IPK)	0.384
20	Center of Medical Genetics	0.304
21	Laboratory of Synthetic Antigens (LAGS)	0.193
22	Banco Exterior de Cuba	0.160
23	Quimefa Group	0.160
24	Ministry for Science and Technology (CIT)	0.152
25	Ministry for Public Health	0.127
26	Llorad Lab	0.103
27	Novatec Lab	0.103
28	Placental Histotherapy Center	0.103
29	Heber Biotec	0.075
30	Vacunas Finlay	0.073
31	Tecnosuma	0.072
32	CIMAB	0.071
33	COMBIOMED	0.063
34	Center of Isotopes (CENTIS)	0.063
35	Dalmer	0.061
36	Electronic Group	0.055
37	Neuronic	0.053
38	Aica Lab	0.049
39	ENCOMED	0.027
40	MedSol Lab	0.016
41	"R.G" Lab	0.016
42	"8 M" Lab	0.016
43	"J.T" Lab	0.016
44	"C.J.F" Biological Products	0.016
45	"R.E" Lab	0.016
46	"S.D" Lab	0.016
47	"A.P" Blood Products	0.016
48	FARMACUBA	0.015
49	State Council	0.011
50	Import Medicament Unit (UEBMI)	0.010
51	Ministry for Agriculture	0.010
52	Ministry of Basic Industry	0.007
53	Ministry of Informatic and Communication	0.003

Authority centrality

Rank	Nodes	Value
1	Centre for Genetic Engineering and Biotech	1.000
2	Finlay Institute	0.964
3	Centre for Immunoessays (CIE)	0.951
4	National Centre for Bioproduccion (BIOCE	0.934
5	Centre for Molecular Immunology (CIM)	0.929
6	National Centre for Scientific Research	0.911
7	National Centre for Animal and Plant Health	0.855
8	National Centre of Production of Laboratory	0.843
9	Institute for Digital Research (ICID)	0.817
10	Pharmaceutical Chemistry Center (CQF)	0.816
11	Centre for Neurosciences (CNC)	0.791
12	Kourí Institute (IPK)	0.774
13	Ministry for Science and Technology (CIT	0.560
14	Laboratory of Synthetic Antigens (LAGS)	0.313
15	Ministry for Public Health	0.289
16	Center of Medical Genetics	0.285
17	FARMACUBA	0.241
18	"A.P" Blood Products	0.238
19	Center of Isotopes (CENTIS)	0.227
20	Llorad Lab	0.215
21	Aica Lab	0.215
22	Novatec Lab	0.215
23	Placental Histotherapy Center	0.215
24	MedSol Lab	0.180
25	"R.G" Lab	0.180
26	"8 M" Lab	0.180
27	"J.T" Lab	0.180
28	"C.J.F" Biological Products	0.180
29	"R.E" Lab	0.180
30	Heber Biotec	0.176
31	Servicex Department 4	0.162
32	Wholesale Havanna (UEBMM)	0.152
33	Tecnosuma	0.151
34	Import Medicament Unit (UEBMI central fr	0.151
35	LABIOFAM Group	0.150
36	"S.D" Lab	0.148
37	Vacunas Finlay	0.148
38	Dalmer	0.146
39	CIMAB	0.146
40	COMBIOMED	0.141
41	Banco Exterior de Cuba	0.131
42	Neuronic	0.126
43	Regulation agency (CECMED)	0.112
44	Biomundi	0.111
45	Quimefa Group	0.101
46	Center for Medical Research and Developm	0.093
47	ENCOMED	0.091
48	National Coordinating Center of Clinical	0.089
49	CEADEN	0.078

50	Ministry for Agriculture	0.053
51	Electronic Group	0.051
52	Ministry of Basic Industry	0.022
53	State Council	0.013
54	Ministry of Informatic and Communication	0.004

Information centrality

Rank	Nodes	Value	Unscaled
1	Regulation agency (CECMED)	0.030	2.044
2	National Coordinating Center of Clinical	0.030	2.007
3	Center for Medical Research and Development	0.029	1.951
4	CEADEN	0.028	1.906
5	Servicex Department 4	0.028	1.880
6	Pharmaceutical Chemistry Center (CQF)	0.027	1.862
7	LABIOFAM Group	0.027	1.841
8	Finlay Institue	0.027	1.822
9	Centre for Genetic Engineering and Biotech	0.027	1.804
10	Centre for Molecular Immunology (CIM)	0.026	1.803
11	National Centre for Scientific Research	0.026	1.802
12	Centre for Immunoessays (CIE)	0.026	1.801
13	Biomundi	0.026	1.795
14	Quimefa Group	0.026	1.789
15	Institute for Digital Research (ICID)	0.026	1.785
16	National Centre for Animal and Plant Health	0.026	1.777
17	National Centre for Bioproduccion (BIOCE	0.026	1.763
18	Banco Exterior de Cuba	0.026	1.752
19	National Centre of Production of Laboratory	0.026	1.746
20	Centre for Neurosciences (CNC)	0.025	1.718
21	Ministry for Science and Technology (CIT	0.024	1.629
22	Kourí Institute (IPK)	0.023	1.590
23	Ministry for Public Health	0.023	1.580
24	Center of Medical Genetics	0.021	1.454
25	ENCOMED	0.018	1.243
26	Llorad Lab	0.018	1.236
27	Novatec Lab	0.018	1.236
28	Placental Histotherapy Center	0.018	1.236
29	Laboratory of Synthetic Antigens (LAGS)	0.018	1.209
30	FARMACUBA	0.017	1.135

31	Heber Biotec	0.015	1.035
32	Aica Lab	0.015	1.028
33	Center of Isotopes (CENTIS)	0.015	1.020
34	Vacunas Finlay	0.015	1.012
35	COMBIOMED	0.015	1.010
36	Tecnosuma	0.015	1.010
37	CIMAB	0.015	1.010
38	State Council	0.010	0.704
39	MedSol Lab	0.010	0.699
40	"R.G" Lab	0.010	0.699
41	"8 M" Lab	0.010	0.699
42	"R.E" Lab	0.010	0.699
43	"J.T" Lab	0.010	0.699
44	"C.J.F" Biological Products	0.010	0.699
45	"S.D" Lab	0.010	0.699
46	"A.P" Blood Products	0.010	0.689
47	Import Medicament Unit (UEBMI Central Fr	0.010	0.685
48	Electronic Group	0.010	0.679
49	Dalmer	0.010	0.678
50	Ministry for Agriculture	0.010	0.657
51	Ministry of Basic Industry	0.010	0.656
52	Neuronic	0.010	0.651
53	Ministry of Informatic and Communication	0.006	0.412

Clique membership count

Rank	Nodes	Value
1	Regulation Agency (CECMED)	35.000
2	National Coordinating Center of Clinical	24.000
3	FARMACUBA	23.000
4	Centre for Genetic Engineering and Biotech	19.000
5	Finlay Institute	19.000
6	National Centre for Scientific Research	17.000
7	Centre for Immunoessays (CIE)	15.000
8	Pharmaceutical Chemistry Center (CQF)	14.000
9	Centre for Molecular Immunology (CIM)	13.000
10	Center for Medical Research and Development	12.000
11	National Centre for Bioproduccion (BIOCE	11.000
12	Kourí Institute (IPK)	10.000
13	Institute for Digital Research (ICID)	9.000
14	CEADEN	8.000
15	Quimefa Group	8.000
16	Servicex Department 4	8.000
17	National Centre for Animal and Plant Health	7.000
18	Biomundi	6.000
19	National Centre of Production of Laboratory	6.000

20	Centre for Neurosicences (CNC)	5.000
21	MedSol Lab	4.000
22	"R.G" Lab	4.000
23	"8 M" Lab	4.000
24	"J.T" Lab	4.000
25	"C.J.F" Biological Products	4.000
26	"R.E" Lab	4.000
27	Ministry for Science and Technology (CIT	3.000
28	"S.D" Lab	3.000
29	"A.P" Blood Products	3.000
30	Ministry for Public Health	3.000
31	LABIOFAM Group	3.000
32	Llorad Lab	2.000
33	Aica Lab	2.000
34	Novatec Lab	2.000
35	Placental Histotherapy Center	2.000
36	Import Medicament Unit (UEBMI central fr	2.000
37	Wholesale Havana (UEBMM)	2.000
38	Banco Exterior de Cuba	2.000
39	Center of Isotopes (CENTIS)	1.000
40	ENCOMED	1.000
41	Laboratory of Synthetic Antigens (LAGS)	1.000
42	Center of Medical Genetics	1.000
43	State Council	1.000
44	CIMAB	1.000
45	Tecnosuma	1.000
46	Neuronic	1.000
47	Vacunas Finlay	1.000
48	Heber Biotec	1.000
49	COMBIOMED	1.000
50	Dalmer	1.000

Simmelian ties

Rank	Nodes	Value	Unscaled
1	Centre for Genetic Engineering and Biotech	0.245	13.000
2	Centre for Molecular Immunology (CIM)	0.226	12.000
3	Finlay Institute	0.226	12.000
4	Centre for Immunoessays (CIE)	0.226	12.000
5	National Centre for Scientific Research	0.208	11.000
6	National Centre for Bioproduccion (BIOCE	0.208	11.000
7	Centre for Neurosicences (CNC)	0.189	10.000
8	National Centre for Animal and Plant Health	0.189	10.000
9	National Centre of Production of Laboratory	0.189	10.000

10	Institute for Digital Research (ICID)	0.189	10.000
11	Pharmaceutical Chemistry Center (CQF)	0.189	10.000
12	Kourí Institute (IPK)	0.113	6.000
13	Center of Medical Genetics	0.075	4.000
14	Laboratory of Synthetic Antigens (LAGS)	0.057	3.000
15	Ministry for Public Health	0.038	2.000
16	Regulation Agency (CECMED)	0.038	2.000
17	National Coordinating Center of Clinical	0.038	2.000

Clustering coefficient

Rank	Nodes	Value
1	State Council	1.000
2	Center of Medical Genetics	0.967
3	Laboratory of Synthetic Antigens (LAGS)	0.700
4	Biomundi	0.659
5	LABIOFAM Group	0.624
6	National Centre of Production of Laboratory	0.621
7	Centre for Neurosciences (CNC)	0.619
8	National Centre for Animal and Plant Health	0.555
9	Centre for Immunoessays (CIE)	0.545
10	Import Medicament Unit (UEBMI Central Fr	0.500
11	Wholesale Havana (UEBMM)	0.500
12	Neuronic	0.500
13	National Centre for Bioproduccion (BIOCE	0.497
14	National Centre for Scientific Research	0.489
15	Kourí Institue (IPK)	0.486
16	Centre for Molecular Immunology (CIM)	0.471
17	Institute for Digital Research (ICID)	0.471
18	"A.P" Blood Products	0.450
19	Finlay Institue	0.426
20	Centre for Genetic Engineering and Biotech	0.422
21	Ministry for Science and Technology (CIT	0.358
22	Servicex Department 4	0.338
23	Ministry for Public Health	0.333
24	Pharmaceutical Chemistry Center (CQF)	0.321
25	National Coordinating Center of Clinical	0.288
26	Center for Medical Research and Development	0.255
27	MedSol Lab	0.250
28	"R.G" Lab	0.250
29	"8 M" Lab	0.250
30	"J.T" Lab	0.250
31	"C.J.F" Biological Products	0.250
32	"R.E" Lab	0.250
33	"S.D" Lab	0.250
34	ENCOMED	0.250
35	Center of Isotopes (CENTIS)	0.200

36	FARMACUBA	0.173
37	CIMAB	0.167
38	Tecnosuma	0.167
39	Vacunas Finlay	0.167
40	COMBIOMED	0.167
41	Dalmer	0.167
42	Regulation Agency (CECMED)	0.151
43	CEADEN	0.096
44	Quimefa Group	0.068
45	Llorad Lab	0.067
46	Aica Lab	0.067
47	Novatec Lab	0.067
48	Placental Histotherapy Center	0.067
49	Heber Biotec	0.024
50	Banco Exterior de Cuba	0.018

Key nodes table

This shows the top scoring nodes side-by-side for selected measures.

Rank	Betweenness centrality	Closeness centrality	Eigenvector centrality	In-degree centrality	Out-degree centrality	Total degree centrality
1	FARMACUBA	Regulation agency (CECMED)	Regulation agency (CECMED)	Centre for Genetic Engineering and Biotechnology (CIGB)	Regulation agency (CECMED)	Regulation agency (CECMED)
2	National Coordinating center of clinical trials (CENCEC)	National Coordinating center of clinical trials (CENCEC)	National Coordinating center of clinical trials (CENCEC)	Finlay Institue	National Coordinating center of clinical trials (CENCEC)	Center for Genetic Engineering and Biotechnology (CIGB)
3	Pharmaceutical Chemistry Center (CQF)	Center for Medical Research and Development (CIDEM)	Centre for Genetic Engineering and Biotechnology (CIGB)	Pharmaceutical Chemistry Center (CQF)	Center for Medical Research and Development (CIDEM)	Pharmaceutical Chemistry Center (CQF)
4	Banco Exterior de Cuba	CEADEN	Finlay Institue	Centre for Molecular Immunology (CIM)	Pharmaceutical Chemistry Center (CQF)	Finlay Institue

5	Quimefa Group	Ministry for Public Health	Centre for Immunoessays (CIE)	National Centre for Scientific Research (CNIC)	CEADEN	Centre for Molecular Immunology (CIM)
6	Ministry for Science and Technology (CITMA)	Pharmaceutical Chemistry Center (CQF)	National Centre for Scientific Research (CNIC)	Centre for Immunoessays (CIE)	Centre for Genetic Engineering and Biotechnology (CIGB)	National Centre for Scientific Research (CNIC)
7	Institute for Digital Research (ICID)	Biomundi	Centre for Molecular Immunology (CIM)	National Centre for Bioproduccion (BIOCEN)	Finlay Instiue	Centre for Immunoessays (CIE)
8	Center for Medical Research and Development (CIDEM)	LABIOFAM Group	National Centre for Bioproduccion (BIOCEN)	Institute for Digital Research (ICID)	Servicex Department 4	National Coordinating center of clinical trials (CENCEC)
9	Ministry for Public Health	Centre for Genetic Engineering and Biotechnology (CIGB)	National Centre for Animal and plant Health (CENSA)	National Centre for Animal and plant Health (CENSA)	Centre for Molecular Immunology (CIM)	National Centre for Bioproduccion (BIOCEN)
10	Regulation agency (CECMED)	Finlay Instiue	Pharmaceutical Chemistry Center (CQF)	Centre for Neurosicences (CNC)	National Centre for Scientific Research (CNIC)	Institute for Digital Research (ICID)
11	Kourí Institue (IPK)	Centre for Molecular Immunology (CIM)	National Centre of production of laboratory animals (CENPALAB)	National Centre of production of laboratory animals (CENPALAB)	Centre for Immunoessays (CIE)	National Centre for Animal and plant Health (CENSA)
12	Centre for Genetic Engineering and Biotechnology (CIGB)	National Centre for Scientific Research (CNIC)	Institute for Digital Research (ICID)	Kourí Institue (IPK)	LABIOFAM Group	Centre for Neurosicences (CNC)
13	Finlay Instiue	Centre for Immunoessays (CIE)	Centre for Neurosicences (CNC)	Ministry for Science and Technology (CITMA)	Institute for Digital Research (ICID)	National Centre of production of laboratory animals (CENPALAB)
14	National Centre for Scientific Research (CNIC)	National Centre for Animal and plant Health (CENSA)	Center for Medical Research and Development (CIDEM)	FARMACUBA	National Centre for Bioproduccion (BIOCEN)	Center for Medical Research and Development (CIDEM)

15	LABIOFAM Group	Institute for Digital Research (ICID)	LABIOFAM Group	Banco Exterior de Cuba	National Centre for Animal and plant Health (CENSA)	Ministry for Science and Technology (CITMA)
16	Electronic Group	Quimefa Group	Kouri Institue (IPK)	Heber Biotec	Biomundi	Kouri Institue (IPK)
17	Centre for Neurosicences (CNC)	Kouri Institue (IPK)	Servicex Department 4	Llorad Lab	Quimefa Group	Banco Exterior de Cuba
18	Centre for Molecular Immunology (CIM)	FARMACUBA	Ministry for Science and Technology (CITMA)	Aica Lab	Banco Exterior de Cuba	Servicex Department 4
19	Centre for Immunoessays (CIE)	Ministry for Science and Technology (CITMA)	Biomundi	Novatec Lab	Centre for Neurosicences (CNC)	CEADEN
20	National Centre for Animal and plant Health (CENSA)	National Centre for Bioproduccion (BIOCEN)	CEADEN	Placental Histotherapy Center	National Centre of production of laboratory animals (CENPALAB)	LABIOFAM Group
21	Servicex Department 4	National Centre of production of laboratory animals (CENPALAB)	Center of Medical Genetics	Center of Isotopes (CENTIS)	Ministry for Science and Technology (CITMA)	Quimefa Group
22	Heber Biotec	Servicex Department 4	Ministry for Public Health	Ministry for Public Health	Kouri Institue (IPK)	FARMACUBA
23	National Centre for Bioproduccion (BIOCEN)	Centre for Neurosicences (CNC)	Laboratory of Synthetic Antigens (LAGS)	Laboratory of Synthetic Antigens (LAGS)	Ministry for Public Health	Biomundi
24	ENCOMED	Banco Exterior de Cuba	FARMACUBA	Center of Medical Genetics	Center of Medical Genetics	Ministry for Public Health
25	Biomundi	Center of Isotopes (CENTIS)	Llorad Lab	Wholesale Havanna (UEBMM)	Llorad Lab	Center of Medical Genetics
26	Center of Isotopes (CENTIS)	Llorad Lab	Aica Lab	Quimefa Group	Novatec Lab	Heber Biotec
27	National Centre of production of laboratory animals (CENPALAB)	Novatec Lab	Novatec Lab	MedSol Lab	Placental Histotherapy Center	Llorad Lab

28	COMBIOMED	Placental Histotherapy Center	Placental Histotherapy Center	"R.G" Lab	ENCOMED	Novatec Lab
29	Llorad Lab	Vacunas Finlay	Center of Isotopes (CENTIS)	"8 M" Lab	Laboratory of Synthetic Antigens (LAGS)	Placental Histotherapy Center
30	Novatec Lab	Heber Biotec	"A.P" Blood Products	"J.T" Lab	Aica Lab	Laboratory of Synthetic Antigens (LAGS)
31	Placental Histotherapy Center	CIMAB	Heber Biotec	"C.J.F" Biological Products	Center of Isotopes (CENTIS)	Aica Lab
32	Aica Lab	Tecnosuma	Banco Exterior de Cuba	"R.E" Lab	Electronic Group	Center of Isotopes (CENTIS)
33	Vacunas Finlay	Center of Medical Genetics	Quimefa Group	"A.P" Blood Products	CIMAB	MedSol Lab
34	Tecnosuma	COMBIOMED	MedSol Lab	Servicex Department 4	Tecnosuma	"R.G" Lab
35	CIMAB	Aica Lab	"R.G" Lab	Center for Medical Research and Development (CIDEM)	Vacunas Finlay	"8 M" Lab
36	CEADEN	Laboratory of Synthetic Antigens (LAGS)	"8 M" Lab	Import Medicament Unit (UEBMI central freezing)	Heber Biotec	"J.T" Lab
37	Ministry of Basic Industry	Ministry for Agriculture	"J.T" Lab	"S.D" Lab	COMBIOMED	"C.J.F" Biological Products
38	Dalmer	ENCOMED	"C.J.F" Biological Products	Regulation agency (CECMED)	FARMACUBA	"R.E" Lab
39	MedSol Lab	Electronic Group	"R.E" Lab	National Coordinating center of clinical trials (CENCEC)	Import Medicament Unit (UEBMI central freezing)	ENCOMED
40	"R.G" Lab	Dalmer	Import Medicament Unit (UEBMI central freezing)	LABIOFAM Group	Ministry of Basic Industry	"A.P" Blood Products
41	"8 M" Lab	MedSol Lab	Wholesale Havanna (UEBMM)	CIMAB	MedSol Lab	CIMAB

42	"J.T" Lab	"R.G" Lab	"S.D" Lab	Tecnosuma	"R.G" Lab	Tecnosuma
43	"C.J.F" Biological Products	"8 M" Lab	Vacunas Finlay	Vacunas Finlay	"8 M" Lab	Vacunas Finlay
44	"R.E" Lab	"J.T" Lab	Tecnosuma	COMBIOMED	"J.T" Lab	COMBIOMED
45	"A.P" Blood Products	"C.J.F" Biological Products	Dalmer	Dalmer	"C.J.F" Biological Products	Import Medicament Unit (UEBMI central freezing)
46	Import Medicament Unit (UEBMI central freezing)	"R.E" Lab	CIMAB	Biomundi	"R.E" Lab	Wholesale Havanna (UEBMM)
47	Wholesale Havanna (UEBMM)	"S.D" Lab	COMBIOMED	Ministry of Basic Industry	"S.D" Lab	"S.D" Lab
48	"S.D" Lab	Ministry of Basic Industry	Neuronic	ENCOMED	"A.P" Blood Products	Electronic Group
49	Laboratory of Synthetic Antigens (LAGS)	"A.P" Blood Products	ENCOMED	Electronic Group	Ministry for Agriculture	Dalmer
50	Center of Medical Genetics	State Council	State Council	Neuronic	Ministry of Informatic and Communications (MIC)	Ministry of Basic Industry
51	Ministry for Agriculture	Neuronic	Electronic Group	CEADEN	State Council	Neuronic
52	Ministry of Informatic and Communications (MIC)	Ministry of Informatic and Communications (MIC)	Ministry for Agriculture	Ministry for Agriculture	Neuronic	Ministry for Agriculture
53	State Council	Import Medicament Unit (UEBMI central freezing)	Ministry of Basic Industry	Ministry of Informatic and Communications (MIC)	Dalmer	Ministry of Informatic and Communications (MIC)
54	Neuronic	Wholesale Havanna (UEBMM)	Ministry of Informatic and Communications (MIC)	State Council	Wholesale Havanna (UEBMM)	State Council

Source: Produced by ORA developed at CASOS – Carnegie Mellon University

Notes

1 Commenting on the high litigation cost in Europe, a very well documented study on the European patent system (the most expensive in the world according this report) states that, only putting in place a "single patent court in Europe would produce savings of €148 to €289 million for business." See B Pottelsberghe (2009), Lost property: the European patent system and why it doesn't work, Bruegel Blueprint Series, Brussels, p. 14.

2 It is also stated that 30 top pharmaceutical firms concentrate on producing low-risk me-too drugs, which cost twice as much in promotion and advertising they do in R&D. In actual fact, it is said that 50 percent of the R&D costs are spent on

advertising drugs, which does not result from innovation (see M Boldrin and D Levine (2008), *Against Intellectual Monopoly*, Cambridge University Press, chapter 9).

3 Between 1989 and 2000, 54 percent of FDA-approved drug applications contained ingredients already on the market. From a medical point of view, about 77 percent of what FDA approves is redundant. Between 1995 and 2000 R&D employees at firms making patented drugs declined slightly, while the number of employees in marketing rose by 59 percent (ibid., p. 231).

4 See CIGB's Negotiation Policy at http://gndp.cigb.edu.cu/index.html#

5 The surveyed firms worked in the health biotech sector in six developing countries – Brazil, China, Cuba, Egypt, India and South Africa. These countries were selected on the basis of their position as southern leaders in the field, as identified through previous research on health biotech in developing countries. The survey followed a broad definition of "collaboration," considering it to be any work jointly undertaken by firms and organizations in developed and developing countries that contributes to the production of knowledge, products or services in health biotech. See C Melon et al. (2009), A survey of South–North health biotech collaboration, *Nature Biotechnology* 27: 229–32.

6 http://gndp.cigb.edu.cu/index.html#

7 www.moneycontrol.com/company-facts/panaceabiotec/history/PB02

8 Bussines monitor international, EMS signs JV with Cuba's Herber Biotec, Jan. 7, 2010, http://store.businessmonitor.com/article/318588/; see also www.investe. sp.gov.br/noticias/lenoticia.php?id=10441&c=6&lang=3

9 Business Monitor International, EMS signs JV with Cuba's Herber Biotec, Jan. 7, 2010, http://store.businessmonitor.com/article/318588/

10 http://biovac.co.za/partnerships.html

11 www.lithahealthcare.co.za/

12 This information is extracted from several press reports. No information is available in the public profiles of BIOVEN or HeberBiotec. Therefore some further confirmation may be needed. The press reports can be found in: www.allbusiness. com/caribbean/300959-1.html, http://goliath.ecnext.com/coms2/gi_0199-2128 182/BIOTECH-JOINT-VENTURE.html, www.accessmylibrary.com/coms2/ summary_0286-26137646_ITM,

13 www.cim.co.cu/productos_ing.asp

14 J Buckley et al. (2006), Off the beaten path, *Nature Biotechnology* 24: 309–15; see also Technology; U.S. Permits 3 Cancer Drugs from Cuba, New York Times, July 2004, www.nytimes.com/2004/07/15/business/technology-us-permits-3-cancer-drugs-from-cuba.html

15 Business Monitor International, EMS signs JV with Cuba's Herber Biotec, Jan. 7, 2010, http://store.businessmonitor.com/article/318588/; see also Clinical Trial.gov, http://clinicaltrials.gov/ct2/show/NCT00600054, and the article: Cuban cancer drug undergoes rare U.S. trial, Miami Herald, August 2009, www.miamiherald. com/living/health/story/1207536.html

16 The countries are Brazil, China, Cuba, Egypt, India, South Africam, South Korea. See the study U Quach et al. (2006), Biotechnology patenting takes off in developing countries, *Int. J. Biotechnology* 8(1/2): 43–59.

17 The 1995 World Trade Organization's (Geneva) Agreement on Trade-Related Aspects of Intellectual Property Rights (TRIPS), poses almost insurmountable entry barriers for the biopharmaceutical industry in developing countries. Paying the prohibitive fees required by multinationals is close to impossible. Cuba, as a

signatory of this agreement, had to find some IP strategy to overcome this disadvantage and take some advantage of the existing loopholes in the legislation.

18 We refer here mostly to inferential statistics.

19 Networks are formally studied in a branch of mathematics called Graph Theory. The formal abstraction called *network* in the social sciences is often named *graph* in Graph Theory, while the term "network" in Graph Theory is reserved for a specific type of graph.

For more detailed information see S Wasserman and K Faust (1994), *Social Network Analysis*, Cambridge, MA: Cambridge University Press; see also L Freeman (1979), Centrality in social networks: Conceptual clarification, *Social Networks* 1: 215–39.

20 The use of the network analysis here makes sense, because the evidence and the theoretical framework employed here fit with the tool. In this study networking is a synonym of national (sectoral) system of innovation. The network tool helps to represent (not to explain) this state of affairs. Within this research, it is seen more in a methodological/descriptive sense, i.e. attempting to support (not to confirm) the logic of the research than as a conceptual point of departure in itself. For more information about this issue, the reader can see F Schweitzer et al. (2009), Economic networks: The new challenges, *Science* 325 (July 24): 422–5; see also S Borgatti (2009), Network analysis in social sciences, *Science* 13 (Feb.): 892–5.

21 Public web sources of the organizations involved in the research can be consulted anytime for further information. However, it is important to remain aware of the time-lags and updating and may be not reflective of the date being dealt with; to prove the relational data it would be much more important to retain the name of the organization and doing the necessary research in order to make sure that the right period is considered. Another issue is that the original (raw) relational data of the research have been registered in XML format, which might be uncomfortable for many readers. That is the reason why they have not been included here; yet they are available after request. In any case, as mentioned in the introductory part of the book, notice that this quantification attempt is merely a very preliminary, experimental exploration that will need a lot of refinement, change, correction and development. It should not in any case be seen as a mandatory step in order to prove or to qualify the qualitative arguments advanced in this research. These qualitative arguments are intended to be the main part of this book and stand by themselves, independently of the vagaries that this quantification approach might hold. Any replication attempt should take the abovementioned caveats into consideration. For further questions and enquiries please feel free to contact the author.

22 www.casos.cs.cmu.edu/projects/ora/software.php

23 The case of using co-patents as proxy for collaboration provides a very instructive example of the above-mentioned. In the Cuban biotechnology it would be inaccurate to assume an industrial sector independent of the research sector. In actual fact, public research institutes are the industrial actors at the same time, and therefore domestic linkages cannot be measured by co-patenting between research institutions and industry in Cuba. Consequently, identifying the patents shared between industry and research agents would not reflect the extent of R&D collaborations within the industry. The examples can go on, but the point is that it could be misleading to identify each organization with only one type of resource or function.

24 In a binary network links are either present or absent. By adding the weight of a tie is generally a function of duration and the intensity of the exchange. We assume that

building this intensity in the Cuban case is relatively easy given the management structure of the industry. For more on weighted networks, see T Opsahl et al., Node centrality in weighted networks: Generalizing degree and shortest paths, *preprint submitted to Social Networks*, April 2010.

25 One of the important *specificities* of the Cuban biotech is the absence of ownership fragmentation of complementary assets (see Annex 4). This fragmentation, basically expressed in the mutual blocking of property rights through exclusive licensing of patents, is one of the most pervasive, perverse and expensive mechanisms of the prevailing model in the industry worldwide. Had the Cuban industry companies worked under this prevailing model, they would have not been able to provide affordable medicaments, or perhaps to develop an industry at all.

26 Social network analysis provides a number of graph-theoretic properties that characterize (a) network structures (at the network level of analysis), (b) network positions (at the node level of analysis), and (c) dyadic properties (at the dyad level). We focus on (b).

27 In the contexts related to network theory, this essay uses the terms *knowledge* and *information* as interchangeable concepts. In economic term, however, it is necessary to establish a differentiation between the two. For example, from the point of view of innovation economics; there is a difference between simple information and knowledge.

28 Mathematically, a network can be represented by an adjacency *matrix* A (usually a square matrix) with n number of vertices. The adjacency matrix may be symmetric or asymmetric depending on the type of links between vertices i and j. In general mathematical terms, total degree centrality CD of a node i is CD = degree of i

$$= \sum_{j=1}^{n} Ai\,j$$

The undirected network will be represented by a symmetric matrix since if there is an edge between i and j then clearly there is also an edge between j and i. Thus $Ai\,j = Aji$.. If Aij = 1 then there is an edge between vertices i and j, if 0 otherwise. On the other hand, directed networks can be represented by an asymmetric adjacency matrix in which $Ai\,j = 1$ implies the existence (conventionally) of an edge pointing from j to i (-1, 0, and +1 depending on the direction), which does not imply the existence of an edge from i to j. By convention, in a directed (i.e. asymmetric) matrix, the sender of a tie is the row and the target of the tie is the column. Given that the network under study does not consider link weights, only 1 and 0 will be employed in the measurement.

Then the absolute value of centrality needs to be normalized, so its value can be independent of the network size. Then we have that **CD′= degree of i/n-1**, where CD′ is the relative centrality being calculated here.

29 In graph theory can be found different concepts describing the way in which flow processes take place. These concepts are *walks, trails, path* and *cycles*. The walks are the most general type of sequence of vertexes and edges and describe the situation where the same vertex or edge can be traversed many times. The trail is a type of walk where each edge can be traversed only once; but a vertex several times. The path (or open walk) allows vertexes and edges to be traversed only once. The cycle (or closed walk) starts and end in the same vertex but has no repeated vertices or edges.

30 As explained in Chapter 7, we call the strategic network of the Cuban biotech a small group of *in-house modular* companies (vertical integrated working under horizontal regime), which represent the core of the industry given their critical contribution to the innovation rate of the industry.

31 $n-1 \Big/ \sum_{i=1}^{n} d(ai,aj) i \neq j$. Where d (ai, aj) represent the sum of the shortest path from the node ai to the rest of the nodes of the network and n the total number of nodes of the network.

32 Eigenvector centrality scores correspond to the values of the first eigenvector of the graph adjacency matrix. In mathematical terms the eigenvector is a vector that remains parallel to the original vector after being multiplied by a matrix. In the equation $\lambda C = AC$ A represents the adjacency matrix, λ the eigenvalue of the eigenvector and C an eigenvector of the adjacency matrix.

This could be interpreted as $CDi = 1 / \lambda \sum_{j=1}^{n} Ai\,j\,CDj,$

where CDi is the degree centrality of the node i expressed as proportional to the average of the centralities of *i*'s network neighbors. The eigenvalue is the factor by which the vector is scaled when multiplied by the matrix. In the first equation C is the vector of the network centralities (CD1, CD2, CD3…) For a mathematical definition see Newman (2008). A foundational definition can be found in Bonacich, Factoring and weighting approaches to status scores and clique identification, *Journal of Mathematical Sociology* 2: 113–20, 1972. According to Borgatti (2005) this measure is consistent with a mechanism in which each node affects all of its neighbors simultaneously, as in a parallel duplication process. Hence, the eigenvector centrality measure is ideally suited for *influence type* processes.

33 The probability that a node ak falls on a randomly selected geodesic connecting the nodes ai and aj is
$bij(ak) = gij(ak)/gij$ (partial betweenness), where gij is the number of geodesics linking ai and aj (1/gij is the probability of choosing one of them) gij(ak) is the number of geodesics linking ai and aj that contain ak. The overall betweenness centrality of a node ak, will be the sum of its partial betweenness values for all unordered

pairs of points where $i \neq j \neq k$: $CB(ak) = bj \sum_{i<j}^{n} \sum^{n} j(ak),$

normalized betweeness is defined as $CB'(ak) = 2CB(ak)/n^2\text{-}3n+2.$

34 In a case like this, it would be completely inappropriate to use Freeman's centrality measure as an index of the importance of a given node for the spread of information because traffic does not seem to be copied or broadcasted from a node

35 Out-degree centrality of node (row) ai is
$Co(ai) = 1/n - 1 \sum_{j=1}^{n} Aij,$ where n is the number of nodes (or columns of the matrix A)

36 In-degree centrality of node (column) ai is
$CI(ai) = 1/n - 1 \sum_{j=1}^{n} Aij$ where n is the number of nodes(or rows of the matrix A)

37 To accomplish that, an iterative algorithm was developed, in order to identify hubs and authorities for each web page. However the techniques employed here could apply to the analysis of many other hyperlinked environments.

38 Similarly to other measures, clique membership count has been carried out by using the software ORA, which offers a measure based on a clique detection algorithm that only considers undirected networks. See C Bron and J Kerbosch, Algorithm 457: Finding all cliques of an undirected graph, *Communications of the ACM* 16(9), ACM Press: New York, 1973. See also Finding all cliques of an undirected graph, Seminar notes by Michaela Regneri, January 11, 2007.

39 Note that, in this work, we are assuming that the case under study fits somewhat with the definition. However, a more rigorous formal demonstration must be advanced. This would include, finding out if the case follows the power law (scale free network), which would prove preferential attachment.

General references

Abate J (1999), *Inventing the Internet*. MIT Press.

Abramovitz M (1986), Catching up, forging ahead and falling behind, *Journal of Economic History* 66: 385–406.

Abramovitz M (1989), *Thinking about Growth and Other Essays on Economic Growth and Welfare*. Cambridge: Cambridge University Press.

Abramovitz M and David PA (1994), Convergence and deferred catch-up productivity leadership and the waning of American exceptionalism. Prepared for publication as Chapter 1. In: Landau R et al. (eds.), *Growth and Development: The Economics of the 21st Century*. Stanford CA: Stanford University Press.

Abreu G et al. (2011), Cuba's strategy for childhood tuberculosis control, 1995–2005, *MEDICC Review* 13(3): 29–34.

Acha V et al. (2007), Exploring the miracle: Strategy and the management of knowledge bases in the aeronautics industry, *International Journal of Innovation and Technology Management* 1(4): 1–25.

Ackoff R (1971), Toward a system of systems concepts, *Management Science* 17(11): 661–71.

Ackoff R and Emery F [1972](2006), *On Purposeful Systems*. Aldine-Transaction, Fourth Paperback printing.

Andreoni A and Chang HJ (2019), The political economy of industrial policy: Structural interdependencies, policy alignment and conflict management, *Structural Change and Economic Dynamics*. Volume 48, March, pp. 136–50.

Aghion P and Howitt P (1992), A model of growth through creative destruction, *Econometrica* 60: 323–51.

Allen R (1983), Collective invention, *Journal of Economic Behavior and Organization* 4: 1–24.

Altieri M and Funes-Monzote F (2012), The paradox of Cuban agriculture, *Monthly Review* 63(8) (January).

Álvares EC (1998), Cuba, un Modelo De desarrollo con justicia social, Instituto Nacional de Investigaciones Económicas, La Habana: paper presented at XI Congress of the Latin American Studies Association, The Palmer House Hilton Hotel, Chicago, Illinois, September 24–26.

Amaral L and Ottino J (2004), Complex networks: Augmenting the framework for the study of complex systems, *Eur. Phys. J.* B **38**: 147–62.

Amatori F, Millward R and Toninelli A (2005), Reappraising State-Owned Enterprise: A Comparison of the UK and Italy. New York: Routledge.

Amirahmadi H and W Wu (1995), Export processing zones in Asia, *Asian Survey* 35(9): 828–49.

Amsden AH (1989). *Asia's Next Giant: South Korea and Late Industrialization*. New York: Oxford University Press

Anderson G (2001), To Change China: A Tale of Three Reformers, *Asia Pacific: Perspectives* 1(1): 1–19, May.

Andreoni A and Chang HJ (2019), The political economy of industrial policy: Structural interdependencies, policy alignment and conflict management, *Structural Change and Economic Dynamics* 48 (March): 136–50.

Andrew R et al. (2011), Dimensions of publicness and organizational performance: A review of the evidence, *Journal of Public Administration Research and Theory* 21(3i): 301–19.

Aoki M (1990), Toward an economic model of the Japanese firm, *Journal of Economic Literature* 28 (March): 1–27.

Aoki M (1999), Information and Governance in the Silicon Valley Model. *Discussion Paper* #99DOF31, Stanford University, July.

Archibald GC, Simon H and Samuelson P (1963), Problem of methodology: Discussion, *The American Economic Review*, Papers and Proceedings of the Seventy-Fifth Annual Meeting of the American Economic Association 53 (2): 227–36.

Arrow K (1962), The economic implications of learning by doing, *Review of Economic Studies* 29(3): 155–73.

Arthur B (1989), Competing technologies, increasing returns, and lock-in by historical events, *The Economic Journal* 99(394): 116–31 (March).

Arthur B (1999), Complexity and the economy, *Science* 284: 107–9.

Arthur B (2009), *The Nature of Technology: What It Is and How It Evolves*. New York: Free Press.

Arthur B (ed.) (2015), *Complexity and the Economy*. New York: Oxford University Press.

Babbage C (1832) (2010), *On the Economy of Machinery and Manufactures*. Cambridge: Cambridge University Press.

Bairoch P (1995), *Economics and World History: Myths and Paradoxes*. Chicago: University of Chicago Press.

Baldarraín-Chaple E (2005), Cambio y Revolución: El surgimiento del Sistema Nacional Único de Salud en Cuba, 1959–1970, *DYNAMIS. Acta Hispanica ad Medicinae Scientiarumque Historiam Illustrandam* 25: 257–78.

Barabási A and Albert R (1999), Emergence of scaling in random networks, *Science* 286, 15 Oct., 509–12

Barabási L et al. (1999), Emergence of scaling in random networks, *Science* **286**(5439): 509–12.

Barnes L (2005), *Needles, Herbs, Gods, and Ghosts: China, Healing, and the West to 1848*. Cambridge MA: Harvard University Press.

Barney J (1991), Firm Resources and Sustained Competitive Advantage, *Journal of Management* March 1991 vol. 17 no. 1 99–120

Barro R and Sala-i-Martin (2003), *Economic Growth*. Cambridge, MA and London: The MIT Press.

Bartels H et al. (2013), *Promoting Access to Medical Technologies and Innovation: Intersections between Public Health, Intellectual Property and Trade*. Geneva: WHO, WIPO and the WTO.

Bastiat F [1845] (1996), *Economic Sophisms, Foundation for Economic Education*, trans. A Goddard, Irvington-on-Hudson, available at The Online Library of Liberty, http://oll.libertyfund.org, last accessed in July 2018.

Bateman M and Chang H-J (2012), Microfinance and the illusion of development: From hubris to nemesis in thirty years, *World Economic Review* 1: 13–36.

Baumol W and Bowen W (1966), *Performing Arts, The Economic Dilemma: A Study of Problems Common to Theater, Opera, Music, and Dance.* Cambridge, MA: MIT Press.

Beaussart ML et al. (2013), Creative liars: The relationship between creativity and integrity, *Thinking Skills and Creativity* 9: 129–34, August.

Beinhocker E (2006), *The Origin of Wealth: Evolution, Complexity, and the Radical Remaking of Economics.* Boston, MA: Harvard Business School Press.

Bell M and Pavitt K (1993), Technological accumulation and industrial growth: Contrasts between developed and developing countries, *Industrial and Corporate Change* 2(1): 157–210.

Bermúdez-Lugo O (2004), Minerals Yearbook. 2004. In: *Minerals Yearbook, Vol. 3: Area Reports, International: Latin America and Canada.* Geological Survey (USGS), pp. 91–4.

Bernier F (1891), *Travels in the Mogul Empire: A.D 1656–1668.* London: Constable. Electronic reproduction, New York, N.Y., Columbia University Libraries, 2006, available at www.columbia.edu/cu/lweb/digital/collections/cul/texts/ldpd_6093710_000/index.html.

Bessen J and Maskin E (2000), Sequential Innovation, Patents, and Imitation, MIT *Working Paper* No. 00-01, Revised March 2006.

Bessen J and Nuvolari A (2016), Knowledge sharing among inventors: Some historical perspectives. In: D Harhoff and K Lakhani (eds.), *Revolutionizing Innovation: Users, Communities and Open Innovation.* Cambridge, MA: MIT Press, pp. 135–55.

Bessen J and Nuvolari A (2017), Diffusing new technology without dissipating rents: some historical case studies of knowledge sharing, LED *Working Paper Series*, 2017/28, November.

Bhaskar R (1978), *A Realist Theory of Science.* Hassocks: Harvester Press.

BioCubaFarma (2018), Main Projects Portfolio.

Biomedicine and health innovation: Synthesis report, OECD Innovation Strategy, November 2010.

Biotechnology and Intellectual Property: Reinventing the Commons Workshop Report, McGill Centre for Intellectual Property Policy Montreal, Canada, September 25–27, 2005.

Block F (2008), Swimming against the current: The rise of a hidden developmental state in the United States, *Politics & Society* 36(2): 169–206, June.

BMI Reseach Group (2016), Cuba's Pharmaceutical & Healthcare Report Q4 2016, Part of BMI's *Industry Report & Forecast Series*, BMI Research, London

Boldrin M and Levine D (2008), *Against Intellectual Monopoly.* Cambridge: Cambridge University Press.

Bolin S (ed.) (2002), *The Standard Edge.* Ann Arbor, MI: Sheridan Books.

Bonacich P (1972), Factoring and weighting approaches to status scores and clique identification, *Journal of Mathematical Sociology* 2: 113–20.

Bonacich P (1987), Power and centrality: A family of measures, *Amer. J. Sociol.* 92(5): 1170–82.

Bonacich P (2007), Some unique properties of eigenvector centrality, *Soc. Networks* 29(4): 555–64.

Borgatti S and Foster P (2003), The network paradigm in organizational research: A review and typology. *J. Management* 29(6): 991–1013.

Borgatti S (2005), Centrality and network flow, *Social Networks* 27: 55–71.

Borgatti S and Halgin D (2011), On network theory, *Organization Science*, Articles in Advance, 1–14.

Borgatti S et al. (2009), Network analysis in social sciences, *Science* 13, February, 892–95.

Borman S and Washington C (2004), Carbohydrate vaccines: Novel chemical and enzymatic oligosaccharide synthesis techniques could lead to a new generation of carbohydrate-based vaccine agents, *Chemical & Engineering News* 82(32) (Aug. 9): 31–5.

Bossche P (2005), *The Origins of the WTO, The Law and Policy of the World Trade Organization: Text, Cases and Materials.* New York: Cambridge University Press.

Braunerhjelm P and Feldman M (eds.) (2006), *Cluster Genesis: Technology Based Industrial Development.* New York: Oxford University Press.

Bravo E (1998), *Development within Underdevelopment. New Trends in Cuban Medicine.* La Habana: Editorial José Martí / Elfos Scientae.

Breschi S and Malerba F (1997), Sectoral systems of innovation: Technological regimes, Schumpeterian dynamics and spatial boundaries. In: C Edquist (ed.), *Systems of Innovation*. London: Frances Pinter.

Brisco N (1907), *The Economic Policy of Robert Walpole.* New York: Columbia University Press.

Bron C and Kerbosch J (1973), Algorithm 457: Finding all cliques of an undirected graph, *Communications of the ACM* 16(9): 575–9.

Brown R and Mawson S (2019), Entrepreneurial ecosystems and public policy in action: a critique of the latest industrial policy blockbuster, *Cambridge Journal of Regions, Economy and Society* 12: 347–68.

Brundenius, C. (2002), Tourism as an Engine of Growth: Reflections on Cuba's New Development Strategy, Working Paper 02.10. Copenhagen: Centre for Development Research.

Brusoni S and Prencipe A (2001), Unpacking the black box of modularity: Technologies, products, organisations, *Industrial and Corporate Change* 10(1): 179–205.

Brusoni S et al. (2001), Knowledge specialisation and the boundaries of the firm: Why firms know more than they make, *Administrative Science Quarterly* 46: 597–621.

Bryson J et al. (eds.) (2001), *Knowledge, Space, Economy.* London: Routledge.

Buchanan J (1979), *What Should Economists Do?*, Indianapolis, Liberty Press

Buchanan J (1986), *Liberty, Market and State.* Brighton, UK: Wheatsheaf Books Ltd.

Buchanan J and Tullock G (1962) (1990), *The Calculus of Consent.* Ann Arbor: University of Michigan Press.

Buchanan J et al. (1980), *Toward a Theory of the Rent-Seeking Society.* College Station, Texas: A&M University Press.

Burlamaqui L et al. (eds.) (2000), *Institution and the Role of State.* Massachusetts, USA, Cheltenham, UK: Edward Elgar.

Burns R (ed.) (2005), *The Business of Healthcare Innovation.* Cambridge: Cambridge University Press.

Burt R (2005), The social capital of structural holes. In: M Guillén et al. (eds.), *The New Economic Sociology*, New York: Russell Sage Foundation, pp. 148–93.

Bush V (1945), Science the Endless Frontier, A Report to the President by the Director of the Office of Scientific Research and Development, United States Government Printing Office, Washington, July, available at https://nsf.gov/od/lpa/nsf50/vbush1945.htm, last accessed in August 2018.

Cacioppo JT (2002), Social neuroscience: Understanding the pieces fosters understanding the whole and vice versa, *American Psychologist* 57(11): 831–4, December.

Caldwell B (1997), Hayek and socialism, *Journal of Economic Literature* XXXV: 1856–90, December

Campion E and Morrissey S (2013), A different model – medical care in Cuba, *New England Journal of Medicine* 368: 297–9.

Caplan P (2003), Patents and open standards, *Information Standards Quarterly* 4(4), October.

Cárdenas A (2009), The Cuban Biotechnology Industry: Innovation and Universal Health Care, theAIRnet Working Paper # 2009-01. Available at www.theairnet.org/V2/healthcare-technology.php (last accessed December 6, 2012).

Cárdenas-O'Farrill A (2009), The Cuban Biotechnology Industry: Innovation and universal health care, *theAIRnet Working Paper* # 2009-01

Cárdenas-O'Farrill A (2014), State and innovative enterprises: The case of the Cuban pharmaceutical industry, *Business and Economic History On-line (BEH)*, Vol. 12.

Carey G et. al. (2015), Systems science and systems thinking for public health: a systematic review of the field, *BMJ Open* 5: e009002. doi:10.1136/bmjopen-2015-009002.

Cargill C (2002), Intellectual property rights and standards settings organizations: An overview of failed evolution, Submitted to the Department of Justice and the Federal Trade Commission, Version 2.

Carlsson, B et al. (2002), Innovation systems: analytical and methodological issues. *Research Policy,* 31(2), 233–245.

Casanueva J (2007), Role of the National Regulatory Authority in Prequalification of Vaccines. Experience of CECMED, Developing Countries Vaccine Manufactures Network (DCVMN) mimeo.

Castro F (1960), Speech of Dr. Fidel Castro at U.N. General Assembly, September 26, 1960, Source: Embassy of Cuba, Report NBR-FBIS, Report Date: 19600926, available at http://lanic.utexas.edu/project/castro/db/1960/19600926.html, last accessed, June 13, 2019, Original text in Spanish available at www.cubadebate.cu/especiales/2018/09/23/texto-completo-del-historico-discurso-de-fidel-en-la-onu-el-26-de-setiembre-de-1960/, last accessed, June 13, 2019

Chandler A (1977), *The Visible Hand.* Cambridge, MA and London: The Belknap Press, Harvard University Press.

Chandler A (2004), *Scale and Scope: The Dynamics of Industrial Capitalism*, Cambridge, MA: Belknap Press of Harvard University Press.

Chang HJ (1999), The developmental state. In: M. Woo-Cumings (ed.), *The Developmental State*. Ithaca and London: Cornell University Press, pp. 182–99.

Chang HJ (1999), The economic theory of the developmental state. In: M Woo-Cumings (ed.), *The Developmental State*. Ithaca and London: Cornell University Press, pp. 182–99.

Chang HJ (2002), Breaking the mould: An institutionalist political economy alternative to the neo-liberal theory of the market, *Cambridge Journal of Economics* 26(5): 539–59.

Chang HJ (2003a), *Kicking Away the Ladder.* London: Anthem Press.

Chang HJ (2003b), *Globalisation, Economic Development and the Role of the State.* London: Zed Books.

Chang HJ (2007) (ed.), *Institutional Change and Economic Development.* London: Anthem Press.

Chang HJ (2007), *State Owned Enterprise.* New York: United Nations DESA.

Chang HJ (2008), *Bad Samaritans: The Myth of Free Trade and Secret History of Capitalism.* New York: Bloomsbury.

Chang HJ (2009), Industrial Policy: Can We Go Beyond an Unproductive Confrontation?, APlenary Paper for ABCDE (Annual World Bank Conference on Development Economics) Seoul, South Korea, June 22–24.

Chang HJ (2010), *23 Things They Don't Tell You about Capitalism*. London: Penguin Group.

Chang HJ (2010), Institutions and economic development: theory, policy and history, *Journal of Institutional Economics*, 7(4): 1–26, pre-published copy.

Chang HJ (2011), Reply to the comments on "Institutions and Economic Development: Theory, Policy and History," *Journal of Institutional Economics* 7(4): 595–613.

Chang HJ (2016), *Transformative Industrial Policy for Africa*, United Nations, Economic Commission for Africa, Addis Ababa, Ethiopia.

Chaptal JA (1893), *Mes souvenirs sur Napoléon,* Librairie Plon, Paris.

Chavance B (2012), John Commons's organizational theory of institutions: A discussion, *Journal of Institutional Economics* 8(1): 27–47.

Chesbrough H et al. (eds.) (2006), *Open Innovation: Researching a New Paradigm.* Oxford: Oxford University Press.

Chiu-Pu C (2005), Ownership and management issues in Taiwanese public enterprises, *The Asia Pacific Journal of Public Administration* 27(2) (December): 163–80.

Chomsky N (1986), The Soviet Union versus socialism, *Our Generation*, Spring/Summer.

Christensen A (2003), Cuba's jewel of tropical medicine, *Perspectives in Health Magazine*, The Magazine of the Pan American Health Organisation 8(2): 22–5.

Christensen CM (1997), *The Innovator's Dilemma: When New Technologies Cause Great Firms to Fail.* Cambridge, MA: Harvard Business School Press.

CIGB, Business Portfolio 2012–2013.

CIGB, Business Portfolio 2016–2017.

Cimoli M et al. (2006), Institutions and Policies Shaping Industrial Development: An Introductory Note, LEM, *Working Paper Series*, No. 2, January.

Cimoli M et al. (eds.) (2009), *Industrial Policy and Economic Development: The Political Economy of Capabilities Accumulation.* Oxford: Oxford University Press.

Cimoli M et al. (eds.) (2009), *The Political Economy of Capabilities Accumulation: The Past and Future of Policies for Industrial Development.* New York: Oxford University Press.

Clark I (2010), Cuba. In: UNESCO Science Report. Paris: UNESCO Publishing, pp. 123–31.

Clark J et al. (2000), Patent Pools: A Solution to the Problem of Access in Biotechnology Patents, United States Patent and Trademark Office, Research Paper, December.

Clay H (1832), In Defense of the American System, Classic Senate Speeches, February 2, 3, and 6, available at www.senate.gov/artandhistory/history/common/generic/Speeches_ClayAmericanSystem.htm

Clithero JA et al. (2008), Foundations of neuroeconomics: From philosophy to practice. *PLoS Biol* 6(11): e298.

Coan RW (2017), *A History of American State and Local Economic Development.* Cheltenham UK, Northampton US: Edward Elgar.

Coe N et al. (2008), Global production networks: realizing the potential, *Journal of Economic Geography* 8(3): 271–95.

Cohen M et al. (2000), Protecting Their Intellectual Assets: Appropriability Conditions and Why U.S. Manufacturing Firms Patent (or Not), NBER *Working Paper* No. 7552, February.

Cohen S and DeLong J B (2016), *Concrete Economics: The Hamilton Approach to Economic Growth and Policy.* Cambridge, MA and London: Harvard Business Review Press.

Colander D and Kupers R (2014), *Complexity and the Art of Public Policy: Solving Society's Problems from the Bottom Up.* Princeton and Oxford: Princeton University Press.

Colander D (ed.) (1984), *Neoclassical Political Economy: An Analysis of Rent-Seeking and DUP Activities.* Cambridge, MA: Ballinger.

Colclough C and Manor J (1991), *States or Markets: Neo-Liberalism and the Development Policy Debate.* Oxford: Clarendon Press.

Commons J (1924), *Legal Foundations of Capitalism.* New York: Macmillan.

Commons J (1934), *Institutional Economics.* New York: Macmillan.

Conner KR and Prahalad CK (1996), A resource-based theory of the firm: Knowledge vs. opportunism. *Organization Science* 7(5): 477–501.

Cooper R et al. (2006), Health in Cuba, *International Journal of Epidemiology* 35: 817–24.

Cuba Health Statistics Yearbook, Anuario Estadistico de Salud 2019 in original Spanish.

Cuba's Biotech Boom, *Nature* 457: 130, January 8, 2009.

Curtis G ed. (1996), *Russia: A Country Study.* Washington, D.C.: GPO for the Library of Congress.

Dandamudi SP (2005), *Guide to RISC Processors for Programmers and Engineers.* New York: Springer Science.

Danermark B et al. (2002), Explaining Society: Critical *Realism* in *Social Sciences.* Routledge, London and New York.

David P (1985), Clio and the economics of QWERTY, *The American Economic Review* 75(2), Papers and Proceedings of the Ninety-Seventh Annual Meeting of the American Economic Association, May 1985, pp. 332–7.

Davidov F et al. (2001), Sponsorship, authorship and accountability, *Canadian Medical Association Journal*, 165(6), September 18: pp. 786–8.

De Vos P (2009), The right to health in times of economic crisis: Cuba's way, *The Lancet* 374 (Nov. 7): 1575–6.

De Vos P et al. (2008a), Commentary: Cuba's health system: challenges ahead, *Health Policy and Planning* 23(4): 288–90.

De Vos P et al. (2008b), Uses of the first line emergency services in Cuba, *Health Policy* 85(1) (Jan.) 94–104.

Dekker D (2006), Measures of simmelian tie strength, simmelian brokerage, and simmelianly brokered, *Journal of Social Structure* 7(1): 1–22.

Delfin M et al. (2000), Epidemiology of hypertension in Cuba, *MEDICC Review*, Vol II, No. 2.

Delgado G et al. (2003), Vaccination Strategies Against Hepatitis B and Their Results: Cuba and the United States, *MEDICC Review* V(1).

DeLong J B (1992), Productivity and machinery investment: a long run look 1870–1980, *Journal of Economic History* 53: 2 (June), 307–24.

Demirel P and Mazzucato M (2012), Innovation and firm growth: Is R&D worth it?, *Industry & Innovation* 19(1): 45–62.

Denhardt J and Denhardt R (2007), *The New Public Service: Serving, Not Steering.* New York, London: M.E. Sharp Armonk.

Denzin N (2006), *Sociological Methods: A Sourcebook,* 5th edition. New Brunswick, N.J.: Aldine Transaction.

Dewhurst M et. al. (2009), Motivating people: Getting beyond money, *McKinsey Quarterly*, November.

Di Maio M (2009), Industrial policies in developing countries. In: Cimoli et al. (eds.), *The Political Economy of Capabilities Accumulation: the Past and Future of Policies for Industrial Development.* Oxford: Oxford University Press, pp. 95–114.

Dierickx I and Cool K (1989), Asset stock accumulation of competitive advantage, *Management Science* 35(12), December: 1504–11.

DiMasi J et al. (2003), The price of innovation: new estimates of drug development costs, *Journal of Health Economics* 22: 151–85.

Dominguez J et al. (2004), *The Cuban Economy at the Start of the Twenty-First Century.* Cambridge, Mass., London: Harvard University Press.

Dopfer et al. (2004), Micro–meso–macro, *J Evol Econ* 14: 263–79.

Dopfer K and Potts J (2008), *The General Theory of Economic Evolution.* London and New York: Routledge.

Dopfer K (2005), Economics, Evolution and the State: The *Governance* of *Complexity.* UK, USA: Edward Elgar.

Dorfman J (1949), *The Economic Mind in American Civilization*, Part III, 1865–1918, New York: Viking Press.

Dosi G (1988), Sources, procedures and microeconomics effects of innovation, *Journal of Economic Literature* XXVI, September: 1120–71.

Dosi G et al. (1994), The process of economic development: Introducing some stylized facts and theories on technologies, firms and institutions, *Industrial and Corporate Change* 3(1): 1–45

Dosi G et al. (2003), The economics of systems integration: Towards an evolutionary interpretation. In: A Prencipe et al. (eds.), *The Business of Systems Integration.* Oxford: Oxford University Press, pp. 95–114.

Dosi G et al. (2006), The relationships between science, technologies and their industrial exploitation: An illustration through the myths and realities of the so-called "European Paradox," *Research Policy* 35: 1450–64.

Drechsler W and Randma-Liiv T (2014), The new public management then and now: Lessons from the transition in Central and Eastern Europe, *Working papers on Technology Governance and Economic Dynamics* 57, May.

Duncan L and Perry A (1949), A method of matrix analysis of group structure, *Psychometrika* 14(2): 95–116.

Dy J et al. (2009), A Comparative Analysis on the Healthcare Systems of China and Cuba: Treatment of Cancer Patients, De La Salle-College of Saint Benilde, Manila, Philippines, available in: www.scribd.com/doc/55417998/Comparative-Analysis-on-Healthcare-Systems-Between-China-and-Cuba, last accessed Sep. 2018.

Dye AD and Sicotte R (1999), U.S.-Cuban trade cooperation and its unraveling, *Business and Economic History* 28(2), Winter.

Dye AD and Sicotte R (2004), The US sugar program and the Cuban revolution, *Journal of Economic History* 64(3): 673–704.

Ebbinghaus B and Manow P (eds) (2001), *Comparing Welfare Capitalism: Social Policy and Political Economy in Europe.* Japan and New York: Routledge.

Eckstein H (1975), Case studies and theory in political science. In: FI Greenstein and NW Polsby (eds.), *Handbook of Political Science*, vol. 7. *Political Science: Scope and Theory.* Reading, MA: Addison-Wesley, pp. 94–137.

Eckstein S (1989), Foreign Aid Cuban Style, *The Multinational Monitor* 10(4): Economics, April.

Eckstein S (2003), *Back from the Future: Cuba under Castro,* Second edition. New York: Routledge.

Economist Intelligence Unit (EUI) (2007), Cuba Country Report, Economist 1st-4th Quarter, Available at www.eiu.com (last accessed 10 December 2007).

Economist Intelligence Unit (EUI) (2010a), Country Report Cuba August 2010: Outlook for 2010–11: External Sector.

Economist Intelligence Unit (EUI) (2010b), *Cuba Economy: Structure of Exports Shifts*, July 8, 2010. New York, NY: Alacra Store (retrieved Dec 6, 2012 from www. alacrastore.com).

Edquist C. (2001), The Systems of Innovation Approach and Innovation Policy: An account of the state of the art, Lead paper presented at the DRUID Conference, Aalborg, June 12–15, 2001, under theme F: National Systems of Innovation, Institutions and Public Policies, National Systems of Innovation, Institutions and Public Policies, Draft of 2001-06-01.

Elsner W (2010), The process and a simple logic of "meso". Emergence and the co-evolution of institutions and group size, *Journal of Evolutionary Economics* 20(3): 445–77.

Erdös P and Renyi A (1959), On random graphs, *Publicationes Mathematicae* 6: 290–7.

Erdös P and Renyi A (1960), On the evolution of random graphs, *Publications of the Mathematical Institute of the Hungarian Academy of Sciences* 5: 17–61.

Ernst & Young (2008), Beyond Borders: Global Biotechnology Report.

Ernst & Young (2009), Beyond Borders: Global Biotechnology Report.

Ernst & Young (2010), Beyond borders: Global Biotechnology Report.

Ernst & Young (2011), Beyond Borders: Global Biotechnology Report.

Ernst & Young (2012), Beyond Borders: Global Biotechnology Report.

Espicom Business Intelligence (2011), Cuba, A World Pharmaceutical Market Report, Q4 2011.

Espino M (2008), Internacional tourism in Cuba: An update, Cuba in Transition, ASCE, available at www.ascecuba.org/publications/ proceedings/volume18/pdfs/espino. pdf (last accessed December 6, 2012).

Estudio económico de América Latina y el Caribe 2009–2010: Cuba, Report Economic commission for Latin America and the Caribbean (ECLAC), available at www.one. cu/publicaciones/cepal/ Estudio%202009_2010/Nota%20de%20Cuba.pdf (last accessed December 6, 2012).

Evans P (1995), *Embedded Autonomy: States and Industrial Transformation*. Princeton, NJ: Princeton University Press.

Evans P and Rauch J E (1999), Bureaucracy and Growth: A Cross-National Analysis of the Effects of "Weberian" State Structures on Economic Growth, *American Sociological Review* 64(5), October: 748–65.

Evans P et al. (eds) [1985] (1999), *Bringing the State Back In*. Cambridge: Cambridge University Press.

Everleny O (2002), "Cuba: An Overview of Foreign Direct Investment." Carleton working papers. Carleton, Canada, 16–18. Available at www1.carleton.ca/economics/ ccms/wp-content/ccms-files/ cep02-04.pdf (last accessed December 6, 2012).

Everleny O (ed.) (2006), *Reflexiones sobre economía cubana*. La Habana: Editorial ciencias sociales.

Everleny O (2009), The Cuban Economy: A Current Evaluation and Proposals for Necessary Policy Changes, Institute of Developing Economies – JETRO, Discussion paper 217, www.ide.go.jp/ English/Publish/Download/Dp/pdf/217.pdf, last accessed at December 6, 2012.

Eyo, S (2011), A Comparison of Biotechnology Industry in Japan and Other Developed Countries (April 23), Available at SSRN: http://ssrn.com/abstract=1878599 or http://dx.doi.org/10.2139/ssrn.1878599

Fallick B et al. (2005). Job hopping in Silicon Valley: Some evidence concerning the micro-foundations of a high technology cluster (October 2005). IZA *Discussion Paper* No. 1799.

Farley J (2009), *The Rejuvenating Power of Buena Vista Social Club*. Online-Publikationen des Arbeitskreis Studium Populärer Musik e.V. (ASPM).

Fehr E and Gächter S (2000), Fairness and retaliation: The economics of reciprocity, *Journal of Economic Perspectives* 14(3): 159–81, Summer.

Feinsilver J (2006), Cuban Medical Diplomacy: When the Left has Got it Right, Washington: Council of Hemispheric Affairs (COHA). Available at www.coha.org/cuban-medical-diplomacy-when-theleft-has-got-it-right/ (last accessed December 6, 2012).

Ferlie E (2017), The new public management and public management studies. *Oxford Research Encyclopedia of Business and Management,* March 29, Retrieved June 26, 2019, from https://oxfordre.com/business/view/10.1093/acrefore/9780190224851.001.0001/acrefore-9780190224851-e-129.

Festré A and Garrouste P (2009), The economic analysis of social norms: A reappraisal of Hayek's legacy, *Rev Austrian Econ* 22(3): 259–79.

Figueras MA (2001), International Tourism and the Formation of Productive Clusters in the Cuban Economy, Paper prepared to the Latin American Studies Association (LASA) 22nd Congress, Washington, D.C., September 2001.

Fitzgerald- Bocarsly P (1997), The History of Interferon: An Interview with Sid Pestka, ISICR, Issue 4:2, available at: www.isicr.org/newsletter/isicr4.2.pdf (last accessed July 2019).

Flochel P and Kumli F (2011), Pharma 3.0: delivering on health outcomes, *Journal of Business Chemistry* 7(3): 155–63.

Flyvbjerg B (2011), Case study. In: N Denzin and Y Lincoln (eds.), *The Sage Handbook of the Qualitative Research,* 4th edition. Thousand Oaks, CA: Sage, pp. 301–16.

Foley D (2003), *Unholy Trinity: Labour, Land and Capital.* London: Routledge.

Foster J (2005), From simplistic to complex systems in economics, *Cambridge J Econ* 29(6): 873–92.

Frankel JA (1982), The 1807–1809 embargo against Great Britain, *Journal of Economic History* 42(2): 291–308.

Frankel PE (1980), Laissez faire in nineteenth-century Britain: Fact or myth?, *Literature of Liberty* iii(4): 5–38.

Freeman Ch (1987), *Technology Policy and Economic Performance: Lesson from Japan.* London: Pinter Publishers.

Freeman Ch (1995), National system of innovation in a historical perpective. *Cambridge Journal of Economics* 19: 5–24.

Freeman Ch (2004), Technological infrastructure and international competitiveness, *Industrial and Corporate Change* 13(3): 541–69.

Freeman Ch (2008), *System of Innovation.* Cheltenham, UK; Northampton, USA: Edward Elgar.

Freeman L (1977, 1979), A set of measures of centrality based on betweenness, *Sociometry* 40: 3541.

Freeman L (1979), Centrality in social networks: Conceptual clarification, *Social Networks*, 1 (1978, 1979): 215–39.

Frey B (1997), *Not Just for the Money: An Economic Theory of Personal Motivation.* Cheltenham, UK: Edward Elgar.

Frey B (2007), Awards as compensation, *European Management Review* 4: 6–14.

Friedewald M (2000),The beginnings of radio communication in Germany, 1897–1918, *Journal of Radio Studies* 7(2): 441–63.

Friedman M (1962) [2002], *Capitalism and Freedom*. Chicago: The University Chicago Press.

Gandhi M (1930), *The Indian Cotton Textile Industry: Its Past, Present and Future*, The Book Company Limited, available at http://archive.org/details/indiancottontext 031792mbp

García-Molina J (2005), La economía cubana desde el siglo XVI al XX: del colonialismo al socialismo con mercado, *Serie Estudios y perspectivas 28*, CEPAL, Mexico D.F.

Gasperini L (2000), The Cuban Education System: Lessons and Dilemmas, *Country Studies Education Reform and Management Publication Series* I (5) (July), 21752, World Bank.

Gastón MW et al. (1957) [2001], Por Qué Reforma Agraria, *Serie B-Apologética*, Folleto No. 23. La Habana: Buró de Información y Propaganda, Agrupación Católica Universitaria.

Gaulé, P (2006),Towards Patent Pools in Biotechnology?, CEMI-REPORT-2006–010, *Working Papers Series*,April.

George AL and Bennett A (2005), *Case Studies and Theory Development in the Social Sciences*. Cambridge, MA: MIT Press.

Georgescu-Roegen N (1971), *The Entropy Law and the Economic Process* (1971). Cambridge, MA: Harvard University Press.

Gereffi G (2005), The global economy: Organization, governance and development. In: N Smelser and R Swedberg (eds.), *Handbook of Economic Sociology*. Princeton: Princeton University Press, pp. 160–82.

Gerlach C (2002), *Wu-Wei in Europe. A Study of Eurasian Economic Thought*, Department of Economic History, London School of Economics, Working Paper No. 12/05.

Gerring J (2007), *Case Study Research Principles and Practices*. Cambridge: Cambridge University Press.

Gerschenkron A (1962), *Economic Backwardness in Historical Perspective, a Book of Essays*. Cambridge, MA: Belknap Press of Harvard University Press.

Gilbert R (2004),Antitrust for patent pools: A century of policy evolution, 2004 *Stan. Tech. L. Rev.* 3. http://stlr.stanford.edu/STLR/Articles/04_STLR_3

Gindis D (2009), From fictions and aggregates to real entities in the theory of the firm, *Journal of Institutional Economics* 5(1),April, 25–46.

Gintis H (2006), The economy as a complex adaptive system, Review of the 2006 book of Eric D. Beinhocker: The Origins of Wealth: Evolution, Complexity, and the Radical Remaking of Economics, *Journal of Economic Literature* XLIV, December, 1018–31.

Giraldo G (2008), Interview with Pedro Ordúñez, *Medicc Review* 10(1),Winter: 15–17.

Giudici G and Roosenboom P (2004), *The Rise and Fall of Europe's New Stock Market*, Series: Advances in Financial Economics, Vol. 10, Emerald Group Publishing Limited.

Godin B (2007), National Innovation Systems: The system approach in historical perspective, Project on the History and Sociology of STI Statistics, *Working Paper* No. 36.

Godínez F (1998), Cuba's tourism industry: Sol Meliá as a case study, *Cuba in Transition*, ASCE, University of Miami, pp. 50–9.

474   *General references*

Gorry C (2007), Interview with Vicente Vérez Bencomo. Director of the Center for the Study of Synthetic Antigens, University of Havana, *MEDICC Review* 9(1), Fall: 14–15.

Gorry C (2012), Biotech: The magic pill? Cuba's burgeoning biopharmaceutical sector helps keep the island economy afloat, *Scientific American Worldview*, 68–9.

Gorter H et al. (2007), *Non-Leninist Marxism: Writings on the Workers Councils* Red and Black Publishers, St Petersburg, Florida.

Granovetter M (1973), The strength of the weak tie, *American Journal of Sociology* 78(6): 1360–80.

Grattan KP (2008), *The Cellular Empire, Dominion To Democracy: A Policy Analysis Of Open Access on Innovation*. Ann Arbor, MI: UMI Dissertation Publishing.

Graz J Ch (2016), The Havana Charter: when state and market shake hands. In Reinert E et al., *Handbook of Alternative Theories of Economic Development*, Cheltenham, UK, Northampton, MA, USA, Edward Elgar, pp. 281–90.

Groppo P et al. (2003), Land reform, Land settlement and cooperatives, FAO Report, 2003/3 Special Edition.

Guevara E (2006), *Apuntes críticos a la economía política*, Editorial Ciencias Sociales, La Habana.

Gutiérrez-Castillo O and Gancedo-Gaspar N (2002), Tourism development: Locomotive for the Cuban economy, *ReVista*, Harvard Review for Latin America, Winter: 76–8.

Guzmán M (2005), Deciphering dengue: The Cuban experience, *Science* 309 (5740) (Sep. 2): 1495–7.

Hadad J (2005), International Workshop on Epidemic Neuropathy in Cuba: Report summary. *MEDICC Review* VII(7): 27–30.

Hall B and Ham R (2001), The patent paradox revisited: an empirical study of patenting in the U.S. semiconductor industry, 1979–1995, *RAND Journal of Economics* 32(1), Spring: 101–28.

Hall D (1998), Public Enterprise in Europa, Paper presented at: IPPR Conference November 24, 1997 "What Future for Public Enterprise?" London, Institute for Public Policy Research (IPPR).

Hamilton A [1791] (2001), *Report on Manufacturers*, available in: www.constitution.org/ah/rpt_manufactures.pdf

Hanneman R and Riddle M (2005), *Introduction to Social Network Methods*. Riverside, CA, University of California, Riverside (published in digital form at http://faculty.ucr.edu/~hanneman/).

Hauknes J and Smith K (2003), Corporate Governance and Innovation in Mobile Telecommunications: How Did the Nordic Area Become a World Leader? STEP Report R-12, Institute for New Technologies United Nations, University Maastricht, Oslo.

Hawkins R et al. (eds.) (1995) *Standards, Innovation and Competitiveness: Politics and Economics of Standards in Natural and Technical Environments*. Cheltenham: Edward Elgar.

Hayek FA [1944] (2007), *The Road to Serfdom: Text and Documents*, The Definitive Edition. Routledge: The University of Chicago Press.

Hayek FA [1960] (2008), *The Constitution of Liberty*. London: Routledge Classics.

Hayek FA (1966), The principles of a liberal social order, *Il Politico* 31(4): 601–18.

Hayek FA (1973), *Law, Legislation and Liberty*. Chicago: University of Chicago Press.

Hayter CS et al. (2018), Public-sector entrepeneurship, *Oxford Review of Economic Policy* 34(4): 676–94.

Hébert-Dufresne L et al (2015), Complex networks as an emerging property of hierarchical preferential attachment, *Phys. Rev. E* 92, 062809.

Hechavarría-Nuñez Y et al. (2009). A methodology to elaborate regulatory guidelines, *Biotecnología Aplicada* 26(02): 122–6.

Heller M (1998), The tragedy of the anticommons: Property in the transition from Marx to markets, *Harvard Law Review* 111: 621.

Heller M and Eisenberg R (1998), Can patents deter innovation? The anticommons in biomedical research, *Science* 280(5364): 698–701.

Henry J (2008), The ideology of the laissez faire program, *Journal Economic Issues* XLII(1), March: 209–24.

Herrera R (2005), Cuba's National Program for Chronic Kidney Disease, Dialysis and Renal Transplantation, *MEDICC Review* VII(5): 2–5.

Hirschman A (1958), *The Strategy of Economic Development*. New Haven: Yale University Press.

Hobday M and Colpan A (2010), Technological innovations and business groups. In: A. Colpan et al. (eds.), *The Oxford Handbook of Business Groups*. New York: Oxford University Press, pp. 763–83.

Hobson J (2004), *The Eastern Origins of Western Civilization*. Cambridge: Cambridge University Press.

Hodgson G (2000), Form micro to macro: the concept of emergence and the role of institutions. In: L Burlamaqui et al. (eds.), *Institutions and the Role of the State*. UK, USA: Edward Elgar, pp. 103–28.

Hodgson G (2001), *How Economics Forgot History: The Problem of Historical Specificity in Social Science*. London/New York: Routledge.

Hodgson G (2002), Darwinism in economics: From analogy to antology, *Journal of evolutionary economics*, 12: 259–281

Hodgson G (2006), What are institutions, *Journal of Economic Issues* Vol XL(1): 1–25

Hodgson G (2009), On the institutional foundation of law: The insufficiency of custom and private ordering, *Journal of Economic Issues* XLIII(1): 143–66.

Holland S (1972), *The State as Entrepreneur: New Dimensions for Public Enterprise: The IRI State Shareholding*. London: Weidenfeld and Nicolson.

Hughes et al. (1999), *Funding a Revolution: Government Support for Computing Research*. Washington, D.C.: National Academy Press.

Hughes S (2003), Scientist at Genentech, CEO at Tularik, Program in the History of the Biological Sciences and Biotechnology, Regional Oral History Office, The Bancroft Library, University of California, Berkeley.

Hughes T et al. (1999), *Funding a Revolution: Government Support for Computing Research*. Washington, D.C.: National Academy Press.

Impagliazzo J and Lee J (eds.) (2008), *History of Computing and Education*. Dordrecht, The Netherlands: Kuwer Academic Publishers.

Informe de Comercio Exterior Uruguay-Cuba: Exportaciones e Importaciones, Uruguay XXI, 2009, available at http://aplicaciones.uruguayxxi. gub.uy/innovaportal/file/523/1/uruguay_-_cuba.pdf (last accessed December 6 2012).

Iniguez L (2013), Overview of evolving changes in Cuba's health services, *MEDICC Review* 15(2) (Apr.): 45–51.

Irving D (2005), The welfare cost of autarky: Evidence from the Jeffersonian trade embargo, 1807–09, *Review International Economics* 13(4), September: 631–45.

Izquierdo L and Hanneman R (2006), *Introduction to the Formal Analysis of Social Networks Using Mathematica*, Published in digital form at www.luis.izquierdo.name. Burgos,

Spain. Also available from the Mathematica Information Center: http://library.wolfram.com

Jackson M and Sambo L (2020), Health systems research and critical systems thinking: the case for partnership, *System Research and Behavioral Sciences* 37: 3–22.

Jacobo O (2007), Role of the National Regulatory Authority in Prequalification of Vaccines. Experience of CECMED, Developing Countries Vaccine Manufactures Network (DCVMN) mimeo.

Jäntti M and Vartiainen J (2009), The Finnish Developmental State and its Growth Regime, UNU-WIDER, United Nations University, Helsinki, *Research Paper* No. 2009/35.

Jessop B (1990), *State Theory: Putting Capitalist States in Their Place.* Cambridge: Polity Press.

Jessop B (2003a), Globalization: It's About Time Too!, *Political Science Series,* Institute for Advanced Studies, 85, Vienna.

Jessop B (2003b), Capitalism and the state. In: S Buckel et al. (eds.), *Formen und Felder politischer Intervention, Zur Relevanz von Staat und Steuerung,* Munster, Germany: Westfälischer Dampfboot, pp. 30–49.

Jessop B (2010), Redesigning the state, reorienting state power, and rethinking state theory. In: C Jenkins and K Leicht (eds.), *Handbook of Politics: State and Society in Global Perspective.* New York: Springer, pp. 41–61.

Johnson C (1982), *MITI and the Japanese Miracle: The Growth of Industrial Policy, 1925–1975.* Redwood City, CA: Stanford University Press.

Juma C and Yee-Cheong L (2005), Innovation: Applying knowledge in development, UN Millenium Project Task Force on Science, Technology and Innovation.

Kahneman D et al. (1982), *Judgment under Uncertainty: Heuristics and Biases.* New York: Cambridge University Press.

Kaldor N (1967), *Strategic Factors in Economic Development.* New York, Ithaca: Cornell University.

Kamenica E (2012), Behavioral economics and psychology of incentives, *Annu. Rev. Econ.* 4: 13.1–13.26.

Kaplan W, Laing R (2005), Local Production of Pharmaceuticals: Industry Policy and Access to Medicines. Health, Nutrition and Population, Discussion Paper, The World Bank, Jan. 16.

Kapur D (2001), Diasporas and Technology Transfer, *Journal of Human Development* 2(2): 265–86.

Katzenstein, P. (1987), *Corporatism and Change: Austria, Switzerland and the Politics of Industry.* Ithaca: Cornell University Press.

Kauffman S (1993), *Origins of Order: Self-Organization and Selection in Evolution.* Oxford: Oxford University Press.

Keck C and Reed G (2012), The curious case of Cuba, *American Journal of Public Health* 102(8) (Aug.): 13–e22.

Kesselheim AS (2010), Using market-exclusivity incentives to promote pharmaceutical innovation, *N Engl J Me* 363(19): 1855–62.

Kim JY (2010), Information diffusion and closeness centrality, *Sociological Theory and Methods* 25(1): 95–106.

Kim L (1997), The dynamics of Samsung's technological learning in semiconductors, *California Management Review* 39(3), Spring; ABI/INFORM Global.

Kirman A (2011), *Complex Economics: Individual and Collective Rationality.* London and New York: Routledge.

Kleinberg J (1998), Authoritative Sources in a Hyperlinked Environment, Proceedings of the ACM-SIAM Symposium on Discrete Algorithms, 1998, and as IBM Research Report RJ 10076, May 1997.

Kleinknecht A et al. (2014), Is flexible labour good for innovation? Evidence from firm-level data, *Cambridge Journal of Economics* 38: 1207–19.

Kortum S and Lerner J (1999), What is behind the recent surge in patenting?, *Research Policy* 28: 1–22.

Krackhardt D (1998), Simmelian tie: Super strong and sticky. In: R.M. Kramer and M Neale *Power and Influence in Organizations.* Thousand Oaks, CA: Sage, pp. 21–38.

Krackhardt D (1999), The ties that torture: Simmelian tie analysis in organizations. *Research in the Sociology of Organizations* 16: 183–210.

Krueger A (1974), The political economy of the rent-seeking society, *American Economic Review* 64: 291–303.

Kuczynski J et al. (ed.) (1973), *Monopolios norteamericanos en Cuba.* La Habana: Editorial Ciencias Sociales.

Lage A (2006), Socialism and the knowledge economy: Cuban biotechnology, Monthly Review 58(7) (Dec.): 53–5.

Lage A (2008), Connecting immunology research to public health: Cuban biotechnology. *Nature Immunology* 9(2) (Feb.): 109–12.

Lakhwinder, S (2006), Globalization, national innovation systems and response of public policy, *MPRA Paper* No. 641, November.

Lall S (1992), Technological capabilities and industrialization, *World Development* 20(2): 165–86.

Lall S (2000), Export performance, technological upgrading and foreign direct investment strategies in the Asian newly industrializing economies: With special reference to Singapur, Investment and Corporate Strategies, *Desarrollo Productivo 88,* CEPAL.

Langlois R (2002), Modularity in technology and organization, *Journal of Economic Behavior & Organization* 49: 19–37.

Lavezzi A (2001), Division of Labor and Economic Growth: from Adam Smith to Paul Romer and Beyond. Paper prepared for the Conference: Old and New Growth Theories: an Assessment. Pisa, October 5–7, 2001.

Lazonick W (2002), Innovative enterprise and historical transformation, *Enterprise & Society* 3 (March): 3–47.

Lazonick W (2006), Corporate Governance, Innovative Enterprise, and Economic Development, UNU WIDER, *Research Paper* No. 2006/71, July.

Lazonick W (2008), *Sustainable Prosperity in the New Economy? Business Organisation and High-Tech Employment in the United States.* Kalamazoo, Michigan: W.E. Upjohn Institute for Employment Research.

Lazonick W (2011), The Innovative Enterprise and the Developmental State: Toward an Economics of "Organizational Success." Paper prepared for: Institute for New Economic Thinking Annual 2011 conference Crisis and Renewal: International Political Economy at the Crossroads Mount Washington Hotel Bretton Woods, NH, April 8–11, 2011.

Lazonick W and Mazzucato M (2012), The risk-reward nexus, pre-print copy, later published in *Industrial and Corporate Change* 22(4) (August 2013): 1093–1128.

Lazonick W and Mazzucato M (2012), The Risk–Reward Nexus. *Discussion Paper.* Policy Network.

Lazonick W and O'Sullivan M (2000), Perspectives on corporate governance, innovation, and economic performance. The European Institute of Business Administration, Fontainebleau Cedex, France.

Lazonick W and Tulum Ö (2011), The US biopharmaceutical finance and the sustainability of the biotech business model, *Research Policy* 40(9), November: 1170–87.

Lazonick W et al. (2007), Boston's Biotech Boom: A "New Massachusetts Miracle"?, Research Paper, Center for Industrial Competitiveness University of Massachusetts Lowell, May.

Le Riverend J (1975), *Historia económica de Cuba*. La Habana: Editorial Pueblo y Educación.

Lee DH et al. (1991), Performance and adaptive roles of the government supported research institutes in South Korea. *World Development* 19(10): 1421–40.

Lee J and Kim S. (2011), Exploring the role of social networks in affective organizational commitment: Network centrality, strength of ties, and structural holes, The American Review of Public Administration 41(2): 205–23.

Lee P et al. (2012), *Continuing Innovation in Information Technology*. Washington, D.C.: National Academy Press.

Lenin V [1920] (1964) *"Left-Wing" Communism: an Infantile Disorder*, Collected Works, Volume 31, Progress Publishers, USSR, pp. 17–118.

Lequin R (2005), Enzyme Immunoassay (EIA)/Enzyme-Linked Immunosorbent Assay (ELISA), *Clinical Chemistry* 51(12) (Dec.): 2415–18.

Lerner J et al. (2005), The design of patent pools: The determinants of licensing rules, The *RAND Journal of Economics* 38(3), 610–25, November.

Levinthal D (1998), The slow pace of rapid technological change: gradualism and punctuation in technological change, *Industrial and Corporate Change* 7: 217–47.

Levinthal D (2006), The neo-Schumpeterian theory of the firm and the strategy field, *Industrial and Corporate Change* 15(2): 391–4.

Libicki M (1994), Standards: The Rough Road to the Common Byte, Harvard University, Center for Information Policy Research, P-94–6.

Light D (ed.) (2010), *The Risks of Prescription Drugs*. New York: Columbia University Press.

Light D and Lexchin J (2005) Foreign free riders and the high price of US medicines. *BMJ* 331(7522): 958–60.

Light D and Lexchin J (2012), Pharmaceutical research and development: What do we get for all that money?, *BMJ* 345: e4348.

Light D and Warburton R (2011), Demythologizing the high costs of pharmaceutical research, *BioSocieties* 6 34–50.

Light D et al. (2011), Longer exclusivity does not guarantee better drugs, *Health Affairs* 30(4): 798.

List F (1856), *National System of Political Economy*. Philadelphia: J.B. Lippincott & Co.

Loewenberg S (2009), The Bayh–Dole Act: A model for promoting research translation?, *Molecular Oncology* 3(2): 91–3.

Lopez E (2002), Development of Cuban biotechnology, *Journal of Commercial Biotechnology* 9(2) (Dec.): 1–5.

Lopez E et al. (2006), Biotechnology in Cuba: 20 years of scientific, social and economic progress, *Journal of Commercial Biotechnology* 13, 1–11.

Lopez E et al. (2007), Taking stock of Cuban biotech, *Nature Biotechnology* 25(11): 1215–16.

Lopez T et al. (2008), Cuban experience on computing and education. In: J Impagliazzo ed., History of Computing and Education. New York: Springer, pp. 57–74.

Lucas R (2005), International migrations and economic development: Lessons from low-income countries , Stockholm, Sweden: Ministry of Foreign Affairs.

Lundvall B (2002), *Innovation, Growth and Social Cohesion.* Cheltenham, UK, Northampton; USA: Edward Elgar.

Lundvall B (2007), National Innovation System: Analytical Focusing Device and Policy Learning Tool, Swedish Institute for Growth Policy Studies, *Working paper* R2007:004.

MacKay T [1891](1981), *A Plea for Liberty: An Argument against Socialism and Socialistic Legislation,* Liberty Classics, Indianapolis. Available at http://oll.libertyfund.org/titles/313, last accessed July 2018

Maddison A (2007), *Contours of the World Economy, 1-2030 AD: Essays in Macro-economic History.* Oxford: Oxford University Press.

Mako W and Zhang C (2003), *Management of China's State-Owned Enterprises Portfolio,* World Bank, Beijing, available at: www.thepresidency.gov.za/ElectronicReport/downloads/volume_4/business_case_viability/BC1_Research_Material/302500_CHAO_Management_enterprises.pdf

Malerba F (1992), Learning by firms and incremental technical change, *The Economic Journal* 102(413) (July): 845–59.

Malerba F (1999), Sectoral systems of innovation and production, DRUID Conference on: National Innovation Systems, Industrial Dynamics and Innovation Policy Rebuild, June 9–12, 1999.

Malerba F (2002), Sectoral systems of innovation and production, *Research Policy* 31: 247–64.

Malerba F et al. (2006), Vertical Integration and Dis-integration of Computer Firms: A History Friendly Model of the Co-evolution of the Computer and Semiconductor Industries, CESPRI *Working Paper* No. 191,

Marcheco B (2009), Cuba's National Medical Genetics Program, *MEDICC Review* 11(1), Winter: 11–13.

Marengo L et al. (2009), Appropriability, Patents, and Rates of Innovation in Complex Products Industries, LEM, *Working Paper Series,* No. 5, April.

Marqués-Dolz MA (2006), *Las industrias menores: empresarios y empresas en Cuba (1880–1920).* La Habana: Editorial de Ciencias Sociales.

Marquetti H (2006), La restructuración del sistema empresarial en Cuba: Tendencias principales. In: Evenly O (ed.) *Reflexiones sobre economía cubana,* Ciencias Sociales, Editorial de Ciencias sociales, Ciudad de la Habana, pp. 297–338.

Marshall A (1927) [1890], *Principles of Economics.* London: Macmillan, Reprint.

Marx M (2007), Noncompetes and inventor mobility: Specialists, stars, and the Michigan experiment, *Management Science* 55(6): 875–89.

Mazzucato M (2011), The *Entrepreneurial State.* London: Demos.

Mazzucato M (2013), *The Entrepeneurial State: Debunking Public vs. Private Sector Myths.* London, New York: Anthem Press.

McKelvey M et al. (eds.) (2004), *The Economic Dynamics of Modern Biotechnology.* Cheltenham, UK, Northhampton, MA, USA: Edward Elgar.

McKinley W (1890), The value of protection, *The North American Review* 150.

Melon CC et al. (2009), A survey of South-North health biotech collaboration, *Nature Biotechnology* 27: 229–32.

Merges R and Sonsini W (2004), From Medieval Guilds to Open Source Software: Informal Norms, Appropriability Institutions, and Innovation, Conference on the Legal History of Intellectual Property, November 13, Madison Wisconsin

Mesa-Lago C (2000), *Market, Socialist, and Mixed Economies: Comparative Policy and Performance, Chile, Cuba, and Costa Rica.* Baltimore/London: The Johns Hopkins University Press.

Metcalfe JS (1994), Evolutionary economics and technology policy, *Economic Journal* 104: 931–94.

Metcalfe JS (1995), Technology systems and technology policy in an evolutionary framework, *Cambridge Journal of Economics* 19: 25–46.

Metcalfe JS (1995), Technology systems and technology policy in an evolutionary framework, *Cambridge Journal of Economics* 19: 25–46.

Micheisen K and Kuisma M (1992), Nationalism and Industrial. Development in Finland, *Business and Economic History*, Second Series, Volume 21.

Miles RE et al. (1997), Organizing in the knowledge era: Anticpating the cellular form, *Academy of Management Executive* 11(4): 7–20.

Mill JS (1848) (1871), *Principles of Political Economy*. London: Longmans, Green, Reader and Dyer, available at https://archive.org/details/principleseconom01milluoft, last accessed in July 2018

Millward R (2005), *Private and Public Enterprise in Europe: Energy, Telecommunications and Transport, 1830–1990*. Cambridge: Cambridge University Press.

Molina E (2009), Cuba: Economic Restructuring, Recent Trends and Major Challenges, The IDEA *Working Paper Series* 02/2009.

Monreal P (2005), The problem of development in contemporary Cuba, *Journal of the Faculty of International Studies*, 19, Japan: Utsunomiya University, pp. 59–71.

Mookerji R (2013), *Local Government in Ancient India*. Hong Kong: Forgotten Books. (Original work published by Oxford University Press, 1920.)

Morales J and Nápoles S (1991), Cuba: el proceso de industrialización y su dimensión regional, *Problemas del Desarrollo* 22(85) (April–June): 199–227.

Morel C et al. (2005), Health innovation networks to help developing countries address neglected diseases, *Science* 39 (July): 401–3.

Moretti E (2010), Local multipliers, *American Economic Review: Papers & Proceedings*, 100 (May 2010), 1–7.

Moretti E and Thulin P (2013), Local multipliers and human capital in the United States and Sweden, *Industrial and Corporate Change* 22(1): 339–62.

Morris E (2014), Unexpected Cuba, *New Left Review* 88 (July-Aug.): 5–45.

Moser P (2013), Patents and innovation: Evidence from economic history, *Journal of Economic Perspectives* 27(1), Winter: 23–44.

Mowery D and Nelson R (1999), *The Sources of Industrial Leadership*. Cambridge: Cambridge University Press,

Mowery D and Simcoe T (2002), Is the Internet a US invention? an economic and technological history of computer networking, *Research Policy* 31: 1369–87.

Mun T (1664) (1895), *England Treasure by Foraign Trade*. Norwood, MA: Norwood Press.

Munos B (2009), Lessons from 60 years of pharmaceutical innovation, *Nature Reviews Drug Discovery* 8 (Dec.): 959–68.

Myrdal G (1944), *American Dilemma: The Negro Problem and Modern Democracy*. Harper & Row, New York/London:

Naqvi SN (1994), *Islam, Economics and Society*. London and New York: Kegan Paul International.

National Research Council (2011), *Measuring the Impacts of Federal Investments in Research: A Workshop Summary*. Washington, DC: The National Academies Press. National Science Foundation (2012), National Patterns of R&D Resources: 2009 Data Update, *NCSES*, NSF 12–321, Arlington, VA. Available at www.nsf.gov/statistics/nsf12321/.

Navarro V (1972), Health, health services, and health planning in Cuba, *International Journal of Health Services* 2(3): 397–432.

Nelson R (1993), *National Innovation Systems: A Comparative Study*. Oxford: Oxford University Press.

Nelson R and Rosenberg N (1993), Technical innovation and national systems. In: R Nelson (ed.), *National Innovation Systems*. Oxford: Oxford University Press, pp. 3–23.

Nelson R and Winter S (1982), *An Evolutionary Theory of Economic Change*. Cambridge, MA: The Belknap Press.

Newman M (2003), The structure and function of complex networks, *SIAM Review* 45: 167–256.

Newman M (2005), A measure of betweenness centrality based on random walks, *Social Networks* 27: 39–54.

Newman M (2008), Mathematics of networks. In: SN Durlauf and LE Blume (eds.), *The New Palgrave Dictionary of Economics, Second Edition*, London: Palgrave Macmillan.

Newman M (2010), *Networks: An Introduction*. Oxford: Oxford University Press.

Nightingale P (2004), Technological Capabilities, Invisible Infrastructure & the Unsocial Construction of Predictability: The Overlooked Fixed Costs of Useful Research. Paper to be presented at the DRUID Summer Conference 2004 on Industrial dynamics, innovation and, Elsinore, Denmark, June 14–16.

Nonaka I and Krogh G (2009), Tacit knowledge and knowledge conversion: Controversy and advancement in organizational knowledge creation theory, *Organization Science* 20(3), May–June: 635–52.

Nonaka I and Takeuchi H (1995), *The Knowledge-Creating Company: How Japanese Companies Create the Dynamics of Innovation*. Oxford: Oxford University Press.

Nova A (2006), Redimensionamiento y diversificación de la industria azucarera. In: Everleny O (ed.), *Reflexiones sobre economía cubana*. La Habana: Editorial Ciencias Sociales, pp. 108–57.

Nozick R (1974), *Anarchy, State, and Utopia*. New York: Basic Books.

O'Connor J (1970), *The Origins of Socialism in Cuba*. Ithaca, London: Cornell University Press.

OECD, Eurostat, WHO (2011), *A System of Health Accounts*. OECD Publishing.

Oficina Nacional de Estadistica (2009), Republica de Cuba.

Oficina Nacional de Estadísticas (ONE) (2010), Anuario estadístico de Cuba 2010.

Oficina Nacional de Estadísticas (ONE) (2019), Cuentas Nacionales.

Olson S and Downey A (2013) (eds.), *Sharing Clinical Research Data: Workshop Summary*. Washington, D.C.: The National Academy Press.

Open Society Archives (1973), The system of government in socialist Cuba, Online: www.osaarchivum.org/files/holdings/300/8/3/text/14-2-118.shtml, last accessed July 2019.

Opsahl T et al. (2010), Node centrality in weighted networks: Generalizing degree and shortest paths, *Social Networks* 32(3), July: 245–51.

Opsahl T et al. (2010), Node Centrality in Weighted Networks: Generalizing Degree and Shortest Paths. Preprint submitted to Social Networks, April.

Ostrom E (2010), Beyond markets and states: Polycentric governance of complex economic systems, *American Economic Review* 100, June: 1–33.

Ostry J et al. (2014), Redistribution, Inequality, and Growth, *IMF Staff Discussion Note*, February.

Palla G et al. (2007), Directed networks: Directed network modules, *New J. Phys.* 9: 186. Palma J (2009), Flying Geese and waddling ducks: The different capabilities of East Asia and Latin America to "demand-adapt" and "supply-upgrade" their export productive capacity. In: M Cimoli et al. (eds), *The Political Economy of Capabilities Accumulation: The Past and Future of Policies for Industrial Development.* Oxford: Oxford University Press, pp. 203–38.

Pannekoek A [1938] (2003), *Lenin as Philosopher: A Critical Examination of the Philosophical Basis of Leninism.* Marquette University Press.

Panzar J and Willig R(1981), Economies of scope, *American Economic Review* 71(2): 268–72.

Parker-Willis H. (1903), Reciprocity with Cuba, *Annals of the American Academy of Political and Social Science,* Vol. 22, The United States and Latin America (July), pp. 129–147

Pascual M et al. (2011), Cuba's National Clinical Trials Coordinating Center: Emergence, evolution, and main results, *MEDICC Review* 13(1) (Jan.): 46–51.

Pavitt K (1984), Sectoral patterns of technical change: towards a taxonomy and a theory, *Research Policy* 13: 343–73.

Pease L (1996), David Atlee Phillips, Clay Shaw and Freeport, Sulphur, *Probe Magazine* 3(3) (March–April): 16–24.

Pelikan P and Wegner G (eds.) (2003), *The Evolutionary Analysis of Economic Policy.* Cheltenham, UK: Edward Elgar.

Penrose E (1959), *The Theory of the Growth of the Firm.* New York: Oxford University Press.

Pérez A et al. (1999), Impact of antimeningococcal B vaccinacion, *Mem Inst Oswaldo Cruz* 94(4): 433–40.

Perez C and Soete L (1988), Catching up in technology: Entry barriers and windows of opportunity. In: G Dosi et al., *Technological Change and Economic Theory.* London: Pinter Publishers, pp. 458–79.

Perez O et al. (2008), Cuba's New export commodity: A framework. In: M Font et al. (eds.), *A Changing Cuba in a Changing World.* New York: Bildner Center for Western Hemisphere Studies, City University of New York, pp. 327–44.

Pérez R and Sanchez C (2008), Capacity building: NRA assessment/benchmark system and institutional development plan: Experience of the Cuban National Regulatory Authority, *XIII International Conference of Regulatory Authorities, September 16–19, 2008, Bern.*

Pérez-Diaz I (2010), *Niquel + cobalto en Cuba: Lo que fui como ingeniero,* Ciencias Sociales, La Habana

Perez-Lopez J (2002), The Cuban Economy in an Unending Special Period, ASCE, Miami.

Peters P (2001), State Enterprise Reform in Cuba: An Early Snapshot. Arlington, Virginia: Lexington Institute.

Peters P (2003), Cutting Losses: Cuba Downsize its Sugar Industry. Arlington, Virginia: Lexington Institute.

Pineiro Hanecker C (2012), Non-state enterprises in Cuba current situation and prospects. Paper presented at the Bildner Center, City University of New York, May 21.

Pisano G (2006), *Science Business: The Premise, the Reality, and the Future of Biotech.* Boston, MA: Harvard Business School Press.

Polanyi K [1944] (2001), *The Great Transformation: The Political and Economic Origin of Our Time.* Boston: Beacon Press.

Polanyi K, Arensberg C and Pearson H (eds.) (1957), *Trade and Market in the Early Empires. Economies in History and theory,* The Free Press, Glencoe Illinois

Polanyi M [1962](1983), *The Tacit Dimension.* Gloucester, MA: Peter Smith Publisher Inc. Anchor Books.

Polanyi M [1966] (1983), *The Tacit Dimension.* New York: Doubleday & Co. Reprinted Gloucester, Mass: Peter Smith.

Pons T et al. (2007), Computational biology in Cuba: An opportunity to promote science in a developing country, *Plos Computational Biology* 3(11), e277 (Nov.): 2047–51.

Porter K et al. (eds.) (2005), *Clusters, Networks, and Innovation.* Oxford: Oxford University Press.

Pottelsberghe B (2009), *Lost Property: The European Patent System and Why It Doesn't Work.* Brussels: Bruegel Blueprint Series.

Poulantzas N (1978), *Political Power and Social Classes.* London and New York: NLB.

Powell W et al. (1996), Interorganizational collaboration and the locus of innovation: networks of learning in biotechnology. *Administrative Science Quarterly* 41(1): 116-45.

Powell W et al. (2005), Network dynamics and field evolution: The growth of inter-organizational collaboration in the life science, *American Journal of Sociology* 110(4): 1132–1205.

Prahalad CK and Hamel G (1990), The core competence of the corporation, *Harvard Business Review* 68: 79–91.

Prencipe A. (2000), Breadth and depth of technological capabilities in complex product systems: The case of the aircraft engine control system, *Research Policy* 29: 895–911.

Prencipe A et al. (eds.) (2005), *The Business of Systems Integration.* Oxford: Oxford University Press,

Pretty J (2008), Agricaulture sustainability: concepts, principles and evidence, *Philosophical Transactions of the Royal Society B: Biological Sciences* 363: 447–65.

Pu C (2005), Ownership and Management Issues in Taiwanese Public Enterprises, *Asia Pacific Journal of Public Administration* 27(2): 163–80.

PwC (2015), State-Owned Enterprises Catalysts for public value creation?, http://www.psrc.pwc.com

Quach, U et al. (2006), Biotechnology patenting takes off in developing countries, *Int. J. Biotechnology* 8(1/2): 43–59.

Raby D (2009), Why Cuba still matters, *Monthly Review* 60(08), January, available online at https://monthlyreview.org/2009/01/01/why-cuba-still-matters/.

Rapoport A (1957), Contribution to the theory of random and biased nets, *Bulletin of Mathematical Biophysics* 19: 257–77.

Ravasz E and Barabási A-L (2003), Hierarchical organization in complex networks, *Phys. Rev. E* 67: 026112.

Reed G (2009), Generating appropriate technologies for health equity: Interview with José Luis Fernández Yero, Director of the Immunoassay Center, Havana, *MEDICC Review* 11(1) (Winter): 14–17.

Reed G and Torres J (2008), Riding the brainwaves of Cuban science: Interview with Pedro Valdés Sosa, Vice Director for Research and Director of Neuroinformatics Cuban Neuroscience Center, Havana, *MEDICC Review* 10(2) (Spring): 11–13.

Reinert E (1999), The role of the state in economic growth, *Journal of Economic Studies* 26(4/5): 268–326.

Reinert E (2007), *How Rich Countries got Rich… and Why Poor Countries Stay Poor.,* London: Constable.

Reinert E (2012), Economics and the Public Sphere, *Working Papers in Technology Governance and Economic Dynamics*, no. 40.

Reinert E (2016), Giovanni Botero (1588) and Antonio Serra (1613): Italy and the birth of development economics. In Reinert E et al. (eds.), *Handbook of Alternative Theories of Economic Development*, Edward Elgar, Cheltenham, UK, Northampton, MA, USA, pp. 3–41.

Remarks of Senator John. F. Kennedy at democratic dinner, Cincinnati, Ohio, October 6, 1960, Source: Papers of John F. Kennedy. Pre-Presidential Papers. Senate Files. Series 12. Speeches and the Press. Box 912, Folder: "Democratic dinner, Cincinnati, Ohio, 6 October 1960," available at www.jfklibrary.org/archives/other-resources/john-f-kennedy-speeches/cincinnati-oh-19601006-democratic-dinner, last accessed 6/2019

Reminga J and Carley K (2003), *Measures for ORA (Organizational Risk Analyzer)*, Carnegie Mellon University, March 22, Available at: www.casos.cs.cmu.edu/publications/papers/reminga_2003_ora.pdf

Ritchie F (2014), Resistance to change in government: risk, inertia and incentives, Economics Working Paper Series 1412, University of the West of England, Bristol.

Roberts C (1996), *The Logic of Historical Explanation*. Pennsylvania: The Pennsylvania State University Press.

Rocha L (2000), Syntactic autonomy, cellular automata, and RNA editing: or why self-organization needs symbols to evolve and how it might evolve them, In: JLR Chandler and G Van de Vijver (eds.), *Closure: Emergent Organizations and Their Dynamics.* New York: Annals of the New York Academy of Sciences, Vol. 901, pp. 207–23.

Rodríguez A et al. (1999), Impact of antimeningococcal B vaccinacion, *Mem Inst Oswaldo Cruz*, Rio de Janeiro, 94(4): 433–40.

Rodriguez JL (2014), The frontier of change in the Cuban economy, *Latin American Perspectives* 41(197/4) (July): 64–73.

Rodrik D (2004), Industrial Policy for the Twenty-First Century. Paper prepared for UNIDO, Harvard University.

Rodrik D (2006), What's So Special about China's Exports? Paper prepared for the project on "China and the Global Economy 2010" of the China Economic Research and Advisory Programme, Harvard University.

Romer P (1986), Increasing returns and long-run growth, *The Journal of Political Economy* 94(5): 1002–37.

Romer P (1990), Endogenous technological change, *Journal of Political Economy* 98: 71–102.

Romero C (2009), South-South Cooperation between Venezuela and Cuba, The Reality of Aid Network, pp. 107–14. Available at http:// realityofaid.org/userfiles/roareports/roareport_e48ca78931.pdf (last accessed December 6, 2012).

Rosenberg N (1976), *Perspectives on Technology.* Cambridge: Cambridge University Press.

Rothwell R (1992), Successful industrial innovation: critical factors for the 1990s, *R&D Management* 22: 221–39.

Rowe W and Brook T (2009), *China's Last Empire: The Great Qing.* Cambridge, MA: The Belknap Press of Harvard University Press.

Rumelt RP (1984), Towards a strategic theory of the firm. In: RB Lamb (ed.), *Competitive Strategic Management.* Englewood Cliffs, NJ: Prentice Hall.

Rusoja E et al. (2018), Thinking about complexity in health: A systematic review of the key systems thinking and complexity ideas in health. *Journal of Evaluation in Clinical Practice*, 24(3) pp. 600–606.

Russell A (2005), Standardization in history: A review essay with an eye to the future. In: S Bolin (ed.), *The Standards Edge: Future Generations*. Ann Arbor, MI: Sheridan Books, available in: www.arussell.org/papers/futuregeneration-russell.pdf

Ruttan V (2006), Is war necessary for economic growth?, *Historically Speaking-Issues* (merged papers), Clemons Lecture, University of Minnesota, October 9.

Rutter HR et al. (2017), The need for a complex systems model of evidence for public health, *The Lancet* 390(10112) (Dec. 9): 2602–4.

Sako M (2004), Supplier development at Honda, Nissan and Toyota: A historical case study of organizational capability enhancement, *Industrial and Corporate Change* 13(2) (April): 281–308.

Sánchez J and Triana J (2008), Un panorama actual de la economía cubana, las transformaciones en curso y sus retos perspectivos, Instituto Real Instituto Elcano Documento de Trabajo 31, Madrid.

Sanchez R and Mahoney JT (1996), Modularity, flexibility, and knowledge management in product and organisation design, *Strategic Management Journal* 17, Winter Special Issue: 63–76.

Sanguinetti J (1998), Comments on "Economic Reform in Latin America and the Caribbean and Possible Implications for Cuba," *Cuba in Transition*, ASCE, November: 20–22.

Savioli A (1961), L'Unita interview with Fidel Castro: The nature of Cuban socialism, L'Unita, Rome, 32, February 1: 1–2.

Scher M (2001), Bank-firm cross shareholding in Japan: What is it, why does it matter, is it winding down? United Nations' Department of Economic and Social Affairs (DESA), Discussion Paper, No. 15.

Schiff E (1971), *Industrialization without National Patents – the Netherlands 1869–1912; Switzerland 1850–1907*. Princeton, NJ: Princeton University Press.

Schilling M (2000), Toward a general modular systems theory and its application to interfirm product modularity, *Academy of Management Review* 25(2): 312–34.

Schilling M and Steensma K (2001), The use of modular organizational forms: an industry-level analysis, *Academy of Management Journal* 44(5): 1149–68.

Schweitzer F et al. (2009), Economic networks: The new challenges, *Science* 325: 422–5, July 24.

Senge P (1990), *The Fifth Discipline: The Art and Practice of the Learning Organization*. New York: Doubleday.

Senker J et al. (2000), European exploitation of biotechnology: Do government policies help?, *Nature Biotechnology* 18(6) (June): 605–8.

Séror A (2006), A case analysis of INFOMED: The Cuban National Health Care Telecommunications Network and Portal, *Journal of Medical Internet Research* 8(1) (Jan.–Mar.): e1.

Shapiro C (2004), *Navigating the Patent Thicket: Cross Licenses, Patent Pools, and Standard Settings*. Cambridge, MA, London: The MIT Press.

Shaw A (1999), *A Guide to Performance Measurements and Non-Financial Indicator*, The Foundation for Performance Measurement, Mattison Public Relations.

Shengxiang S et al. (2017), Fear, anger, and risk preference reversals: An experimental study on a Chinese sample, *Frontiers in Psychology* 8: 1371.

Shih S et al. (2006), Building global competitiveness in a turbulent environment: Acer's journey of transformation. In: W Mobley and E Weldon (eds.), *Advances in Global Leadership*, Volume 4. Wagon Lane, Bingley, UK: Emerald, pp. 201–17.

Shinohara M (1976), MITI's industrial policy and Japanese industrial organization, *IDE-RETRO* 14(4) (December): 319–487.

Shipman A (1999), *The Market Revolution and Its Limits: A Price for Everything*. New York: Routledge.

Siepmann T (2005), The global exportation of the U.S. Bay-Dole Act, *University of Dayton Law Review* 30(2): 210–43.

Simon H (1955), On a class of skew distribution functions, *Biometrika* 42: 425–40.

Simon H (1962), The architecture of complexity, *Proceedings of the American Philosophical Society* 106(6) (Dec. 12): 467–82.

Simon H (1981), *The Sciences of the Artificial*. Cambridge, MA: MIT Press.

Simon H (1991), Organizations and markets, *Journal of Economic Perspectives* 5: 25–44.

Skocpol T (1979), State and revolution: Old regimes and revolutionary crises in France, Russia, and China, *Theory and Society* 7(½), Special Double Issue on State and Revolution (Jan.- Mar.): 7–95.

Slembeck P (2003), Ideologies, beliefs, and economic advice: A cognitive–evolutionary view on economic policy-making. In P Pelikan and G Wegner (eds.), *The Evolutionary Analysis of Economic Policy*. Cheltenham: Edward Elgar, pp. 121–68.

Smith A (1776) (2005), *The Wealth of Nations*, Pennsylvania State University, Electronic Classics Series.

Smith A (1776) (2005), *Wealth of Nations*. Electronic Classics Series. Pennsylvania: The Pennsylvania State University.

Smith A (1776) (2005), *Wealth of the Nation*. The Pennsylvania State University, Electronic Classics Series

So AD et al. (2008), Is Bayh-Dole good for developing countries? Lessons from the US experience. *PLoS Biol* 6(10): e262.

Solow R (1957), Technical change and the aggregate production function, *The Review of Economics and Statistics* 39(3) (Aug.): 312–20.

Sotolongo F (2009), Meningococcal Vaccine Production and Vaccine Research in Cuba, Presentation at the 4th Conference on Global Health on Vaccination Research, Oslo, 2009.

Sotolongo F et al. (2007), Cuban meningococcal BC vaccine: Experiences and contributions from 20 years of application, *MEDICC Review* 9(1) (Fall): 16–22.

Sredojević D et al. (2016), Technological changes in economic growth theory: Neoclassical, endogenous, and evolutionary- institutional approach, *Economic Themes* 54(2): 177–94.

Steele D (1987), Hayek's theory of cultural group selection, *The Journal of Libertarian Studies* III(2): 171–95.

Steinmueller W (1995), The U.S. software industry: An analysis and interpretive history, *MERIT Research Memoranda* 9(006), UNU-MERIT.

Steinmueller W (1996), The U.S. software industry: An analysis and interpretative history. In Mowery (ed.), *The International Computer Software Industry*. Oxford: Oxford University Press.

Stephenson K and Zelen M (1989), Rethinking centrality: methods and examples, *Social Networks* 11: 1–37.

Stuart T and Sorenson O (2003), Liquidity events and the geographic distribution of entrepreneurial activity, *Administrative Science Quarterly* 48: 175–201.

Sudgen R (1993), Normative judgments and spontaneous order: The contractarian element in Hayek's thought, *Constitutional Political Economy* 4(3): 393–424.

Sung L and Pelto D (1998), Greater predictability may result in patent pools; as the Federal Circuit refines scope of biotech claims, use of collective rights becomes likely, *The National Law Journal,* ISSN: 0162-7325.

Sunita K and Aishetu K (2006), State enterprises what remains? *The World Bank Group,* Number 304, February.

Teece D (1980), Economies of scope and the scope of the enterprise, Journal of Economic Behavior & Organization 1(3) 223–47. Reprinted in D Faulkner, ed. (2002), Strategy: Critical Perspectives on Business and Management. New York: Routledge.

Teece D (2007), Explicating dynamic capabilities: the nature and microfoundations of (sustainable) enterprise performance, *Strat. Mgmt. J.* 28(13) (December): 1319–50.

Teece D et al. (1997), Dynamic capabilities and strategic management, *Strategic Management Journal* 18(7) (August): 509–33.

Teichova A and Matis H (eds.) (2003), *Nation, State and the Economy in History.* New York: Cambridge University Press.

Teubner G and Febbrajo A (eds.) (1992), *State, Law, and Economy as Autopoietic Systems.* Milan: Giuffrè.

Thaler RH and Sunstein CR (2008), *Nudge: Improving Decisions about Health, Wealth, and Happiness.* New Haven, CO: Yale University Press.

Thomas P (1926), *Mercantilism and East Indian Trade: An Early Phase of the Protection vs. Free Trade Controversy.* London: P.S King & Son Ltd.

Thompson G (2003), *Between Hierarchies and Markets: The Logic and Limits of Network Forms of Organization.* Oxford: Oxford University Press.

Thorsteinsdóttir H et al. (2004), Cuba–innovation through synergy, *Nature Biotechnology* 22, Supplement (Dec.): 19–24.

Toussaint E (2007), *The World Bank: A Critical Primer.* London: Pluto Press.

Travieso-Díaz M (2001), Cuba's Perfeccionamiento Empresarial Law: A Step towards Privatization? Miami: ASCE.

Truslow FA et al. (ed.) (1951), *Report on Cuba,* IBRD Special Publication, Washington, D.C.

Ure A (1835), *The Philosophy of Manufactures: or, An Exposition of the Scientific, Moral, and Commercial Economy of the Factory System of Great Britain.* London: Charles Knight.

Usselman S (2002), *Regulating Railroad Innovation: Business, Technology and Politics in America, 1840–1920.* New York: Cambridge University Press.

Valdés P and Obrador A (2009), Stratified active screening: Where neurotechnology meets public health, *MEDICC Review* 11(1) (Winter): 7–10.

Valverde S and Solé R (2006), Self-organization and Hierarchy in Open Source Social Networks, SFI Working Paper: 2006-12-053.

Vasconcelos G (2010), From Hayek's spontaneous orders to Luhmann's autopoietic systems, *Studies in Emergent Order* 3: 50–81.

Vasconcelos G (2010), From Hayek's spontaneous orders to Luhmann's autopoietic systems. *Studies in Emergent Order* 3: 50–81.

Vaskela G (1996), The Land Reform of 1919–1940: Lithuania and the Countries of East and Central Europe, *Lithuanian Historical Studies,* Lithuanian Institute of History, V.1.P. 116–32.

Veblen T (1898), Why is economics not an evolutionary science, *Quarterly Journal of Economics,* July, 373–97.

Veblen T [1899](1994), *The Theory of the Leisure Class.* New York: Dover Publications Inc.

Vega-Redondo F (2006), *Complex Social Networks.* New York: Cambridge University Press.

Vidal P (2010), Cuban Economic Policy under the Raúl Castro Government, Institute of Developing Economies of Japan's External Trade, available at www.ide.go.jp/ Japanese/Publish/Download/Report/2009/pdf/2009_408_ch2

Viner J (1927), Adam Smith and laissez faire, *Journal of Political Economy* 35(2), April, 198–232.

von Hippel E (2005), Democratizing *Innovation*. Cambridge: MIT Press.

von Hippel E and von Krogh G (2006), Free revealing and the private-collective model for innovation incentives, *R&D Management* 36: 295–306.

von Mises L [1922] (1981), *Socialism: An Economic and Sociological Analysis.*, Indianapolis: Yale University Press. Full text from Yale University edition, English Edition (1951).

von Mises L [1929] (2011), *Critique of Interventionism*. Alabama: Ludwig von Mises Institute.

von Neumann J (1966), *The Theory of Self-Reproducing Automata*. Champaign, IL: University of Illinois Press.

Wade R (1990) (2003), *Governing the Market: Economic Theory and the Role of Government in East Asia's Industrialization*. Princeton, NJ: Princeton University Press.

Wasserman S and Faust K (1994), *Social Network Analysis: Methods and Applications*. Cambridge University Press, Cambridge, UK; New York, US; Melbourne, Australia.

Watts D and Strogatz S (1998), Collective dynamics of "small-world" networks, *Nature*, June (6684): 440–2.

Wellman B (1988), Structural analysis: From method and metaphor to theory and substance. In: B Wellman and SD Berkowitz (eds.), *Social Structures: A Network Approach*. Cambridge: Cambridge University Press, pp. 19–61.

Wernerfelt B (2002), Why should the boss own the assets?, *Journal of Economics and Management Strategy* 11: 473–85.

Wessner C et al. (eds.) (2001), *Capitalizing on New Needs and New Opportunities: Government-Industry Partnerships in Biotechnology and Information Technologies*. Washington, D.C.: National Academy Press.

WHO (2010), Indicator Code Book.

WHO (2011), Global Health Indicators.

WHO Global Report (year unavailable), Preventing chronic diseases: A vital investment, available in: www.who.int/chp/chronic_disease_report/part1/en/index.html (last accessed Sep. 2018).

Wilber C and Harrison R (1978), The methodological basis of institutional economics: Pattern models, storytelling and holism. *Journal of Economic Issues* XII(1): 61–89.

Williamson O (1975), *Markets and Hierarchies*. Free Press, New York World Bank Data.

Winter S (2006), The logic of appropriability: From Schumpeter to Arrow to Teece, *Research Policy* 35(8) (October): 1100–6.

Witt U (2003), Economic policy making in evolutionary perspective, *J Evol Econ* 13: 77–94.

Woo-Cumings M (ed.) (1999), *The Developmental State*. Ithaca and London: Cornell University Press.

World Bank (2008), The Growth Report: Strategies for Sustained Growth and Inclusive Development, Commission on Growth and Development, Conference Edition (available at www.ycsg.yale.edu/ center/forms/growthReport.pdf).

Yaffe H (2009), Che Guevara: *The Economics of the Revolution*, London: Palgrave Macmillan.

Yero LF (2008), Chronic vascular diseases in Cuba: Strategies for 2015, *MEDICC Review* 10(2) (Spring): 5–7.

Yglesia Martinez T and Capote Nestor (1993), *The Americas,* The History of Cuba and its Interpreters, 1898–1935 49(3) (January): 369–85.

Yin R (2003a), *Applications of Case Study Research*, 2nd edition. Thousand Oaks, CA: Sage.

Yin R (2003b), *Case Study Research: Design and Methods*, 3rd edition. Thousand Oaks, CA: Sage.

Young A (1928), Increasing returns and economic progress, *The Economic Journal* 38(152): 527–42.

Zablocki EM (2007), Formation of a business incubator. In A Krattiger et al. (eds.), *Intellectual Property Management in Health and Agricultural Innovation: A Handbook of Best Practices.* Oxford, UK: MIHR and PIPRA, Davis, USA, pp. 1305–14.

Zaman H (1991), *Economic Fuctions of an Islamic State: The Early Experience.* Markfield, UK: The Islamic Foundation.

Zimbalist A (1989), Cuba's revolutionary economy, *The Multinational Monitor* 10(4).

Zywicki T (2004), Reconciling Group Selection and Methodological Individualism. *Research Paper,* George Mason Law & Economics, No. 04-12. April. Available at SSRN: http://ssrn.com/abstract=524402 or http://dx.doi.org/10.2139/ssrn.524402

Index

8 de Marzo Lab 321

ACINOX 241–42
Ackoff, Russell 36, 95, 100, 101
Advanced Research Projects Agency
  (ARPA/DARPA) 92, 98–99, 110n36,
  110n42, 146, 147, 156n9, 161–62n41,
  216, 336n99, 362
aggregation fallacy 42
Agilent Technologies Foundation Health
  Award 277
Agre, Peter 272
Aica Lab 320, 323, 349n196
ALBA 250, 259n88
Albarrán, Joaquín 295
Alienes, Julián 190
American Institutionalist School 16, 40, 41
American Standards Association 110n35
Amgen 283, 285, 334n86
ancient civilizations 107–08n21, 208n35
Apple 124, 143, 147
artificial intelligence technology 330–31n60
AT&T 88, 103, 108n28, 108–09n29
Austria 73, 80, 192
Austrian School: anti-historicism 22n21;
  anti-interventionist theories 67–68, 72,
  78; founder of 22n25; minimal state
  29–30; neo-Austrians 29, 62, 72, 78,
  81, 82–83; neoliberalism and 108n26;
  overly focused on organic institutions 37;
  self-organization 36
autopoiesis 30, 53n7

Babbage, Charles 71
Bastiat, Frédéric 67, 105n10
Batista, Fulgencio 180, 182, 190
Bentham, Jeremy 17, 66, 104n3
Betancourt, Juan NicolásDávalos 295
Biogen Idec 285, 335n88

Biological Front 289, 310
Biomundi 322, 349n198
biopharmaceutical industry (international):
  asset fragmentation 366; complex
  structures 279, 283; dysfunctional
  business models 280, 283, 284, 285–86,
  308, 330n61; exclusive licensing 280–81,
  286, 308, 331–32n68, 459n25; low R&D
  productivity 279–80, 282, 332–33n72;
  marketing blowout 280, 282, 333n76,
  457–58n2; me-too drugs 280, 281,
  333n76, 457n2, 458n3; negative cash
  flow 279; NFO state funding 284–85;
  patents 281–82, 366; Pharma 3.0
  model 266–67, 286, 297, 298, 304, 404;
  regulation as spur to innovation 303–04;
  standardization inadequate 283, 286,
  304; stock markets 282–83, 285, 333n78,
  334n79, 334n82, 335n92; strategic
  alliances 280–81, 282; technology
  platform companies 280, 282, 283,
  333n77; uncertainty factor 279, 284,
  334n83; venture capital 282–83, 334n80,
  334n84, 336n102; vertical integration
  (FIPCO) 280, 282, 283–84, 308,
  330n63, 333n77
Biotechnological and Pharmaceutical
  Industries Enterprise Group
  (BioCubaFarma) 2, 226, 290–92, 301,
  306, 316, 324, 337n107, 376
Bismarck, Otto von 184
Blumberg, Baruch 344n153
Bolsheviks 181
Bonilla, Raúl Cepero 190
Botero, Giovanni 39, 46, 71
bounded rationality 126
Brazil: absorbing imported knowledge
  341n132; aircraft industry 80, 346n168;
  Cuba and 204, 232, 250, 252, 255n34,

Printed in the United States
by Baker & Taylor Publisher Services